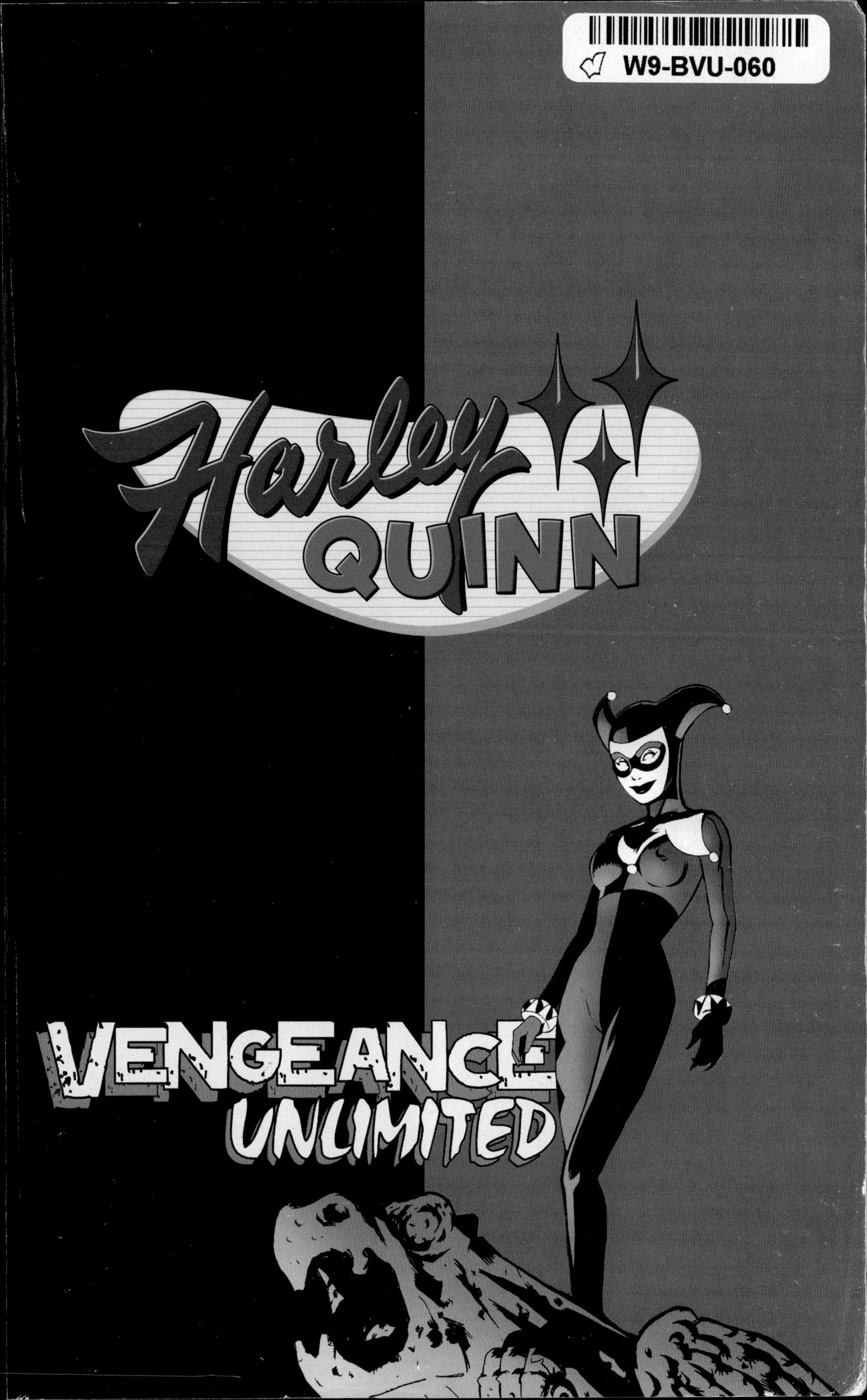
Harley
QUINN
VENGEANCE
UNLIMITED

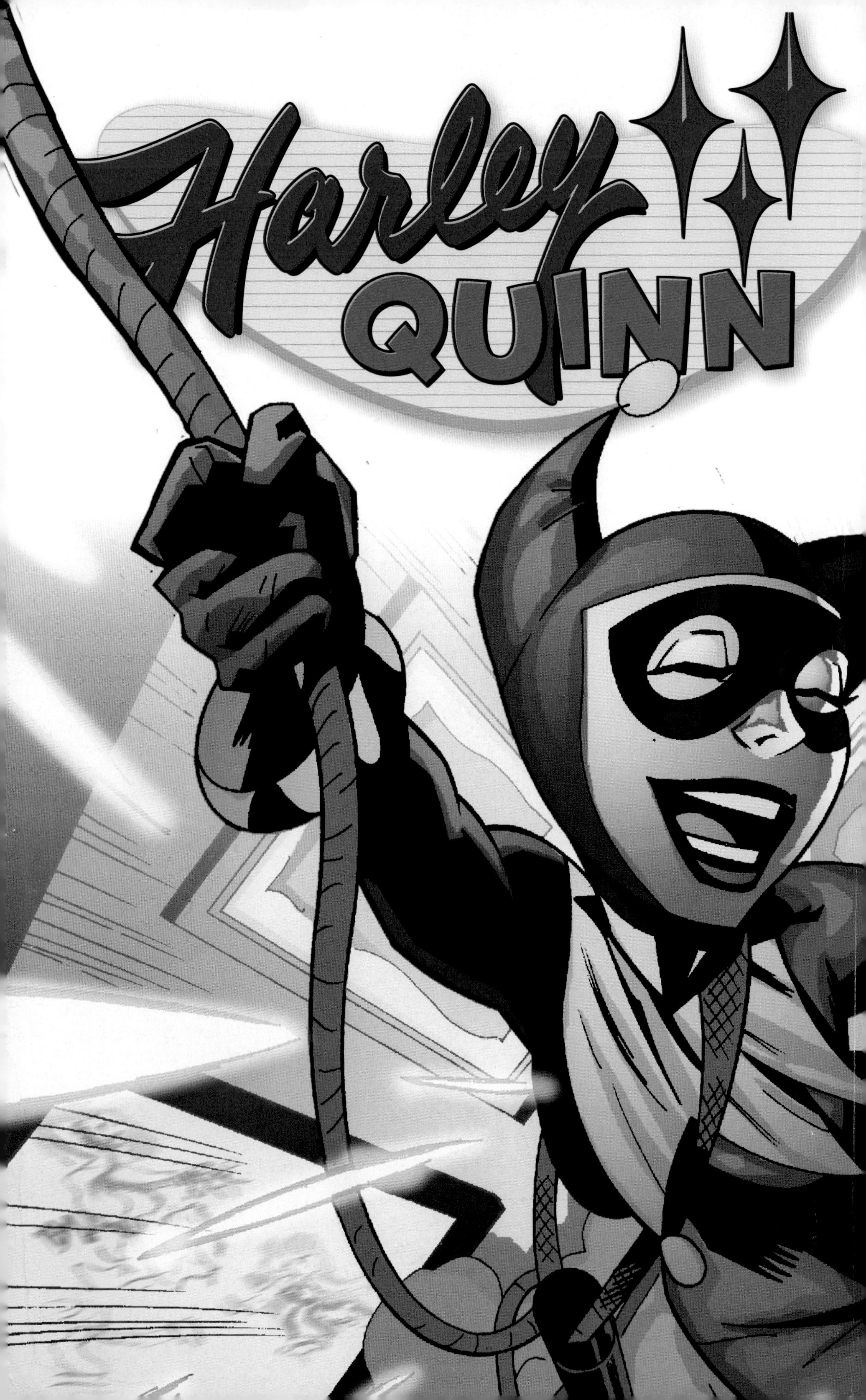
Harley
QUINN

VENGEANCE UNLIMITED

Written by A.J. Lieberman
Pencilled by Mike Huddleston Inked by Troy Nixey
With guest artists Nathan Fox Steve Yeowell Charlie Adlard Colored by Alex Sinclair Joel Benjamin
Lettered by Sean Konot Bob Pinaha Covers by Mike Huddleston & Troy Nixey
Harley Quinn created by Paul Dini and Bruce Timm

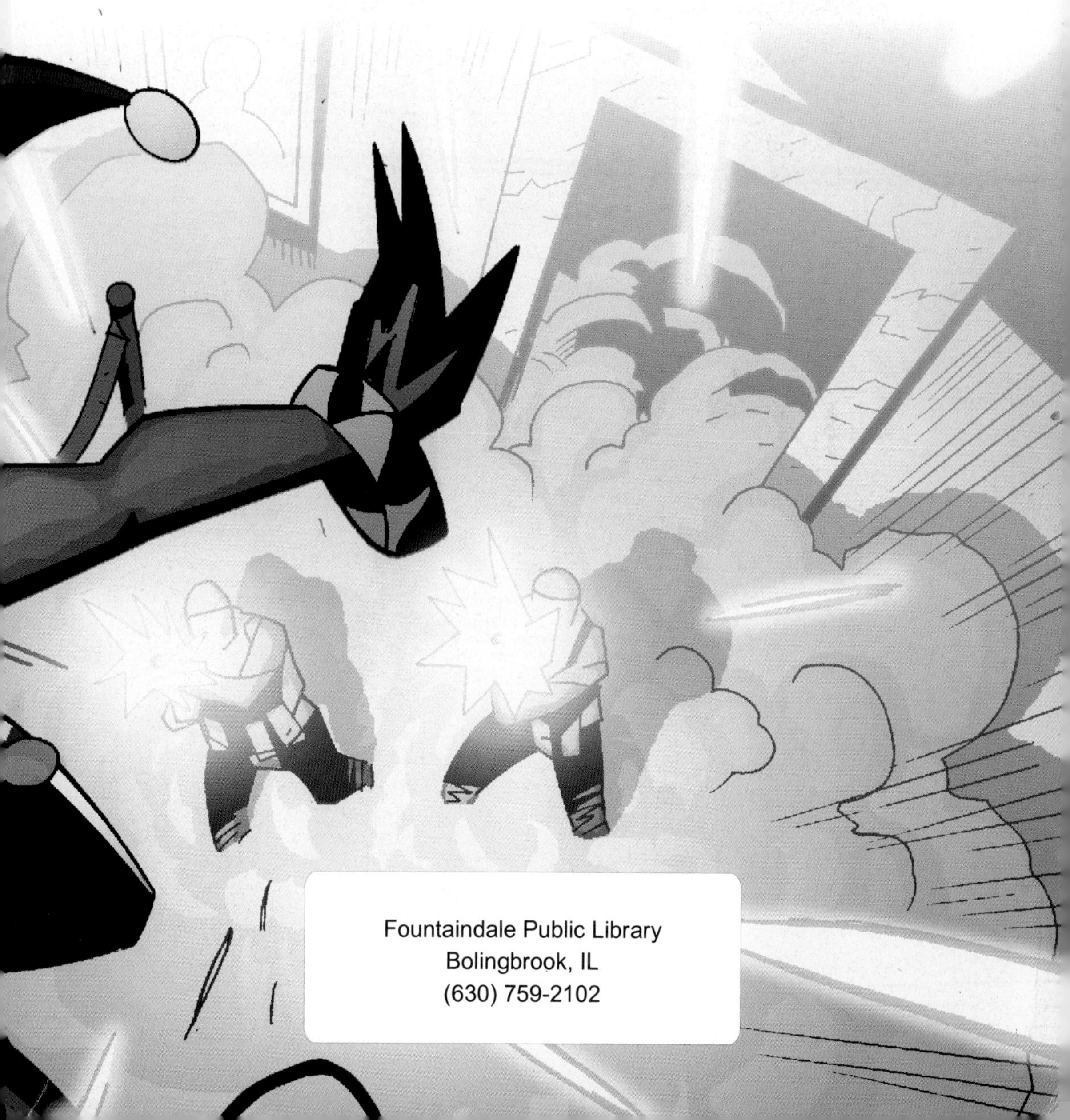

Matt Idelson	Editor – Original Series
Nachie Castro	Assistant Editor – Original Series
Jeb Woodard	Group Editor – Collected Editions
Curtis King Jr.	Publication Design
Bob Harras	Senior VP – Editor-in-Chief, DC Comics
Diane Nelson	President
Dan DiDio and Jim Lee	Co-Publishers
Geoff John	Chief Creative Officer
Amit Desai	Senior VP – Marketing and Global Franchise Management
Nairi Gardiner	Senior VP – Finance
Sam Ades	VP – Digital Marketing
Bobbie Chase	VP – Talent Development
Mark Chiarello	Senior VP – Art, Design & Collected Editions
John Cunningham	VP – Content Strategy
Anne DePies	VP – Strategy Planning & Reporting
Don Falletti	VP – Manufacturing Operations
Lawrence Ganem	VP – Editorial Administration & Talent Relations
Alison Gill	Senior VP – Manufacturing & Operations
Hank Kanalz	Senior VP – Editorial Strategy & Administration
Jay Kogan	VP – Legal Affairs
Derek Maddalena	Senior VP – Sales & Business Development
Dan Miron	VP – Sales Planning & Trade Development
Nick Napolitano	VP – Manufacturing Administration
Carol Roeder	VP – Marketing
Eddie Scannell	VP – Mass Account & Digital Sales
Susan Sheppard	VP – Business Affairs
Courtney Simmons	Senior VP – Publicity & Communications
Jim (Ski) Sokolowski	VP – Comic Book Specialty & Newsstand Sales

HARLEY QUINN: VENGEANCE UNLIMITED

Published by DC Comics. Copyright © 2014 DC Comics. All Rights Reserved.

Originally published in single magazine form in HARLEY QUINN #26-38 © 2003, 2004 DC Comics. All Rights Reserved. All characters, their distinctive likenesses and related elements featured in this publication are trademarks of DC Comics. The stories, characters and incidents featured in this publication are entirely fictional. DC Comics does not read or accept unsolicited ideas, stories or artwork.

DC Comics, 4000 Warner Blvd., Burbank, CA 91522
A Warner Bros. Entertainment Company.
Printed by RR Donnelley, Salem, VA, USA. 8/28/15. Second Printing.
ISBN: 978-1-4012-5068-3

Library of Congress Cataloging-in-Publication Data

Lieberman, A. J., author.
  Harley Quinn : Vengeance Unlimited / A.J. Lieberman, Mike Huddleston, Troy Nixey.
    pages cm
  ISBN 978-1-4012-5068-3 (paperback)
  1. Graphic novels. I. Huddleston, Mike, illustrator. II. Nixey, Troy, illustrator. III. Title. IV. Title: Vengeance Unlimited.
  PN6728.H367L54 2014
  741.5'973—dc23
                                                2014011714

PEFC Certified
Printed on paper from sustainably managed forests, controlled sources
PEFC/29-31-75   www.pefc.org

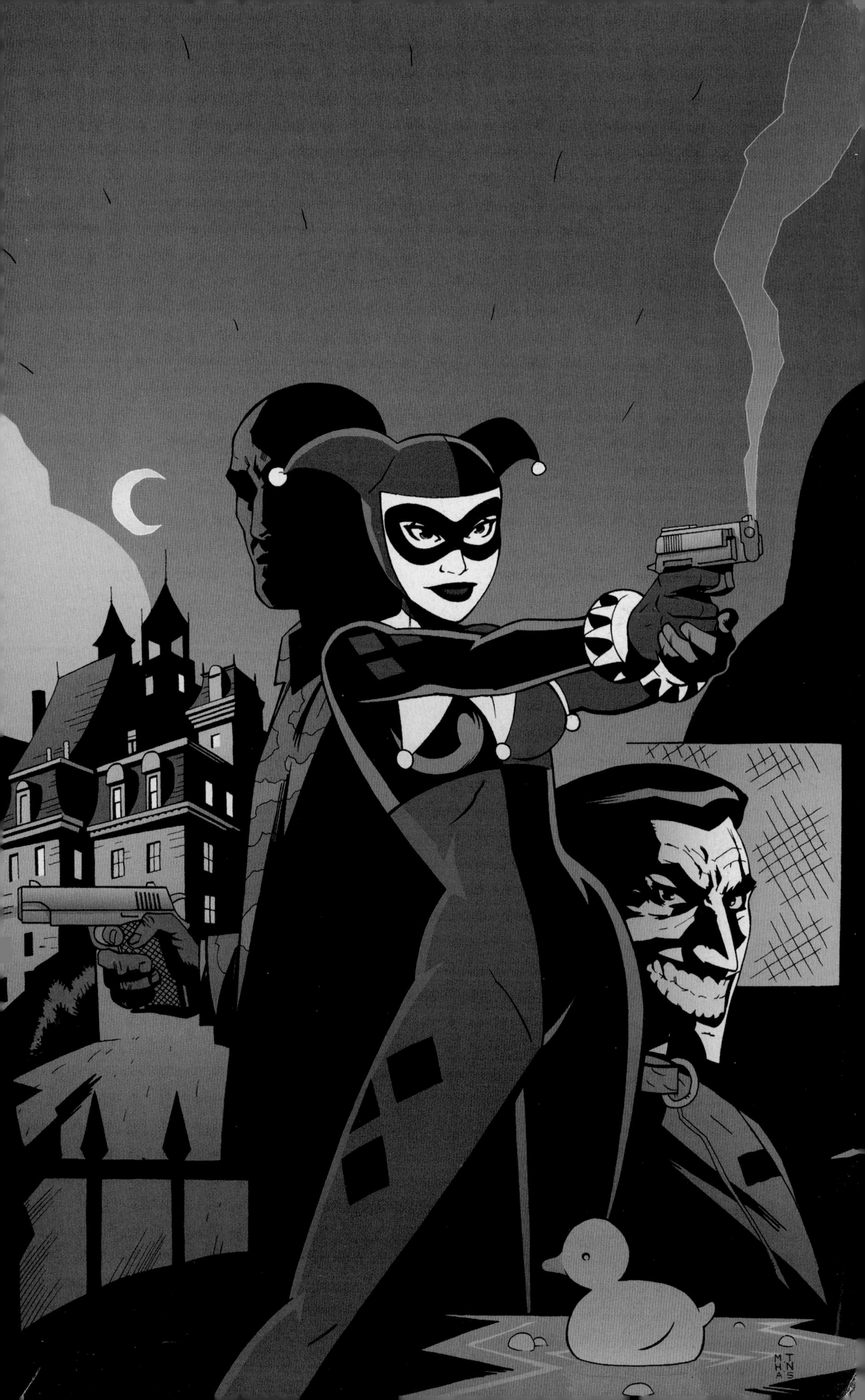

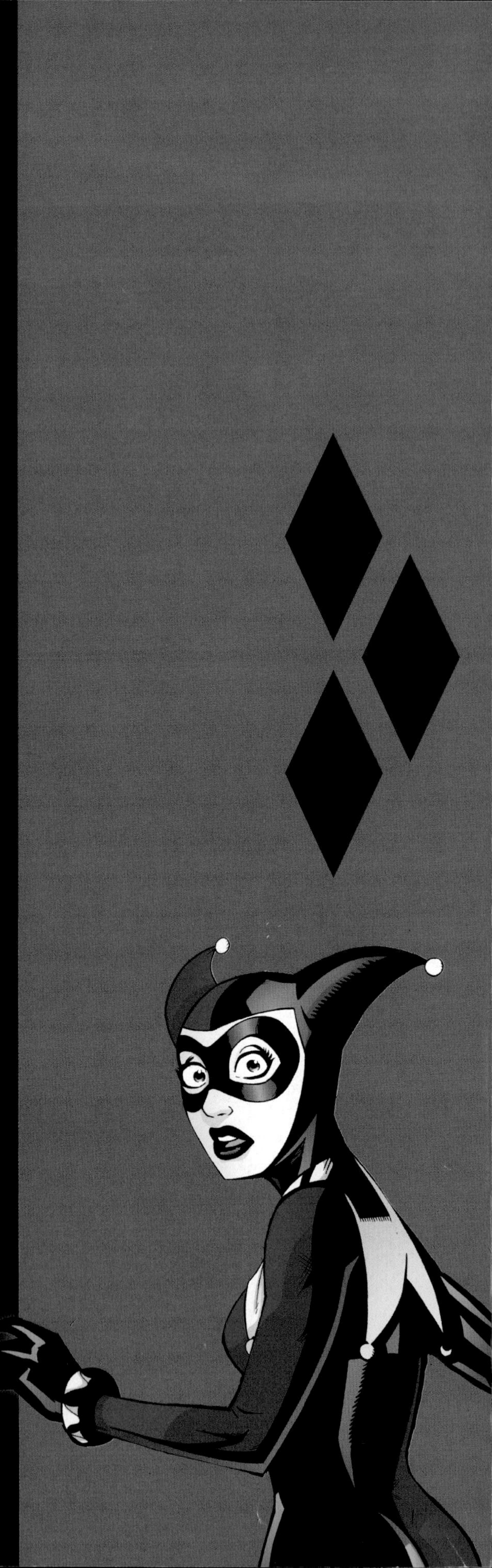

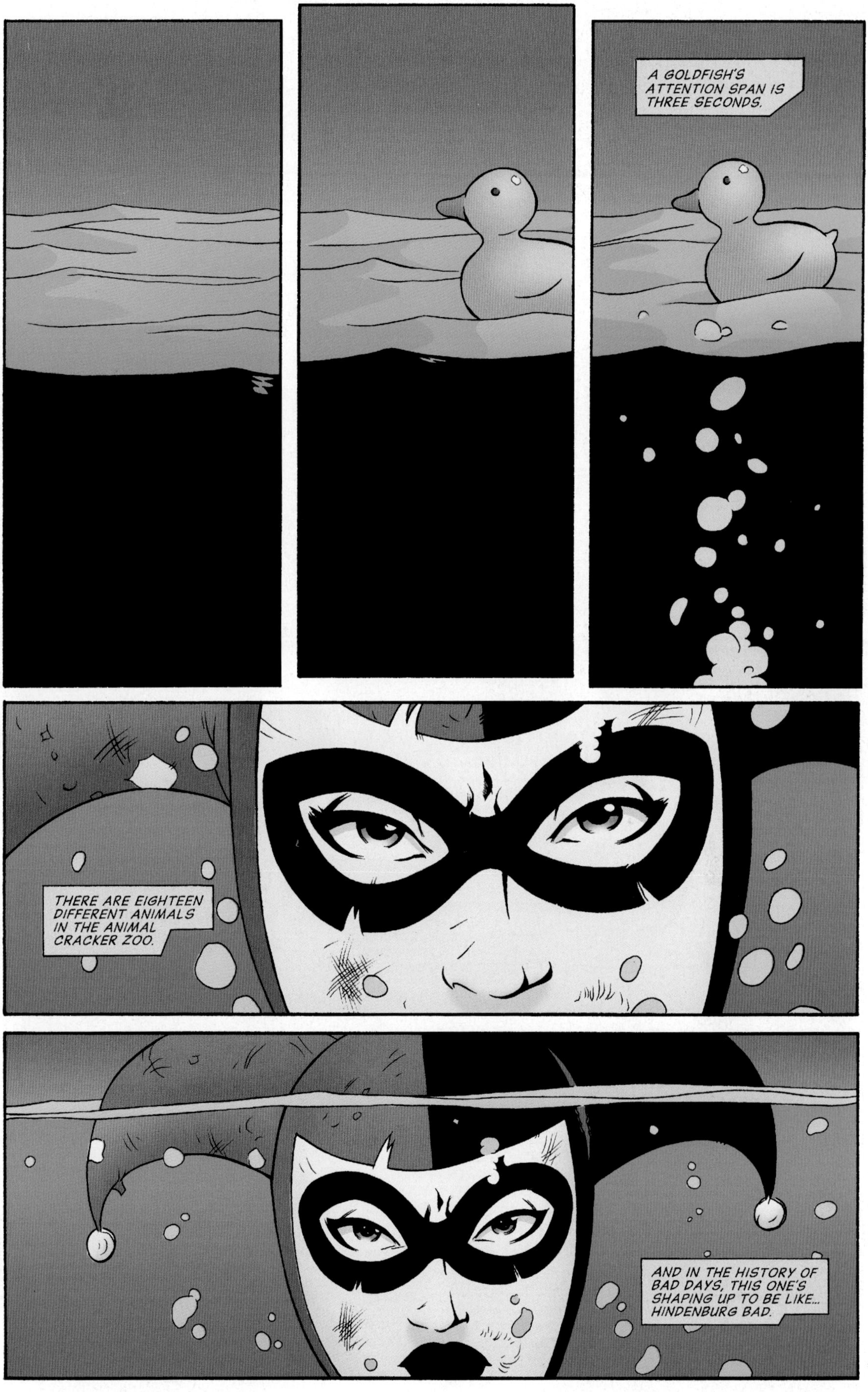
A GOLDFISH'S ATTENTION SPAN IS THREE SECONDS.
THERE ARE EIGHTEEN DIFFERENT ANIMALS IN THE ANIMAL CRACKER ZOO.
AND IN THE HISTORY OF BAD DAYS, THIS ONE'S SHAPING UP TO BE LIKE... HINDENBURG BAD.

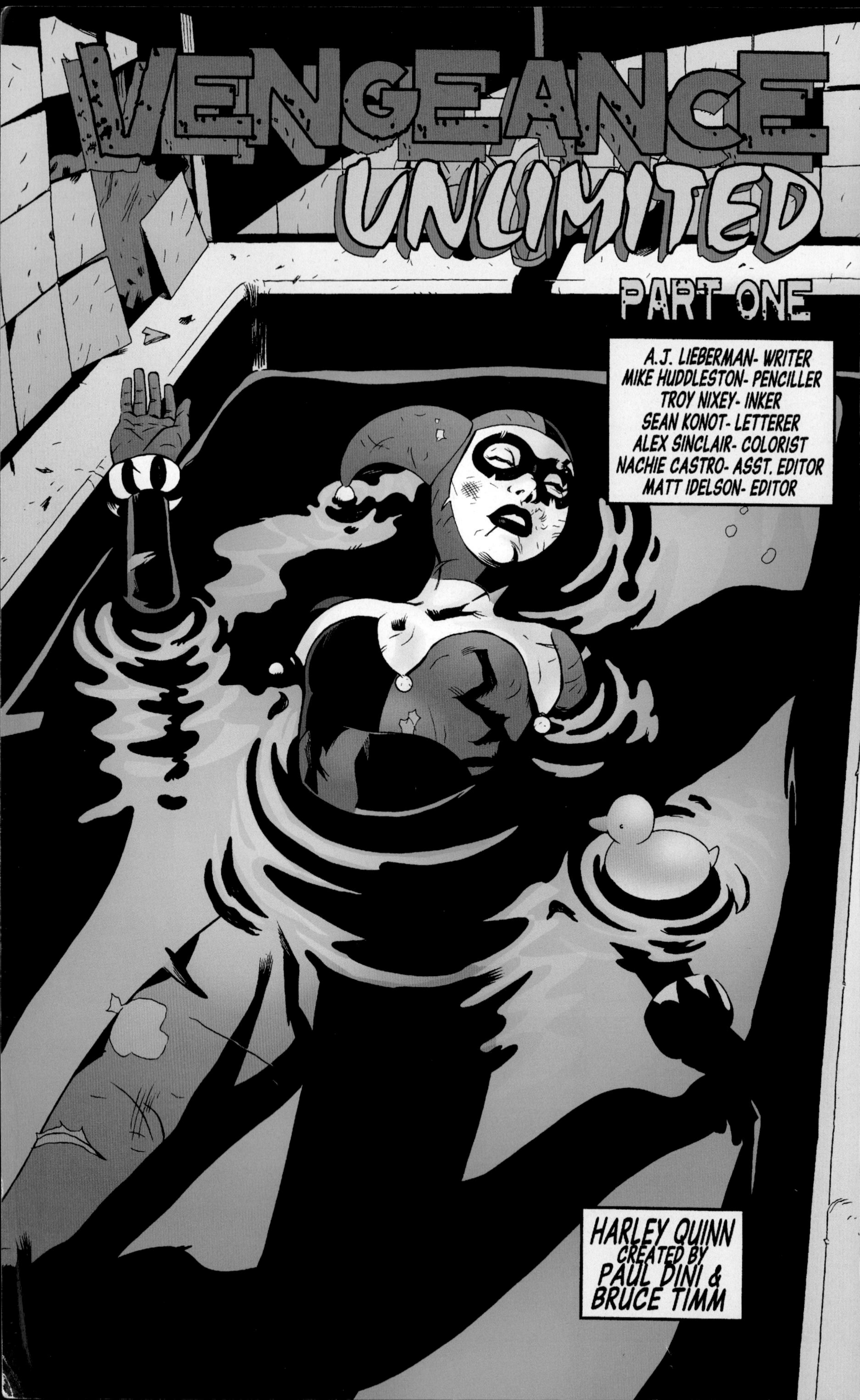
VENGEANCE
UNLIMITED
PART ONE
A.J. LIEBERMAN- WRITER
MIKE HUDDLESTON- PENCILLER
TROY NIXEY- INKER
SEAN KONOT- LETTERER
ALEX SINCLAIR- COLORIST
NACHIE CASTRO- ASST. EDITOR
MATT IDELSON- EDITOR
HARLEY QUINN CREATED BY PAUL DINI & BRUCE TIMM

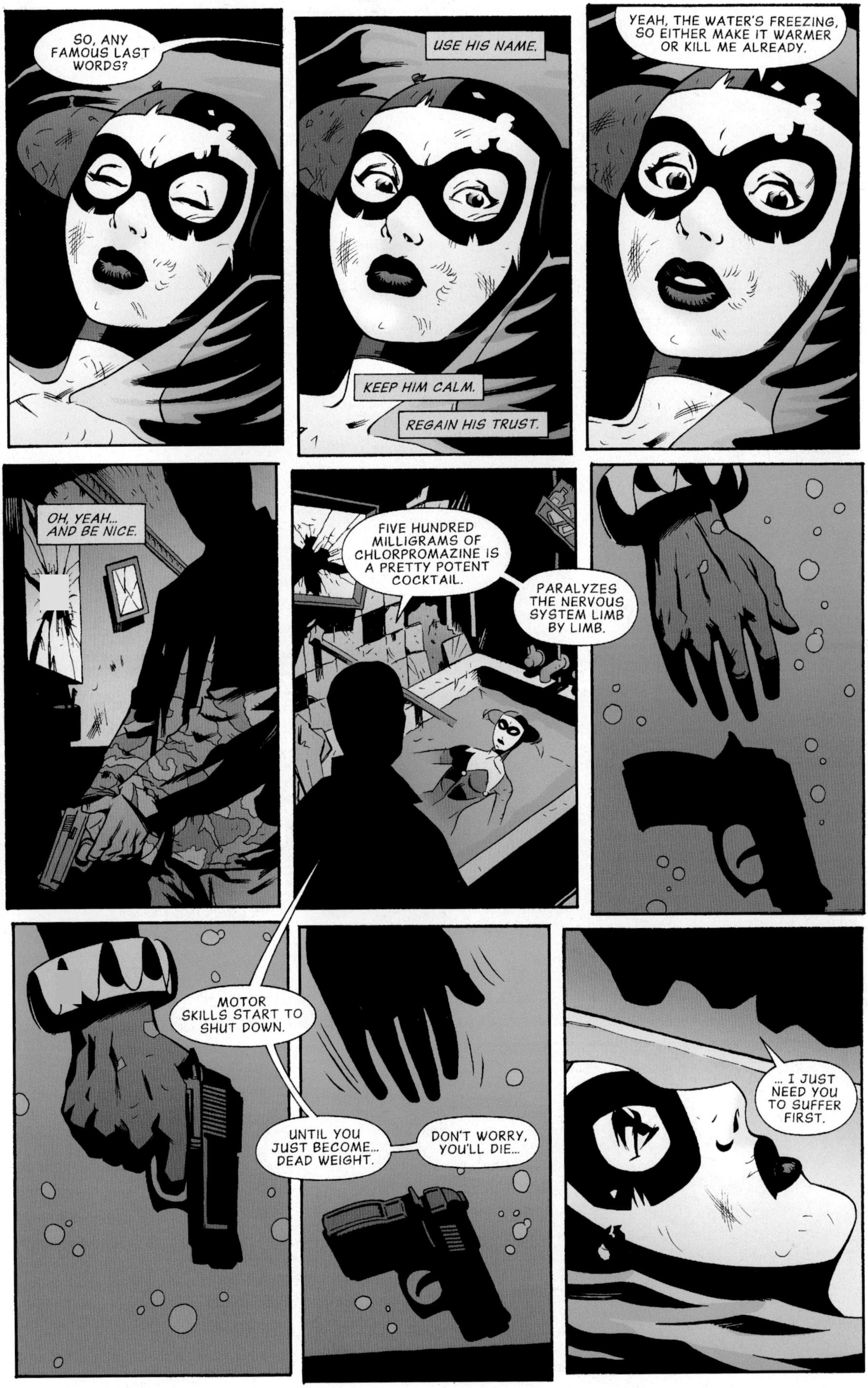
SO, ANY FAMOUS LAST WORDS?
USE HIS NAME.
KEEP HIM CALM.
REGAIN HIS TRUST.
YEAH, THE WATER'S FREEZING, SO EITHER MAKE IT WARMER OR KILL ME ALREADY.
OH, YEAH... AND BE NICE.
FIVE HUNDRED MILLIGRAMS OF CHLORPROMAZINE IS A PRETTY POTENT COCKTAIL.
PARALYZES THE NERVOUS SYSTEM LIMB BY LIMB.
MOTOR SKILLS START TO SHUT DOWN.
UNTIL YOU JUST BECOME... DEAD WEIGHT.
DON'T WORRY, YOU'LL DIE...
... I JUST NEED YOU TO SUFFER FIRST.

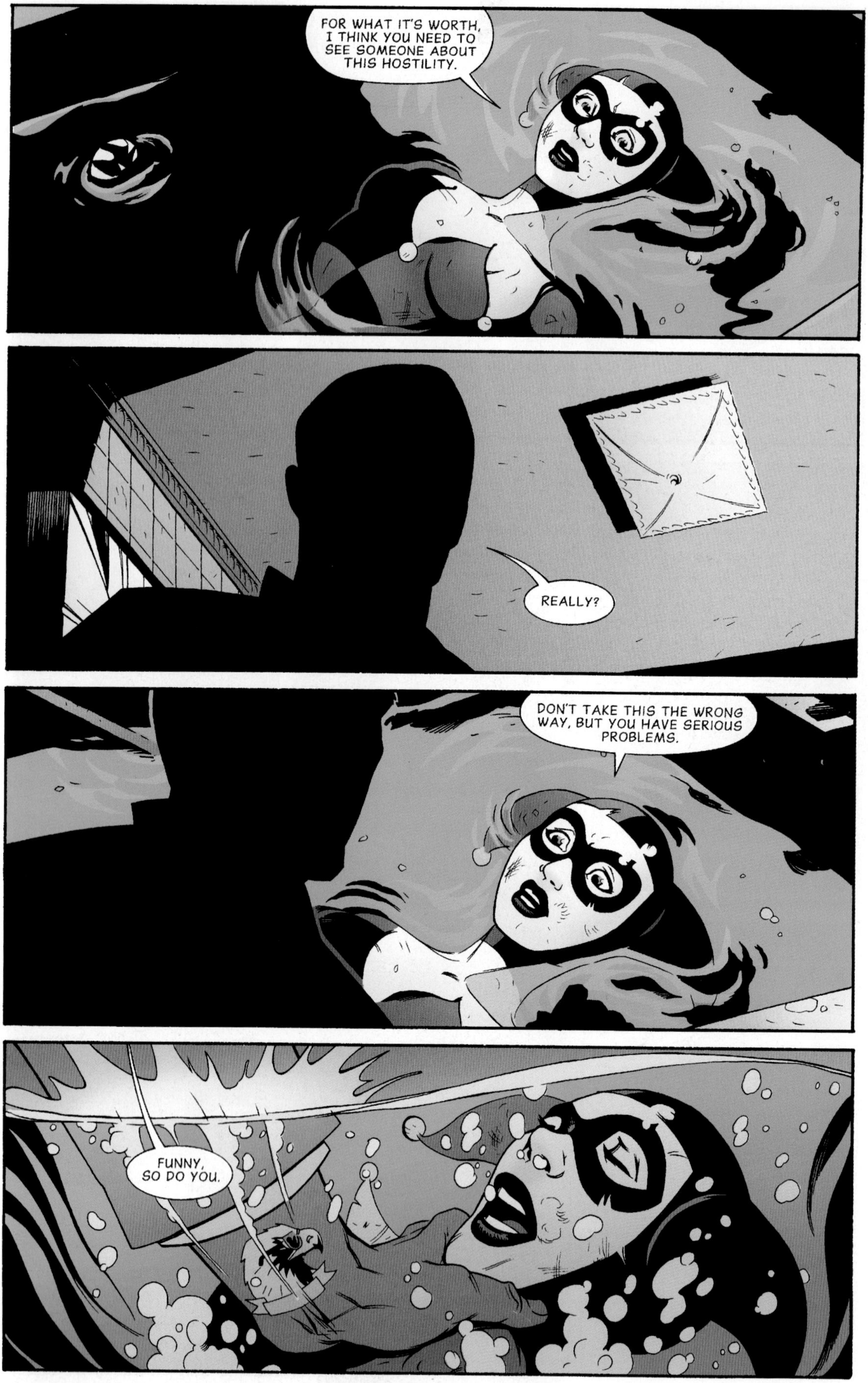
FOR WHAT IT'S WORTH, I THINK YOU NEED TO SEE SOMEONE ABOUT THIS HOSTILITY.
REALLY?
DON'T TAKE THIS THE WRONG WAY, BUT YOU HAVE SERIOUS PROBLEMS.
FUNNY, SO DO YOU.

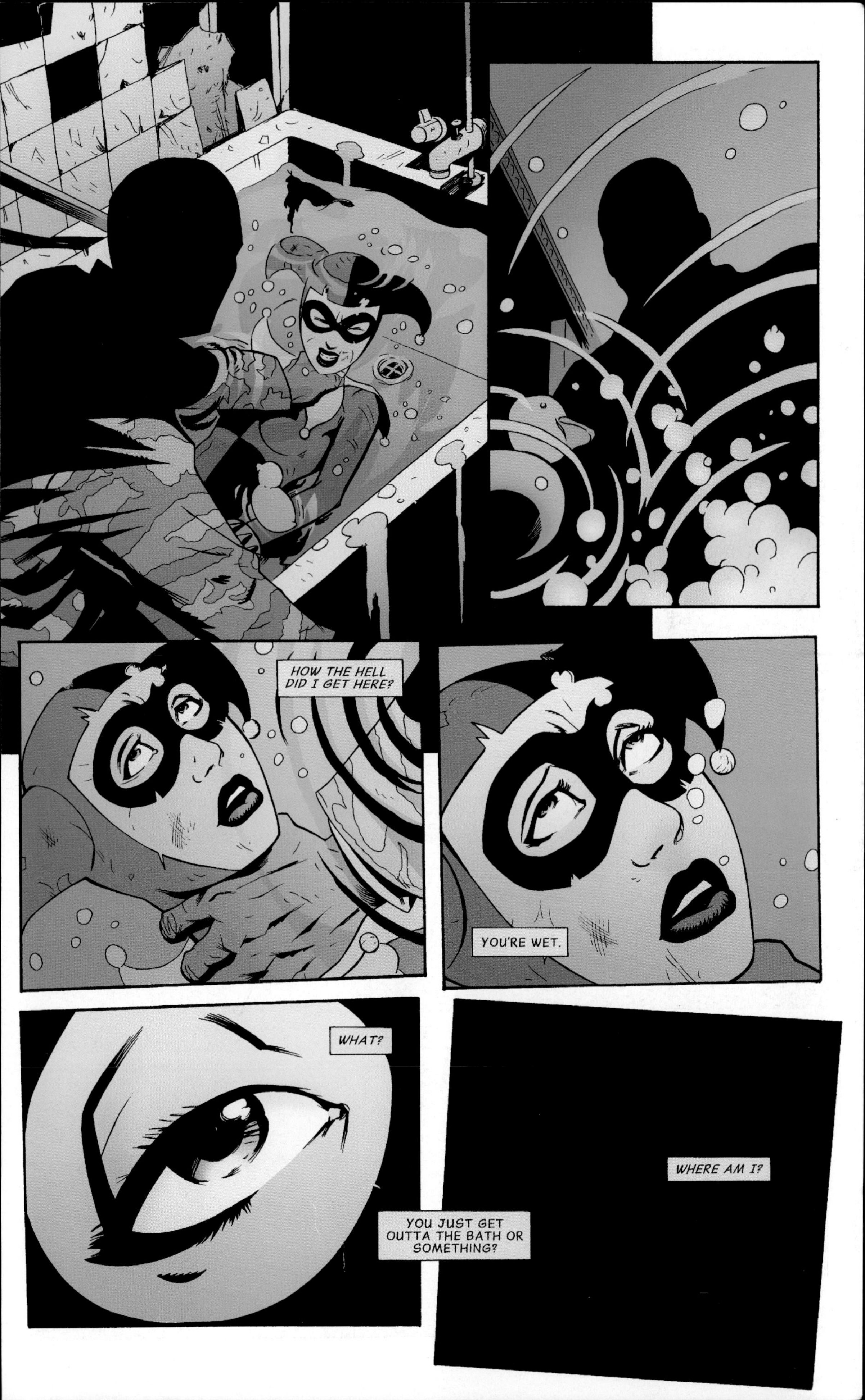
HOW THE HELL DID I GET HERE?
YOU'RE WET.
WHAT?
YOU JUST GET OUTTA THE BATH OR SOMETHING?
WHERE AM I?

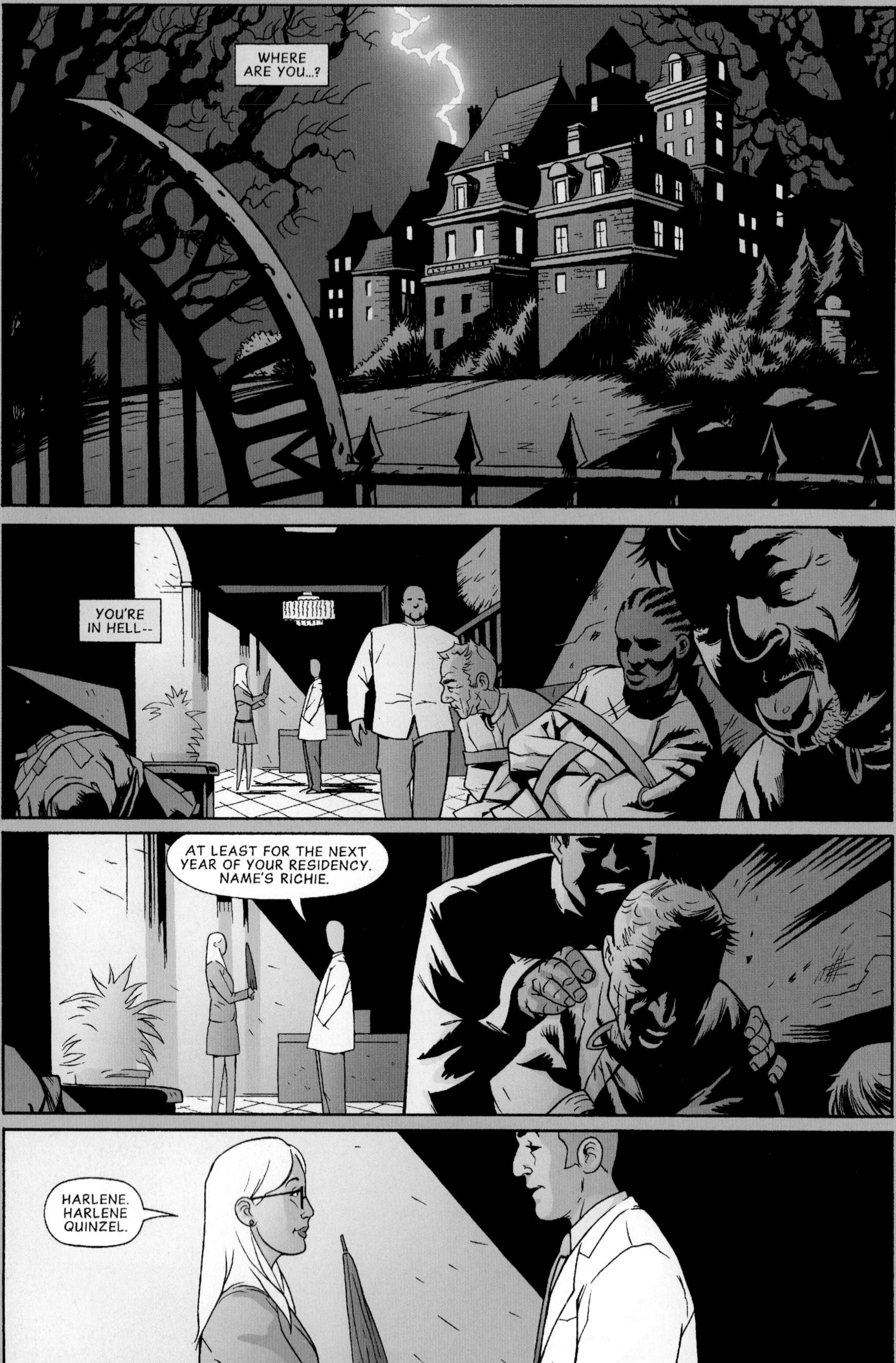
WHERE ARE YOU...?
YOU'RE IN HELL--
AT LEAST FOR THE NEXT YEAR OF YOUR RESIDENCY. NAME'S RICHIE.
HARLENE. HARLENE QUINZEL.

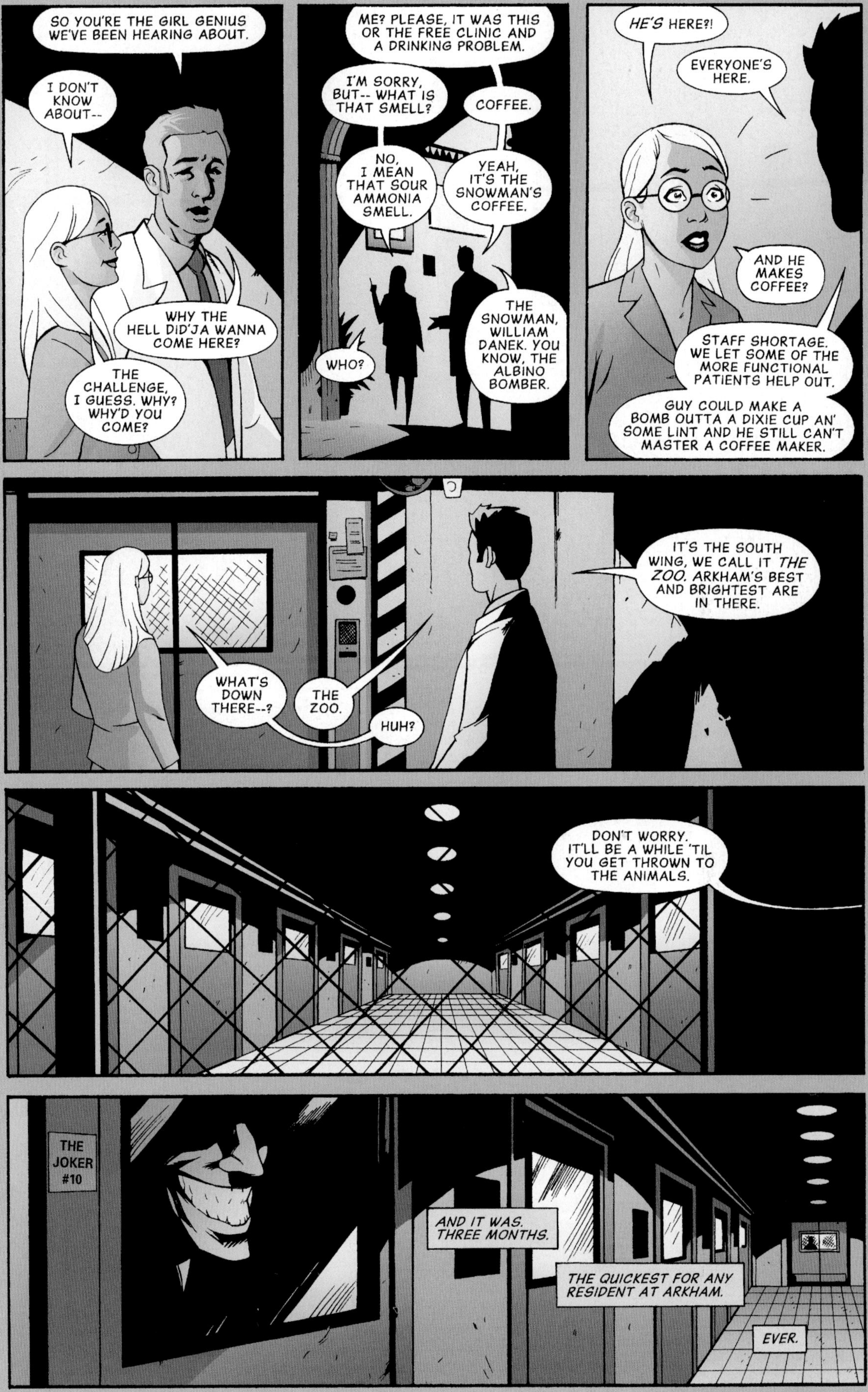

SO YOU'RE THE GIRL GENIUS WE'VE BEEN HEARING ABOUT.
I DON'T KNOW ABOUT--
WHY THE HELL DID'JA WANNA COME HERE?
THE CHALLENGE, I GUESS. WHY? WHY'D YOU COME?
ME? PLEASE, IT WAS THIS OR THE FREE CLINIC AND A DRINKING PROBLEM.
I'M SORRY, BUT-- WHAT IS THAT SMELL?
COFFEE.
NO, I MEAN THAT SOUR AMMONIA SMELL.
YEAH, IT'S THE SNOWMAN'S COFFEE.
WHO?
THE SNOWMAN, WILLIAM DANEK. YOU KNOW, THE ALBINO BOMBER.
HE'S HERE?!
EVERYONE'S HERE.
AND HE MAKES COFFEE?
STAFF SHORTAGE. WE LET SOME OF THE MORE FUNCTIONAL PATIENTS HELP OUT.
GUY COULD MAKE A BOMB OUTTA A DIXIE CUP AN' SOME LINT AND HE STILL CAN'T MASTER A COFFEE MAKER.
WHAT'S DOWN THERE--?
THE ZOO.
HUH?
IT'S THE SOUTH WING, WE CALL IT THE ZOO. ARKHAM'S BEST AND BRIGHTEST ARE IN THERE.
DON'T WORRY. IT'LL BE A WHILE 'TIL YOU GET THROWN TO THE ANIMALS.
THE JOKER #10
AND IT WAS. THREE MONTHS.
THE QUICKEST FOR ANY RESIDENT AT ARKHAM.
EVER.

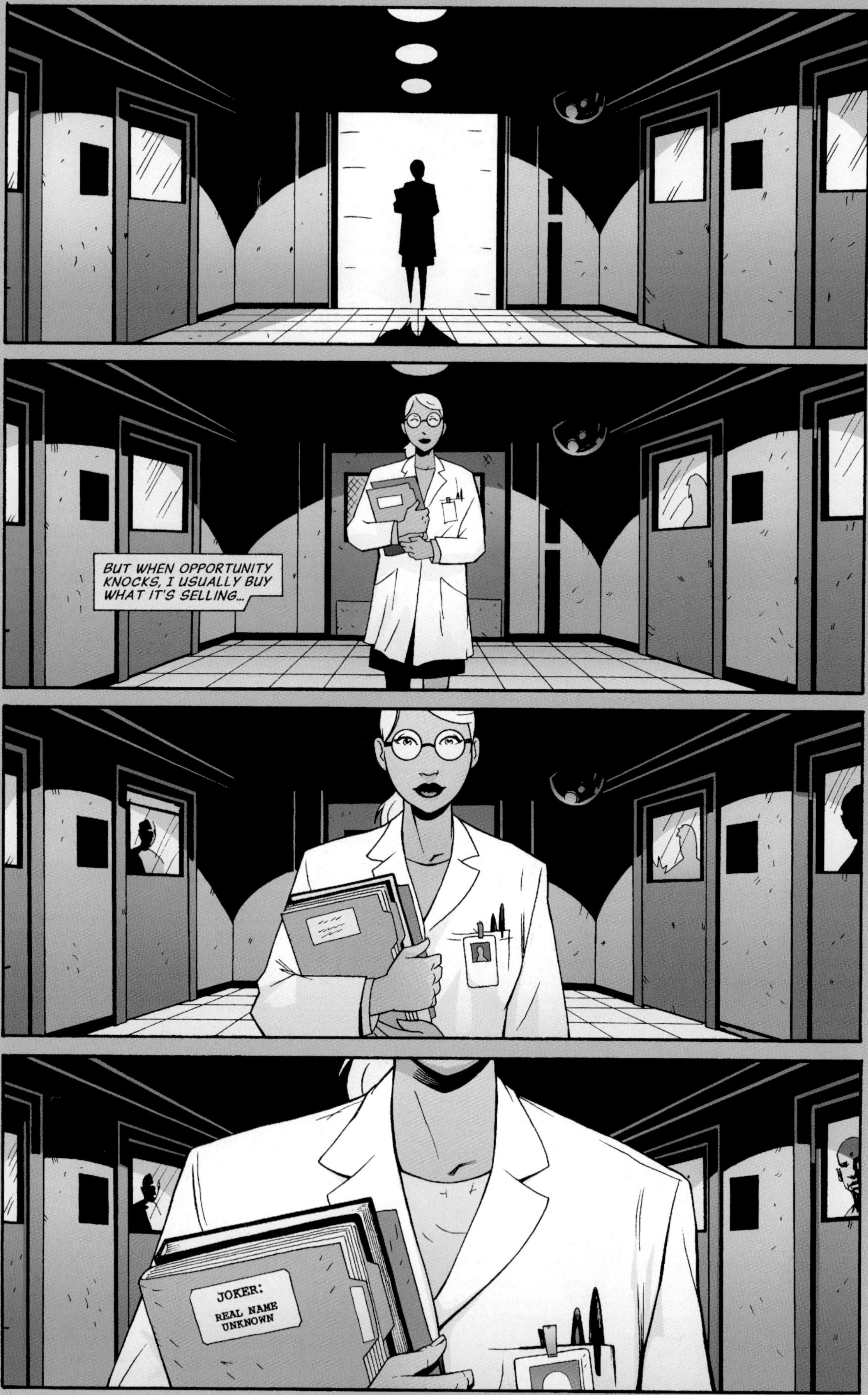
BUT WHEN OPPORTUNITY KNOCKS, I USUALLY BUY WHAT IT'S SELLING...
JOKER:
REAL NAME UNKNOWN

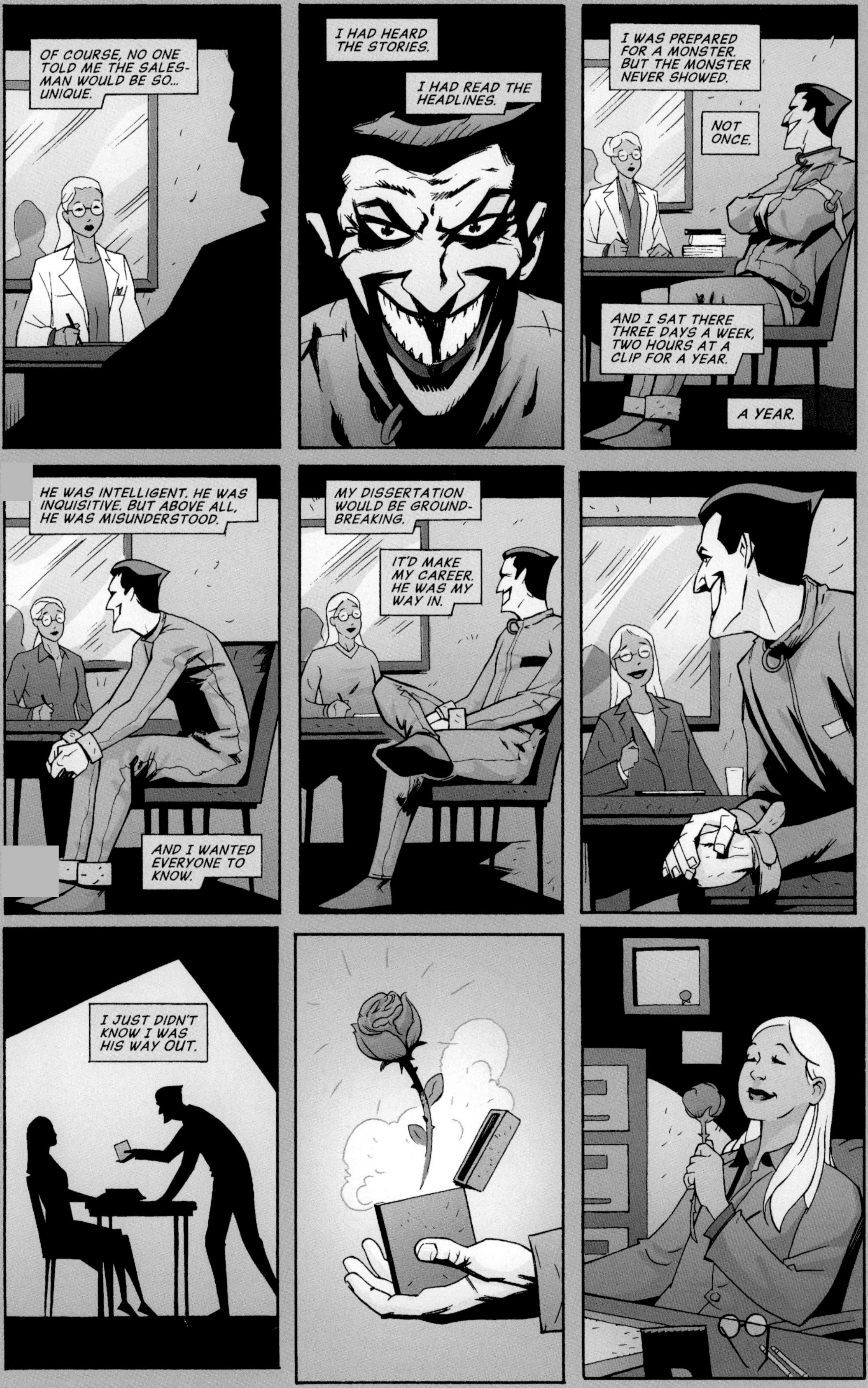
OF COURSE, NO ONE TOLD ME THE SALES-MAN WOULD BE SO... UNIQUE.
I HAD HEARD THE STORIES.
I HAD READ THE HEADLINES.
I WAS PREPARED FOR A MONSTER. BUT THE MONSTER NEVER SHOWED.
NOT ONCE.
AND I SAT THERE THREE DAYS A WEEK, TWO HOURS AT A CLIP FOR A YEAR.
A YEAR.
HE WAS INTELLIGENT. HE WAS INQUISITIVE. BUT ABOVE ALL, HE WAS MISUNDERSTOOD.
AND I WANTED EVERYONE TO KNOW.
MY DISSERTATION WOULD BE GROUND-BREAKING.
IT'D MAKE MY CAREER. HE WAS MY WAY IN.
I JUST DIDN'T KNOW I WAS HIS WAY OUT.

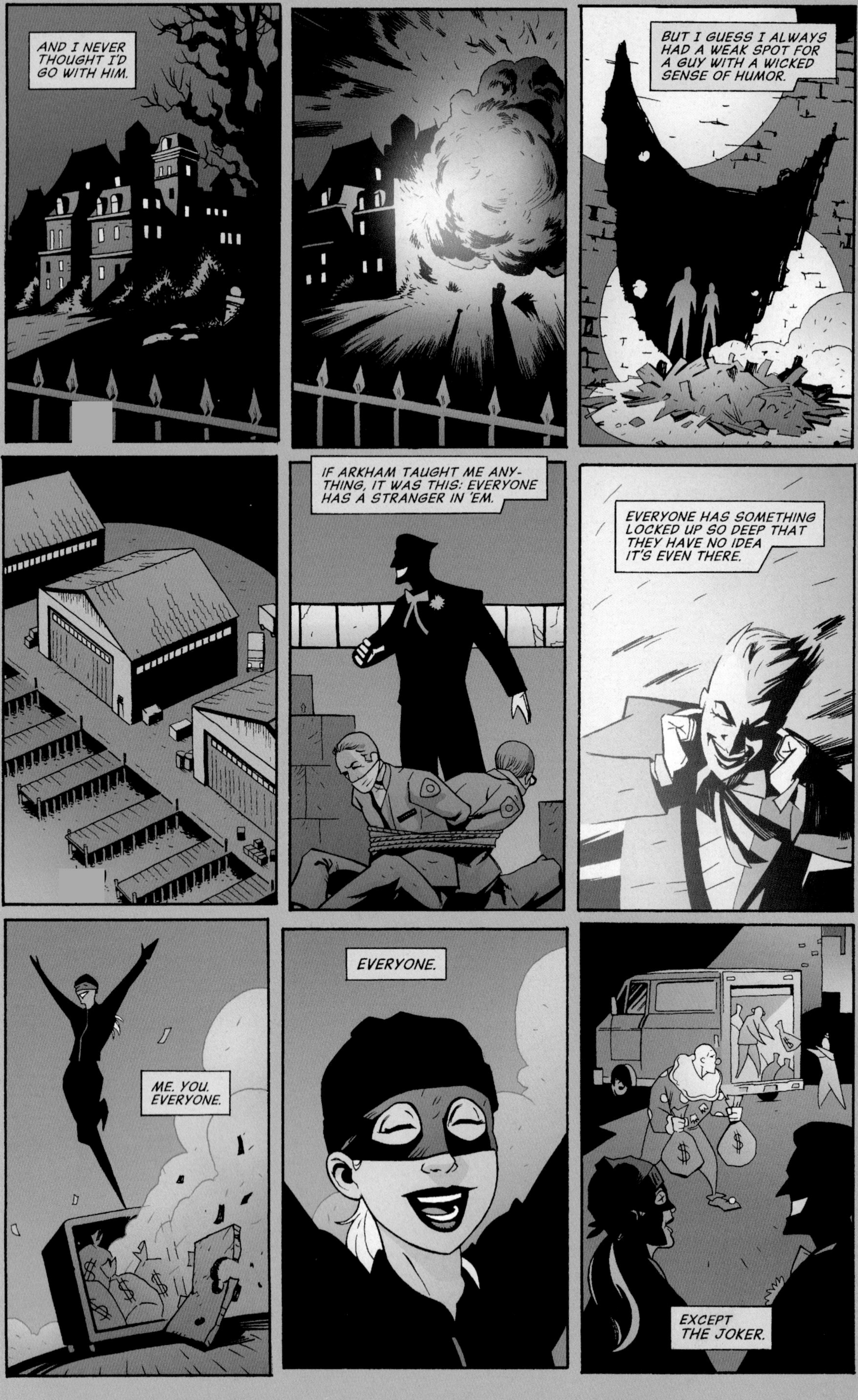
AND I NEVER THOUGHT I'D GO WITH HIM.
BUT I GUESS I ALWAYS HAD A WEAK SPOT FOR A GUY WITH A WICKED SENSE OF HUMOR.
IF ARKHAM TAUGHT ME ANY-THING, IT WAS THIS: EVERYONE HAS A STRANGER IN 'EM.
EVERYONE HAS SOMETHING LOCKED UP SO DEEP THAT THEY HAVE NO IDEA IT'S EVEN THERE.
ME. YOU. EVERYONE.
EVERYONE.
EXCEPT THE JOKER.

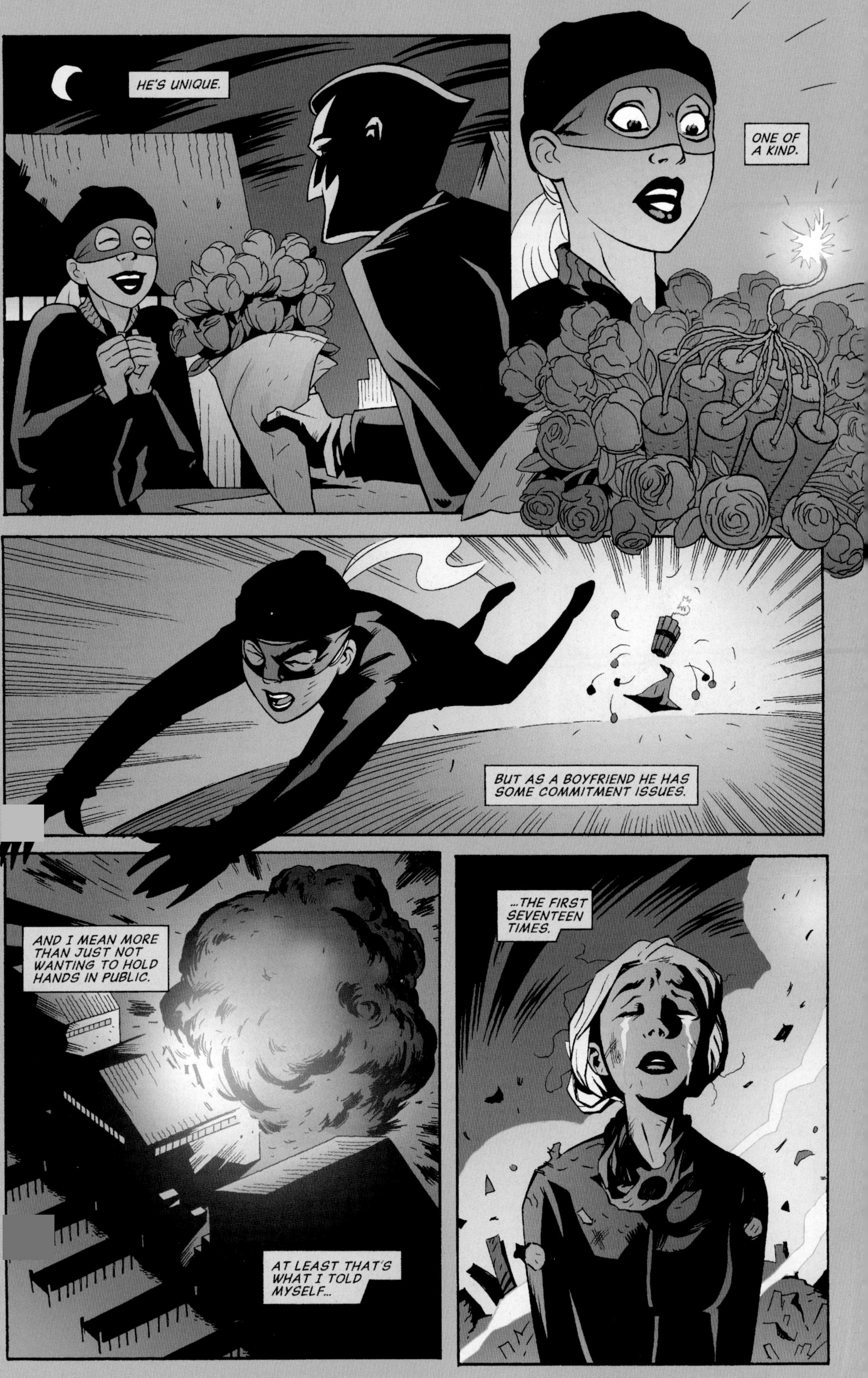
HE'S UNIQUE.
ONE OF A KIND.
BUT AS A BOYFRIEND HE HAS SOME COMMITMENT ISSUES.
AND I MEAN MORE THAN JUST NOT WANTING TO HOLD HANDS IN PUBLIC.
AT LEAST THAT'S WHAT I TOLD MYSELF...
...THE FIRST SEVENTEEN TIMES.

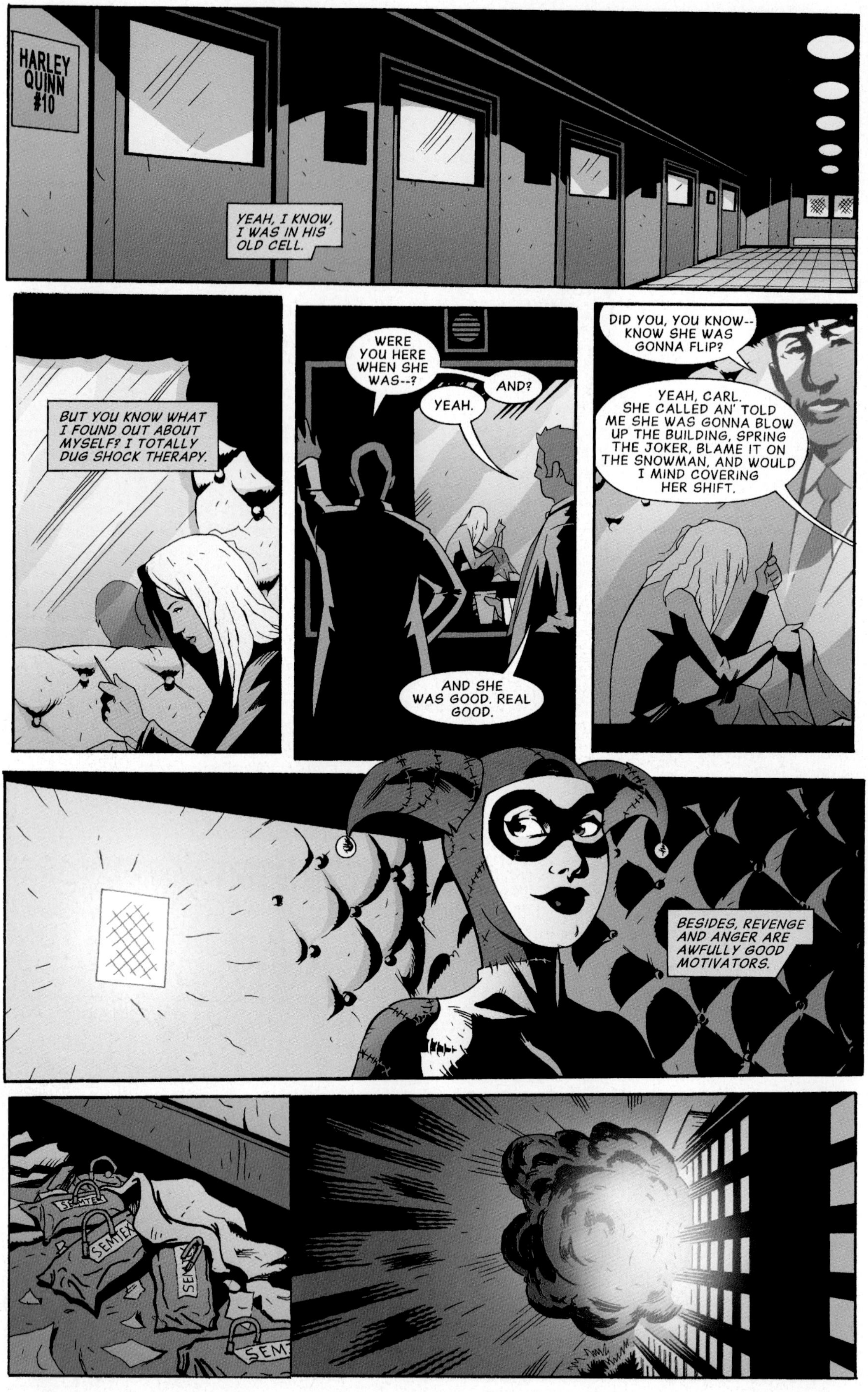
HARLEY QUINN #10
YEAH, I KNOW, I WAS IN HIS OLD CELL.
BUT YOU KNOW WHAT I FOUND OUT ABOUT MYSELF? I TOTALLY DUG SHOCK THERAPY.
WERE YOU HERE WHEN SHE WAS--?
YEAH.
AND?
AND SHE WAS GOOD. REAL GOOD.
DID YOU, YOU KNOW-- KNOW SHE WAS GONNA FLIP?
YEAH, CARL. SHE CALLED AN' TOLD ME SHE WAS GONNA BLOW UP THE BUILDING, SPRING THE JOKER, BLAME IT ON THE SNOWMAN, AND WOULD I MIND COVERING HER SHIFT.
BESIDES, REVENGE AND ANGER ARE AWFULLY GOOD MOTIVATORS.
SEMTEX
SEMTEX
SEMTEX

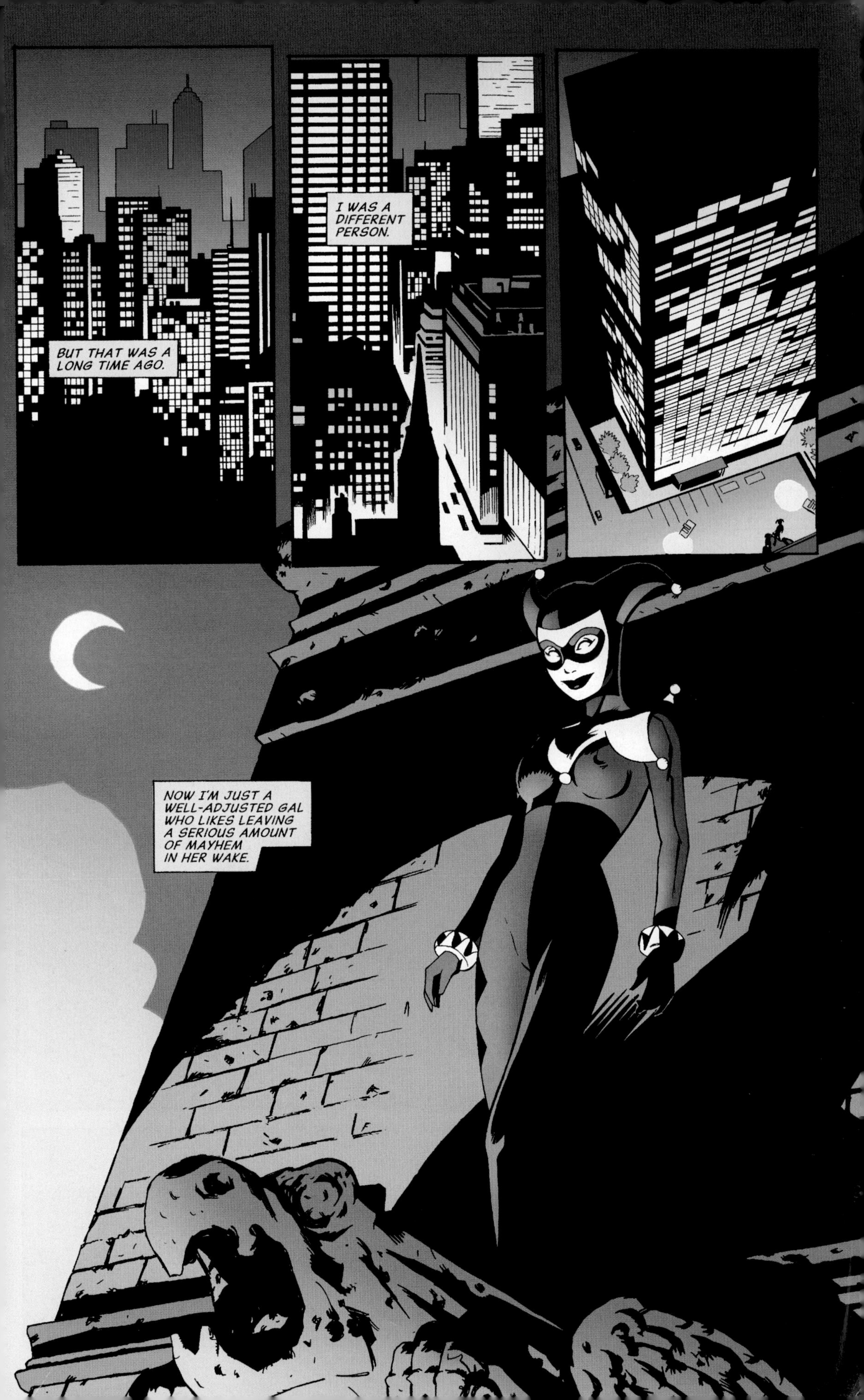
BUT THAT WAS A LONG TIME AGO.
I WAS A DIFFERENT PERSON.
NOW I'M JUST A WELL-ADJUSTED GAL WHO LIKES LEAVING A SERIOUS AMOUNT OF MAYHEM IN HER WAKE.

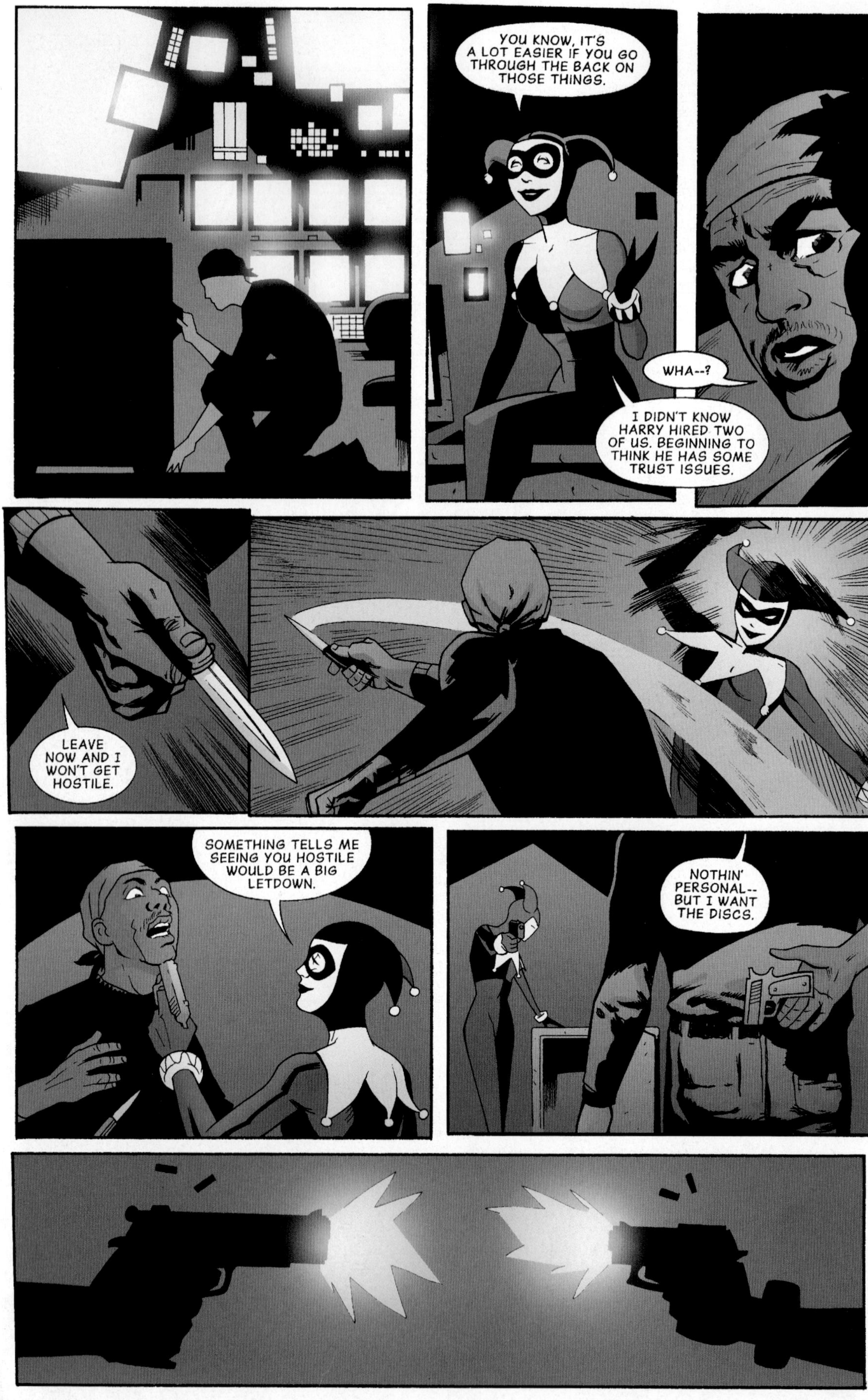

YOU KNOW, IT'S A LOT EASIER IF YOU GO THROUGH THE BACK ON THOSE THINGS.
WHA--?
I DIDN'T KNOW HARRY HIRED TWO OF US. BEGINNING TO THINK HE HAS SOME TRUST ISSUES.
LEAVE NOW AND I WON'T GET HOSTILE.
SOMETHING TELLS ME SEEING YOU HOSTILE WOULD BE A BIG LETDOWN.
NOTHIN' PERSONAL-- BUT I WANT THE DISCS.

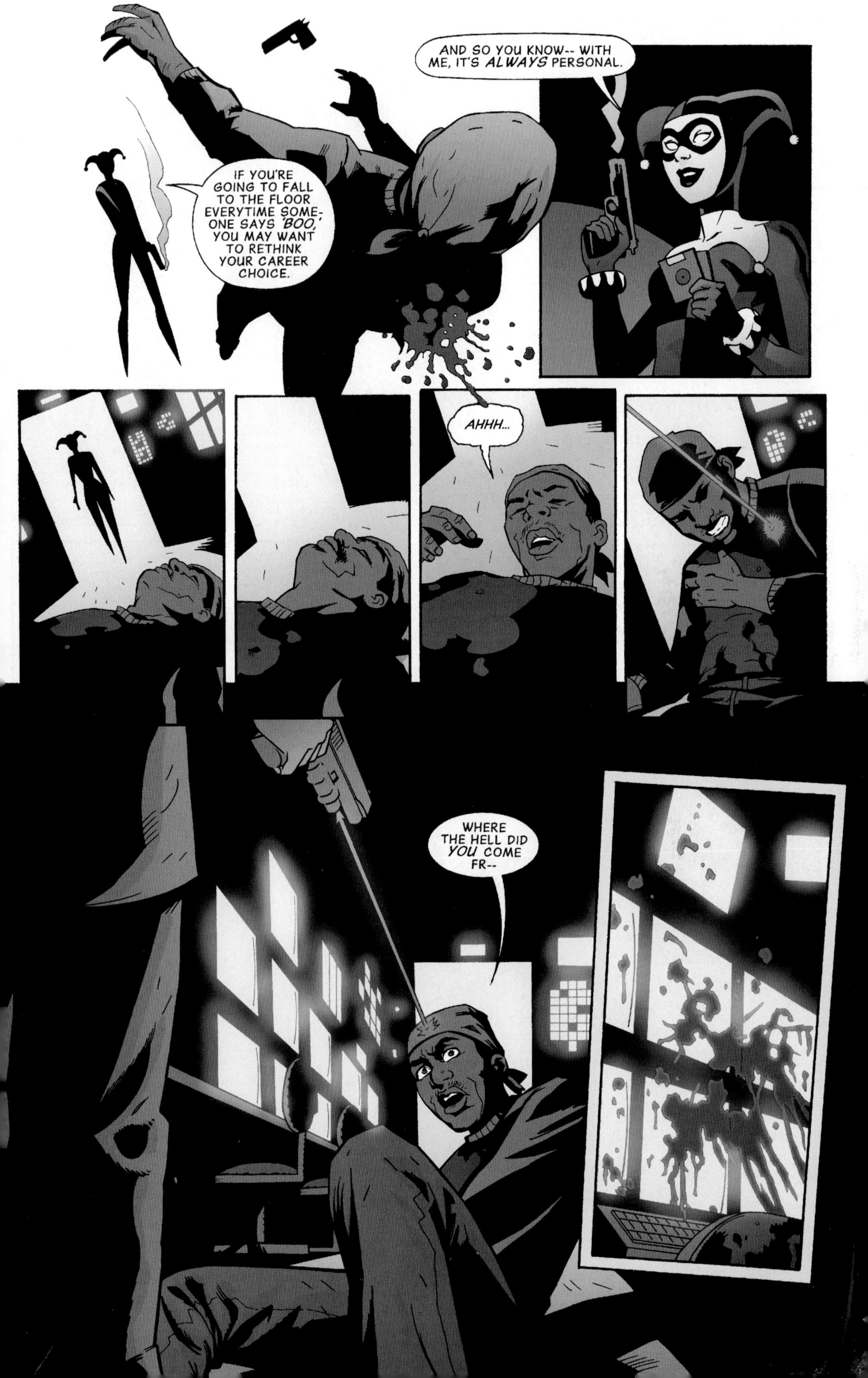
IF YOU'RE GOING TO FALL TO THE FLOOR EVERYTIME SOME-ONE SAYS 'BOO,' YOU MAY WANT TO RETHINK YOUR CAREER CHOICE.
AND SO YOU KNOW-- WITH ME, IT'S ALWAYS PERSONAL.
AHHH...
WHERE THE HELL DID YOU COME FR--

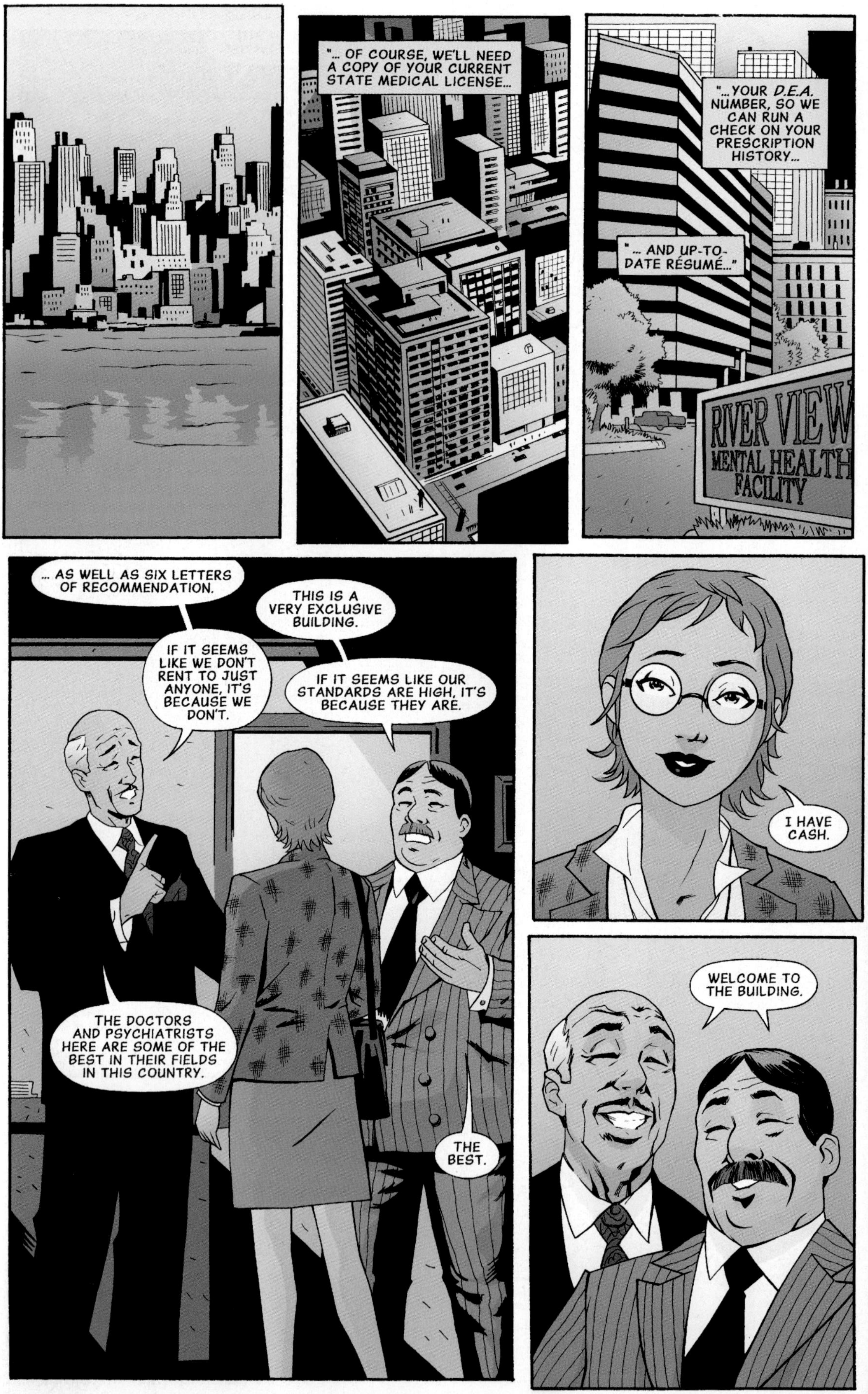
"... OF COURSE, WE'LL NEED A COPY OF YOUR CURRENT STATE MEDICAL LICENSE...
"... YOUR D.E.A. NUMBER, SO WE CAN RUN A CHECK ON YOUR PRESCRIPTION HISTORY...
"... AND UP-TO-DATE RÉSUMÉ..."
RIVER VIEW MENTAL HEALTH FACILITY
... AS WELL AS SIX LETTERS OF RECOMMENDATION.
THIS IS A VERY EXCLUSIVE BUILDING.
IF IT SEEMS LIKE WE DON'T RENT TO JUST ANYONE, IT'S BECAUSE WE DON'T.
IF IT SEEMS LIKE OUR STANDARDS ARE HIGH, IT'S BECAUSE THEY ARE.
THE DOCTORS AND PSYCHIATRISTS HERE ARE SOME OF THE BEST IN THEIR FIELDS IN THIS COUNTRY.
THE BEST.
I HAVE CASH.
WELCOME TO THE BUILDING.

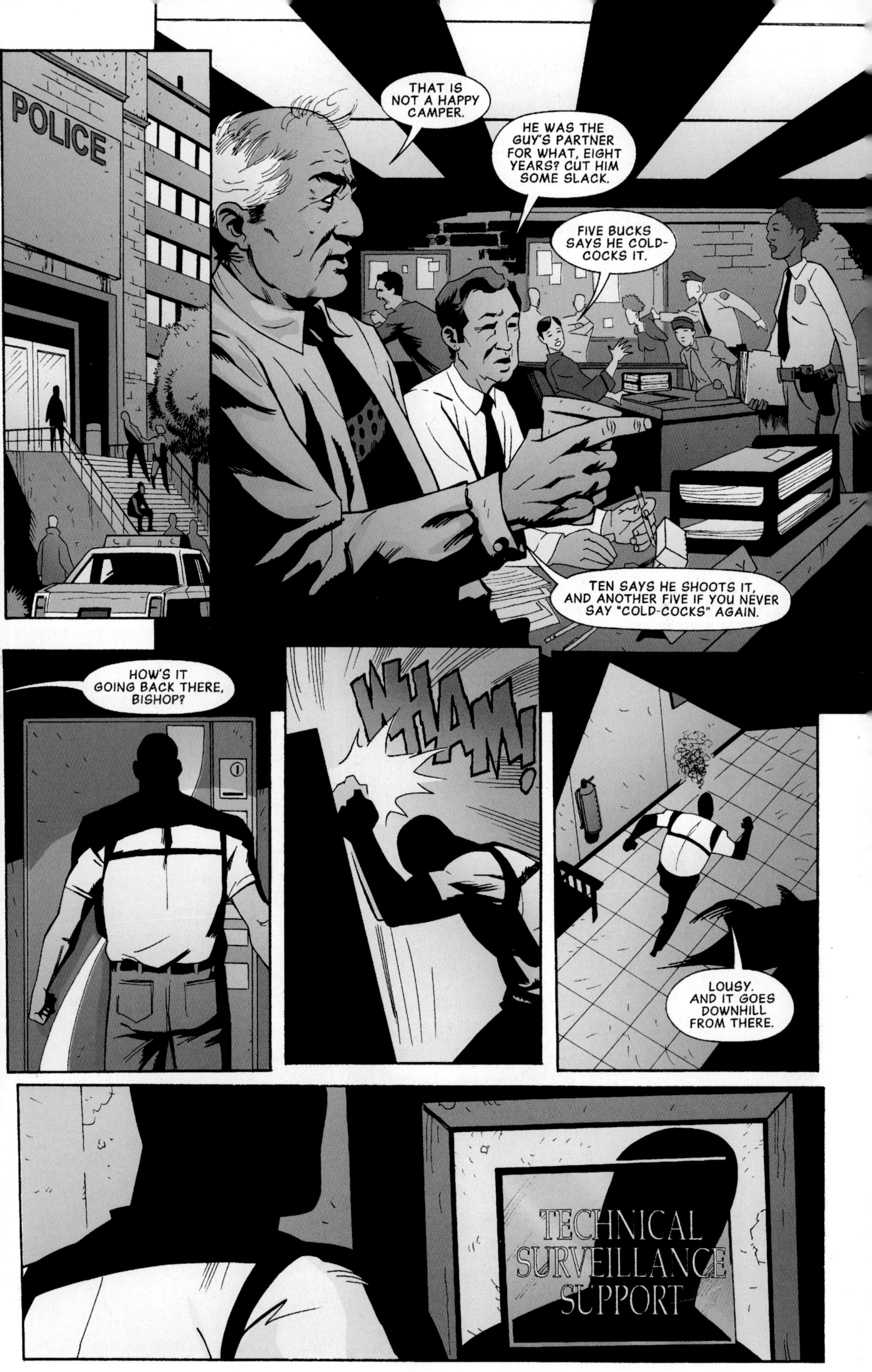
POLICE
THAT IS NOT A HAPPY CAMPER.
HE WAS THE GUY'S PARTNER FOR WHAT, EIGHT YEARS? CUT HIM SOME SLACK.
FIVE BUCKS SAYS HE COLD-COCKS IT.
TEN SAYS HE SHOOTS IT, AND ANOTHER FIVE IF YOU NEVER SAY "COLD-COCKS" AGAIN.
HOW'S IT GOING BACK THERE, BISHOP?
WHAM!
LOUSY. AND IT GOES DOWNHILL FROM THERE.
TECHNICAL SURVEILLANCE SUPPORT

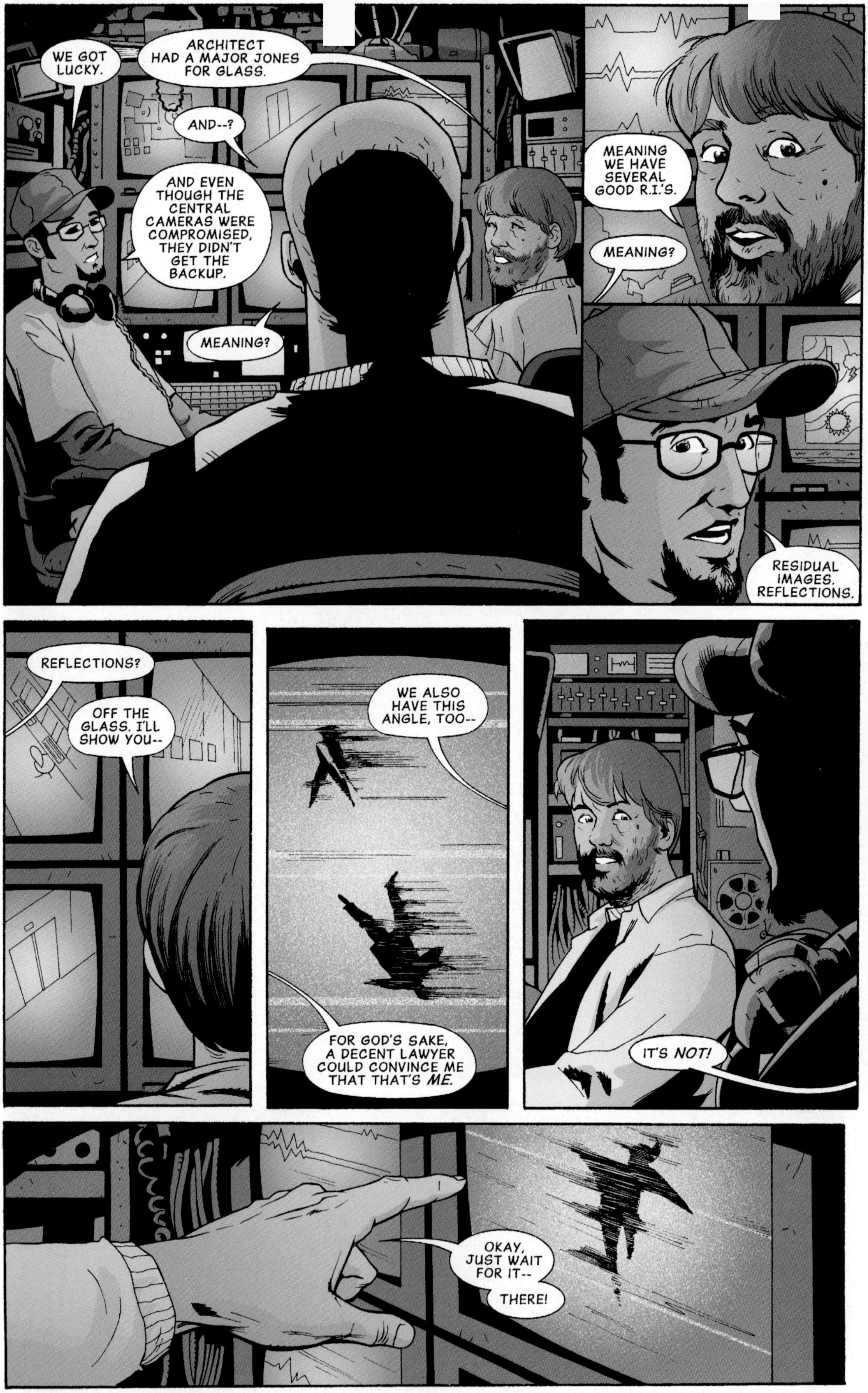
WE GOT LUCKY.
ARCHITECT HAD A MAJOR JONES FOR GLASS.
AND--?
AND EVEN THOUGH THE CENTRAL CAMERAS WERE COMPROMISED, THEY DIDN'T GET THE BACKUP.
MEANING?
MEANING WE HAVE SEVERAL GOOD R.I.'S.
MEANING?
RESIDUAL IMAGES. REFLECTIONS.
REFLECTIONS?
OFF THE GLASS. I'LL SHOW YOU--
WE ALSO HAVE THIS ANGLE, TOO--
FOR GOD'S SAKE, A DECENT LAWYER COULD CONVINCE ME THAT THAT'S *ME*.
IT'S *NOT!*
OKAY, JUST WAIT FOR IT--
THERE!

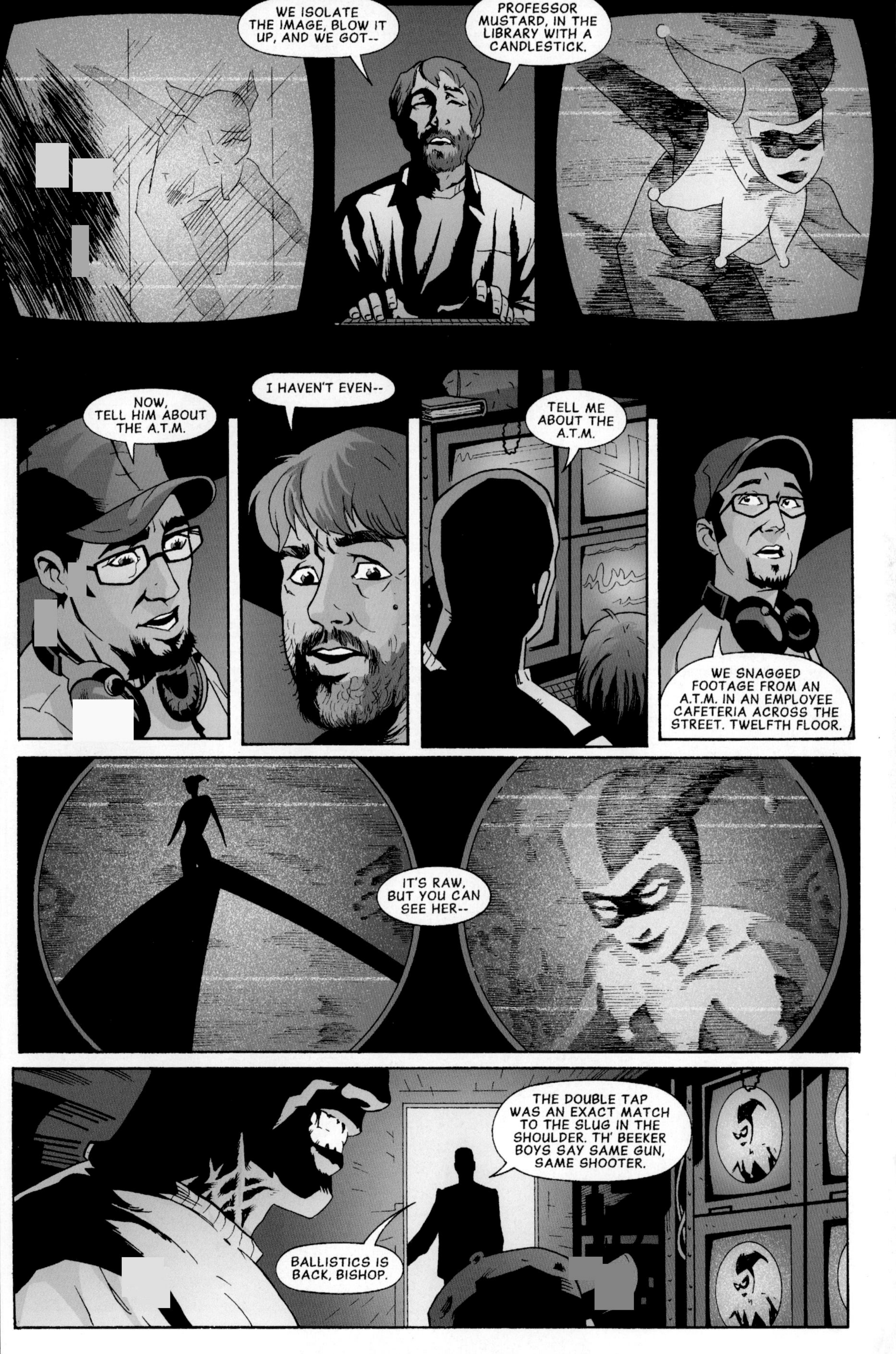
WE ISOLATE THE IMAGE, BLOW IT UP, AND WE GOT--
PROFESSOR MUSTARD, IN THE LIBRARY WITH A CANDLESTICK.
NOW, TELL HIM ABOUT THE A.T.M.
I HAVEN'T EVEN--
TELL ME ABOUT THE A.T.M.
WE SNAGGED FOOTAGE FROM AN A.T.M. IN AN EMPLOYEE CAFETERIA ACROSS THE STREET. TWELFTH FLOOR.
IT'S RAW, BUT YOU CAN SEE HER--
BALLISTICS IS BACK, BISHOP.
THE DOUBLE TAP WAS AN EXACT MATCH TO THE SLUG IN THE SHOULDER. TH' BEEKER BOYS SAY SAME GUN, SAME SHOOTER.

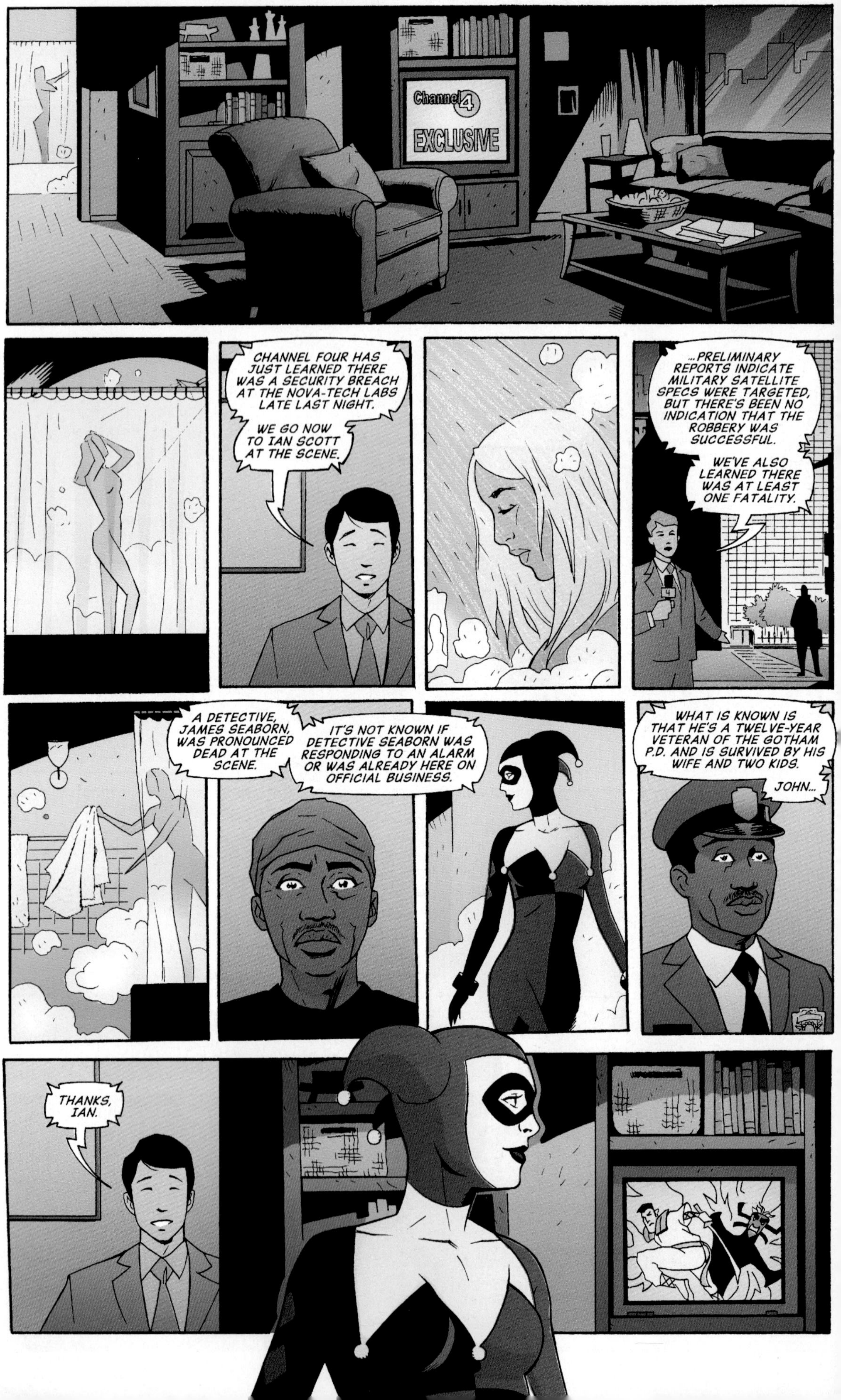
Channel 4
EXCLUSIVE
CHANNEL FOUR HAS JUST LEARNED THERE WAS A SECURITY BREACH AT THE NOVA-TECH LABS LATE LAST NIGHT.
WE GO NOW TO IAN SCOTT AT THE SCENE.
...PRELIMINARY REPORTS INDICATE MILITARY SATELLITE SPECS WERE TARGETED, BUT THERE'S BEEN NO INDICATION THAT THE ROBBERY WAS SUCCESSFUL.
WE'VE ALSO LEARNED THERE WAS AT LEAST ONE FATALITY.
A DETECTIVE, JAMES SEABORN, WAS PRONOUNCED DEAD AT THE SCENE.
IT'S NOT KNOWN IF DETECTIVE SEABORN WAS RESPONDING TO AN ALARM OR WAS ALREADY HERE ON OFFICIAL BUSINESS.
WHAT IS KNOWN IS THAT HE'S A TWELVE-YEAR VETERAN OF THE GOTHAM P.D. AND IS SURVIVED BY HIS WIFE AND TWO KIDS.
JOHN...
THANKS, IAN.

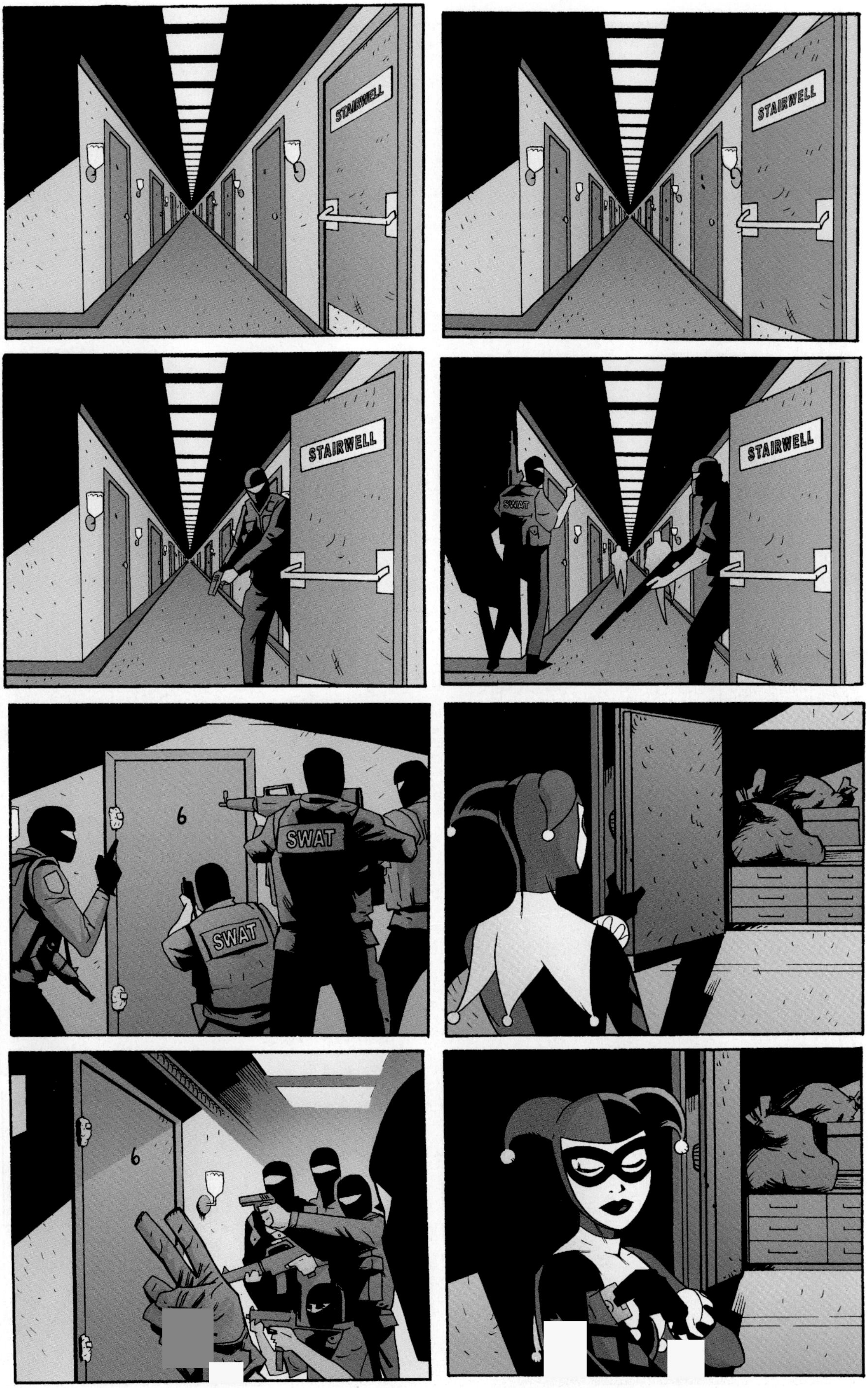
STAIRWELL
STAIRWELL
STAIRWELL
SWAT
STAIRWELL
6
SWAT
SWAT
6

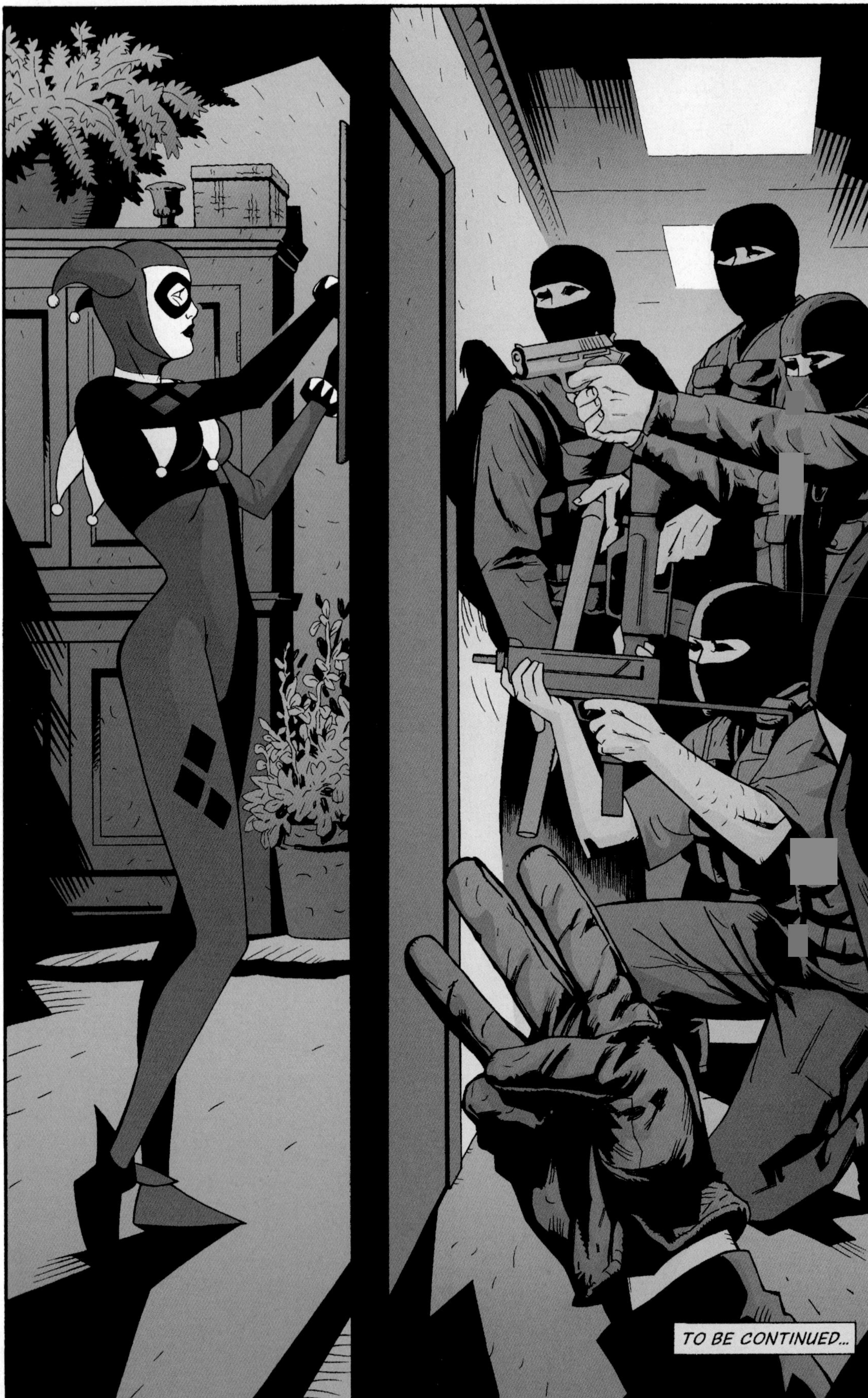
TO BE CONTINUED...

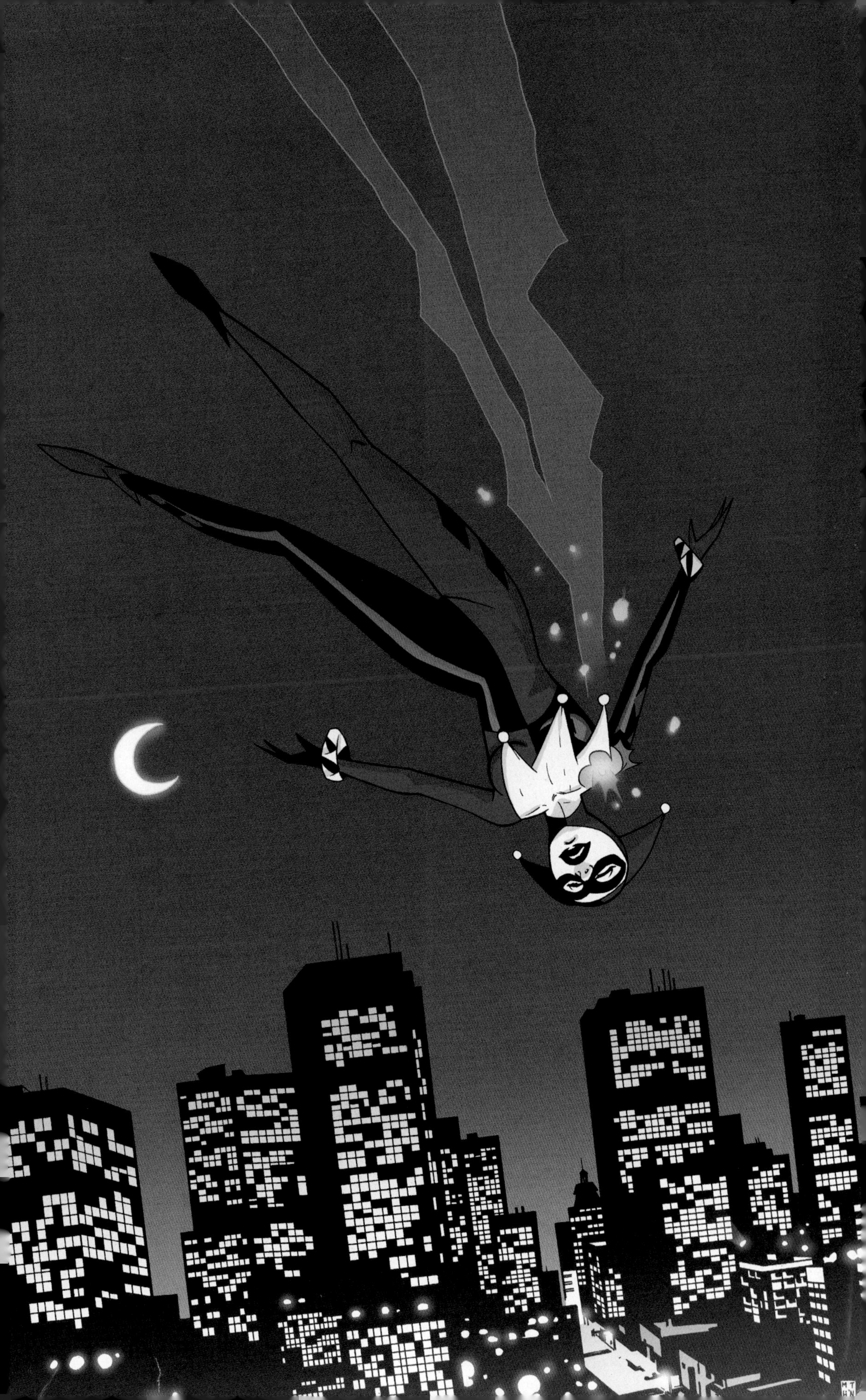

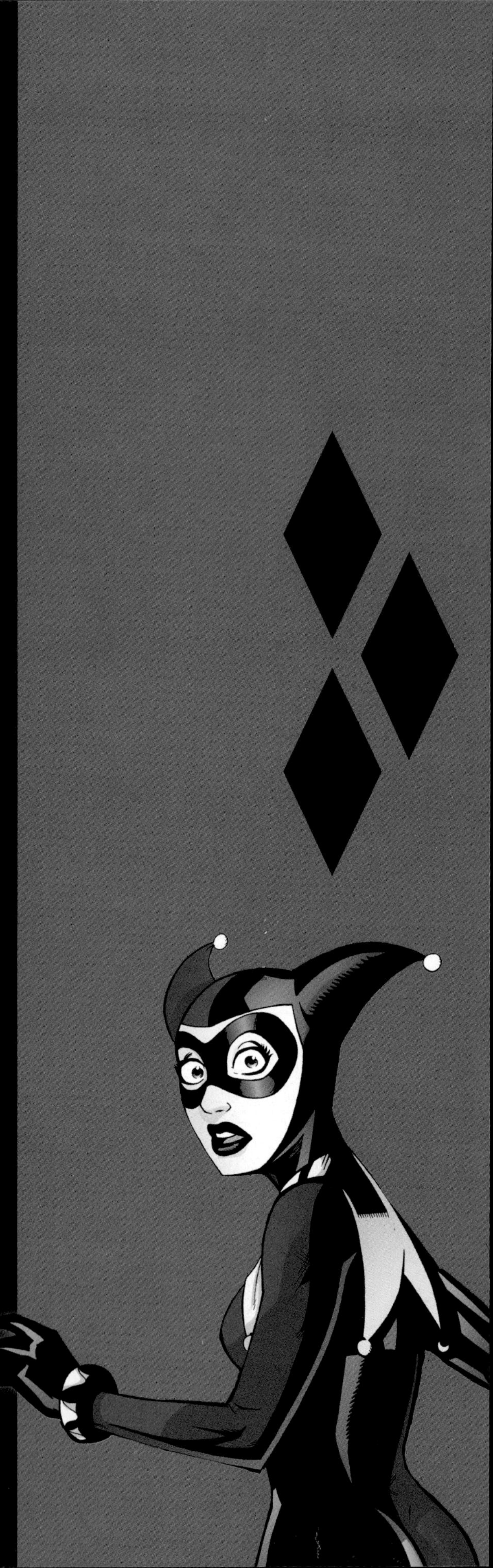

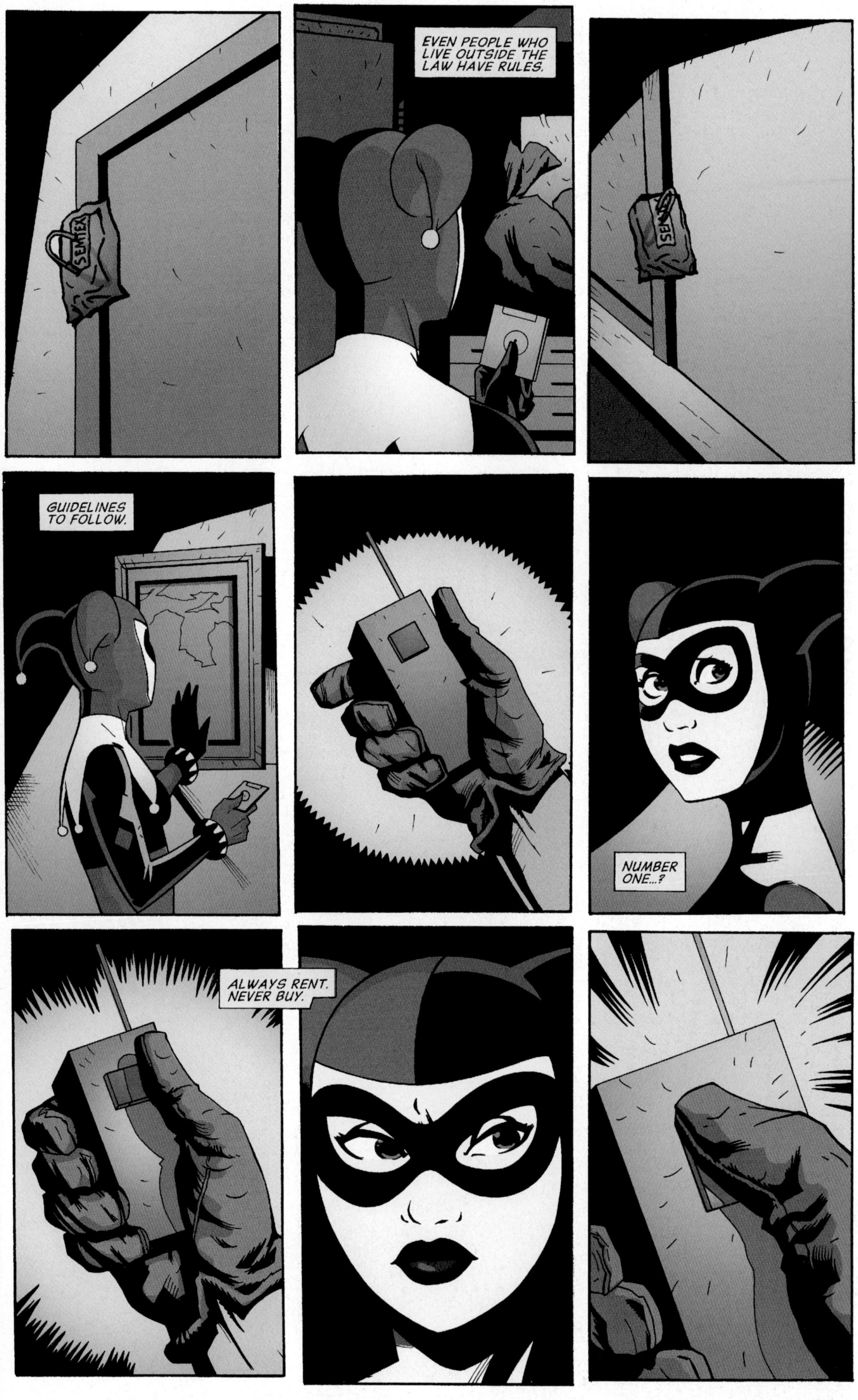
SEMTEX
EVEN PEOPLE WHO LIVE OUTSIDE THE LAW HAVE RULES.
SEMTEX
GUIDELINES TO FOLLOW.
NUMBER ONE...?
ALWAYS RENT. NEVER BUY.

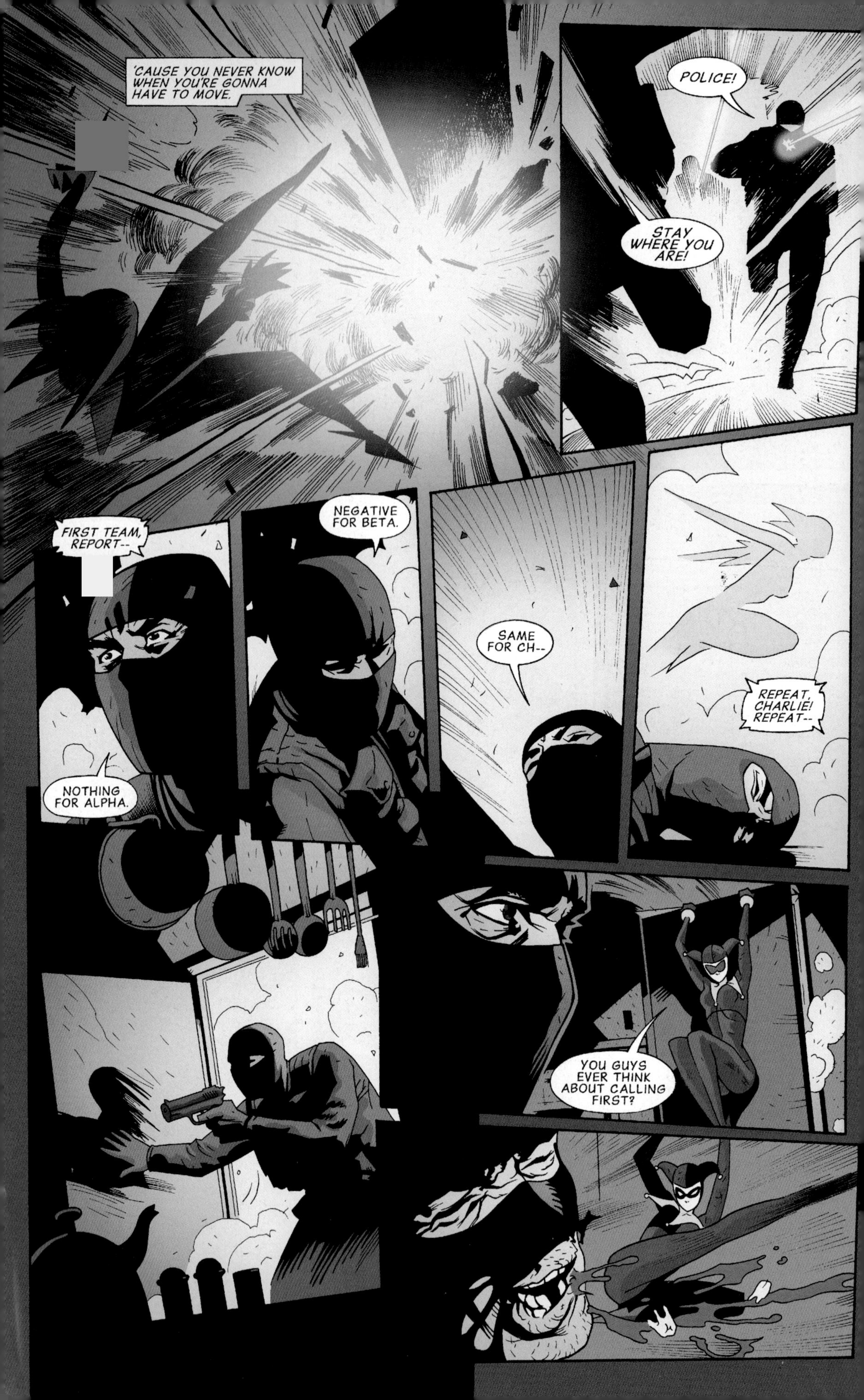
'CAUSE YOU NEVER KNOW WHEN YOU'RE GONNA HAVE TO MOVE.
POLICE!
STAY WHERE YOU ARE!
FIRST TEAM, REPORT--
NOTHING FOR ALPHA.
NEGATIVE FOR BETA.
SAME FOR CH--
REPEAT, CHARLIE! REPEAT--
YOU GUYS EVER THINK ABOUT CALLING FIRST?

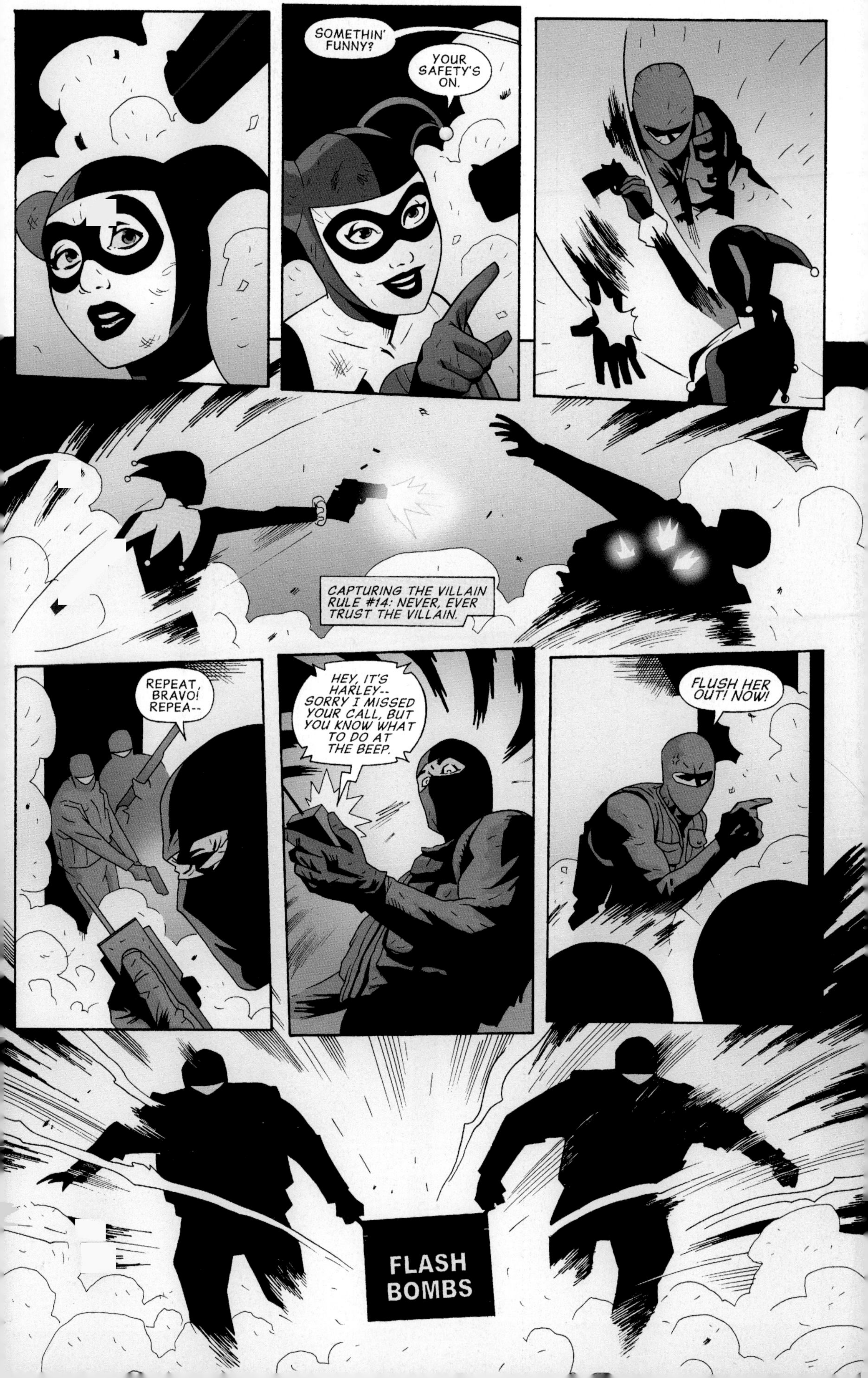
SOMETHIN' FUNNY?
YOUR SAFETY'S ON.
CAPTURING THE VILLAIN RULE #14: NEVER, EVER TRUST THE VILLAIN.
REPEAT, BRAVO! REPEA--
HEY, IT'S HARLEY-- SORRY I MISSED YOUR CALL, BUT YOU KNOW WHAT TO DO AT THE BEEP.
FLUSH HER OUT! NOW!
FLASH BOMBS

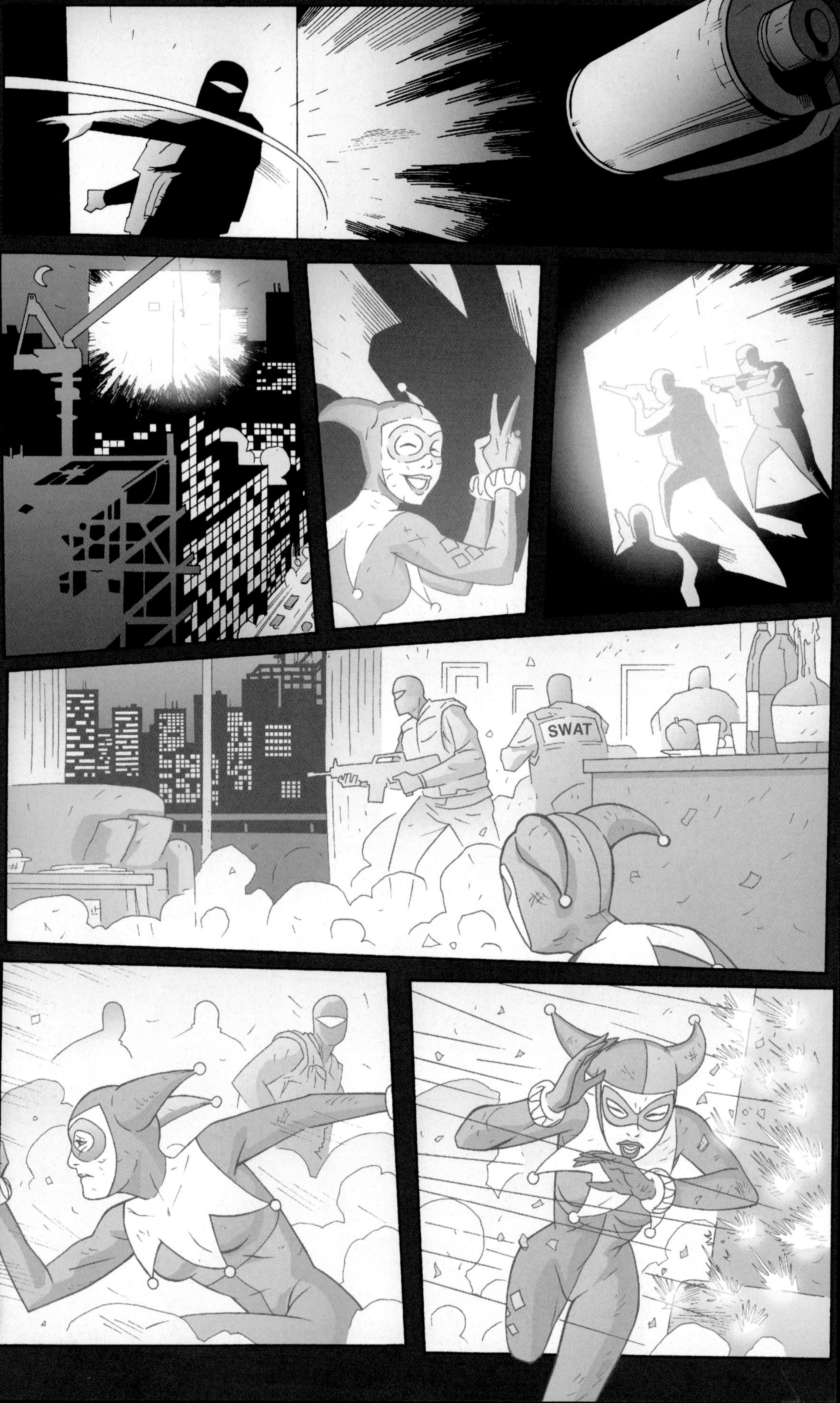
SWAT

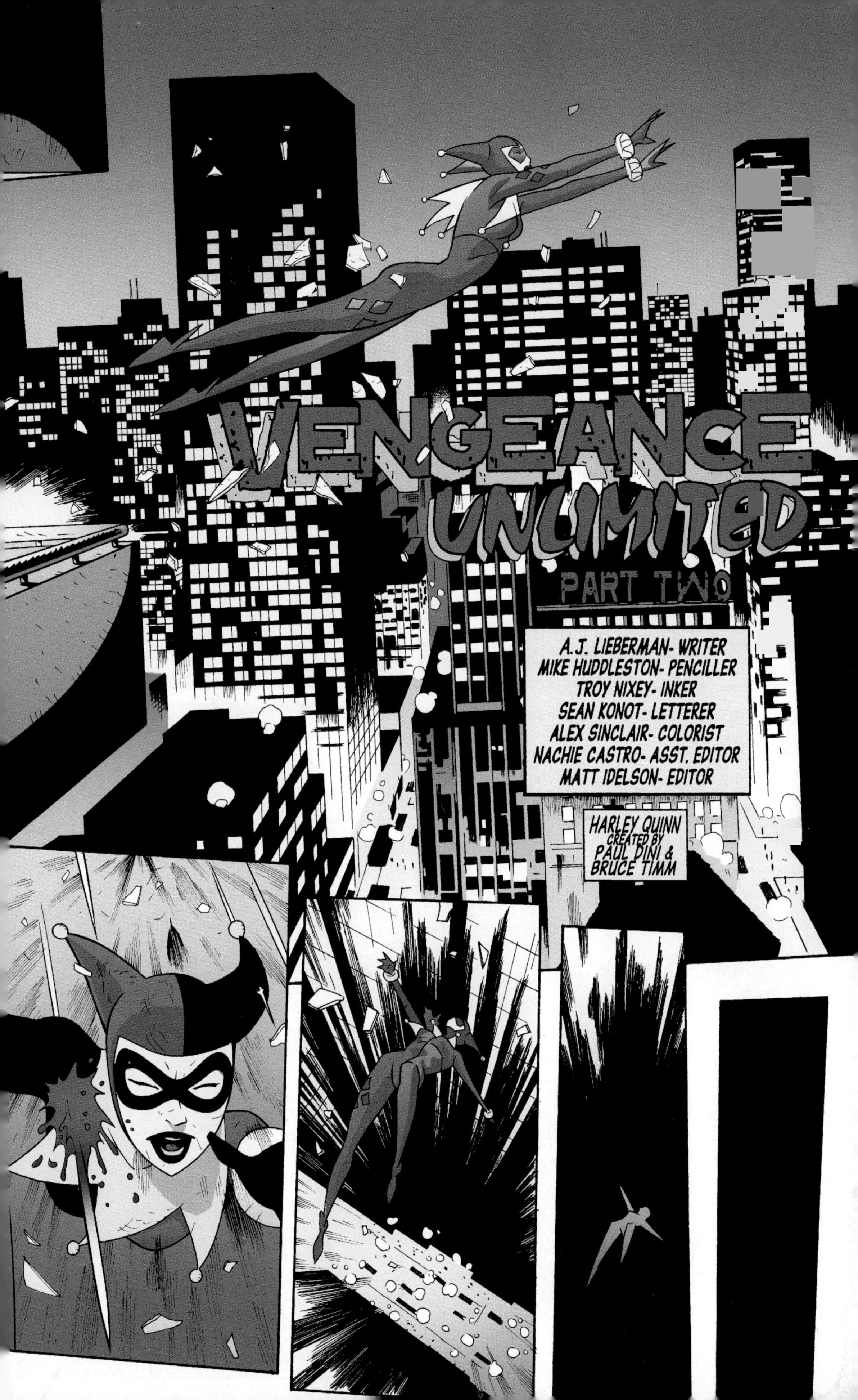
VENGEANCE UNLIMITED
PART TWO
A.J. LIEBERMAN- WRITER
MIKE HUDDLESTON- PENCILLER
TROY NIXEY- INKER
SEAN KONOT- LETTERER
ALEX SINCLAIR- COLORIST
NACHIE CASTRO- ASST. EDITOR
MATT IDELSON- EDITOR
HARLEY QUINN CREATED BY PAUL DINI & BRUCE TIMM

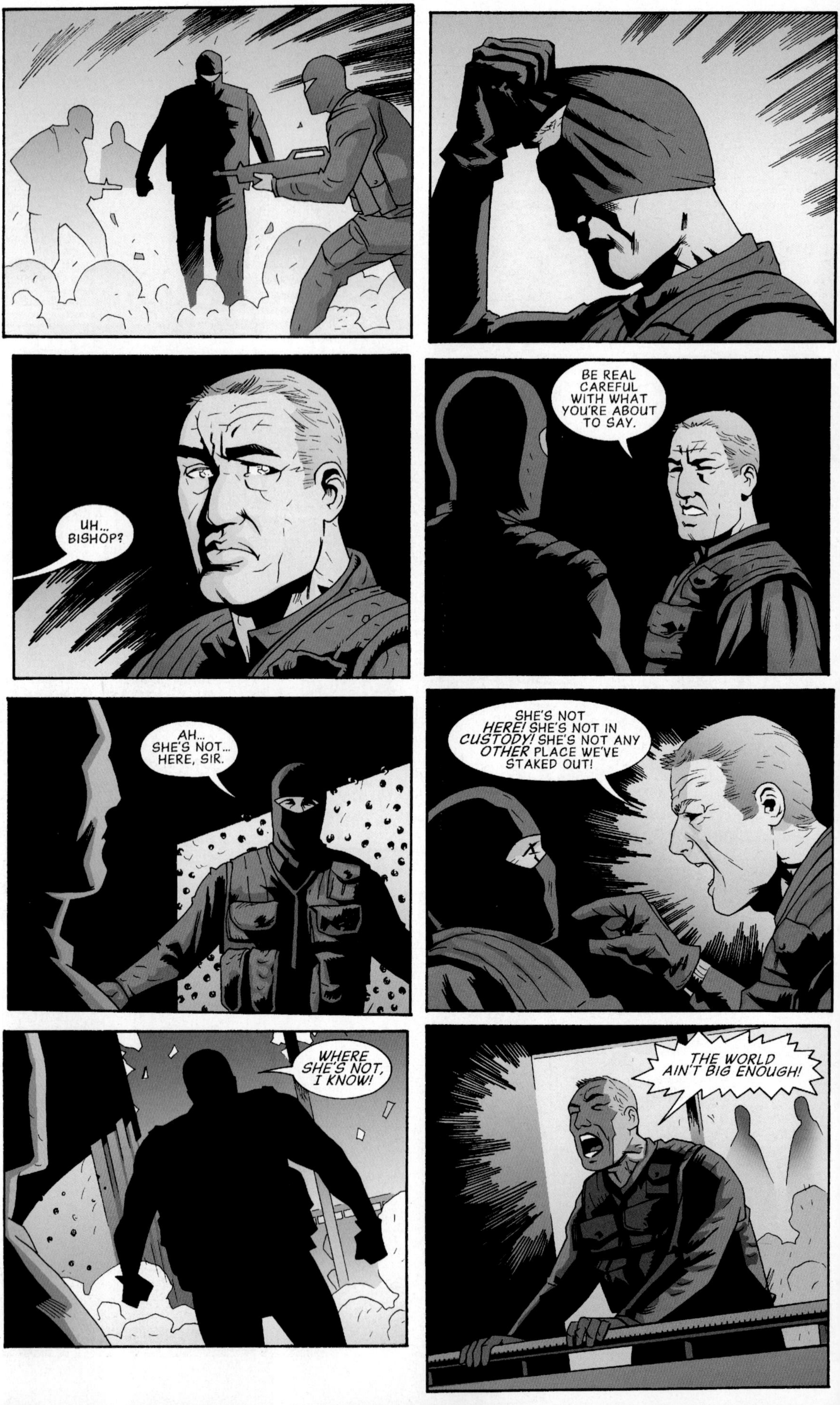
UH... BISHOP?
BE REAL CAREFUL WITH WHAT YOU'RE ABOUT TO SAY.
AH... SHE'S NOT... HERE, SIR.
SHE'S NOT HERE! SHE'S NOT IN CUSTODY! SHE'S NOT ANY OTHER PLACE WE'VE STAKED OUT!
WHERE SHE'S NOT, I KNOW!
THE WORLD AIN'T BIG ENOUGH!

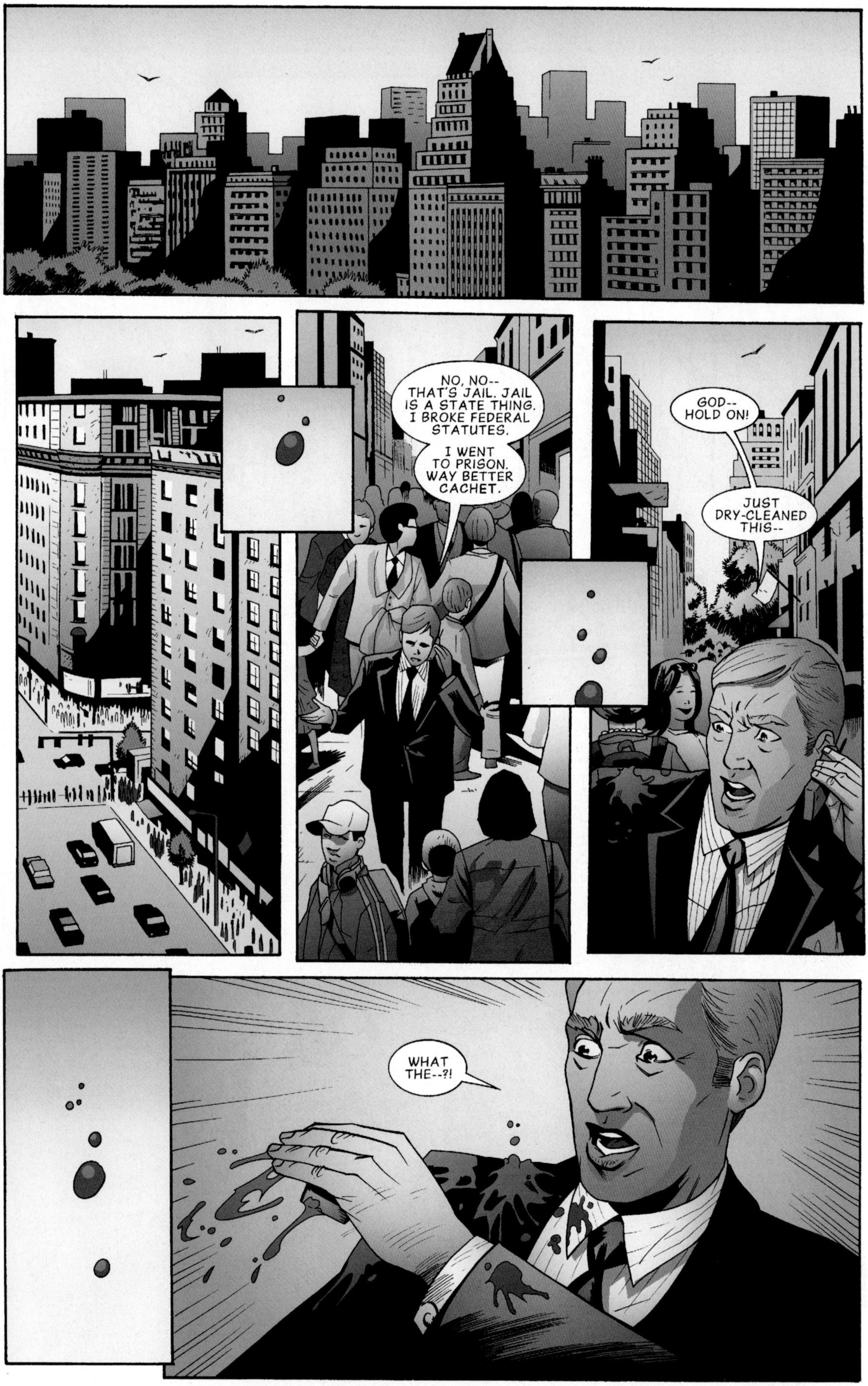

NO, NO-- THAT'S JAIL. JAIL IS A STATE THING. I BROKE FEDERAL STATUTES.
I WENT TO PRISON. WAY BETTER CACHET.
GOD-- HOLD ON!
JUST DRY-CLEANED THIS--
WHAT THE--?!

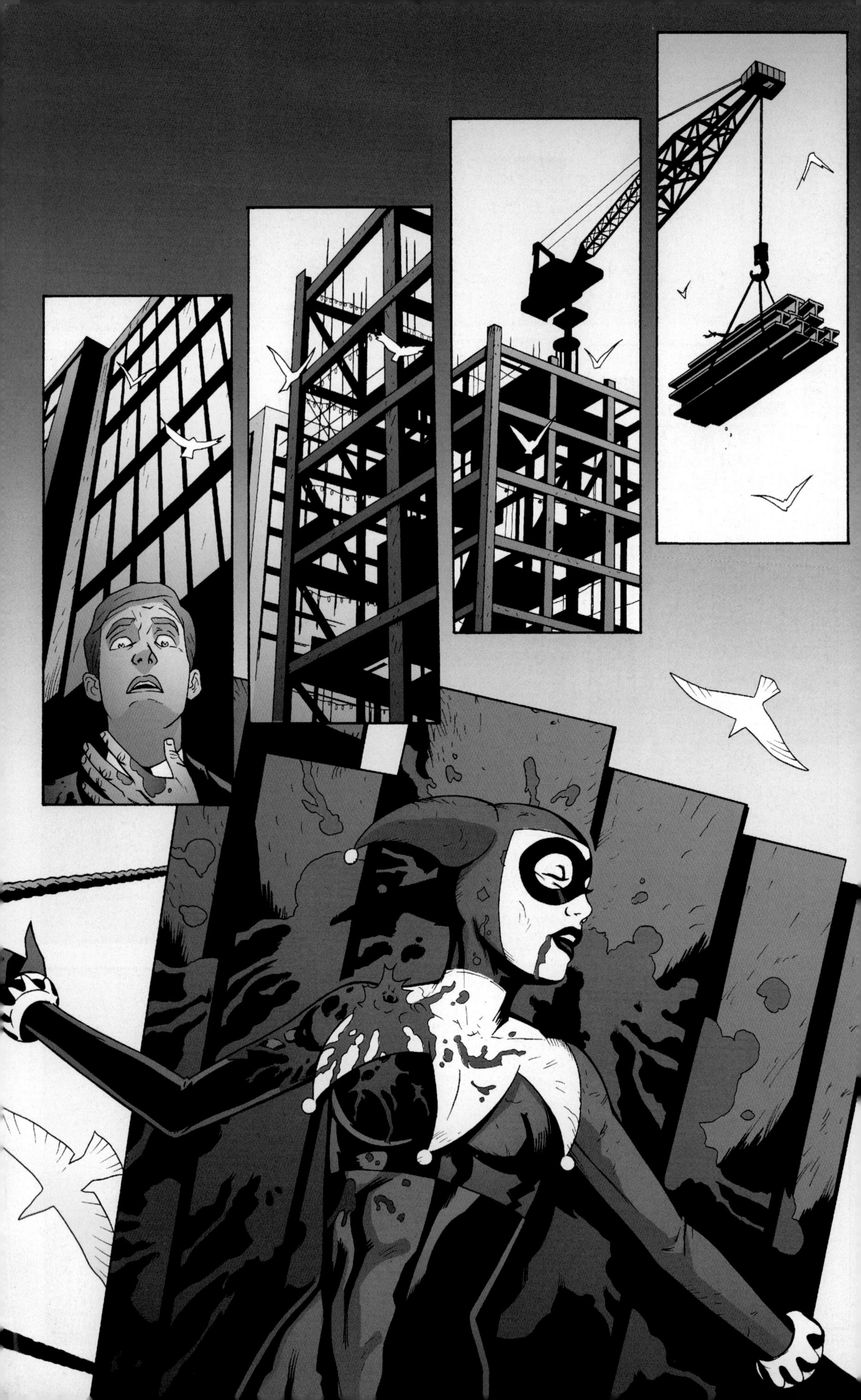

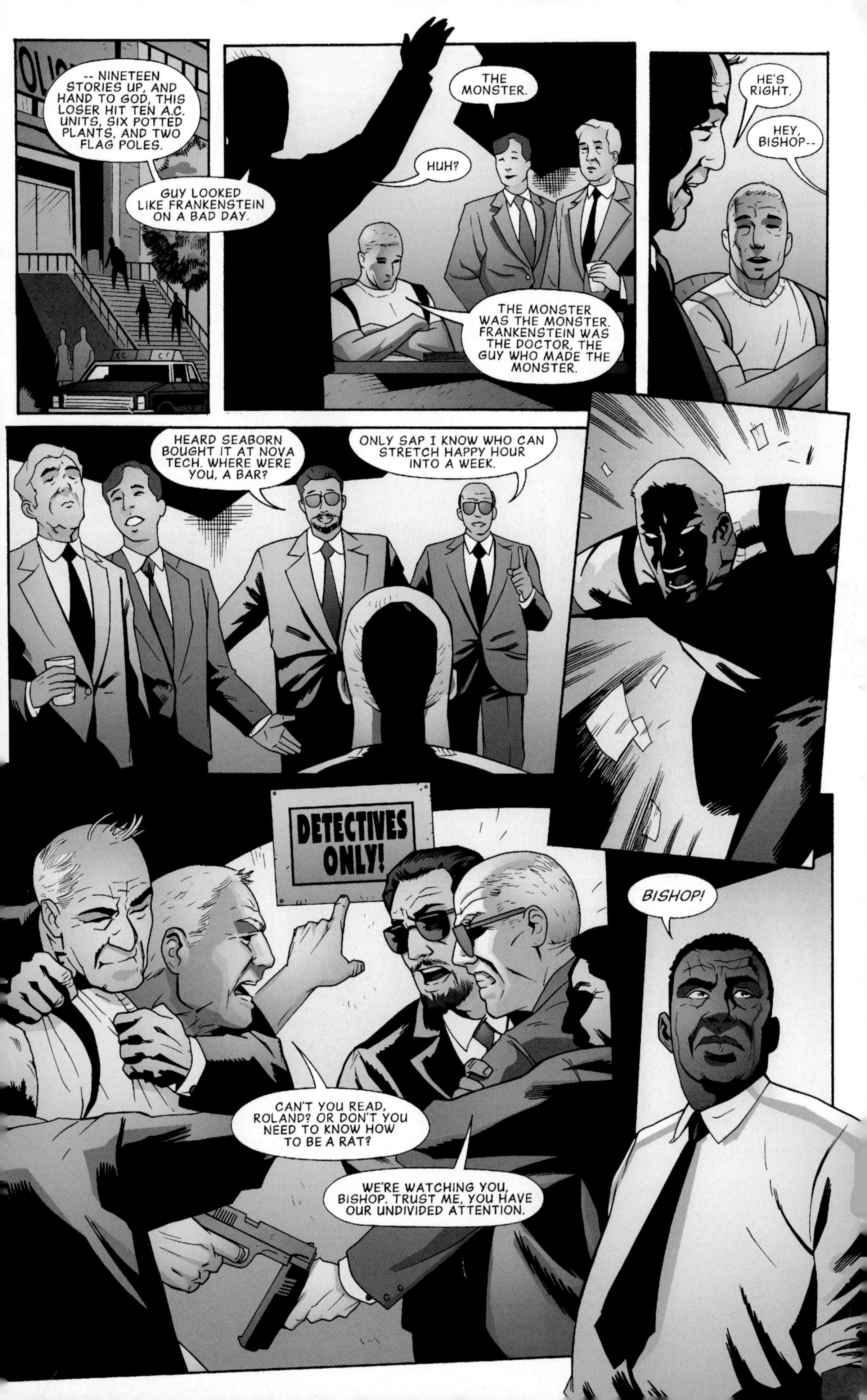
-- NINETEEN STORIES UP, AND HAND TO GOD, THIS LOSER HIT TEN A.C. UNITS, SIX POTTED PLANTS, AND TWO FLAG POLES.
GUY LOOKED LIKE FRANKENSTEIN ON A BAD DAY.
THE MONSTER.
HUH?
THE MONSTER WAS THE MONSTER. FRANKENSTEIN WAS THE DOCTOR, THE GUY WHO MADE THE MONSTER.
HE'S RIGHT.
HEY, BISHOP--
HEARD SEABORN BOUGHT IT AT NOVA TECH. WHERE WERE YOU, A BAR?
ONLY SAP I KNOW WHO CAN STRETCH HAPPY HOUR INTO A WEEK.
DETECTIVES ONLY!
CAN'T YOU READ, ROLAND? OR DON'T YOU NEED TO KNOW HOW TO BE A RAT?
WE'RE WATCHING YOU, BISHOP. TRUST ME, YOU HAVE OUR UNDIVIDED ATTENTION.
BISHOP!

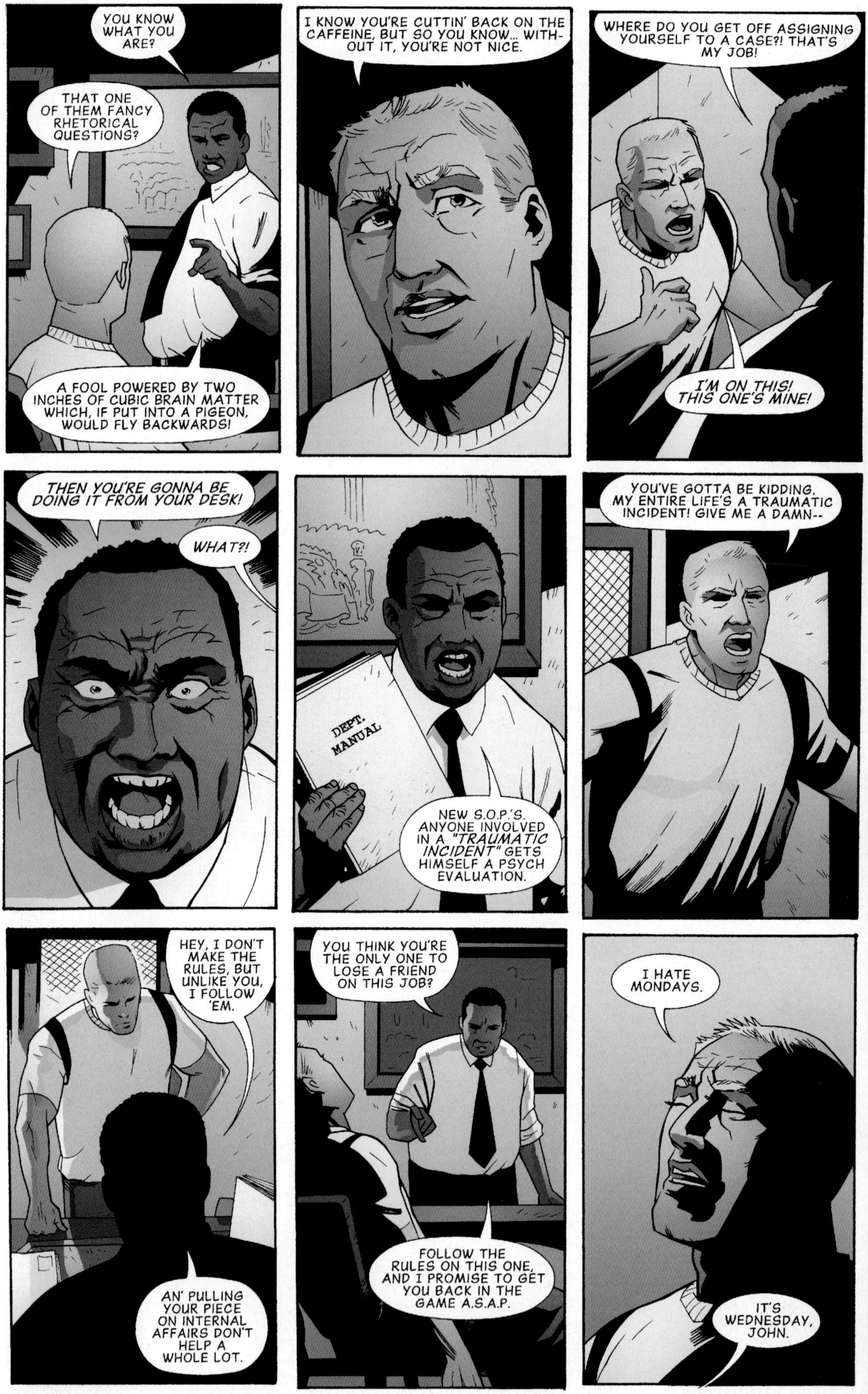
YOU KNOW WHAT YOU ARE?
THAT ONE OF THEM FANCY RHETORICAL QUESTIONS?
A FOOL POWERED BY TWO INCHES OF CUBIC BRAIN MATTER WHICH, IF PUT INTO A PIGEON, WOULD FLY BACKWARDS!
I KNOW YOU'RE CUTTIN' BACK ON THE CAFFEINE, BUT SO YOU KNOW... WITHOUT IT, YOU'RE NOT NICE.
WHERE DO YOU GET OFF ASSIGNING YOURSELF TO A CASE?! THAT'S MY JOB!
I'M ON THIS! THIS ONE'S MINE!
THEN YOU'RE GONNA BE DOING IT FROM YOUR DESK!
WHAT?!
DEPT. MANUAL
NEW S.O.P.'S. ANYONE INVOLVED IN A "TRAUMATIC INCIDENT" GETS HIMSELF A PSYCH EVALUATION.
YOU'VE GOTTA BE KIDDING. MY ENTIRE LIFE'S A TRAUMATIC INCIDENT! GIVE ME A DAMN--
HEY, I DON'T MAKE THE RULES, BUT UNLIKE YOU, I FOLLOW 'EM.
AN' PULLING YOUR PIECE ON INTERNAL AFFAIRS DON'T HELP A WHOLE LOT.
YOU THINK YOU'RE THE ONLY ONE TO LOSE A FRIEND ON THIS JOB?
FOLLOW THE RULES ON THIS ONE, AND I PROMISE TO GET YOU BACK IN THE GAME A.S.A.P.
I HATE MONDAYS.
IT'S WEDNESDAY, JOHN.

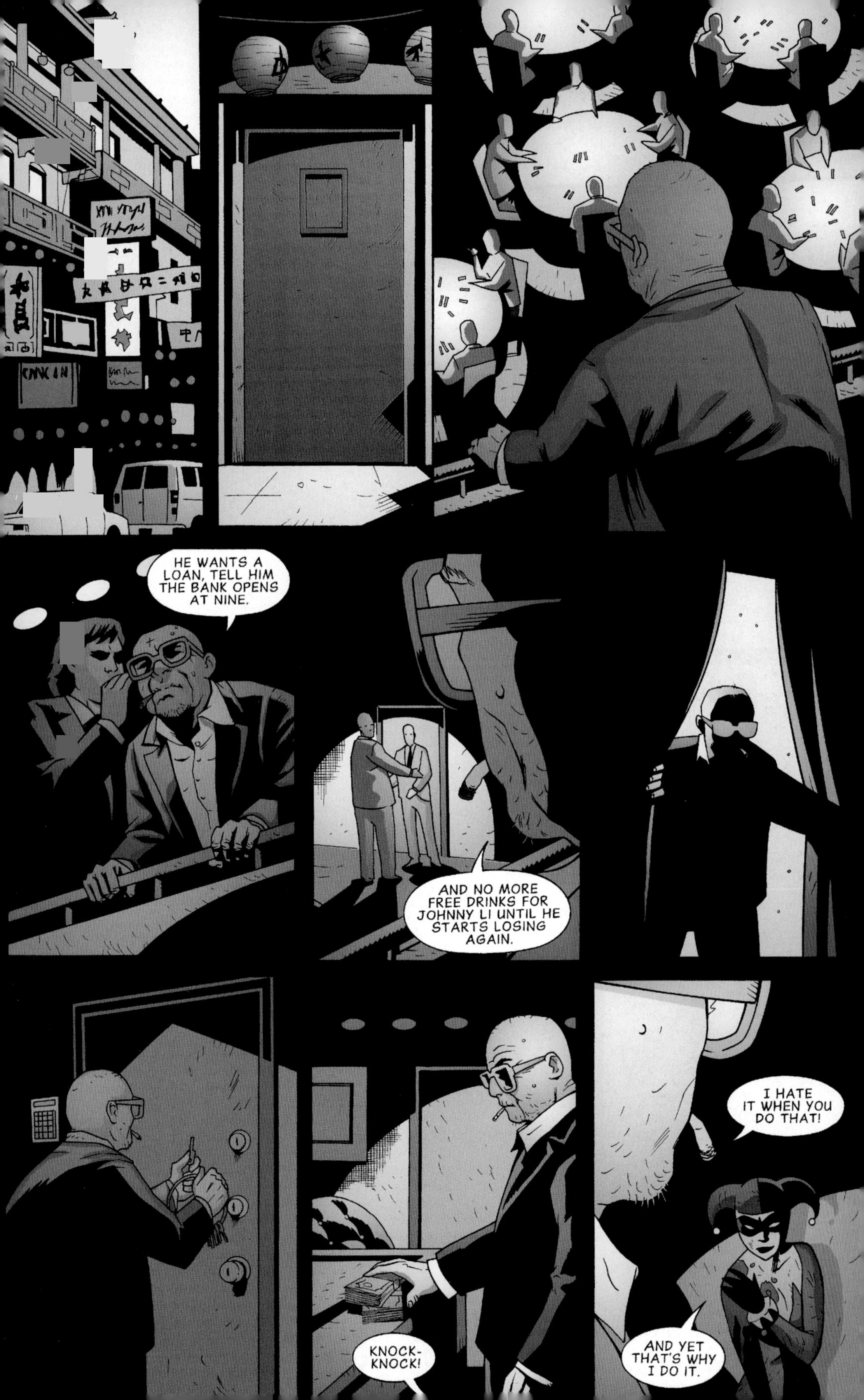
HE WANTS A LOAN, TELL HIM THE BANK OPENS AT NINE.
AND NO MORE FREE DRINKS FOR JOHNNY LI UNTIL HE STARTS LOSING AGAIN.
KNOCK-KNOCK!
I HATE IT WHEN YOU DO THAT!
AND YET THAT'S WHY I DO IT.

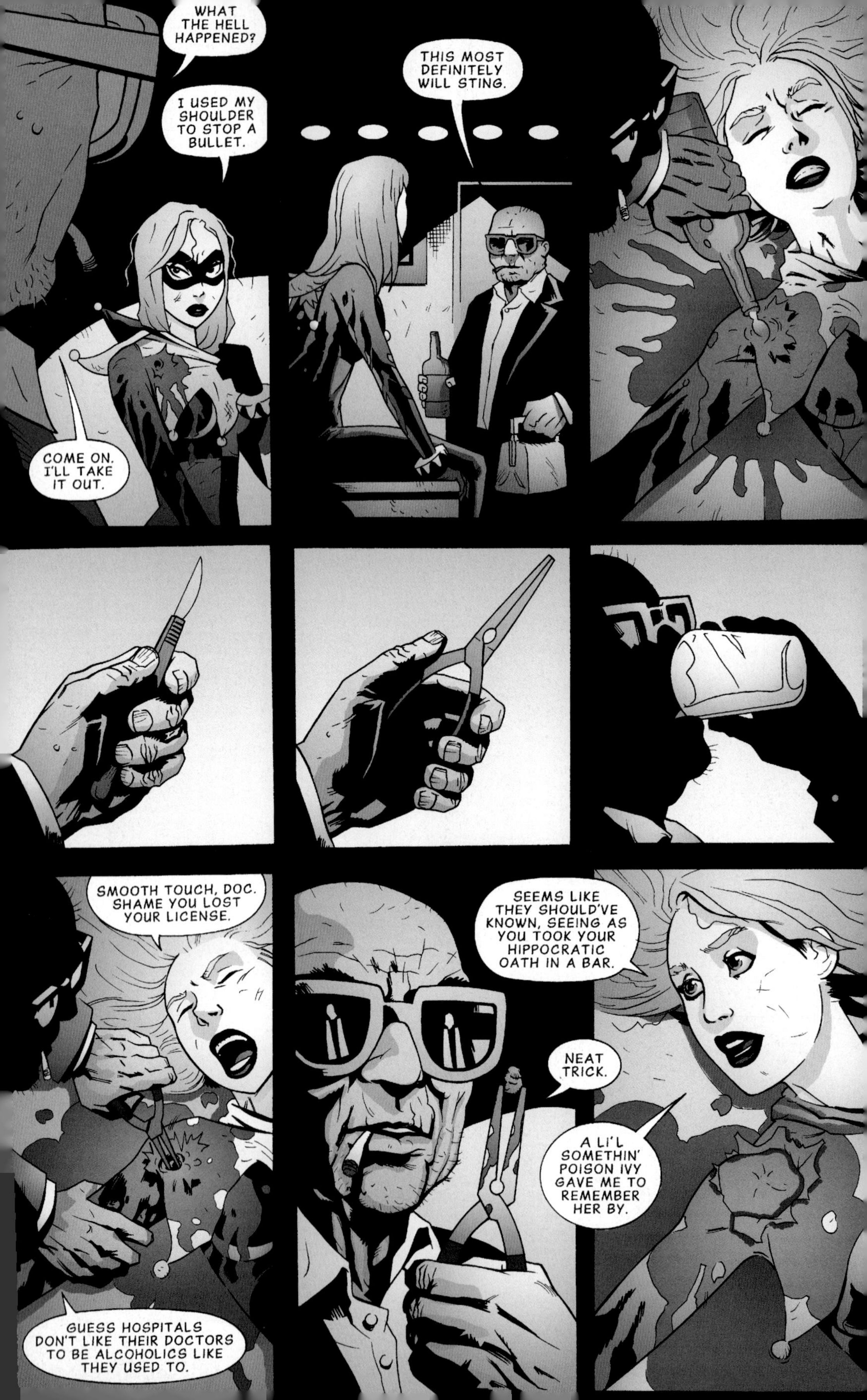
WHAT THE HELL HAPPENED?
I USED MY SHOULDER TO STOP A BULLET.
COME ON. I'LL TAKE IT OUT.
THIS MOST DEFINITELY WILL STING.
SMOOTH TOUCH, DOC. SHAME YOU LOST YOUR LICENSE.
GUESS HOSPITALS DON'T LIKE THEIR DOCTORS TO BE ALCOHOLICS LIKE THEY USED TO.
SEEMS LIKE THEY SHOULD'VE KNOWN, SEEING AS YOU TOOK YOUR HIPPOCRATIC OATH IN A BAR.
NEAT TRICK.
A LI'L SOMETHIN' POISON IVY GAVE ME TO REMEMBER HER BY.

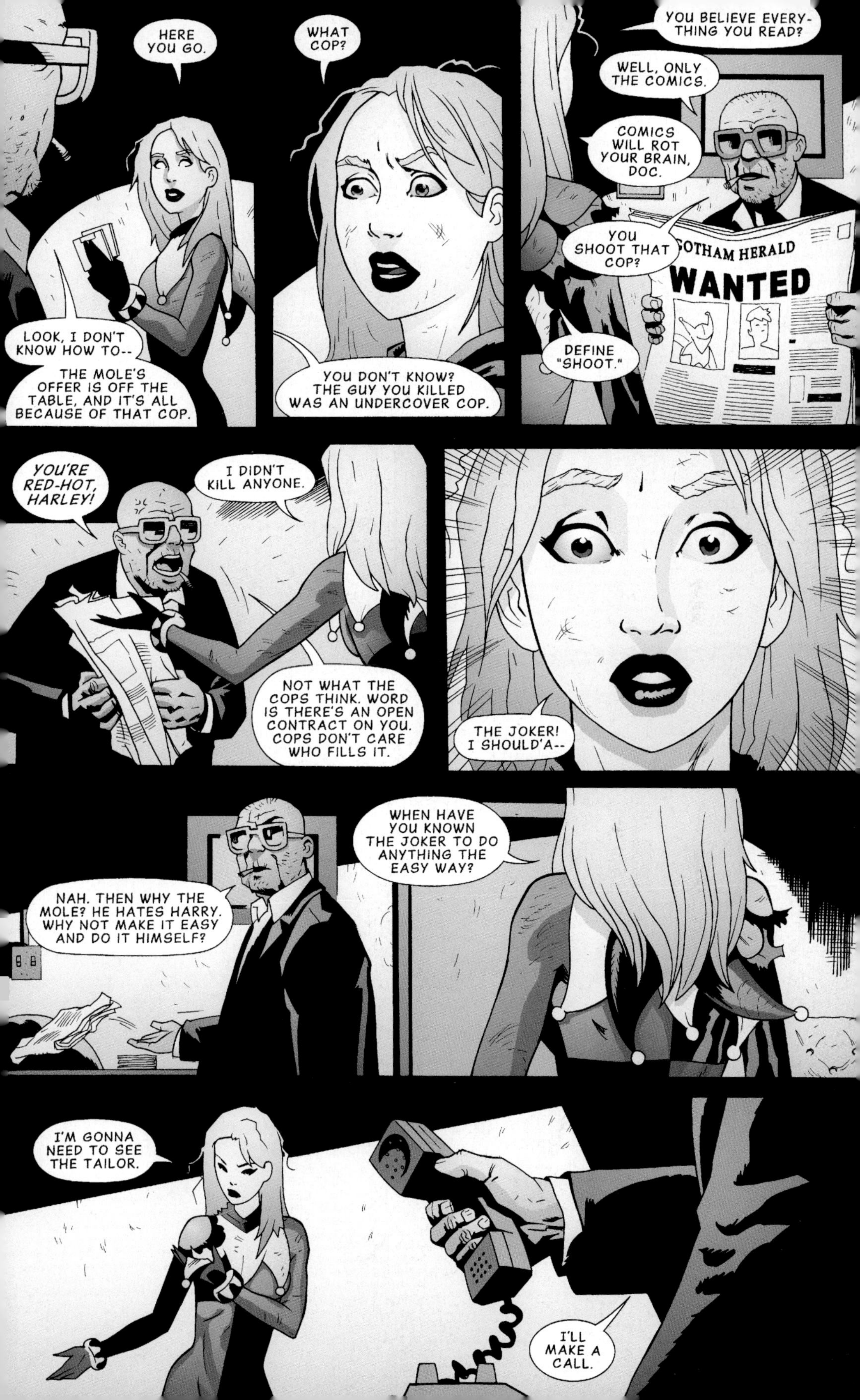
HERE YOU GO.
LOOK, I DON'T KNOW HOW TO--
THE MOLE'S OFFER IS OFF THE TABLE, AND IT'S ALL BECAUSE OF THAT COP.
WHAT COP?
YOU DON'T KNOW? THE GUY YOU KILLED WAS AN UNDERCOVER COP.
YOU BELIEVE EVERY-THING YOU READ?
WELL, ONLY THE COMICS.
COMICS WILL ROT YOUR BRAIN, DOC.
YOU SHOOT THAT COP?
GOTHAM HERALD
WANTED
DEFINE "SHOOT."
YOU'RE RED-HOT, HARLEY!
I DIDN'T KILL ANYONE.
NOT WHAT THE COPS THINK. WORD IS THERE'S AN OPEN CONTRACT ON YOU. COPS DON'T CARE WHO FILLS IT.
THE JOKER! I SHOULD'A--
WHEN HAVE YOU KNOWN THE JOKER TO DO ANYTHING THE EASY WAY?
NAH. THEN WHY THE MOLE? HE HATES HARRY. WHY NOT MAKE IT EASY AND DO IT HIMSELF?
I'M GONNA NEED TO SEE THE TAILOR.
I'LL MAKE A CALL.

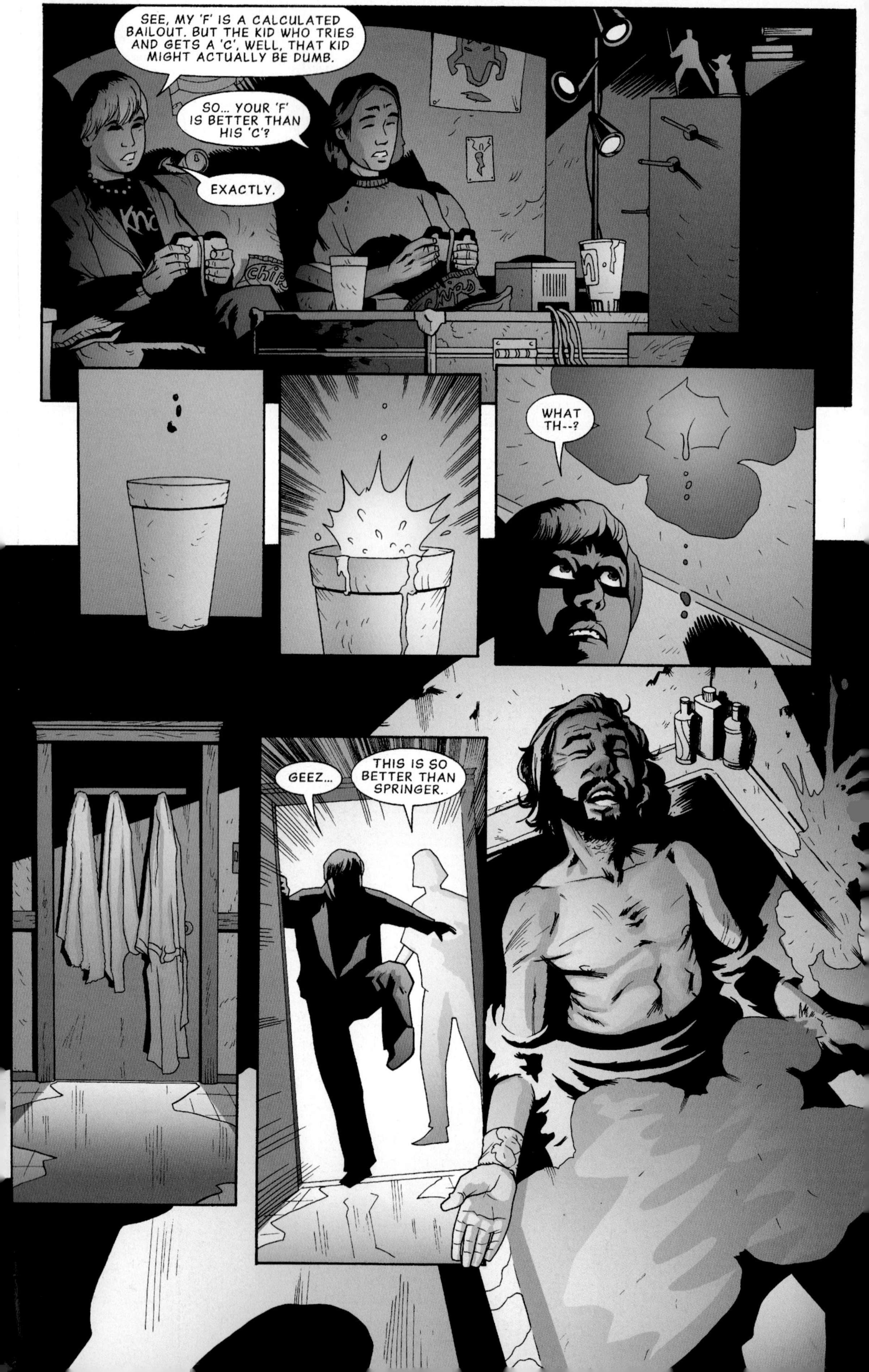
SEE, MY 'F' IS A CALCULATED BAILOUT. BUT THE KID WHO TRIES AND GETS A 'C', WELL, THAT KID MIGHT ACTUALLY BE DUMB.
SO... YOUR 'F' IS BETTER THAN HIS 'C'?
EXACTLY.
WHAT TH--?
GEEZ...
THIS IS SO BETTER THAN SPRINGER.

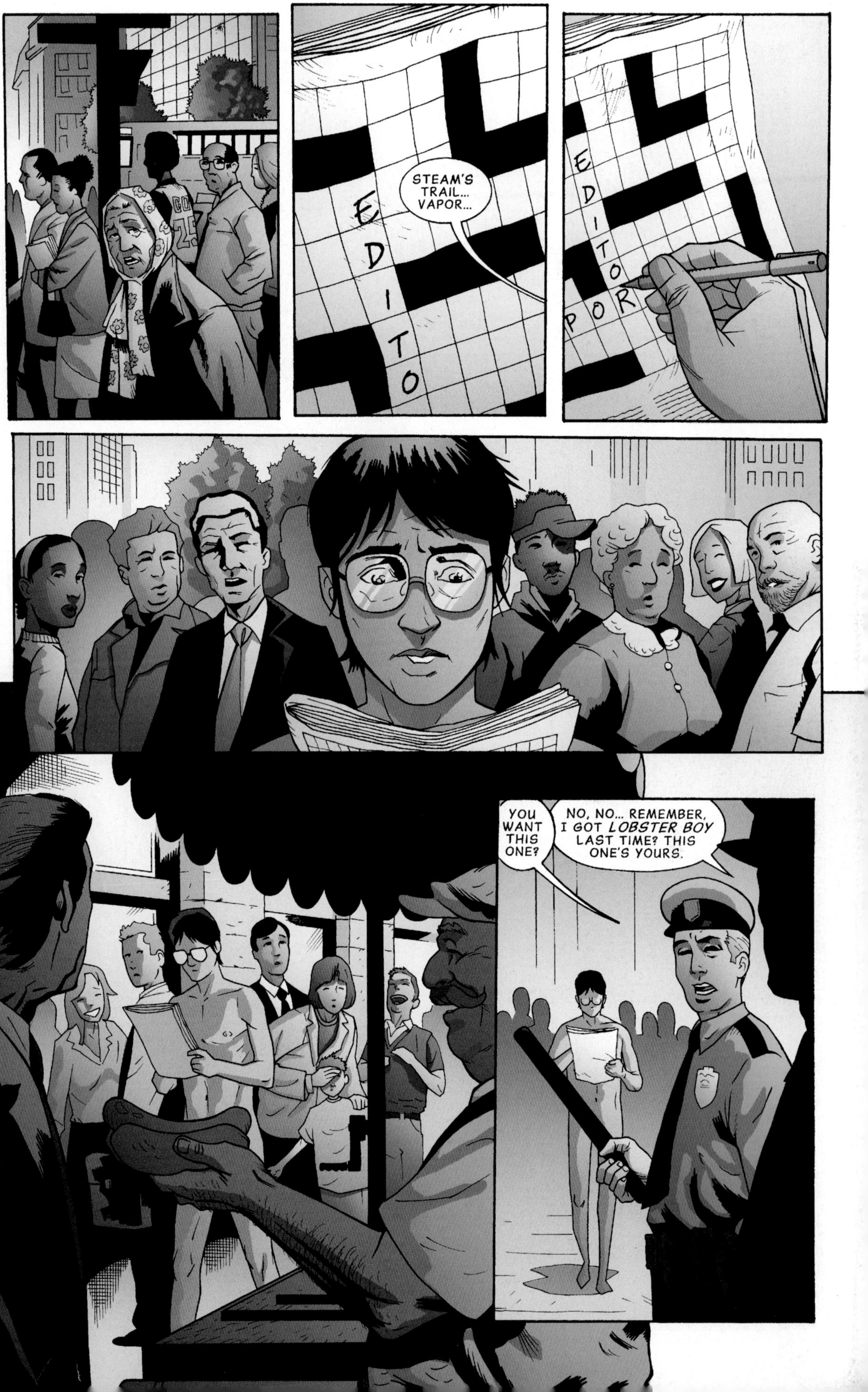
STEAM'S TRAIL... VAPOR...
YOU WANT THIS ONE?
NO, NO... REMEMBER, I GOT *LOBSTER BOY* LAST TIME? THIS ONE'S YOURS.

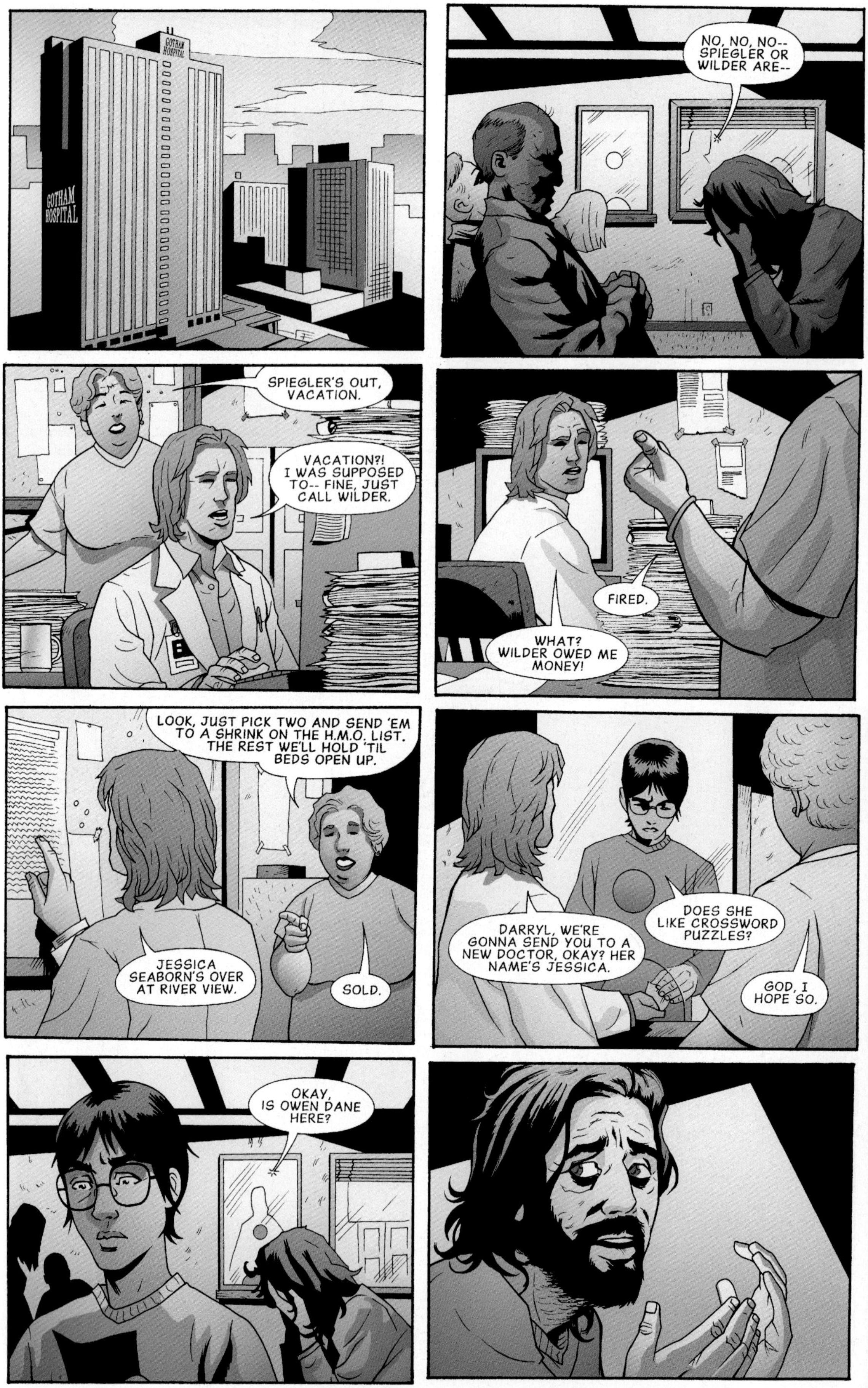
GOTHAM HOSPITAL
GOTHAM HOSPITAL
NO, NO, NO-- SPIEGLER OR WILDER ARE--
SPIEGLER'S OUT, VACATION.
VACATION?! I WAS SUPPOSED TO-- FINE, JUST CALL WILDER.
FIRED.
WHAT? WILDER OWED ME MONEY!
LOOK, JUST PICK TWO AND SEND 'EM TO A SHRINK ON THE H.M.O. LIST. THE REST WE'LL HOLD 'TIL BEDS OPEN UP.
JESSICA SEABORN'S OVER AT RIVER VIEW.
SOLD.
DARRYL, WE'RE GONNA SEND YOU TO A NEW DOCTOR, OKAY? HER NAME'S JESSICA.
DOES SHE LIKE CROSSWORD PUZZLES?
GOD, I HOPE SO.
OKAY, IS OWEN DANE HERE?

"DOCTOR SEABORN...?"

DOCTOR SEABORN, YOUR TEN O'CLOCK IS HERE.

SEND HIM IN.

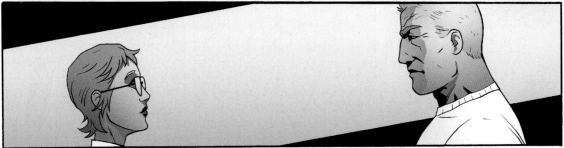

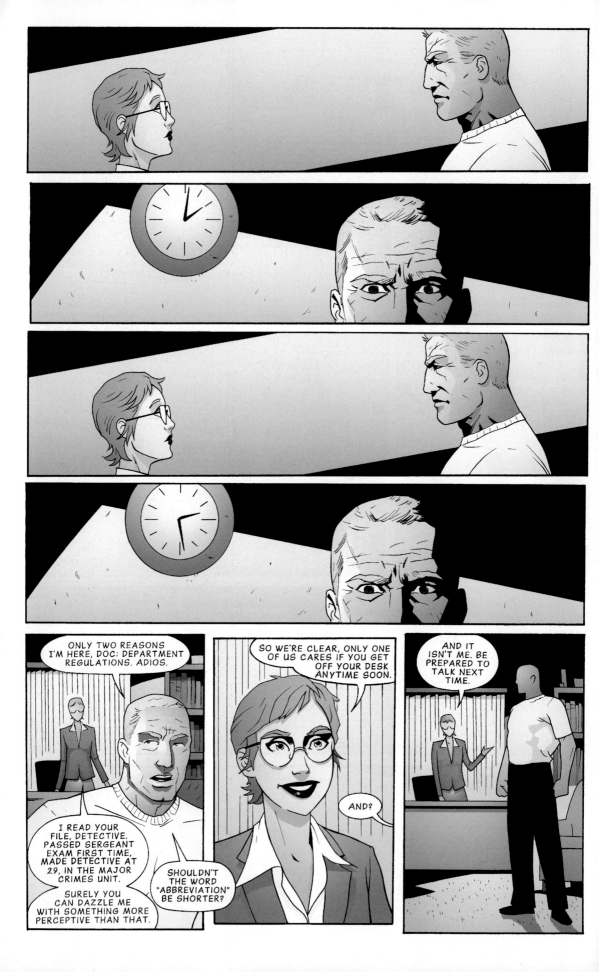

ONLY TWO REASONS I'M HERE, DOC: DEPARTMENT REGULATIONS. ADIOS.

SO WE'RE CLEAR, ONLY ONE OF US CARES IF YOU GET OFF YOUR DESK ANYTIME SOON.

AND IT ISN'T ME. BE PREPARED TO TALK NEXT TIME.

AND?

I READ YOUR FILE, DETECTIVE. PASSED SERGEANT EXAM FIRST TIME, MADE DETECTIVE AT 29, IN THE MAJOR CRIMES UNIT.

SURELY YOU CAN DAZZLE ME WITH SOMETHING MORE PERCEPTIVE THAN THAT.

SHOULDN'T THE WORD "ABBREVIATION" BE SHORTER?

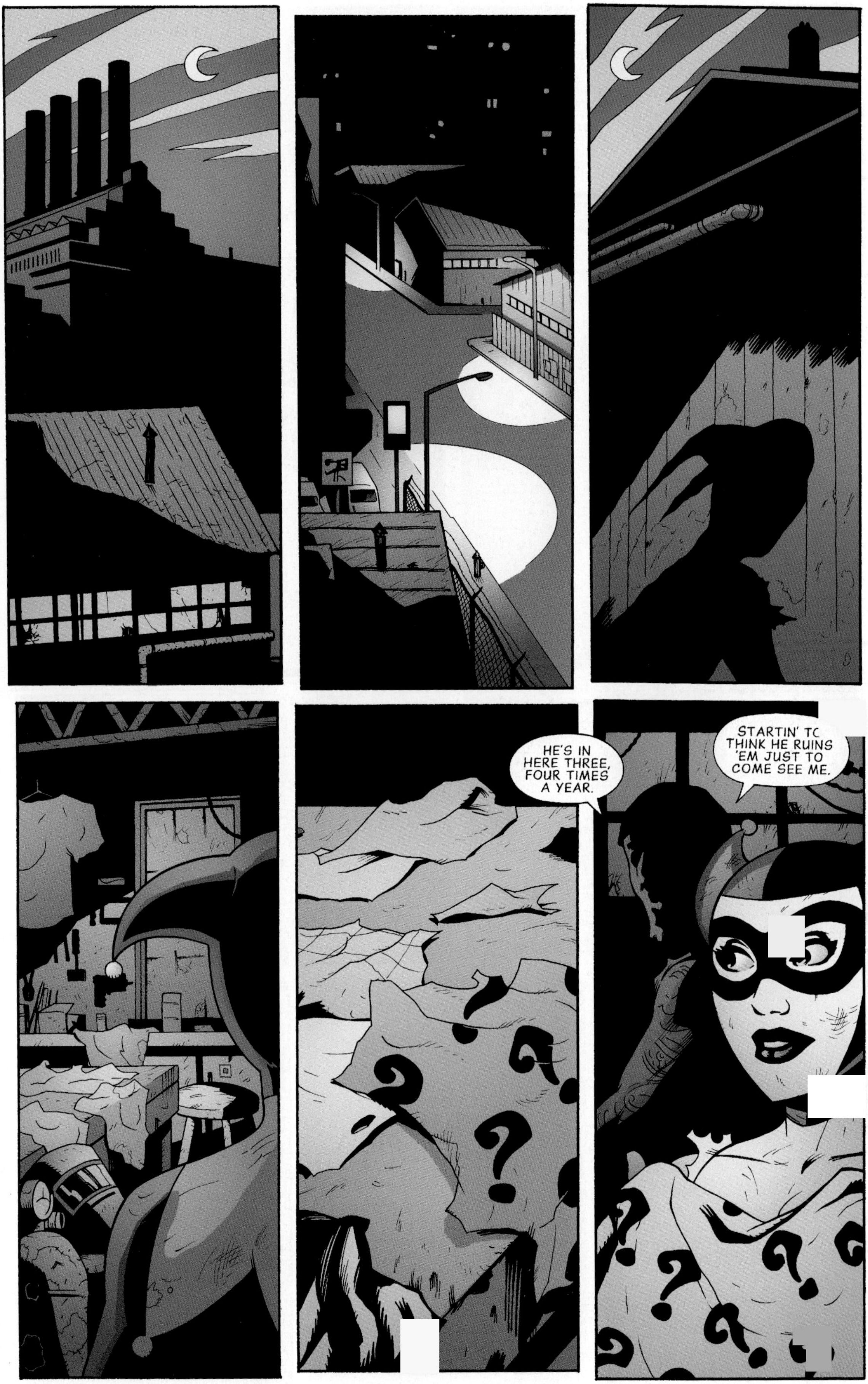
HE'S IN HERE THREE, FOUR TIMES A YEAR.
STARTIN' TO THINK HE RUINS 'EM JUST TO COME SEE ME.

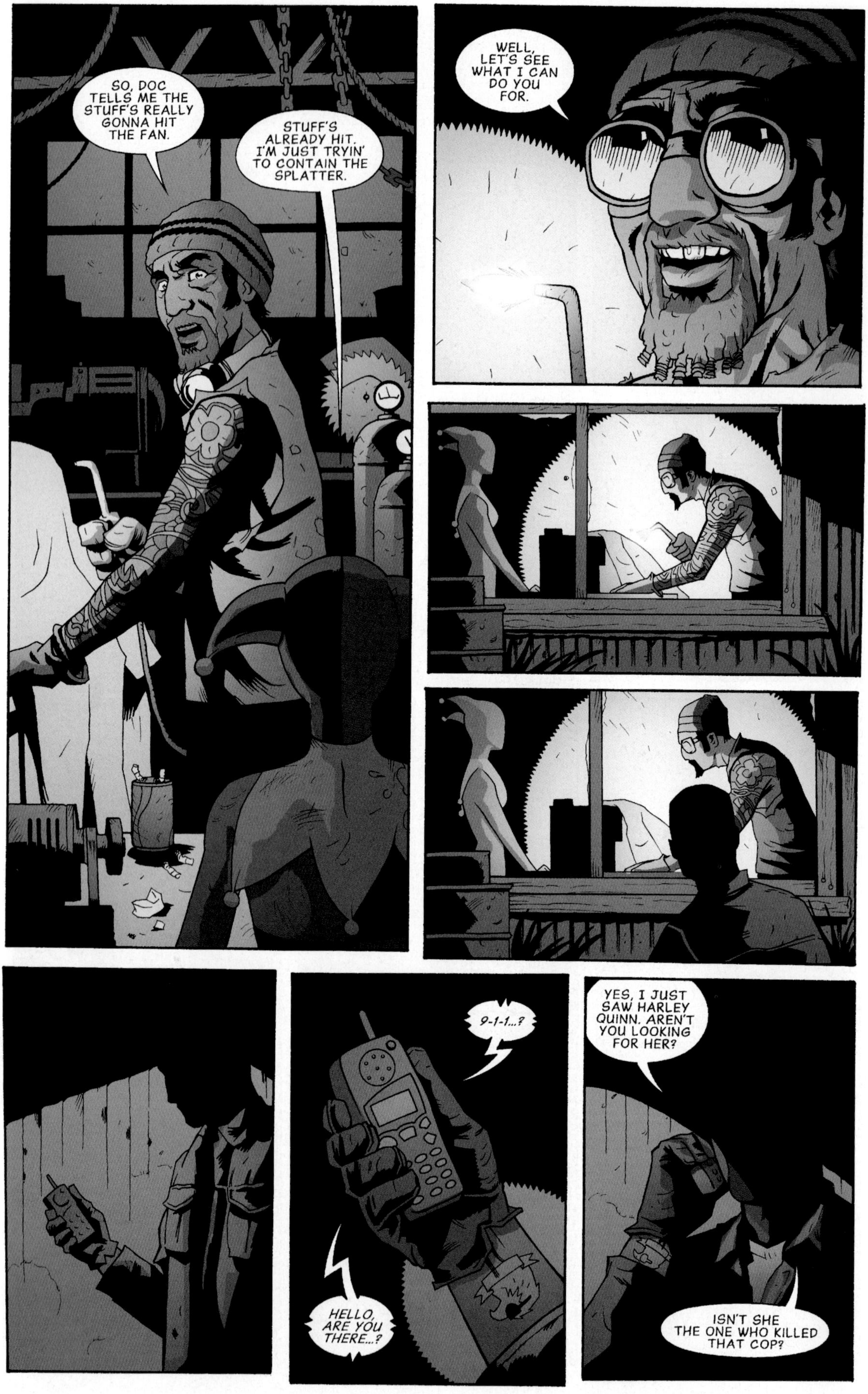
SO, DOC TELLS ME THE STUFF'S REALLY GONNA HIT THE FAN.
STUFF'S ALREADY HIT. I'M JUST TRYIN' TO CONTAIN THE SPLATTER.
WELL, LET'S SEE WHAT I CAN DO YOU FOR.
9-1-1...?
HELLO, ARE YOU THERE...?
YES, I JUST SAW HARLEY QUINN. AREN'T YOU LOOKING FOR HER?
ISN'T SHE THE ONE WHO KILLED THAT COP?

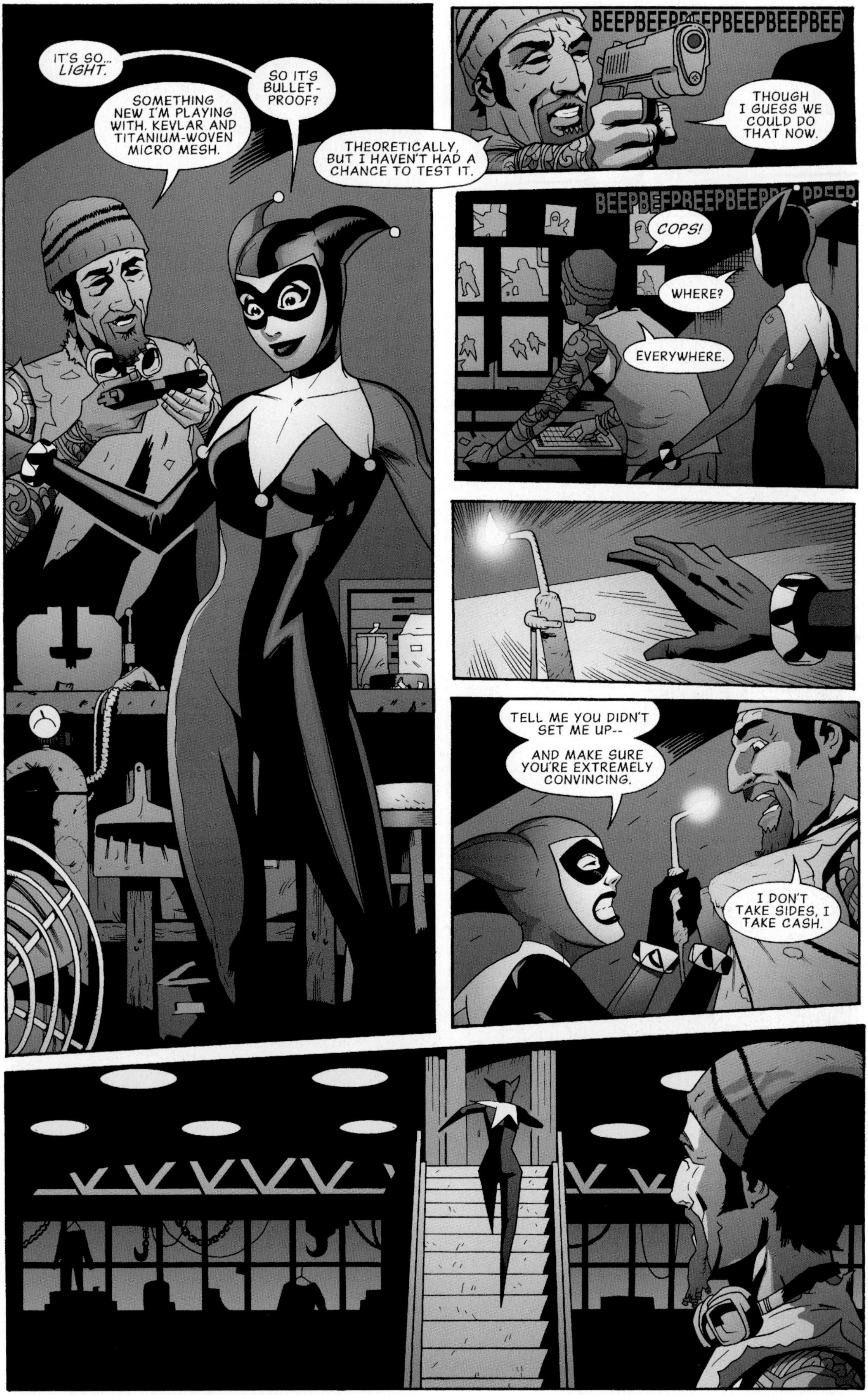
IT'S SO... LIGHT.
SO IT'S BULLET-PROOF?
SOMETHING NEW I'M PLAYING WITH. KEVLAR AND TITANIUM-WOVEN MICRO MESH.
THEORETICALLY, BUT I HAVEN'T HAD A CHANCE TO TEST IT.
BEEPBEEPBEEPBEEPBEEPBEE
THOUGH I GUESS WE COULD DO THAT NOW.
COPS!
WHERE?
EVERYWHERE.
TELL ME YOU DIDN'T SET ME UP--
AND MAKE SURE YOU'RE EXTREMELY CONVINCING.
I DON'T TAKE SIDES, I TAKE CASH.

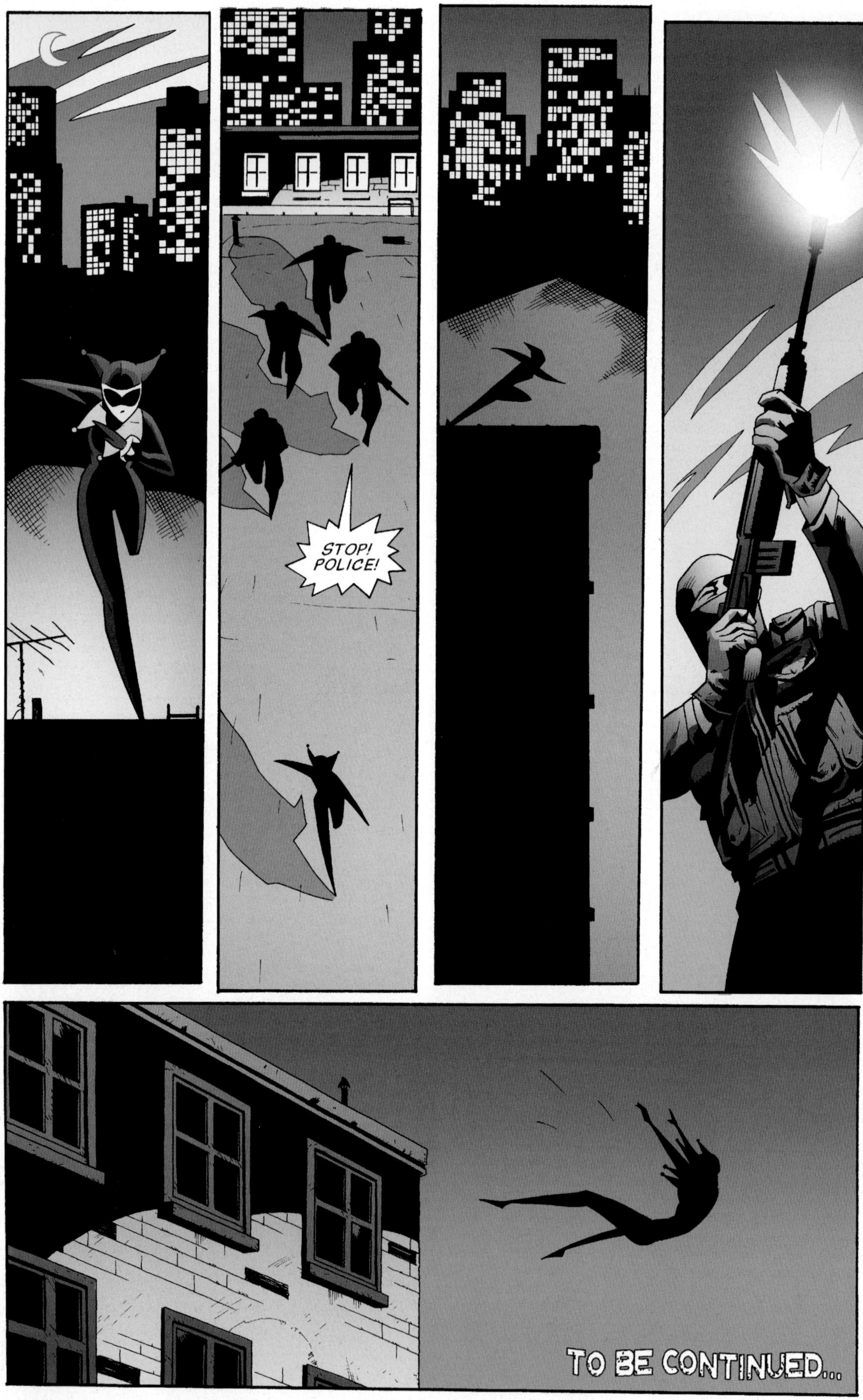
STOP! POLICE!
TO BE CONTINUED...

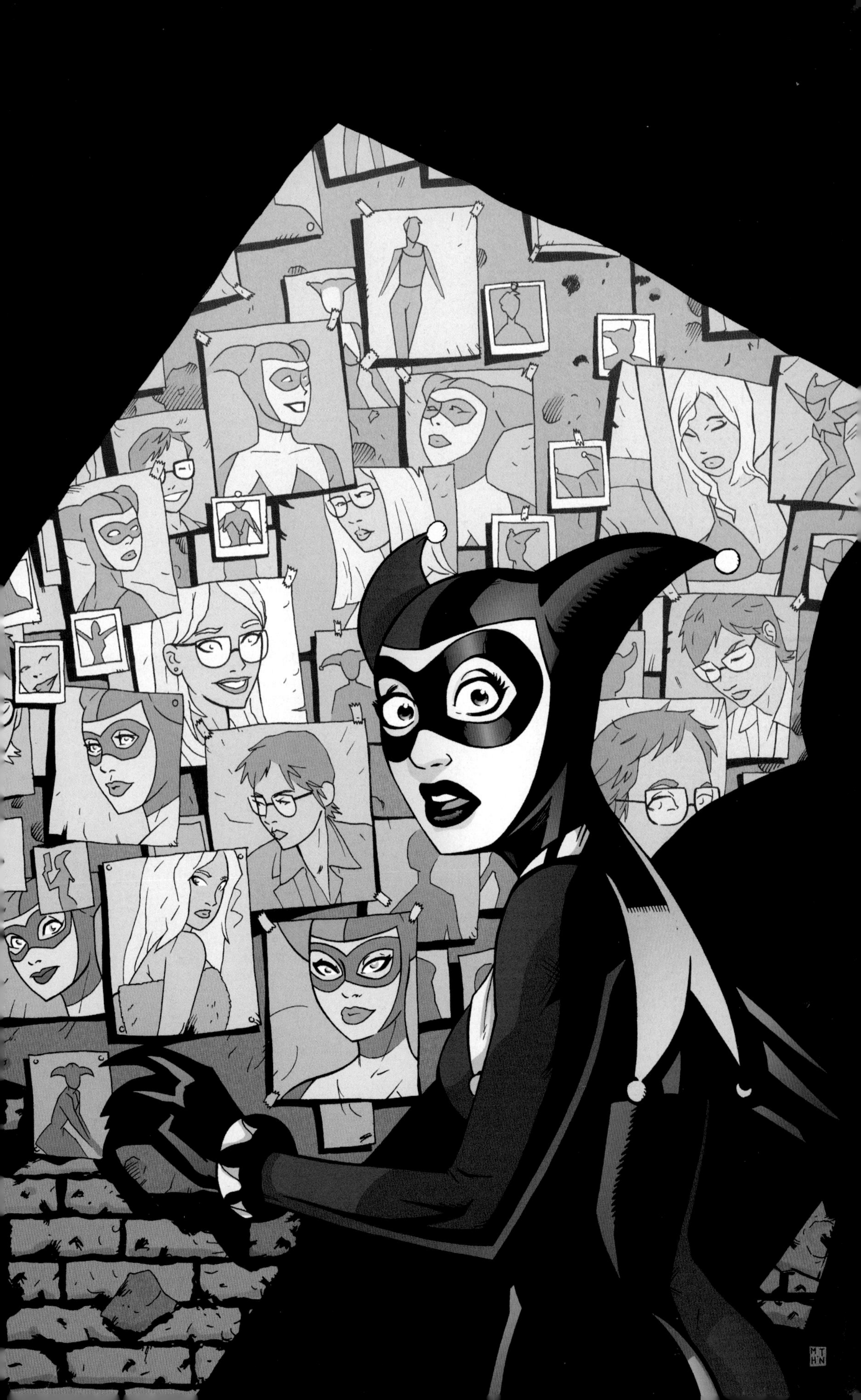

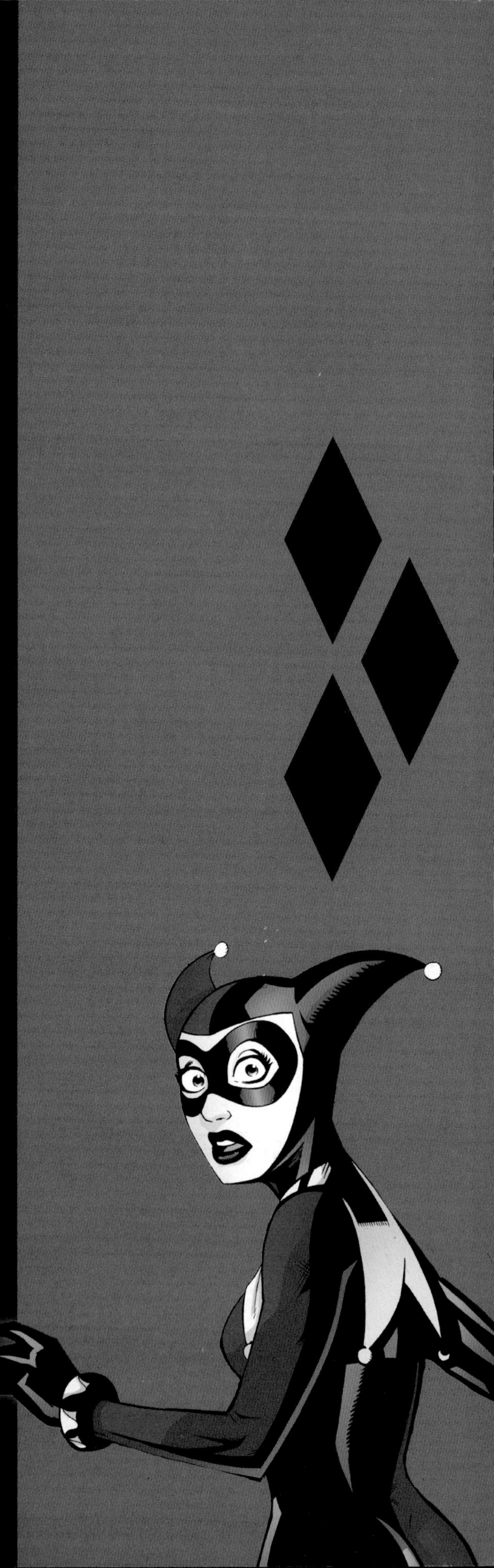

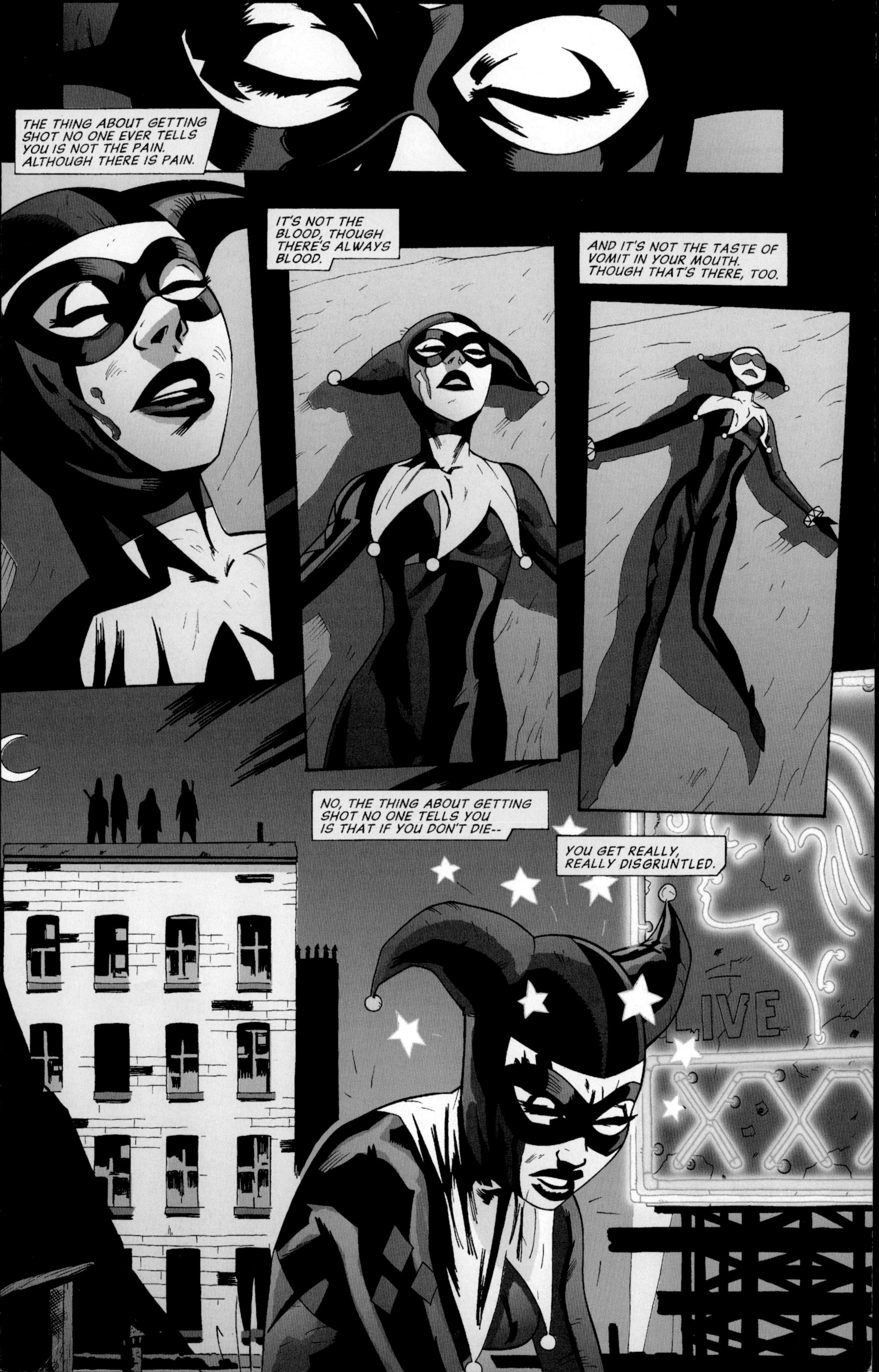
THE THING ABOUT GETTING SHOT NO ONE EVER TELLS YOU IS NOT THE PAIN. ALTHOUGH THERE IS PAIN.
IT'S NOT THE BLOOD, THOUGH THERE'S ALWAYS BLOOD.
AND IT'S NOT THE TASTE OF VOMIT IN YOUR MOUTH. THOUGH THAT'S THERE, TOO.
NO, THE THING ABOUT GETTING SHOT NO ONE TELLS YOU IS THAT IF YOU DON'T DIE--
YOU GET REALLY, REALLY DISGRUNTLED.
LIVE

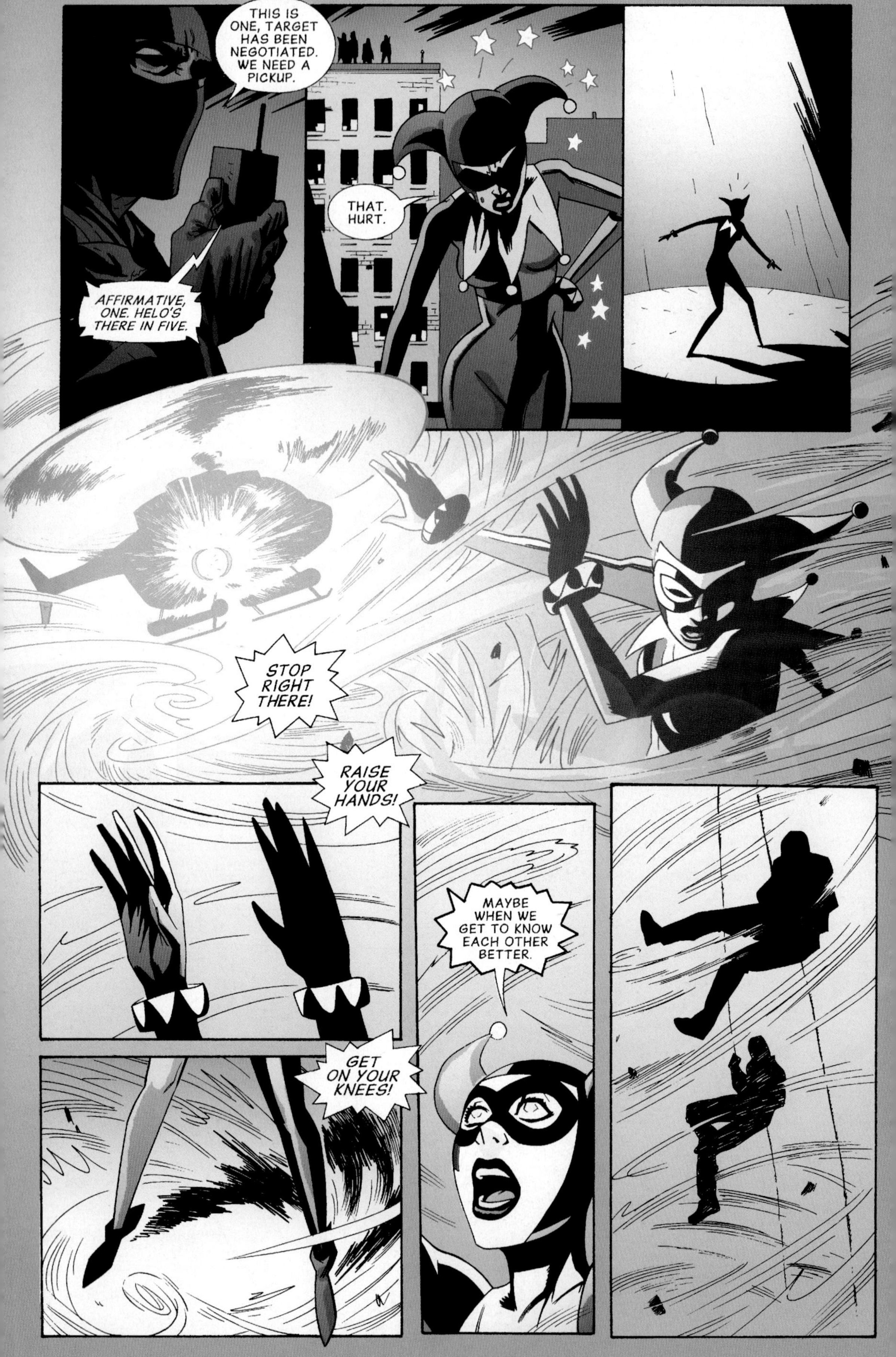
THIS IS ONE, TARGET HAS BEEN NEGOTIATED. WE NEED A PICKUP.
AFFIRMATIVE, ONE. HELO'S THERE IN FIVE.
THAT. HURT.
STOP RIGHT THERE!
RAISE YOUR HANDS!
GET ON YOUR KNEES!
MAYBE WHEN WE GET TO KNOW EACH OTHER BETTER.

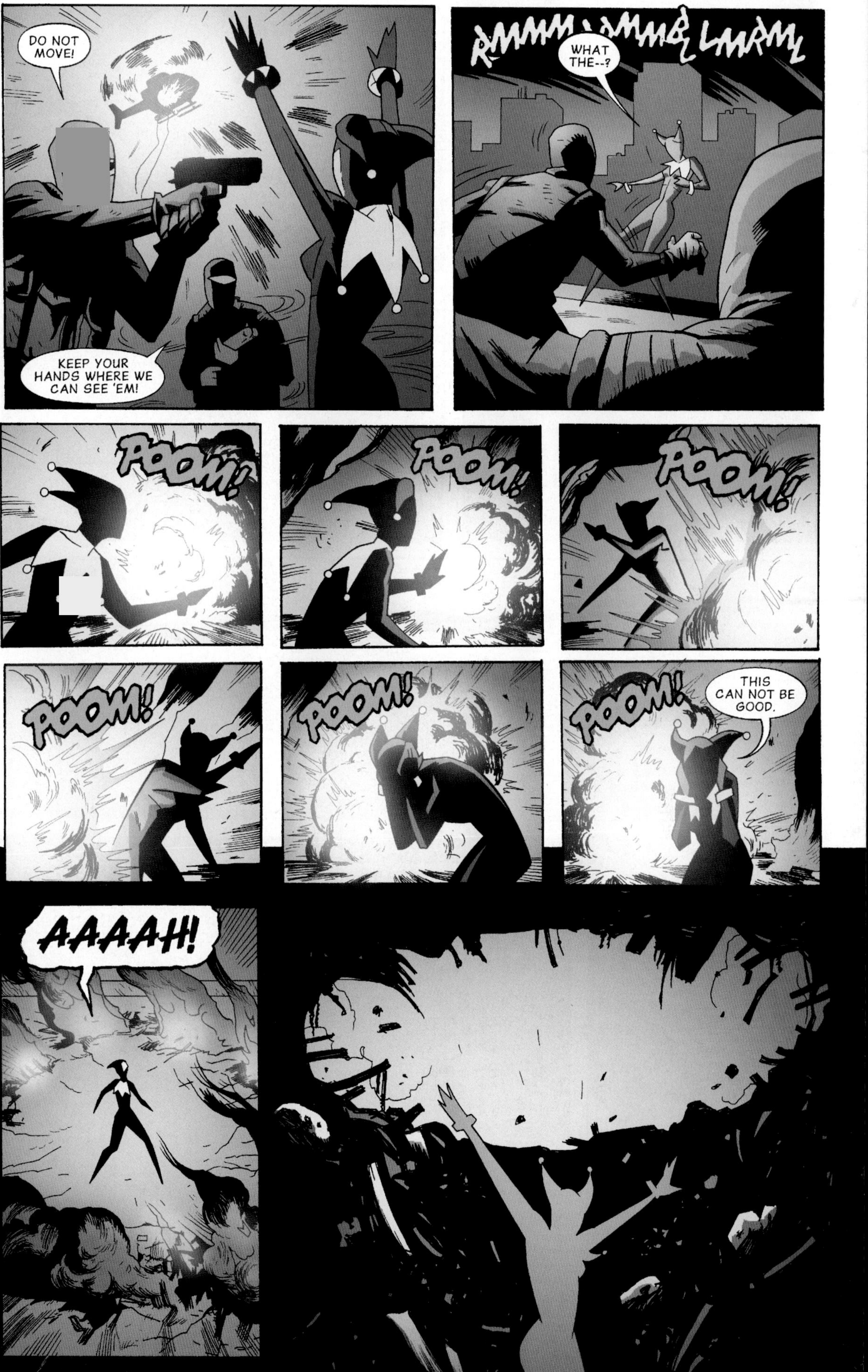
DO NOT MOVE!
KEEP YOUR HANDS WHERE WE CAN SEE 'EM!
WHAT THE--?
POOM!
POOM!
POOM!
POOM!
POOM!
POOM!
THIS CAN NOT BE GOOD.
AAAAH!

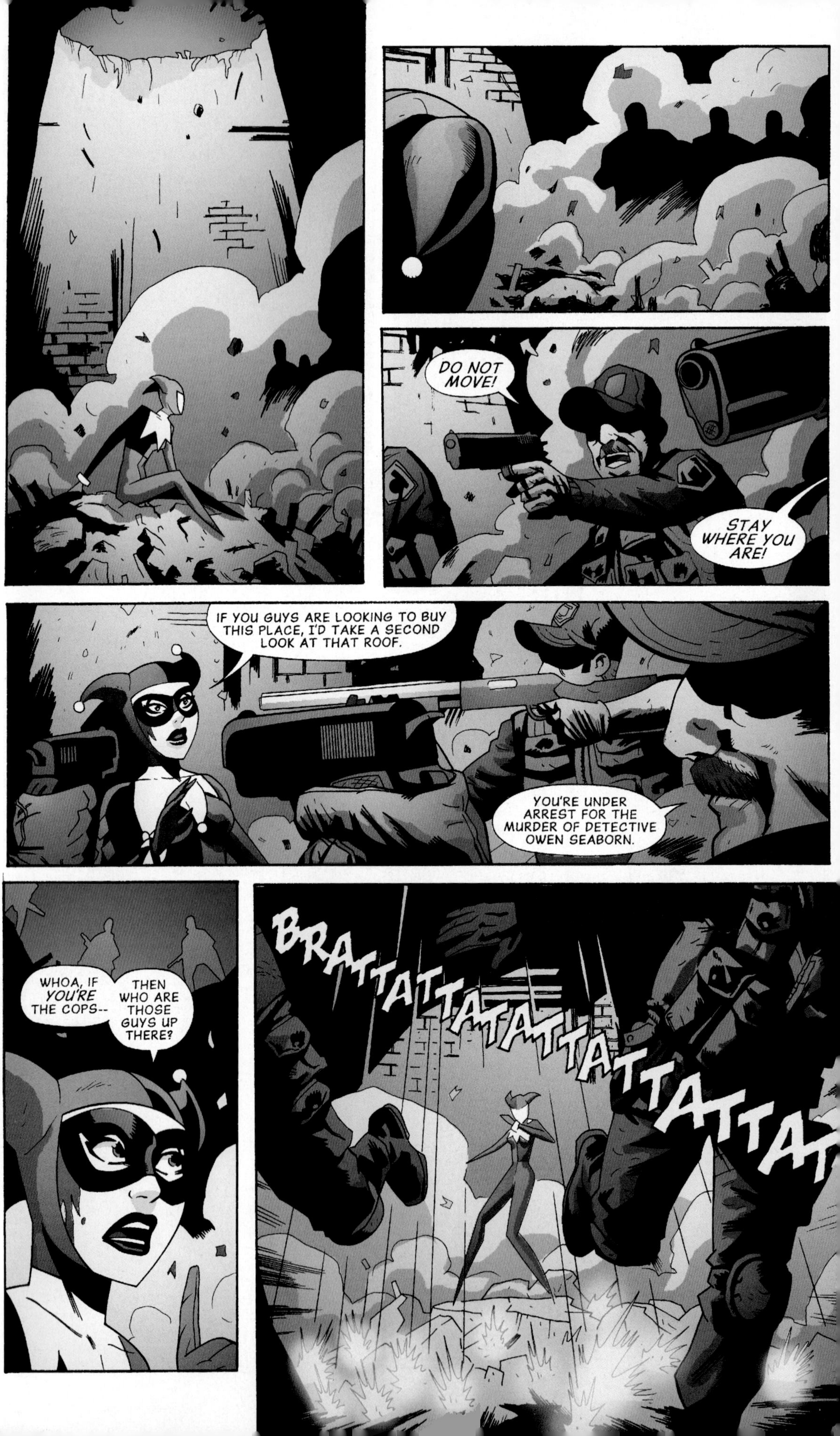
DO NOT MOVE!
STAY WHERE YOU ARE!
IF YOU GUYS ARE LOOKING TO BUY THIS PLACE, I'D TAKE A SECOND LOOK AT THAT ROOF.
YOU'RE UNDER ARREST FOR THE MURDER OF DETECTIVE OWEN SEABORN.
WHOA, IF *YOU'RE* THE COPS--
THEN WHO ARE THOSE GUYS UP THERE?
BRATTATTATATTATTATTATTAT

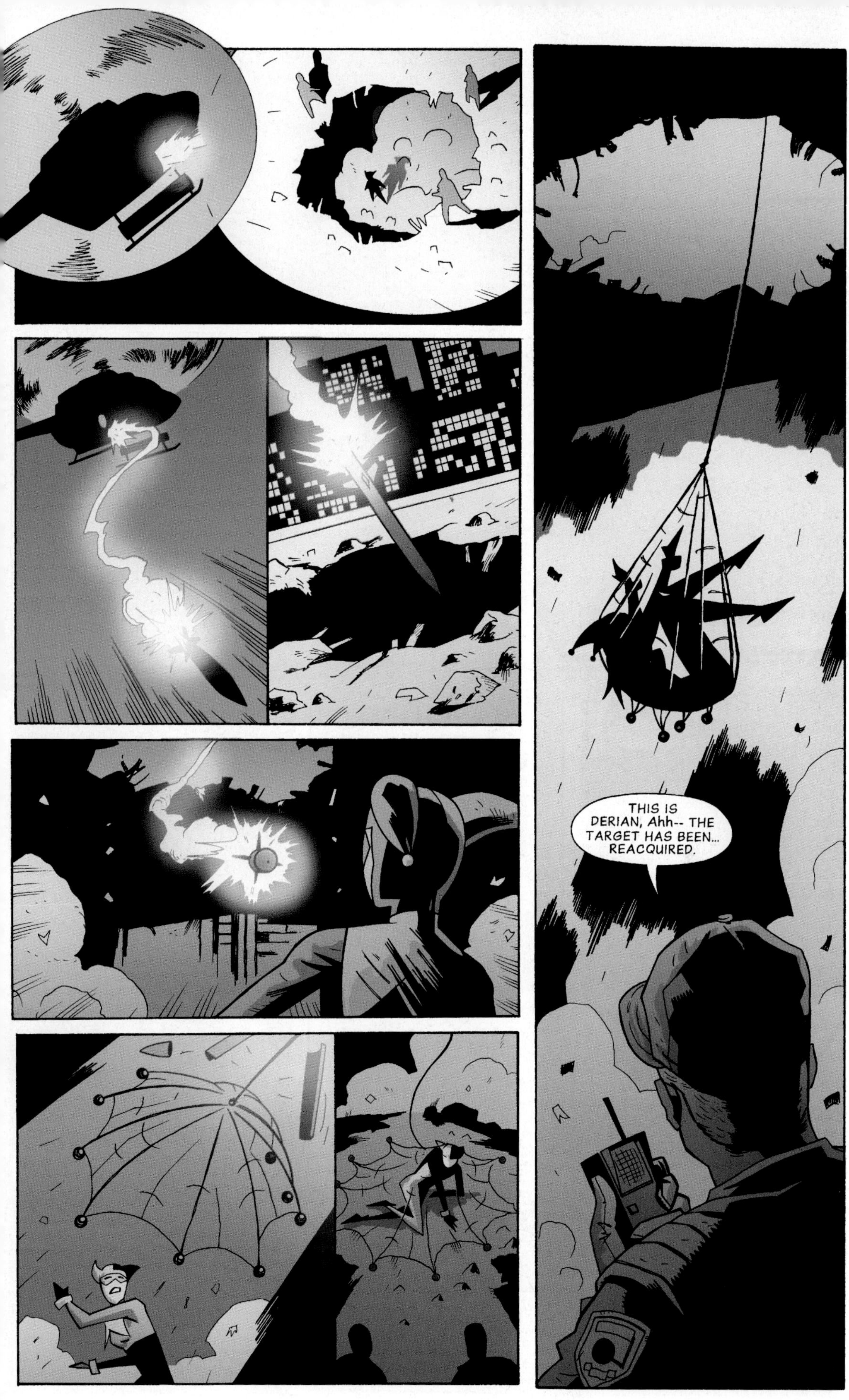
THIS IS DERIAN, Ahh-- THE TARGET HAS BEEN... REACQUIRED.

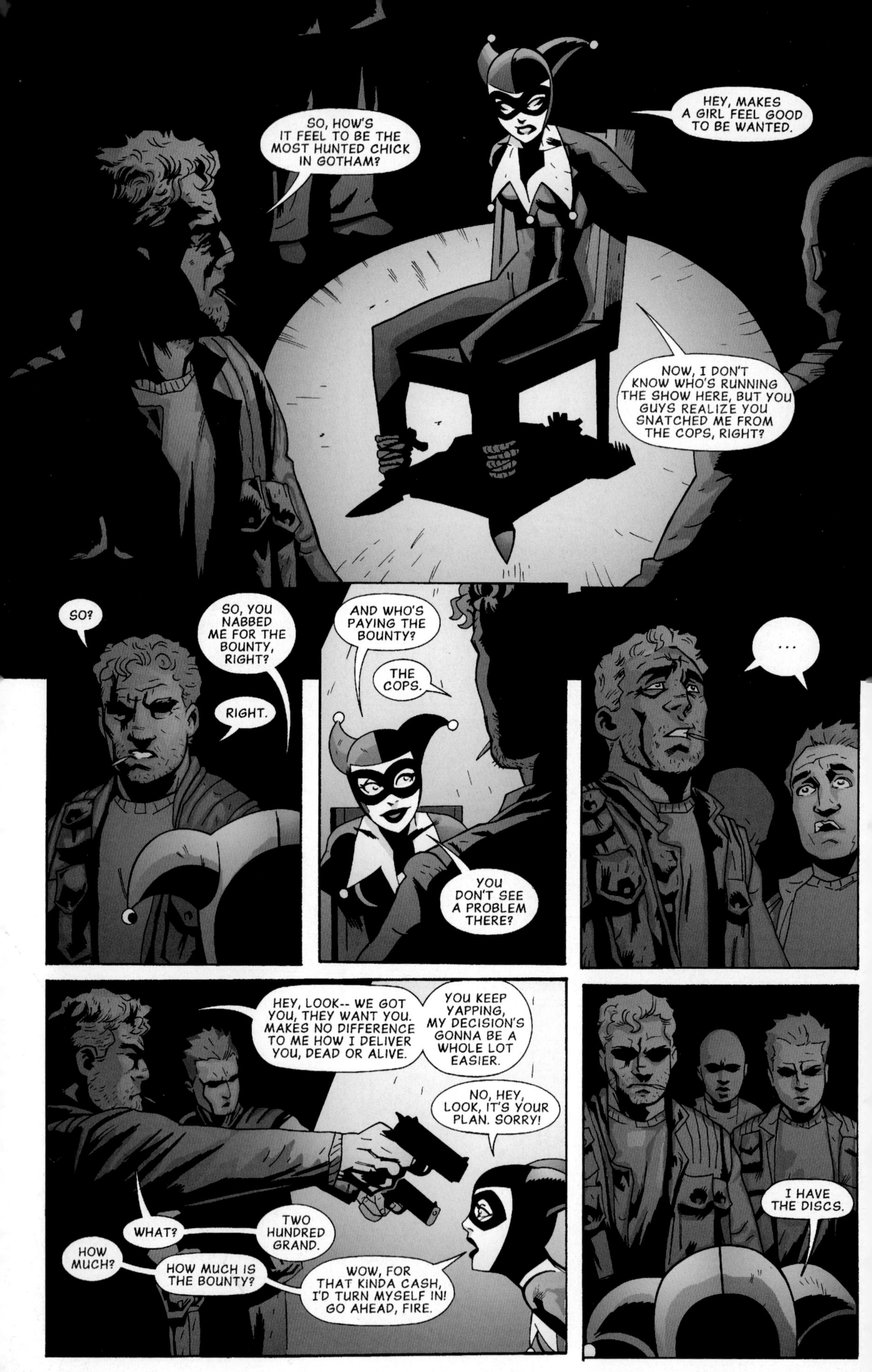

SO, HOW'S IT FEEL TO BE THE MOST HUNTED CHICK IN GOTHAM?
HEY, MAKES A GIRL FEEL GOOD TO BE WANTED.
NOW, I DON'T KNOW WHO'S RUNNING THE SHOW HERE, BUT YOU GUYS REALIZE YOU SNATCHED ME FROM THE COPS, RIGHT?
SO?
SO, YOU NABBED ME FOR THE BOUNTY, RIGHT?
RIGHT.
AND WHO'S PAYING THE BOUNTY?
THE COPS.
YOU DON'T SEE A PROBLEM THERE?
...
HEY, LOOK-- WE GOT YOU, THEY WANT YOU. MAKES NO DIFFERENCE TO ME HOW I DELIVER YOU, DEAD OR ALIVE.
YOU KEEP YAPPING, MY DECISION'S GONNA BE A WHOLE LOT EASIER.
NO, HEY, LOOK, IT'S YOUR PLAN. SORRY!
HOW MUCH?
HOW MUCH IS THE BOUNTY?
WHAT?
TWO HUNDRED GRAND.
WOW, FOR THAT KINDA CASH, I'D TURN MYSELF IN! GO AHEAD, FIRE.
I HAVE THE DISCS.

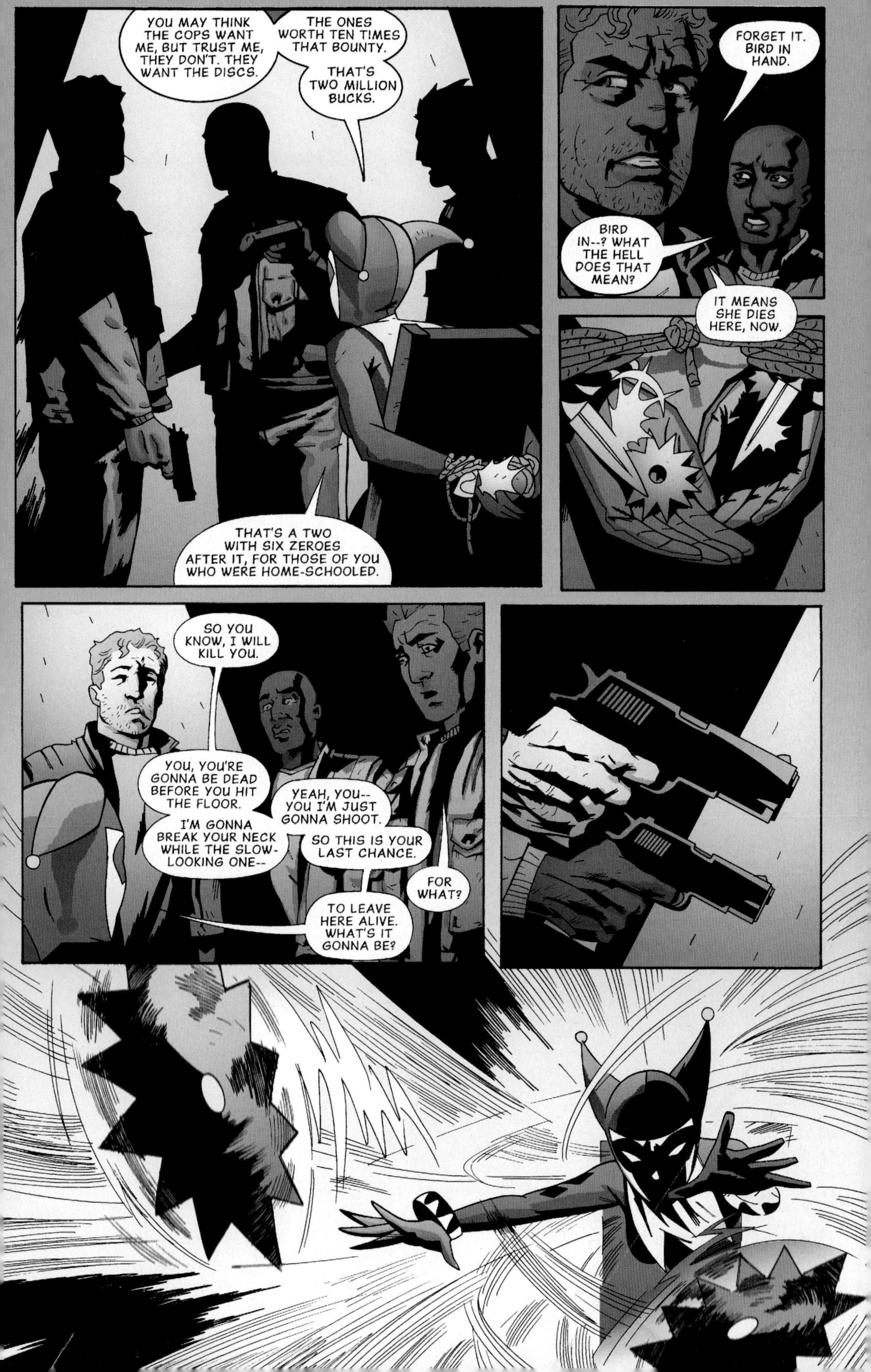
YOU MAY THINK THE COPS WANT ME, BUT TRUST ME, THEY DON'T. THEY WANT THE DISCS.
THE ONES WORTH TEN TIMES THAT BOUNTY.
THAT'S TWO MILLION BUCKS.
THAT'S A TWO WITH SIX ZEROES AFTER IT, FOR THOSE OF YOU WHO WERE HOME-SCHOOLED.
FORGET IT. BIRD IN HAND.
BIRD IN--? WHAT THE HELL DOES THAT MEAN?
IT MEANS SHE DIES HERE, NOW.
SO YOU KNOW, I WILL KILL YOU.
YOU, YOU'RE GONNA BE DEAD BEFORE YOU HIT THE FLOOR.
I'M GONNA BREAK YOUR NECK WHILE THE SLOW-LOOKING ONE--
YEAH, YOU-- YOU I'M JUST GONNA SHOOT.
SO THIS IS YOUR LAST CHANCE.
FOR WHAT?
TO LEAVE HERE ALIVE. WHAT'S IT GONNA BE?

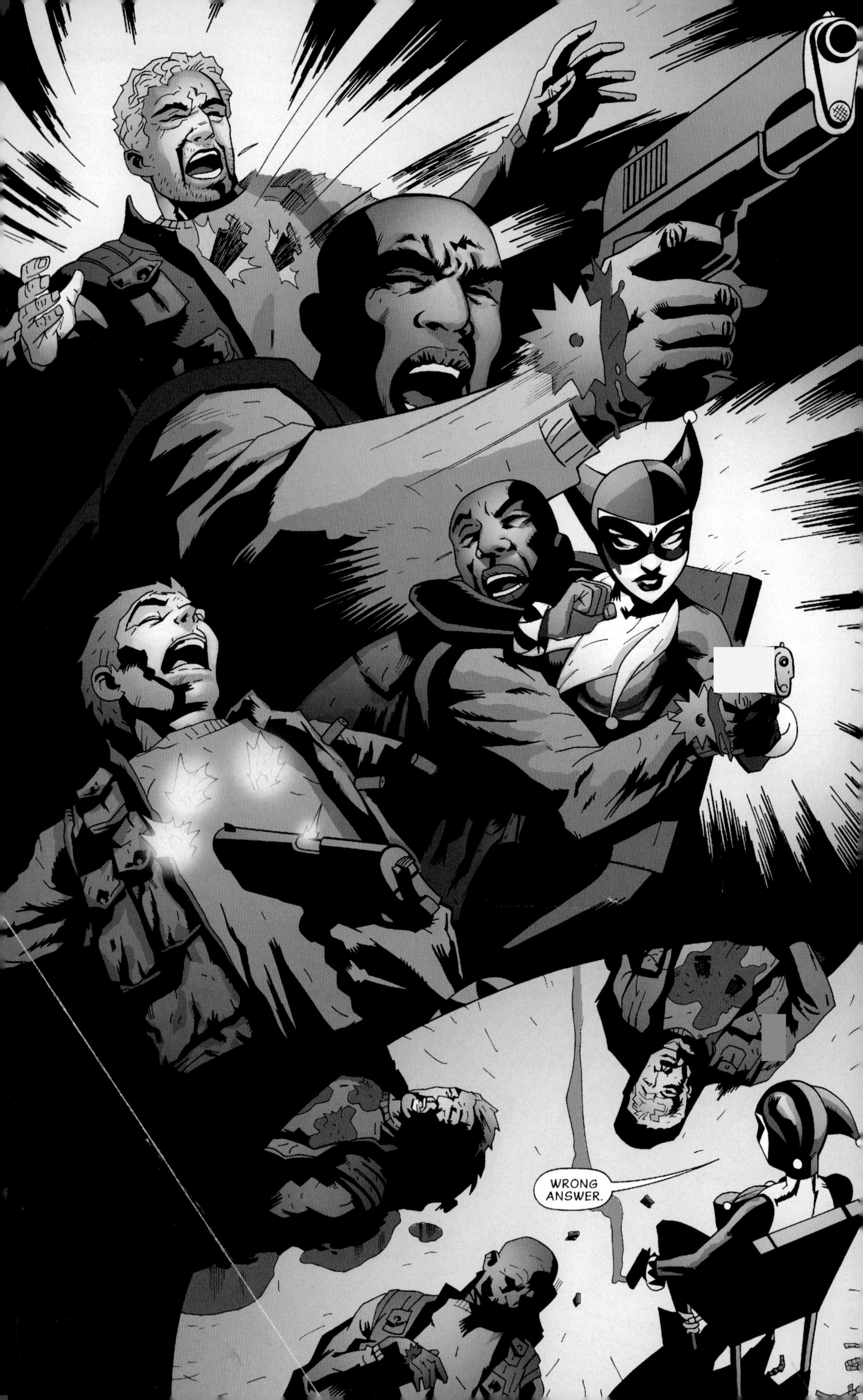
WRONG ANSWER.

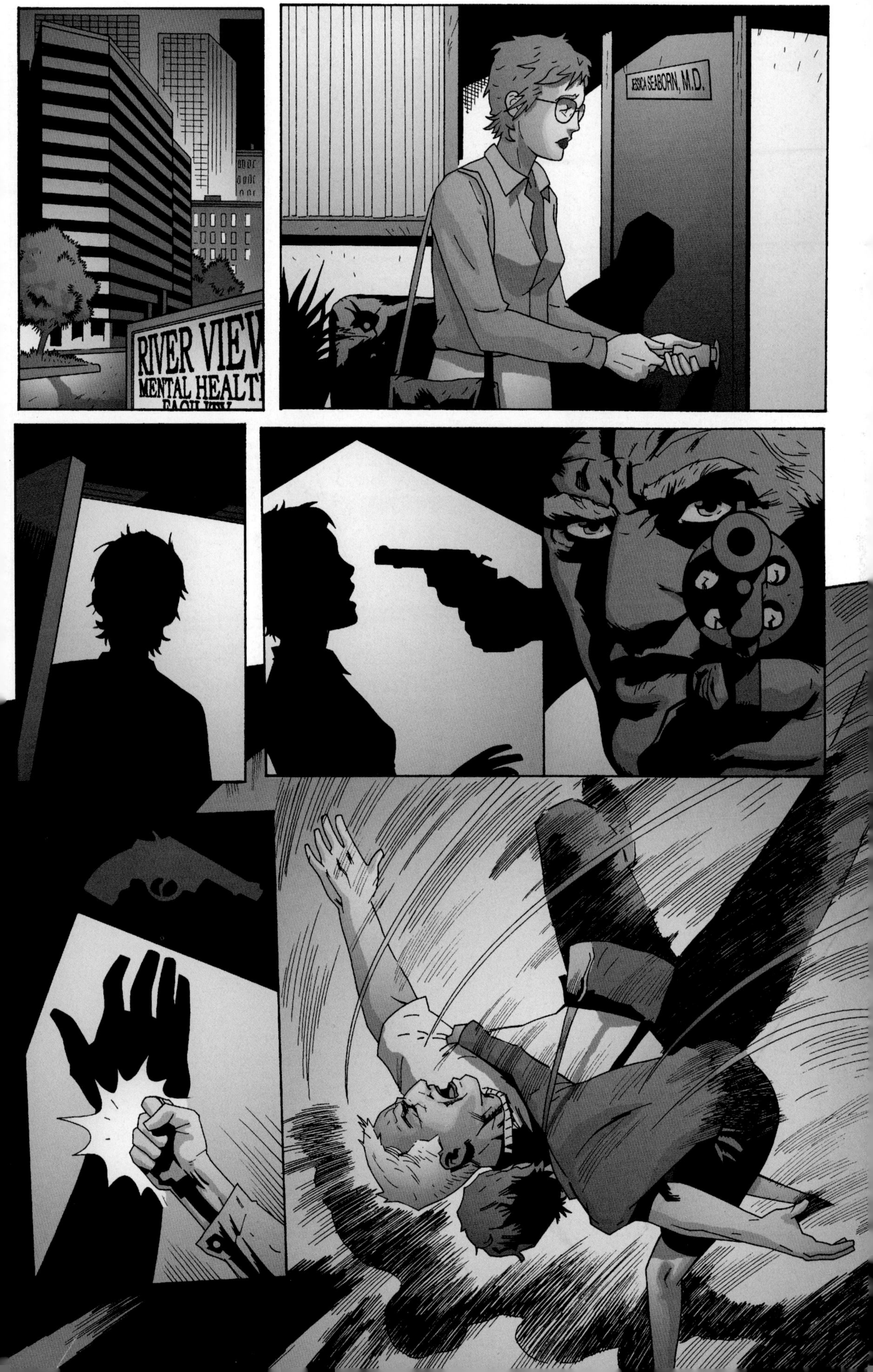
JESSICA SEABORN, M.D.
RIVER VIEW
MENTAL HEALT

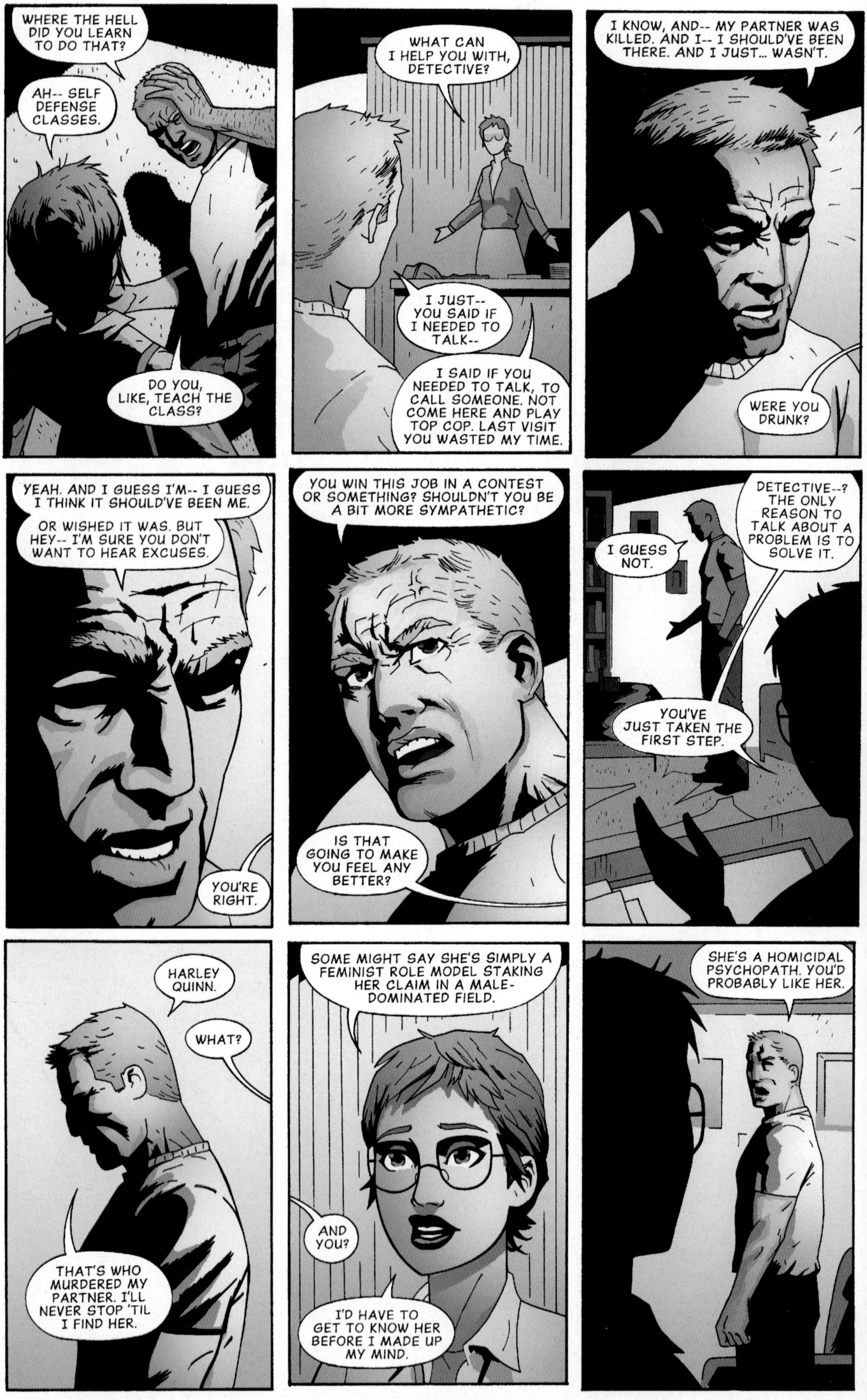
WHERE THE HELL DID YOU LEARN TO DO THAT?
AH-- SELF DEFENSE CLASSES.
DO YOU, LIKE, TEACH THE CLASS?
WHAT CAN I HELP YOU WITH, DETECTIVE?
I JUST-- YOU SAID IF I NEEDED TO TALK--
I SAID IF YOU NEEDED TO TALK, TO CALL SOMEONE. NOT COME HERE AND PLAY TOP COP. LAST VISIT YOU WASTED MY TIME.
I KNOW, AND-- MY PARTNER WAS KILLED. AND I-- I SHOULD'VE BEEN THERE. AND I JUST... WASN'T.
WERE YOU DRUNK?
YEAH. AND I GUESS I'M-- I GUESS I THINK IT SHOULD'VE BEEN ME.
OR WISHED IT WAS. BUT HEY-- I'M SURE YOU DON'T WANT TO HEAR EXCUSES.
YOU'RE RIGHT.
YOU WIN THIS JOB IN A CONTEST OR SOMETHING? SHOULDN'T YOU BE A BIT MORE SYMPATHETIC?
IS THAT GOING TO MAKE YOU FEEL ANY BETTER?
I GUESS NOT.
DETECTIVE--? THE ONLY REASON TO TALK ABOUT A PROBLEM IS TO SOLVE IT.
YOU'VE JUST TAKEN THE FIRST STEP.
HARLEY QUINN.
WHAT?
THAT'S WHO MURDERED MY PARTNER. I'LL NEVER STOP 'TIL I FIND HER.
SOME MIGHT SAY SHE'S SIMPLY A FEMINIST ROLE MODEL STAKING HER CLAIM IN A MALE-DOMINATED FIELD.
AND YOU?
I'D HAVE TO GET TO KNOW HER BEFORE I MADE UP MY MIND.
SHE'S A HOMICIDAL PSYCHOPATH. YOU'D PROBABLY LIKE HER.

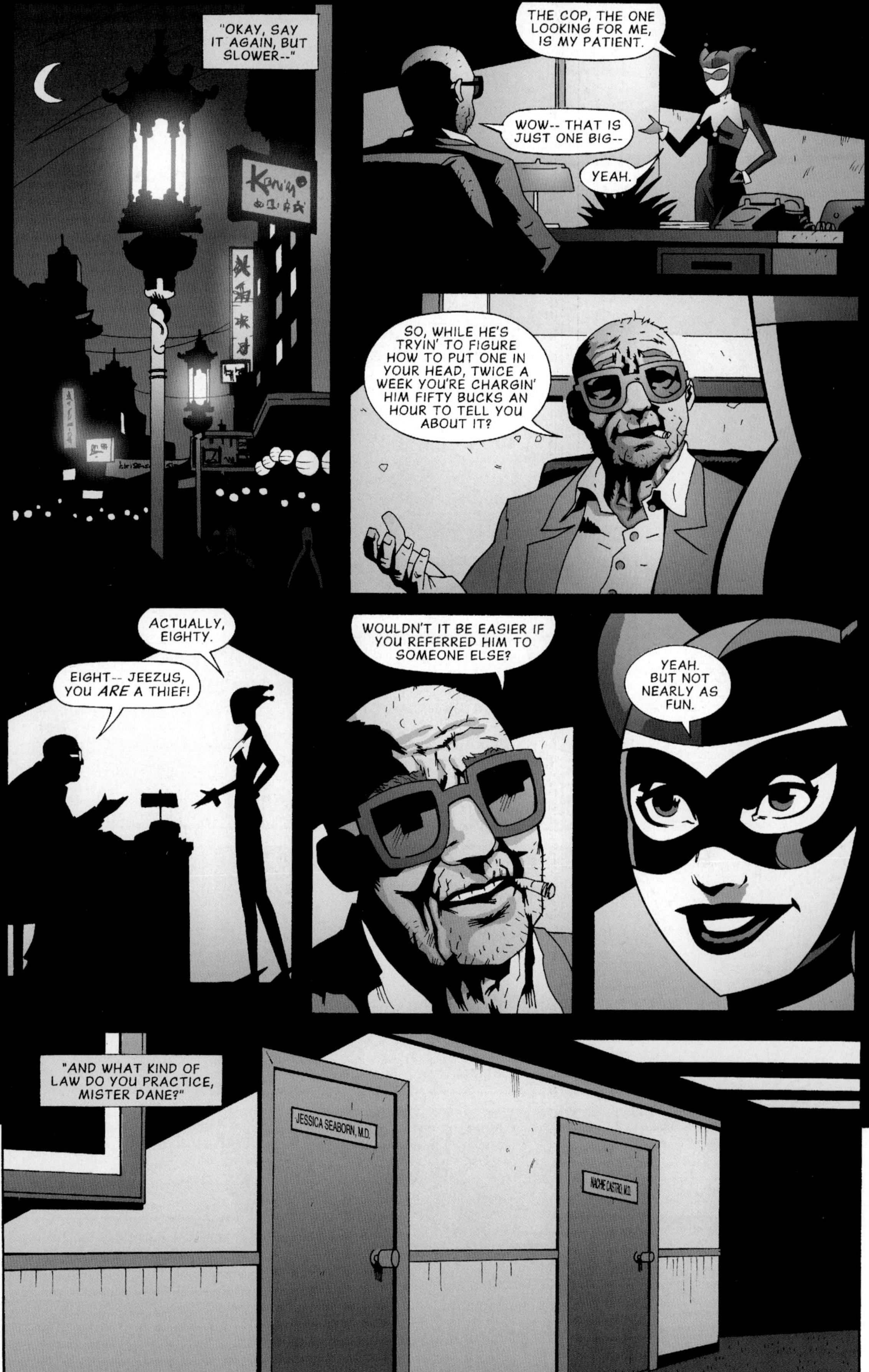
"OKAY, SAY IT AGAIN, BUT SLOWER--"
THE COP, THE ONE LOOKING FOR ME, IS MY PATIENT.
WOW-- THAT IS JUST ONE BIG--
YEAH.
SO, WHILE HE'S TRYIN' TO FIGURE HOW TO PUT ONE IN YOUR HEAD, TWICE A WEEK YOU'RE CHARGIN' HIM FIFTY BUCKS AN HOUR TO TELL YOU ABOUT IT?
ACTUALLY, EIGHTY.
EIGHT-- JEEZUS, YOU *ARE* A THIEF!
WOULDN'T IT BE EASIER IF YOU REFERRED HIM TO SOMEONE ELSE?
YEAH. BUT NOT NEARLY AS FUN.
"AND WHAT KIND OF LAW DO YOU PRACTICE, MISTER DANE?"
JESSICA SEABORN, M.D.
NACHIE CASTRO, M.D.

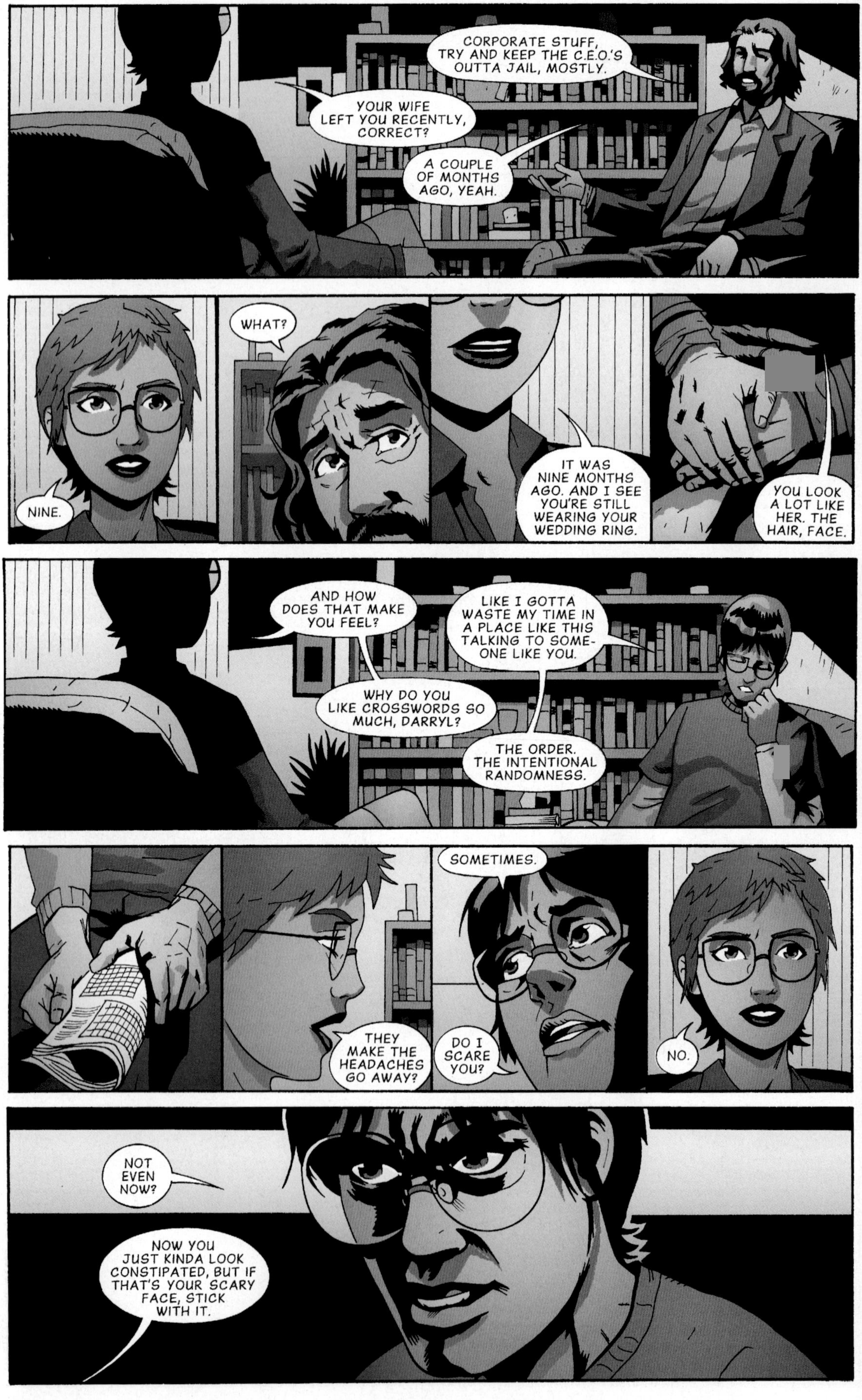
CORPORATE STUFF, TRY AND KEEP THE C.E.O.'S OUTTA JAIL, MOSTLY.
YOUR WIFE LEFT YOU RECENTLY, CORRECT?
A COUPLE OF MONTHS AGO, YEAH.
NINE.
WHAT?
IT WAS NINE MONTHS AGO. AND I SEE YOU'RE STILL WEARING YOUR WEDDING RING.
YOU LOOK A LOT LIKE HER. THE HAIR, FACE.
AND HOW DOES THAT MAKE YOU FEEL?
LIKE I GOTTA WASTE MY TIME IN A PLACE LIKE THIS TALKING TO SOME-ONE LIKE YOU.
WHY DO YOU LIKE CROSSWORDS SO MUCH, DARRYL?
THE ORDER. THE INTENTIONAL RANDOMNESS.
THEY MAKE THE HEADACHES GO AWAY?
SOMETIMES.
DO I SCARE YOU?
NO.
NOT EVEN NOW?
NOW YOU JUST KINDA LOOK CONSTIPATED, BUT IF THAT'S YOUR SCARY FACE, STICK WITH IT.

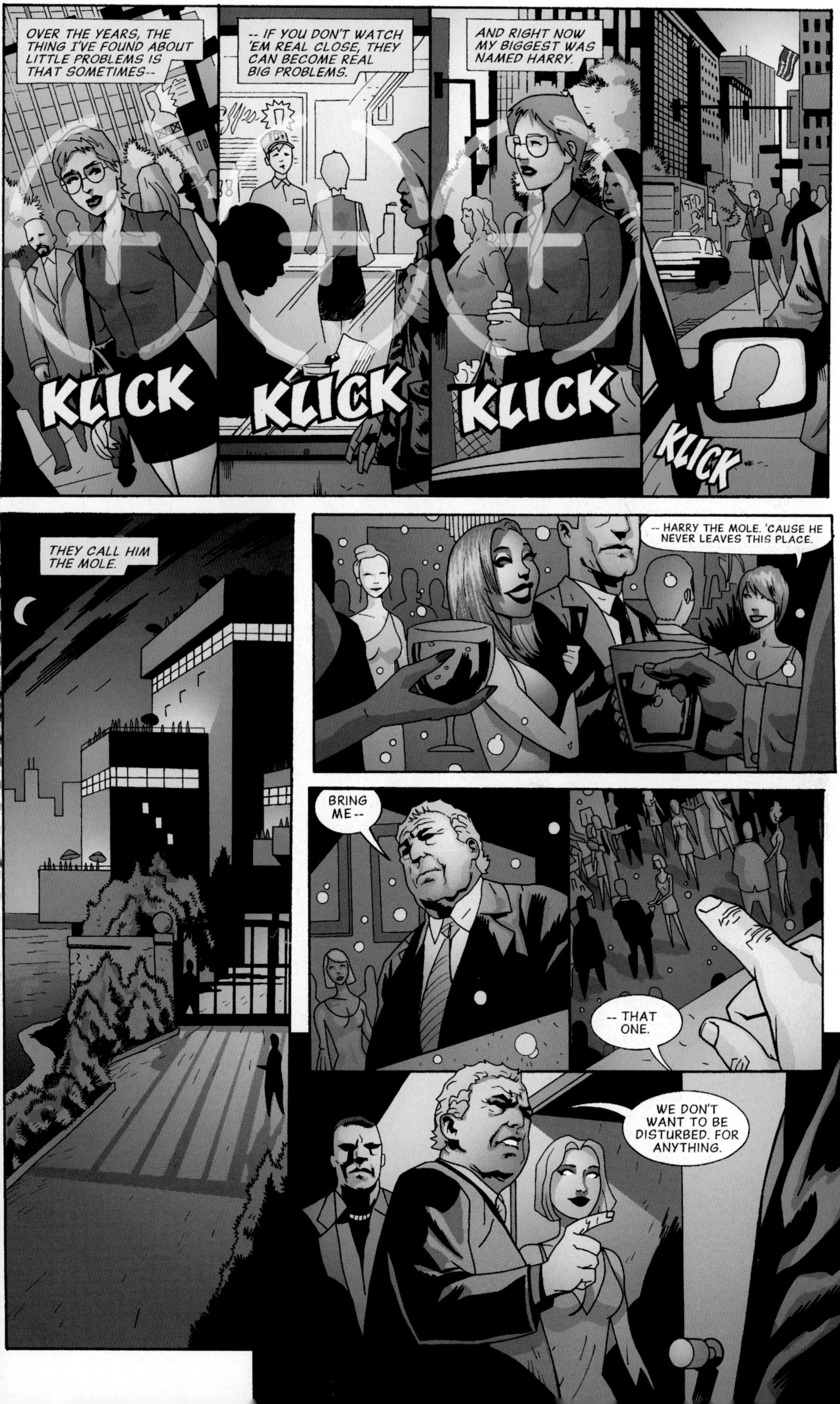
OVER THE YEARS, THE THING I'VE FOUND ABOUT LITTLE PROBLEMS IS THAT SOMETIMES--
KLICK
-- IF YOU DON'T WATCH 'EM REAL CLOSE, THEY CAN BECOME REAL BIG PROBLEMS.
KLICK
AND RIGHT NOW MY BIGGEST WAS NAMED HARRY.
KLICK
KLICK
THEY CALL HIM THE MOLE.
-- HARRY THE MOLE. 'CAUSE HE NEVER LEAVES THIS PLACE.
BRING ME --
-- THAT ONE.
WE DON'T WANT TO BE DISTURBED. FOR ANYTHING.

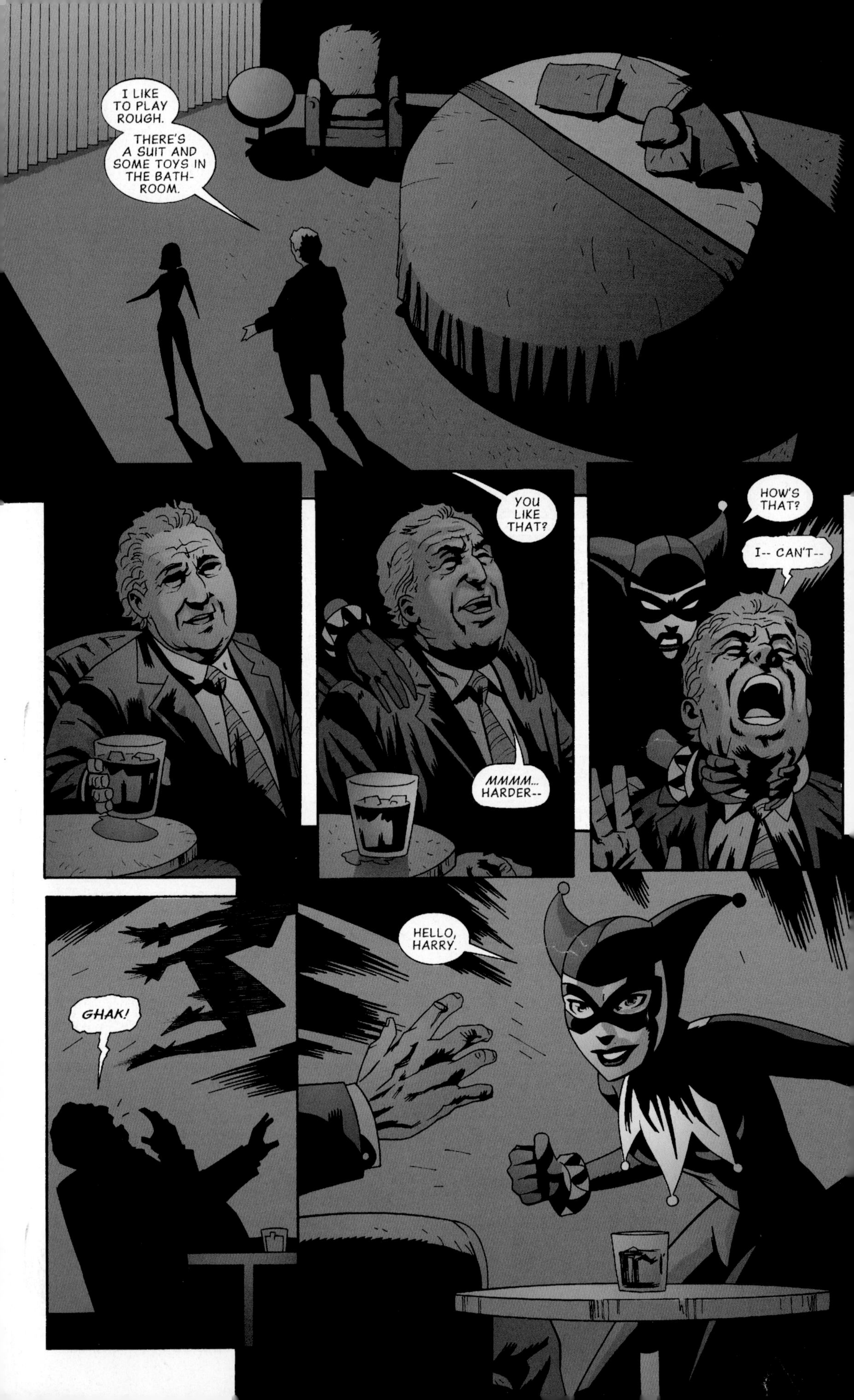
I LIKE TO PLAY ROUGH.
THERE'S A SUIT AND SOME TOYS IN THE BATH-ROOM.
YOU LIKE THAT?
MMMM... HARDER--
HOW'S THAT?
I-- CAN'T--
GHAK!
HELLO, HARRY.

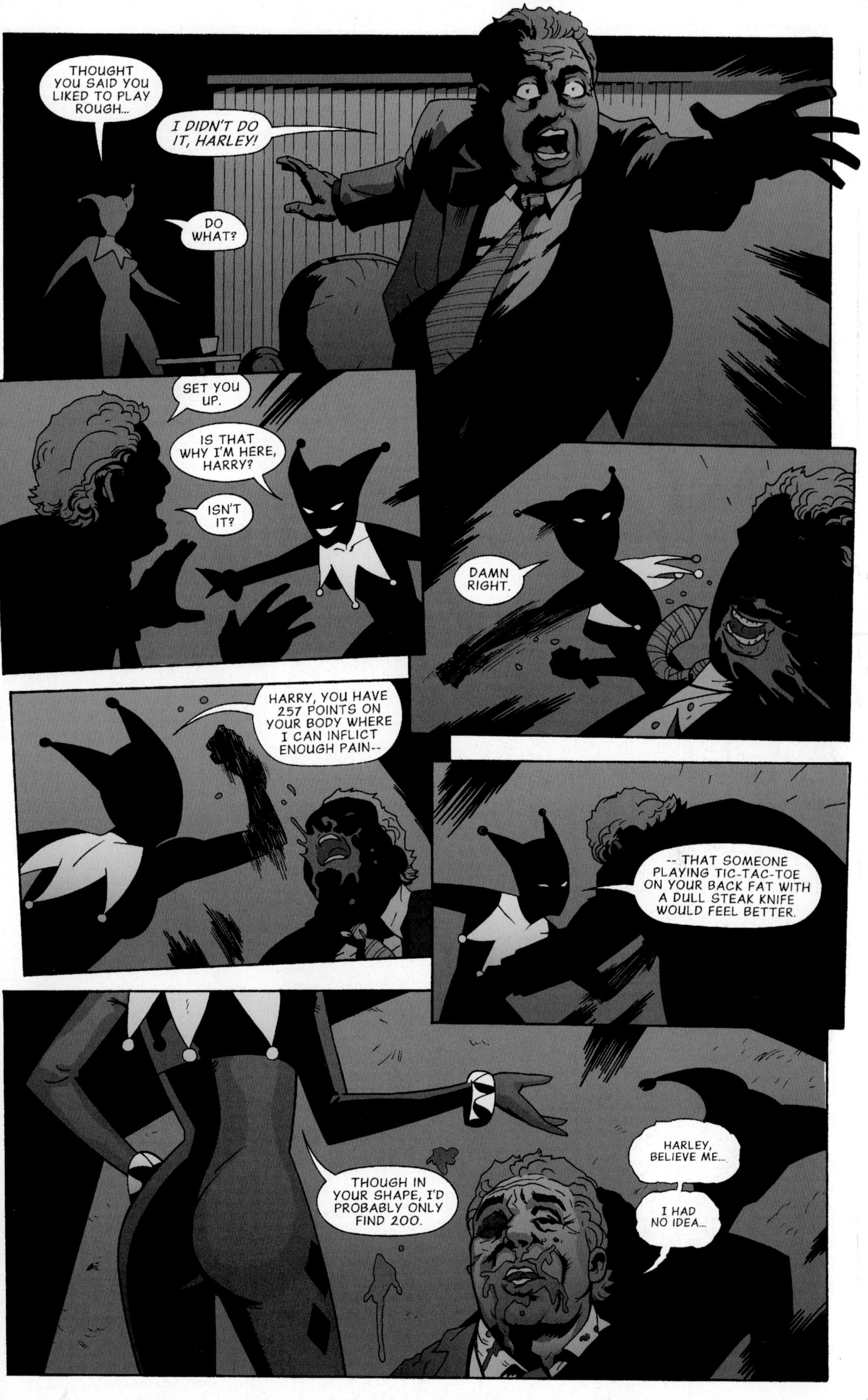
THOUGHT YOU SAID YOU LIKED TO PLAY ROUGH...
I DIDN'T DO IT, HARLEY!
DO WHAT?
SET YOU UP.
IS THAT WHY I'M HERE, HARRY?
ISN'T IT?
DAMN RIGHT.
HARRY, YOU HAVE 257 POINTS ON YOUR BODY WHERE I CAN INFLICT ENOUGH PAIN--
-- THAT SOMEONE PLAYING TIC-TAC-TOE ON YOUR BACK FAT WITH A DULL STEAK KNIFE WOULD FEEL BETTER.
THOUGH IN YOUR SHAPE, I'D PROBABLY ONLY FIND 200.
HARLEY, BELIEVE ME...
I HAD NO IDEA...

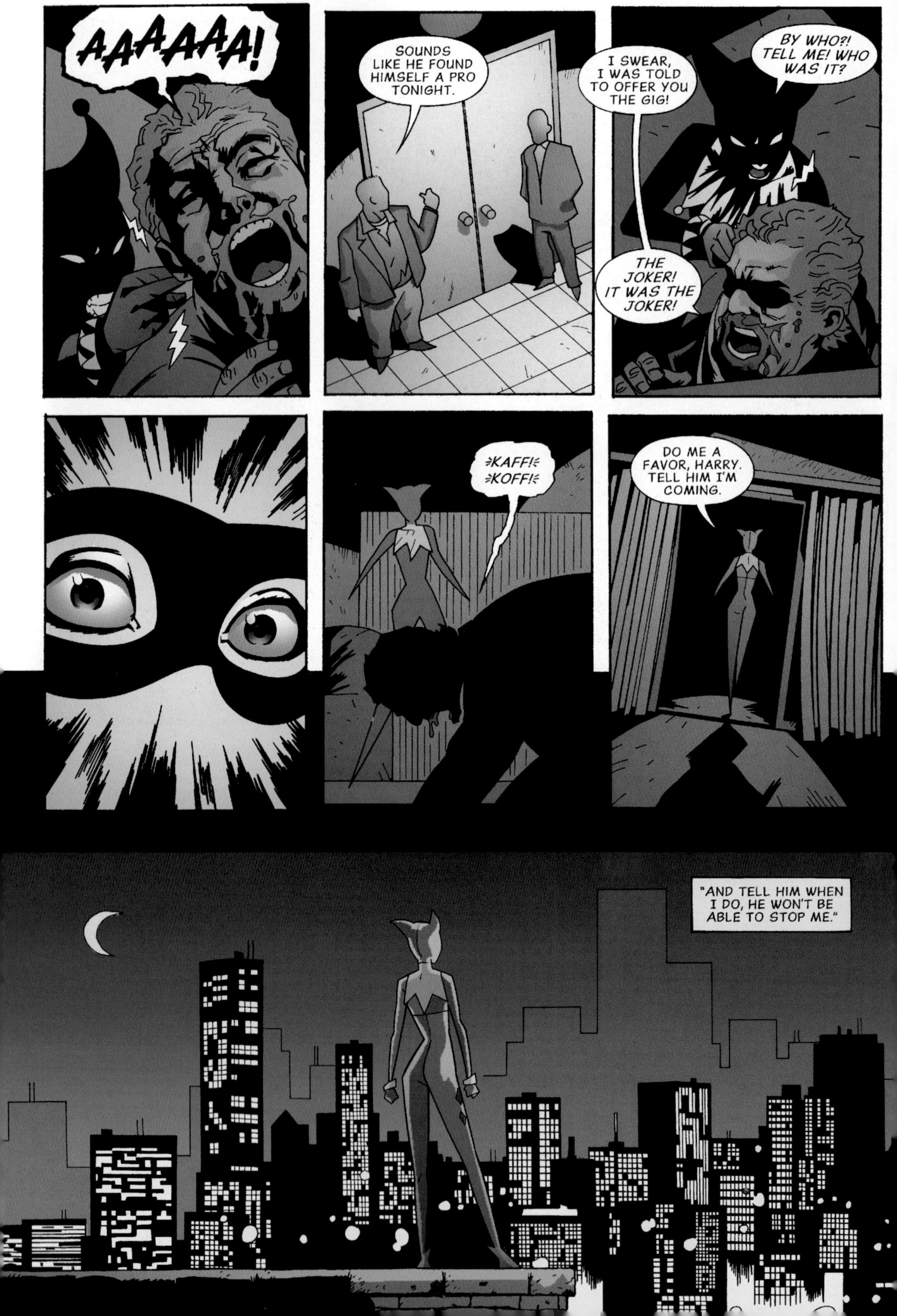
AAAAAA!
SOUNDS LIKE HE FOUND HIMSELF A PRO TONIGHT.
I SWEAR, I WAS TOLD TO OFFER YOU THE GIG!
BY WHO?! TELL ME! WHO WAS IT?
THE JOKER! IT WAS THE JOKER!
KAFF! KOFF!
DO ME A FAVOR, HARRY. TELL HIM I'M COMING.
"AND TELL HIM WHEN I DO, HE WON'T BE ABLE TO STOP ME."

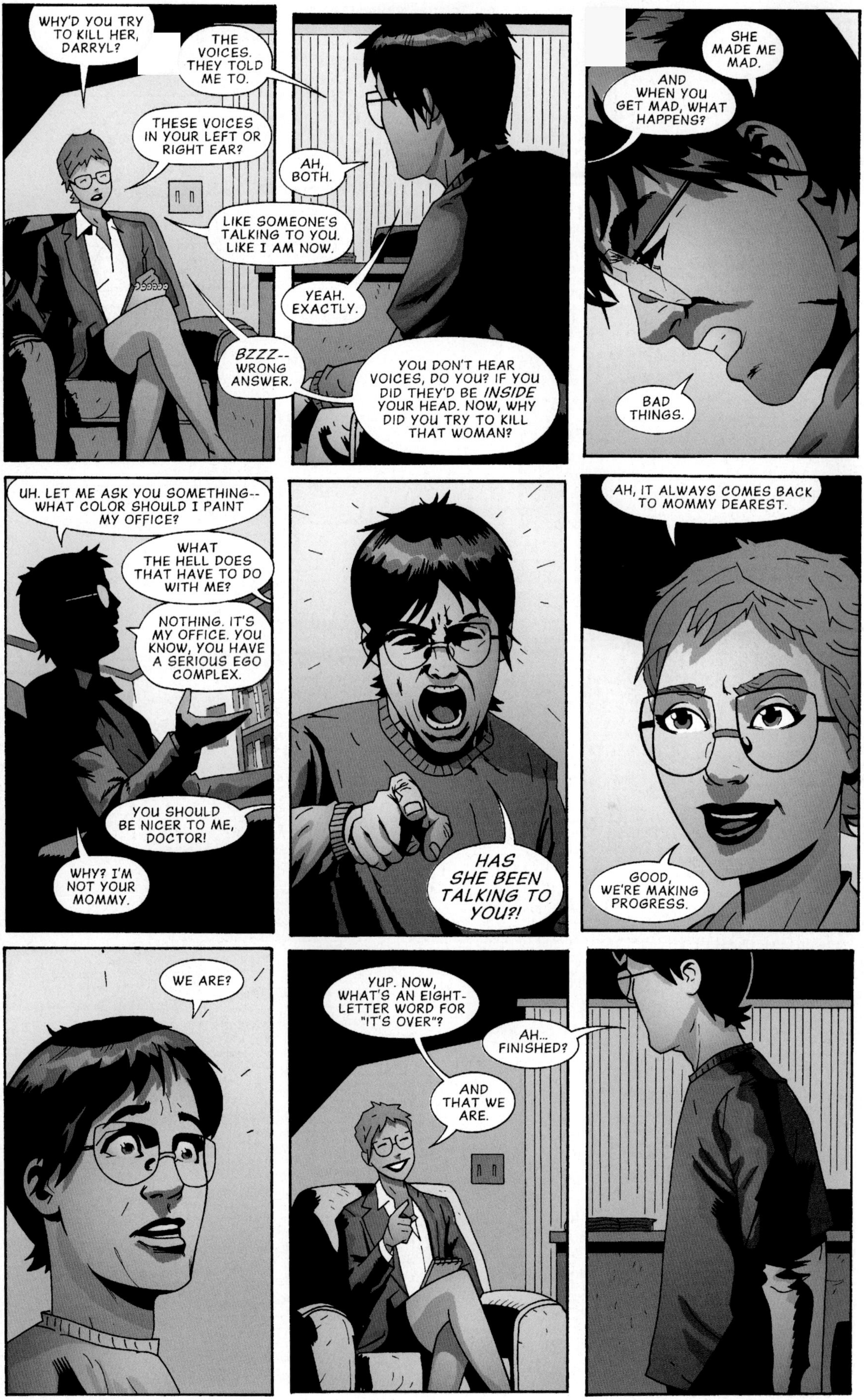
WHY'D YOU TRY TO KILL HER, DARRYL?
THE VOICES. THEY TOLD ME TO.
THESE VOICES IN YOUR LEFT OR RIGHT EAR?
AH, BOTH.
LIKE SOMEONE'S TALKING TO YOU. LIKE I AM NOW.
YEAH. EXACTLY.
BZZZ-- WRONG ANSWER.
YOU DON'T HEAR VOICES, DO YOU? IF YOU DID THEY'D BE INSIDE YOUR HEAD. NOW, WHY DID YOU TRY TO KILL THAT WOMAN?
SHE MADE ME MAD.
AND WHEN YOU GET MAD, WHAT HAPPENS?
BAD THINGS.
UH. LET ME ASK YOU SOMETHING-- WHAT COLOR SHOULD I PAINT MY OFFICE?
WHAT THE HELL DOES THAT HAVE TO DO WITH ME?
NOTHING. IT'S MY OFFICE. YOU KNOW, YOU HAVE A SERIOUS EGO COMPLEX.
YOU SHOULD BE NICER TO ME, DOCTOR!
WHY? I'M NOT YOUR MOMMY.
HAS SHE BEEN TALKING TO YOU?!
AH, IT ALWAYS COMES BACK TO MOMMY DEAREST.
GOOD, WE'RE MAKING PROGRESS.
WE ARE?
YUP. NOW, WHAT'S AN EIGHT-LETTER WORD FOR "IT'S OVER"?
AH... FINISHED?
AND THAT WE ARE.

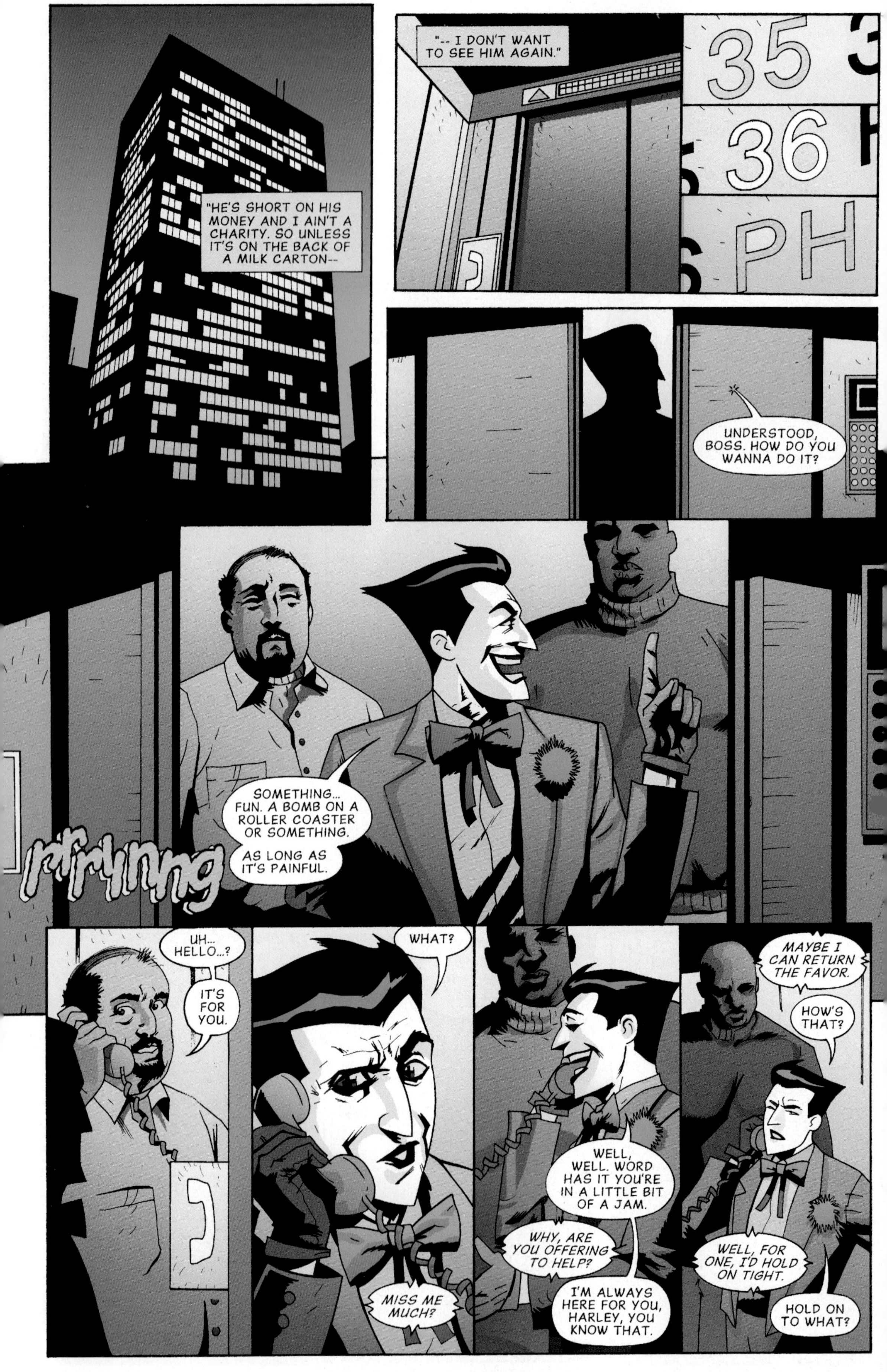
"HE'S SHORT ON HIS MONEY AND I AIN'T A CHARITY. SO UNLESS IT'S ON THE BACK OF A MILK CARTON--
"-- I DON'T WANT TO SEE HIM AGAIN."
35
36
PH
UNDERSTOOD, BOSS. HOW DO YOU WANNA DO IT?
SOMETHING... FUN. A BOMB ON A ROLLER COASTER OR SOMETHING.
AS LONG AS IT'S PAINFUL.
rrrrynnng
UH... HELLO...?
IT'S FOR YOU.
WHAT?
MISS ME MUCH?
WELL, WELL. WORD HAS IT YOU'RE IN A LITTLE BIT OF A JAM.
WHY, ARE YOU OFFERING TO HELP?
I'M ALWAYS HERE FOR YOU, HARLEY, YOU KNOW THAT.
MAYBE I CAN RETURN THE FAVOR.
HOW'S THAT?
WELL, FOR ONE, I'D HOLD ON TIGHT.
HOLD ON TO WHAT?

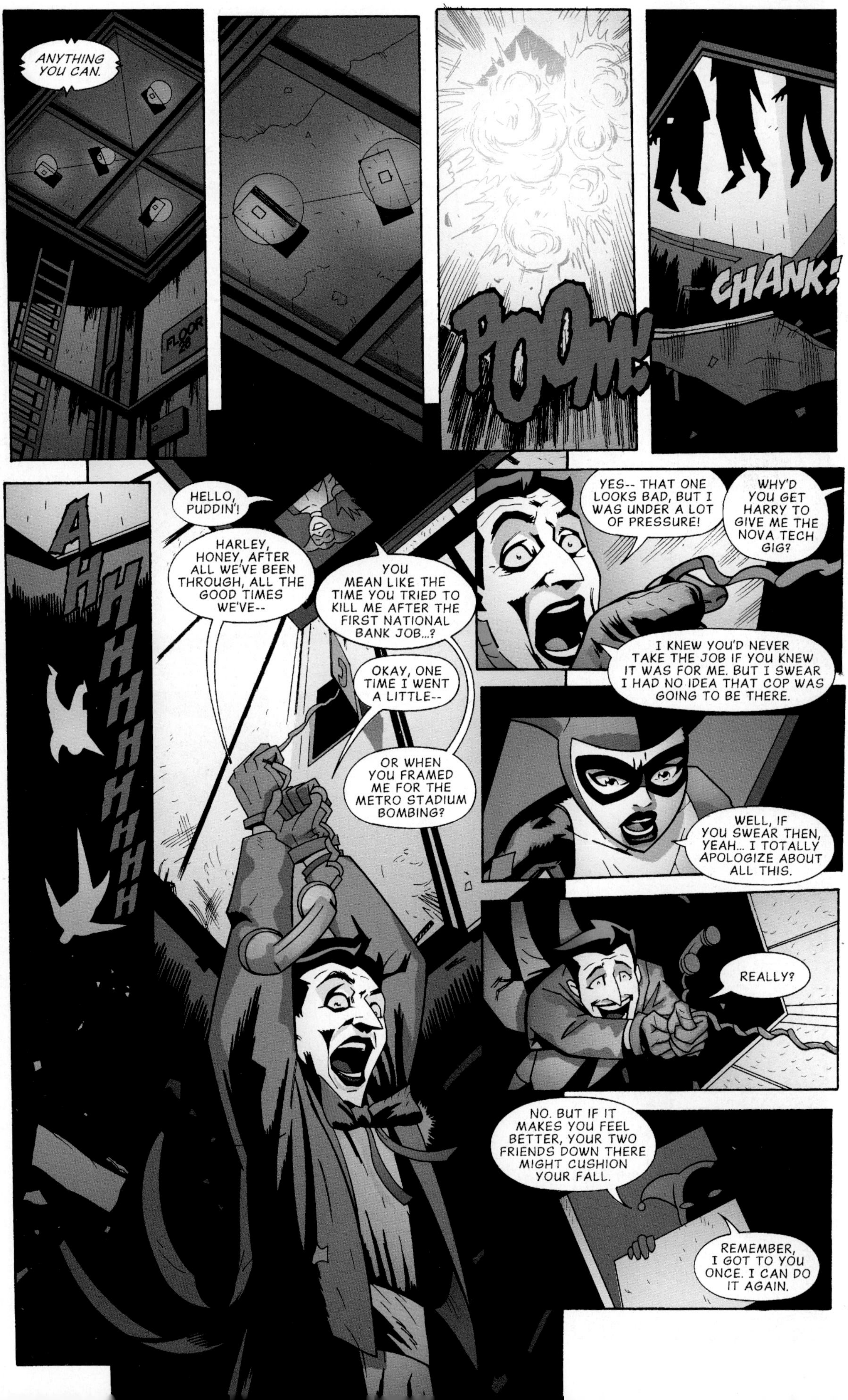

ANYTHING YOU CAN.
FLOOR 28
POOM!
CHANK!
AHHHHHHHHHHH
HELLO, PUDDIN'!
HARLEY, HONEY, AFTER ALL WE'VE BEEN THROUGH, ALL THE GOOD TIMES WE'VE--
YOU MEAN LIKE THE TIME YOU TRIED TO KILL ME AFTER THE FIRST NATIONAL BANK JOB...?
OKAY, ONE TIME I WENT A LITTLE--
OR WHEN YOU FRAMED ME FOR THE METRO STADIUM BOMBING?
YES-- THAT ONE LOOKS BAD, BUT I WAS UNDER A LOT OF PRESSURE!
WHY'D YOU GET HARRY TO GIVE ME THE NOVA TECH GIG?
I KNEW YOU'D NEVER TAKE THE JOB IF YOU KNEW IT WAS FOR ME. BUT I SWEAR I HAD NO IDEA THAT COP WAS GOING TO BE THERE.
WELL, IF YOU SWEAR THEN, YEAH... I TOTALLY APOLOGIZE ABOUT ALL THIS.
REALLY?
NO. BUT IF IT MAKES YOU FEEL BETTER, YOUR TWO FRIENDS DOWN THERE MIGHT CUSHION YOUR FALL.
REMEMBER, I GOT TO YOU ONCE. I CAN DO IT AGAIN.

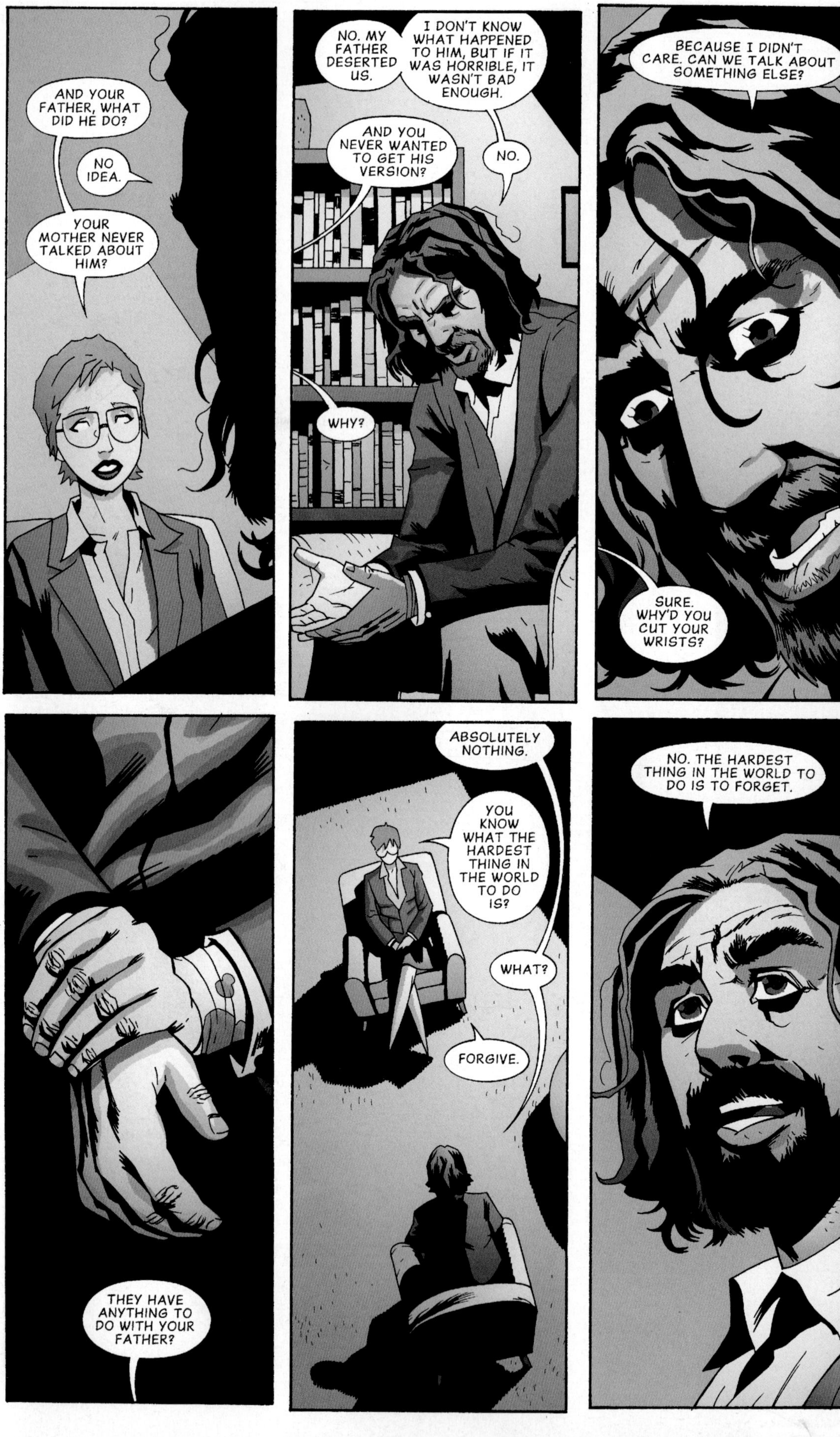
AND YOUR FATHER, WHAT DID HE DO?
NO IDEA.
YOUR MOTHER NEVER TALKED ABOUT HIM?
NO. MY FATHER DESERTED US.
I DON'T KNOW WHAT HAPPENED TO HIM, BUT IF IT WAS HORRIBLE, IT WASN'T BAD ENOUGH.
AND YOU NEVER WANTED TO GET HIS VERSION?
NO.
WHY?
BECAUSE I DIDN'T CARE. CAN WE TALK ABOUT SOMETHING ELSE?
SURE. WHY'D YOU CUT YOUR WRISTS?
THEY HAVE ANYTHING TO DO WITH YOUR FATHER?
ABSOLUTELY NOTHING.
YOU KNOW WHAT THE HARDEST THING IN THE WORLD TO DO IS?
WHAT?
FORGIVE.
NO. THE HARDEST THING IN THE WORLD TO DO IS TO FORGET.

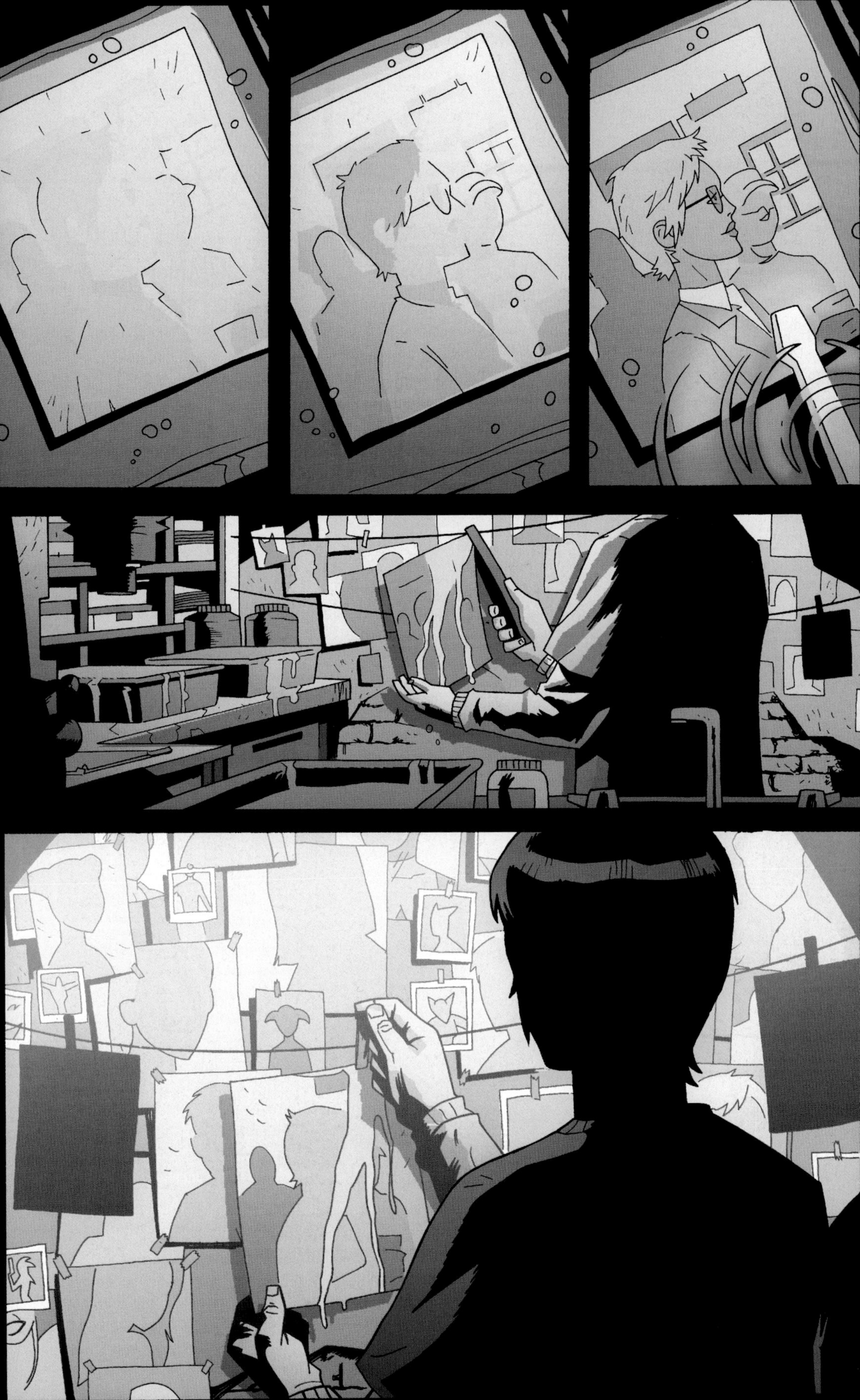

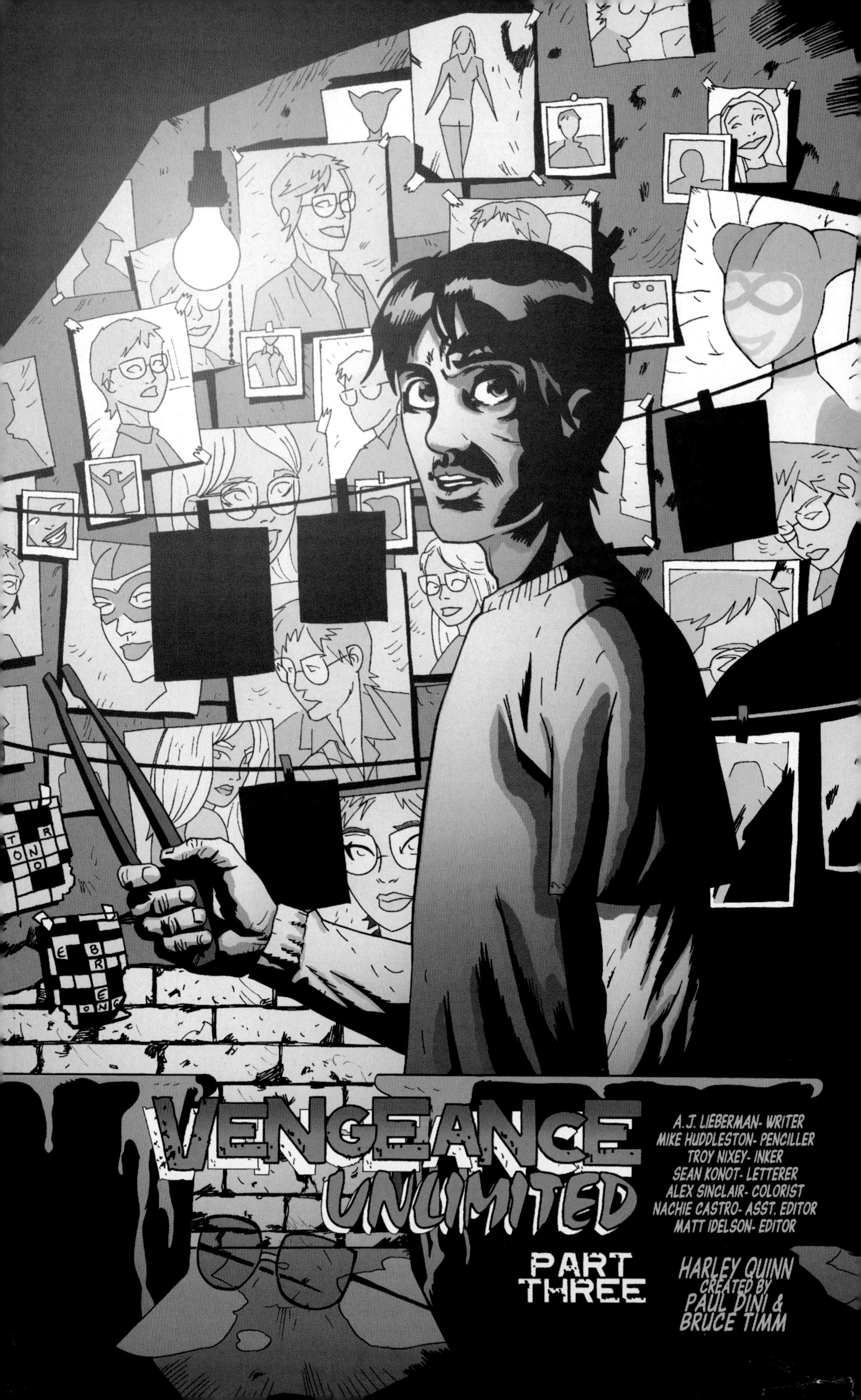
VENGEANCE UNLIMITED
A.J. LIEBERMAN- WRITER
MIKE HUDDLESTON- PENCILLER
TROY NIXEY- INKER
SEAN KONOT- LETTERER
ALEX SINCLAIR- COLORIST
NACHIE CASTRO- ASST. EDITOR
MATT IDELSON- EDITOR
PART THREE
HARLEY QUINN CREATED BY PAUL DINI & BRUCE TIMM

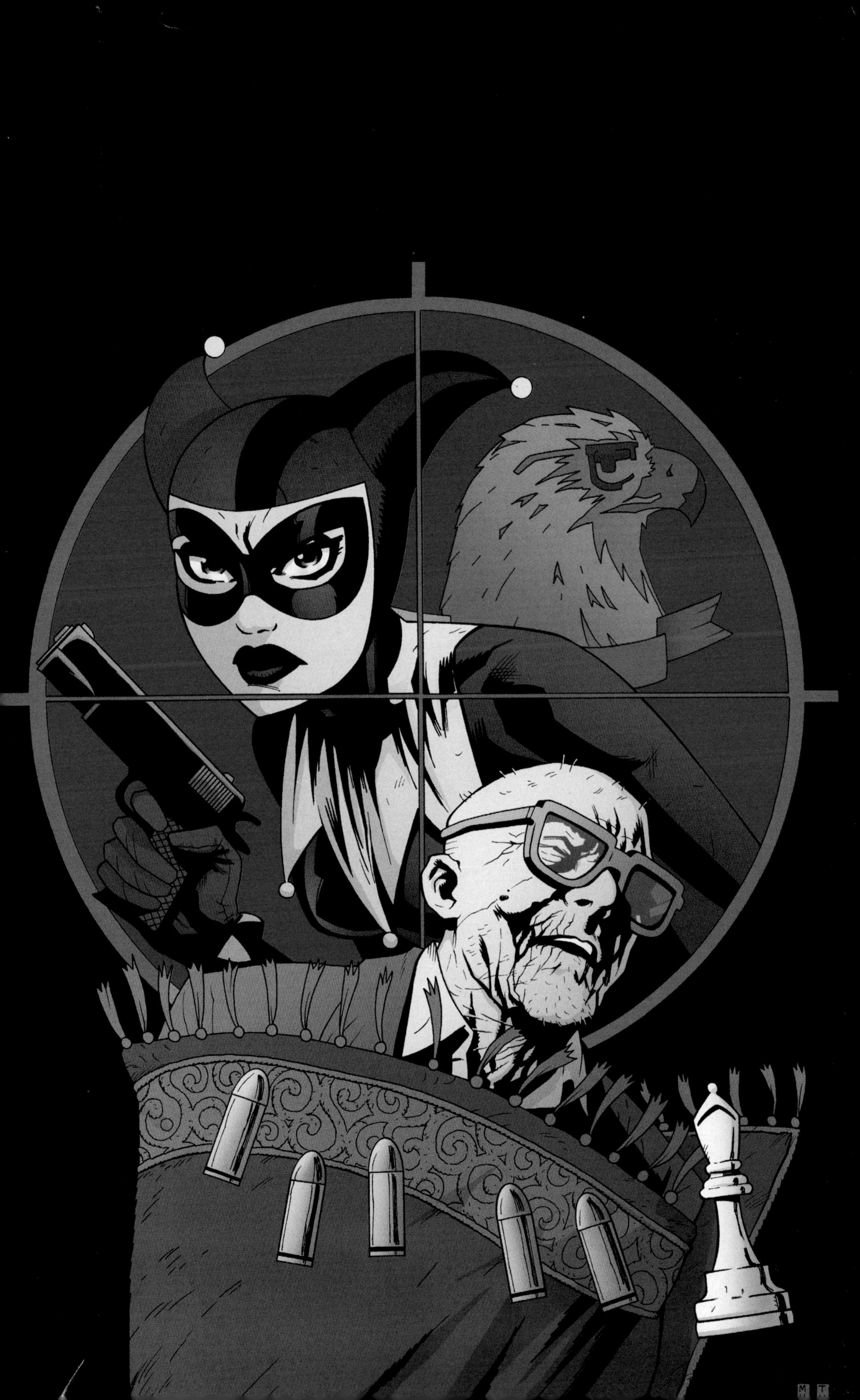

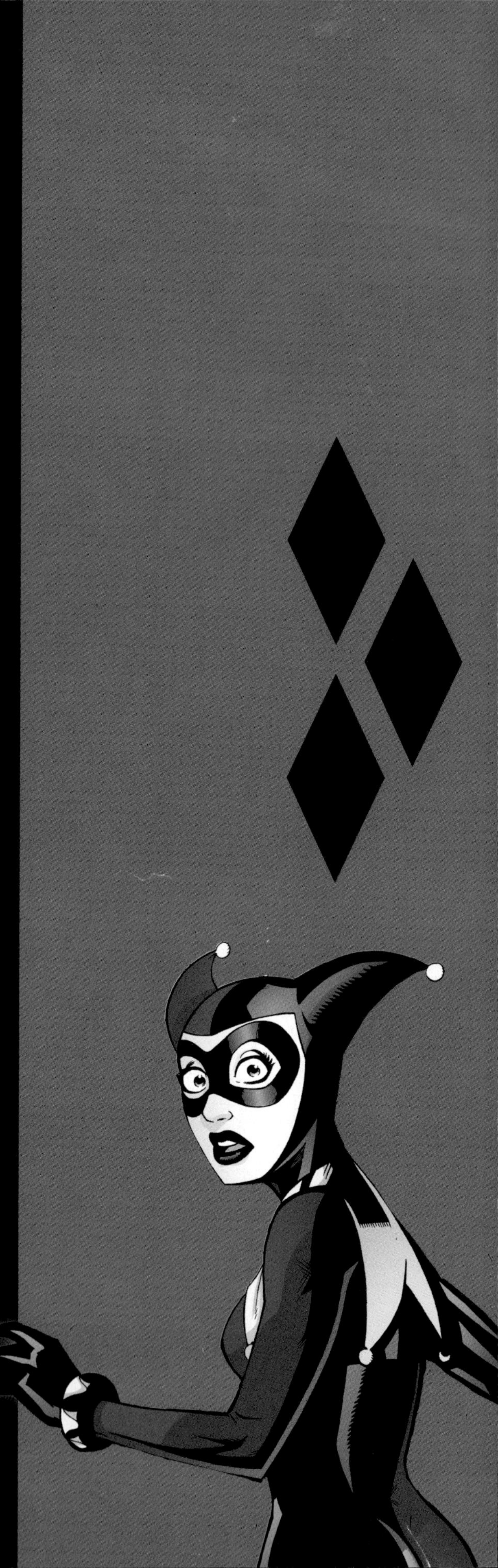

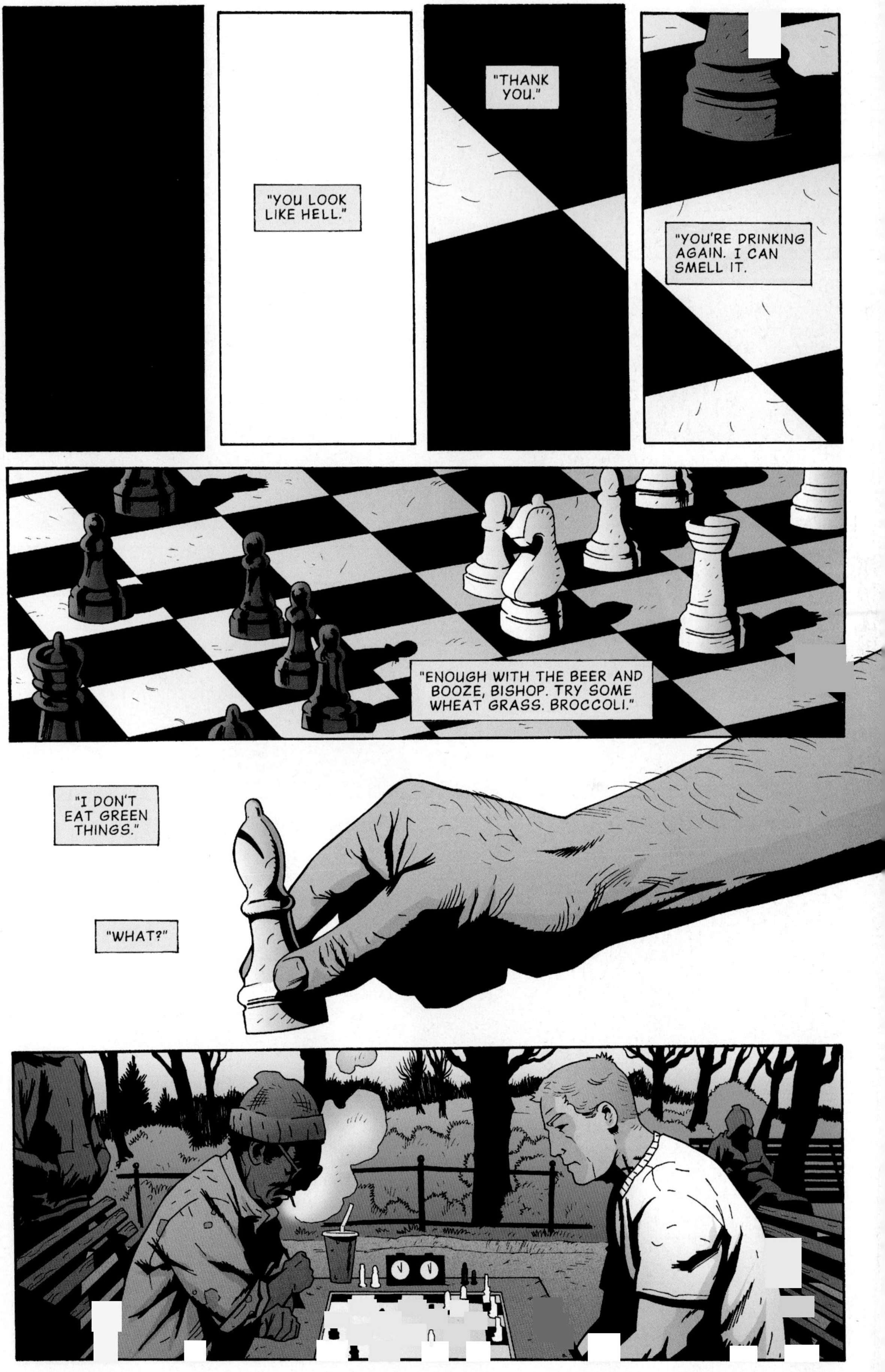
"YOU LOOK LIKE HELL."
"THANK YOU."
"YOU'RE DRINKING AGAIN. I CAN SMELL IT.
"ENOUGH WITH THE BEER AND BOOZE, BISHOP. TRY SOME WHEAT GRASS. BROCCOLI."
"I DON'T EAT GREEN THINGS."
"WHAT?"

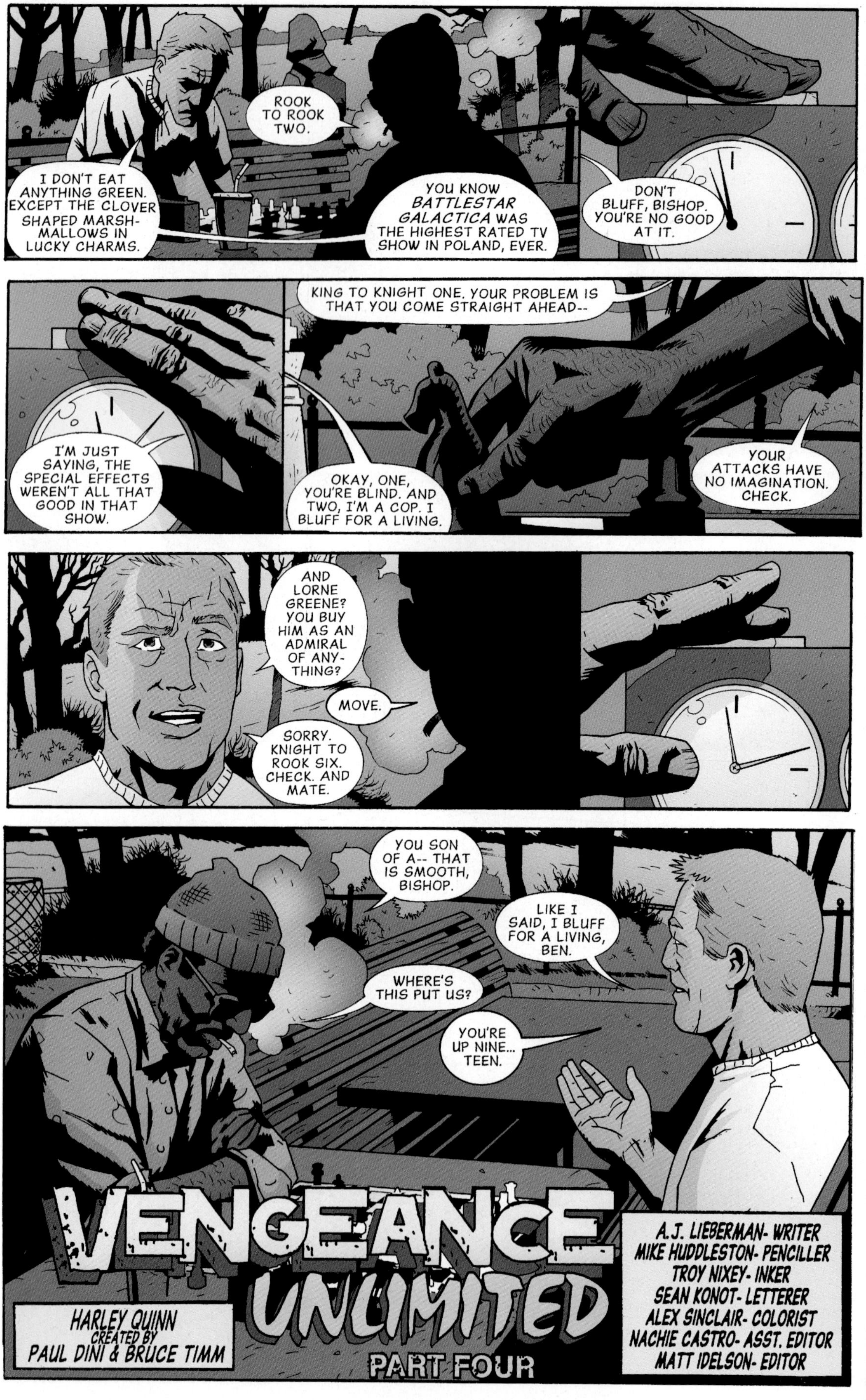
ROOK TO ROOK TWO.
I DON'T EAT ANYTHING GREEN. EXCEPT THE CLOVER SHAPED MARSH-MALLOWS IN LUCKY CHARMS.
YOU KNOW BATTLESTAR GALACTICA WAS THE HIGHEST RATED TV SHOW IN POLAND, EVER.
DON'T BLUFF, BISHOP. YOU'RE NO GOOD AT IT.
I'M JUST SAYING, THE SPECIAL EFFECTS WEREN'T ALL THAT GOOD IN THAT SHOW.
KING TO KNIGHT ONE. YOUR PROBLEM IS THAT YOU COME STRAIGHT AHEAD--
OKAY, ONE, YOU'RE BLIND. AND TWO, I'M A COP. I BLUFF FOR A LIVING.
YOUR ATTACKS HAVE NO IMAGINATION. CHECK.
AND LORNE GREENE? YOU BUY HIM AS AN ADMIRAL OF ANY-THING?
MOVE.
SORRY. KNIGHT TO ROOK SIX. CHECK. AND MATE.
YOU SON OF A-- THAT IS SMOOTH, BISHOP.
LIKE I SAID, I BLUFF FOR A LIVING, BEN.
WHERE'S THIS PUT US?
YOU'RE UP NINE... TEEN.
VENGEANCE UNLIMITED
PART FOUR
HARLEY QUINN CREATED BY PAUL DINI & BRUCE TIMM
A.J. LIEBERMAN- WRITER
MIKE HUDDLESTON- PENCILLER
TROY NIXEY- INKER
SEAN KONOT- LETTERER
ALEX SINCLAIR- COLORIST
NACHIE CASTRO- ASST. EDITOR
MATT IDELSON- EDITOR

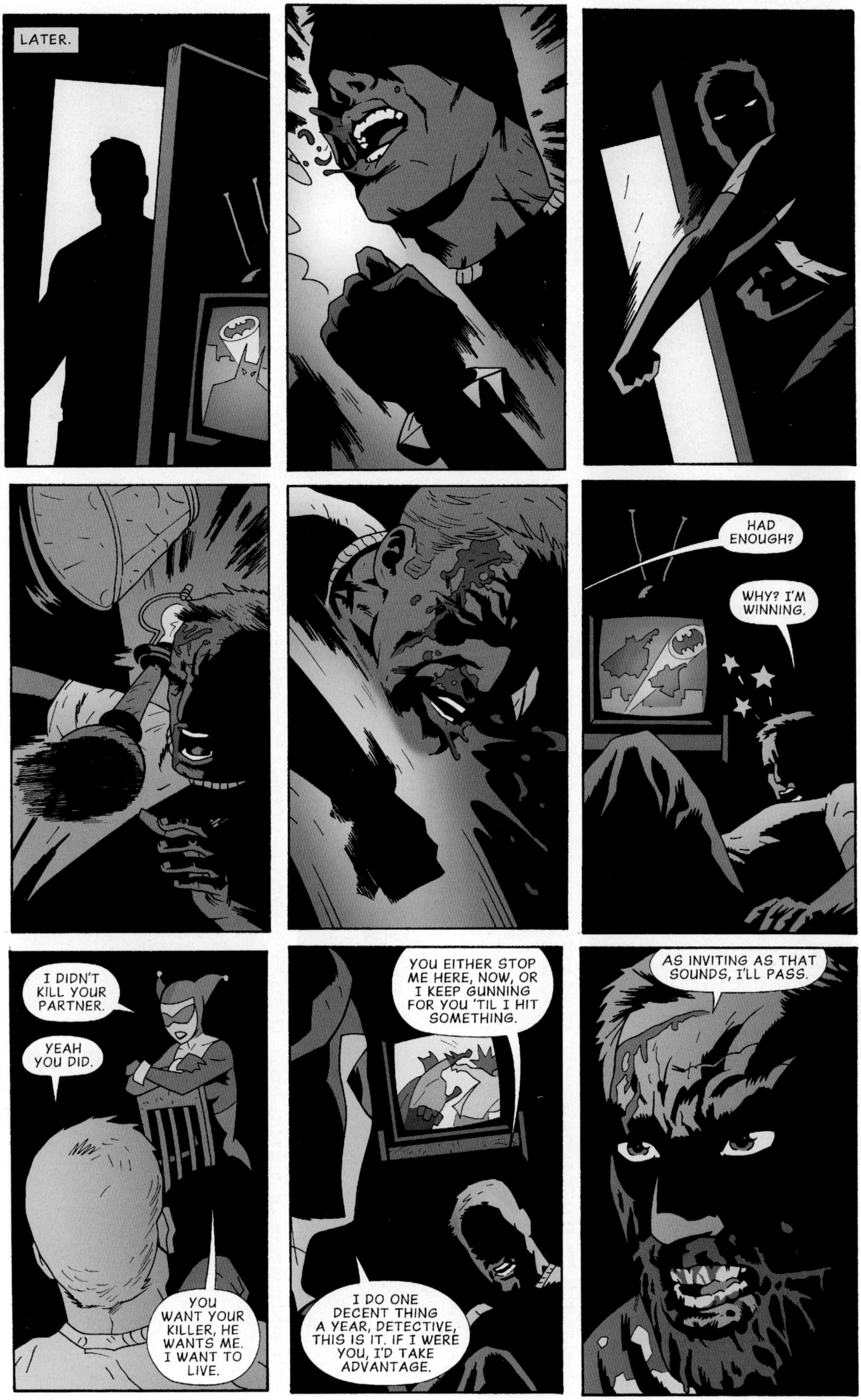

LATER.
HAD ENOUGH?
WHY? I'M WINNING.
I DIDN'T KILL YOUR PARTNER.
YEAH YOU DID.
YOU WANT YOUR KILLER, HE WANTS ME. I WANT TO LIVE.
YOU EITHER STOP ME HERE, NOW, OR I KEEP GUNNING FOR YOU 'TIL I HIT SOMETHING.
I DO ONE DECENT THING A YEAR, DETECTIVE, THIS IS IT. IF I WERE YOU, I'D TAKE ADVANTAGE.
AS INVITING AS THAT SOUNDS, I'LL PASS.

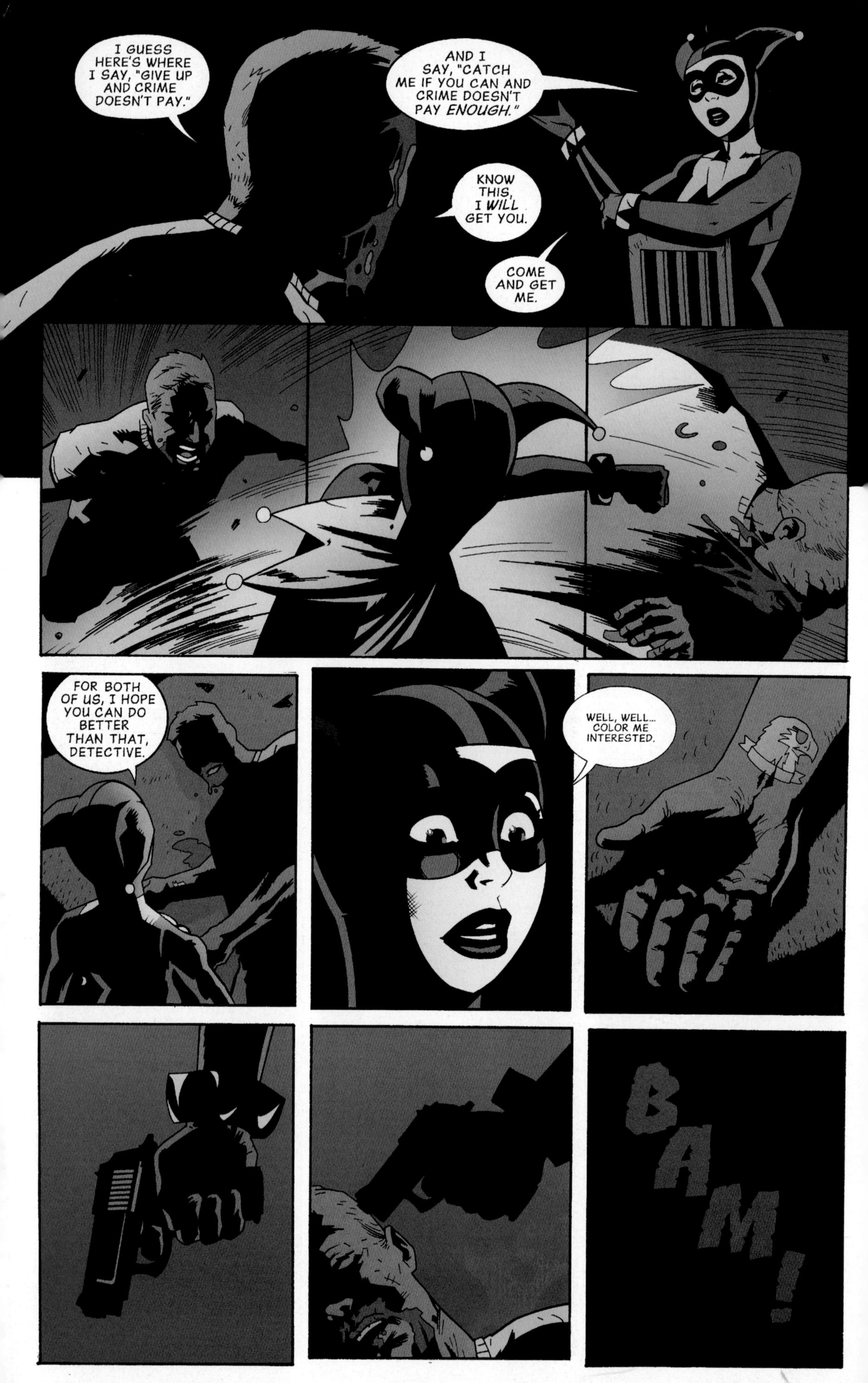
I GUESS HERE'S WHERE I SAY, "GIVE UP AND CRIME DOESN'T PAY."
AND I SAY, "CATCH ME IF YOU CAN AND CRIME DOESN'T PAY *ENOUGH*."
KNOW THIS, I *WILL* GET YOU.
COME AND GET ME.
FOR BOTH OF US, I HOPE YOU CAN DO BETTER THAN THAT, DETECTIVE.
WELL, WELL... COLOR ME INTERESTED.
BAM!

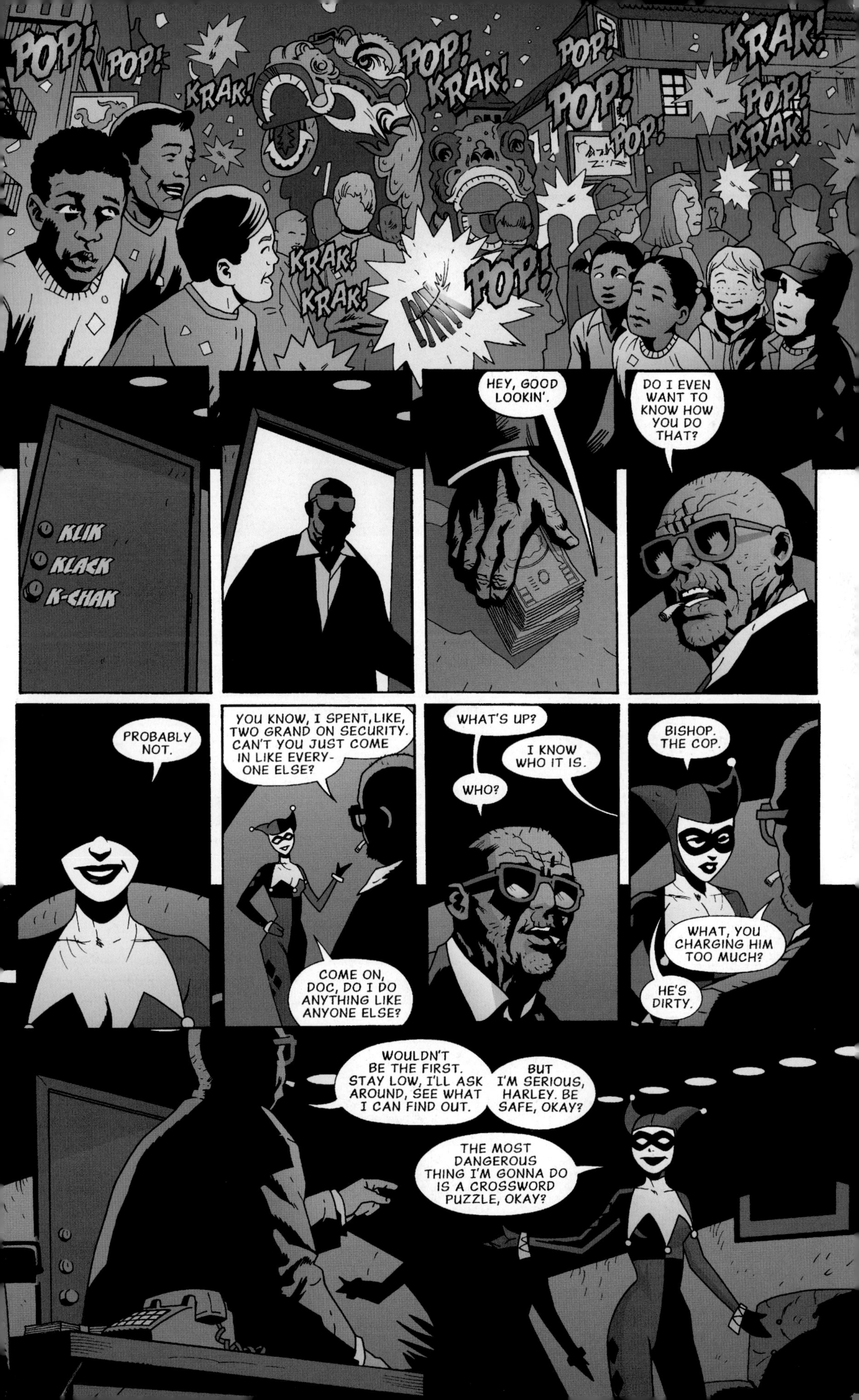
POP! POP!
KRAK!
POP! KRAK!
POP! POP! POP!
KRAK! POP! KRAK!
KRAK! KRAK!
POP!
KLIK
KLACK
K-CHAK
HEY, GOOD LOOKIN'.
DO I EVEN WANT TO KNOW HOW YOU DO THAT?
PROBABLY NOT.
YOU KNOW, I SPENT, LIKE, TWO GRAND ON SECURITY. CAN'T YOU JUST COME IN LIKE EVERY-ONE ELSE?
COME ON, DOC, DO I DO ANYTHING LIKE ANYONE ELSE?
WHAT'S UP?
I KNOW WHO IT IS.
WHO?
BISHOP. THE COP.
WHAT, YOU CHARGING HIM TOO MUCH?
HE'S DIRTY.
WOULDN'T BE THE FIRST. STAY LOW, I'LL ASK AROUND, SEE WHAT I CAN FIND OUT.
BUT I'M SERIOUS, HARLEY. BE SAFE, OKAY?
THE MOST DANGEROUS THING I'M GONNA DO IS A CROSSWORD PUZZLE, OKAY?

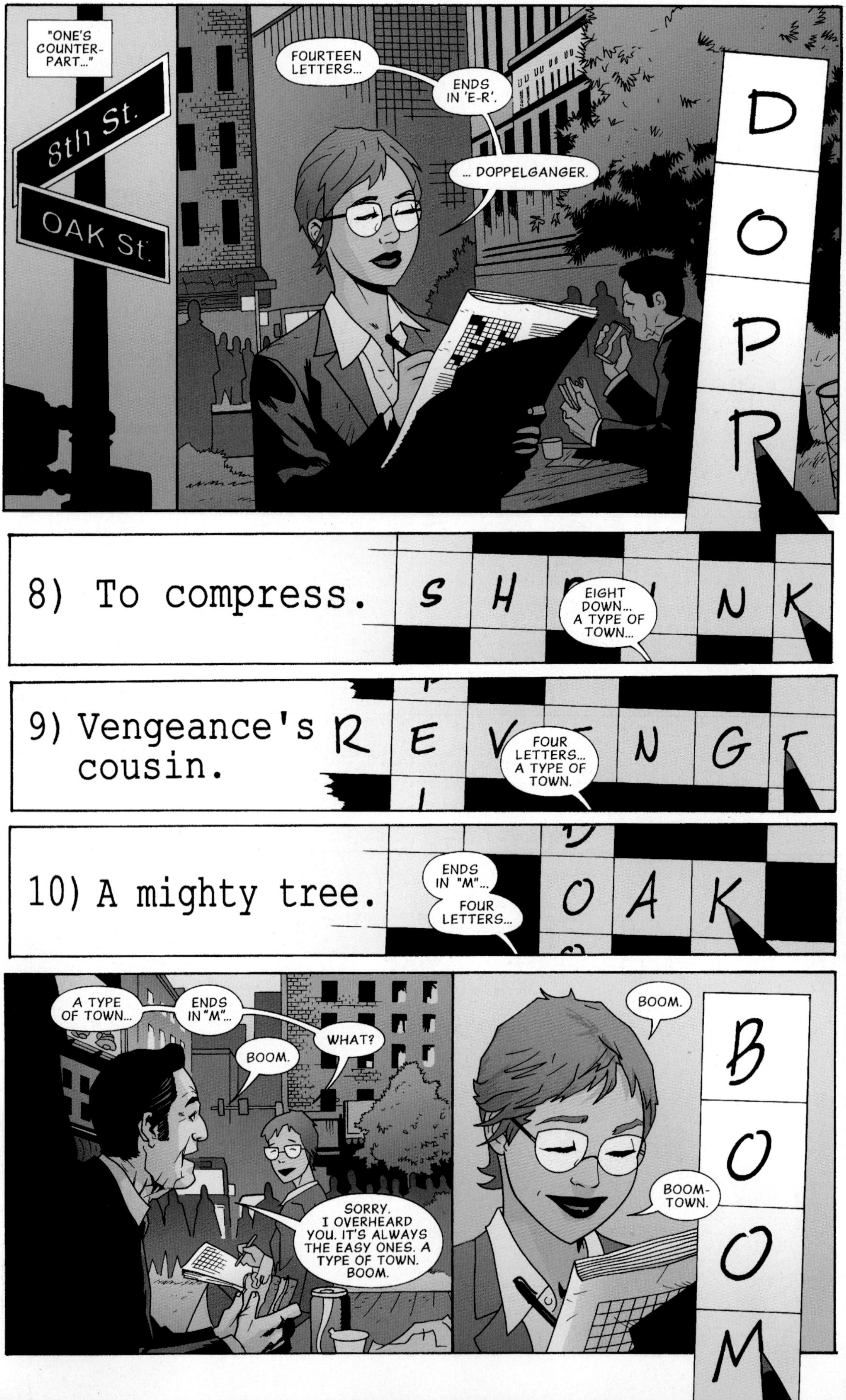
"ONE'S COUNTER-PART..."
8th St.
OAK St.
FOURTEEN LETTERS...
ENDS IN 'E-R'.
... DOPPELGANGER.
8) To compress.
EIGHT DOWN... A TYPE OF TOWN...
9) Vengeance's cousin.
FOUR LETTERS... A TYPE OF TOWN.
10) A mighty tree.
ENDS IN "M"...
FOUR LETTERS...
OAK
A TYPE OF TOWN...
ENDS IN "M"...
WHAT?
BOOM.
SORRY. I OVERHEARD YOU. IT'S ALWAYS THE EASY ONES. A TYPE OF TOWN. BOOM.
BOOM.
BOOM-TOWN.
BOOM

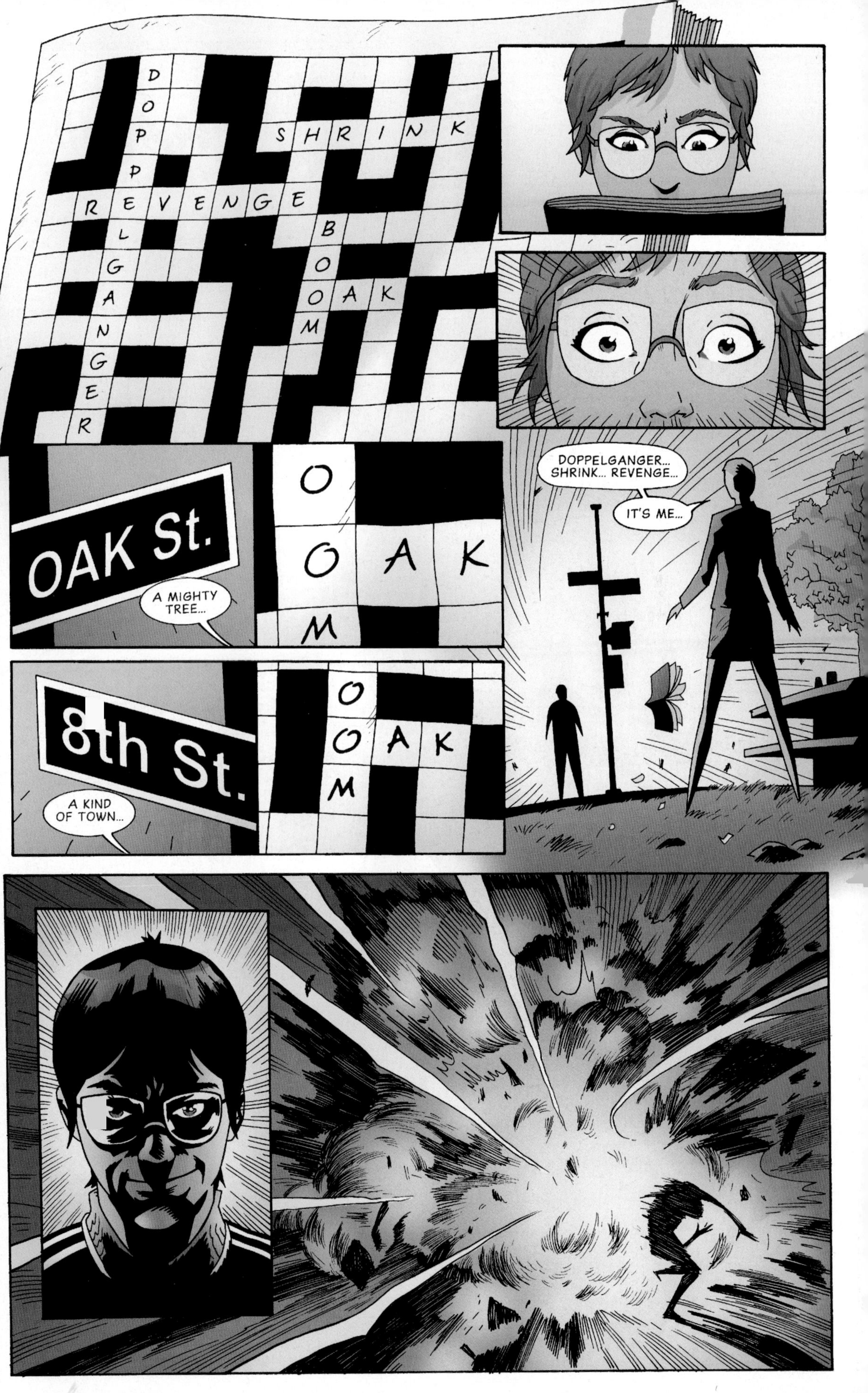
DOPPELGANGER
SHRINK
REVENGE
BOOM
OAK
OAK St.
A MIGHTY TREE...
OAK
8th St.
A KIND OF TOWN...
OAK
DOPPELGANGER... SHRINK... REVENGE...
IT'S ME...

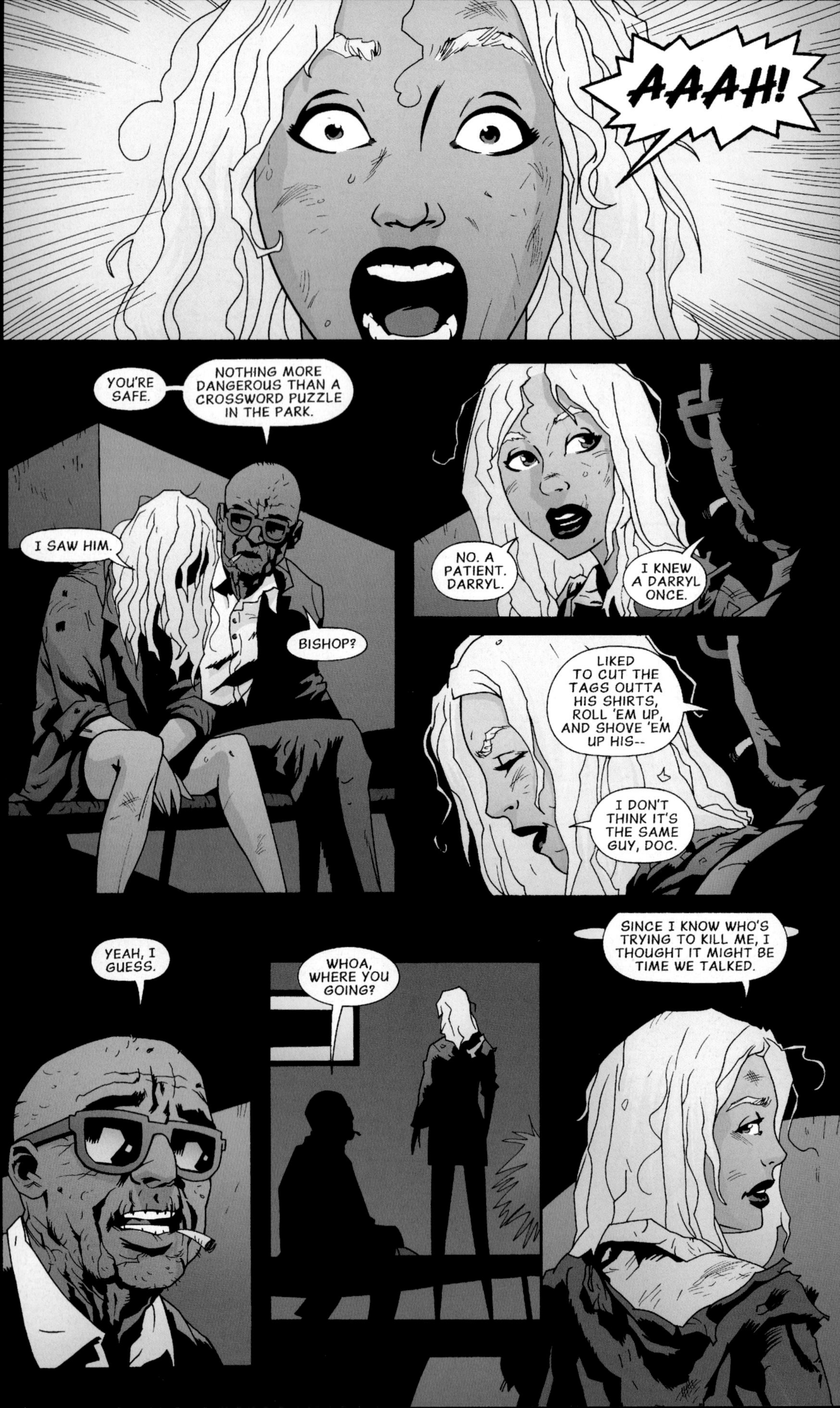
AAAH!
YOU'RE SAFE.
NOTHING MORE DANGEROUS THAN A CROSSWORD PUZZLE IN THE PARK.
I SAW HIM.
BISHOP?
NO. A PATIENT. DARRYL.
I KNEW A DARRYL ONCE.
LIKED TO CUT THE TAGS OUTTA HIS SHIRTS, ROLL 'EM UP, AND SHOVE 'EM UP HIS--
I DON'T THINK IT'S THE SAME GUY, DOC.
YEAH, I GUESS.
WHOA, WHERE YOU GOING?
SINCE I KNOW WHO'S TRYING TO KILL ME, I THOUGHT IT MIGHT BE TIME WE TALKED.

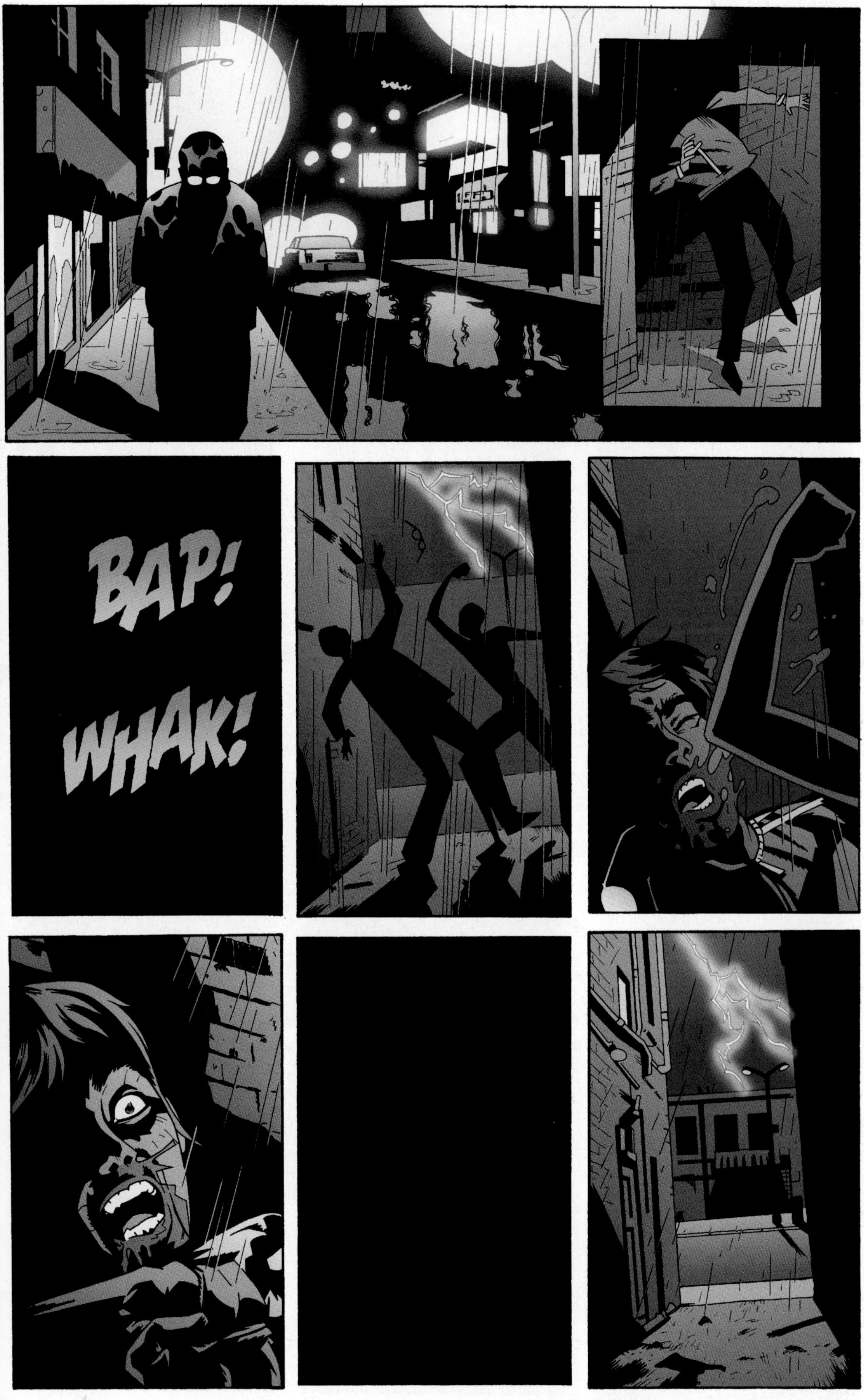
BAP!
WHAK!

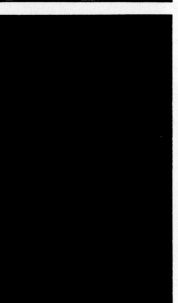

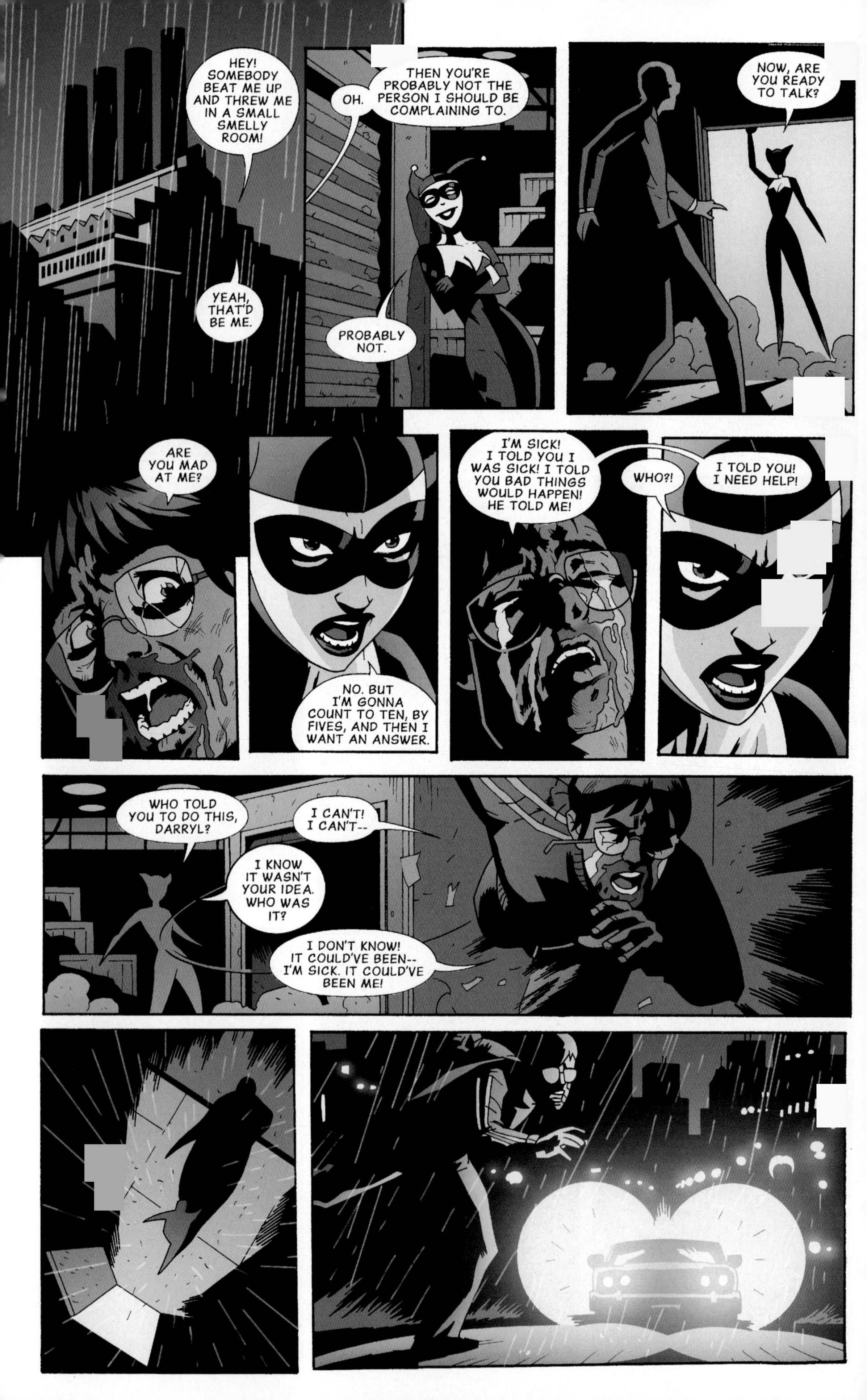
HEY! SOMEBODY BEAT ME UP AND THREW ME IN A SMALL SMELLY ROOM!
YEAH, THAT'D BE ME.
OH.
THEN YOU'RE PROBABLY NOT THE PERSON I SHOULD BE COMPLAINING TO.
PROBABLY NOT.
NOW, ARE YOU READY TO TALK?
ARE YOU MAD AT ME?
NO. BUT I'M GONNA COUNT TO TEN, BY FIVES, AND THEN I WANT AN ANSWER.
I'M SICK! I TOLD YOU I WAS SICK! I TOLD YOU BAD THINGS WOULD HAPPEN! HE TOLD ME!
WHO?!
I TOLD YOU! I NEED HELP!
WHO TOLD YOU TO DO THIS, DARRYL?
I CAN'T! I CAN'T--
I KNOW IT WASN'T YOUR IDEA. WHO WAS IT?
I DON'T KNOW! IT COULD'VE BEEN-- I'M SICK. IT COULD'VE BEEN ME!

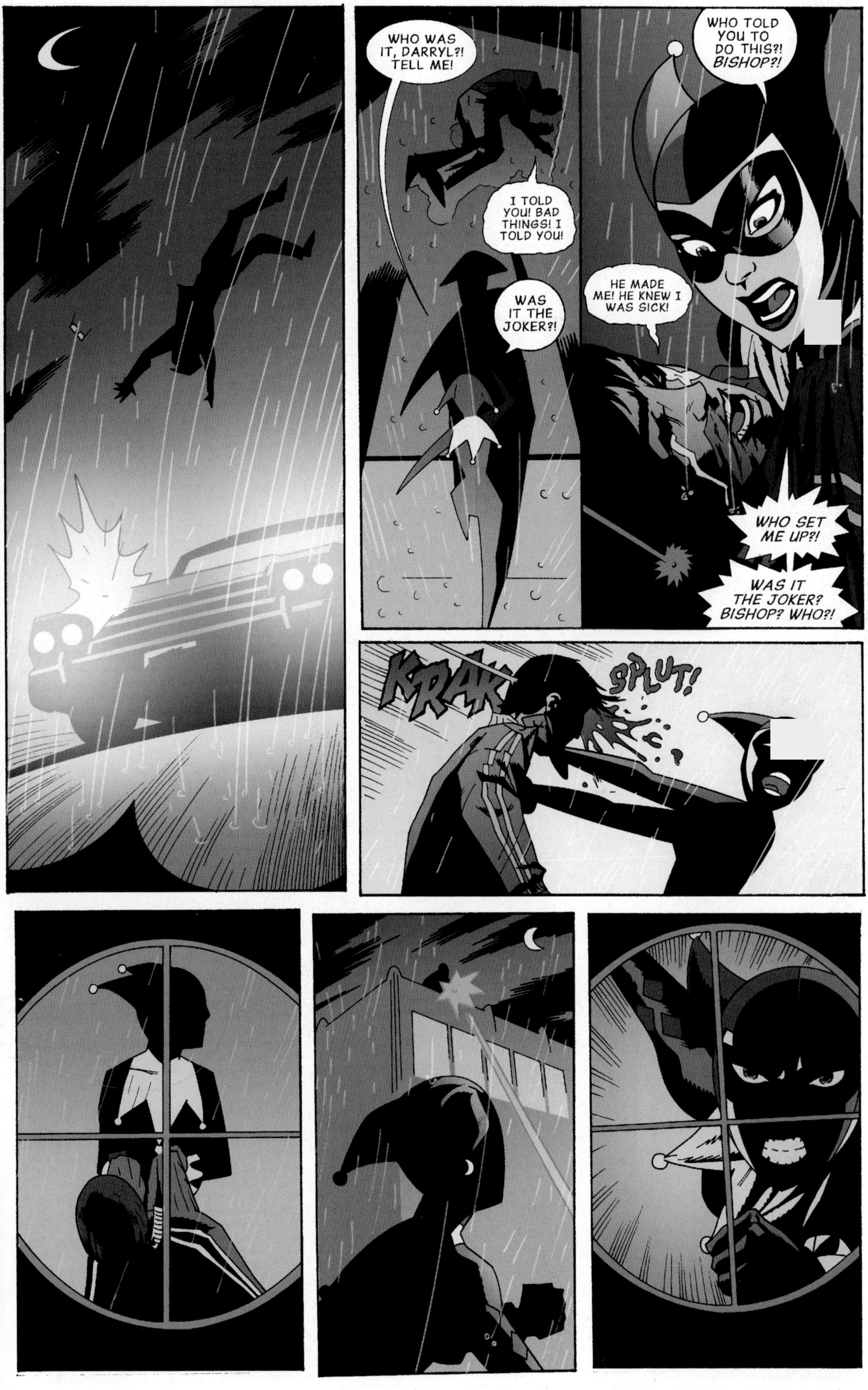
WHO WAS IT, DARRYL?! TELL ME!
I TOLD YOU! BAD THINGS! I TOLD YOU!
WAS IT THE JOKER?!
WHO TOLD YOU TO DO THIS?! BISHOP?!
HE MADE ME! HE KNEW I WAS SICK!
WHO SET ME UP?!
WAS IT THE JOKER? BISHOP? WHO?!
KRAK
SPLUT!

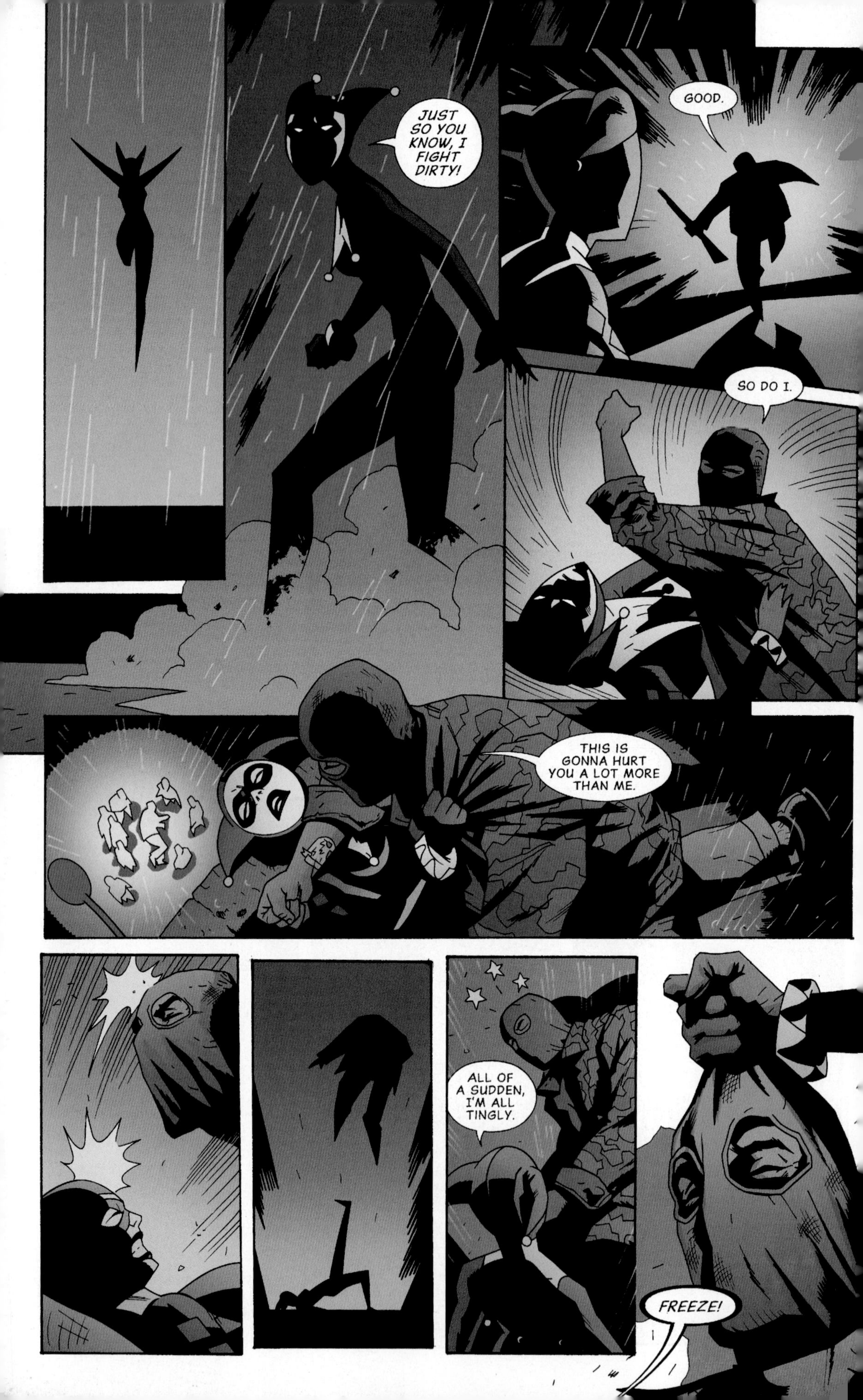
JUST SO YOU KNOW, I FIGHT DIRTY!
GOOD.
SO DO I.
THIS IS GONNA HURT YOU A LOT MORE THAN ME.
ALL OF A SUDDEN, I'M ALL TINGLY.
FREEZE!

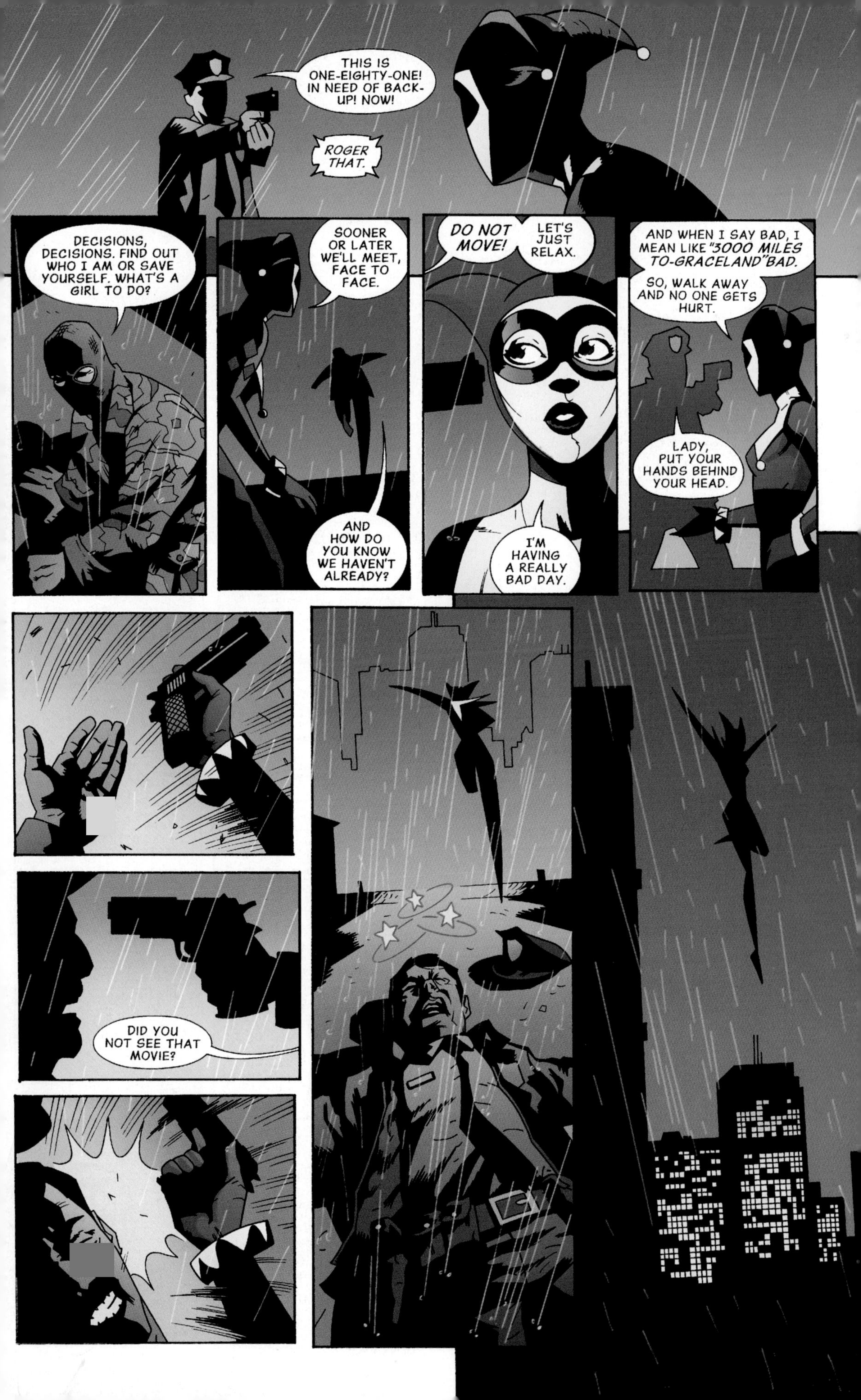
THIS IS ONE-EIGHTY-ONE! IN NEED OF BACK-UP! NOW!
ROGER THAT.
DECISIONS, DECISIONS. FIND OUT WHO I AM OR SAVE YOURSELF. WHAT'S A GIRL TO DO?
SOONER OR LATER WE'LL MEET, FACE TO FACE.
AND HOW DO YOU KNOW WE HAVEN'T ALREADY?
DO NOT MOVE!
LET'S JUST RELAX.
I'M HAVING A REALLY BAD DAY.
AND WHEN I SAY BAD, I MEAN LIKE "3000 MILES TO-GRACELAND" BAD.
SO, WALK AWAY AND NO ONE GETS HURT.
LADY, PUT YOUR HANDS BEHIND YOUR HEAD.
DID YOU NOT SEE THAT MOVIE?

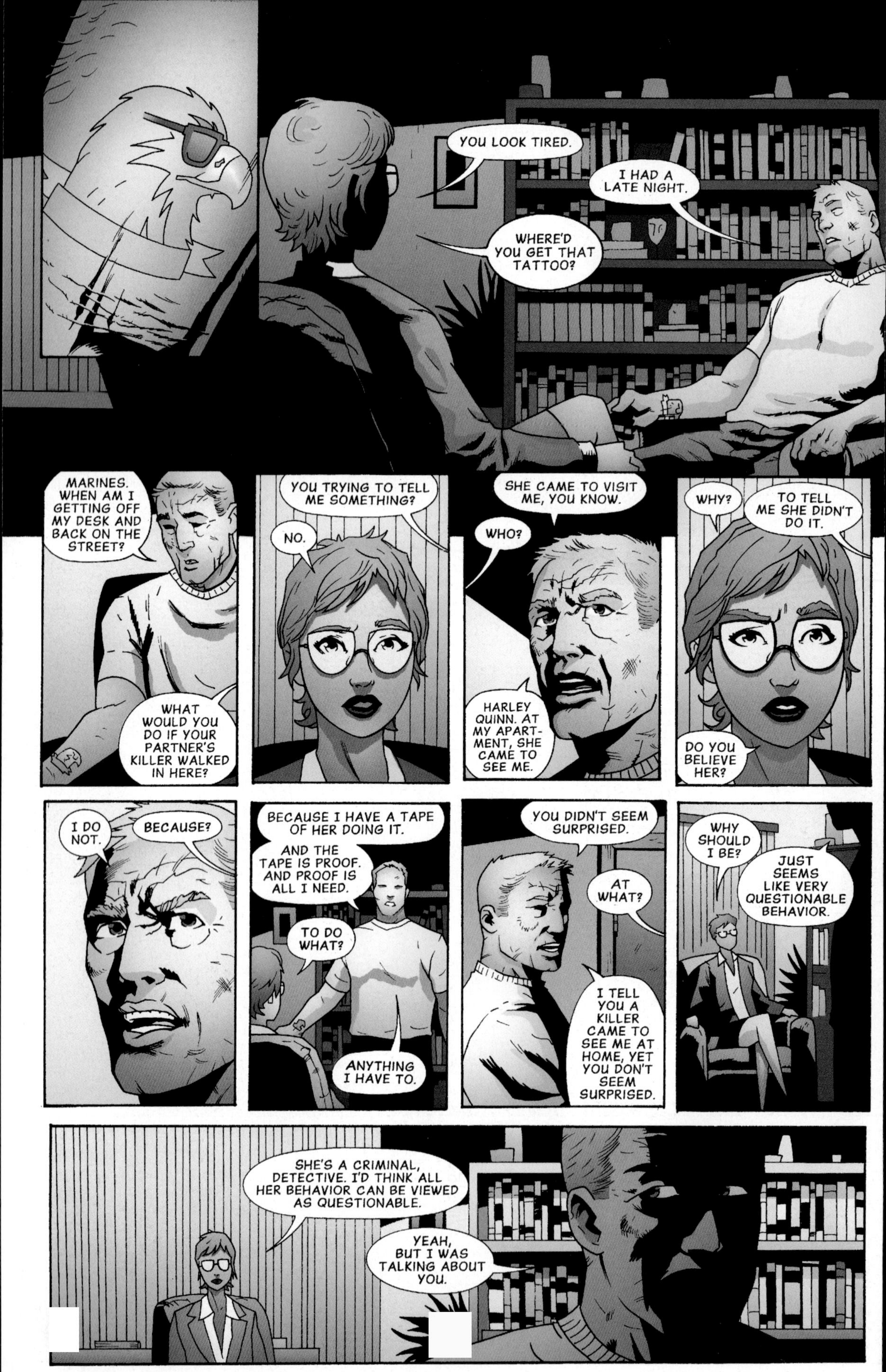
YOU LOOK TIRED.
I HAD A LATE NIGHT.
WHERE'D YOU GET THAT TATTOO?
MARINES. WHEN AM I GETTING OFF MY DESK AND BACK ON THE STREET?
WHAT WOULD YOU DO IF YOUR PARTNER'S KILLER WALKED IN HERE?
YOU TRYING TO TELL ME SOMETHING?
NO.
SHE CAME TO VISIT ME, YOU KNOW.
WHO?
HARLEY QUINN. AT MY APART-MENT, SHE CAME TO SEE ME.
WHY?
TO TELL ME SHE DIDN'T DO IT.
DO YOU BELIEVE HER?
I DO NOT.
BECAUSE?
BECAUSE I HAVE A TAPE OF HER DOING IT.
AND THE TAPE IS PROOF. AND PROOF IS ALL I NEED.
TO DO WHAT?
ANYTHING I HAVE TO.
YOU DIDN'T SEEM SURPRISED.
AT WHAT?
I TELL YOU A KILLER CAME TO SEE ME AT HOME, YET YOU DON'T SEEM SURPRISED.
WHY SHOULD I BE?
JUST SEEMS LIKE VERY QUESTIONABLE BEHAVIOR.
SHE'S A CRIMINAL, DETECTIVE. I'D THINK ALL HER BEHAVIOR CAN BE VIEWED AS QUESTIONABLE.
YEAH, BUT I WAS TALKING ABOUT YOU.

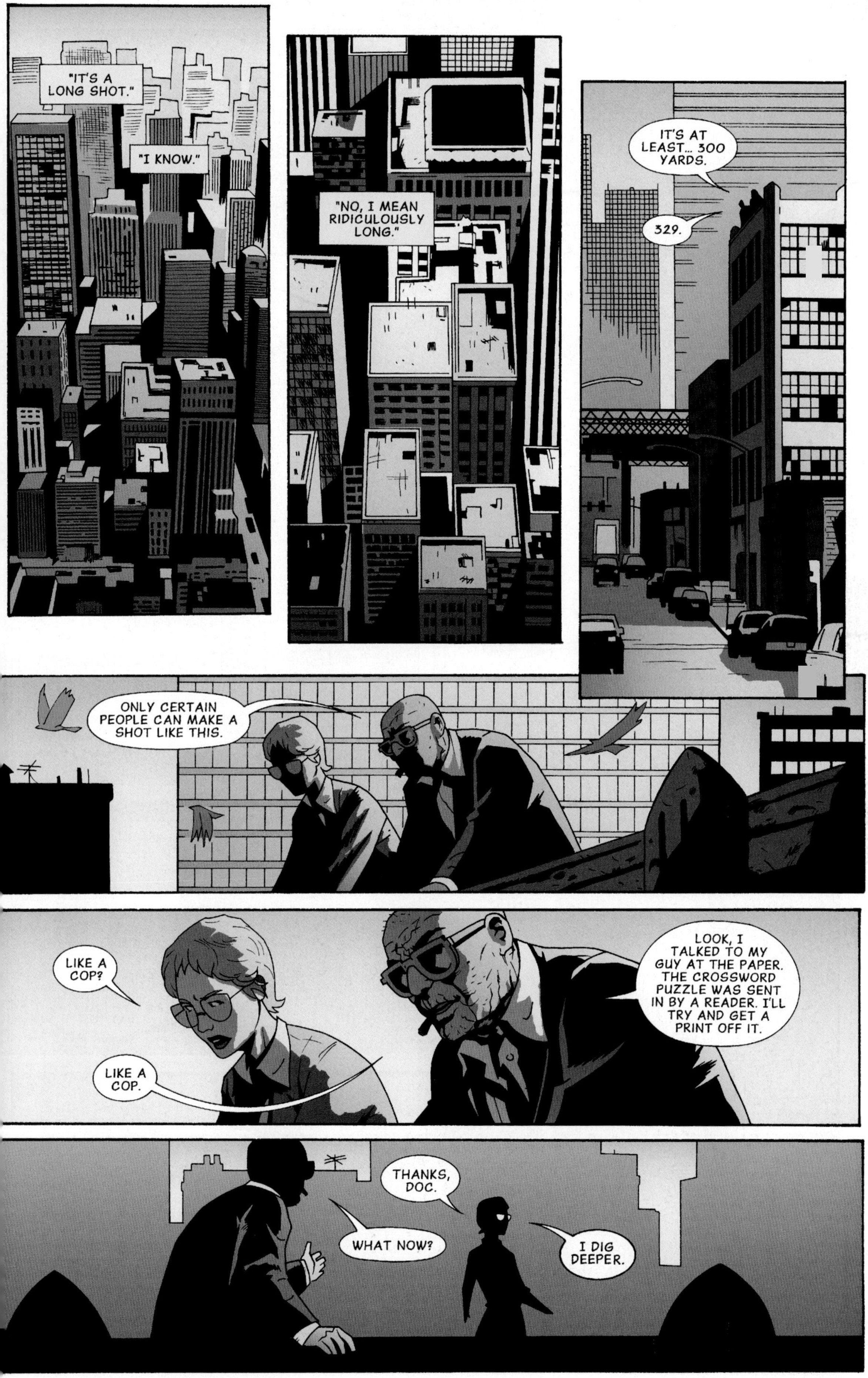

"IT'S A LONG SHOT."
"I KNOW."
"NO, I MEAN RIDICULOUSLY LONG."
IT'S AT LEAST... 300 YARDS.
329.
ONLY CERTAIN PEOPLE CAN MAKE A SHOT LIKE THIS.
LIKE A COP?
LIKE A COP.
LOOK, I TALKED TO MY GUY AT THE PAPER. THE CROSSWORD PUZZLE WAS SENT IN BY A READER. I'LL TRY AND GET A PRINT OFF IT.
THANKS, DOC.
WHAT NOW?
I DIG DEEPER.

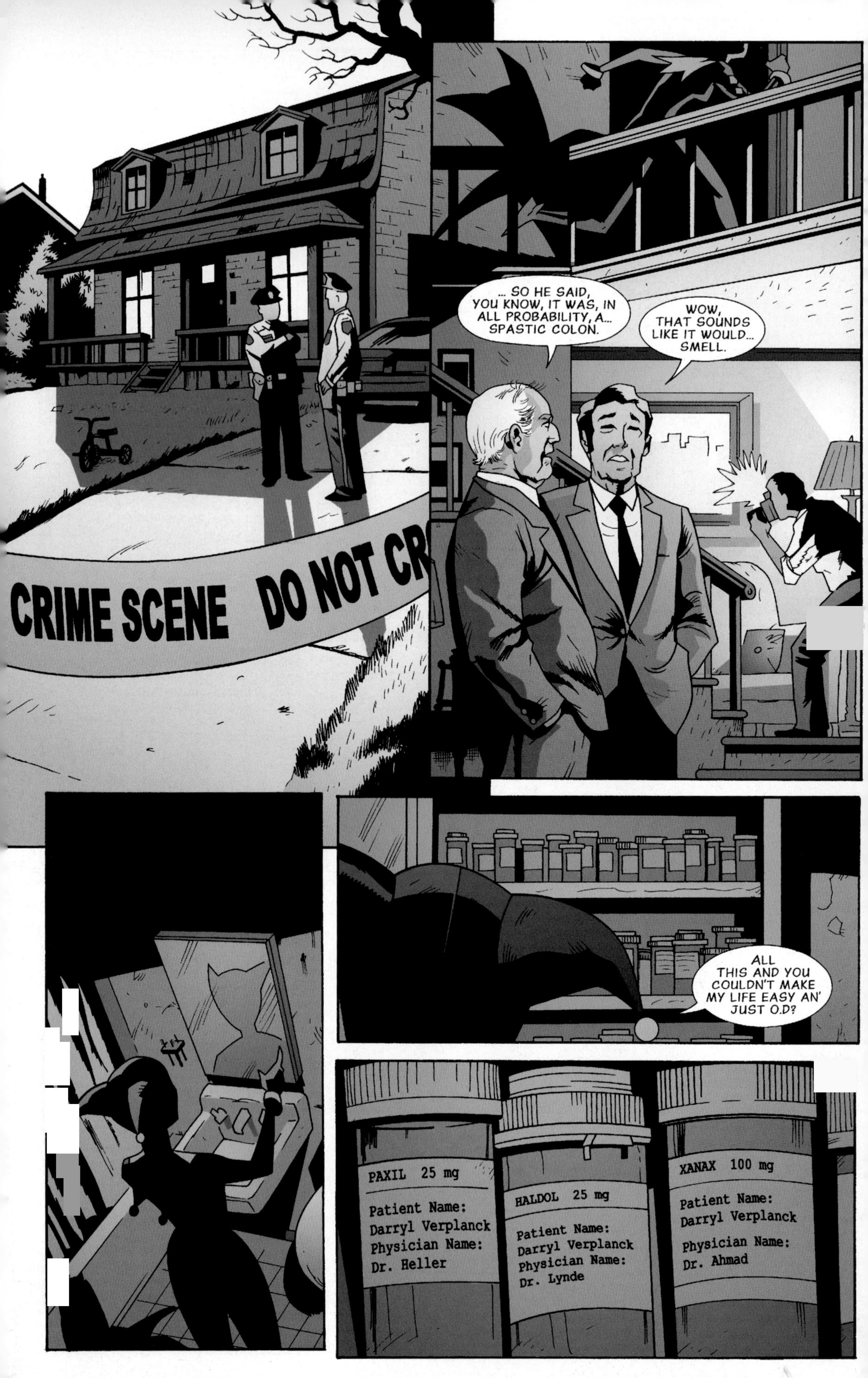
CRIME SCENE DO NOT CR
... SO HE SAID, YOU KNOW, IT WAS, IN ALL PROBABILITY, A... SPASTIC COLON.
WOW, THAT SOUNDS LIKE IT WOULD... SMELL.
ALL THIS AND YOU COULDN'T MAKE MY LIFE EASY AN' JUST O.D?
PAXIL 25 mg
Patient Name: Darryl Verplanck
Physician Name: Dr. Heller
HALDOL 25 mg
Patient Name: Darryl Verplanck
Physician Name: Dr. Lynde
XANAX 100 mg
Patient Name: Darryl Verplanck
Physician Name: Dr. Ahmad

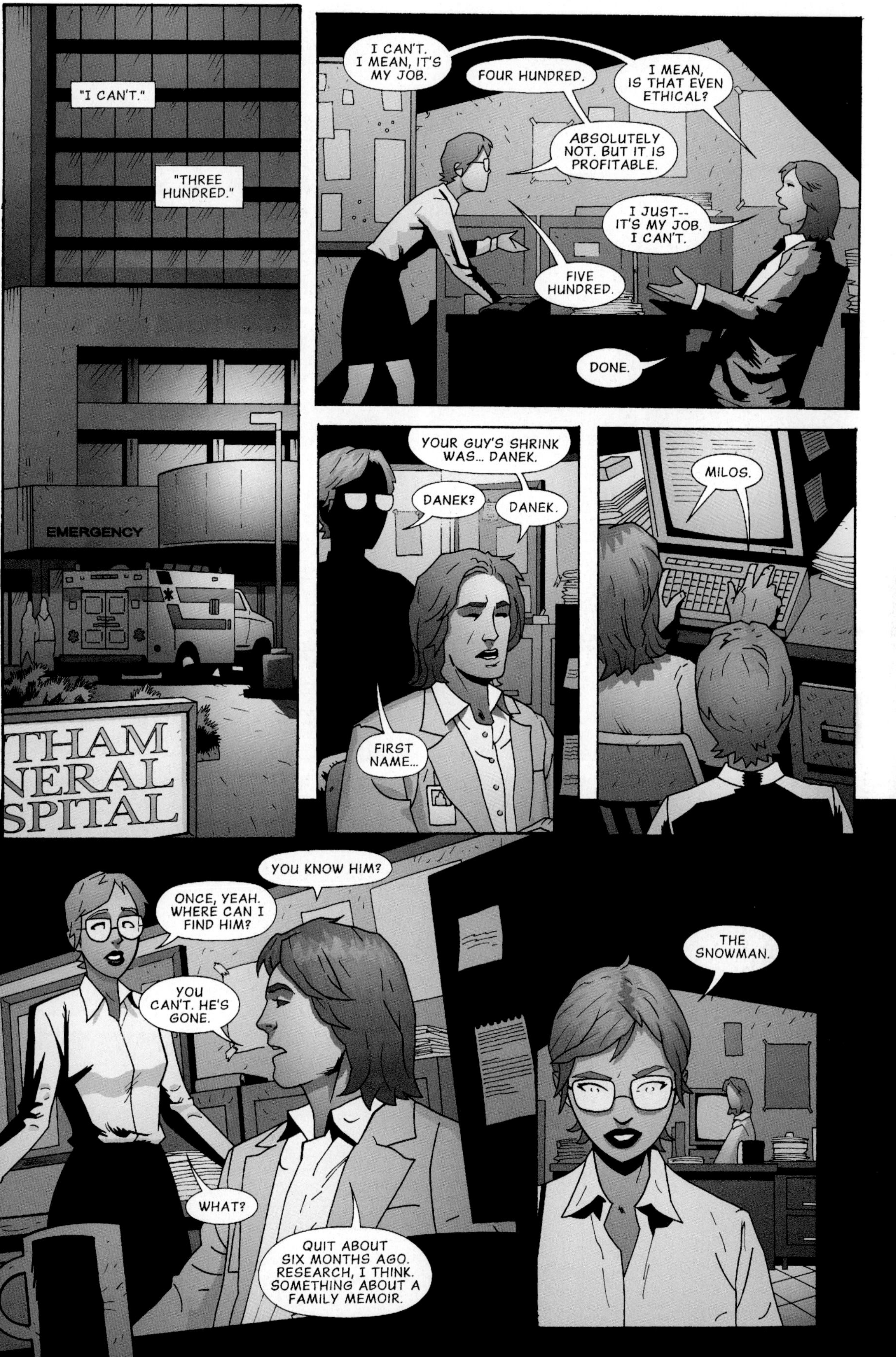
"I CAN'T."
"THREE HUNDRED."
EMERGENCY
THAM
NERAL
SPITAL
I CAN'T. I MEAN, IT'S MY JOB.
FOUR HUNDRED.
I MEAN, IS THAT EVEN ETHICAL?
ABSOLUTELY NOT. BUT IT IS PROFITABLE.
I JUST-- IT'S MY JOB. I CAN'T.
FIVE HUNDRED.
DONE.
YOUR GUY'S SHRINK WAS... DANEK.
DANEK?
DANEK.
FIRST NAME...
MILOS.
YOU KNOW HIM?
ONCE, YEAH. WHERE CAN I FIND HIM?
YOU CAN'T. HE'S GONE.
WHAT?
QUIT ABOUT SIX MONTHS AGO. RESEARCH, I THINK. SOMETHING ABOUT A FAMILY MEMOIR.
THE SNOWMAN.

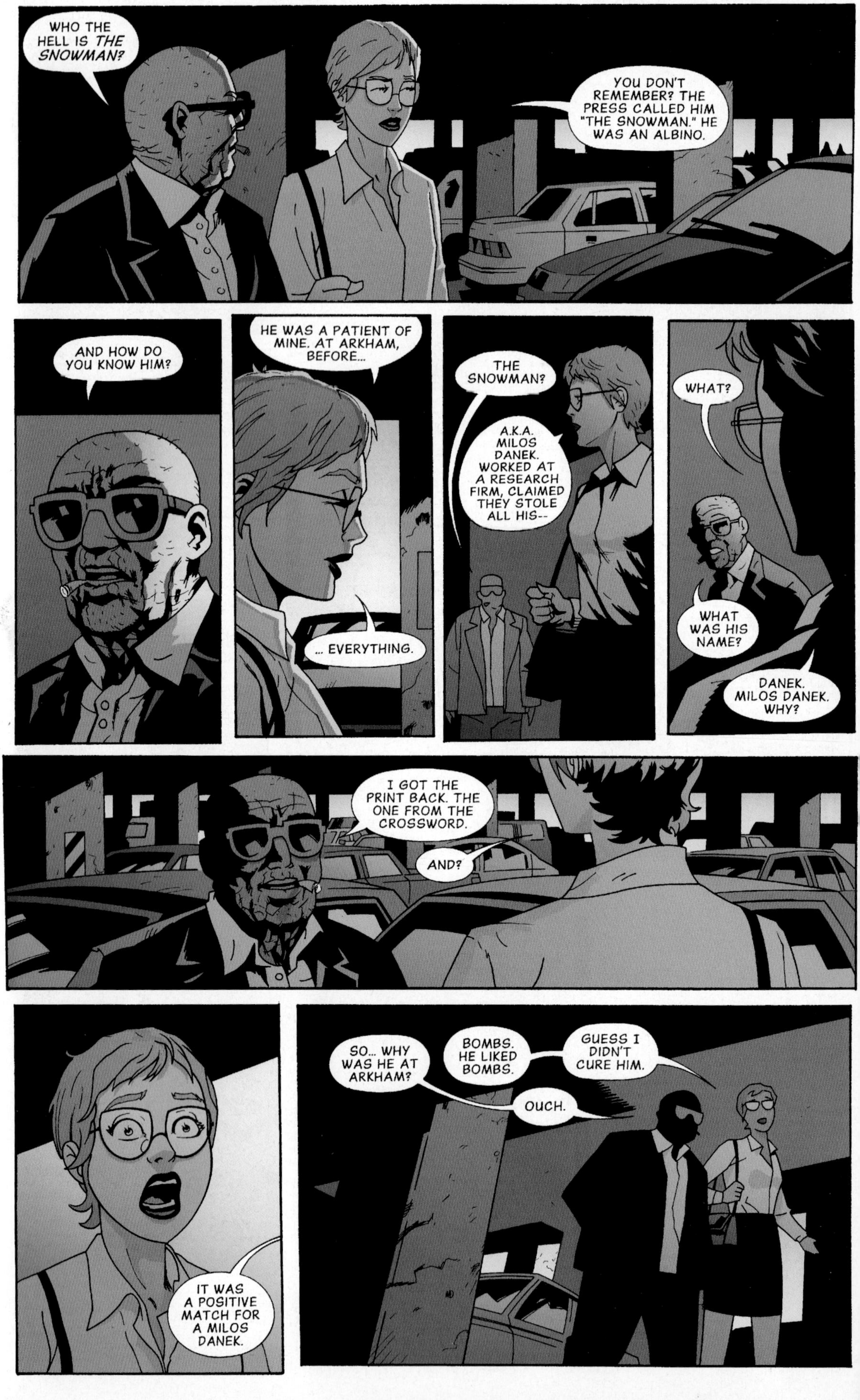
WHO THE HELL IS *THE SNOWMAN?*
YOU DON'T REMEMBER? THE PRESS CALLED HIM "THE SNOWMAN." HE WAS AN ALBINO.
AND HOW DO YOU KNOW HIM?
HE WAS A PATIENT OF MINE. AT ARKHAM, BEFORE...
... EVERYTHING.
THE SNOWMAN?
A.K.A. MILOS DANEK. WORKED AT A RESEARCH FIRM, CLAIMED THEY STOLE ALL HIS--
WHAT?
WHAT WAS HIS NAME?
DANEK. MILOS DANEK. WHY?
I GOT THE PRINT BACK. THE ONE FROM THE CROSSWORD.
AND?
IT WAS A POSITIVE MATCH FOR A MILOS DANEK.
SO... WHY WAS HE AT ARKHAM?
BOMBS. HE LIKED BOMBS.
GUESS I DIDN'T CURE HIM.
OUCH.

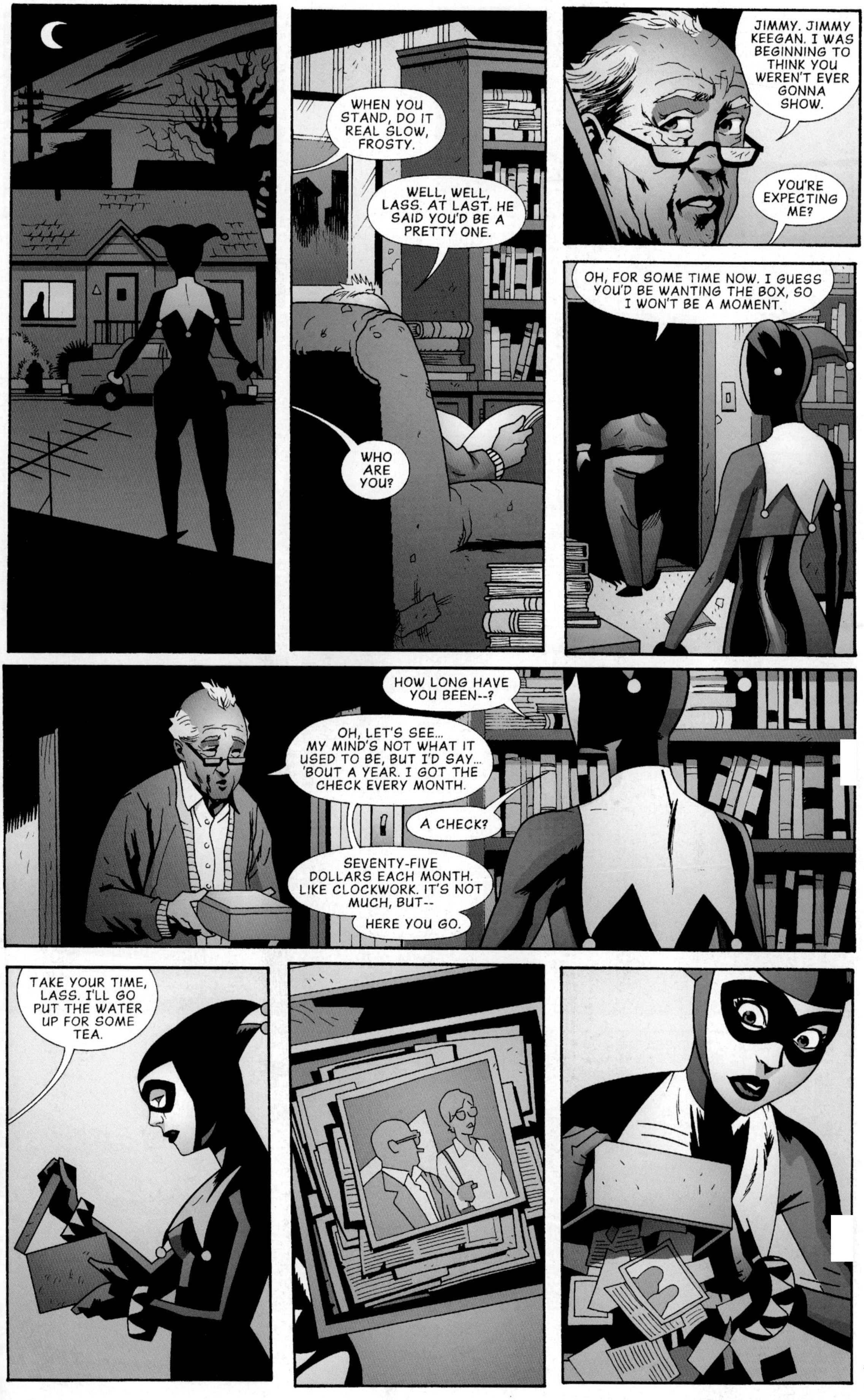
WHEN YOU STAND, DO IT REAL SLOW, FROSTY.
WELL, WELL, LASS. AT LAST. HE SAID YOU'D BE A PRETTY ONE.
WHO ARE YOU?
JIMMY. JIMMY KEEGAN. I WAS BEGINNING TO THINK YOU WEREN'T EVER GONNA SHOW.
YOU'RE EXPECTING ME?
OH, FOR SOME TIME NOW. I GUESS YOU'D BE WANTING THE BOX, SO I WON'T BE A MOMENT.
HOW LONG HAVE YOU BEEN--?
OH, LET'S SEE... MY MIND'S NOT WHAT IT USED TO BE, BUT I'D SAY... 'BOUT A YEAR. I GOT THE CHECK EVERY MONTH.
A CHECK?
SEVENTY-FIVE DOLLARS EACH MONTH. LIKE CLOCKWORK. IT'S NOT MUCH, BUT--
HERE YOU GO.
TAKE YOUR TIME, LASS. I'LL GO PUT THE WATER UP FOR SOME TEA.

PSYCHIATRIST HELPS JOKER ESCAPE

GOTHAM CITY- A late-night brea
at Arkham Asylum last night sa
escape of a handful of dangero
inmates, including The Joker,
was aided by his psychiatrist

HE'S DEAD.

WHAT?

HE'S DEAD. DANEK IS DEAD.

OH, YEAH. SWEET, SWEET MAN.

YOU KNEW HIM?

KNEW HIM? LASS, I RENTED THE ROOM UPSTAIRS TO HIM FOR TEN YEARS.

BUT, I JUST-- I GOT SOMETHING HE SENT ME JUST THE OTHER DAY.

NO, IT WASN'T MILOS. DID'JA TRY HIS SON?

WHAT?

MAYBE Y'GOT THE WRONG DANEK, IS ALL. YOU TRY HIS SON?

SON? HE DIDN'T HAVE ANY CHILDREN.

SURE HE DID. PRIDE AND JOY.

YOU MUST BE MISTAKEN. I WAS HIS PSYCHIATRIST FOR TWO YEARS.

HE NEVER SAID ANY-THING ABOUT A SON.

GAVE 'IM UP FOR ADOPTION, BUT TALKED ABOUT 'IM ALL THE TIME.

A SON.

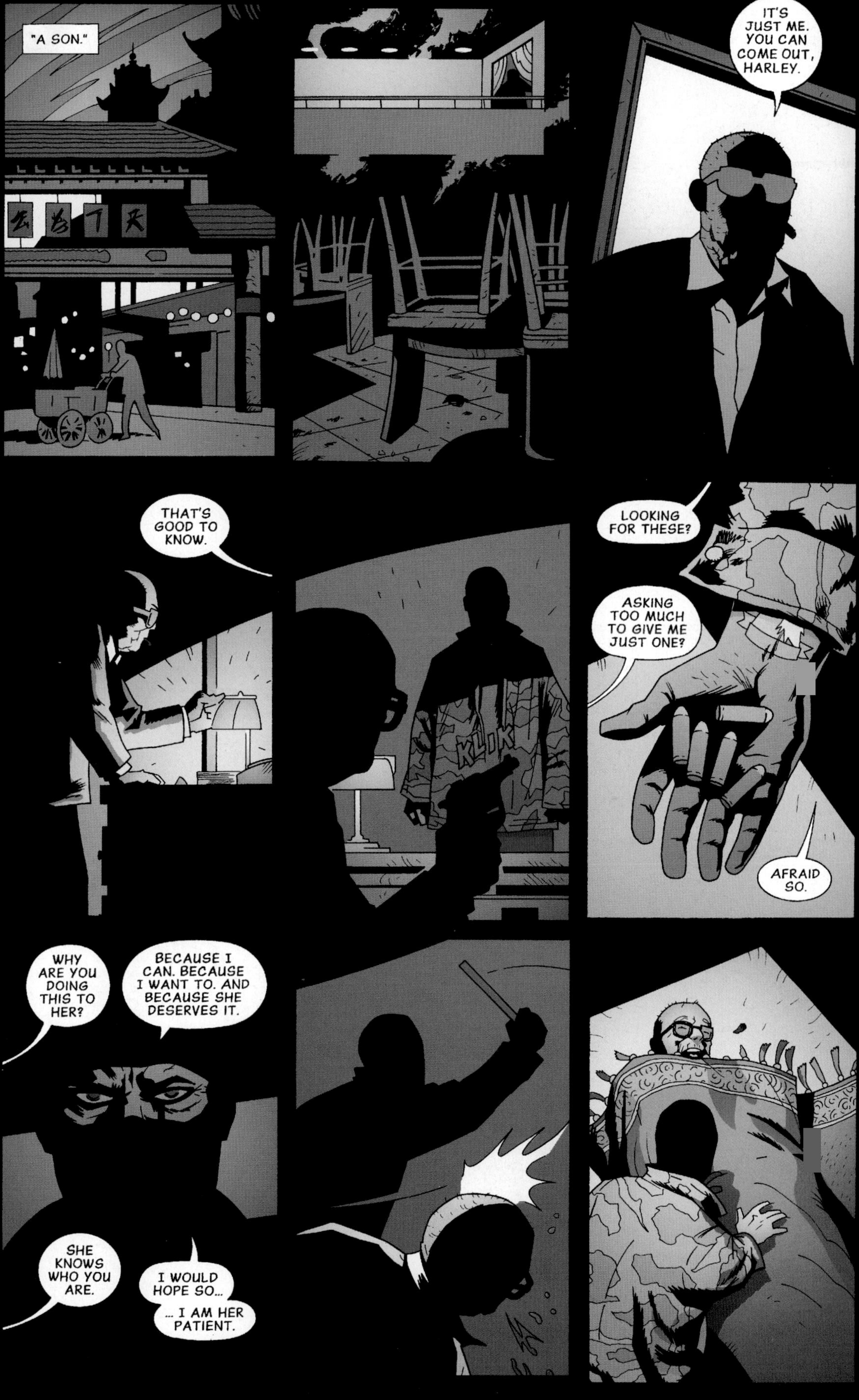
"A SON."
IT'S JUST ME. YOU CAN COME OUT, HARLEY.
THAT'S GOOD TO KNOW.
KLIK
LOOKING FOR THESE?
ASKING TOO MUCH TO GIVE ME JUST ONE?
AFRAID SO.
WHY ARE YOU DOING THIS TO HER?
BECAUSE I CAN. BECAUSE I WANT TO. AND BECAUSE SHE DESERVES IT.
SHE KNOWS WHO YOU ARE.
I WOULD HOPE SO...
... I AM HER PATIENT.

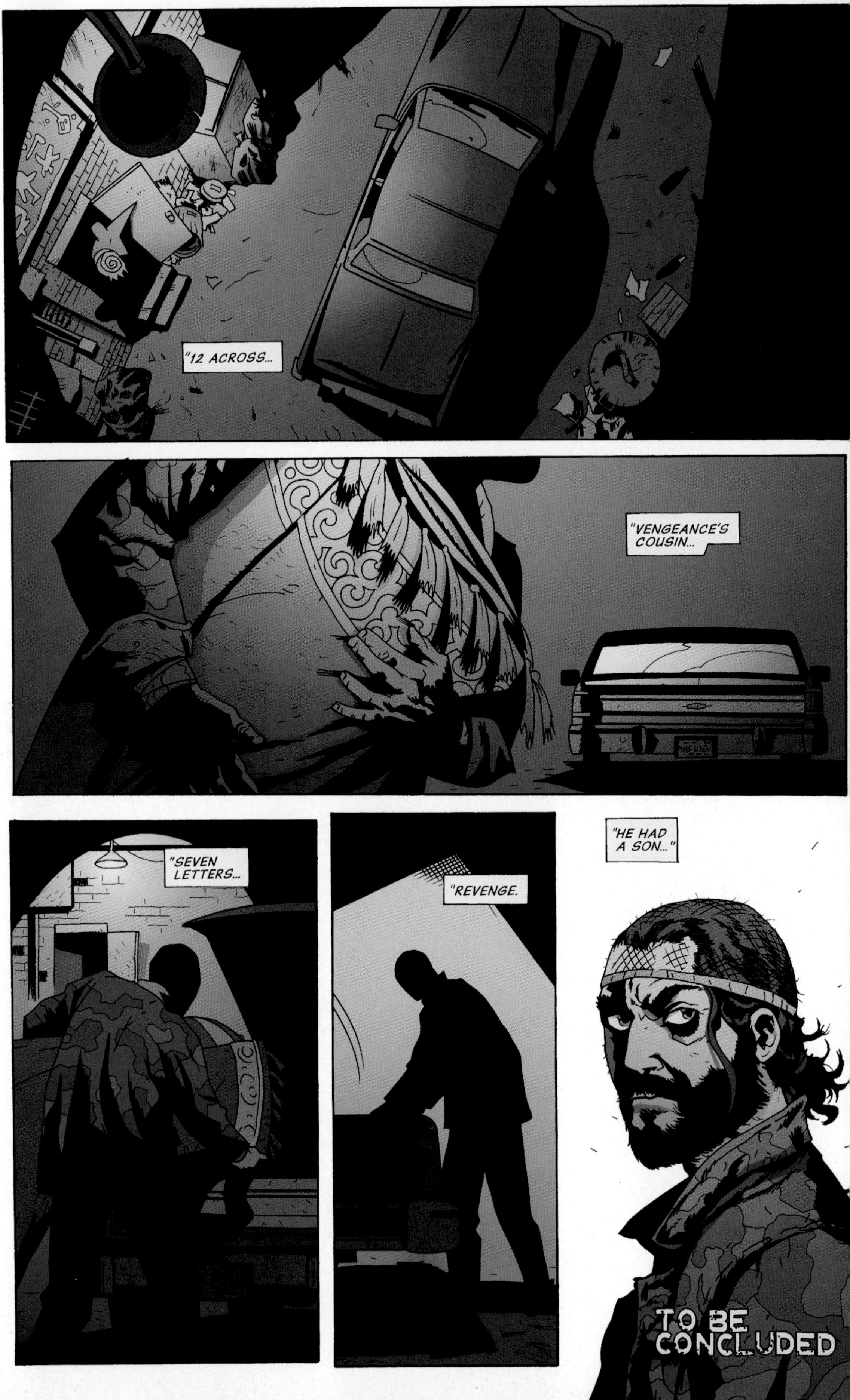
"12 ACROSS...
"VENGEANCE'S COUSIN...
"SEVEN LETTERS...
"REVENGE.
"HE HAD A SON..."
TO BE CONCLUDED

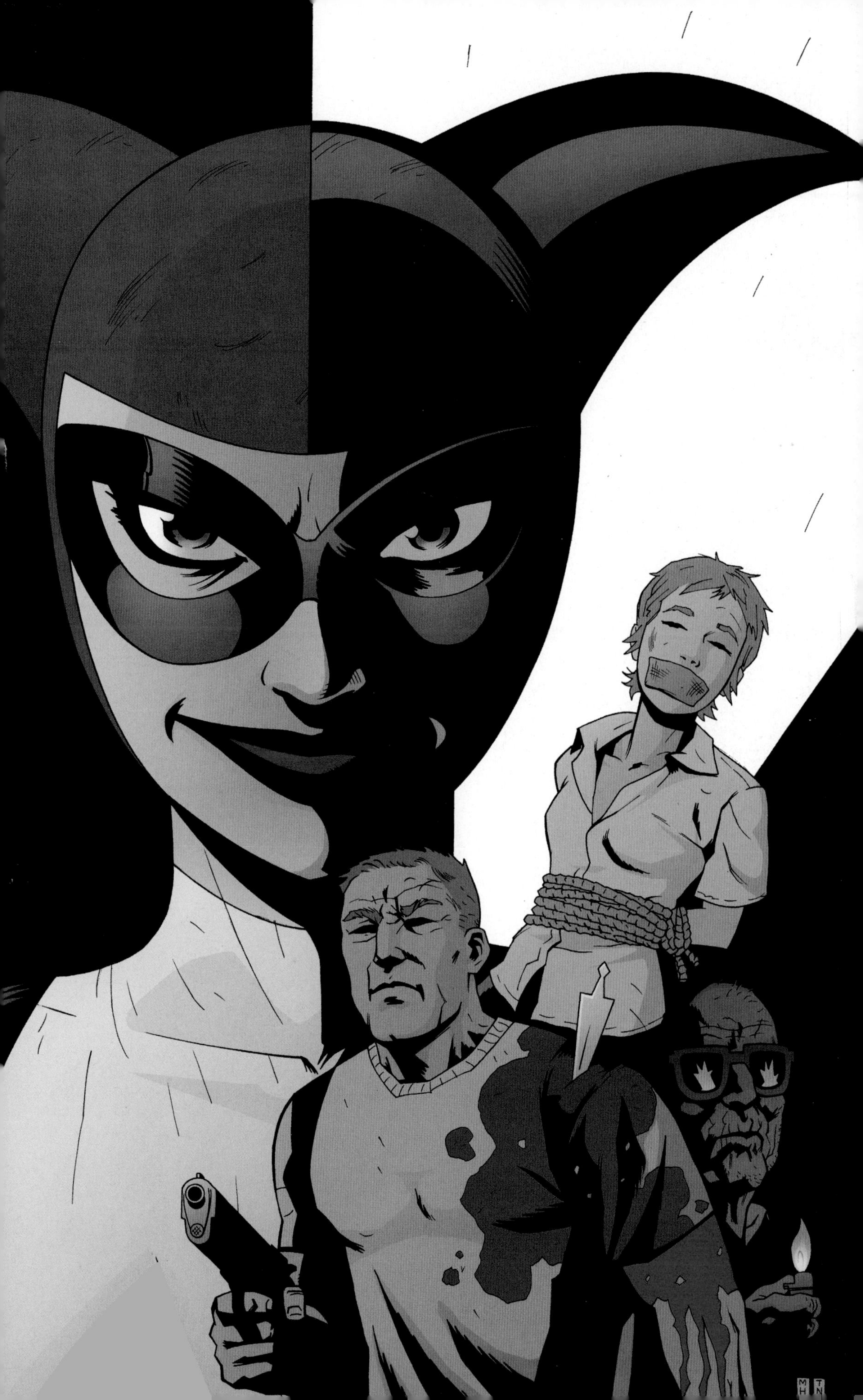

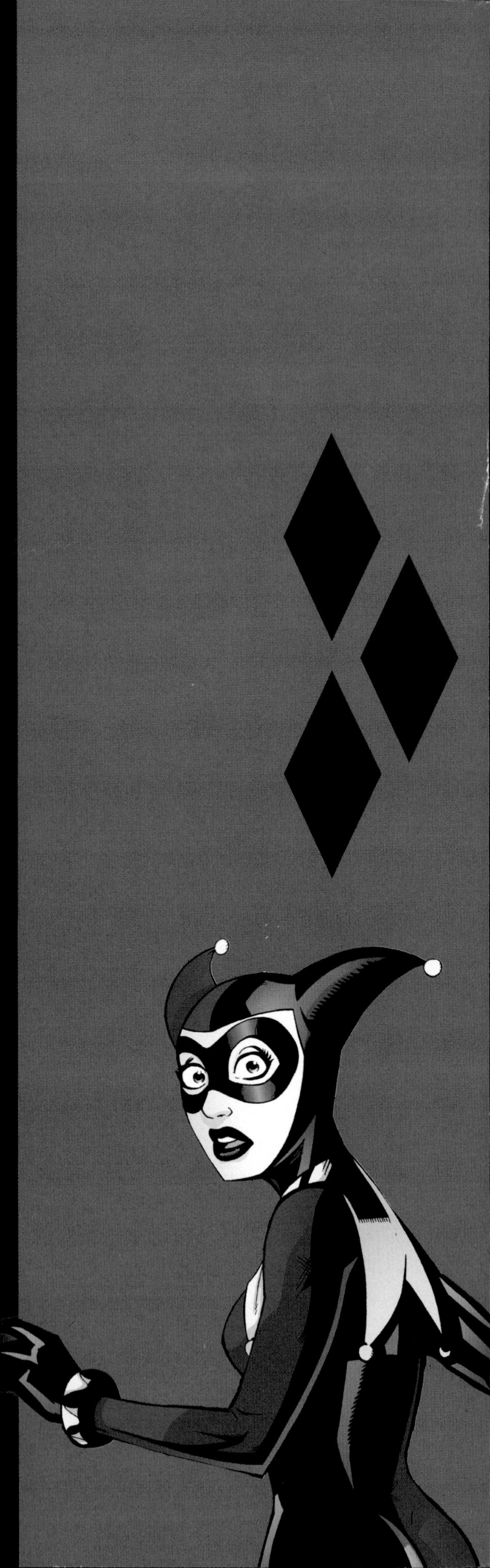

VENGEANCE UNLIMITED

PART FIVE

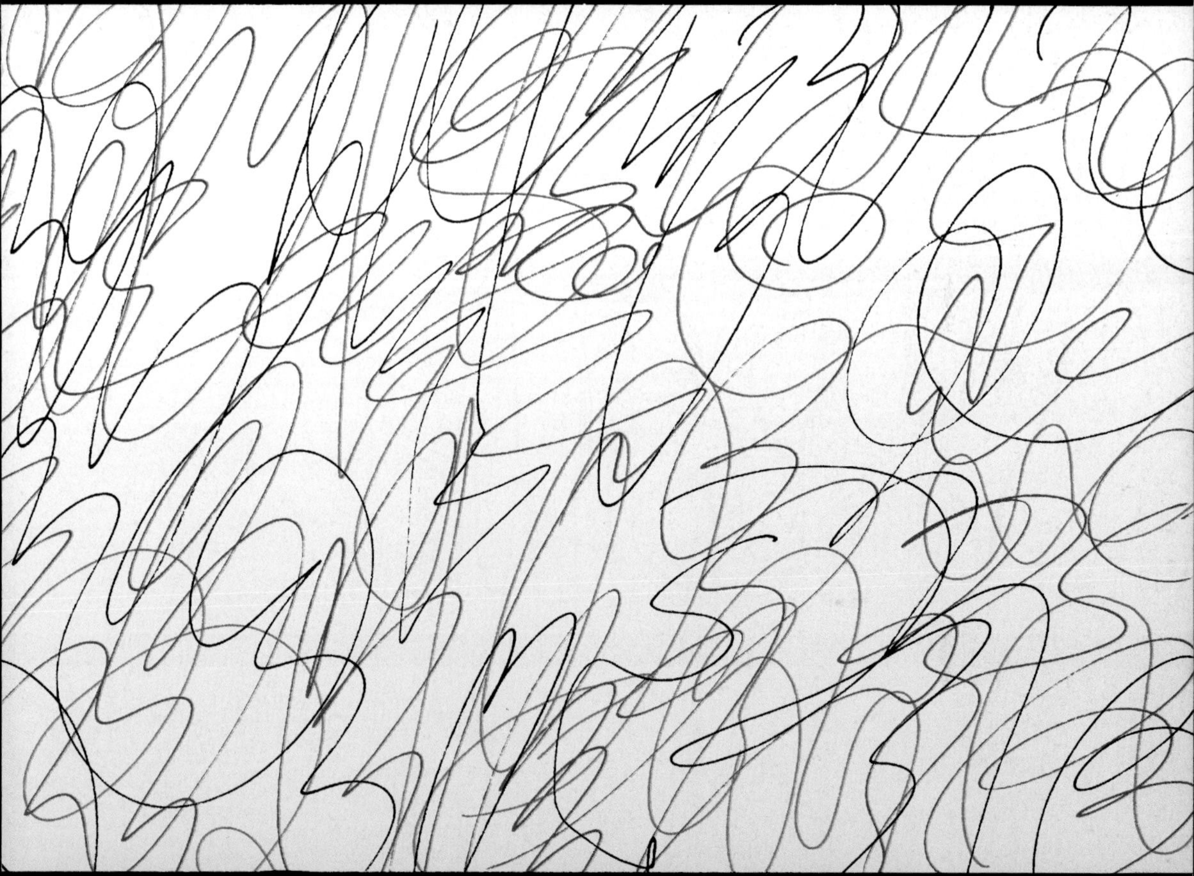

A.J. LIEBERMAN- WRITER MIKE HUDDLESTON- PENCILLER
TROY NIXEY- INKER SEAN KONOT- LETTERER ALEX SINCLAIR- COLORIST
NACHIE CASTRO- ASST. EDITOR MATT IDELSON- EDITOR
HARLEY QUINN CREATED BY PAUL DINI & BRUCE TIMM

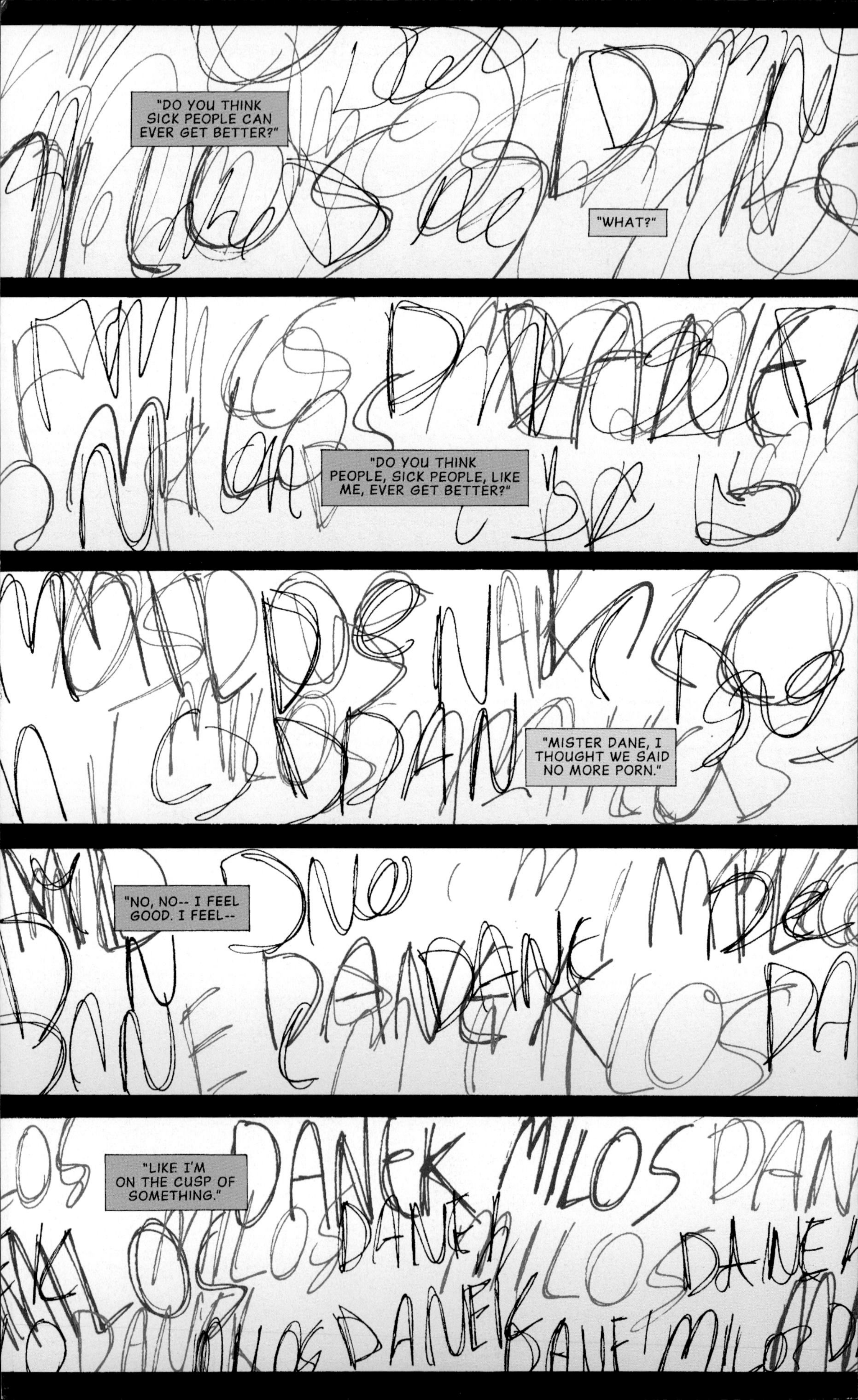
"DO YOU THINK SICK PEOPLE CAN EVER GET BETTER?"
"WHAT?"
"DO YOU THINK PEOPLE, SICK PEOPLE, LIKE ME, EVER GET BETTER?"
"MISTER DANE, I THOUGHT WE SAID NO MORE PORN."
"NO, NO-- I FEEL GOOD. I FEEL--
"LIKE I'M ON THE CUSP OF SOMETHING."

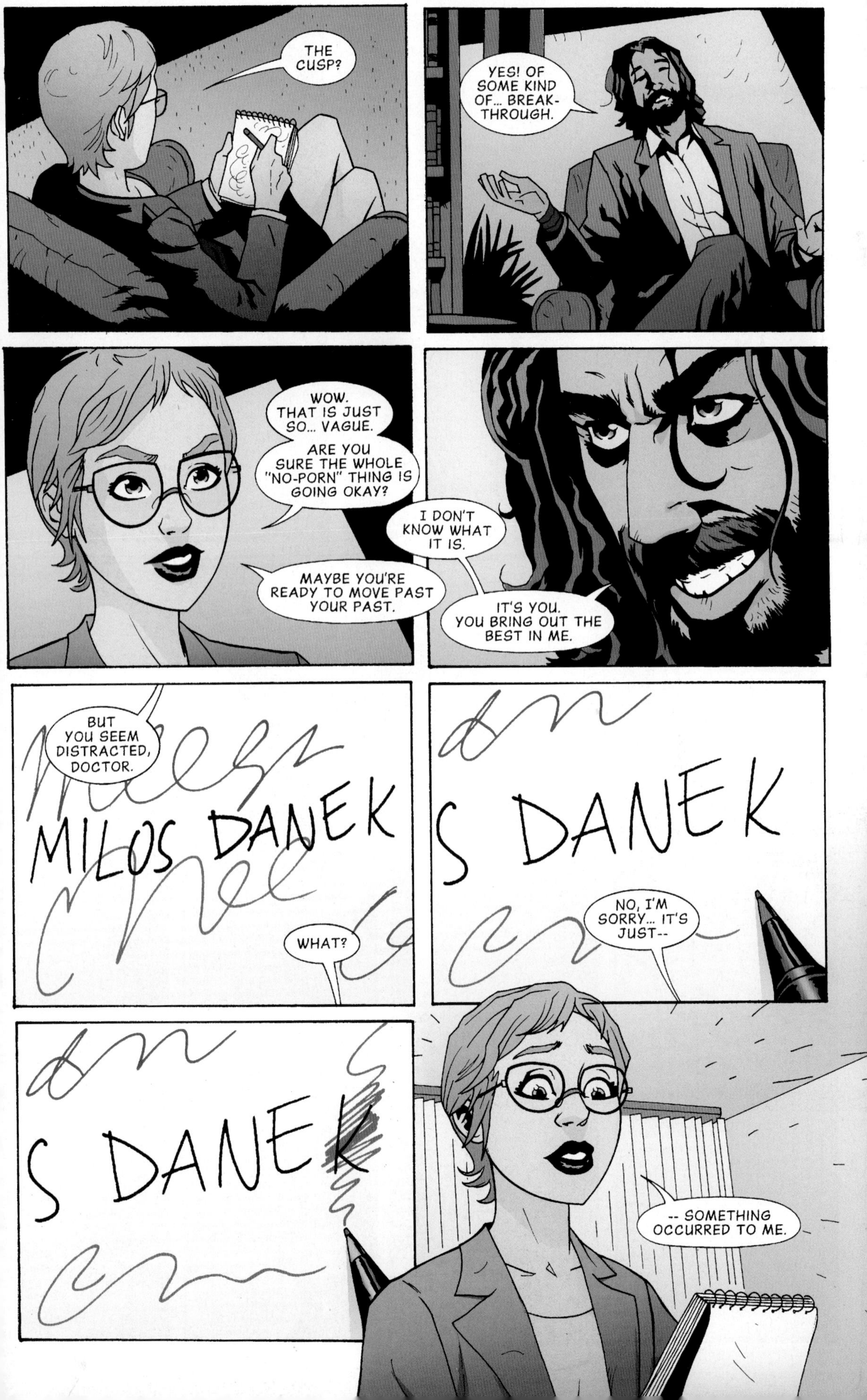
THE CUSP?
YES! OF SOME KIND OF... BREAK-THROUGH.
WOW. THAT IS JUST SO... VAGUE.
ARE YOU SURE THE WHOLE "NO-PORN" THING IS GOING OKAY?
MAYBE YOU'RE READY TO MOVE PAST YOUR PAST.
I DON'T KNOW WHAT IT IS.
IT'S YOU. YOU BRING OUT THE BEST IN ME.
BUT YOU SEEM DISTRACTED, DOCTOR.
MILOS DANEK
WHAT?
S DANEK
NO, I'M SORRY... IT'S JUST--
S DANEK
-- SOMETHING OCCURRED TO ME.

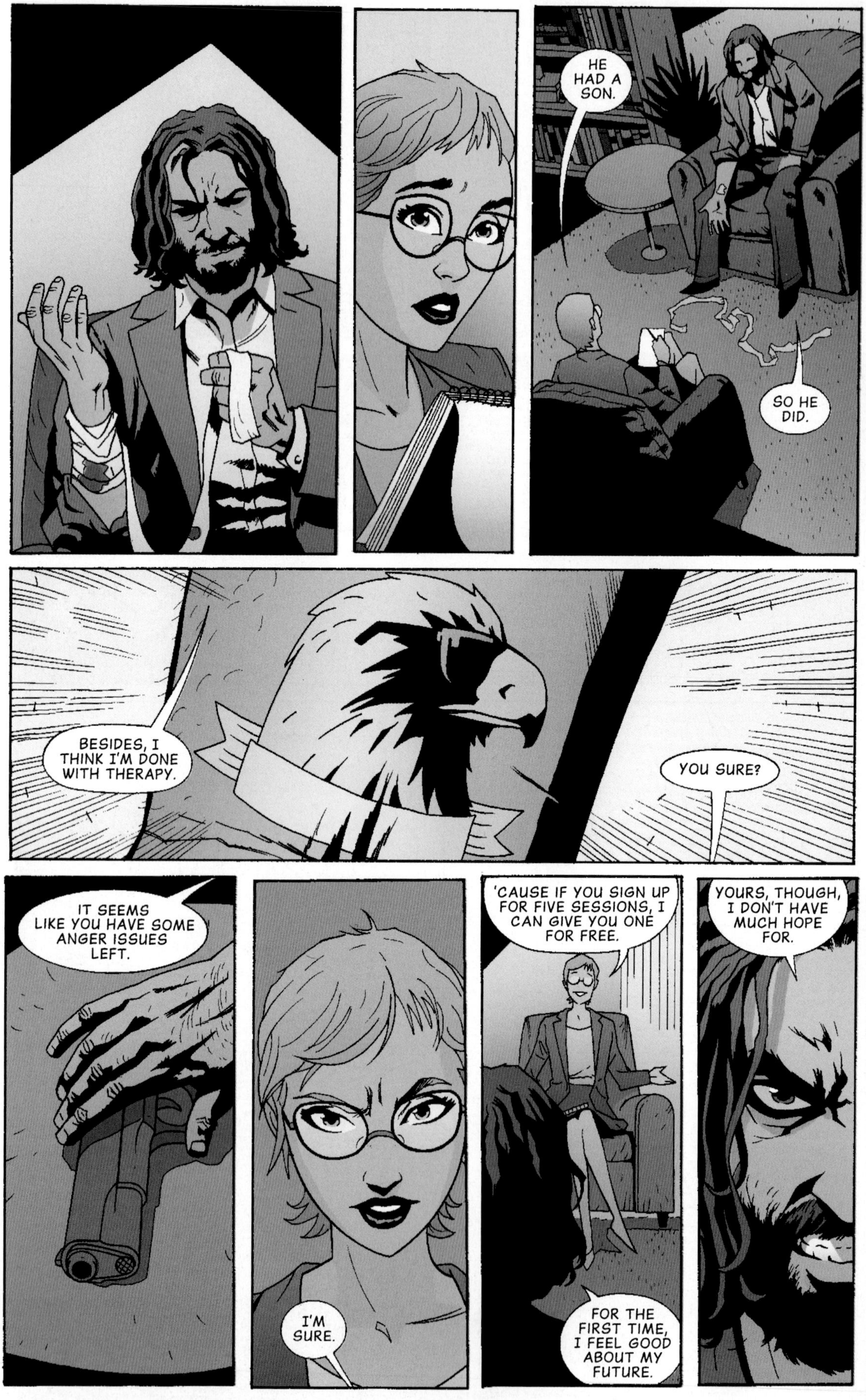
HE HAD A SON.
SO HE DID.
BESIDES, I THINK I'M DONE WITH THERAPY.
YOU SURE?
IT SEEMS LIKE YOU HAVE SOME ANGER ISSUES LEFT.
I'M SURE.
'CAUSE IF YOU SIGN UP FOR FIVE SESSIONS, I CAN GIVE YOU ONE FOR FREE.
FOR THE FIRST TIME, I FEEL GOOD ABOUT MY FUTURE.
YOURS, THOUGH, I DON'T HAVE MUCH HOPE FOR.

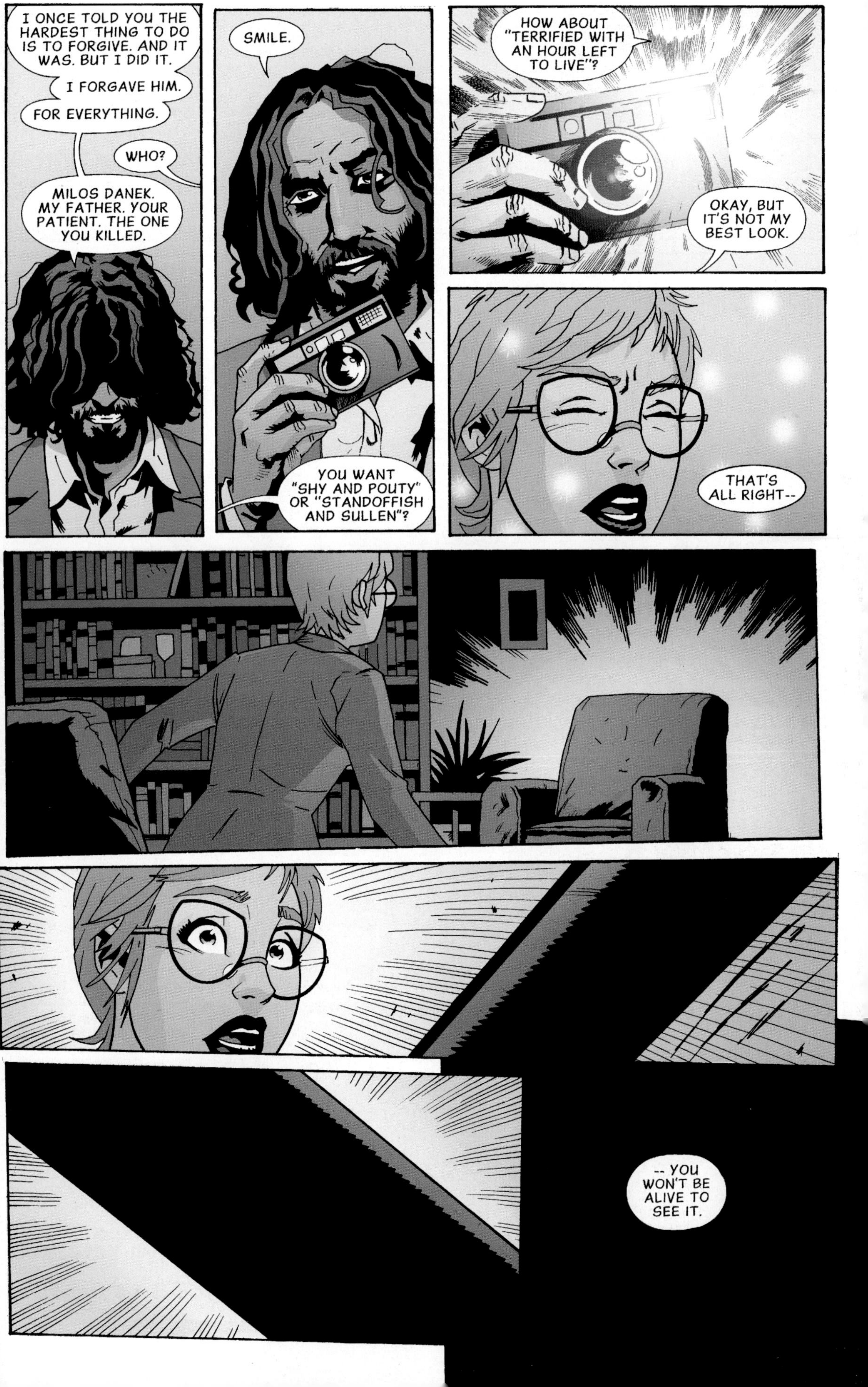
I ONCE TOLD YOU THE HARDEST THING TO DO IS TO FORGIVE. AND IT WAS. BUT I DID IT.
I FORGAVE HIM.
FOR EVERYTHING.
WHO?
MILOS DANEK. MY FATHER. YOUR PATIENT. THE ONE YOU KILLED.
SMILE.
YOU WANT "SHY AND POUTY" OR "STANDOFFISH AND SULLEN"?
HOW ABOUT "TERRIFIED WITH AN HOUR LEFT TO LIVE"?
OKAY, BUT IT'S NOT MY BEST LOOK.
THAT'S ALL RIGHT--
-- YOU WON'T BE ALIVE TO SEE IT.

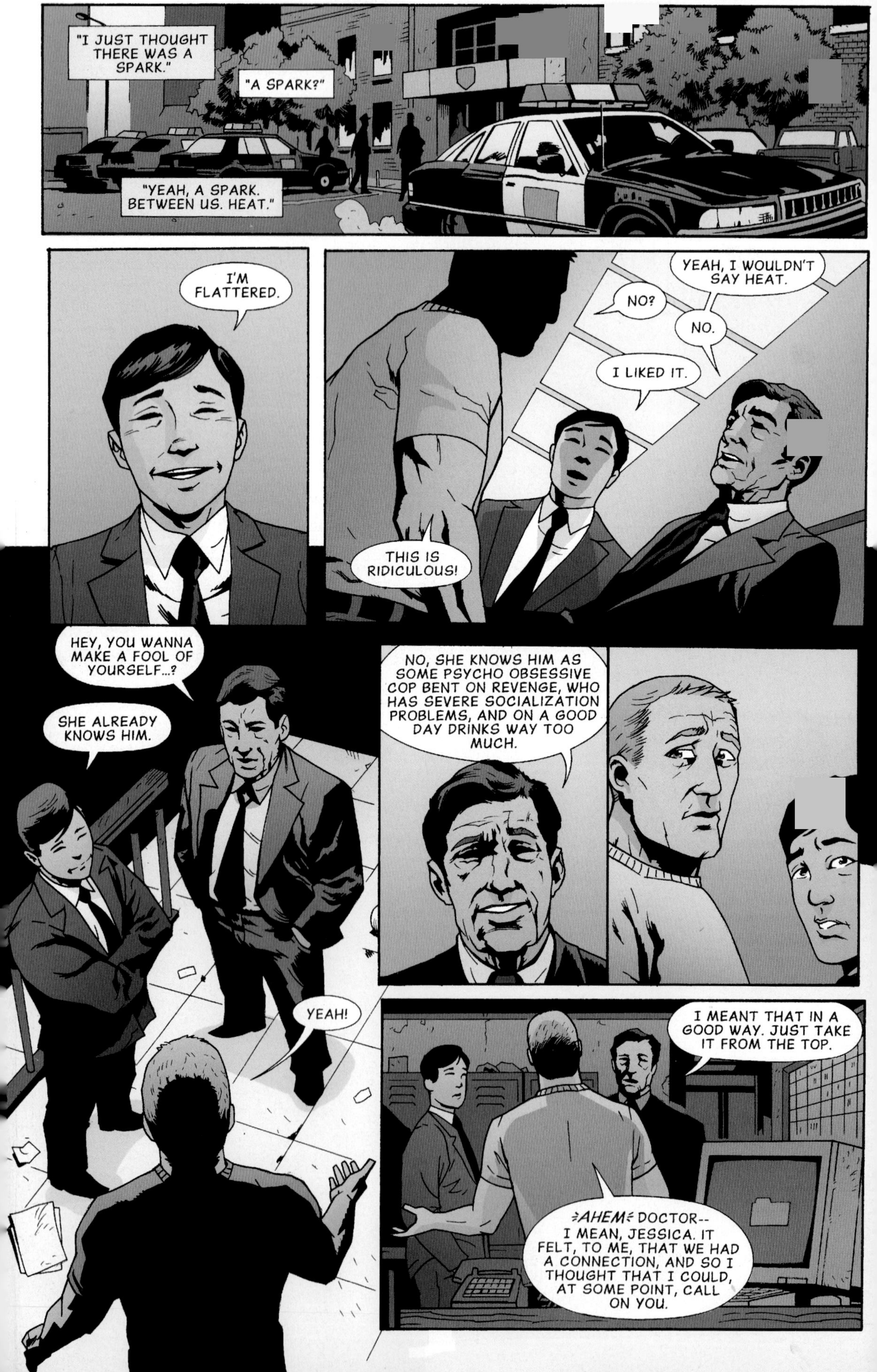
"I JUST THOUGHT THERE WAS A SPARK."
"A SPARK?"
"YEAH, A SPARK. BETWEEN US. HEAT."
I'M FLATTERED.
YEAH, I WOULDN'T SAY HEAT.
NO?
NO.
I LIKED IT.
THIS IS RIDICULOUS!
HEY, YOU WANNA MAKE A FOOL OF YOURSELF...?
SHE ALREADY KNOWS HIM.
YEAH!
NO, SHE KNOWS HIM AS SOME PSYCHO OBSESSIVE COP BENT ON REVENGE, WHO HAS SEVERE SOCIALIZATION PROBLEMS, AND ON A GOOD DAY DRINKS WAY TOO MUCH.
I MEANT THAT IN A GOOD WAY. JUST TAKE IT FROM THE TOP.
AHEM DOCTOR-- I MEAN, JESSICA. IT FELT, TO ME, THAT WE HAD A CONNECTION, AND SO I THOUGHT THAT I COULD, AT SOME POINT, CALL ON YOU.

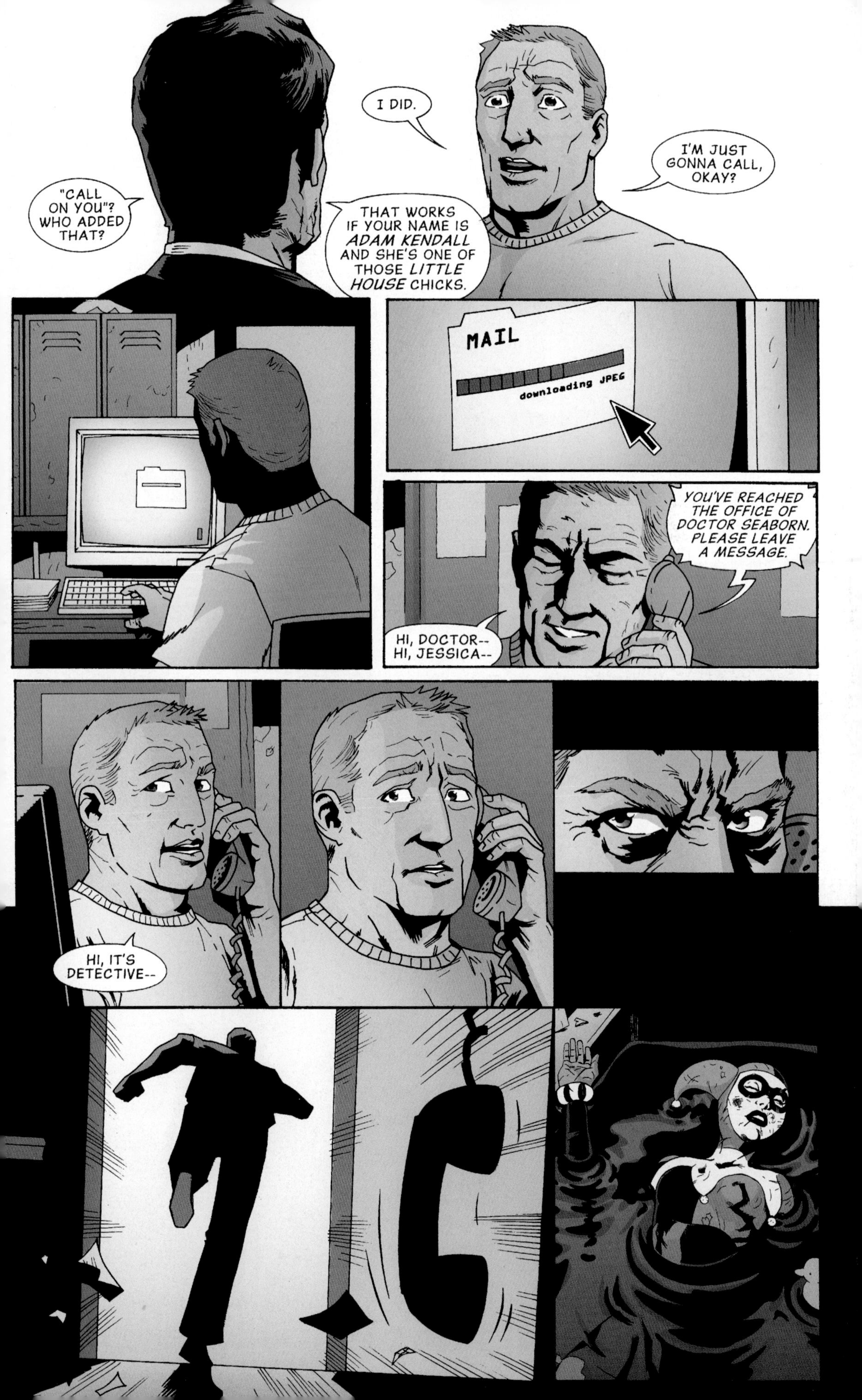
I DID.
"CALL ON YOU"? WHO ADDED THAT?
THAT WORKS IF YOUR NAME IS *ADAM KENDALL* AND SHE'S ONE OF THOSE *LITTLE HOUSE* CHICKS.
I'M JUST GONNA CALL, OKAY?
MAIL
downloading JPEG
YOU'VE REACHED THE OFFICE OF DOCTOR SEABORN. PLEASE LEAVE A MESSAGE.
HI, DOCTOR--
HI, JESSICA--
HI, IT'S DETECTIVE--

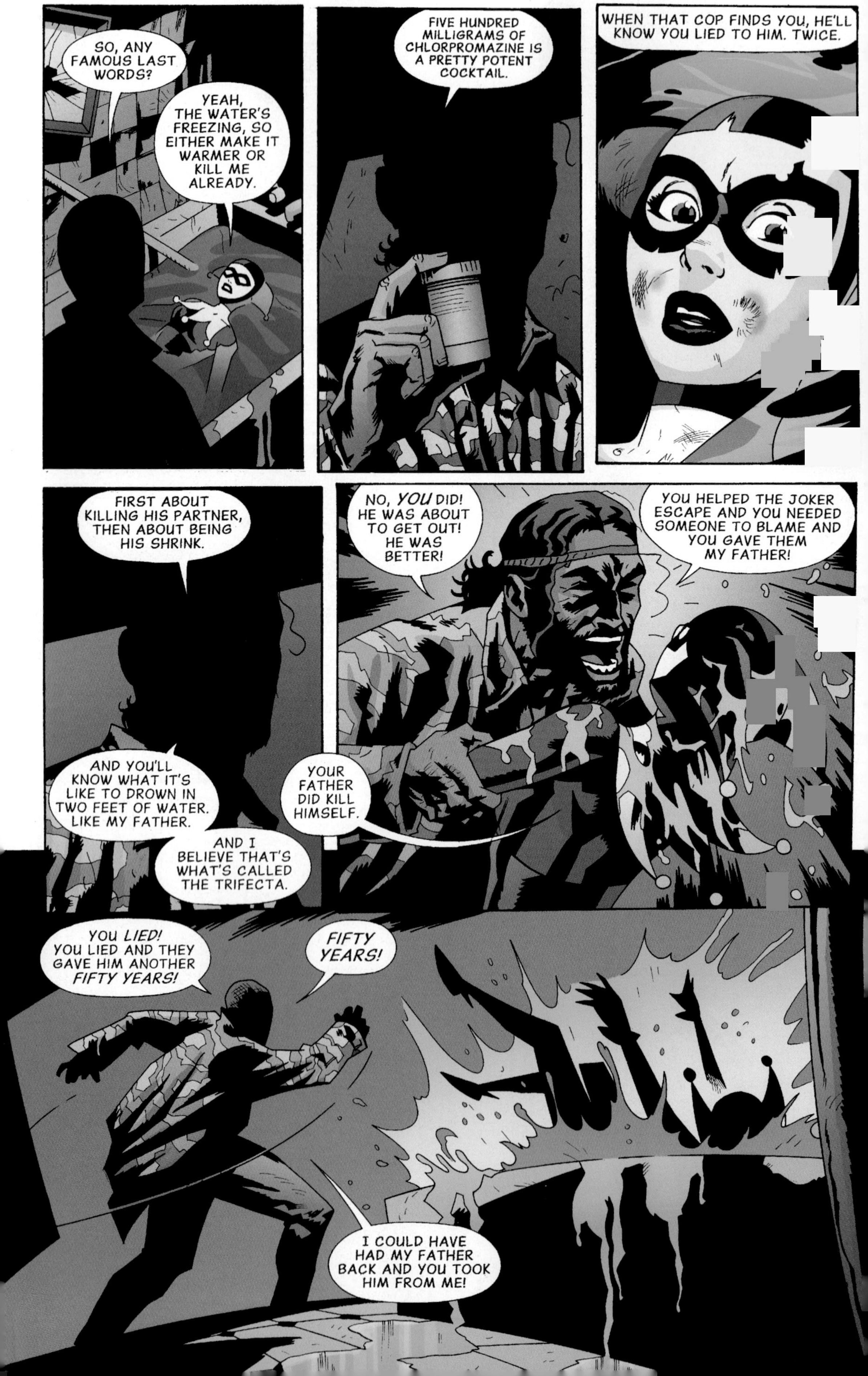
SO, ANY FAMOUS LAST WORDS?
YEAH, THE WATER'S FREEZING, SO EITHER MAKE IT WARMER OR KILL ME ALREADY.
FIVE HUNDRED MILLIGRAMS OF CHLORPROMAZINE IS A PRETTY POTENT COCKTAIL.
WHEN THAT COP FINDS YOU, HE'LL KNOW YOU LIED TO HIM. TWICE.
FIRST ABOUT KILLING HIS PARTNER, THEN ABOUT BEING HIS SHRINK.
AND YOU'LL KNOW WHAT IT'S LIKE TO DROWN IN TWO FEET OF WATER. LIKE MY FATHER.
AND I BELIEVE THAT'S WHAT'S CALLED THE TRIFECTA.
NO, YOU DID! HE WAS ABOUT TO GET OUT! HE WAS BETTER!
YOU HELPED THE JOKER ESCAPE AND YOU NEEDED SOMEONE TO BLAME AND YOU GAVE THEM MY FATHER!
YOUR FATHER DID KILL HIMSELF.
YOU LIED! YOU LIED AND THEY GAVE HIM ANOTHER FIFTY YEARS!
FIFTY YEARS!
I COULD HAVE HAD MY FATHER BACK AND YOU TOOK HIM FROM ME!

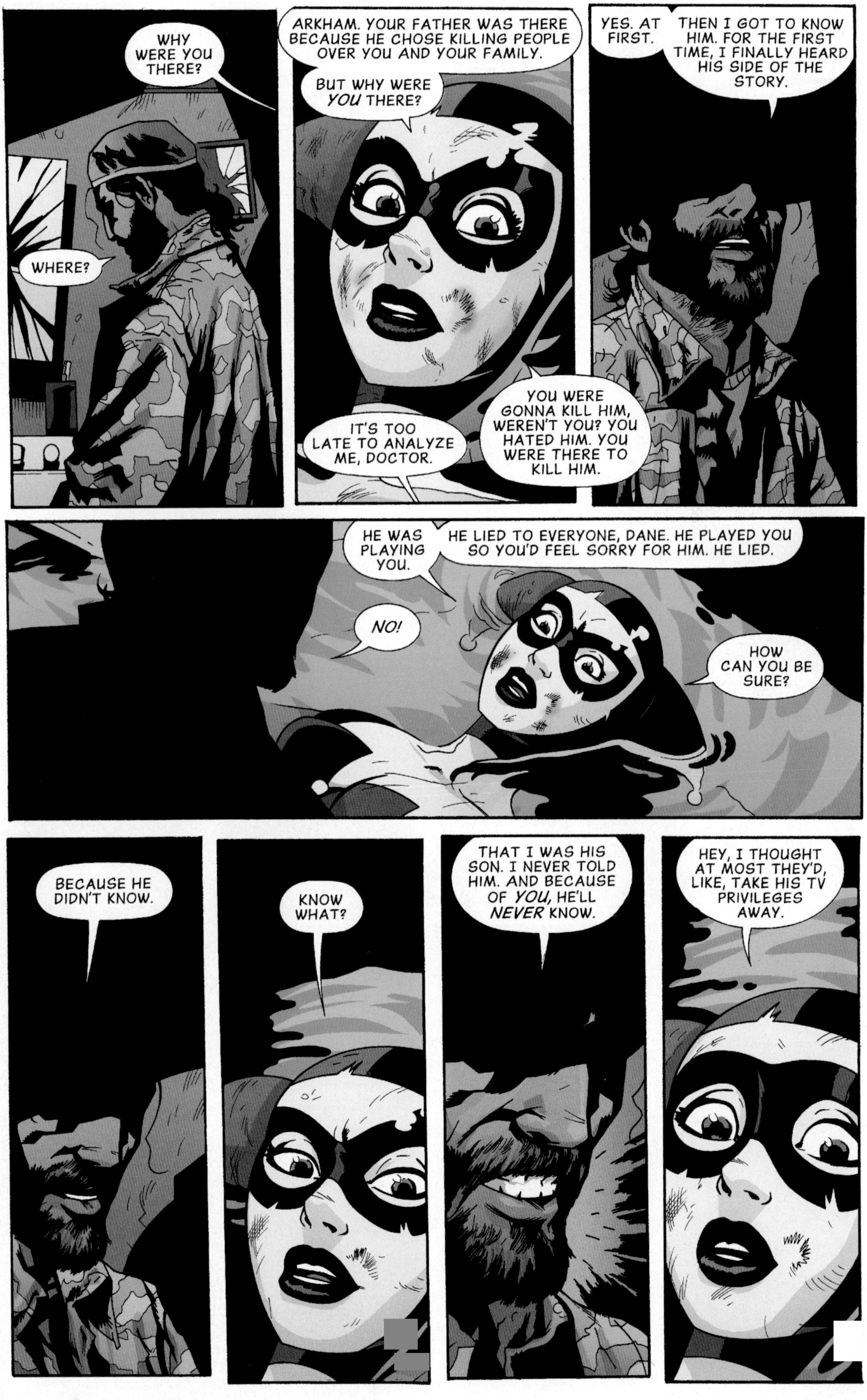

WHY WERE YOU THERE?
WHERE?
ARKHAM. YOUR FATHER WAS THERE BECAUSE HE CHOSE KILLING PEOPLE OVER YOU AND YOUR FAMILY.
BUT WHY WERE *YOU* THERE?
IT'S TOO LATE TO ANALYZE ME, DOCTOR.
YOU WERE GONNA KILL HIM, WEREN'T YOU? YOU HATED HIM. YOU WERE THERE TO KILL HIM.
YES. AT FIRST.
THEN I GOT TO KNOW HIM. FOR THE FIRST TIME, I FINALLY HEARD HIS SIDE OF THE STORY.
HE WAS PLAYING YOU.
HE LIED TO EVERYONE, DANE. HE PLAYED YOU SO YOU'D FEEL SORRY FOR HIM. HE LIED.
NO!
HOW CAN YOU BE SURE?
BECAUSE HE DIDN'T KNOW.
KNOW WHAT?
THAT I WAS HIS SON. I NEVER TOLD HIM. AND BECAUSE OF *YOU,* HE'LL *NEVER* KNOW.
HEY, I THOUGHT AT MOST THEY'D, LIKE, TAKE HIS TV PRIVILEGES AWAY.

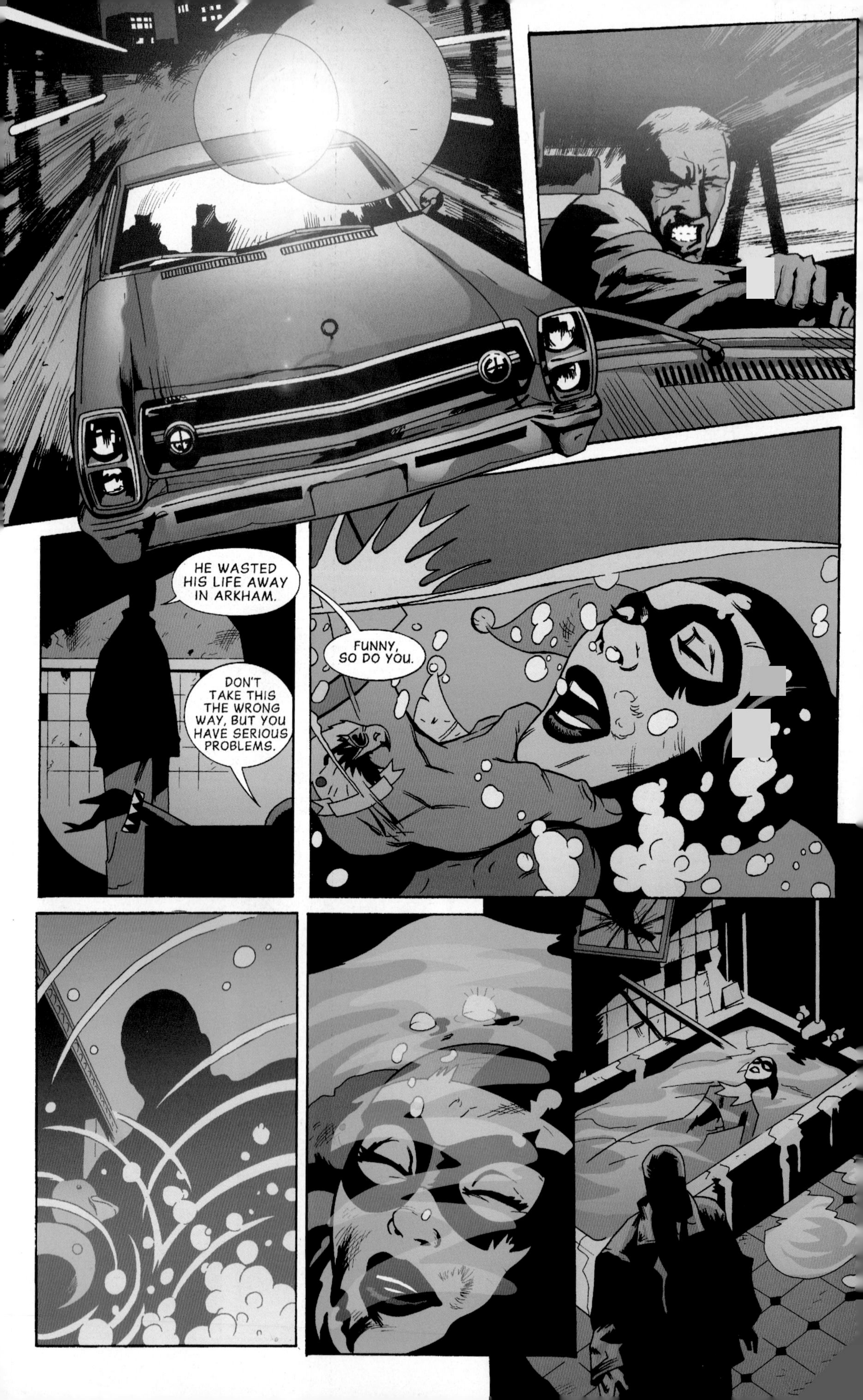
HE WASTED HIS LIFE AWAY IN ARKHAM.
DON'T TAKE THIS THE WRONG WAY, BUT YOU HAVE SERIOUS PROBLEMS.
FUNNY, SO DO YOU.

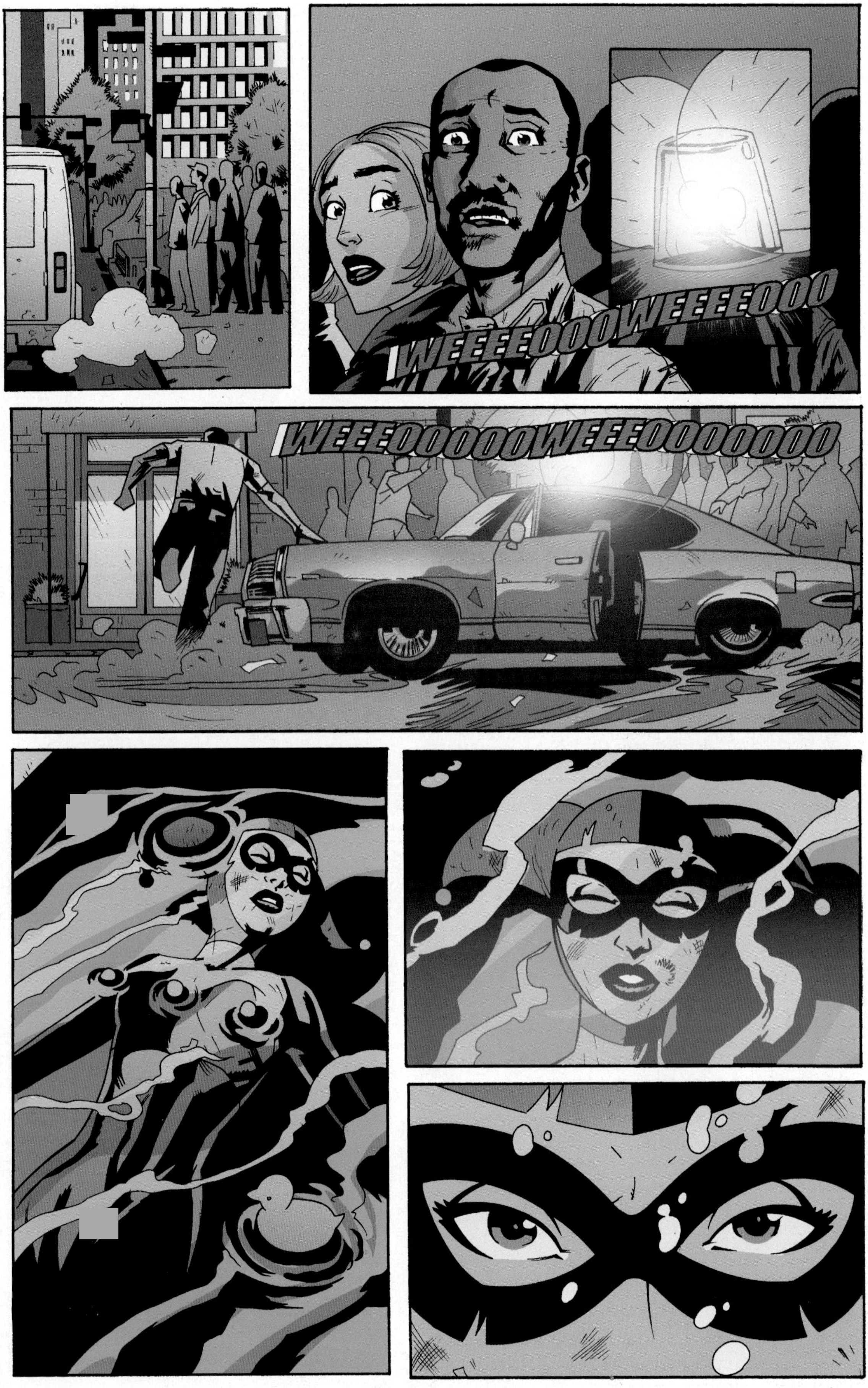
WEEEEOOOWEEEEOOO
WEEEOOOOOOWEEEOOOOOOOO

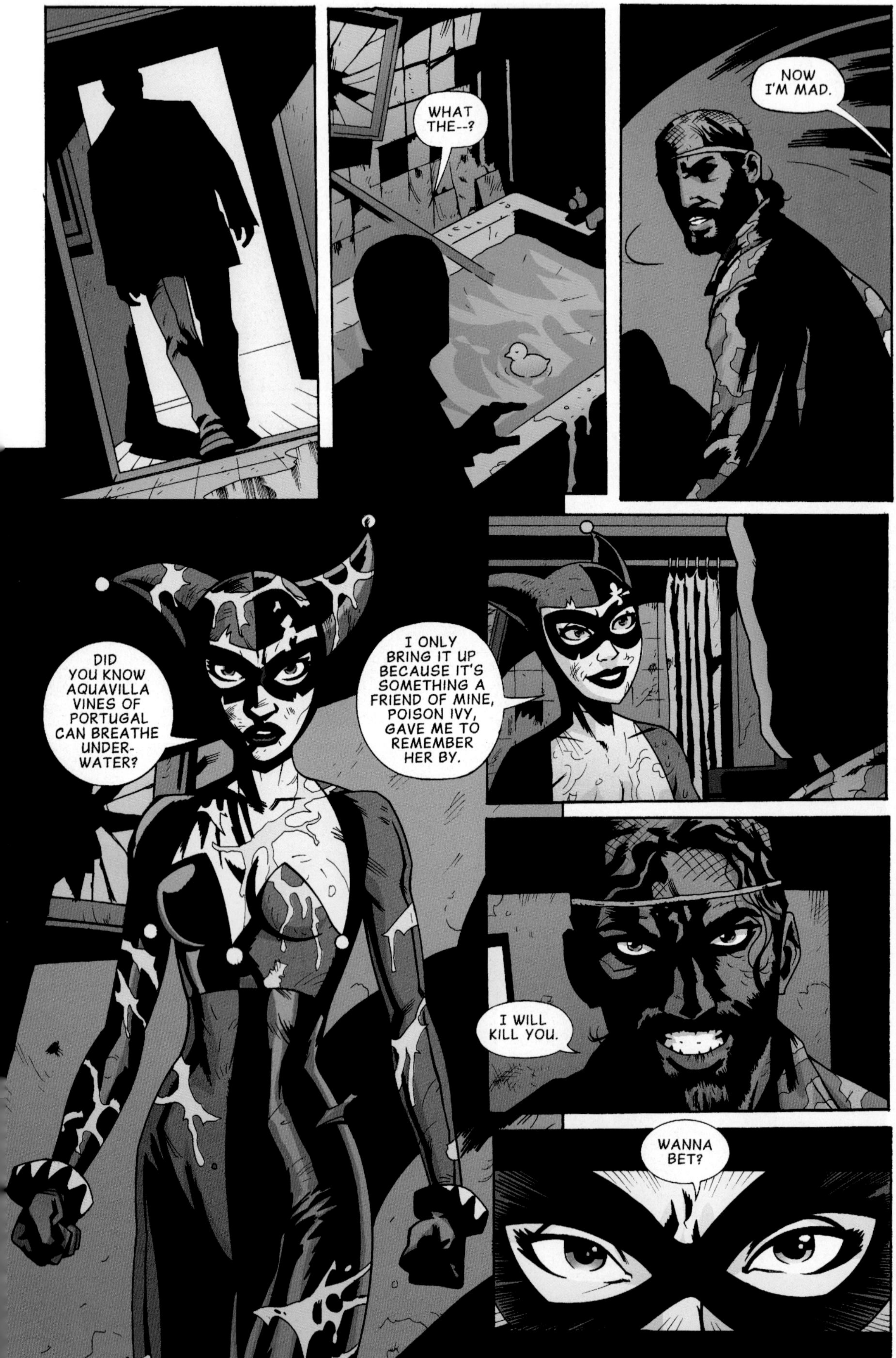
WHAT THE--?
NOW I'M MAD.
DID YOU KNOW AQUAVILLA VINES OF PORTUGAL CAN BREATHE UNDER-WATER?
I ONLY BRING IT UP BECAUSE IT'S SOMETHING A FRIEND OF MINE, POISON IVY, GAVE ME TO REMEMBER HER BY.
I WILL KILL YOU.
WANNA BET?

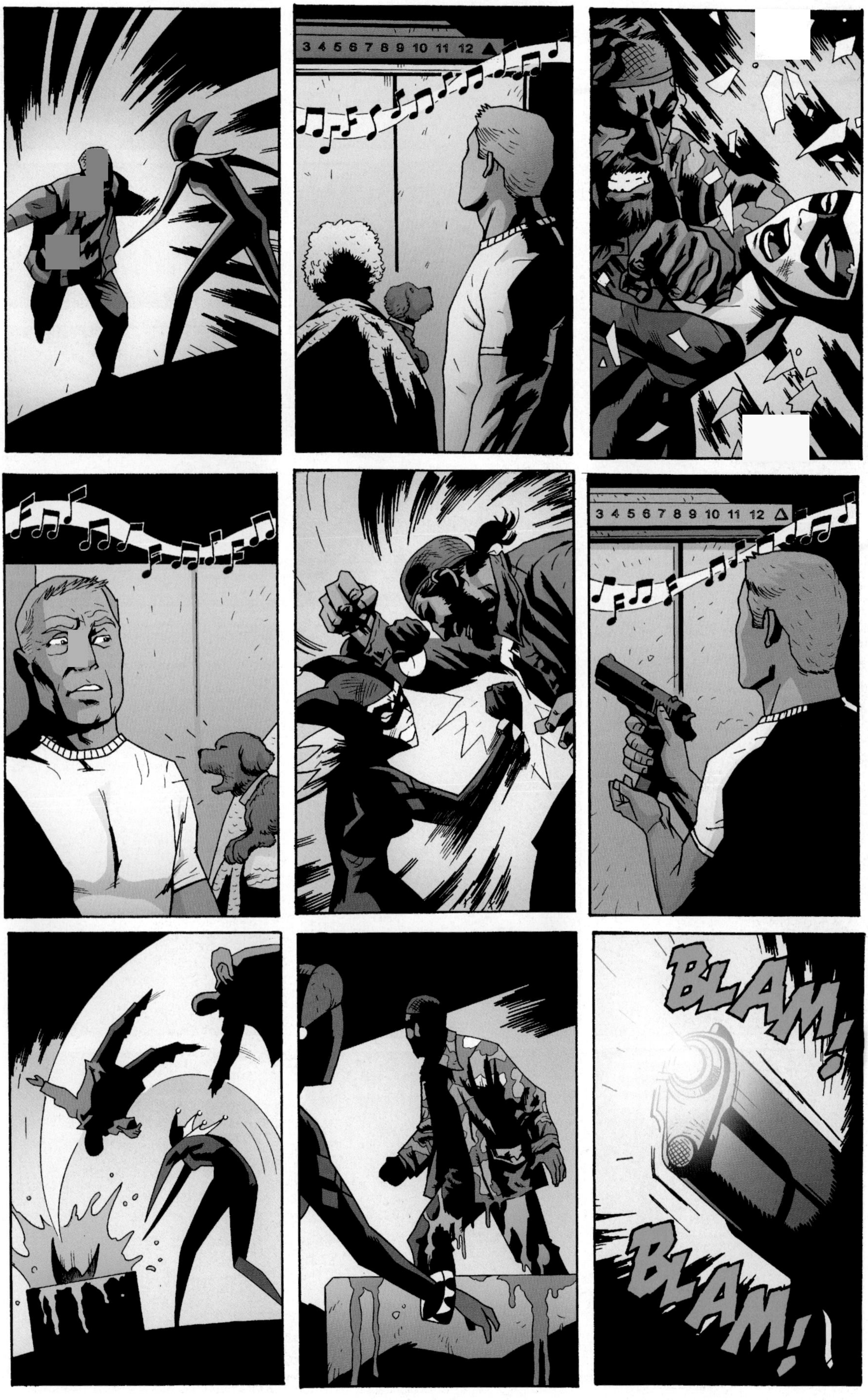
3 4 5 6 7 8 9 10 11 12
3 4 5 6 7 8 9 10 11 12
BLAM!
BLAM!

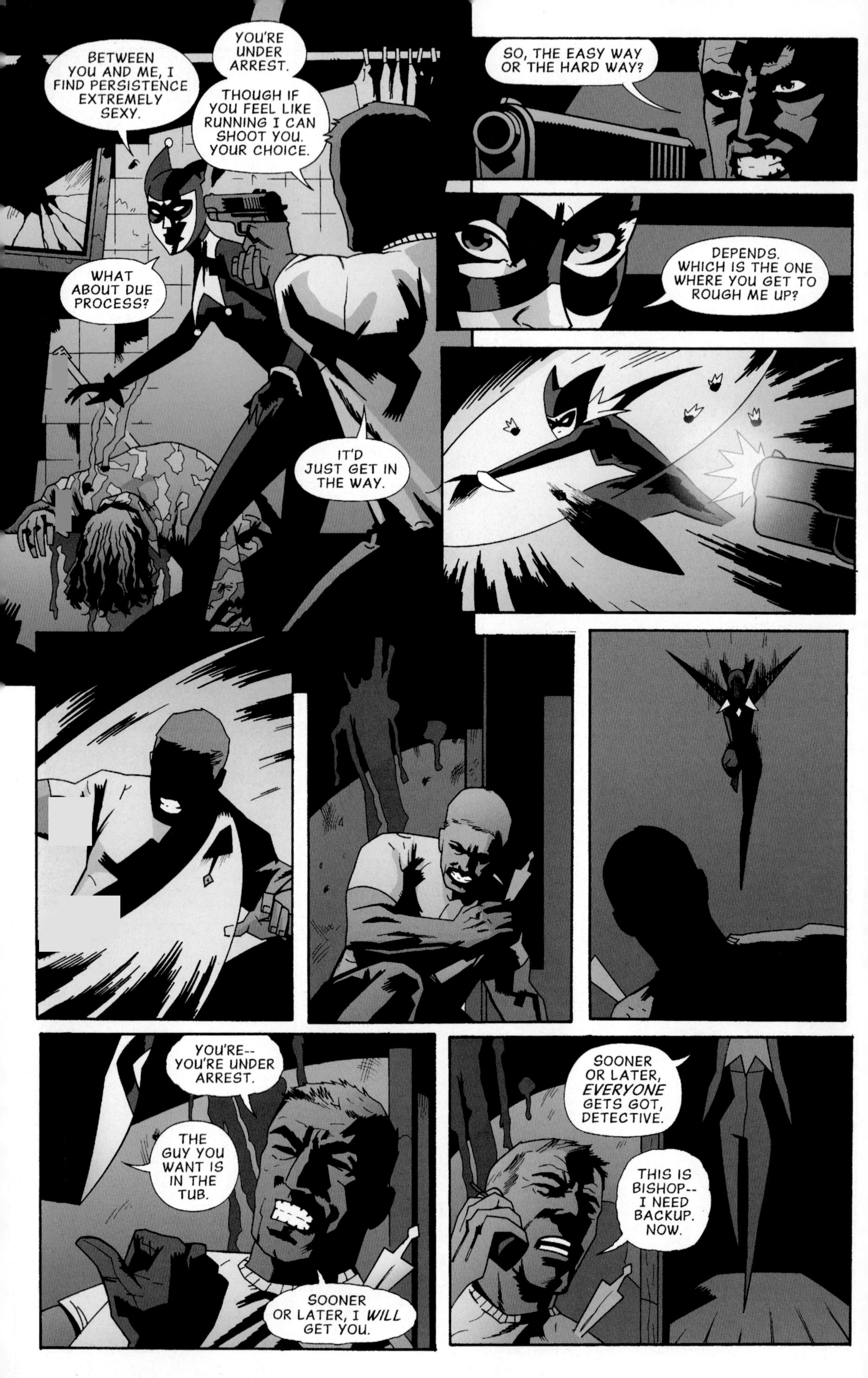
BETWEEN YOU AND ME, I FIND PERSISTENCE EXTREMELY SEXY.
YOU'RE UNDER ARREST.
THOUGH IF YOU FEEL LIKE RUNNING I CAN SHOOT YOU. YOUR CHOICE.
WHAT ABOUT DUE PROCESS?
IT'D JUST GET IN THE WAY.
SO, THE EASY WAY OR THE HARD WAY?
DEPENDS. WHICH IS THE ONE WHERE YOU GET TO ROUGH ME UP?
YOU'RE-- YOU'RE UNDER ARREST.
THE GUY YOU WANT IS IN THE TUB.
SOONER OR LATER, I *WILL* GET YOU.
SOONER OR LATER, *EVERYONE* GETS GOT, DETECTIVE.
THIS IS BISHOP-- I NEED BACKUP. NOW.

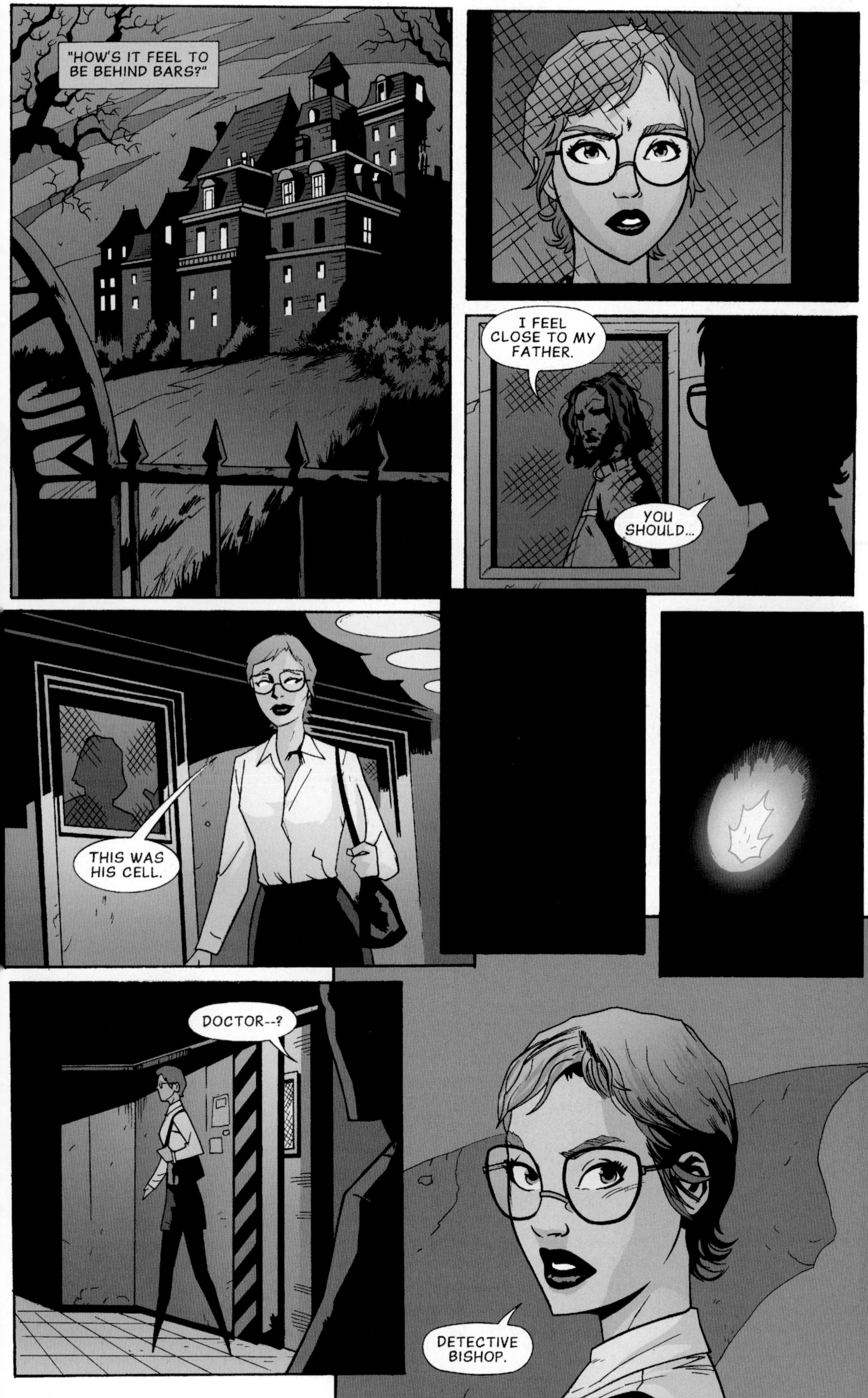
"HOW'S IT FEEL TO BE BEHIND BARS?"
I FEEL CLOSE TO MY FATHER.
YOU SHOULD...
THIS WAS HIS CELL.
DOCTOR--?
DETECTIVE BISHOP.

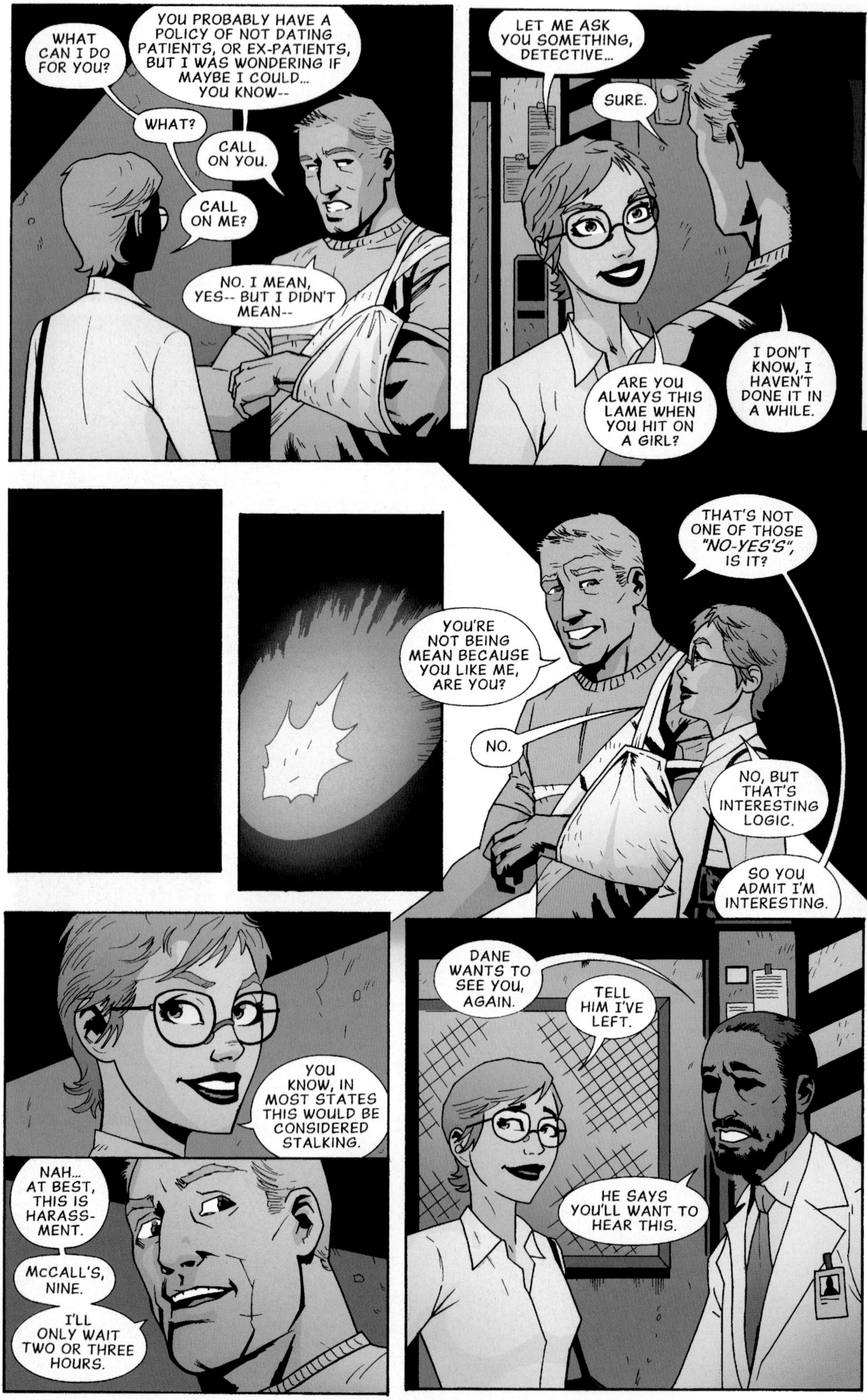
WHAT CAN I DO FOR YOU?
YOU PROBABLY HAVE A POLICY OF NOT DATING PATIENTS, OR EX-PATIENTS, BUT I WAS WONDERING IF MAYBE I COULD... YOU KNOW--
WHAT?
CALL ON YOU.
CALL ON ME?
NO. I MEAN, YES-- BUT I DIDN'T MEAN--
LET ME ASK YOU SOMETHING, DETECTIVE...
SURE.
ARE YOU ALWAYS THIS LAME WHEN YOU HIT ON A GIRL?
I DON'T KNOW, I HAVEN'T DONE IT IN A WHILE.
YOU'RE NOT BEING MEAN BECAUSE YOU LIKE ME, ARE YOU?
NO.
THAT'S NOT ONE OF THOSE "NO-YES'S", IS IT?
NO, BUT THAT'S INTERESTING LOGIC.
SO YOU ADMIT I'M INTERESTING.
YOU KNOW, IN MOST STATES THIS WOULD BE CONSIDERED STALKING.
NAH... AT BEST, THIS IS HARASS-MENT.
McCALL'S, NINE.
I'LL ONLY WAIT TWO OR THREE HOURS.
DANE WANTS TO SEE YOU, AGAIN.
TELL HIM I'VE LEFT.
HE SAYS YOU'LL WANT TO HEAR THIS.

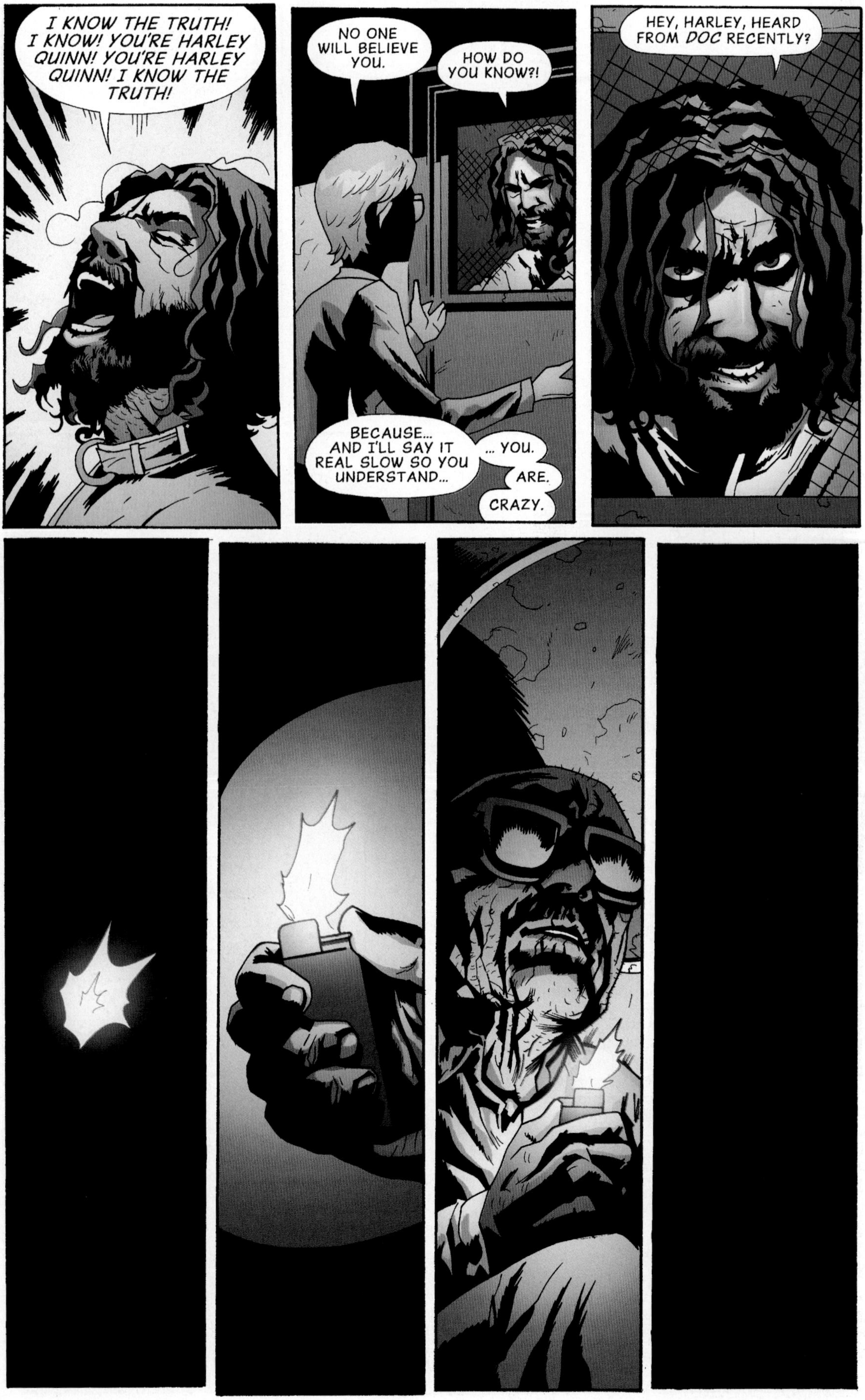
I KNOW THE TRUTH! I KNOW! YOU'RE HARLEY QUINN! YOU'RE HARLEY QUINN! I KNOW THE TRUTH!
NO ONE WILL BELIEVE YOU.
HOW DO YOU KNOW?!
BECAUSE... AND I'LL SAY IT REAL SLOW SO YOU UNDERSTAND...
... YOU.
ARE.
CRAZY.
HEY, HARLEY, HEARD FROM *DOC* RECENTLY?

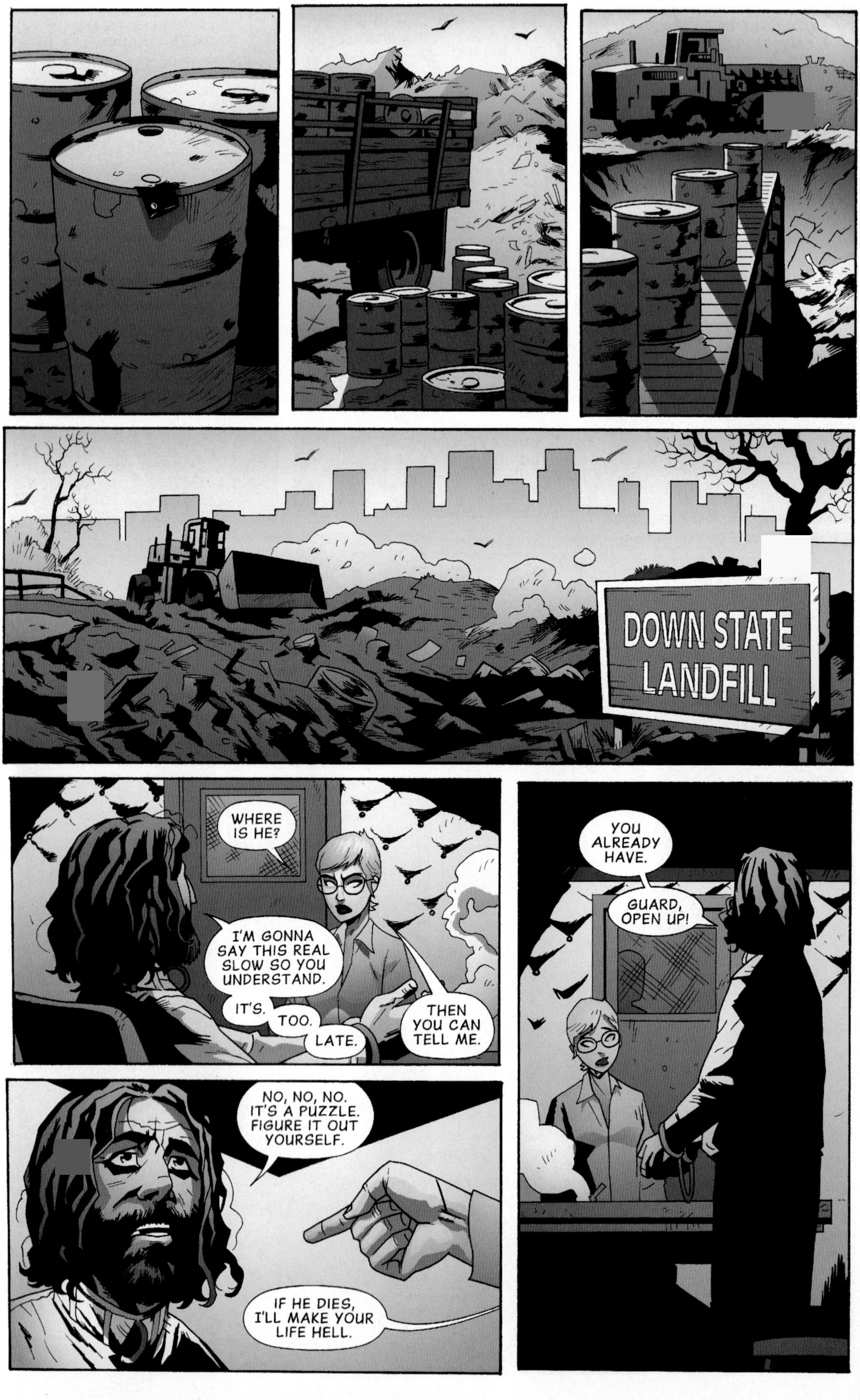
DOWN STATE LANDFILL
WHERE IS HE?
I'M GONNA SAY THIS REAL SLOW SO YOU UNDERSTAND.
IT'S.
TOO.
LATE.
THEN YOU CAN TELL ME.
NO, NO, NO. IT'S A PUZZLE. FIGURE IT OUT YOURSELF.
IF HE DIES, I'LL MAKE YOUR LIFE HELL.
YOU ALREADY HAVE.
GUARD, OPEN UP!

PUZZLE...?

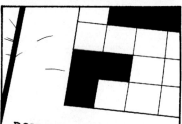

DOWN
1. Some court pract
2. Peace Corps cousi
3. Latin words for "clarification"
4. Five families graveyard
5. Candy dispenser

FIVE FAMILIES... MAFIA... MAFIA'S GRAVEYARD...

LANDFILL!

THWUNK!

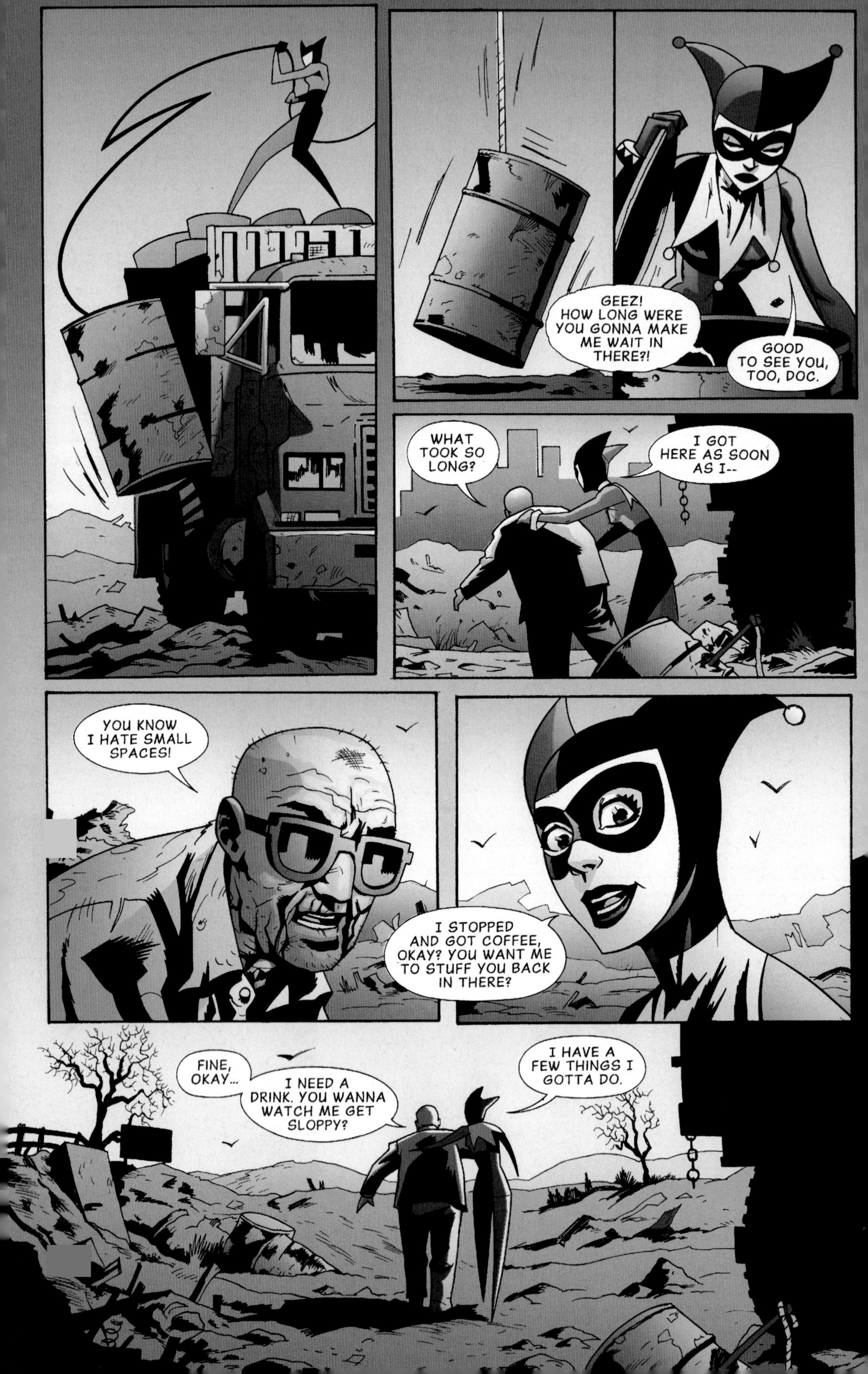
GEEZ! HOW LONG WERE YOU GONNA MAKE ME WAIT IN THERE?!
GOOD TO SEE YOU, TOO, DOC.
WHAT TOOK SO LONG?
I GOT HERE AS SOON AS I--
YOU KNOW I HATE SMALL SPACES!
I STOPPED AND GOT COFFEE, OKAY? YOU WANT ME TO STUFF YOU BACK IN THERE?
FINE, OKAY...
I NEED A DRINK. YOU WANNA WATCH ME GET SLOPPY?
I HAVE A FEW THINGS I GOTTA DO.

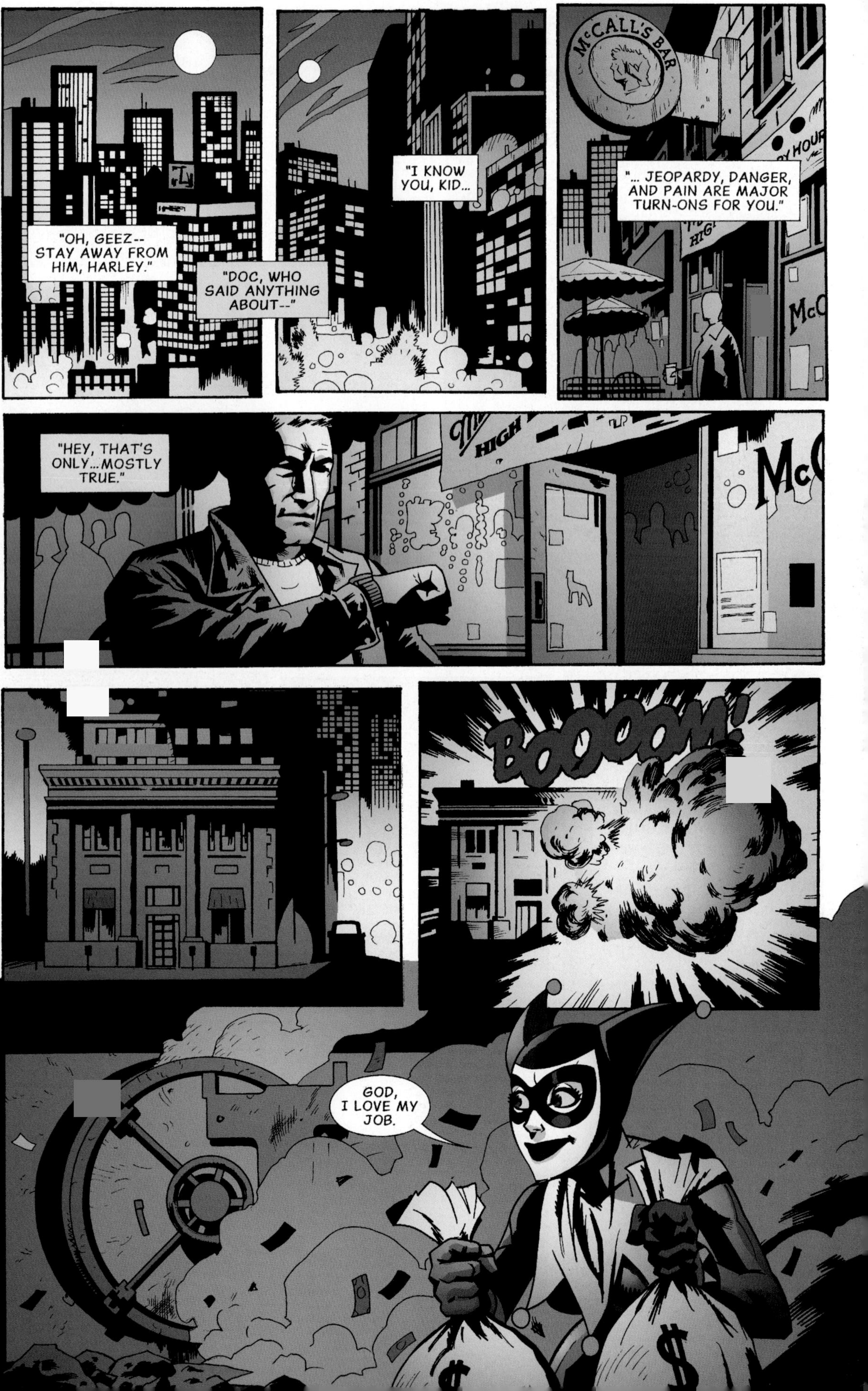
"OH, GEEZ-- STAY AWAY FROM HIM, HARLEY."
"DOC, WHO SAID ANYTHING ABOUT--"
"I KNOW YOU, KID...
McCALL'S BAR
"... JEOPARDY, DANGER, AND PAIN ARE MAJOR TURN-ONS FOR YOU."
"HEY, THAT'S ONLY...MOSTLY TRUE."
BOOOOM!
GOD, I LOVE MY JOB.

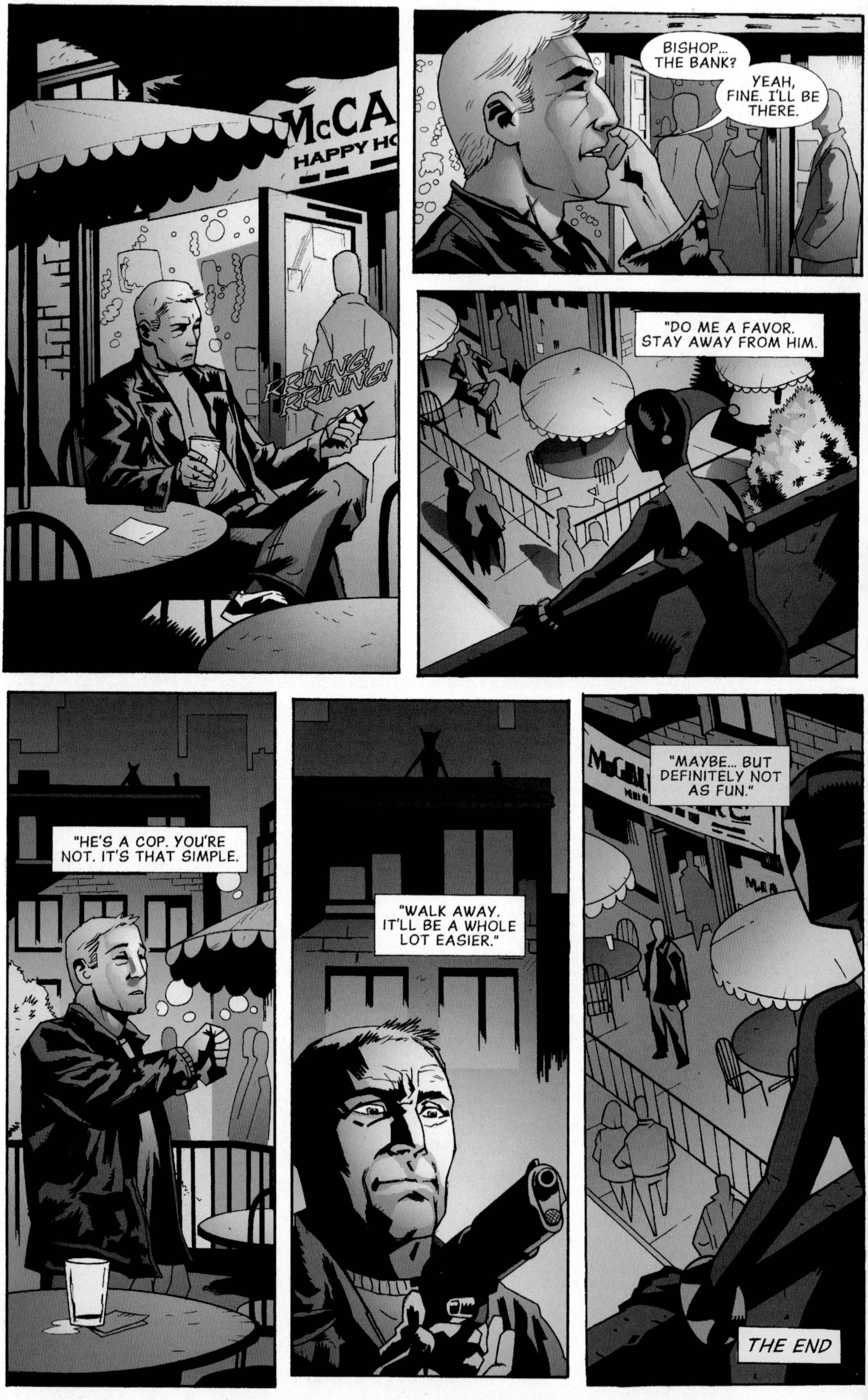
McCA
HAPPY HO
RRINNG! RRINNG!
BISHOP... THE BANK?
YEAH, FINE. I'LL BE THERE.
"DO ME A FAVOR. STAY AWAY FROM HIM.
"HE'S A COP. YOU'RE NOT. IT'S THAT SIMPLE.
"WALK AWAY. IT'LL BE A WHOLE LOT EASIER."
"MAYBE... BUT DEFINITELY NOT AS FUN."
THE END

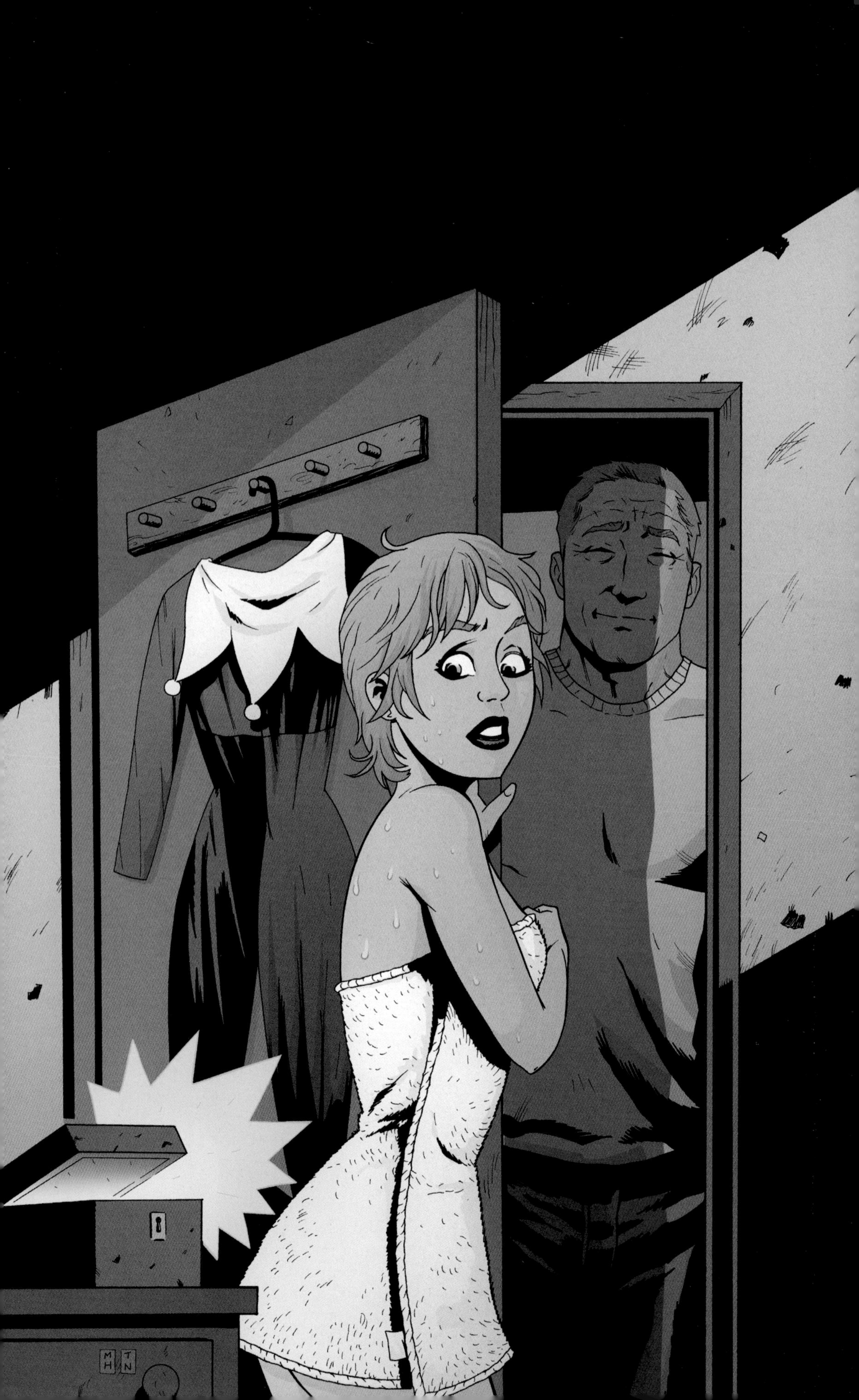
MH TN

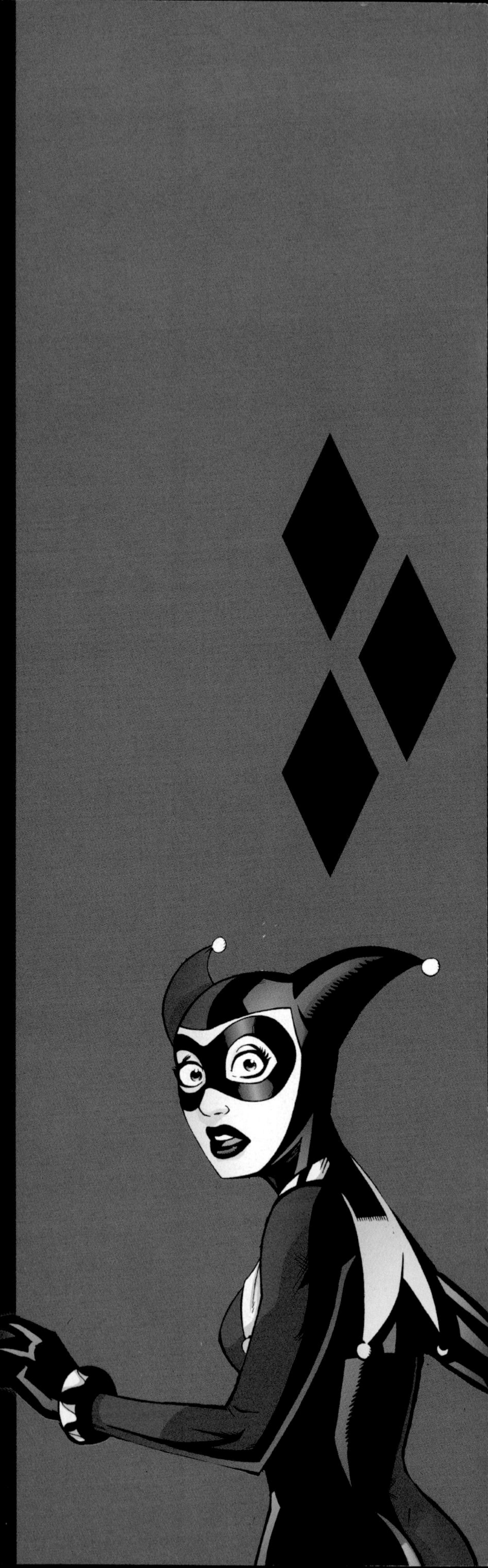

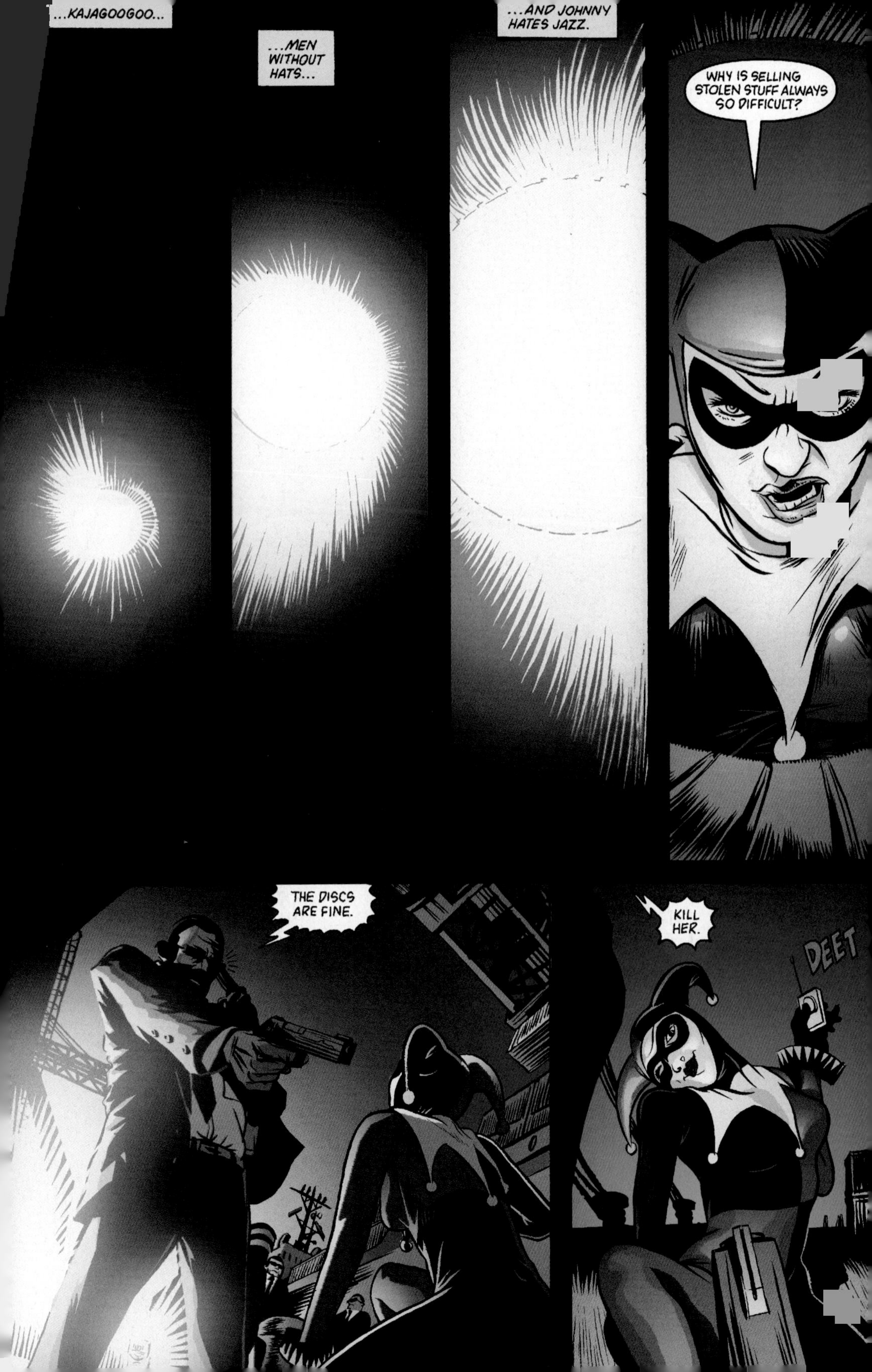
...KAJAGOOGOO...
...MEN WITHOUT HATS...
...AND JOHNNY HATES JAZZ.
WHY IS SELLING STOLEN STUFF ALWAYS SO DIFFICULT?
THE DISCS ARE FINE.
KILL HER.
DEET

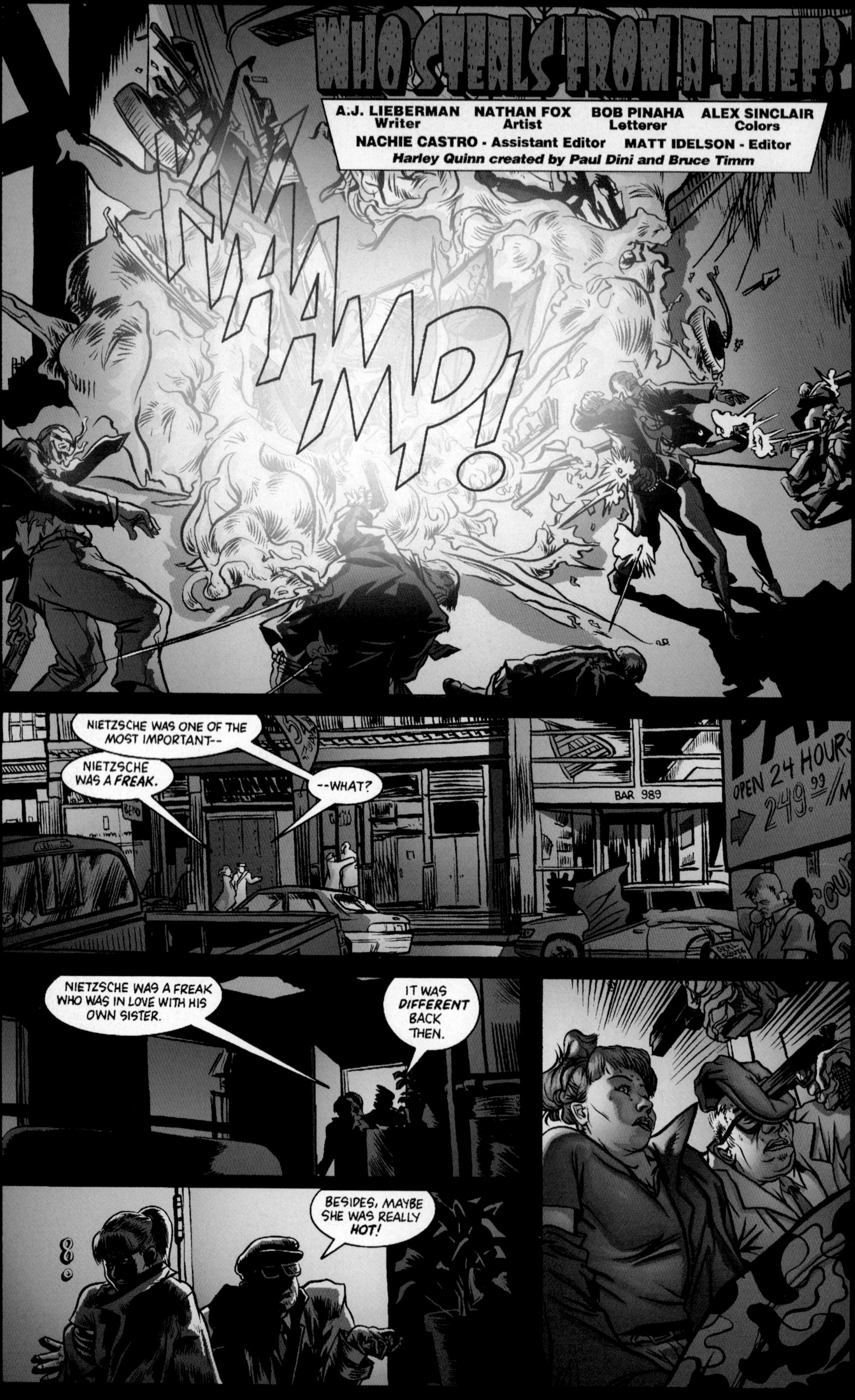
WHO STEALS FROM A THIEF?
A.J. LIEBERMAN Writer
NATHAN FOX Artist
BOB PINAHA Letterer
ALEX SINCLAIR Colors
NACHIE CASTRO - Assistant Editor
MATT IDELSON - Editor
Harley Quinn created by Paul Dini and Bruce Timm
WHAMP!
NIETZSCHE WAS ONE OF THE MOST IMPORTANT--
NIETZSCHE WAS A FREAK.
--WHAT?
BAR 989
OPEN 24 HOURS
249.99
NIETZSCHE WAS A FREAK WHO WAS IN LOVE WITH HIS OWN SISTER.
IT WAS DIFFERENT BACK THEN.
BESIDES, MAYBE SHE WAS REALLY HOT!

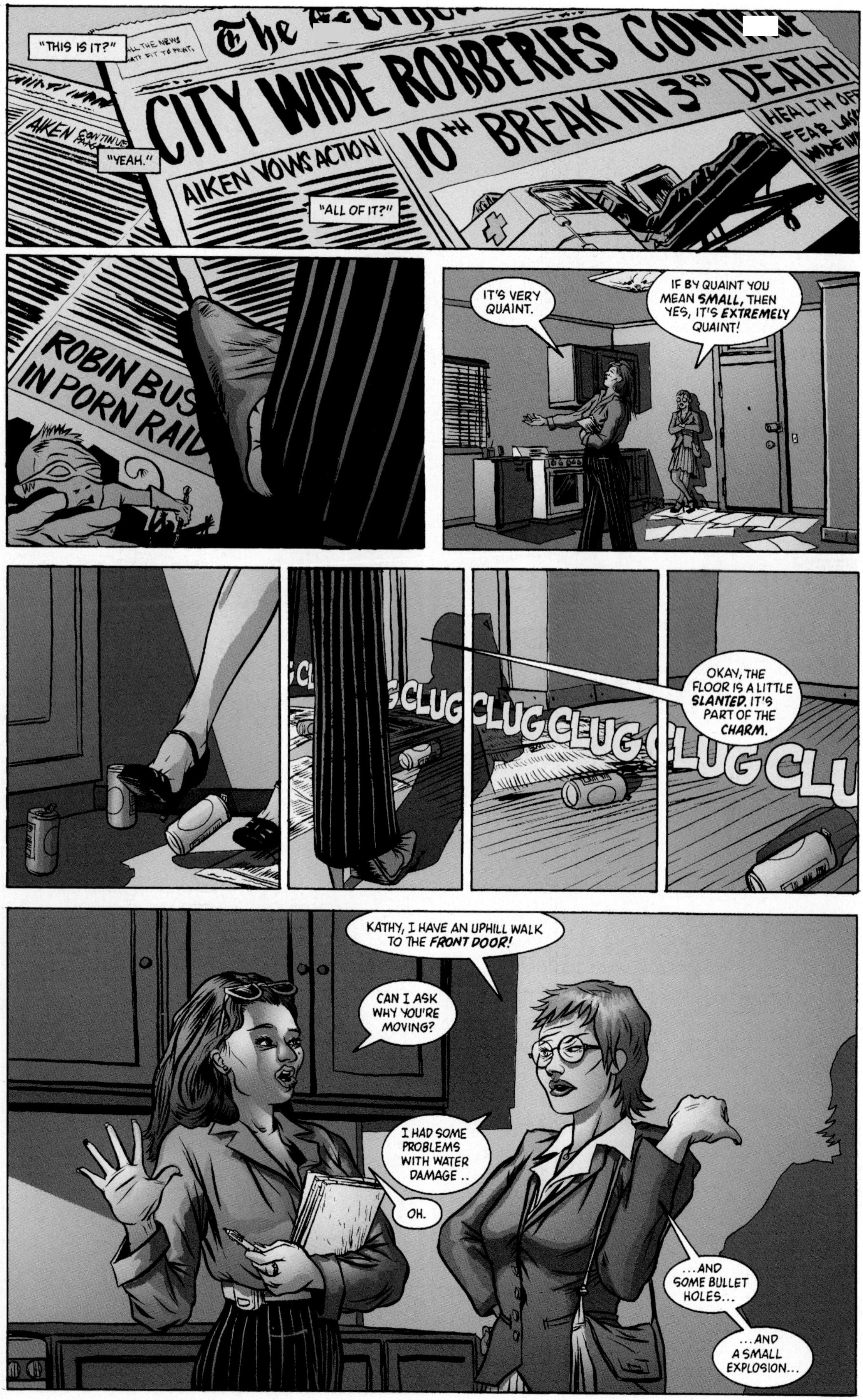
"THIS IS IT?"
CITY WIDE ROBBERIES
10TH BREAK IN 3RD DEATH
AIKEN VOWS ACTION
"YEAH."
"ALL OF IT?"
IN PORN RAID
IT'S VERY QUAINT.
IF BY QUAINT YOU MEAN SMALL, THEN YES, IT'S EXTREMELY QUAINT!
CLUG CLUG CLUG CLUG
OKAY, THE FLOOR IS A LITTLE SLANTED. IT'S PART OF THE CHARM.
KATHY, I HAVE AN UPHILL WALK TO THE FRONT DOOR!
CAN I ASK WHY YOU'RE MOVING?
I HAD SOME PROBLEMS WITH WATER DAMAGE ..
OH.
...AND SOME BULLET HOLES...
...AND A SMALL EXPLOSION...

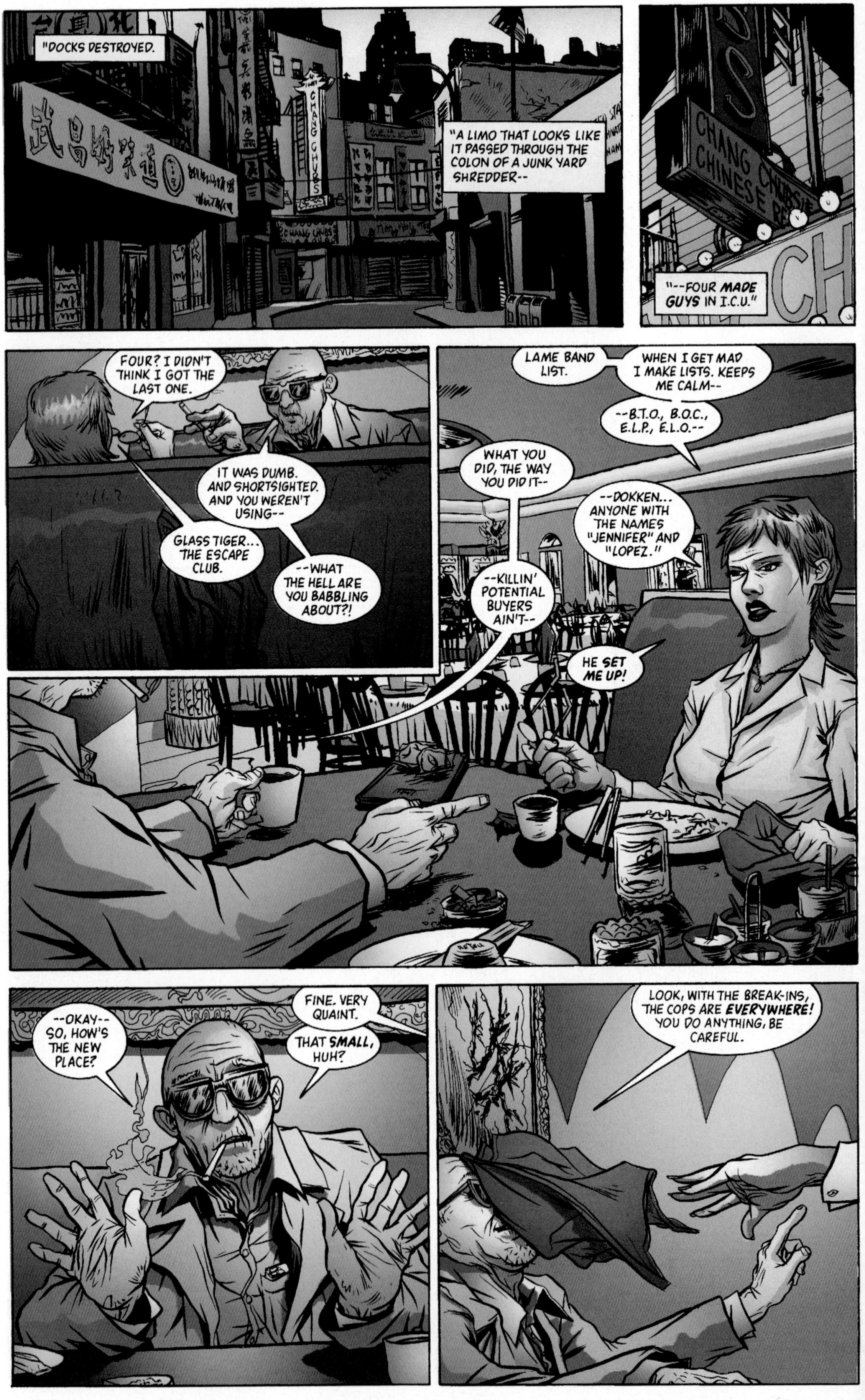
"DOCKS DESTROYED.
"A LIMO THAT LOOKS LIKE IT PASSED THROUGH THE COLON OF A JUNK YARD SHREDDER--
"--FOUR **MADE GUYS** IN I.C.U."
FOUR? I DIDN'T THINK I GOT THE LAST ONE.
IT WAS DUMB. AND SHORTSIGHTED. AND YOU WEREN'T USING--
GLASS TIGER... THE ESCAPE CLUB.
--WHAT THE HELL ARE YOU BABBLING ABOUT?!
WHEN I GET MAD I MAKE LISTS. KEEPS ME CALM--
LAME BAND LIST.
--B.T.O., B.O.C., E.L.P., E.L.O.--
WHAT YOU DID, THE WAY YOU DID IT--
--DOKKEN... ANYONE WITH THE NAMES "JENNIFER" AND "LOPEZ."
--KILLIN' POTENTIAL BUYERS AIN'T--
HE **SET ME UP!**
--OKAY-- SO, HOW'S THE NEW PLACE?
FINE. VERY QUAINT.
THAT **SMALL,** HUH?
LOOK, WITH THE BREAK-INS, THE COPS ARE **EVERYWHERE!** YOU DO ANYTHING, BE CAREFUL.

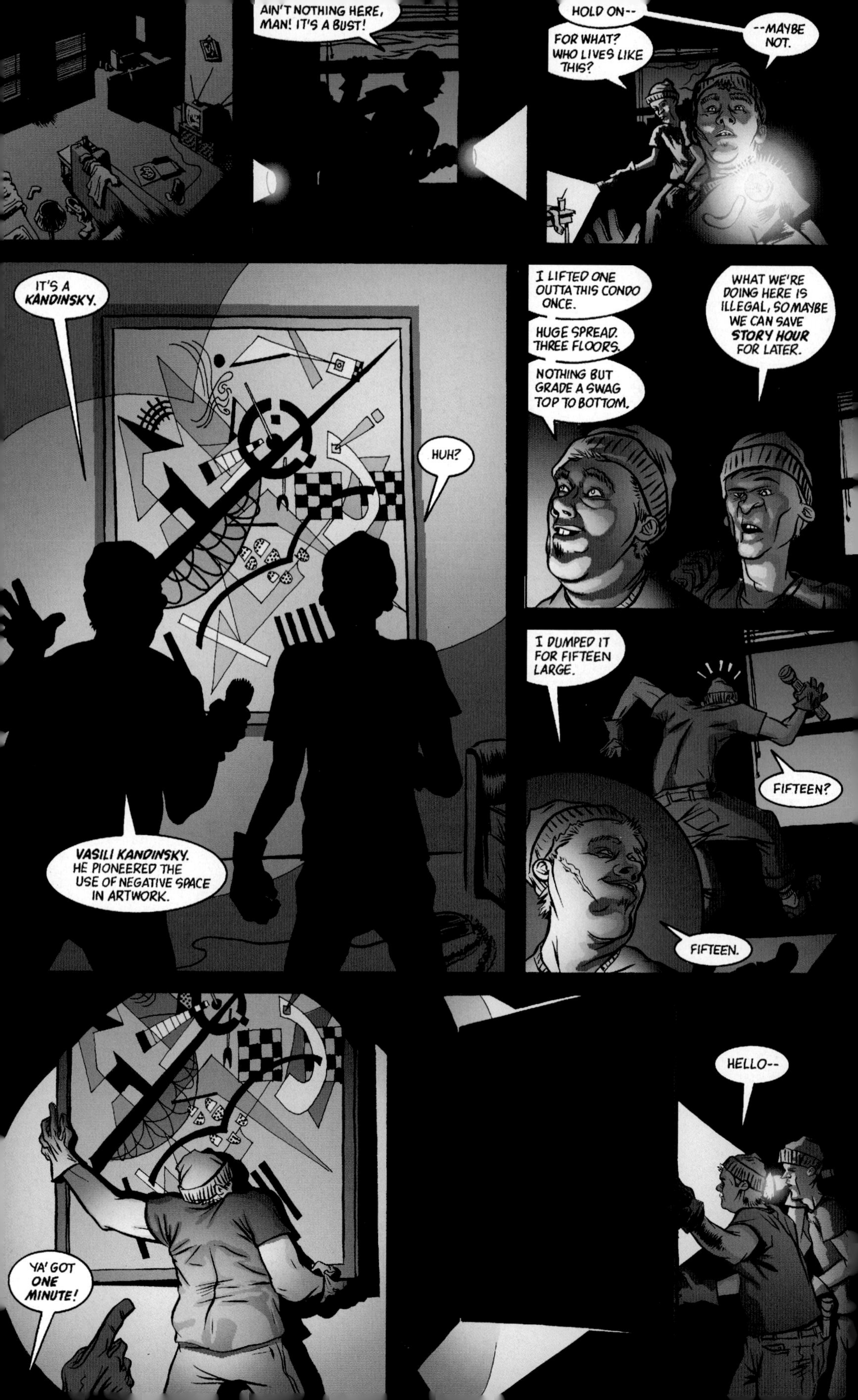
AIN'T NOTHING HERE, MAN! IT'S A BUST!
HOLD ON--
FOR WHAT? WHO LIVES LIKE THIS?
--MAYBE NOT.
IT'S A KANDINSKY.
HUH?
VASILI KANDINSKY. HE PIONEERED THE USE OF NEGATIVE SPACE IN ARTWORK.
I LIFTED ONE OUTTA THIS CONDO ONCE.
HUGE SPREAD. THREE FLOORS.
NOTHING BUT GRADE A SWAG TOP TO BOTTOM.
WHAT WE'RE DOING HERE IS ILLEGAL, SO MAYBE WE CAN SAVE STORY HOUR FOR LATER.
I DUMPED IT FOR FIFTEEN LARGE.
FIFTEEN?
FIFTEEN.
YA' GOT ONE MINUTE!
HELLO--

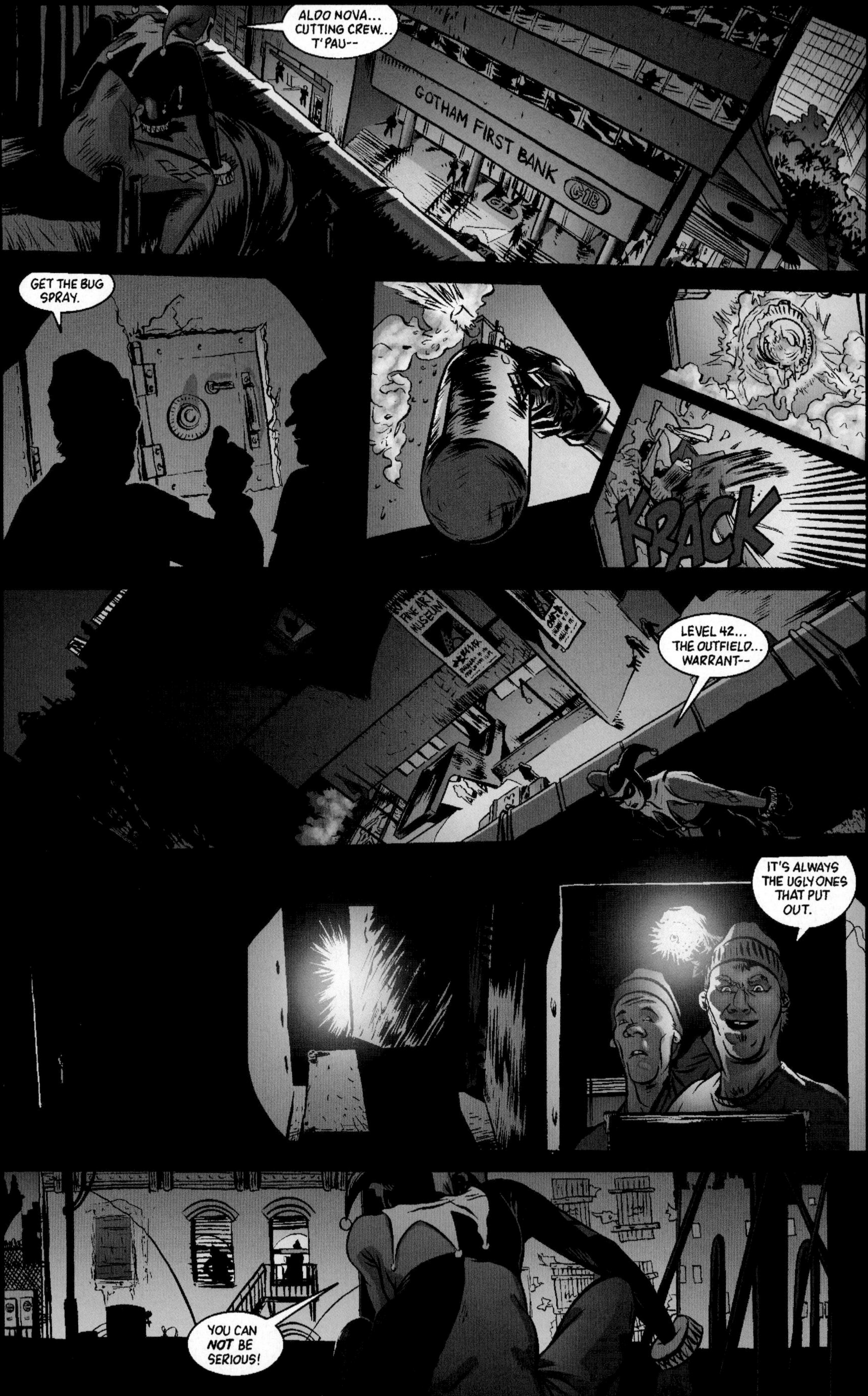
ALDO NOVA...
CUTTING CREW...
T'PAU--
GOTHAM FIRST BANK
GFB
GET THE BUG SPRAY.
KRACK
FINE ART MUSEUM
LEVEL 42... THE OUTFIELD... WARRANT--
IT'S ALWAYS THE UGLY ONES THAT PUT OUT.
YOU CAN NOT BE SERIOUS!

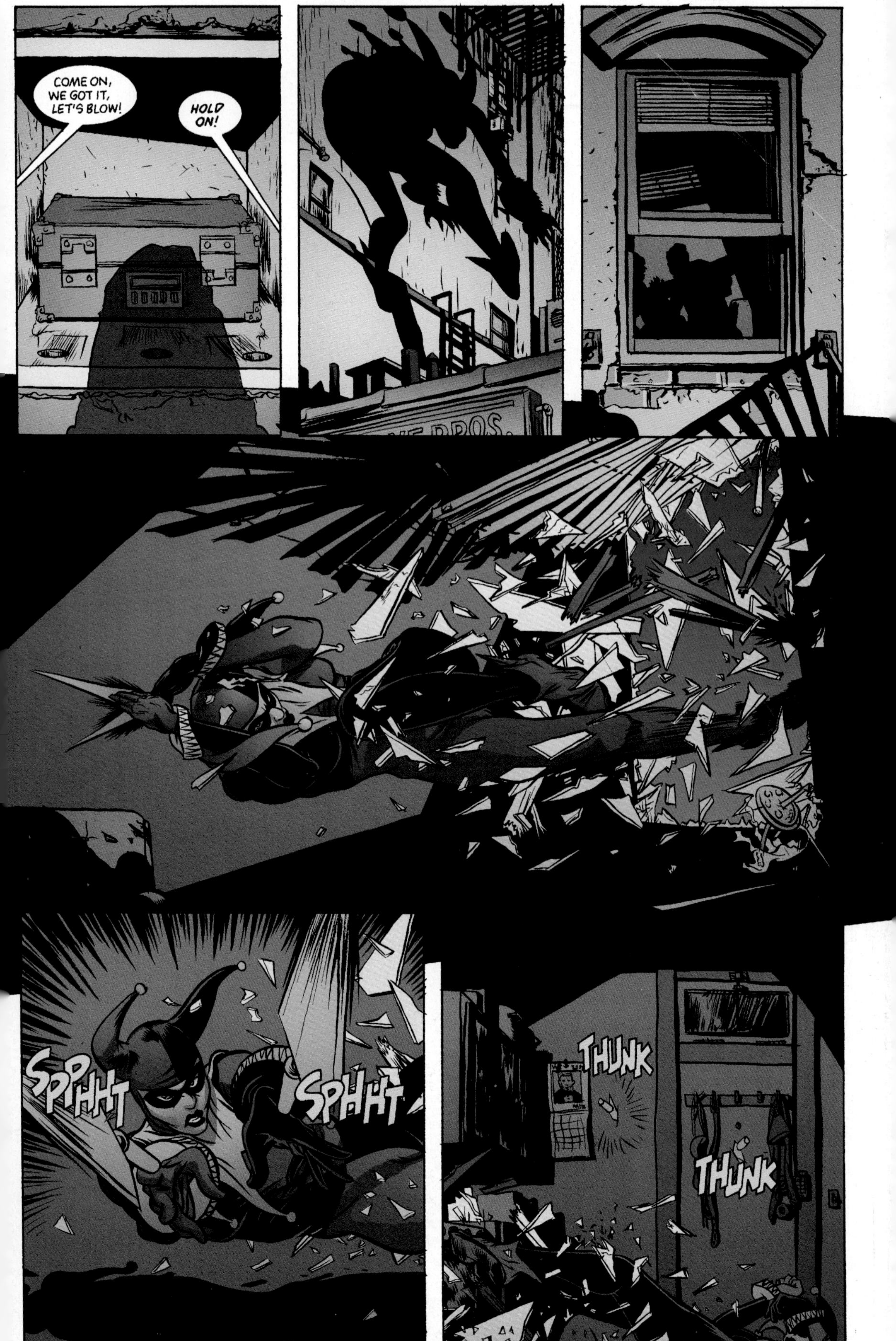
COME ON, WE GOT IT, LET'S BLOW!
HOLD ON!
SPPHHT
SPHHT
THUNK
THUNK

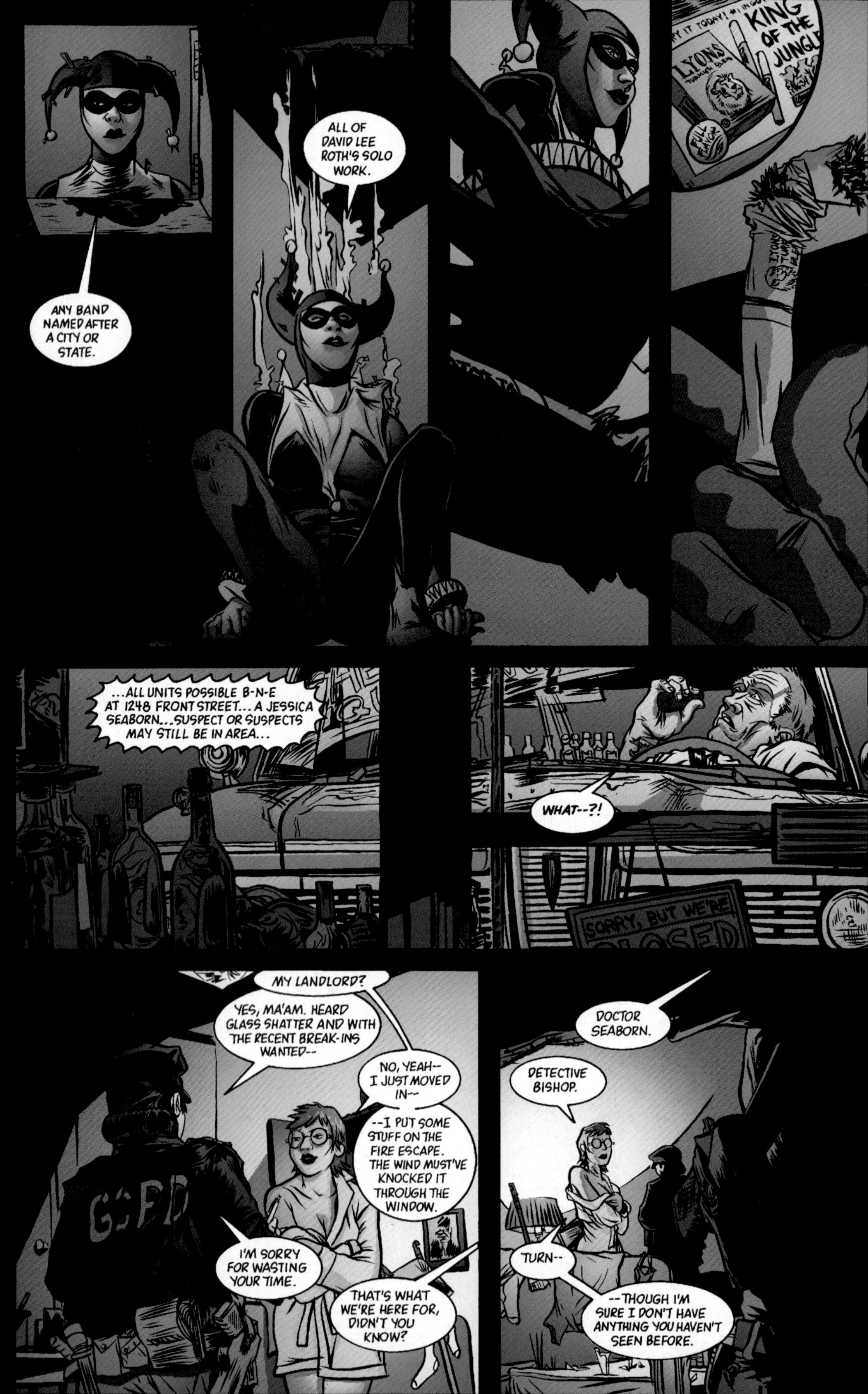
ANY BAND NAMED AFTER A CITY OR STATE.
ALL OF DAVID LEE ROTH'S SOLO WORK.
KING OF THE JUNGLE
LYONS
...ALL UNITS POSSIBLE B-N-E AT 1248 FRONT STREET... A JESSICA SEABORN... SUSPECT OR SUSPECTS MAY STILL BE IN AREA...
WHAT--?!
SORRY, BUT WE'RE
MY LANDLORD?
YES, MA'AM. HEARD GLASS SHATTER AND WITH THE RECENT BREAK-INS WANTED--
NO, YEAH-- I JUST MOVED IN--
--I PUT SOME STUFF ON THE FIRE ESCAPE. THE WIND MUST'VE KNOCKED IT THROUGH THE WINDOW.
I'M SORRY FOR WASTING YOUR TIME.
THAT'S WHAT WE'RE HERE FOR, DIDN'T YOU KNOW?
DOCTOR SEABORN.
DETECTIVE BISHOP.
TURN--
--THOUGH I'M SURE I DON'T HAVE ANYTHING YOU HAVEN'T SEEN BEFORE.

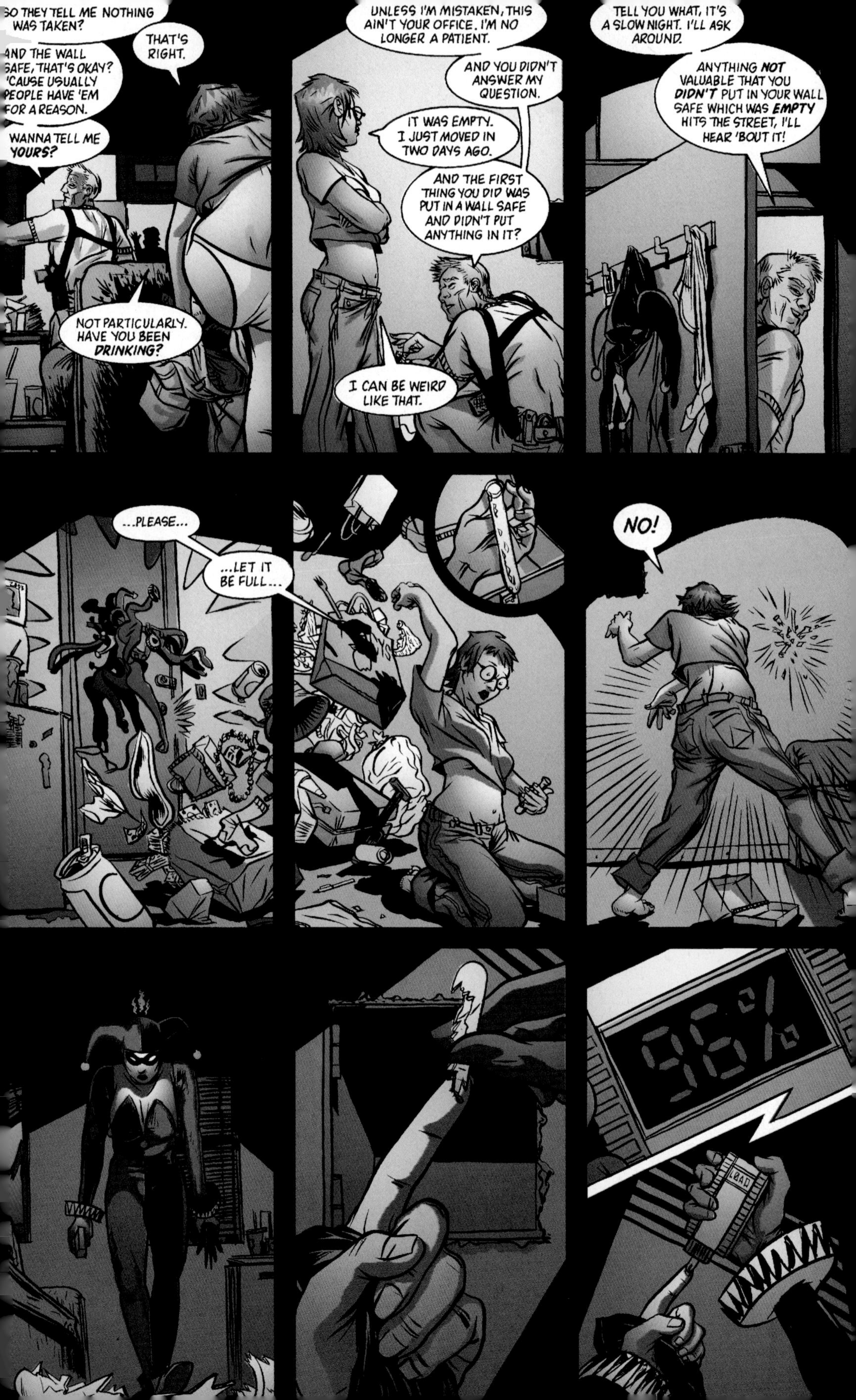
SO THEY TELL ME NOTHING WAS TAKEN?
THAT'S RIGHT.
AND THE WALL SAFE, THAT'S OKAY? 'CAUSE USUALLY PEOPLE HAVE 'EM FOR A REASON.
WANNA TELL ME YOURS?
NOT PARTICULARLY. HAVE YOU BEEN DRINKING?
UNLESS I'M MISTAKEN, THIS AIN'T YOUR OFFICE. I'M NO LONGER A PATIENT.
AND YOU DIDN'T ANSWER MY QUESTION.
IT WAS EMPTY. I JUST MOVED IN TWO DAYS AGO.
AND THE FIRST THING YOU DID WAS PUT IN A WALL SAFE AND DIDN'T PUT ANYTHING IN IT?
I CAN BE WEIRD LIKE THAT.
TELL YOU WHAT, IT'S A SLOW NIGHT. I'LL ASK AROUND.
ANYTHING NOT VALUABLE THAT YOU DIDN'T PUT IN YOUR WALL SAFE WHICH WAS EMPTY HITS THE STREET, I'LL HEAR 'BOUT IT!
...PLEASE...
...LET IT BE FULL...
NO!
96%
LOAD

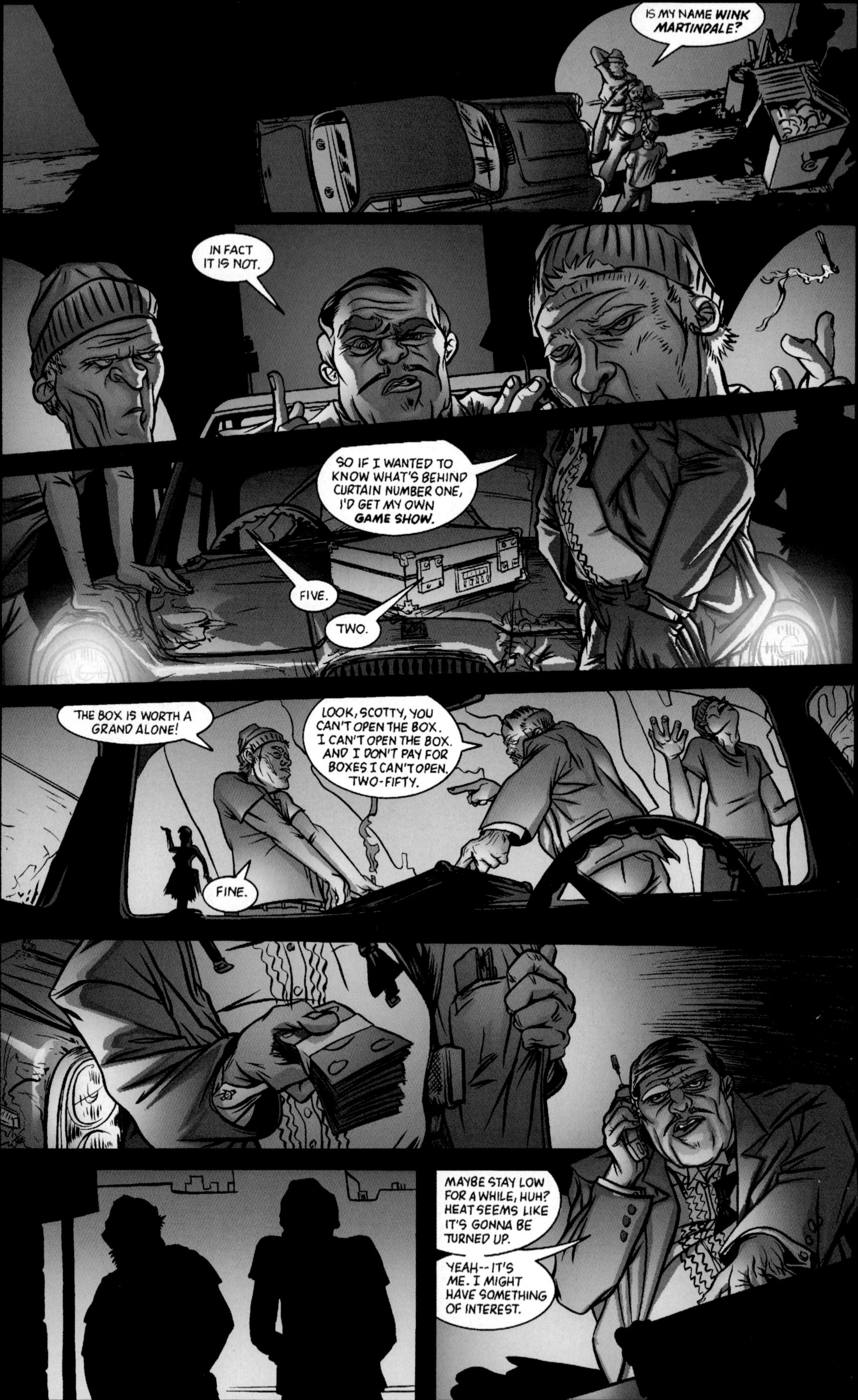
IS MY NAME **WINK MARTINDALE?**
IN FACT IT IS NOT.
SO IF I WANTED TO KNOW WHAT'S BEHIND CURTAIN NUMBER ONE, I'D GET MY OWN **GAME SHOW.**
FIVE.
TWO.
THE BOX IS WORTH A GRAND ALONE!
LOOK, SCOTTY, YOU CAN'T OPEN THE BOX. I CAN'T OPEN THE BOX. AND I DON'T PAY FOR BOXES I CAN'T OPEN. TWO-FIFTY.
FINE.
MAYBE STAY LOW FOR A WHILE, HUH? HEAT SEEMS LIKE IT'S GONNA BE TURNED UP.
YEAH-- IT'S ME. I MIGHT HAVE SOMETHING OF INTEREST.

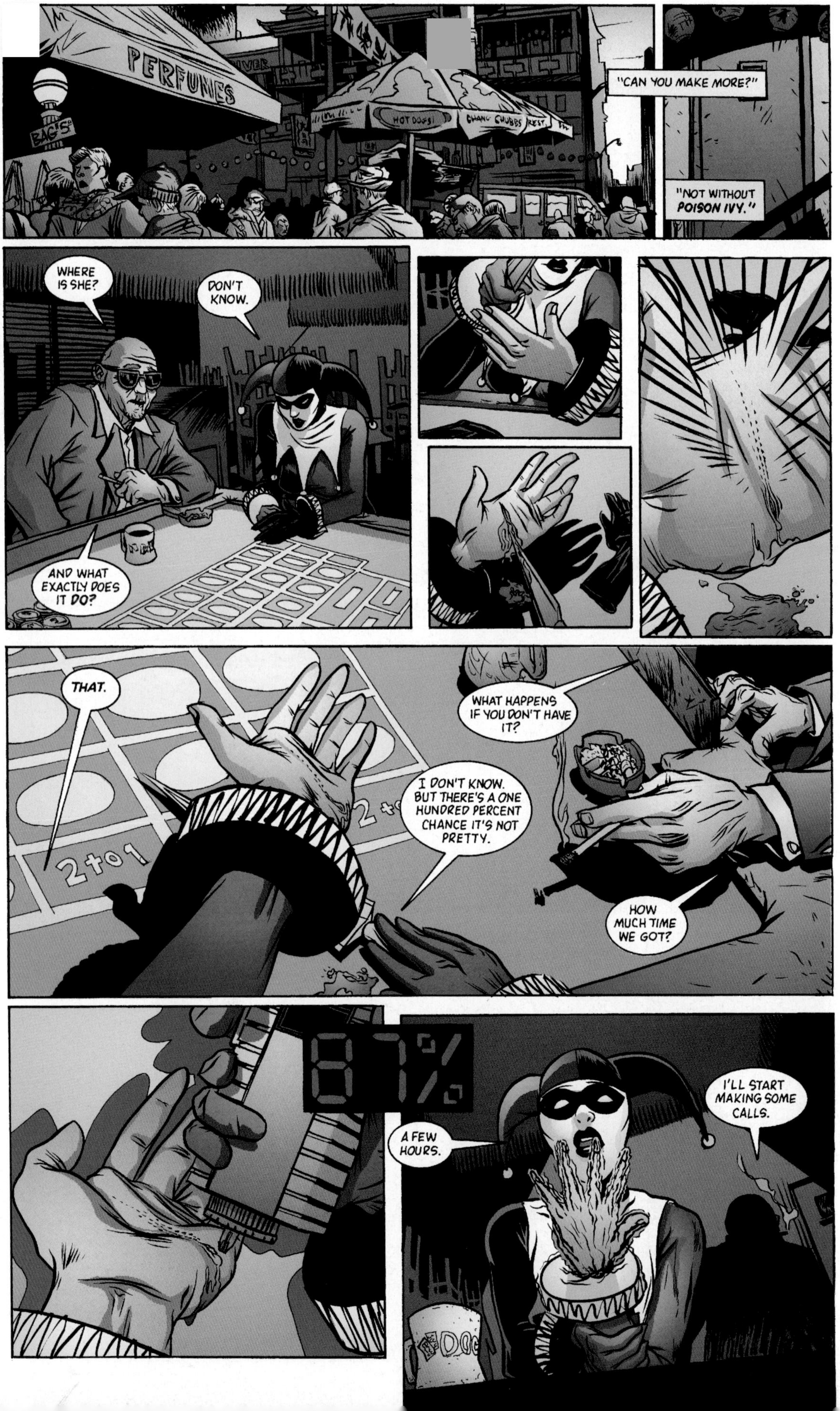
PERFUMES
HOT DOGS!
"CAN YOU MAKE MORE?"
"NOT WITHOUT POISON IVY."
WHERE IS SHE?
DON'T KNOW.
AND WHAT EXACTLY DOES IT DO?
THAT.
WHAT HAPPENS IF YOU DON'T HAVE IT?
I DON'T KNOW. BUT THERE'S A ONE HUNDRED PERCENT CHANCE IT'S NOT PRETTY.
HOW MUCH TIME WE GOT?
2 to 1
87%
A FEW HOURS.
I'LL START MAKING SOME CALLS.

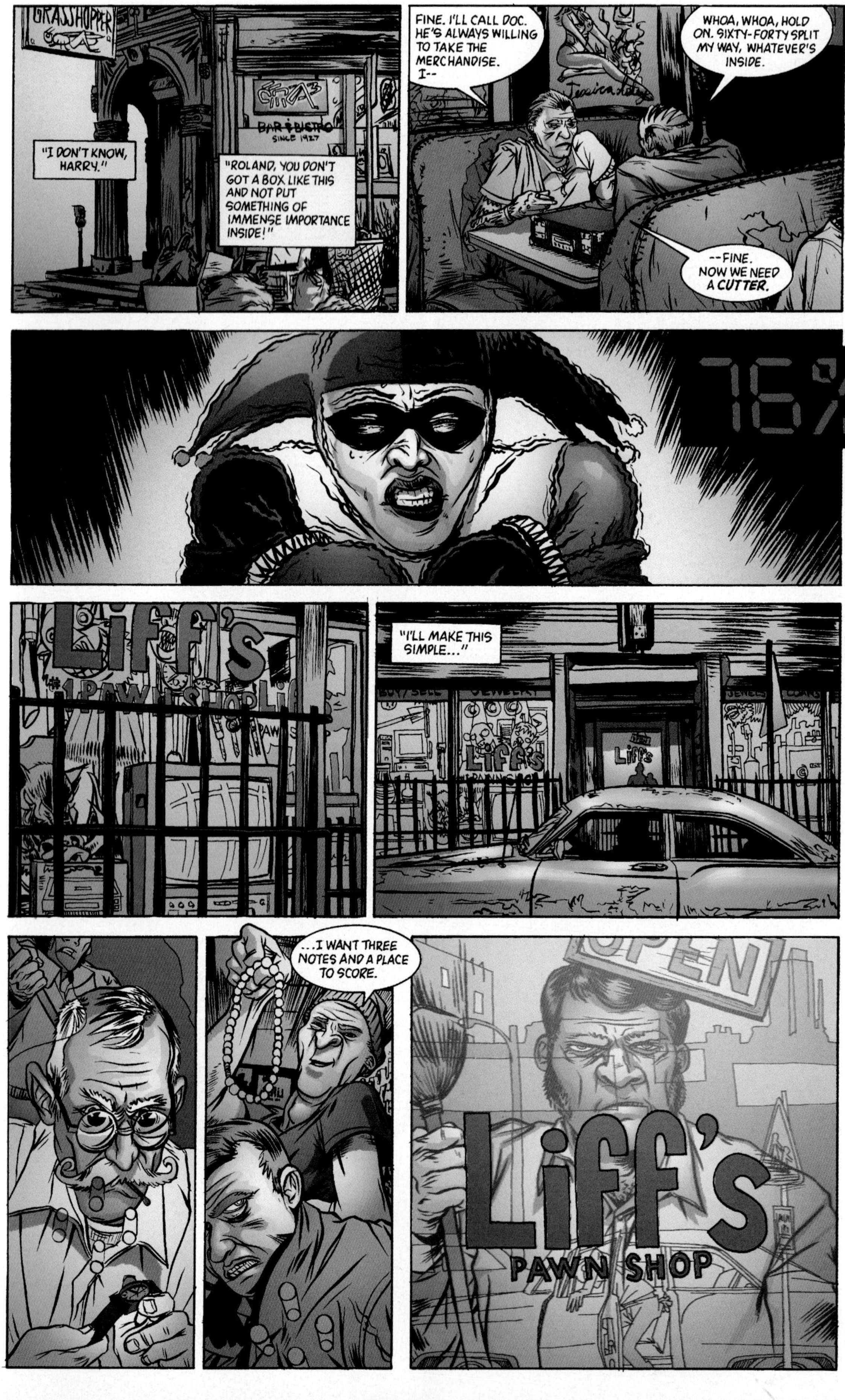
GRASSHOPPER
BAR & BISTRO SINCE 1927
"I DON'T KNOW, HARRY."
"ROLAND, YOU DON'T GOT A BOX LIKE THIS AND NOT PUT SOMETHING OF IMMENSE IMPORTANCE INSIDE!"
FINE. I'LL CALL DOC. HE'S ALWAYS WILLING TO TAKE THE MERCHANDISE. I--
WHOA, WHOA, HOLD ON. SIXTY-FORTY SPLIT MY WAY, WHATEVER'S INSIDE.
--FINE. NOW WE NEED A CUTTER.
76%
LIFF'S
"I'LL MAKE THIS SIMPLE..."
...I WANT THREE NOTES AND A PLACE TO SCORE.
OPEN
LIFF'S
PAWN SHOP

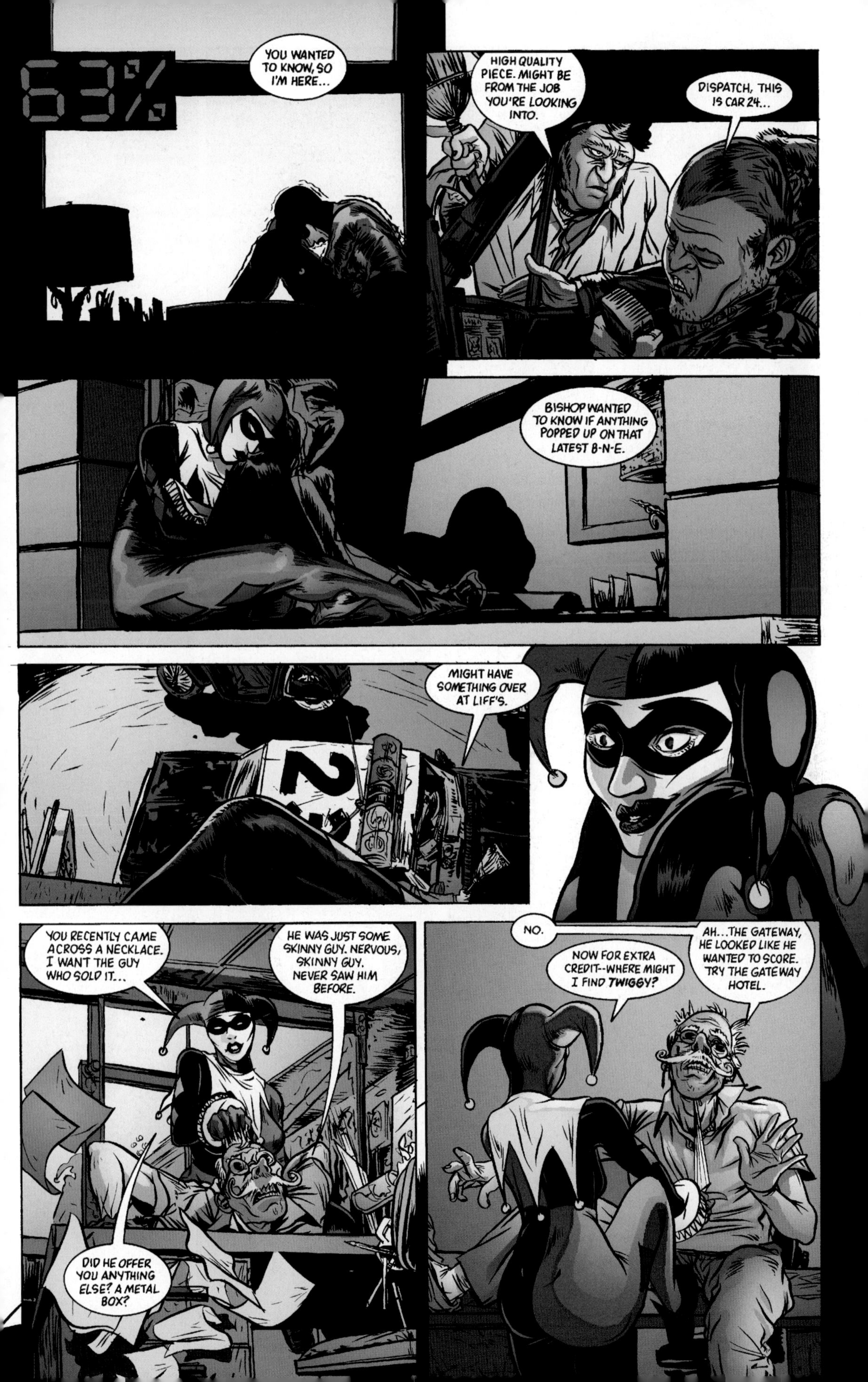
63%
YOU WANTED TO KNOW, SO I'M HERE...
HIGH QUALITY PIECE. MIGHT BE FROM THE JOB YOU'RE LOOKING INTO.
DISPATCH, THIS IS CAR 24...
BISHOP WANTED TO KNOW IF ANYTHING POPPED UP ON THAT LATEST B-N-E.
MIGHT HAVE SOMETHING OVER AT LIFF'S.
YOU RECENTLY CAME ACROSS A NECKLACE. I WANT THE GUY WHO SOLD IT...
HE WAS JUST SOME SKINNY GUY. NERVOUS, SKINNY GUY. NEVER SAW HIM BEFORE.
DID HE OFFER YOU ANYTHING ELSE? A METAL BOX?
NO.
NOW FOR EXTRA CREDIT--WHERE MIGHT I FIND TWIGGY?
AH...THE GATEWAY, HE LOOKED LIKE HE WANTED TO SCORE. TRY THE GATEWAY HOTEL.

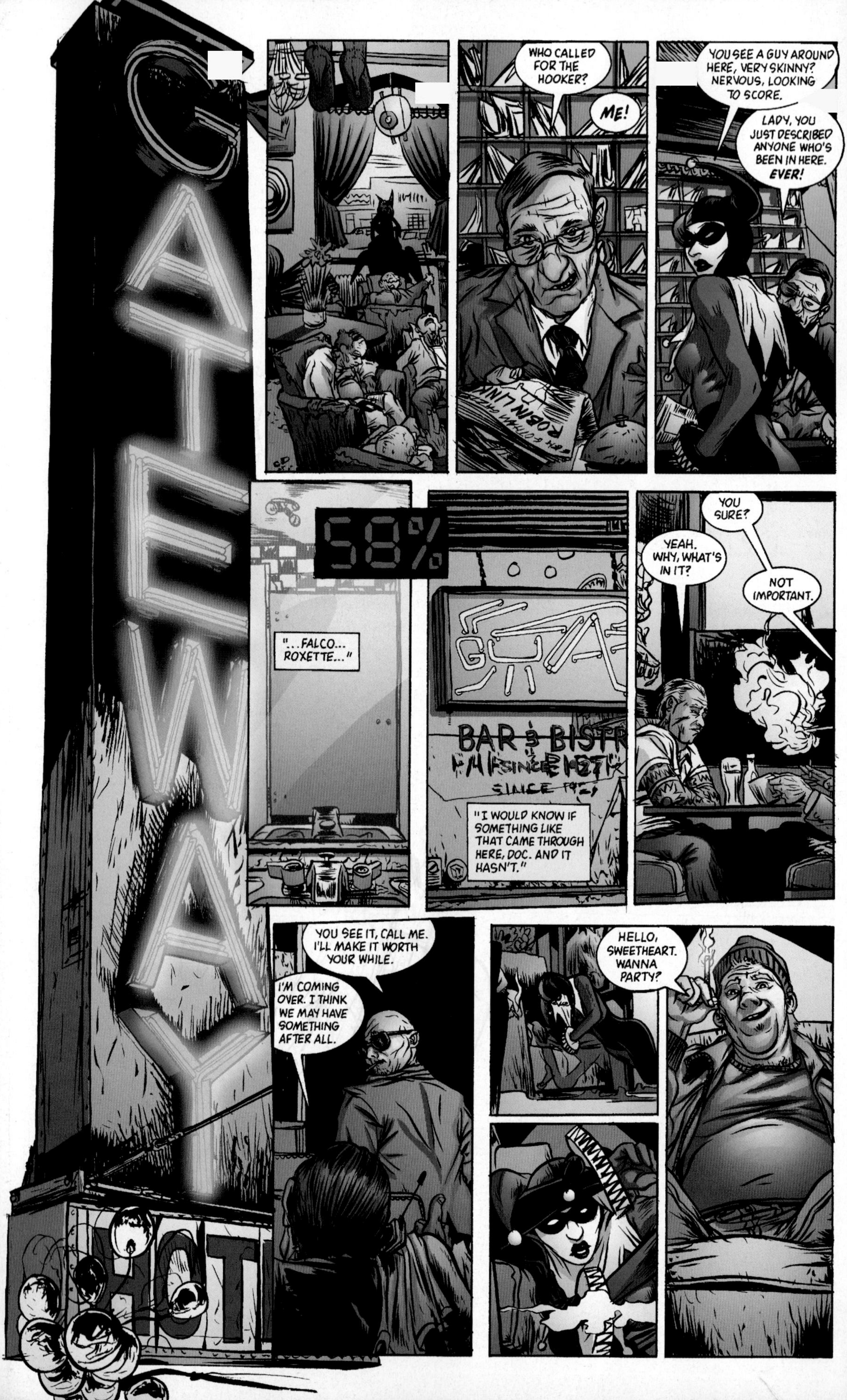

WHO CALLED FOR THE HOOKER?
ME!
YOU SEE A GUY AROUND HERE, VERY SKINNY? NERVOUS, LOOKING TO SCORE.
LADY, YOU JUST DESCRIBED ANYONE WHO'S BEEN IN HERE. EVER!
58%
"...FALCO... ROXETTE..."
"I WOULD KNOW IF SOMETHING LIKE THAT CAME THROUGH HERE, DOC. AND IT HASN'T."
YOU SURE?
YEAH. WHY, WHAT'S IN IT?
NOT IMPORTANT.
YOU SEE IT, CALL ME. I'LL MAKE IT WORTH YOUR WHILE.
I'M COMING OVER. I THINK WE MAY HAVE SOMETHING AFTER ALL.
HELLO, SWEETHEART. WANNA PARTY?

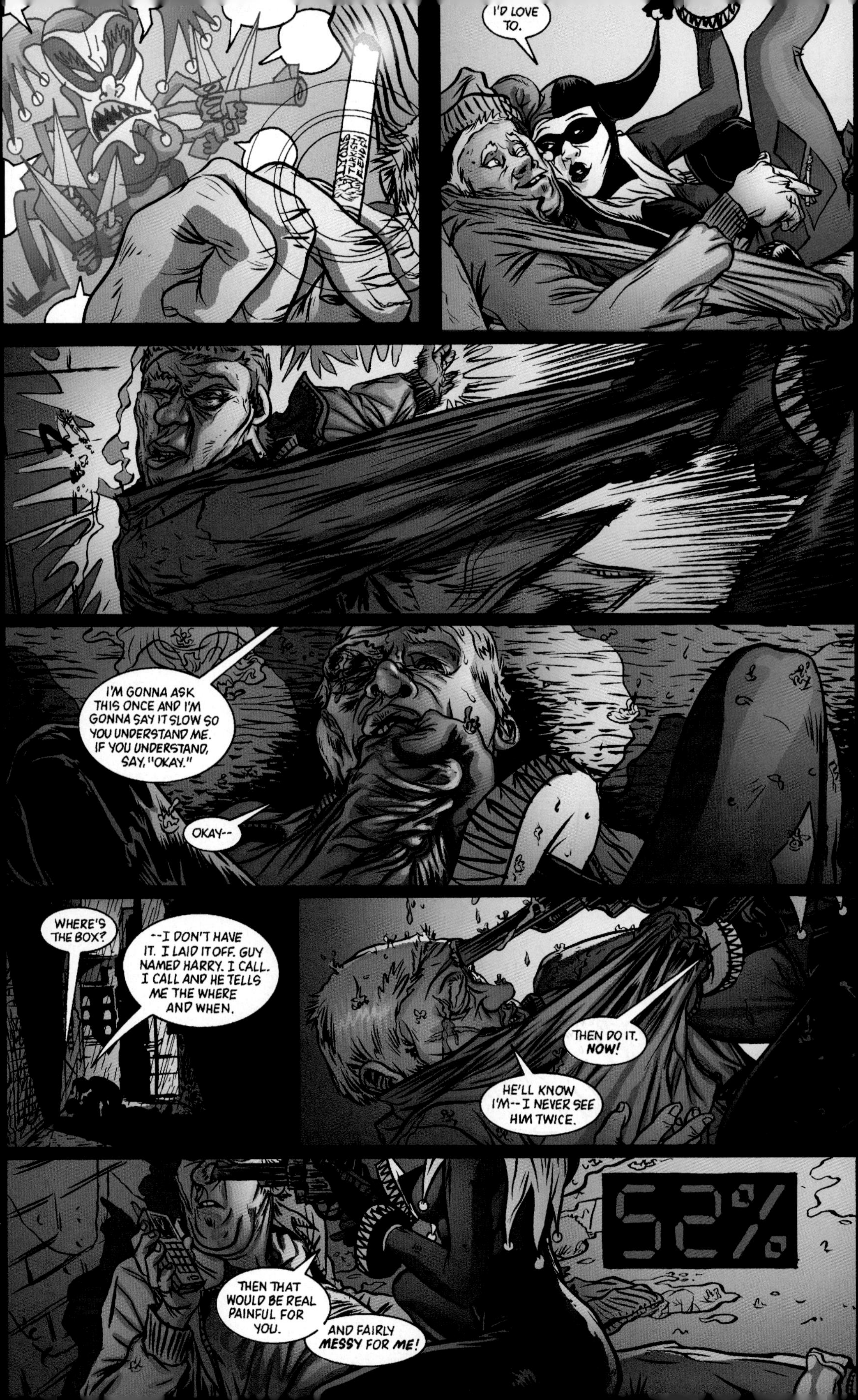
I'D LOVE TO.
I'M GONNA ASK THIS ONCE AND I'M GONNA SAY IT SLOW SO YOU UNDERSTAND ME. IF YOU UNDERSTAND, SAY, "OKAY."
OKAY--
WHERE'S THE BOX?
--I DON'T HAVE IT. I LAID IT OFF. GUY NAMED HARRY. I CALL. I CALL AND HE TELLS ME THE WHERE AND WHEN.
THEN DO IT. NOW!
HE'LL KNOW I'M-- I NEVER SEE HIM TWICE.
52%
THEN THAT WOULD BE REAL PAINFUL FOR YOU.
AND FAIRLY MESSY FOR ME!

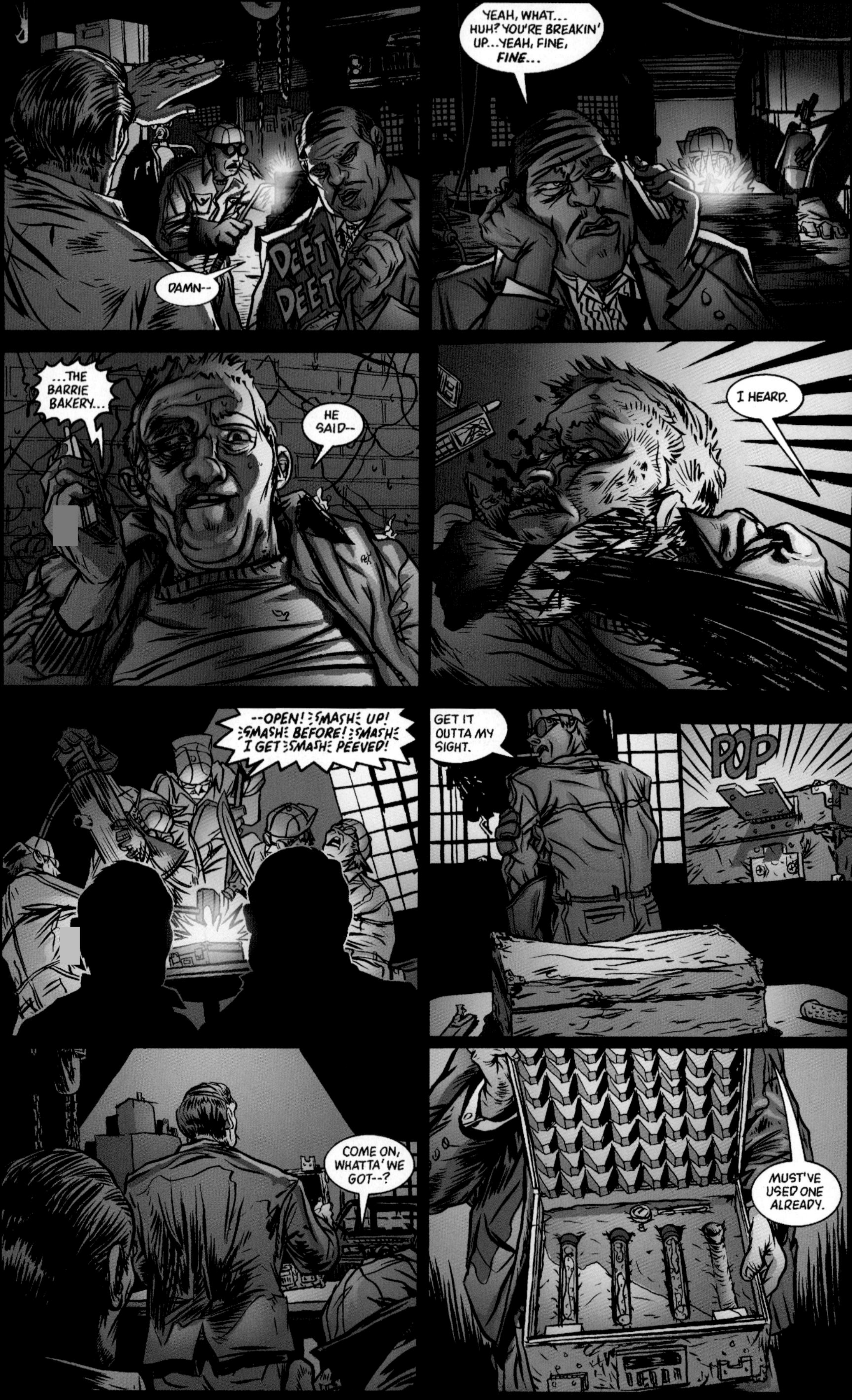
DEET DEET
DAMN--
YEAH, WHAT... HUH? YOU'RE BREAKIN' UP...YEAH, FINE, FINE...
...THE BARRIE BAKERY...
HE SAID--
I HEARD.
--OPEN! SMASH UP! SMASH BEFORE! SMASH I GET SMASH PEEVED!
GET IT OUTTA MY SIGHT.
POP
COME ON, WHATTA' WE GOT--?
MUST'VE USED ONE ALREADY.

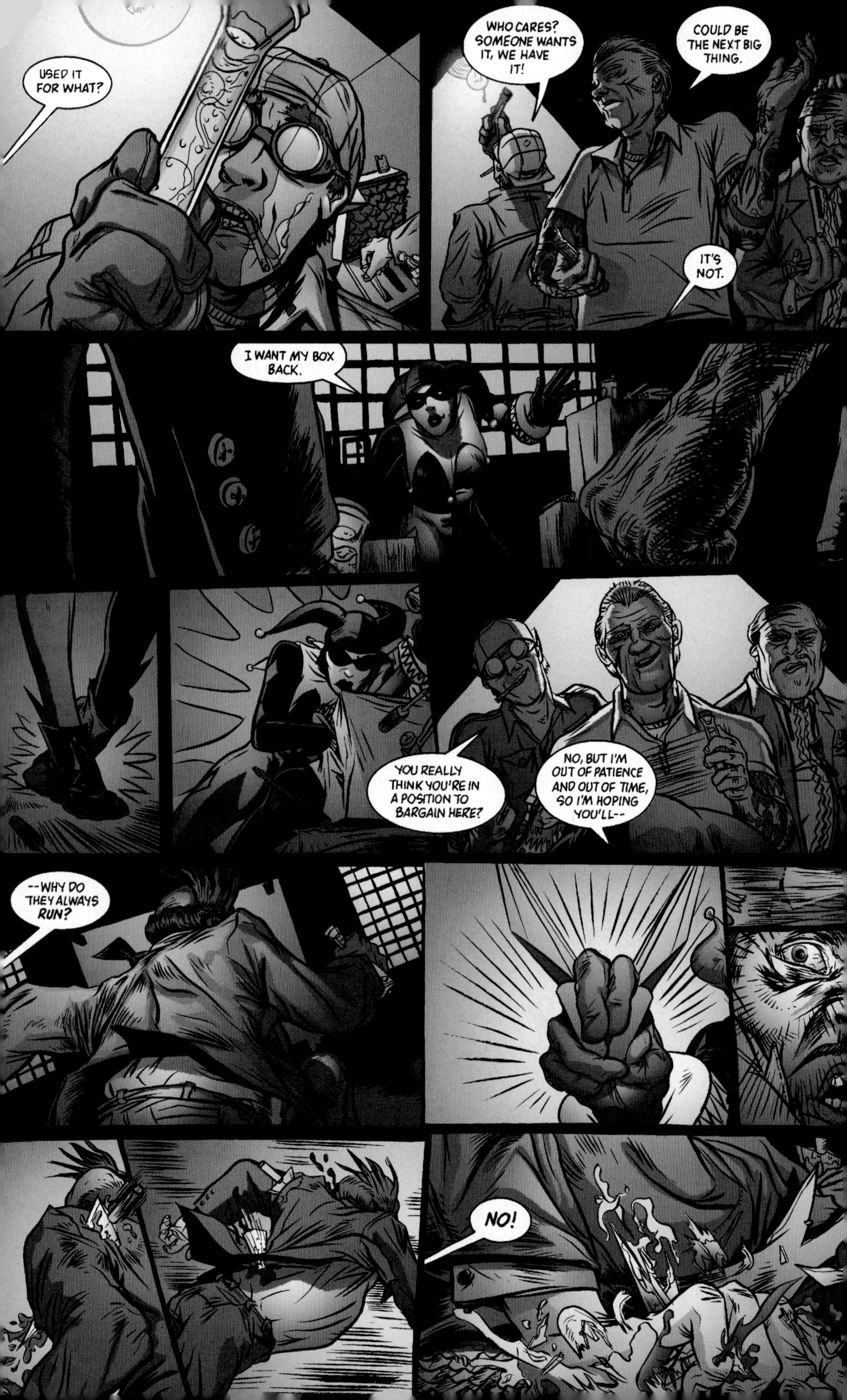
USED IT FOR WHAT?
WHO CARES? SOMEONE WANTS IT, WE HAVE IT!
COULD BE THE NEXT BIG THING.
IT'S NOT.
I WANT MY BOX BACK.
YOU REALLY THINK YOU'RE IN A POSITION TO BARGAIN HERE?
NO, BUT I'M OUT OF PATIENCE AND OUT OF TIME, SO I'M HOPING YOU'LL--
--WHY DO THEY ALWAYS RUN?
NO!

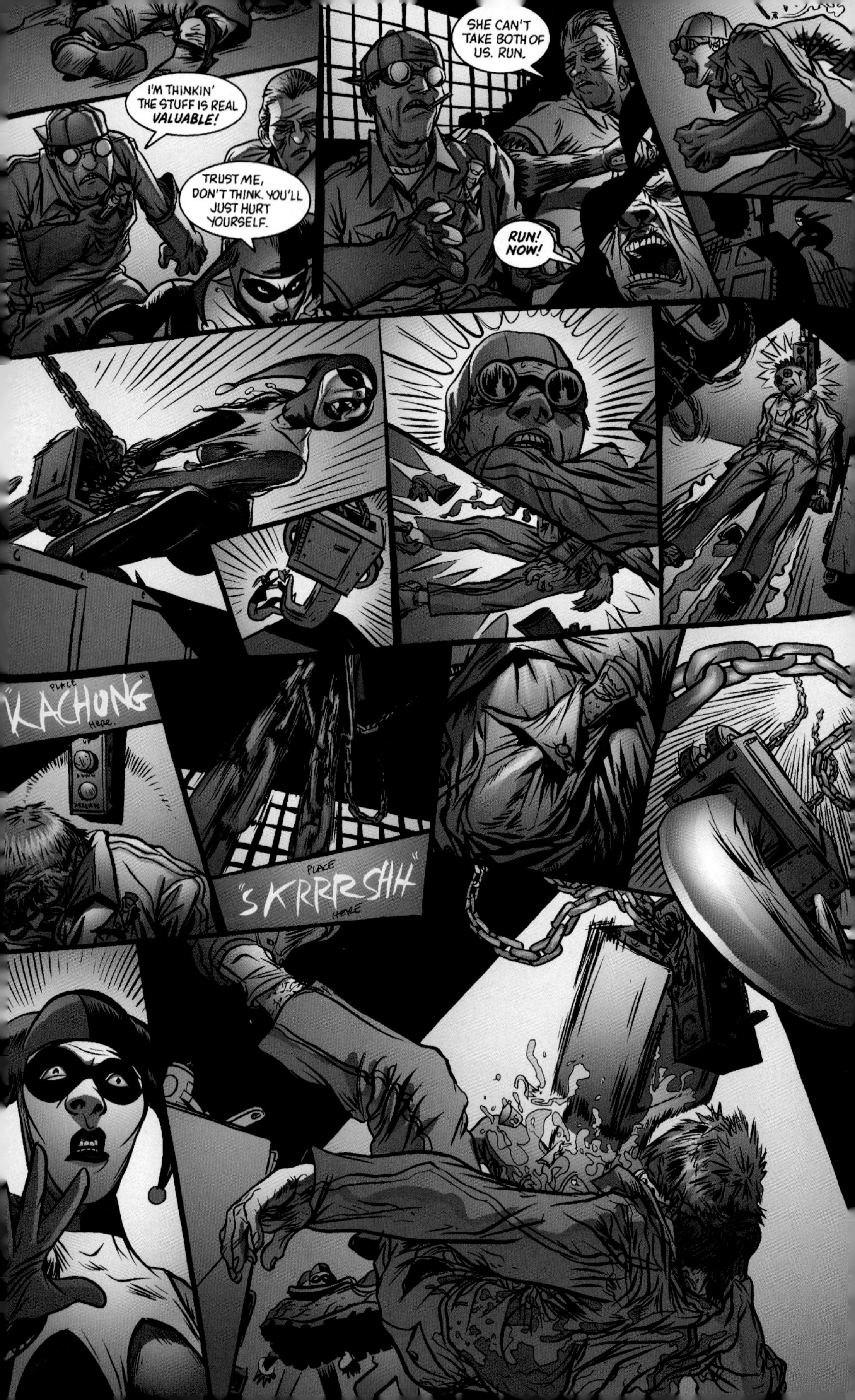

I'M THINKIN' THE STUFF IS REAL VALUABLE!
TRUST ME, DON'T THINK. YOU'LL JUST HURT YOURSELF.
SHE CAN'T TAKE BOTH OF US. RUN.
RUN! NOW!
"PLACE KACHUNG HERE."
"PLACE SKRRRSHH HERE"

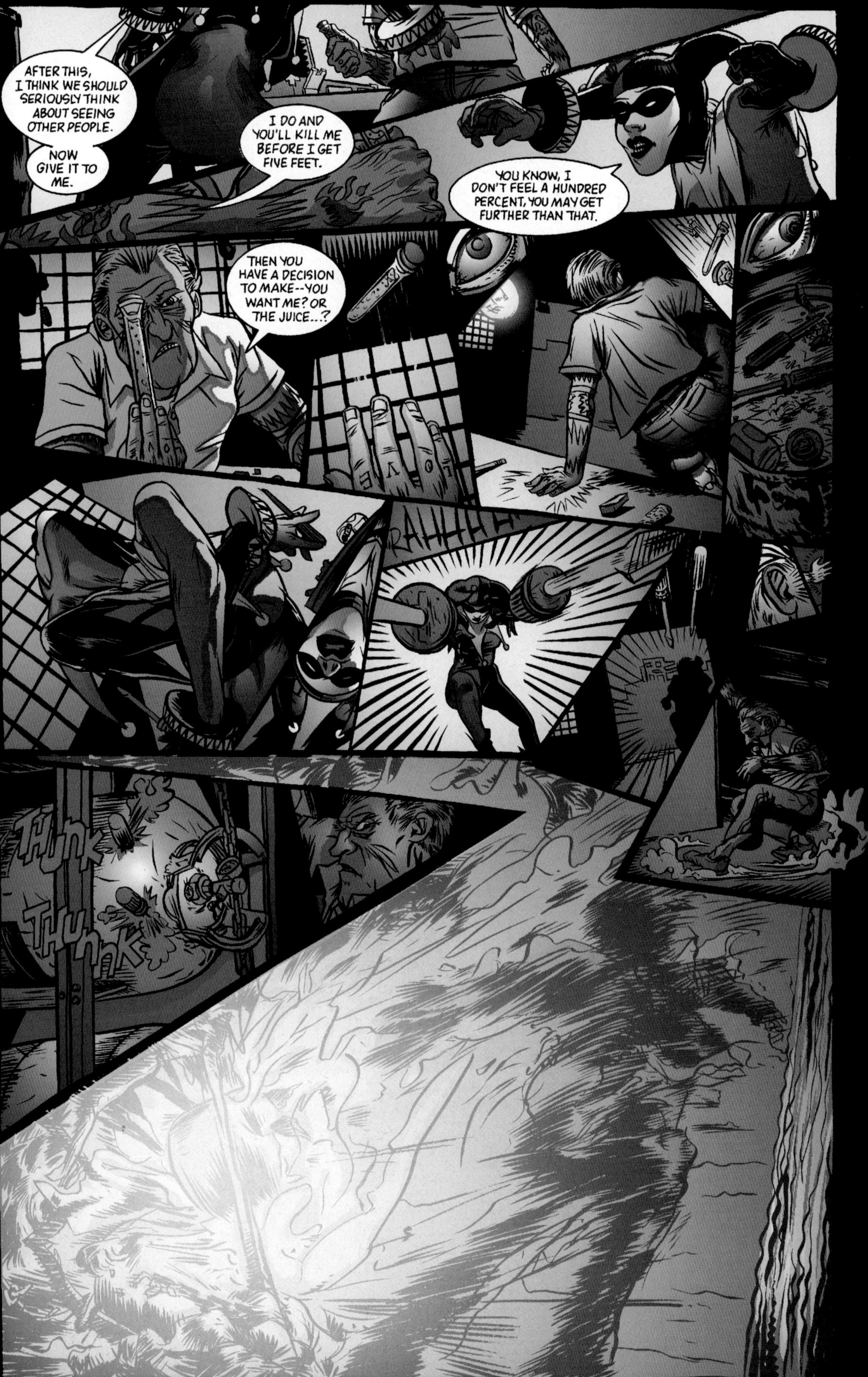
AFTER THIS, I THINK WE SHOULD SERIOUSLY THINK ABOUT SEEING OTHER PEOPLE.
NOW GIVE IT TO ME.
I DO AND YOU'LL KILL ME BEFORE I GET FIVE FEET.
YOU KNOW, I DON'T FEEL A HUNDRED PERCENT, YOU MAY GET FURTHER THAN THAT.
THEN YOU HAVE A DECISION TO MAKE--YOU WANT ME? OR THE JUICE..?
THUNK
THUNK

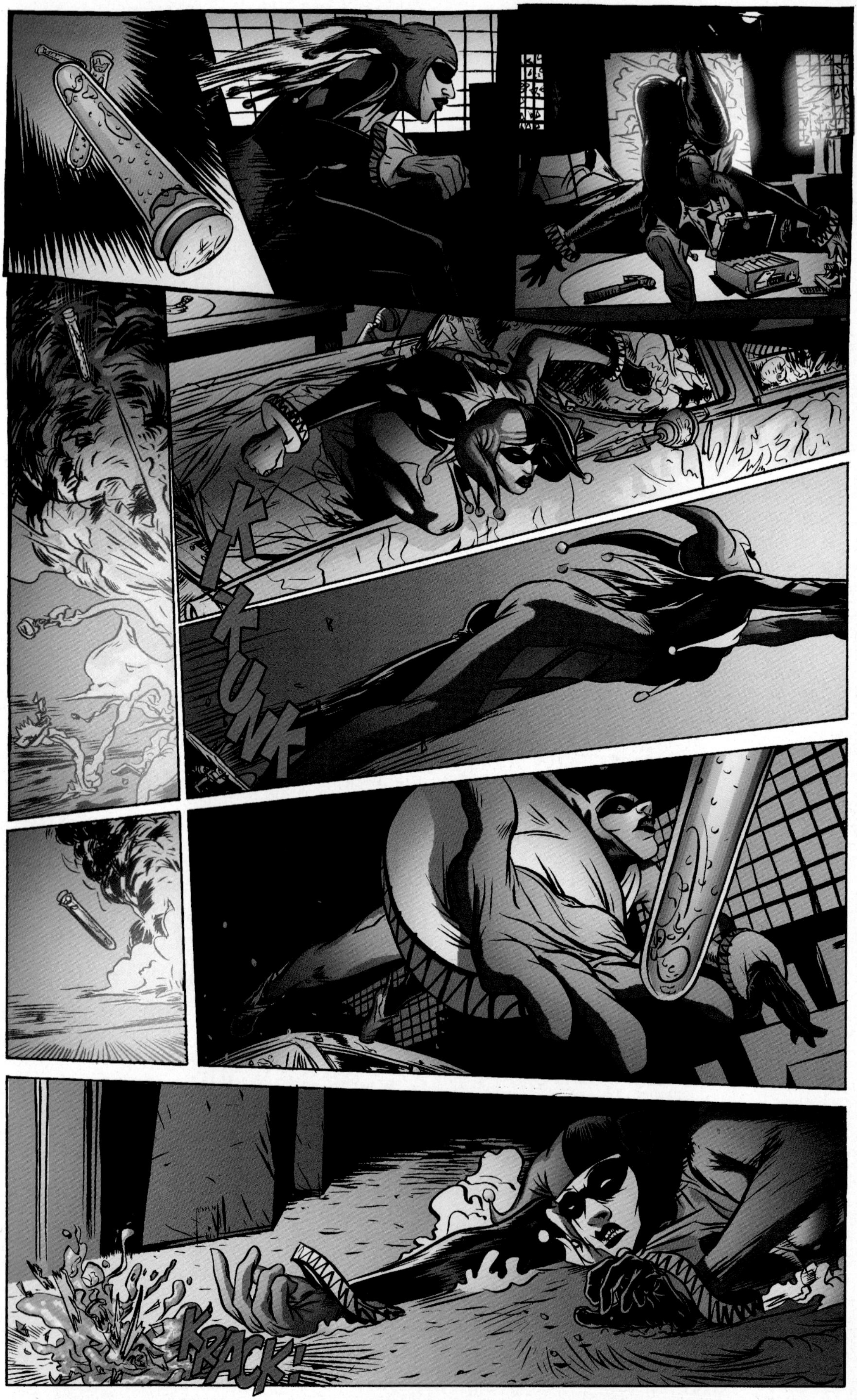
K-KUNK
KRACK!

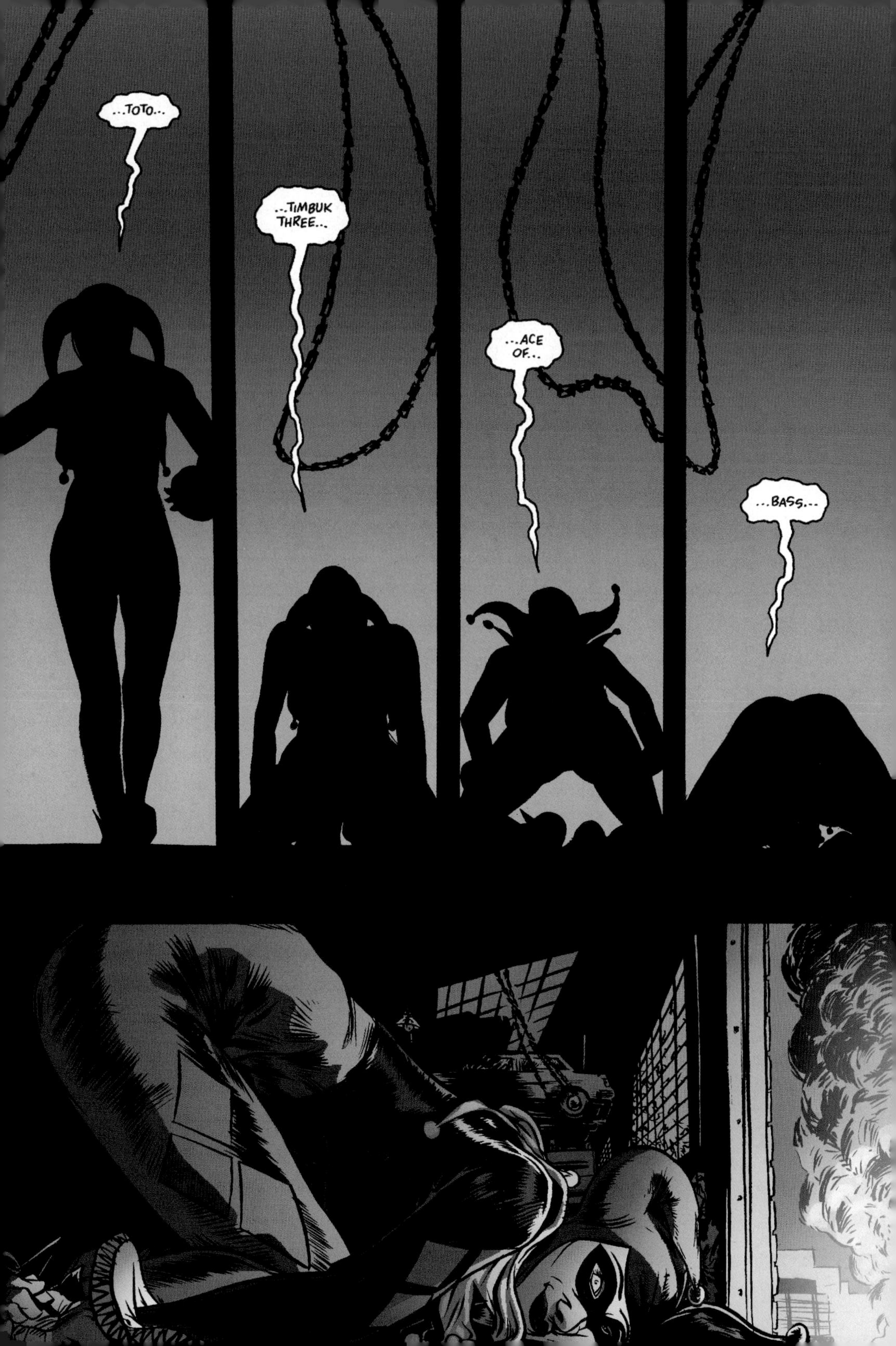
...TOTO...
...TIMBUK THREE...
...ACE OF...
...BASS...

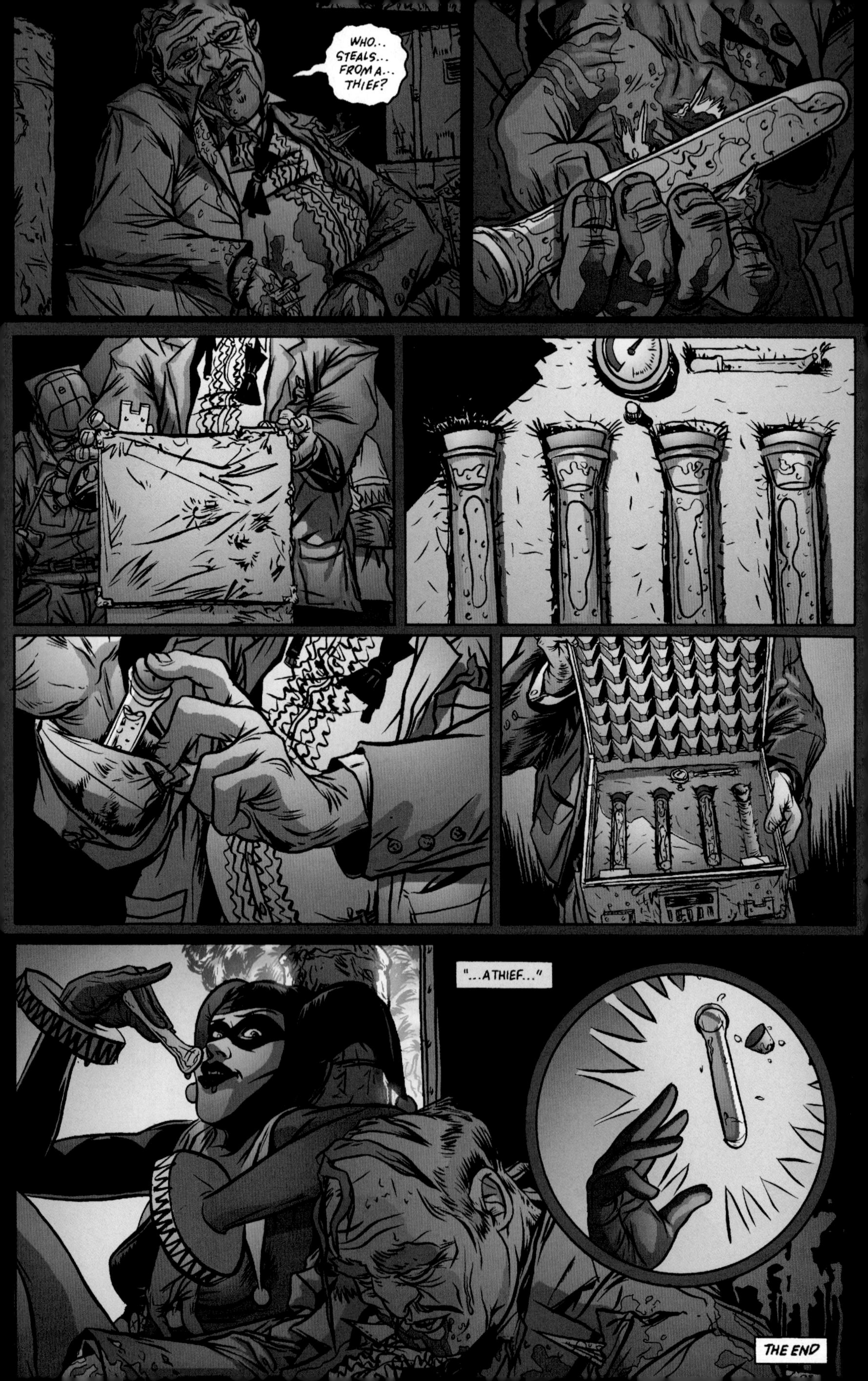
WHO... STEALS... FROM A... THIEF?
"...A THIEF..."
THE END

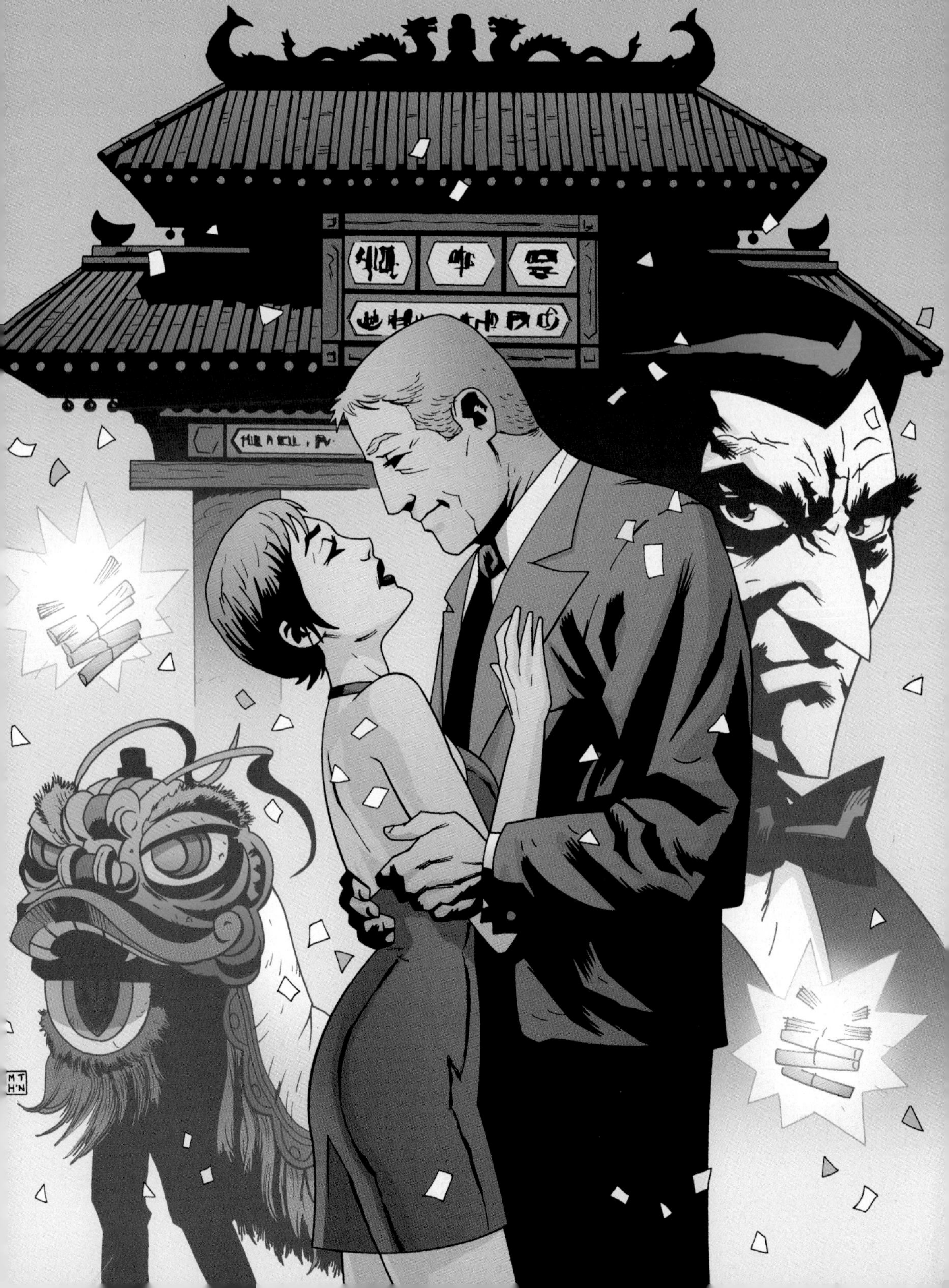

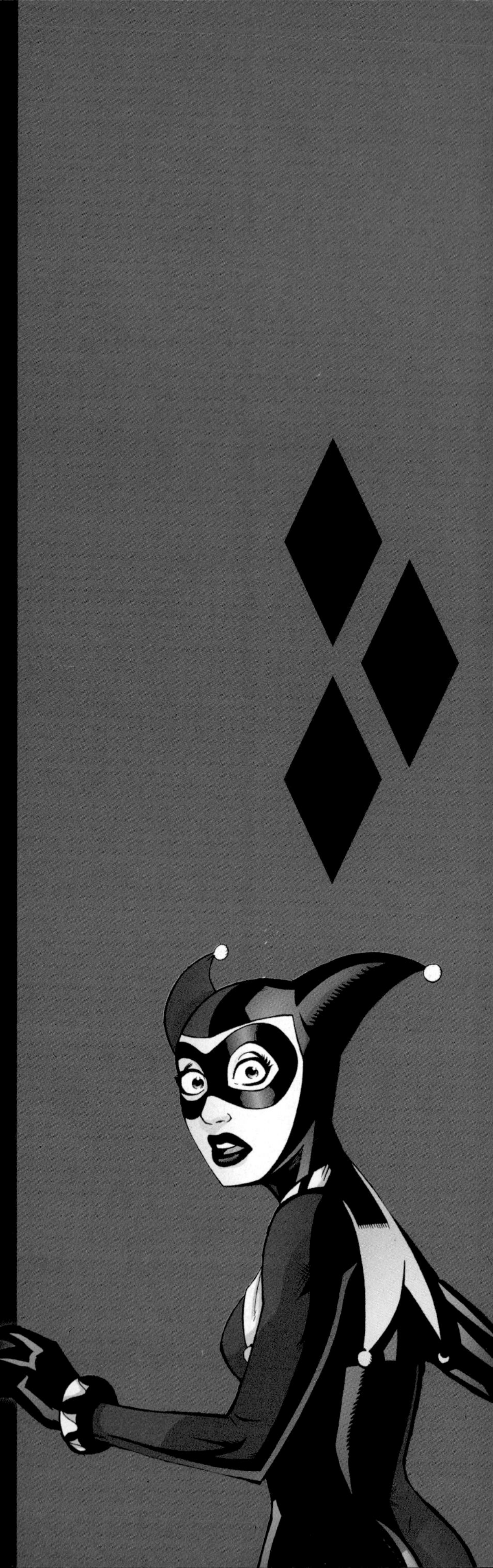

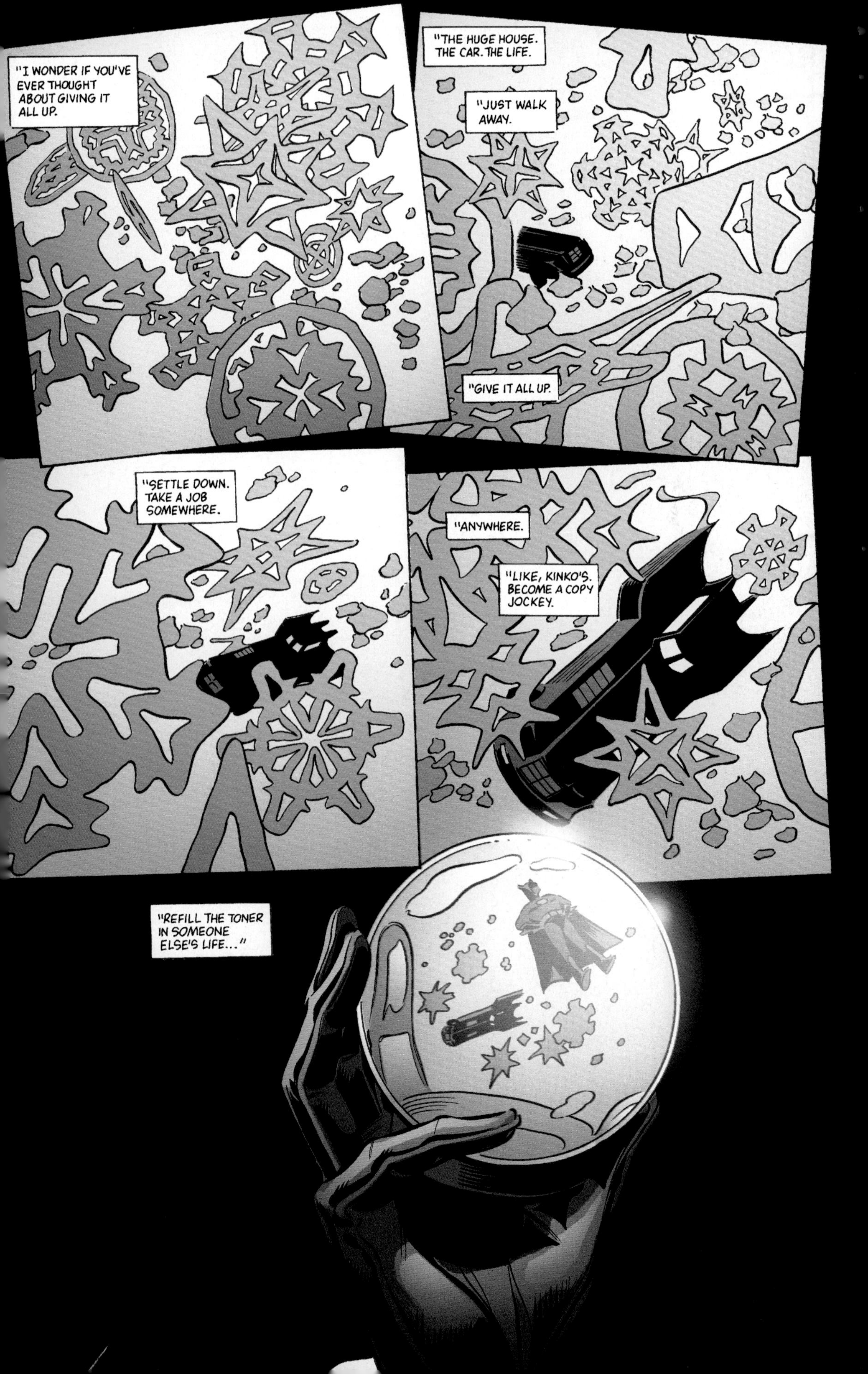
"I WONDER IF YOU'VE EVER THOUGHT ABOUT GIVING IT ALL UP.
"THE HUGE HOUSE. THE CAR. THE LIFE.
"JUST WALK AWAY.
"GIVE IT ALL UP.
"SETTLE DOWN. TAKE A JOB SOMEWHERE.
"ANYWHERE.
"LIKE, KINKO'S. BECOME A COPY JOCKEY.
"REFILL THE TONER IN SOMEONE ELSE'S LIFE..."

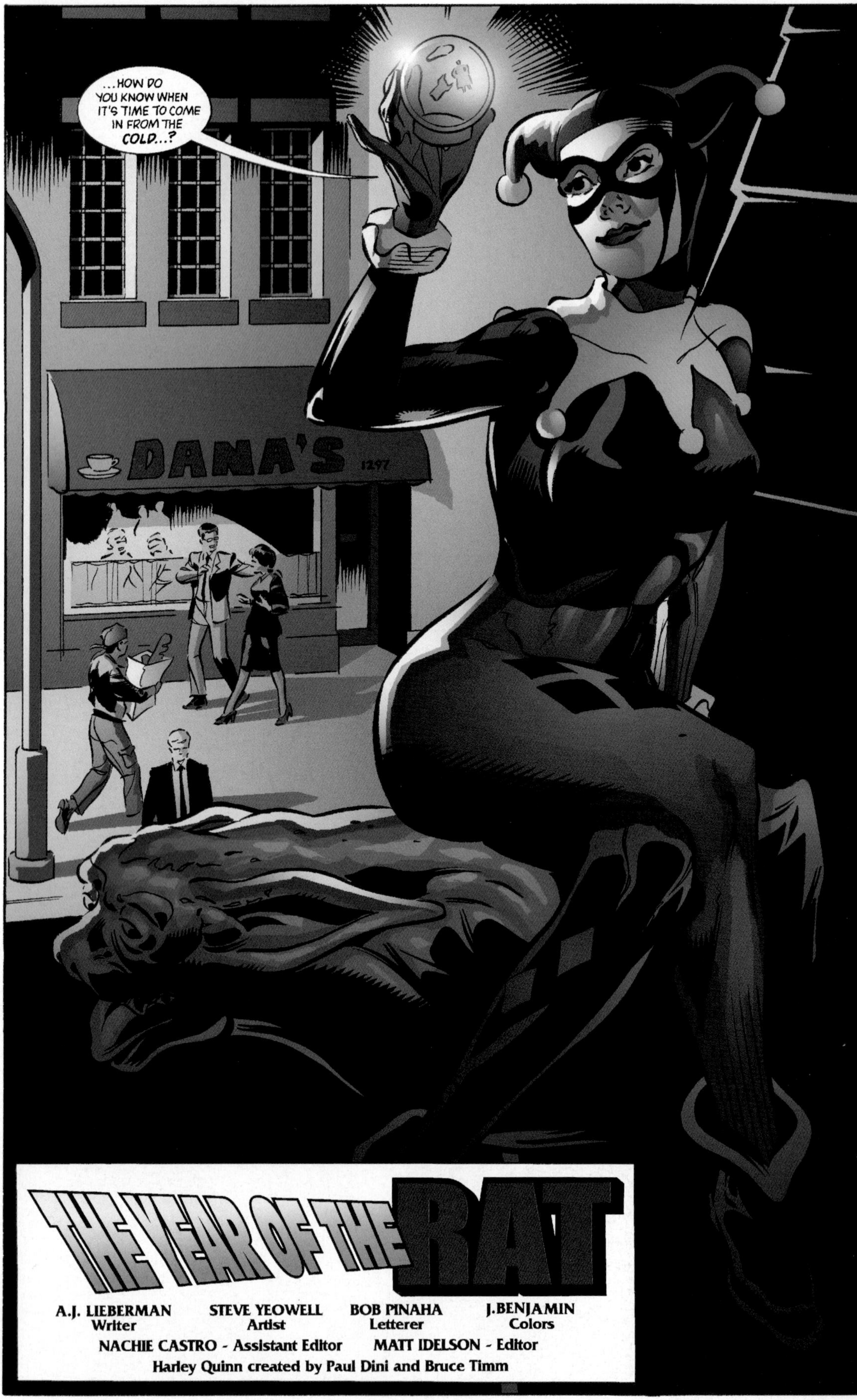
...HOW DO YOU KNOW WHEN IT'S TIME TO COME IN FROM THE COLD...?
DANA'S
1297
THE YEAR OF THE RAT
A.J. LIEBERMAN Writer
STEVE YEOWELL Artist
BOB PINAHA Letterer
J.BENJAMIN Colors
NACHIE CASTRO - Assistant Editor
MATT IDELSON - Editor
Harley Quinn created by Paul Dini and Bruce Timm

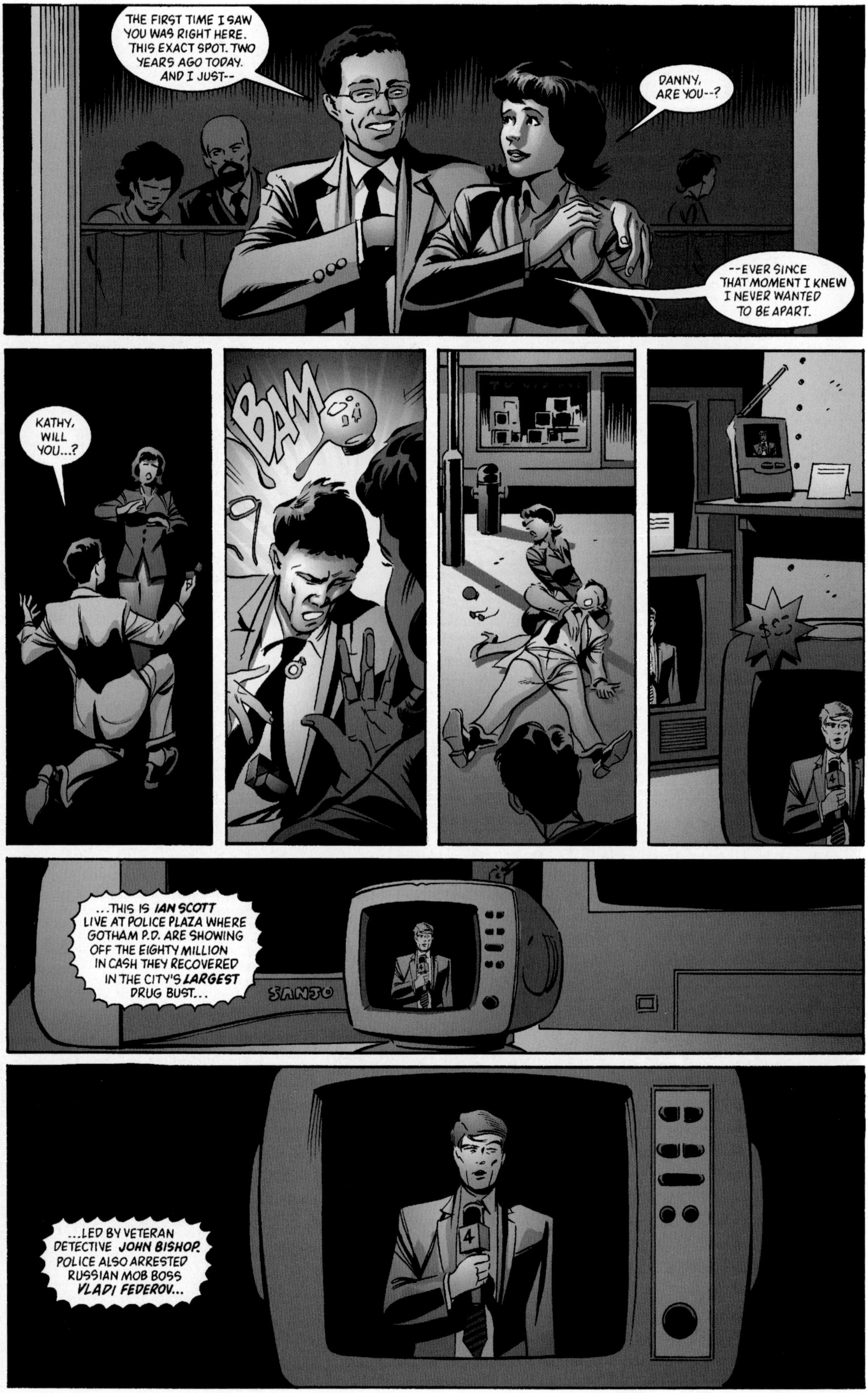
THE FIRST TIME I SAW YOU WAS RIGHT HERE. THIS EXACT SPOT. TWO YEARS AGO TODAY. AND I JUST--
DANNY, ARE YOU--?
--EVER SINCE THAT MOMENT I KNEW I NEVER WANTED TO BE APART.
KATHY, WILL YOU...?
BAM
...THIS IS IAN SCOTT LIVE AT POLICE PLAZA WHERE GOTHAM P.D. ARE SHOWING OFF THE EIGHTY MILLION IN CASH THEY RECOVERED IN THE CITY'S LARGEST DRUG BUST...
SANJO
...LED BY VETERAN DETECTIVE JOHN BISHOP. POLICE ALSO ARRESTED RUSSIAN MOB BOSS VLADI FEDEROV...

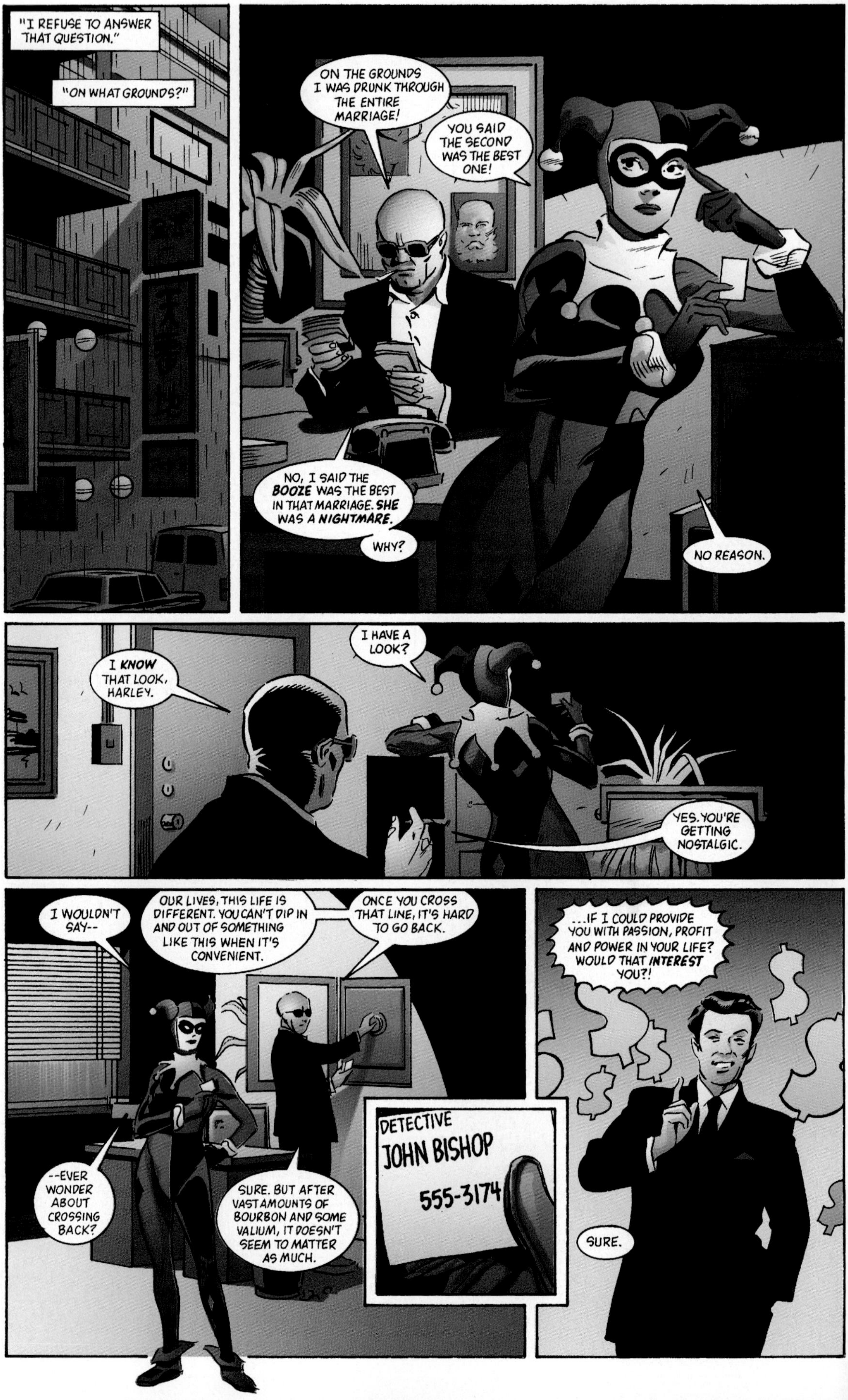
"I REFUSE TO ANSWER THAT QUESTION."
"ON WHAT GROUNDS?"
ON THE GROUNDS I WAS DRUNK THROUGH THE ENTIRE MARRIAGE!
YOU SAID THE SECOND WAS THE BEST ONE!
NO, I SAID THE BOOZE WAS THE BEST IN THAT MARRIAGE. SHE WAS A NIGHTMARE.
WHY?
NO REASON.
I KNOW THAT LOOK, HARLEY.
I HAVE A LOOK?
YES. YOU'RE GETTING NOSTALGIC.
I WOULDN'T SAY--
--EVER WONDER ABOUT CROSSING BACK?
OUR LIVES, THIS LIFE IS DIFFERENT. YOU CAN'T DIP IN AND OUT OF SOMETHING LIKE THIS WHEN IT'S CONVENIENT.
ONCE YOU CROSS THAT LINE, IT'S HARD TO GO BACK.
SURE. BUT AFTER VAST AMOUNTS OF BOURBON AND SOME VALIUM, IT DOESN'T SEEM TO MATTER AS MUCH.
DETECTIVE
JOHN BISHOP
555-3174
...IF I COULD PROVIDE YOU WITH PASSION, PROFIT AND POWER IN YOUR LIFE? WOULD THAT INTEREST YOU?!
SURE.

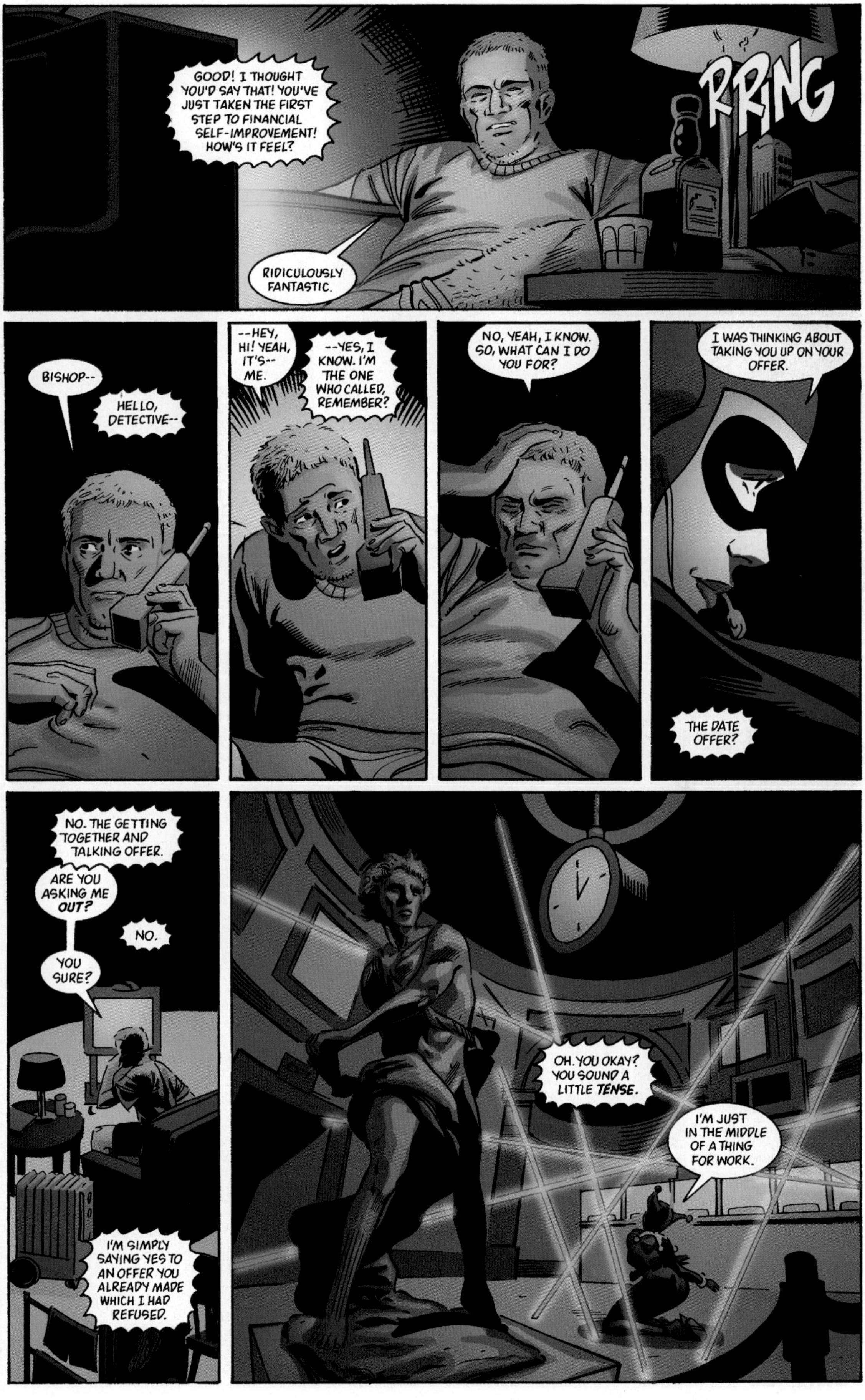
GOOD! I THOUGHT YOU'D SAY THAT! YOU'VE JUST TAKEN THE FIRST STEP TO FINANCIAL SELF-IMPROVEMENT! HOW'S IT FEEL?
RRING
RIDICULOUSLY FANTASTIC.
BISHOP--
HELLO, DETECTIVE--
--HEY, HI! YEAH, IT'S-- ME.
--YES, I KNOW. I'M THE ONE WHO CALLED, REMEMBER?
NO, YEAH, I KNOW. SO, WHAT CAN I DO YOU FOR?
I WAS THINKING ABOUT TAKING YOU UP ON YOUR OFFER.
THE DATE OFFER?
NO. THE GETTING TOGETHER AND TALKING OFFER.
ARE YOU ASKING ME OUT?
NO.
YOU SURE?
I'M SIMPLY SAYING YES TO AN OFFER YOU ALREADY MADE WHICH I HAD REFUSED.
OH. YOU OKAY? YOU SOUND A LITTLE TENSE.
I'M JUST IN THE MIDDLE OF A THING FOR WORK.

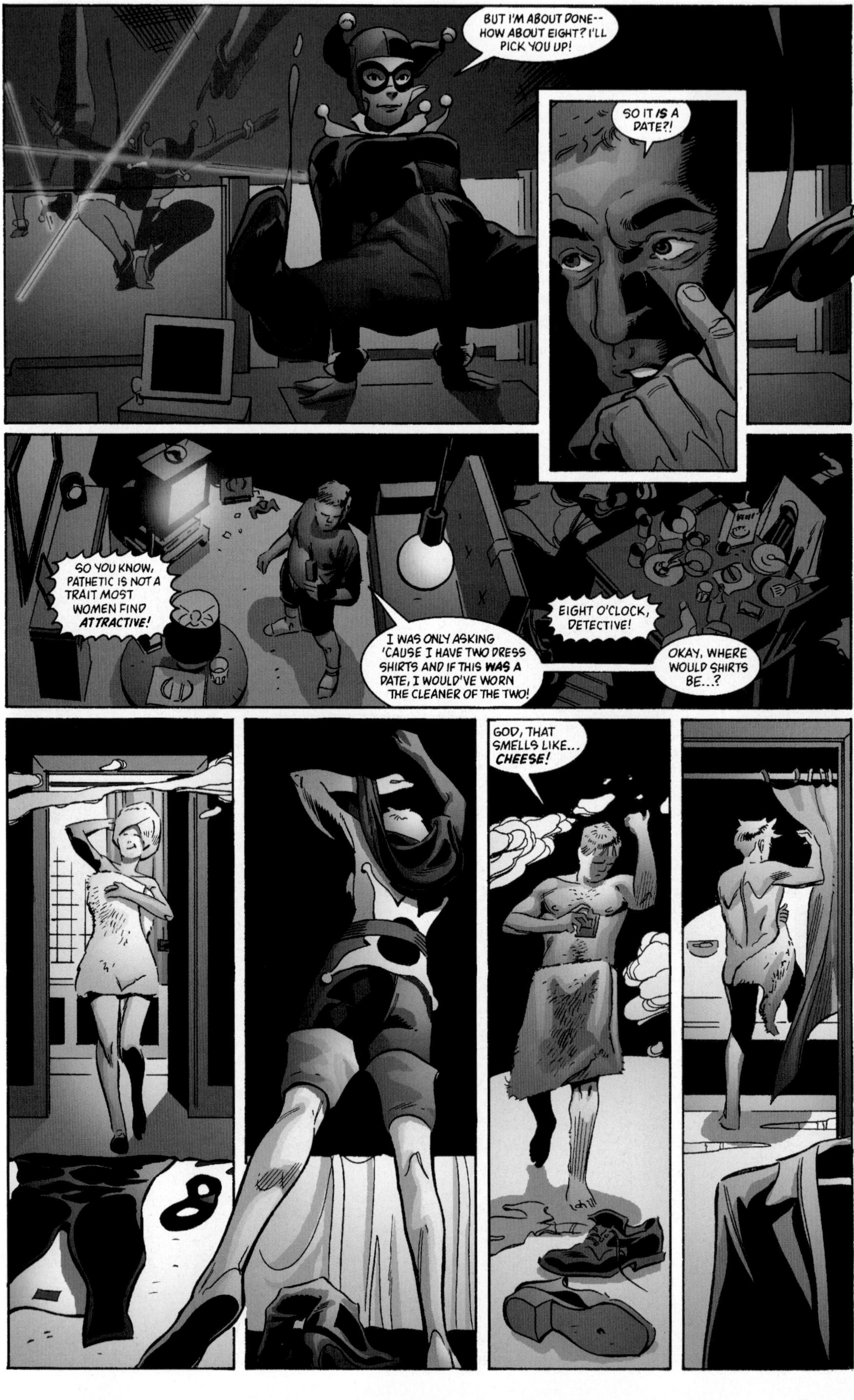
BUT I'M ABOUT DONE-- HOW ABOUT EIGHT? I'LL PICK YOU UP!
SO IT *IS* A DATE?!
SO YOU KNOW, PATHETIC IS NOT A TRAIT MOST WOMEN FIND *ATTRACTIVE!*
I WAS ONLY ASKING 'CAUSE I HAVE TWO DRESS SHIRTS AND IF THIS *WAS* A DATE, I WOULD'VE WORN THE CLEANER OF THE TWO!
EIGHT O'CLOCK, DETECTIVE!
OKAY, WHERE WOULD SHIRTS BE...?
GOD, THAT SMELLS LIKE... *CHEESE!*

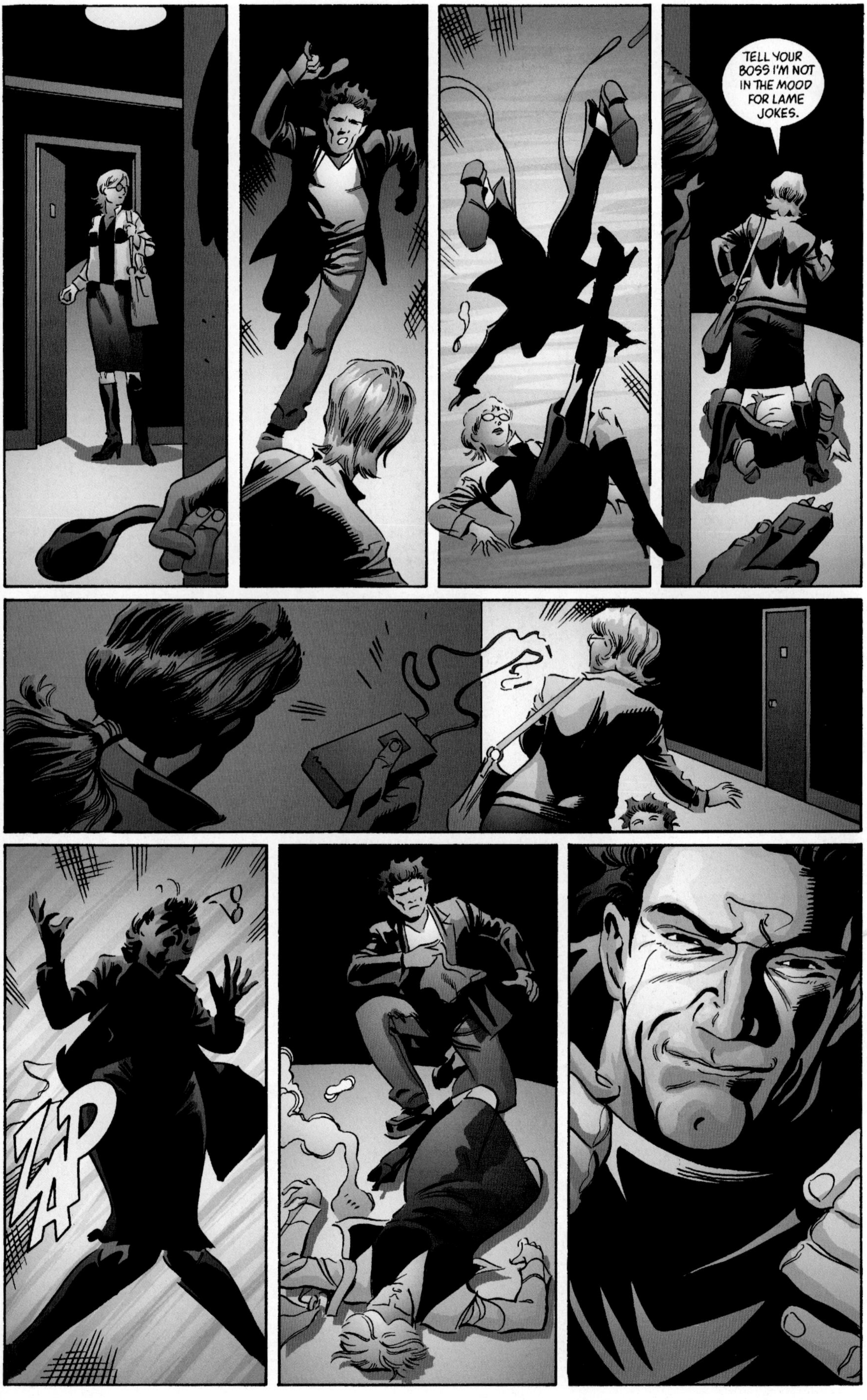
TELL YOUR BOSS I'M NOT IN THE MOOD FOR LAME JOKES.
ZAP

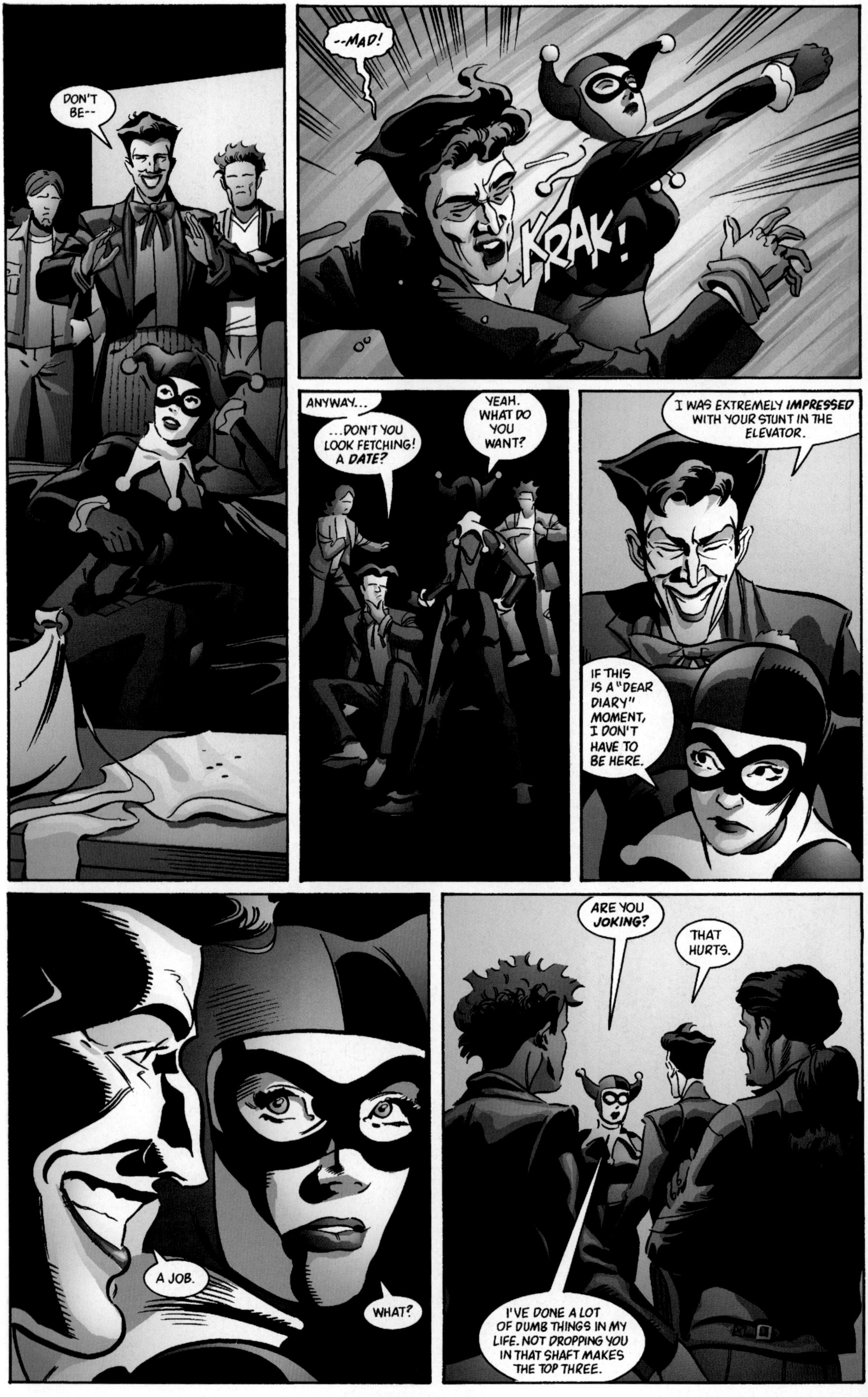
DON'T BE--
--MAD!
KRAK!
ANYWAY...
...DON'T YOU LOOK FETCHING! A DATE?
YEAH. WHAT DO YOU WANT?
I WAS EXTREMELY IMPRESSED WITH YOUR STUNT IN THE ELEVATOR.
IF THIS IS A "DEAR DIARY" MOMENT, I DON'T HAVE TO BE HERE.
A JOB.
WHAT?
ARE YOU JOKING?
THAT HURTS.
I'VE DONE A LOT OF DUMB THINGS IN MY LIFE. NOT DROPPING YOU IN THAT SHAFT MAKES THE TOP THREE.

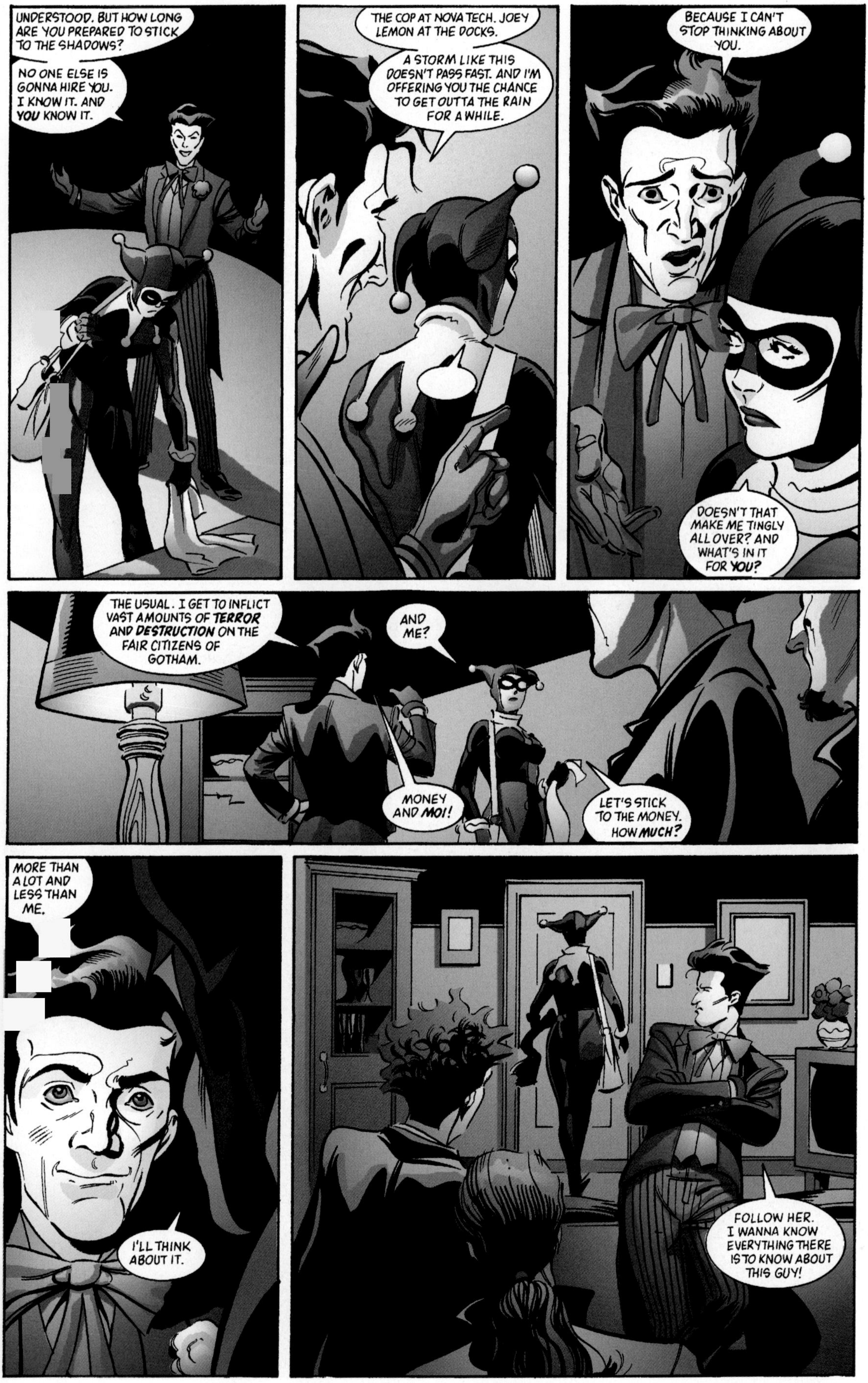
UNDERSTOOD. BUT HOW LONG ARE YOU PREPARED TO STICK TO THE SHADOWS?
NO ONE ELSE IS GONNA HIRE YOU. I KNOW IT. AND YOU KNOW IT.
THE COP AT NOVA TECH. JOEY LEMON AT THE DOCKS.
A STORM LIKE THIS DOESN'T PASS FAST. AND I'M OFFERING YOU THE CHANCE TO GET OUTTA THE RAIN FOR A WHILE.
BECAUSE I CAN'T STOP THINKING ABOUT YOU.
DOESN'T THAT MAKE ME TINGLY ALL OVER? AND WHAT'S IN IT FOR YOU?
THE USUAL. I GET TO INFLICT VAST AMOUNTS OF TERROR AND DESTRUCTION ON THE FAIR CITIZENS OF GOTHAM.
AND ME?
MONEY AND MOI!
LET'S STICK TO THE MONEY. HOW MUCH?
MORE THAN A LOT AND LESS THAN ME.
I'LL THINK ABOUT IT.
FOLLOW HER. I WANNA KNOW EVERYTHING THERE IS TO KNOW ABOUT THIS GUY!

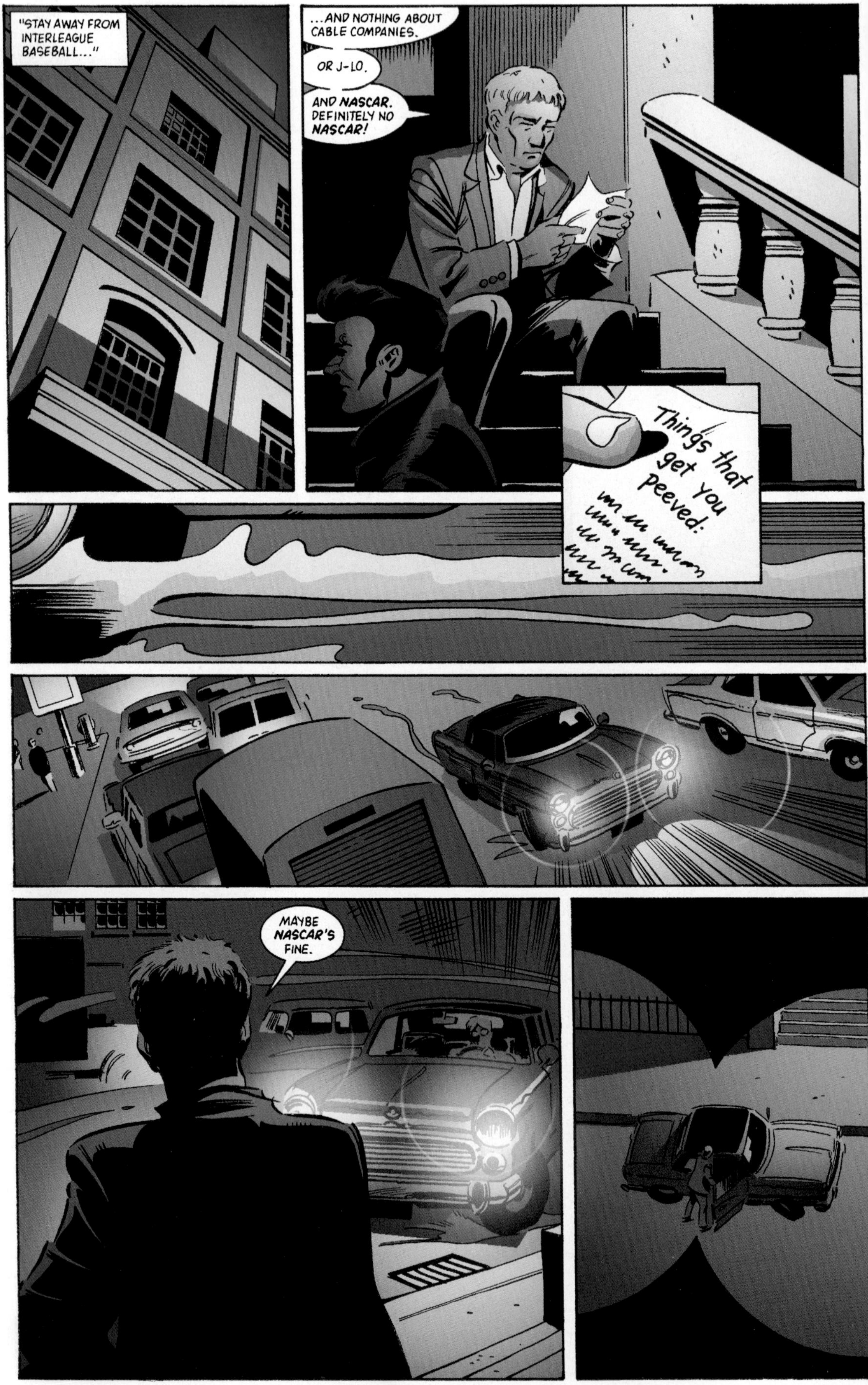
"STAY AWAY FROM INTERLEAGUE BASEBALL..."
...AND NOTHING ABOUT CABLE COMPANIES.
OR J-LO.
AND NASCAR. DEFINITELY NO NASCAR!
Things that get you peeved:
MAYBE NASCAR'S FINE.

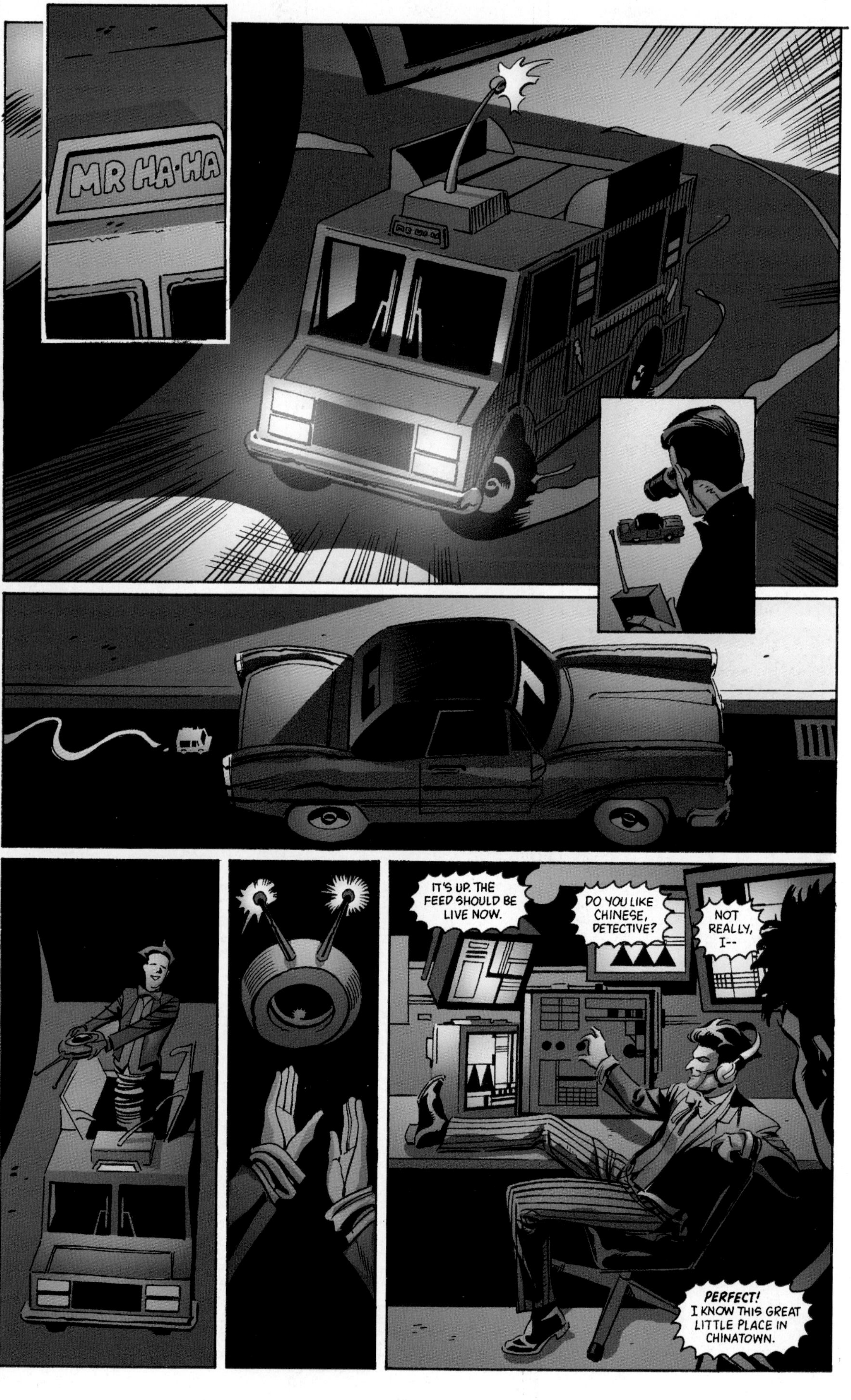
MR HA·HA
IT'S UP. THE FEED SHOULD BE LIVE NOW.
DO YOU LIKE CHINESE, DETECTIVE?
NOT REALLY, I--
PERFECT! I KNOW THIS GREAT LITTLE PLACE IN CHINATOWN.

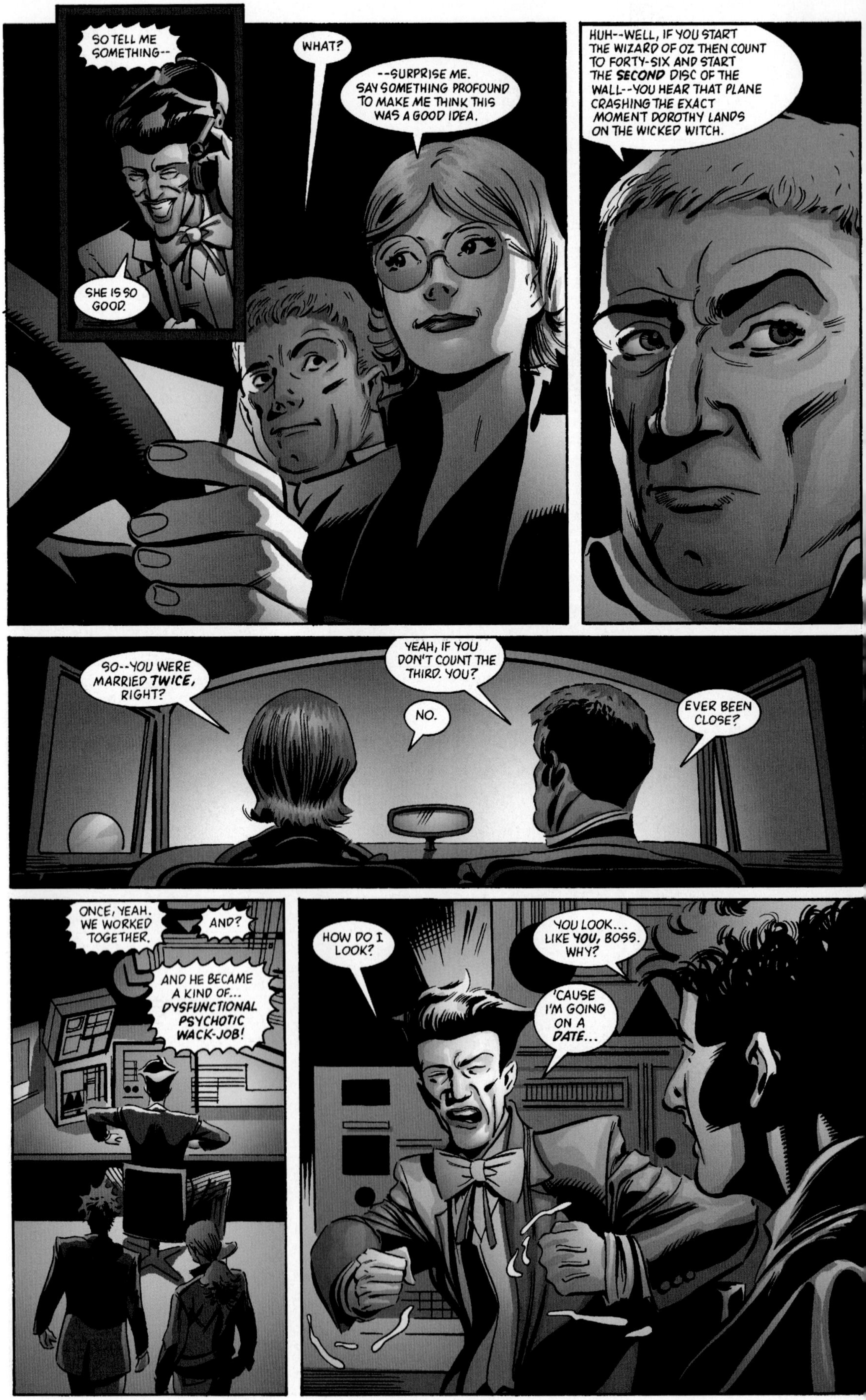
SO TELL ME SOMETHING--
SHE IS SO GOOD.
WHAT?
--SURPRISE ME. SAY SOMETHING PROFOUND TO MAKE ME THINK THIS WAS A GOOD IDEA.
HUH--WELL, IF YOU START THE WIZARD OF OZ THEN COUNT TO FORTY-SIX AND START THE SECOND DISC OF THE WALL--YOU HEAR THAT PLANE CRASHING THE EXACT MOMENT DOROTHY LANDS ON THE WICKED WITCH.
SO--YOU WERE MARRIED TWICE, RIGHT?
YEAH, IF YOU DON'T COUNT THE THIRD. YOU?
NO.
EVER BEEN CLOSE?
ONCE, YEAH. WE WORKED TOGETHER.
AND?
AND HE BECAME A KIND OF... DYSFUNCTIONAL PSYCHOTIC WACK-JOB!
HOW DO I LOOK?
YOU LOOK... LIKE YOU, BOSS. WHY?
'CAUSE I'M GOING ON A DATE...

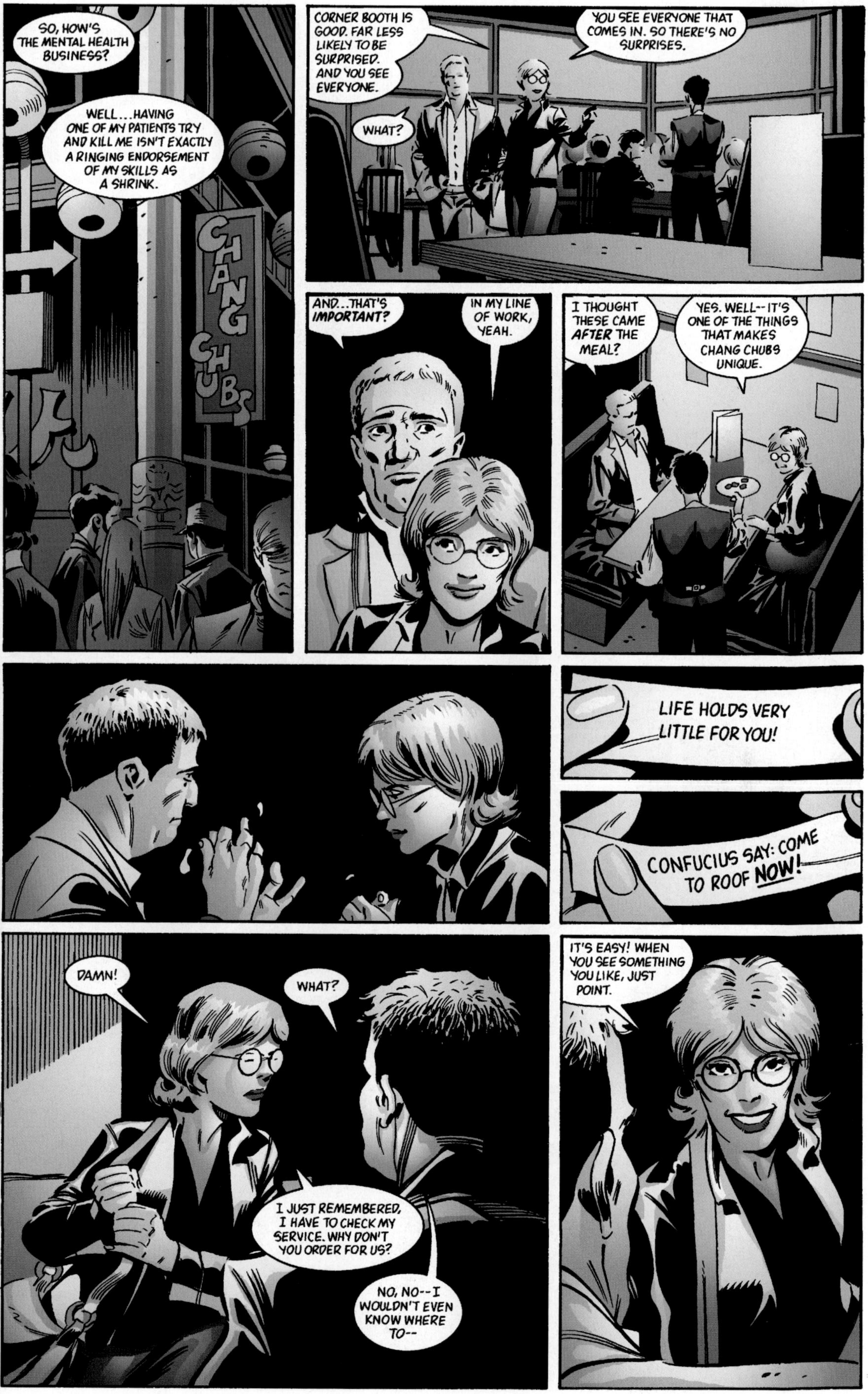
SO, HOW'S THE MENTAL HEALTH BUSINESS?
WELL... HAVING ONE OF MY PATIENTS TRY AND KILL ME ISN'T EXACTLY A RINGING ENDORSEMENT OF MY SKILLS AS A SHRINK.
CHANG CHUBS
CORNER BOOTH IS GOOD. FAR LESS LIKELY TO BE SURPRISED. AND YOU SEE EVERYONE.
WHAT?
YOU SEE EVERYONE THAT COMES IN. SO THERE'S NO SURPRISES.
AND...THAT'S IMPORTANT?
IN MY LINE OF WORK, YEAH.
I THOUGHT THESE CAME AFTER THE MEAL?
YES. WELL--IT'S ONE OF THE THINGS THAT MAKES CHANG CHUBS UNIQUE.
LIFE HOLDS VERY LITTLE FOR YOU!
CONFUCIUS SAY: COME TO ROOF NOW!
DAMN!
WHAT?
I JUST REMEMBERED, I HAVE TO CHECK MY SERVICE. WHY DON'T YOU ORDER FOR US?
NO, NO--I WOULDN'T EVEN KNOW WHERE TO--
IT'S EASY! WHEN YOU SEE SOMETHING YOU LIKE, JUST POINT.

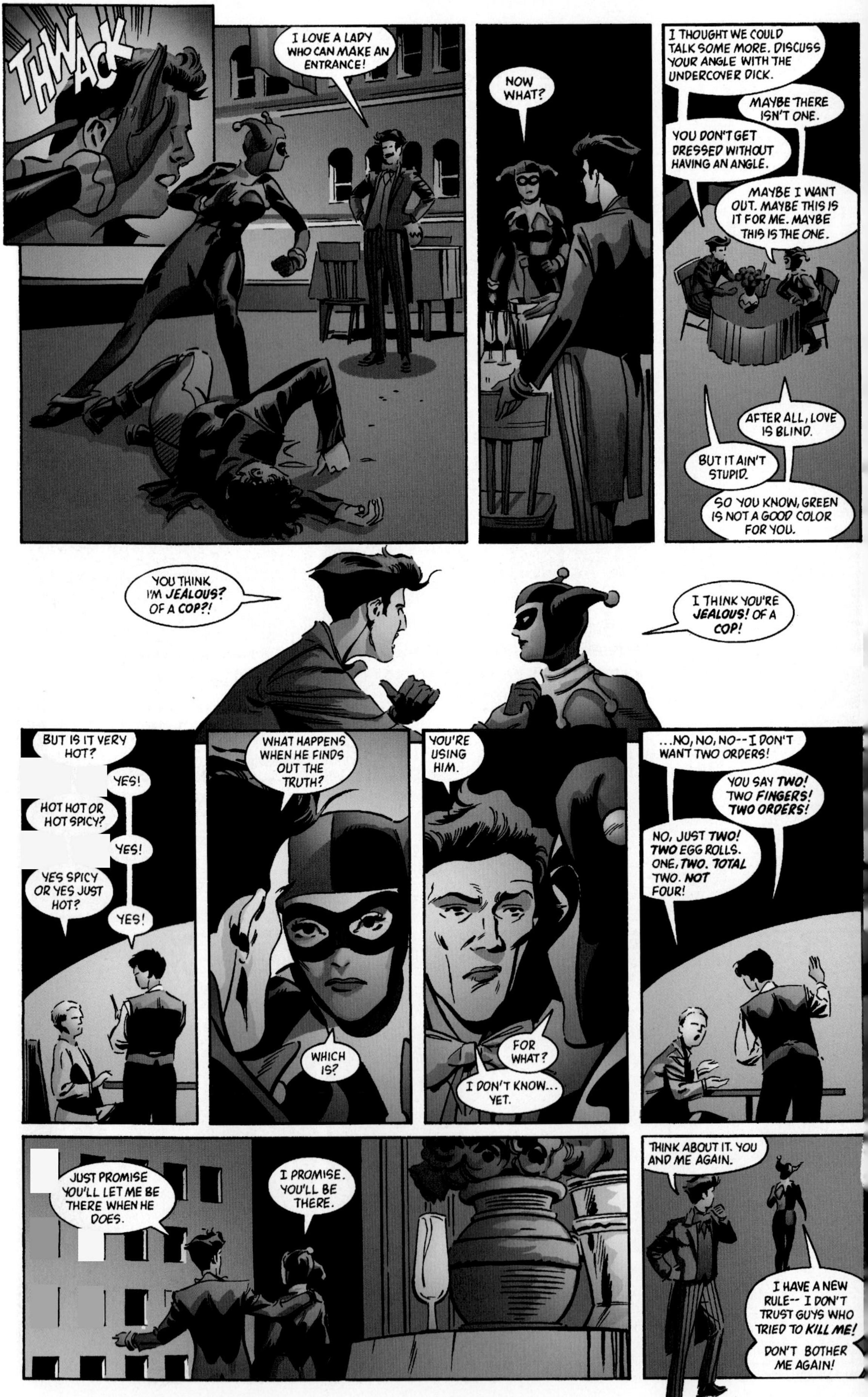
THWACK
I LOVE A LADY WHO CAN MAKE AN ENTRANCE!
NOW WHAT?
I THOUGHT WE COULD TALK SOME MORE. DISCUSS YOUR ANGLE WITH THE UNDERCOVER DICK.
MAYBE THERE ISN'T ONE.
YOU DON'T GET DRESSED WITHOUT HAVING AN ANGLE.
MAYBE I WANT OUT. MAYBE THIS IS IT FOR ME. MAYBE THIS IS THE ONE.
AFTER ALL, LOVE IS BLIND.
BUT IT AIN'T STUPID.
SO YOU KNOW, GREEN IS NOT A GOOD COLOR FOR YOU.
YOU THINK I'M *JEALOUS?* OF A *COP?!*
I THINK YOU'RE *JEALOUS!* OF A *COP!*
BUT IS IT VERY HOT?
YES!
HOT HOT OR HOT SPICY?
YES!
YES SPICY OR YES JUST HOT?
YES!
WHAT HAPPENS WHEN HE FINDS OUT THE TRUTH?
WHICH IS?
YOU'RE USING HIM.
FOR WHAT?
I DON'T KNOW... YET.
...NO, NO, NO--I DON'T WANT TWO ORDERS!
YOU SAY *TWO! TWO FINGERS! TWO ORDERS!*
NO, JUST *TWO! TWO* EGG ROLLS. ONE, *TWO. TOTAL* TWO. *NOT* FOUR!
JUST PROMISE YOU'LL LET ME BE THERE WHEN HE DOES.
I PROMISE. YOU'LL BE THERE.
THINK ABOUT IT. YOU AND ME AGAIN.
I HAVE A NEW RULE-- I DON'T TRUST GUYS WHO TRIED TO *KILL ME!*
DON'T BOTHER ME AGAIN!

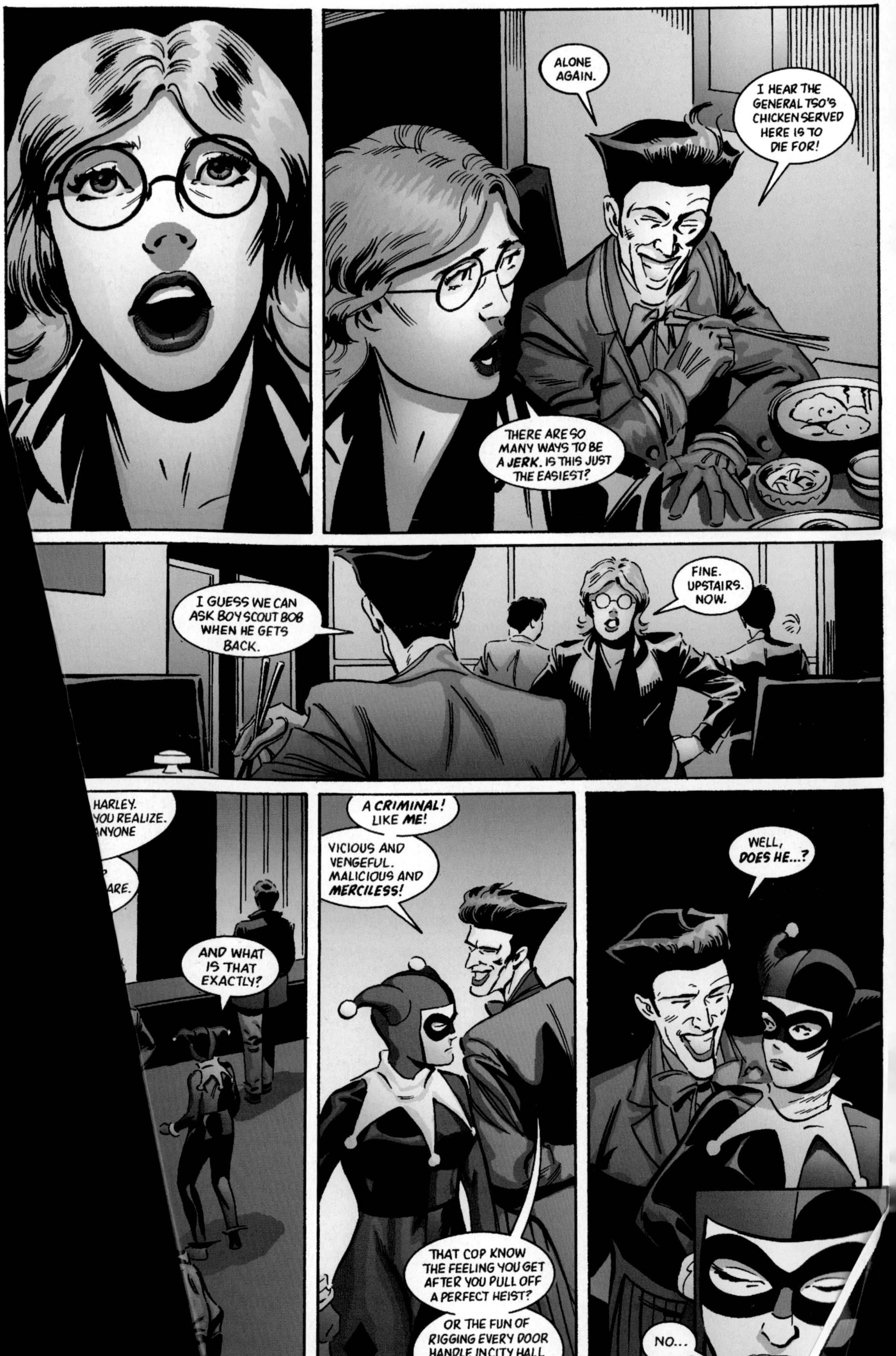
ALONE AGAIN.
I HEAR THE GENERAL TSO'S CHICKEN SERVED HERE IS TO DIE FOR!
THERE ARE SO MANY WAYS TO BE A **JERK**. IS THIS JUST THE EASIEST?
I GUESS WE CAN ASK BOY SCOUT BOB WHEN HE GETS BACK.
FINE. UPSTAIRS. NOW.
HARLEY. YOU REALIZE. ANYONE
ARE.
AND WHAT IS THAT EXACTLY?
A ***CRIMINAL!*** LIKE ***ME!***
VICIOUS AND VENGEFUL. MALICIOUS AND ***MERCILESS!***
THAT COP KNOW THE FEELING YOU GET AFTER YOU PULL OFF A PERFECT HEIST?
OR THE FUN OF RIGGING EVERY DOOR HANDLE IN CITY HALL TO A FIVE HUNDRED AMP CHARGE?
WELL, ***DOES HE...?***
NO...

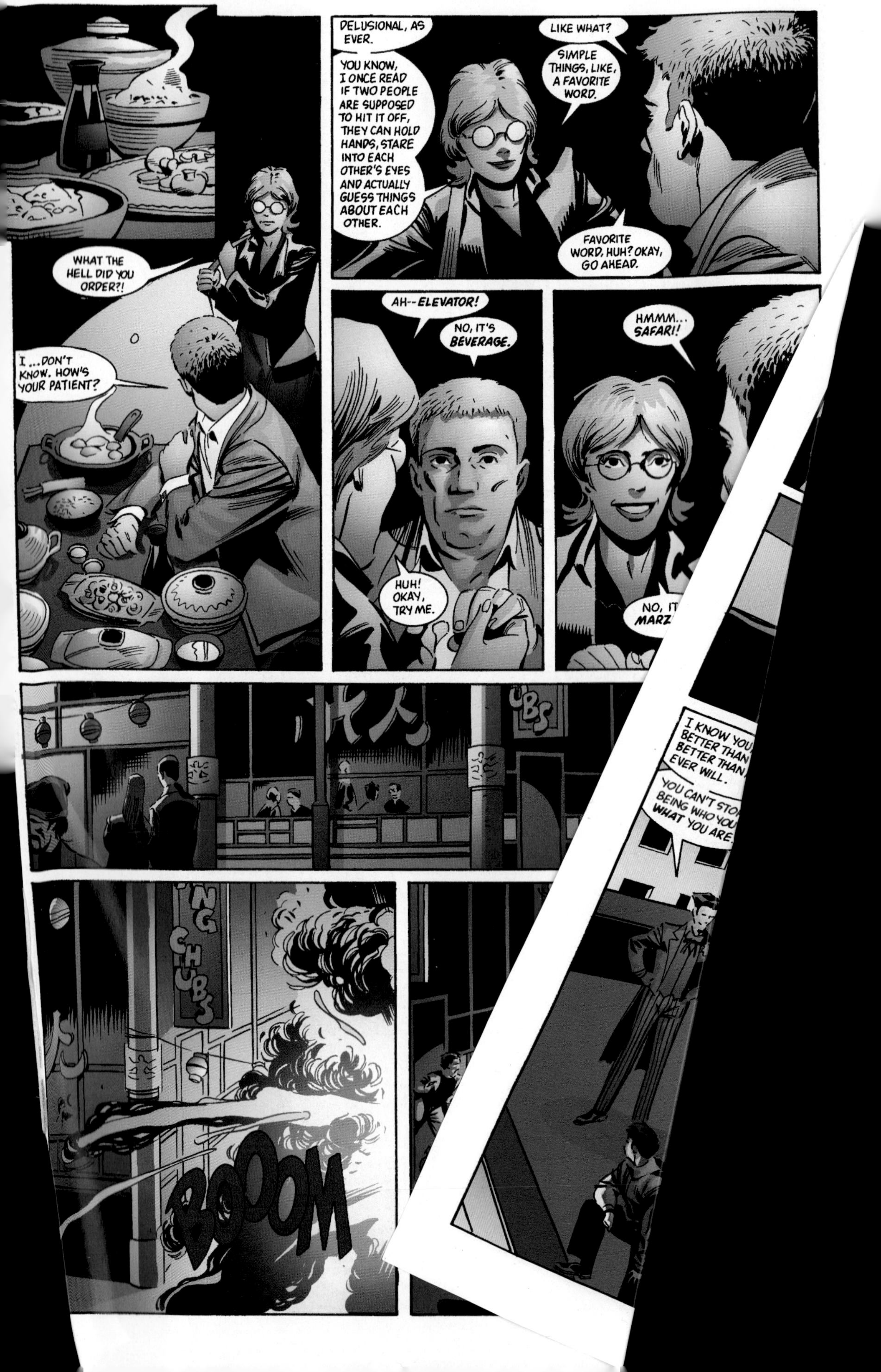

WHAT THE HELL DID YOU ORDER?!
I ...DON'T KNOW. HOW'S YOUR PATIENT?
DELUSIONAL, AS EVER.
YOU KNOW, I ONCE READ IF TWO PEOPLE ARE SUPPOSED TO HIT IT OFF, THEY CAN HOLD HANDS, STARE INTO EACH OTHER'S EYES AND ACTUALLY GUESS THINGS ABOUT EACH OTHER.
LIKE WHAT?
SIMPLE THINGS, LIKE, A FAVORITE WORD.
FAVORITE WORD, HUH? OKAY, GO AHEAD.
HUH! OKAY, TRY ME.
AH--ELEVATOR!
NO, IT'S BEVERAGE.
HMMM... SAFARI!
NO, IT
MARZ
BOOOM
I KNOW YOU
BETTER THAN
BETTER THAN
EVER WILL.
YOU CAN'T STO
BEING WHO YOU
WHAT YOU ARE.

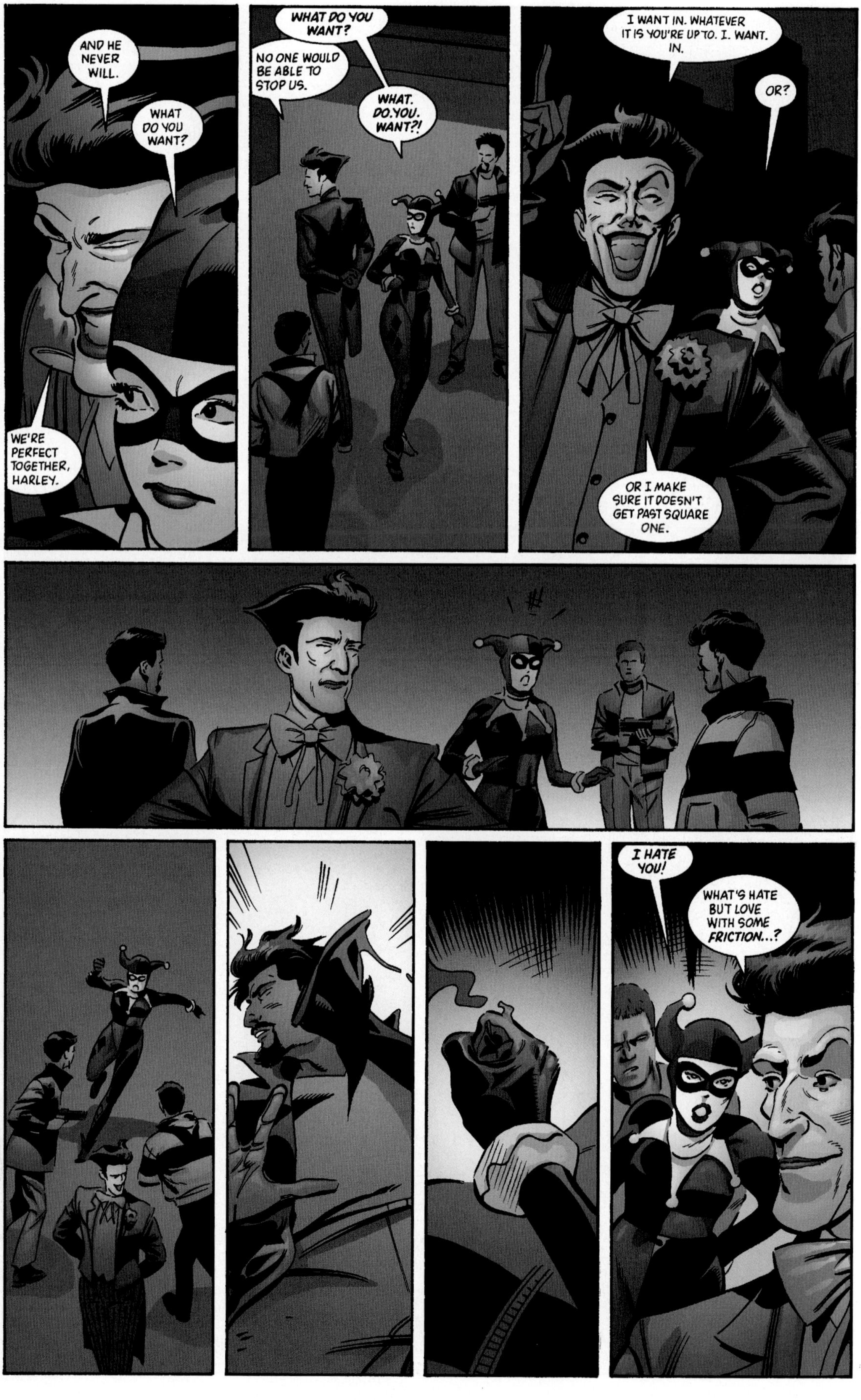
AND HE NEVER WILL.
WHAT DO YOU WANT?
WE'RE PERFECT TOGETHER, HARLEY.
WHAT DO YOU WANT?
NO ONE WOULD BE ABLE TO STOP US.
WHAT. DO.YOU. WANT?!
I WANT IN. WHATEVER IT IS YOU'RE UP TO. I. WANT. IN.
OR?
OR I MAKE SURE IT DOESN'T GET PAST SQUARE ONE.
I HATE YOU!
WHAT'S HATE BUT LOVE WITH SOME FRICTION...?

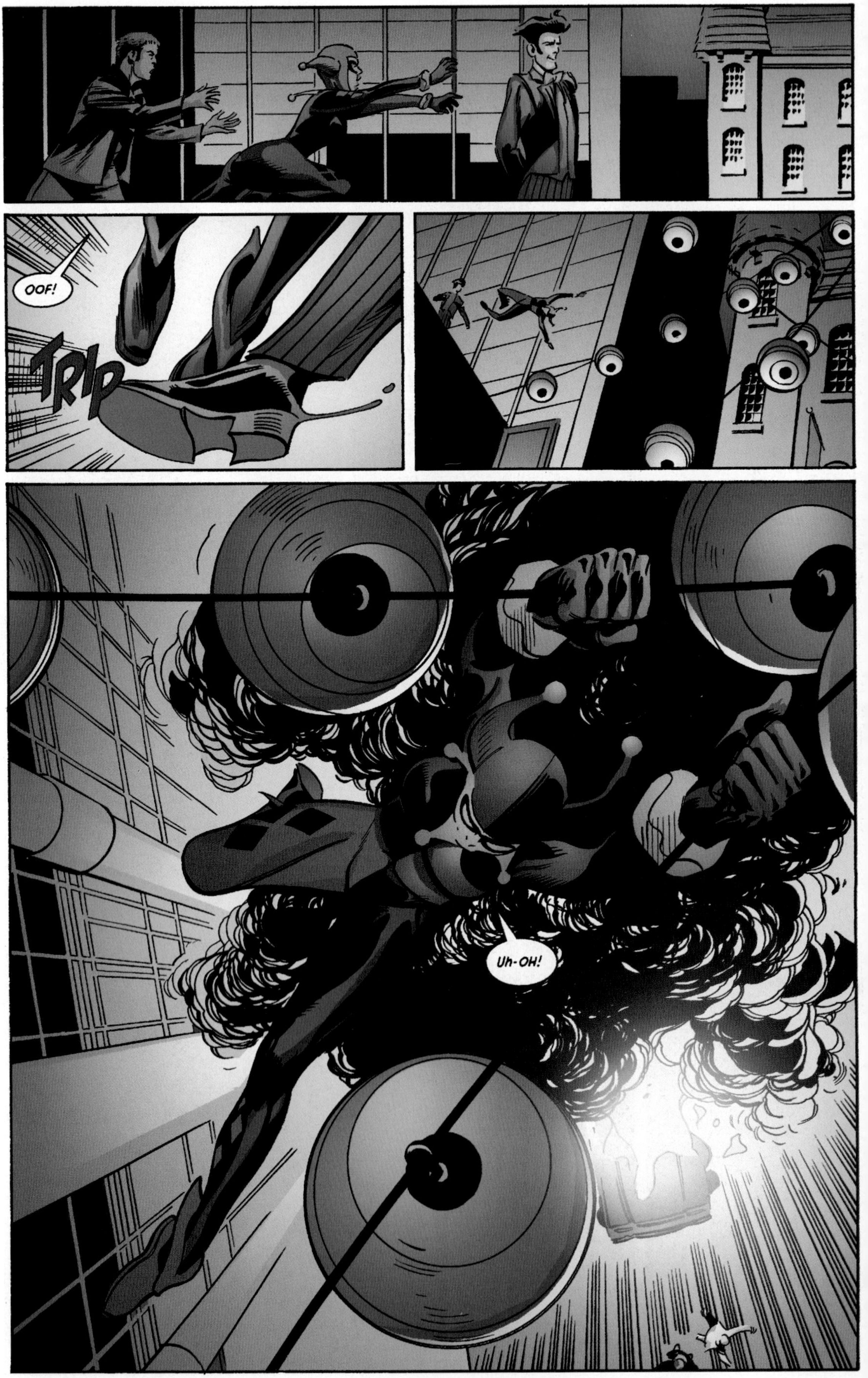
OOF!
TRIP
Uh-OH!

COME ON, PEOPLE, LET'S GO, BACK IT UP!

NOW--EITHER I'M IN OR I CLEAR MY MIND OF EVERY SICK THING IT'S THINKING AND CONCENTRATE ON MAKING YOUR LIFE *MISERABLE.*

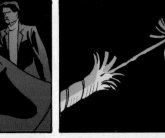

FINE. BUT IT'S *MY* DEAL. IT'S *MY SHOW* AND I'LL CALL THE SHOTS!

YES, MA'AM!

SNAP

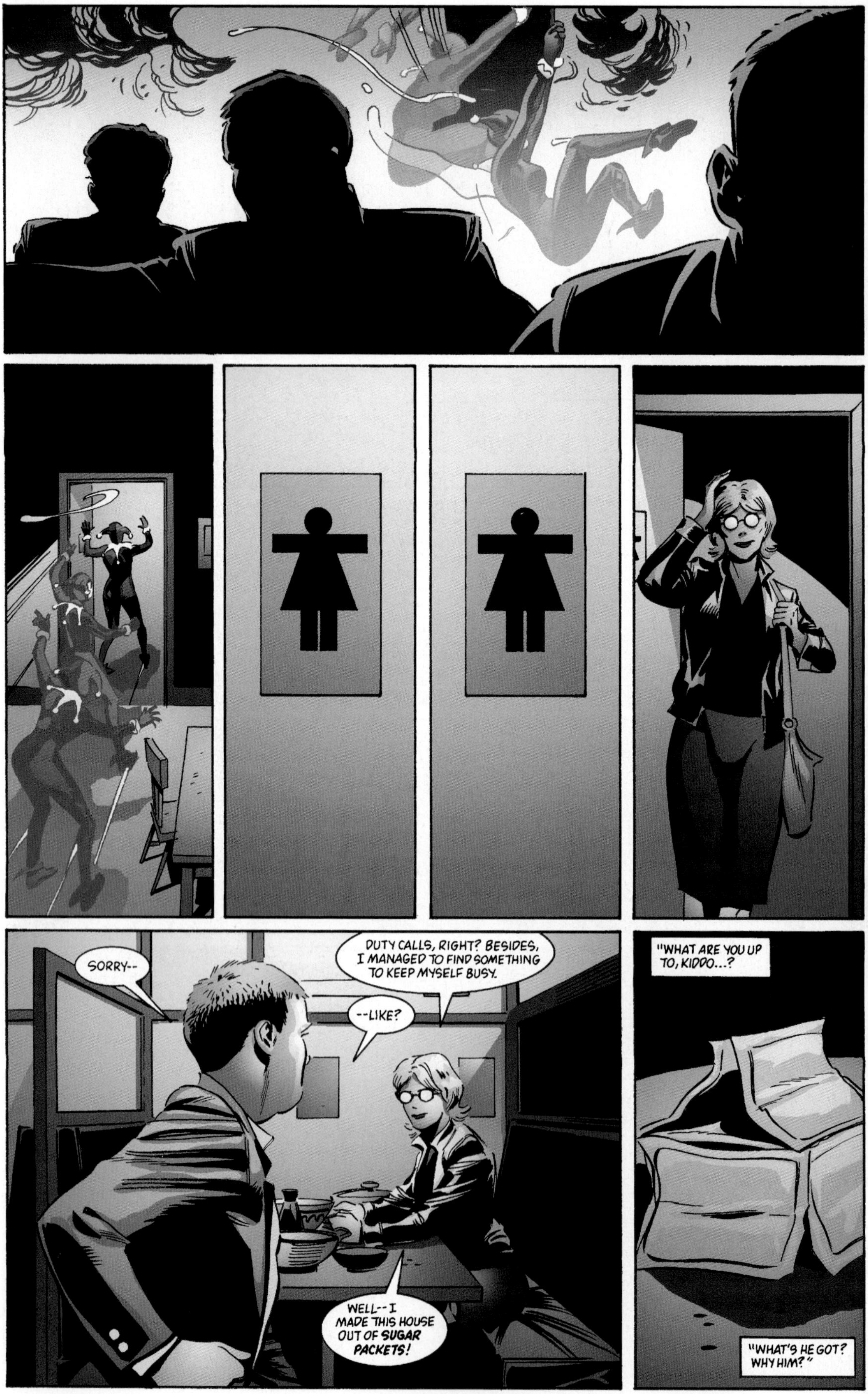
SORRY--
DUTY CALLS, RIGHT? BESIDES, I MANAGED TO FIND SOMETHING TO KEEP MYSELF BUSY.
--LIKE?
WELL--I MADE THIS HOUSE OUT OF SUGAR PACKETS!
"WHAT ARE YOU UP TO, KIDDO...?
"WHAT'S HE GOT? WHY HIM?"

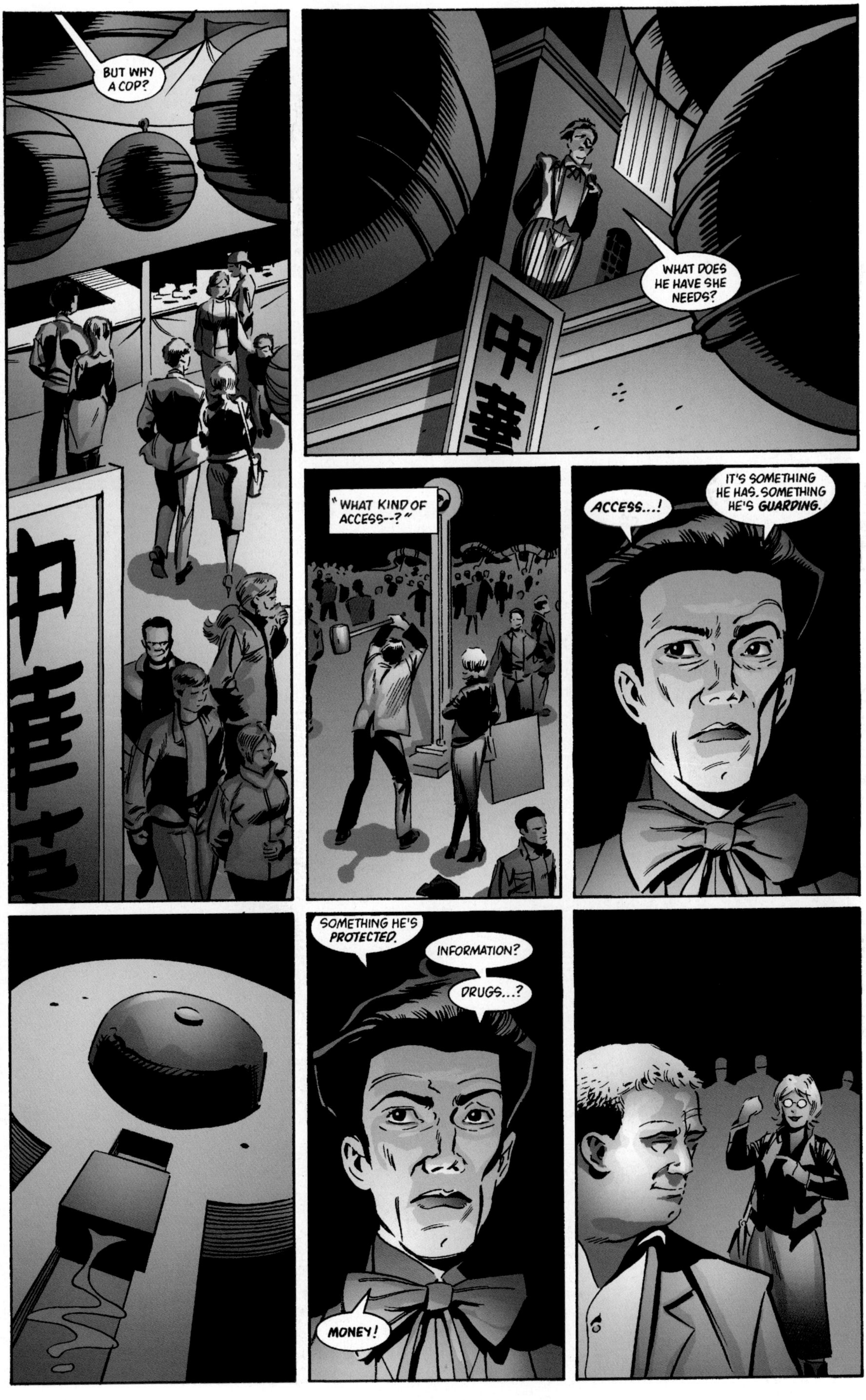
BUT WHY A COP?
WHAT DOES HE HAVE SHE NEEDS?
中華
"WHAT KIND OF ACCESS--?"
ACCESS...!
IT'S SOMETHING HE HAS. SOMETHING HE'S GUARDING.
SOMETHING HE'S PROTECTED.
INFORMATION?
DRUGS...?
MONEY!

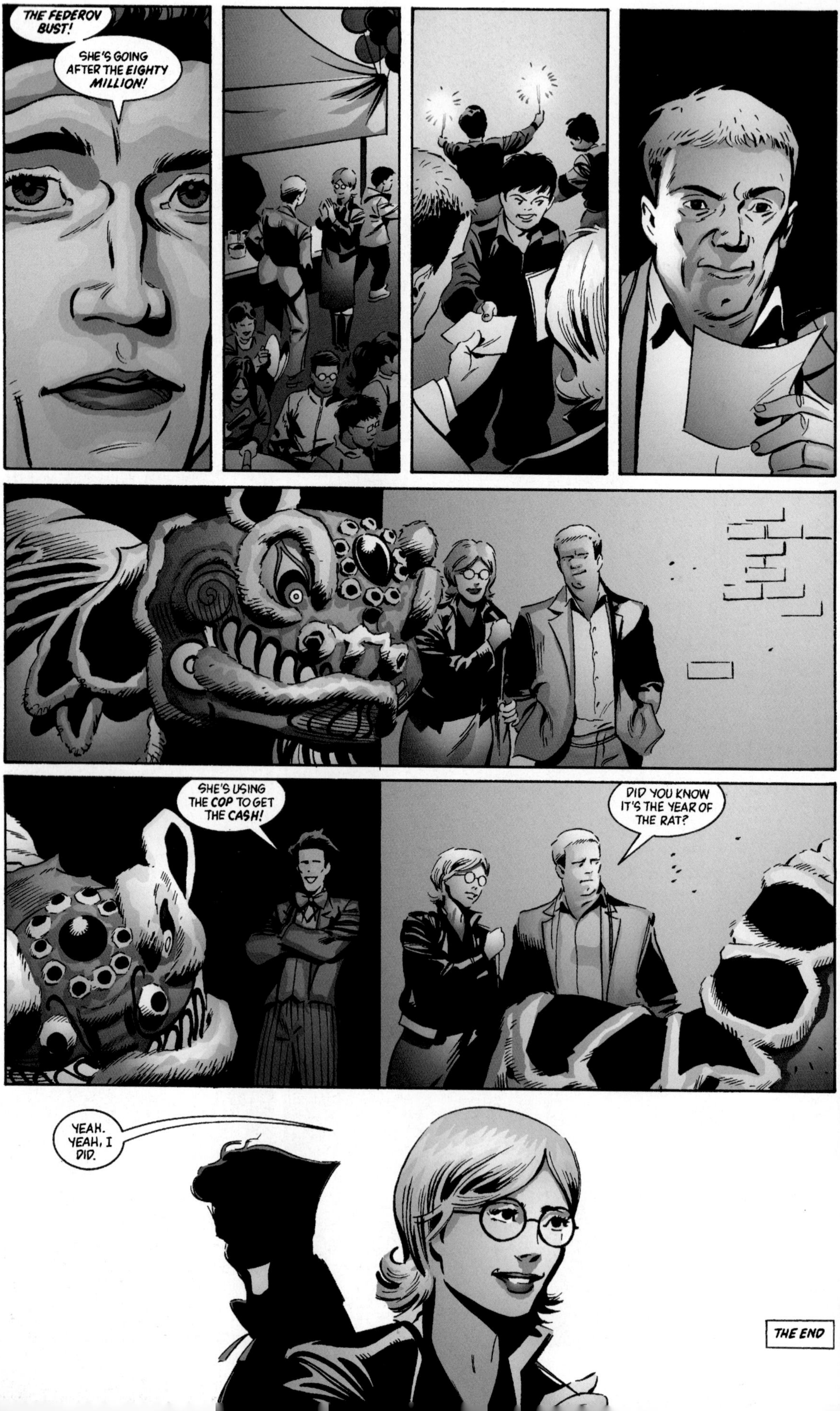
THE FEDEROV BUST!
SHE'S GOING AFTER THE EIGHTY MILLION!
SHE'S USING THE COP TO GET THE CASH!
DID YOU KNOW IT'S THE YEAR OF THE RAT?
YEAH. YEAH, I DID.
THE END

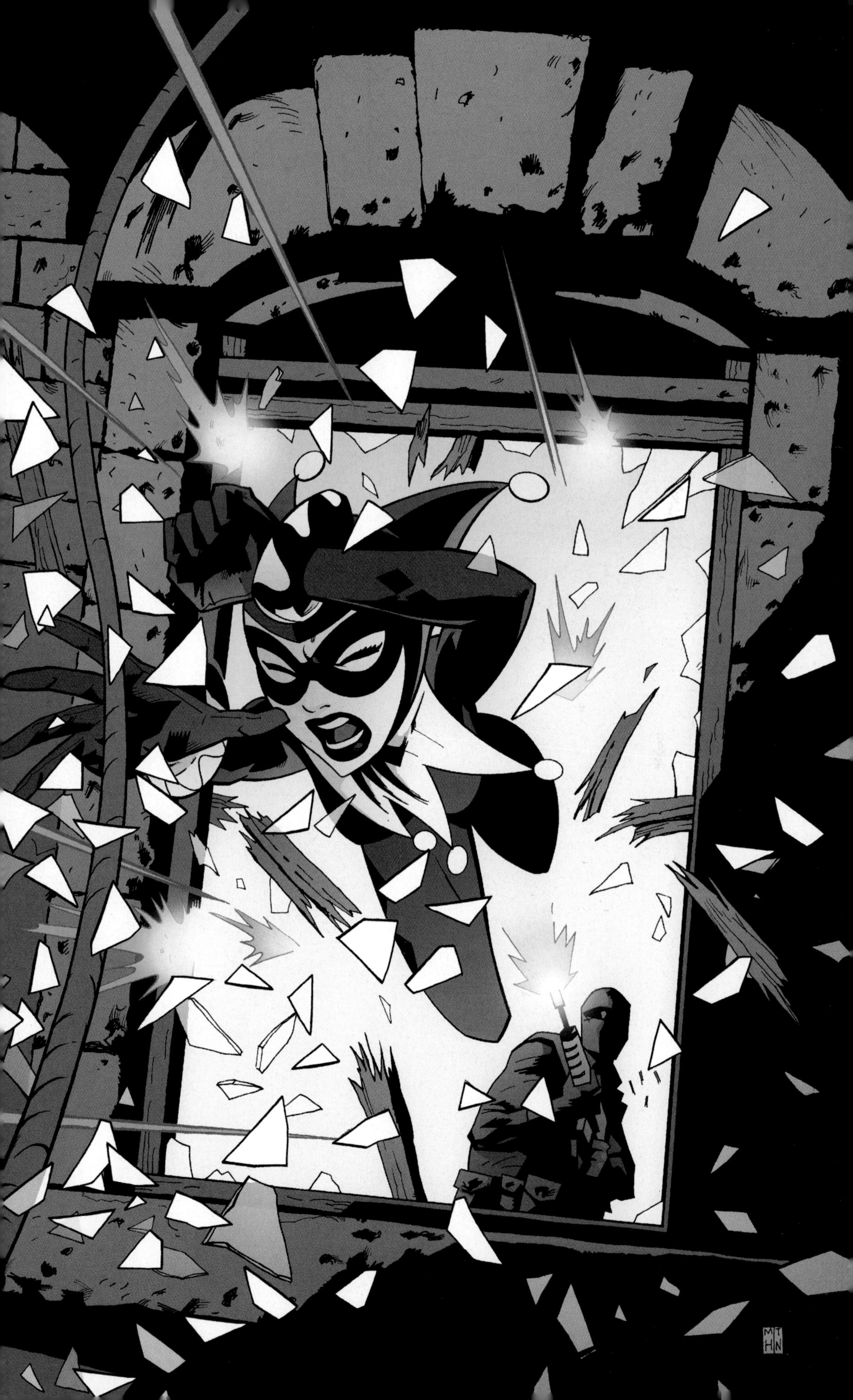

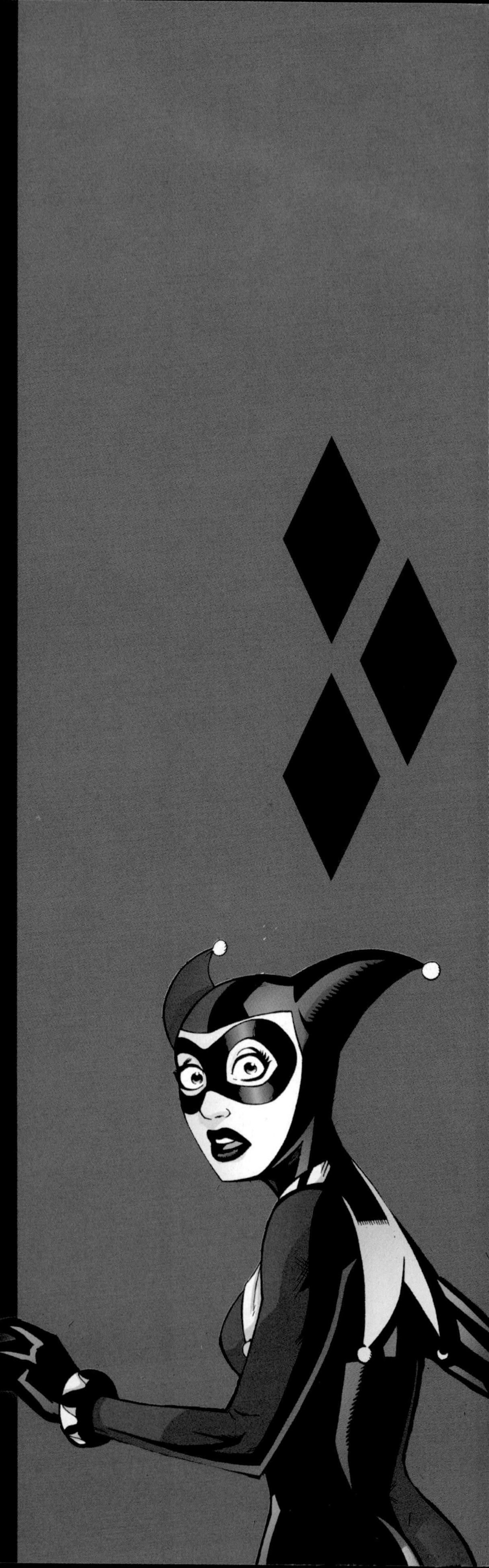

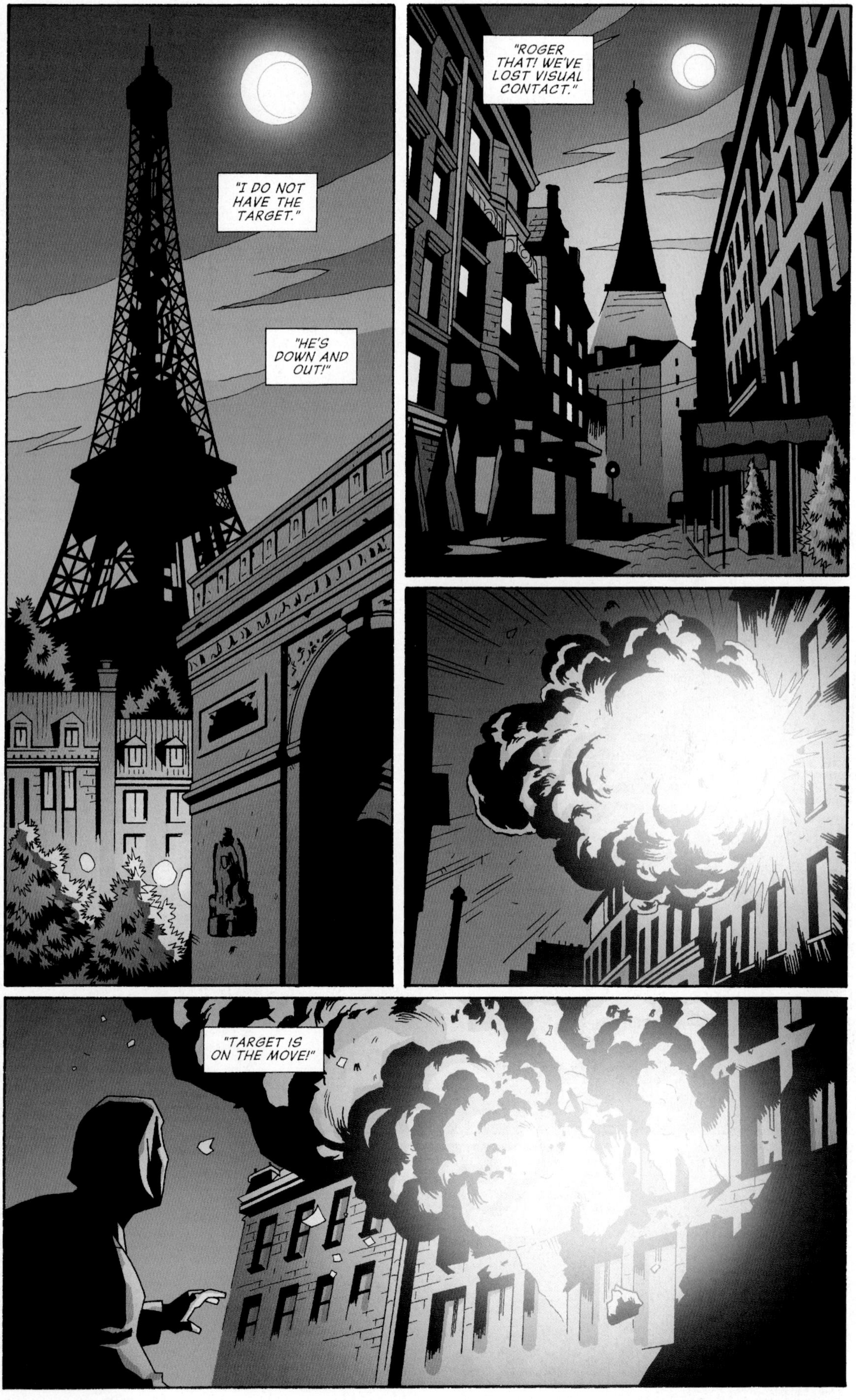
"I DO NOT HAVE THE TARGET."
"HE'S DOWN AND OUT!"
"ROGER THAT! WE'VE LOST VISUAL CONTACT."
"TARGET IS ON THE MOVE!"

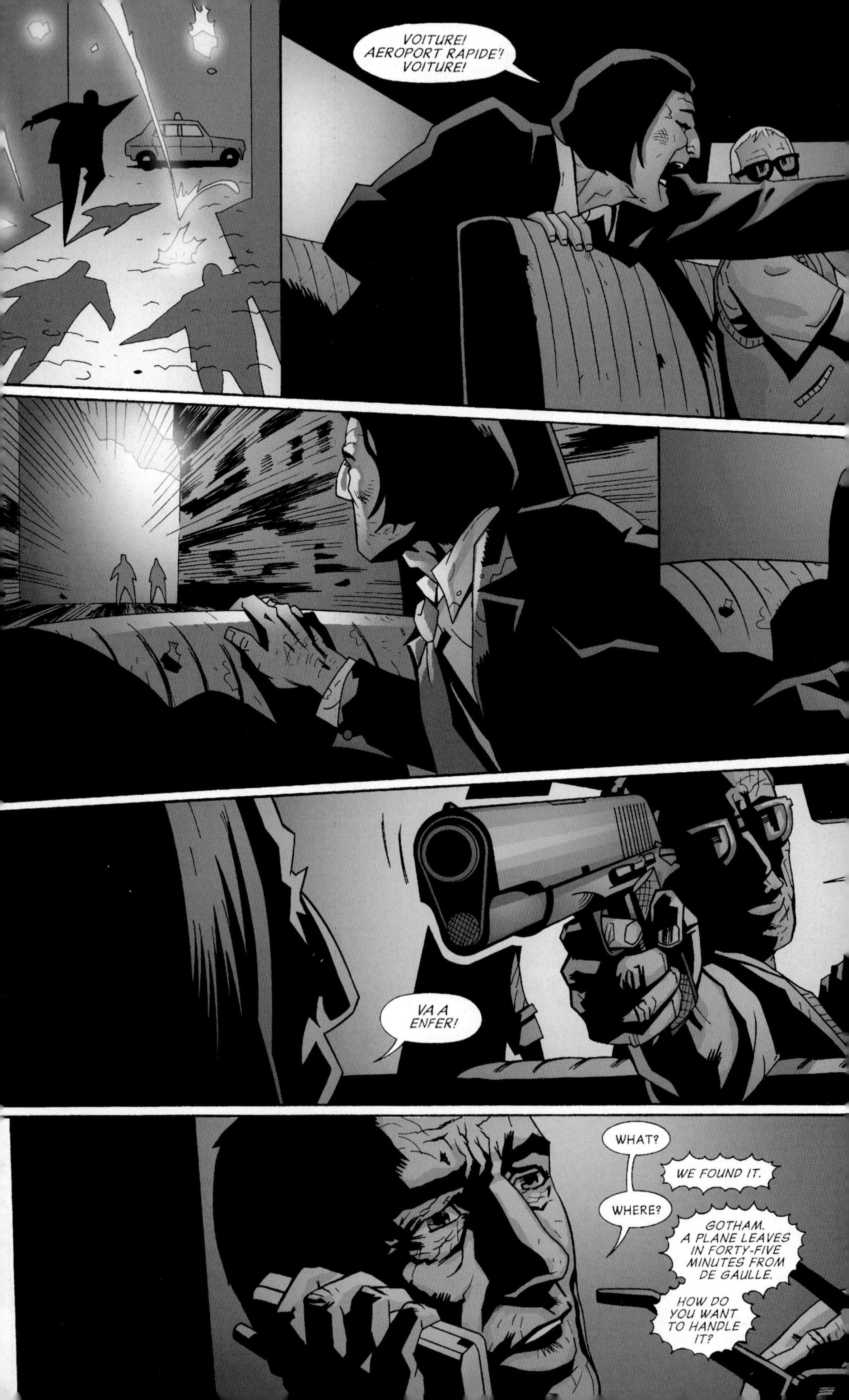

VOITURE! AEROPORT RAPIDE'! VOITURE!
VA A ENFER!
WHAT?
WE FOUND IT.
WHERE?
GOTHAM. A PLANE LEAVES IN FORTY-FIVE MINUTES FROM DE GAULLE.
HOW DO YOU WANT TO HANDLE IT?

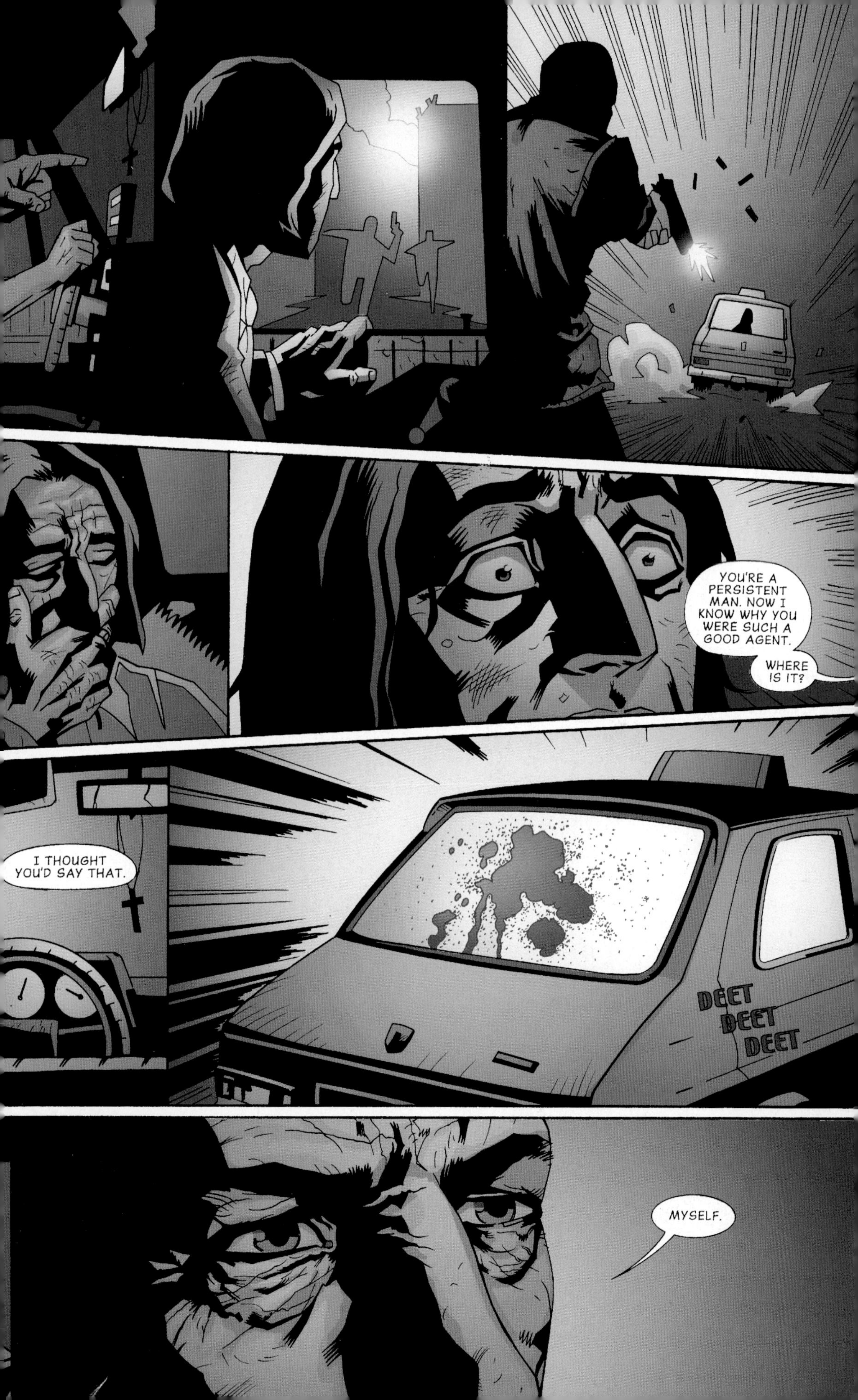
YOU'RE A PERSISTENT MAN. NOW I KNOW WHY YOU WERE SUCH A GOOD AGENT.
WHERE IS IT?
I THOUGHT YOU'D SAY THAT.
DEET DEET DEET
MYSELF.

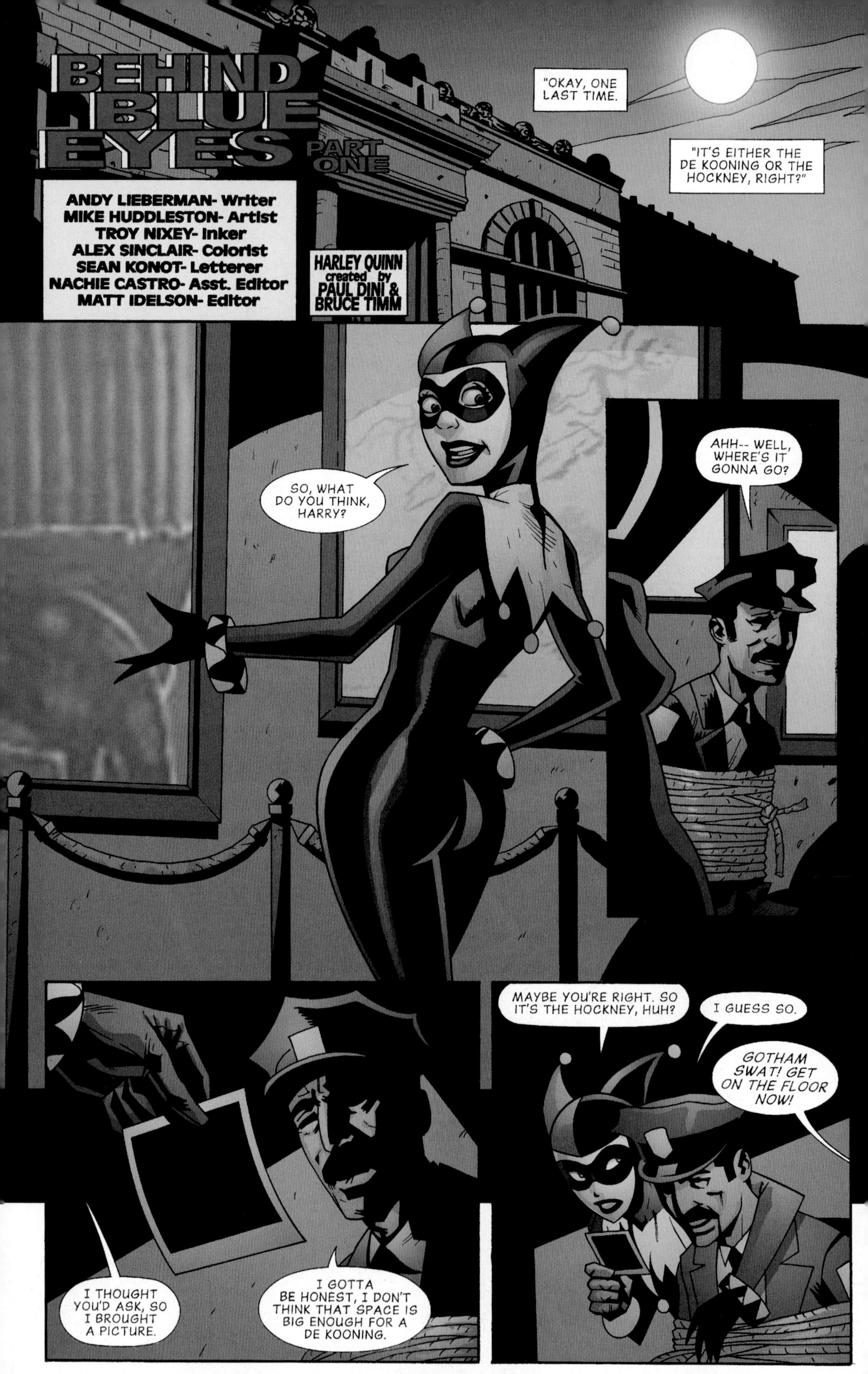
BEHIND BLUE EYES PART ONE
ANDY LIEBERMAN- Writer
MIKE HUDDLESTON- Artist
TROY NIXEY- Inker
ALEX SINCLAIR- Colorist
SEAN KONOT- Letterer
NACHIE CASTRO- Asst. Editor
MATT IDELSON- Editor
HARLEY QUINN created by PAUL DINI & BRUCE TIMM
"OKAY, ONE LAST TIME.
"IT'S EITHER THE DE KOONING OR THE HOCKNEY, RIGHT?"
SO, WHAT DO YOU THINK, HARRY?
AHH-- WELL, WHERE'S IT GONNA GO?
I THOUGHT YOU'D ASK, SO I BROUGHT A PICTURE.
I GOTTA BE HONEST, I DON'T THINK THAT SPACE IS BIG ENOUGH FOR A DE KOONING.
MAYBE YOU'RE RIGHT. SO IT'S THE HOCKNEY, HUH?
I GUESS SO.
GOTHAM SWAT! GET ON THE FLOOR NOW!

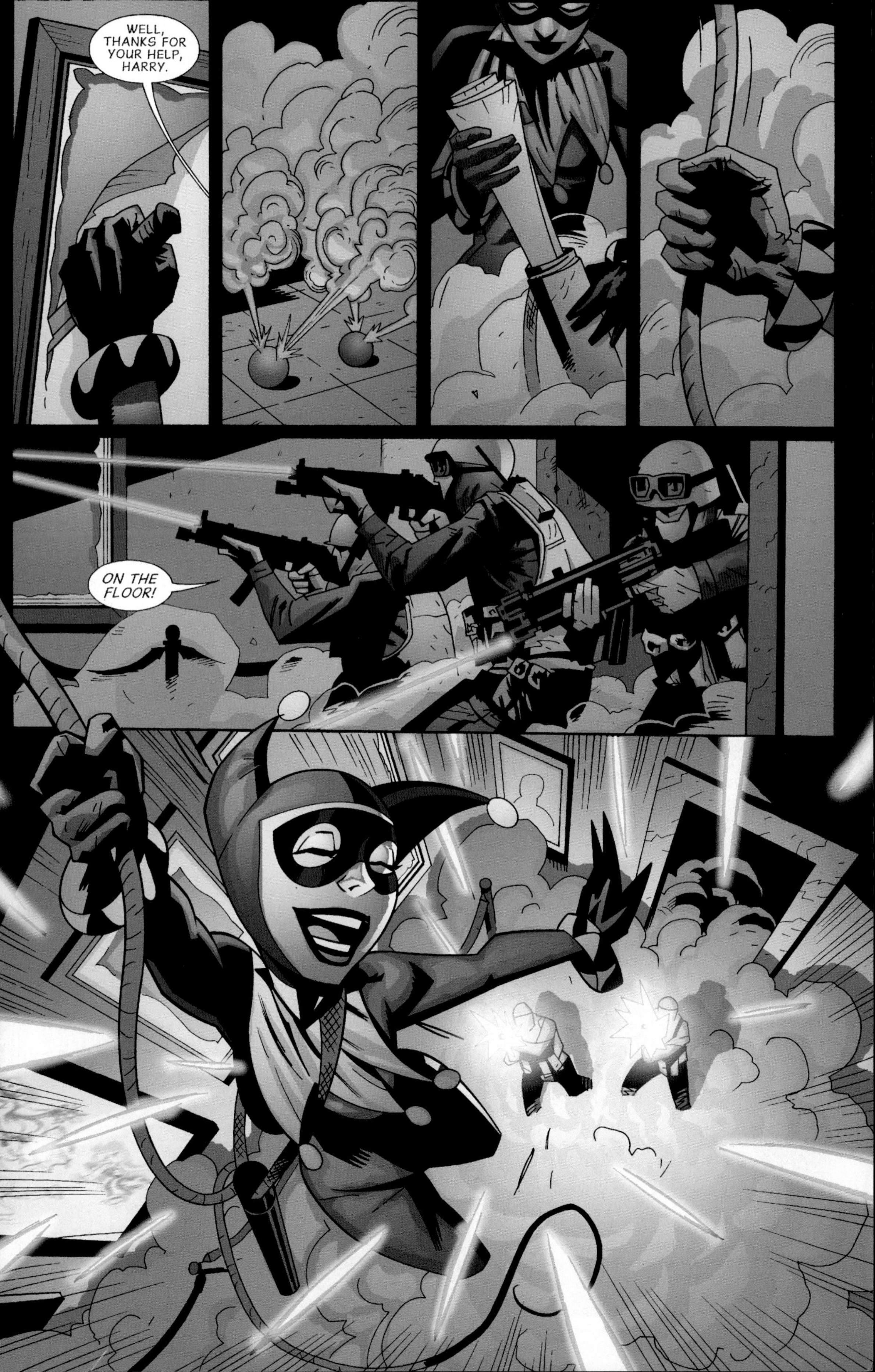
WELL, THANKS FOR YOUR HELP, HARRY.
ON THE FLOOR!

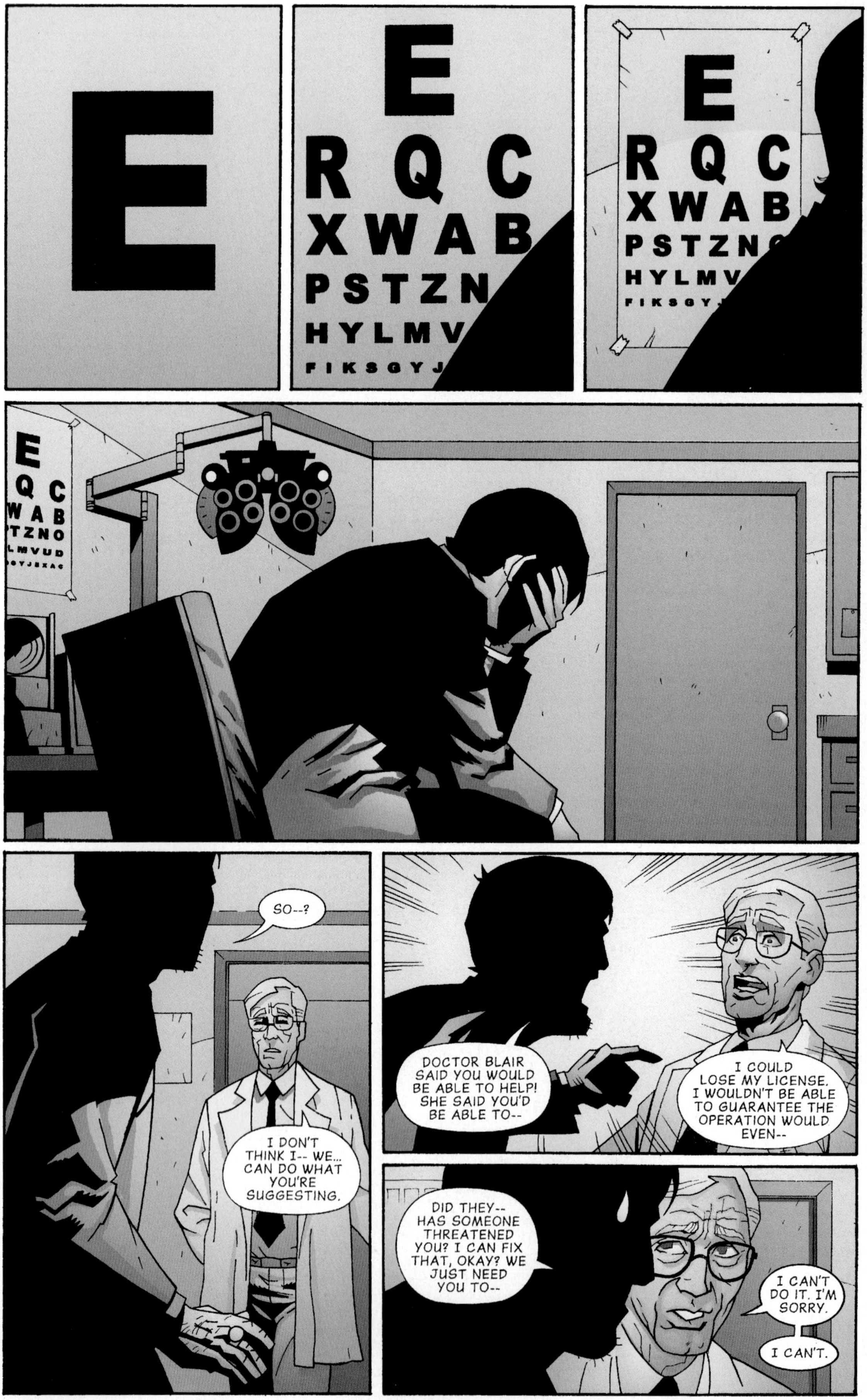
E
E
R Q C
X W A B
P S T Z N
H Y L M V
F I K S G Y J
E
R Q C
X W A B
P S T Z N
H Y L M V
F I K S G Y J
SO--?
I DON'T THINK I-- WE... CAN DO WHAT YOU'RE SUGGESTING.
DOCTOR BLAIR SAID YOU WOULD BE ABLE TO HELP! SHE SAID YOU'D BE ABLE TO--
I COULD LOSE MY LICENSE. I WOULDN'T BE ABLE TO GUARANTEE THE OPERATION WOULD EVEN--
DID THEY-- HAS SOMEONE THREATENED YOU? I CAN FIX THAT, OKAY? WE JUST NEED YOU TO--
I CAN'T DO IT. I'M SORRY.
I CAN'T.

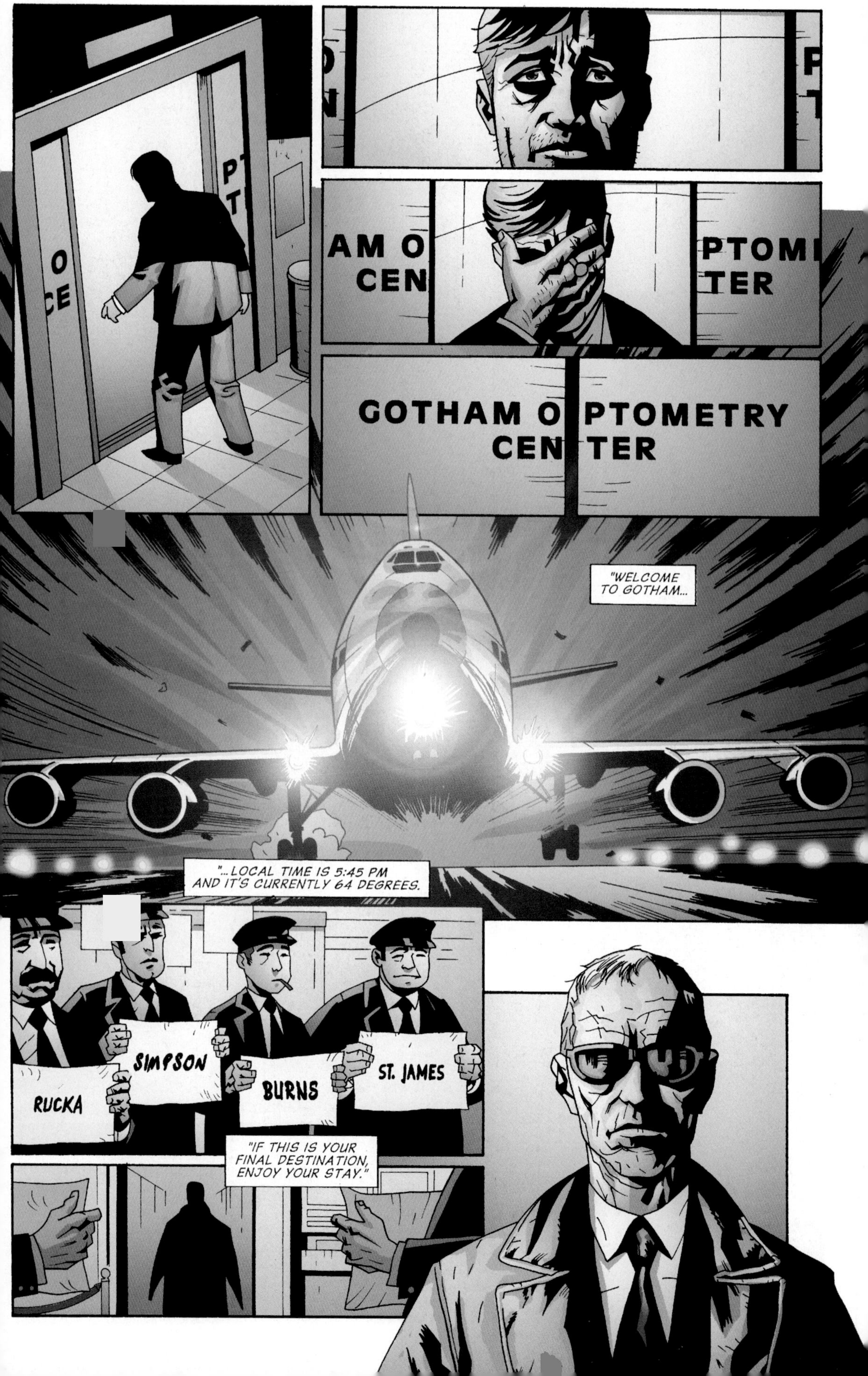
PT
AM O
CEN
PTOM
TER
GOTHAM O PTOMETRY
CEN TER
"WELCOME TO GOTHAM...
"...LOCAL TIME IS 5:45 PM AND IT'S CURRENTLY 64 DEGREES.
SIMPSON
RUCKA
BURNS
ST. JAMES
"IF THIS IS YOUR FINAL DESTINATION, ENJOY YOUR STAY."

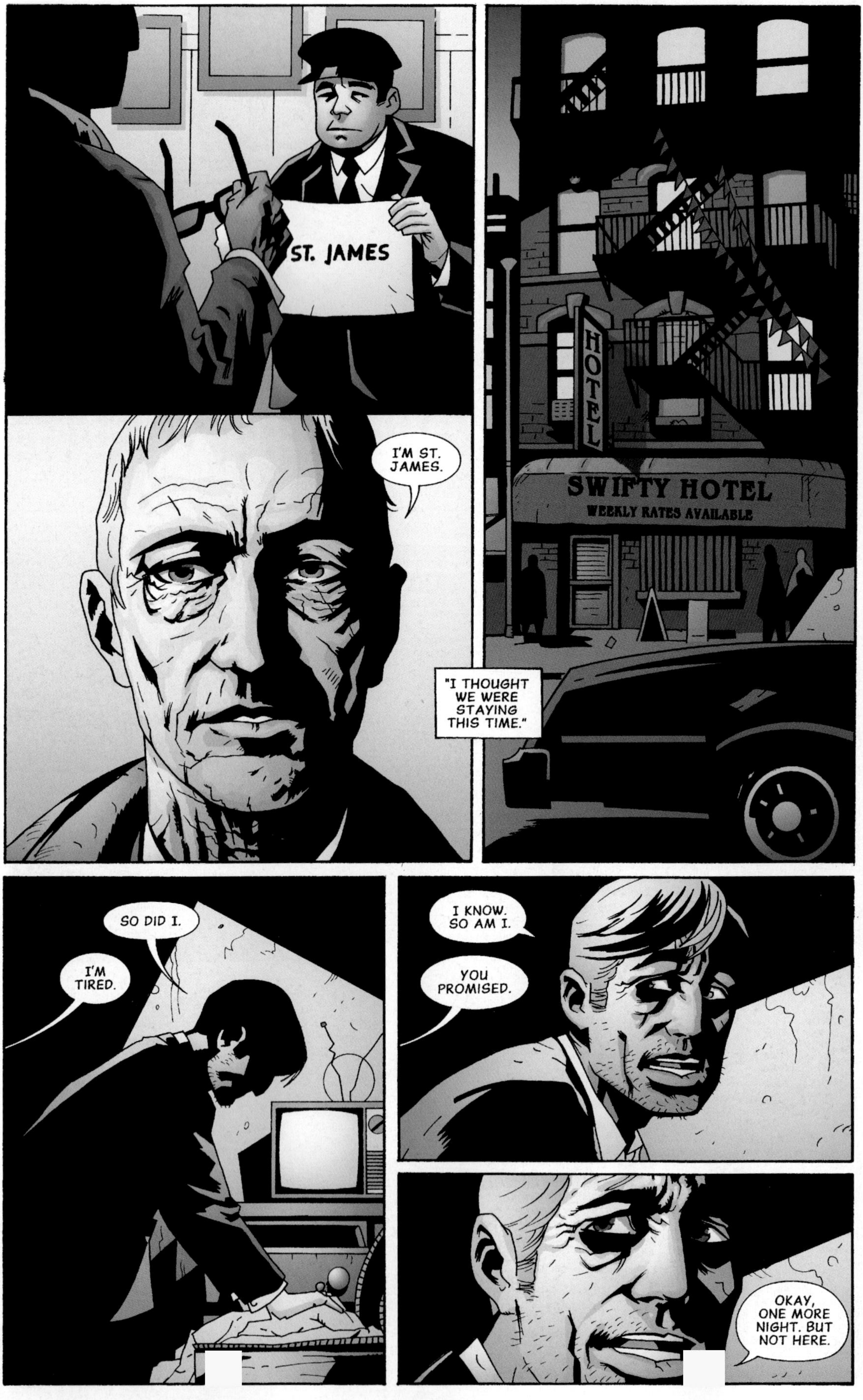
ST. JAMES
HOTEL
SWIFTY HOTEL
WEEKLY RATES AVAILABLE
I'M ST. JAMES.
"I THOUGHT WE WERE STAYING THIS TIME."
I'M TIRED.
SO DID I.
YOU PROMISED.
I KNOW. SO AM I.
OKAY, ONE MORE NIGHT. BUT NOT HERE.

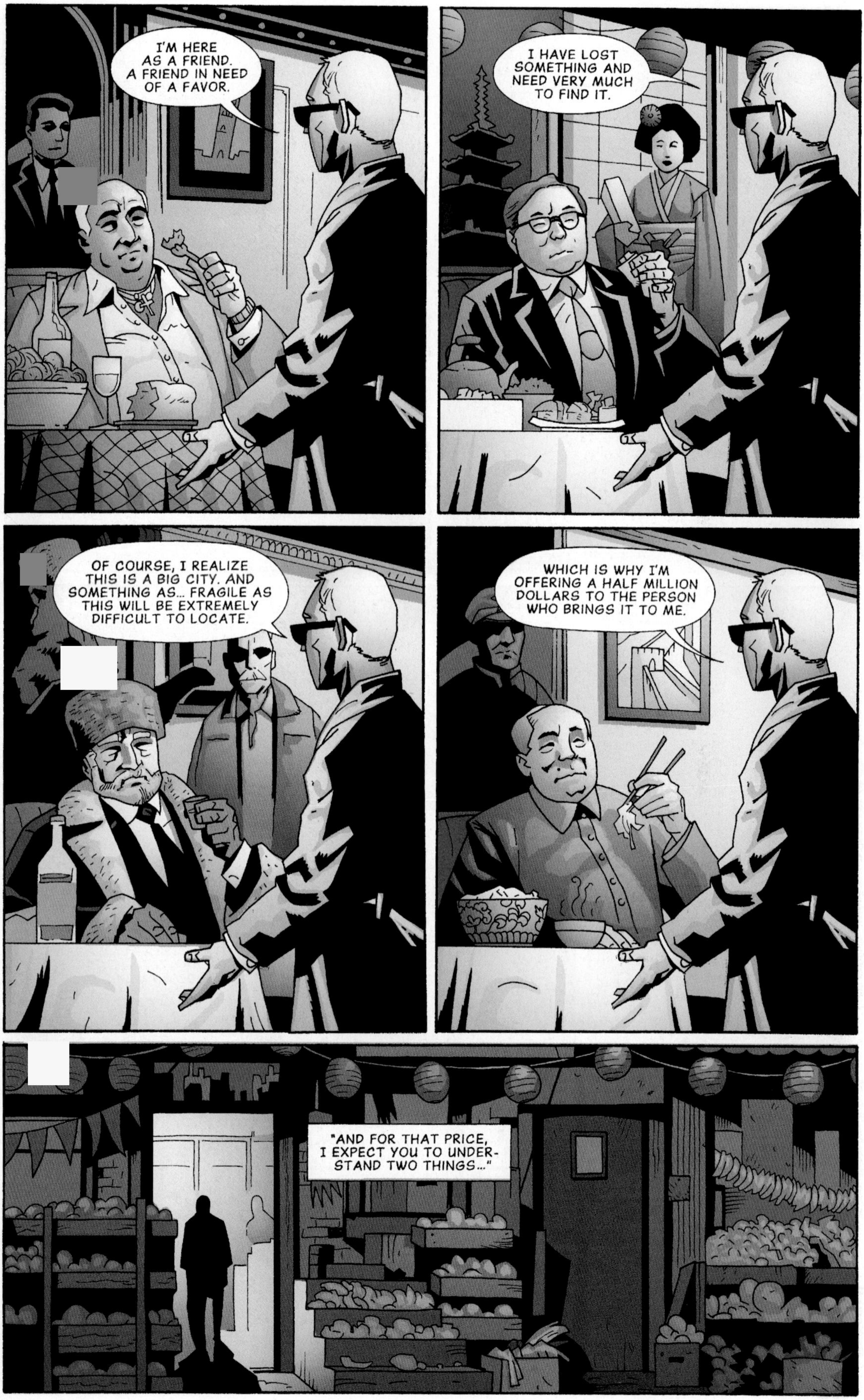
I'M HERE AS A FRIEND. A FRIEND IN NEED OF A FAVOR.
I HAVE LOST SOMETHING AND NEED VERY MUCH TO FIND IT.
OF COURSE, I REALIZE THIS IS A BIG CITY. AND SOMETHING AS... FRAGILE AS THIS WILL BE EXTREMELY DIFFICULT TO LOCATE.
WHICH IS WHY I'M OFFERING A HALF MILLION DOLLARS TO THE PERSON WHO BRINGS IT TO ME.
"AND FOR THAT PRICE, I EXPECT YOU TO UNDERSTAND TWO THINGS..."

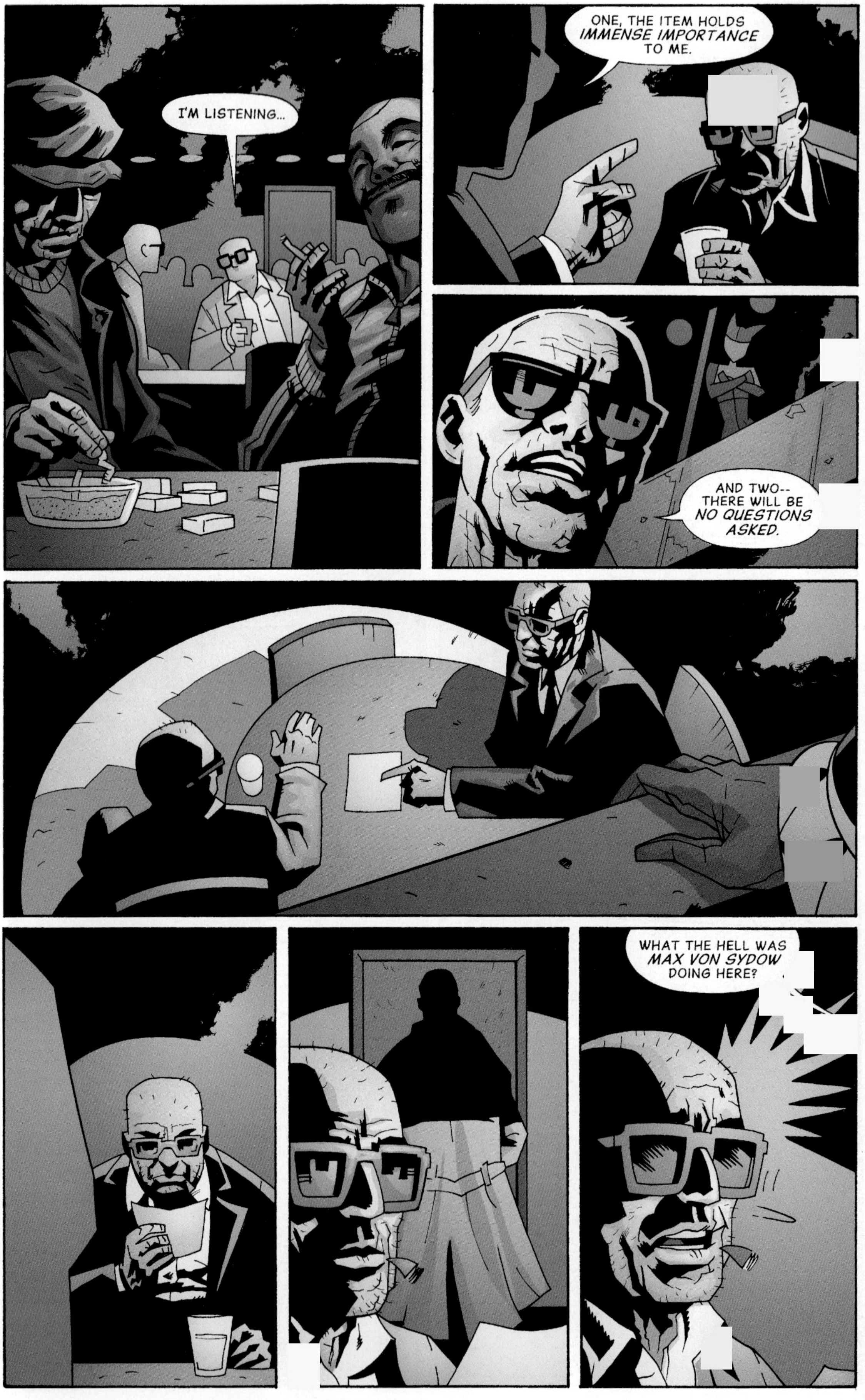
I'M LISTENING...
ONE, THE ITEM HOLDS
IMMENSE IMPORTANCE
TO ME.
AND TWO--
THERE WILL BE
NO QUESTIONS
ASKED.
WHAT THE HELL WAS
MAX VON SYDOW
DOING HERE?

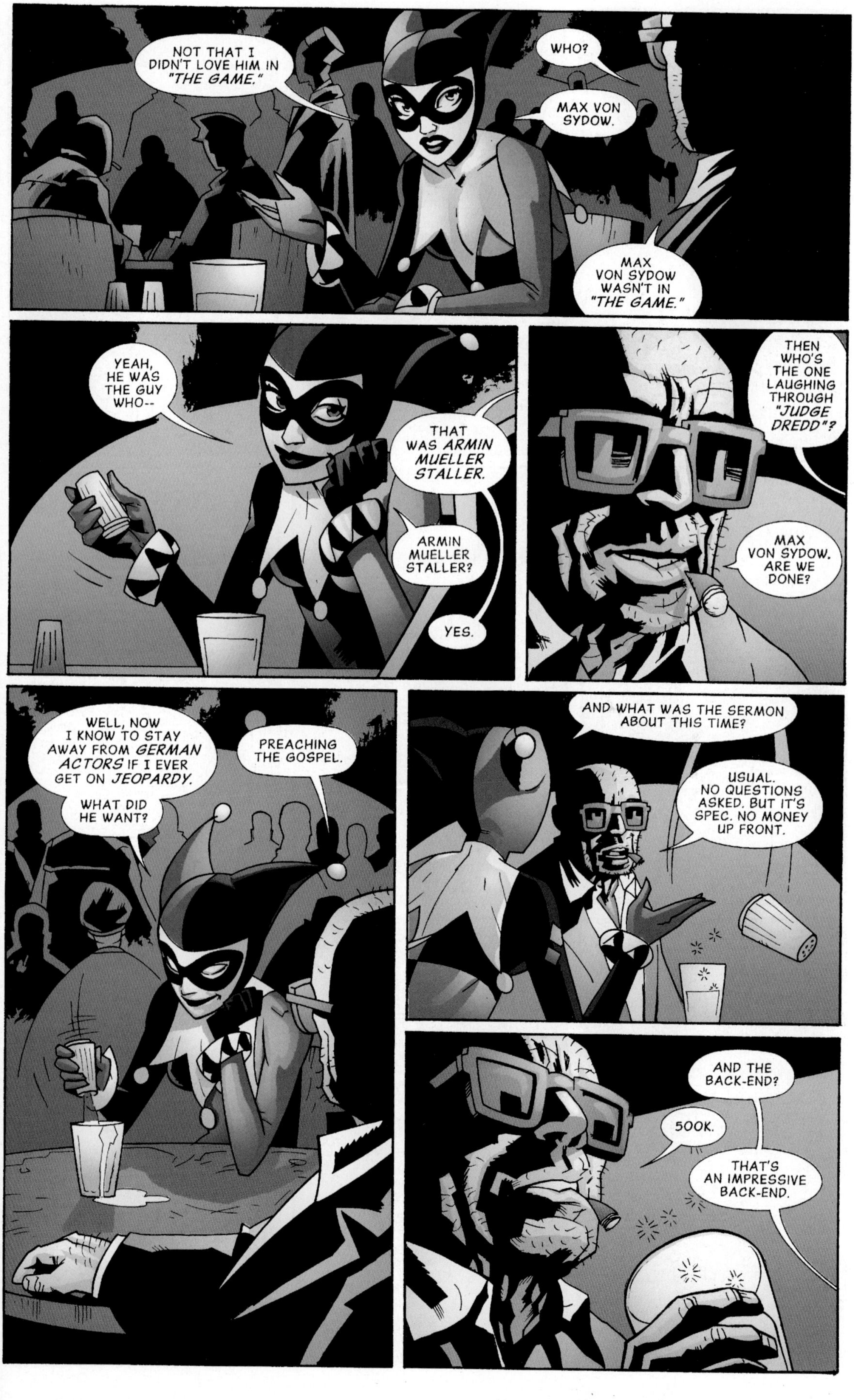
NOT THAT I DIDN'T LOVE HIM IN "THE GAME."
WHO?
MAX VON SYDOW.
MAX VON SYDOW WASN'T IN "THE GAME."
YEAH, HE WAS THE GUY WHO--
THAT WAS ARMIN MUELLER STALLER.
ARMIN MUELLER STALLER?
YES.
THEN WHO'S THE ONE LAUGHING THROUGH "JUDGE DREDD"?
MAX VON SYDOW. ARE WE DONE?
WELL, NOW I KNOW TO STAY AWAY FROM GERMAN ACTORS IF I EVER GET ON JEOPARDY.
WHAT DID HE WANT?
PREACHING THE GOSPEL.
AND WHAT WAS THE SERMON ABOUT THIS TIME?
USUAL. NO QUESTIONS ASKED. BUT IT'S SPEC. NO MONEY UP FRONT.
AND THE BACK-END?
500K.
THAT'S AN IMPRESSIVE BACK-END.

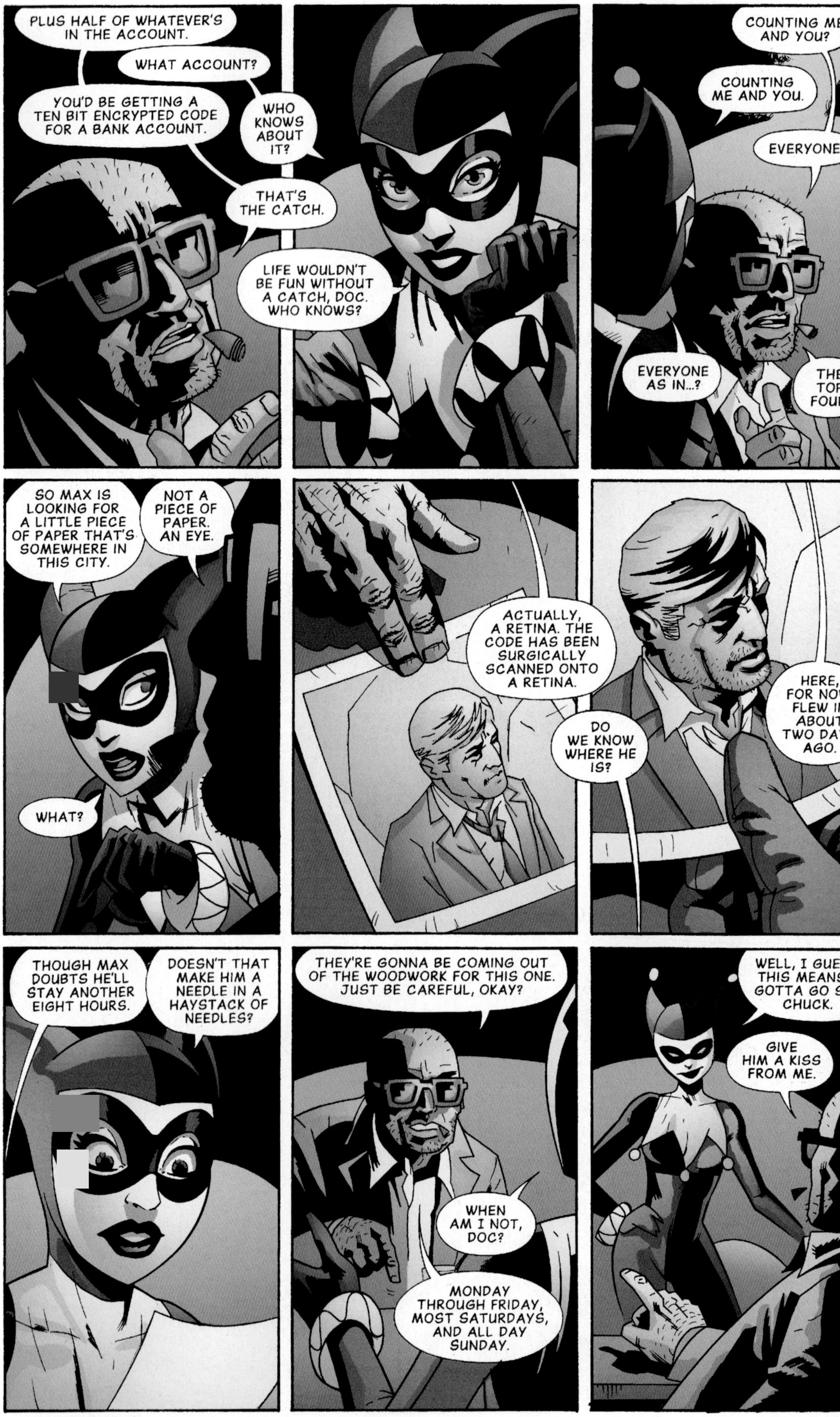
PLUS HALF OF WHATEVER'S IN THE ACCOUNT.
WHAT ACCOUNT?
YOU'D BE GETTING A TEN BIT ENCRYPTED CODE FOR A BANK ACCOUNT.
WHO KNOWS ABOUT IT?
THAT'S THE CATCH.
LIFE WOULDN'T BE FUN WITHOUT A CATCH, DOC. WHO KNOWS?
COUNTING ME AND YOU?
COUNTING ME AND YOU.
EVERYONE.
EVERYONE AS IN...?
THE TOP FOUR.
SO MAX IS LOOKING FOR A LITTLE PIECE OF PAPER THAT'S SOMEWHERE IN THIS CITY.
NOT A PIECE OF PAPER. AN EYE.
WHAT?
ACTUALLY, A RETINA. THE CODE HAS BEEN SURGICALLY SCANNED ONTO A RETINA.
DO WE KNOW WHERE HE IS?
HERE, FOR NOW. FLEW IN ABOUT TWO DAYS AGO.
THOUGH MAX DOUBTS HE'LL STAY ANOTHER EIGHT HOURS.
DOESN'T THAT MAKE HIM A NEEDLE IN A HAYSTACK OF NEEDLES?
THEY'RE GONNA BE COMING OUT OF THE WOODWORK FOR THIS ONE. JUST BE CAREFUL, OKAY?
WHEN AM I NOT, DOC?
MONDAY THROUGH FRIDAY, MOST SATURDAYS, AND ALL DAY SUNDAY.
WELL, I GUESS THIS MEANS I GOTTA GO SEE CHUCK.
GIVE HIM A KISS FROM ME.

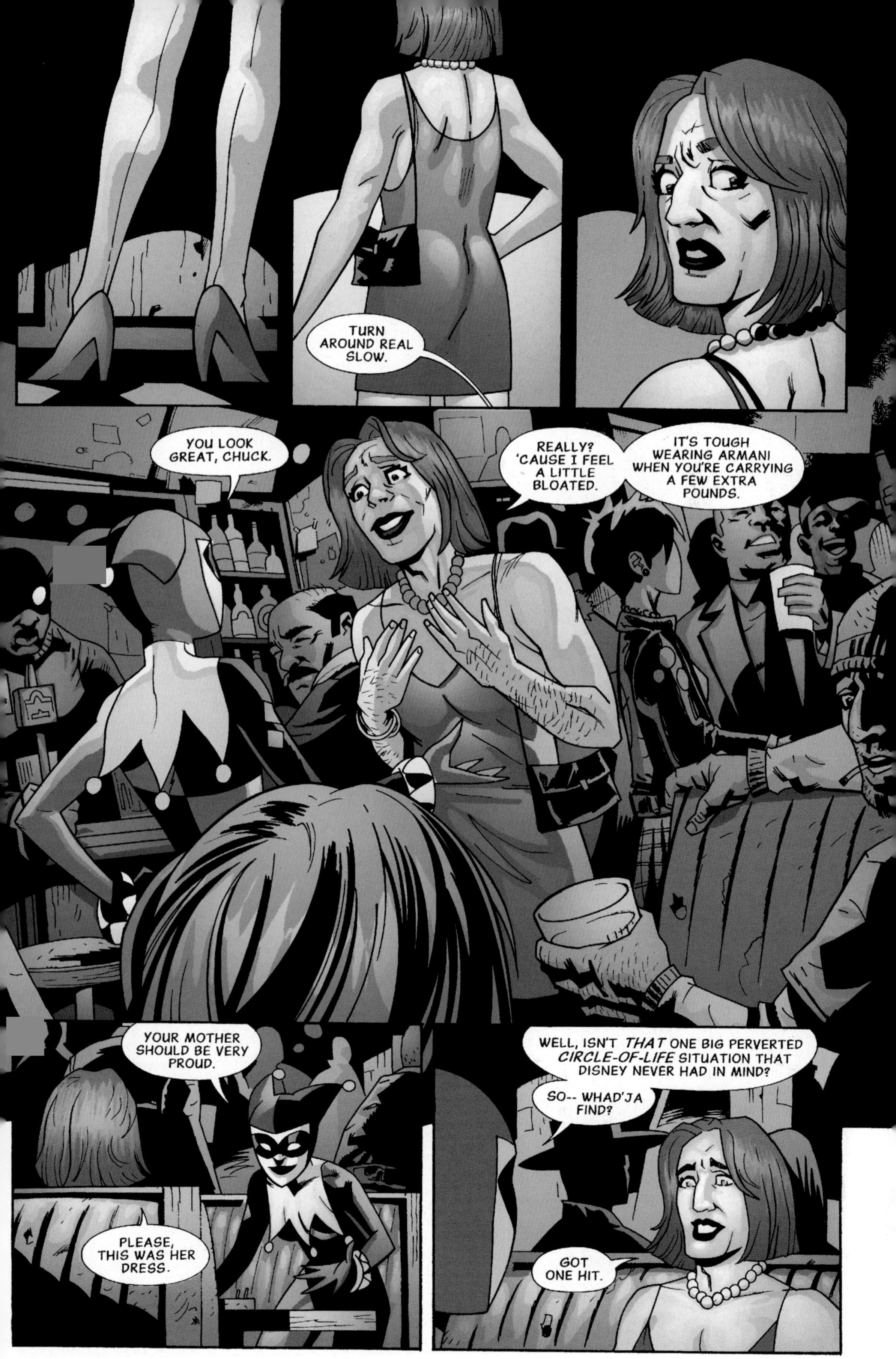
TURN AROUND REAL SLOW.
YOU LOOK GREAT, CHUCK.
REALLY? 'CAUSE I FEEL A LITTLE BLOATED.
IT'S TOUGH WEARING ARMANI WHEN YOU'RE CARRYING A FEW EXTRA POUNDS.
YOUR MOTHER SHOULD BE VERY PROUD.
PLEASE, THIS WAS HER DRESS.
WELL, ISN'T *THAT* ONE BIG PERVERTED *CIRCLE-OF-LIFE* SITUATION THAT DISNEY NEVER HAD IN MIND?
SO-- WHAD'JA FIND?
GOT ONE HIT.

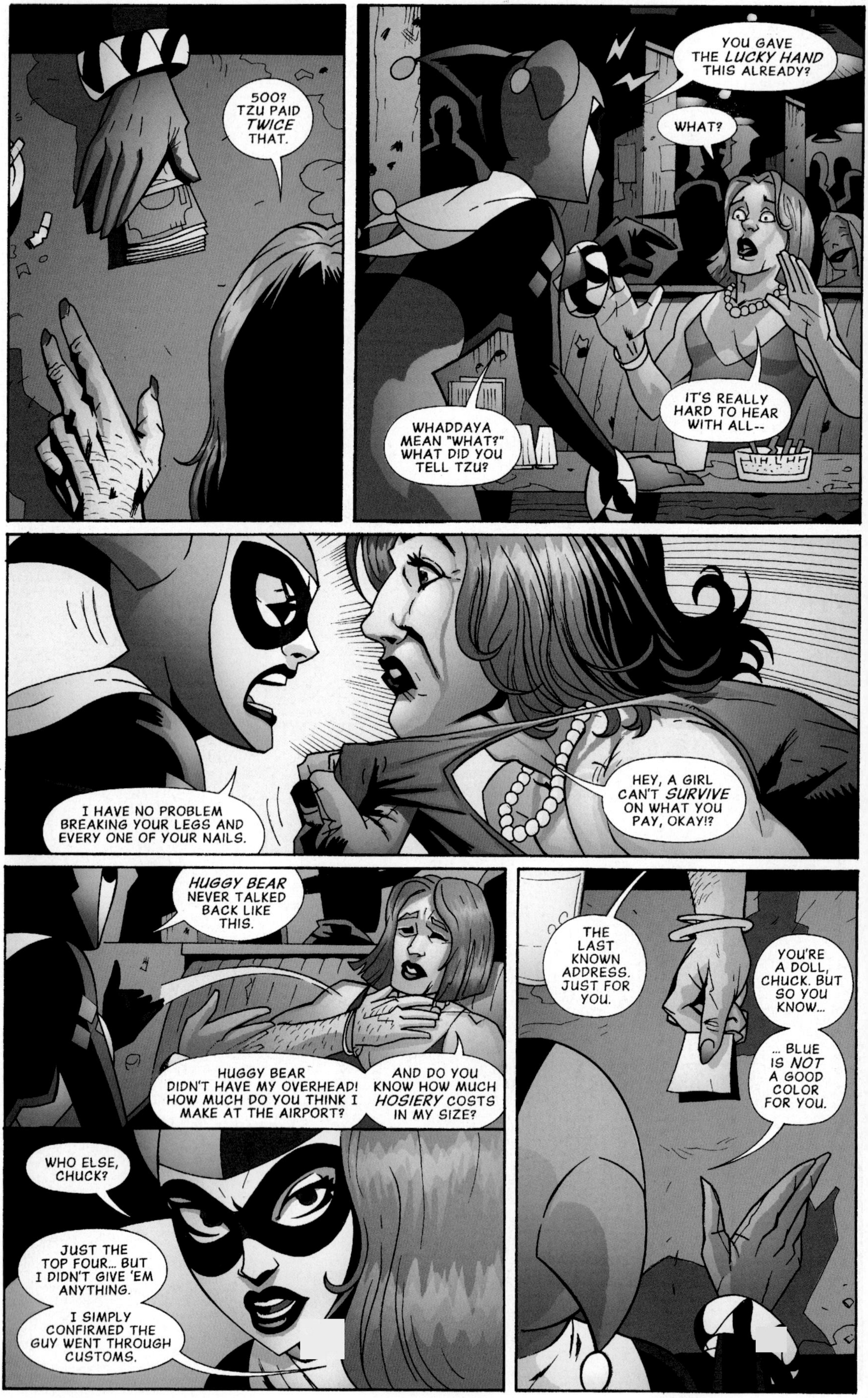
500? TZU PAID TWICE THAT.
YOU GAVE THE LUCKY HAND THIS ALREADY?
WHAT?
WHADDAYA MEAN "WHAT?" WHAT DID YOU TELL TZU?
IT'S REALLY HARD TO HEAR WITH ALL--
I HAVE NO PROBLEM BREAKING YOUR LEGS AND EVERY ONE OF YOUR NAILS.
HEY, A GIRL CAN'T SURVIVE ON WHAT YOU PAY, OKAY!?
HUGGY BEAR NEVER TALKED BACK LIKE THIS.
HUGGY BEAR DIDN'T HAVE MY OVERHEAD! HOW MUCH DO YOU THINK I MAKE AT THE AIRPORT?
AND DO YOU KNOW HOW MUCH HOSIERY COSTS IN MY SIZE?
WHO ELSE, CHUCK?
JUST THE TOP FOUR... BUT I DIDN'T GIVE 'EM ANYTHING.
I SIMPLY CONFIRMED THE GUY WENT THROUGH CUSTOMS.
THE LAST KNOWN ADDRESS. JUST FOR YOU.
YOU'RE A DOLL, CHUCK. BUT SO YOU KNOW...
... BLUE IS NOT A GOOD COLOR FOR YOU.

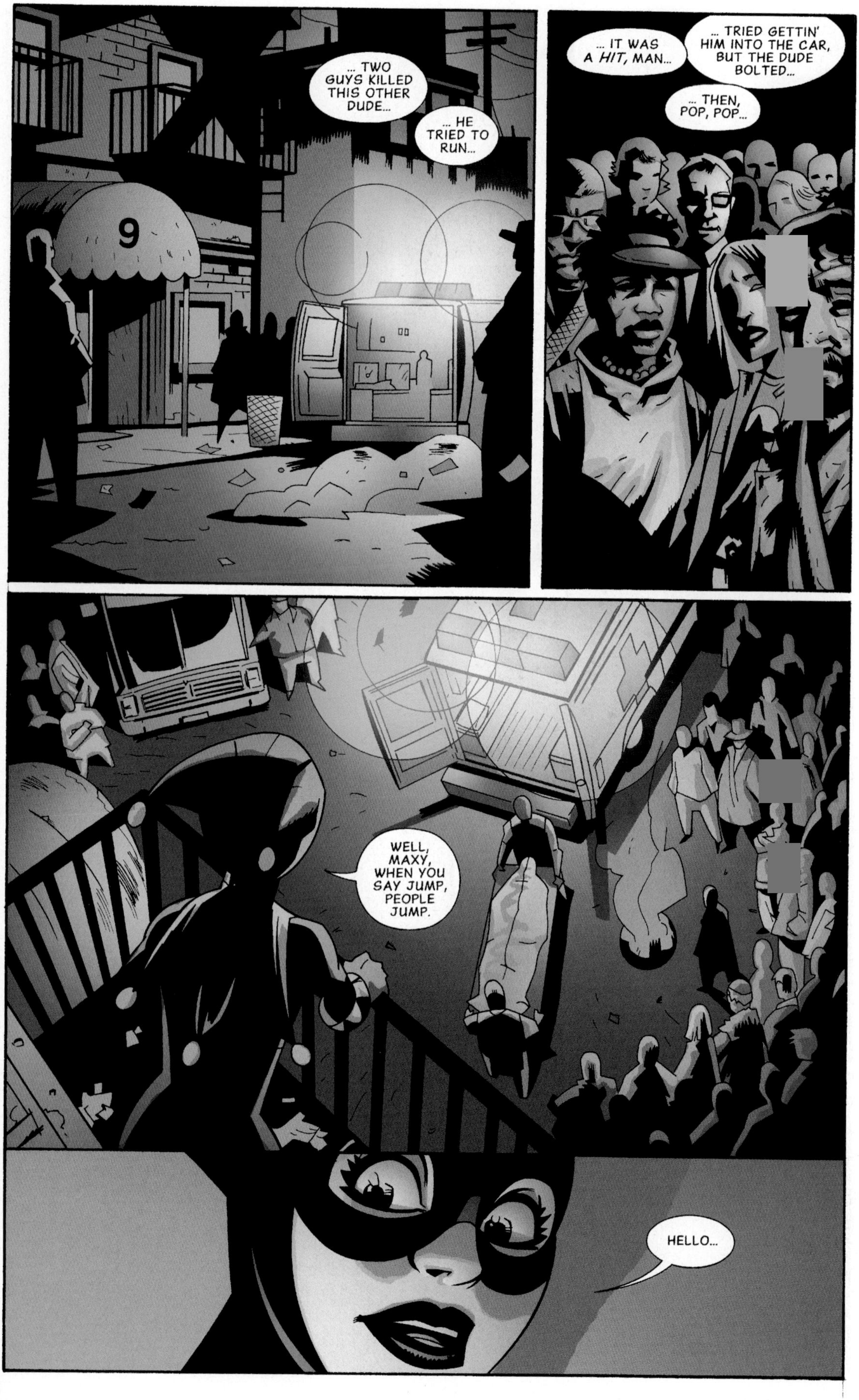
... TWO GUYS KILLED THIS OTHER DUDE...
... HE TRIED TO RUN...
... IT WAS A *HIT*, MAN...
... TRIED GETTIN' HIM INTO THE CAR, BUT THE DUDE BOLTED...
... THEN, POP, POP...
WELL, MAXY, WHEN YOU SAY JUMP, PEOPLE JUMP.
HELLO...

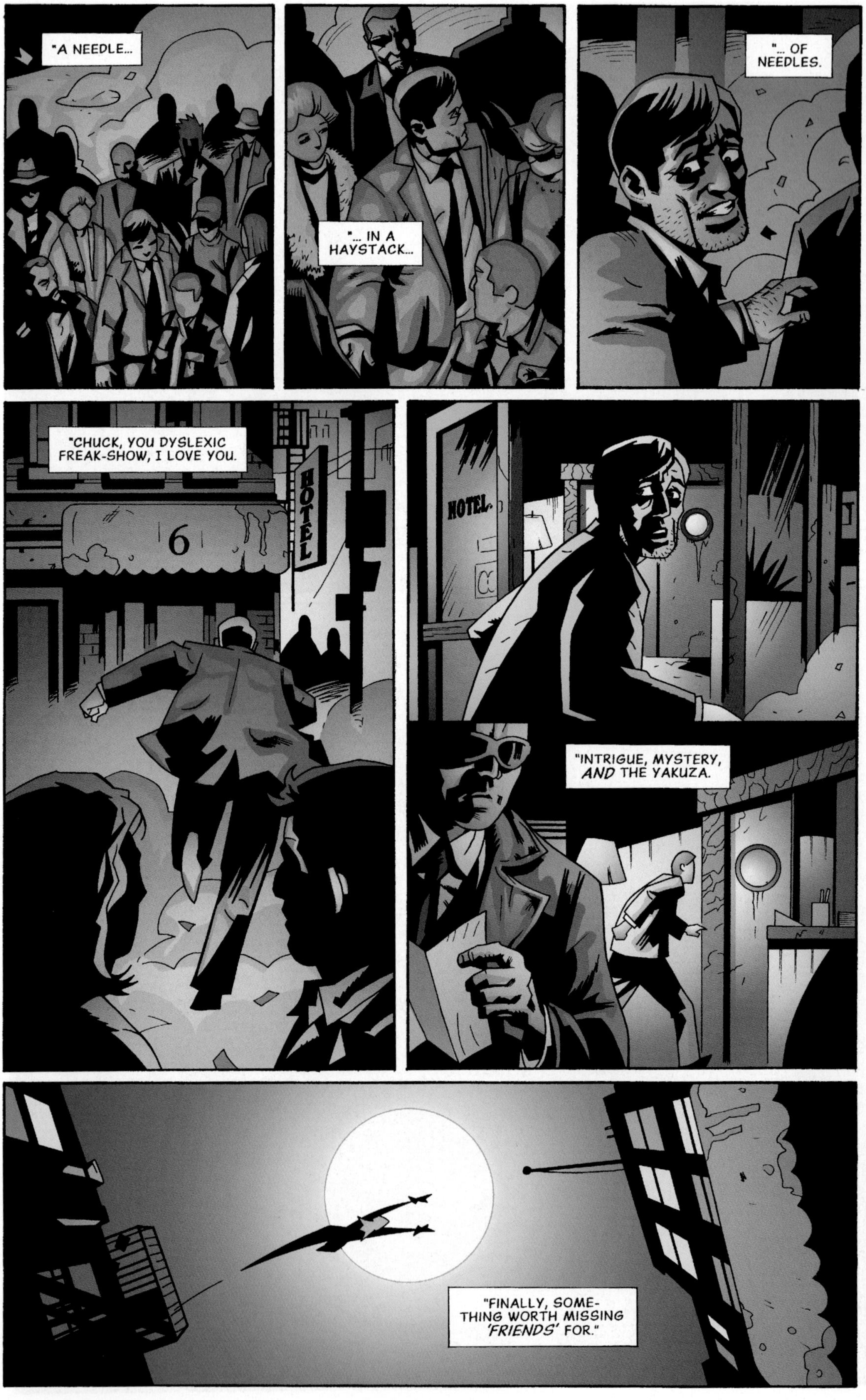
"A NEEDLE...
"... IN A HAYSTACK...
"... OF NEEDLES.
"CHUCK, YOU DYSLEXIC FREAK-SHOW, I LOVE YOU.
6
HOTEL
HOTEL
"INTRIGUE, MYSTERY, AND THE YAKUZA.
"FINALLY, SOME-THING WORTH MISSING 'FRIENDS' FOR."

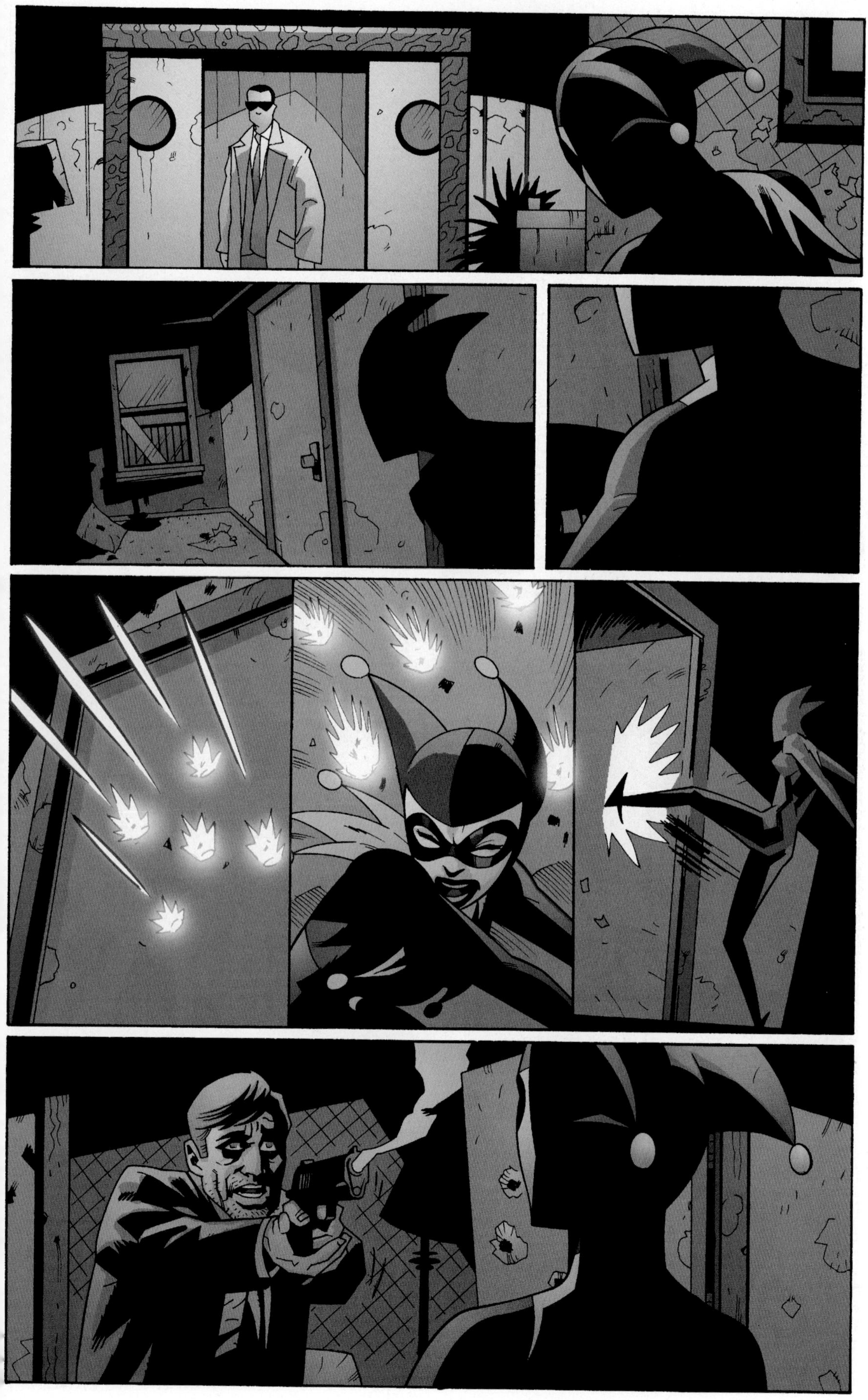

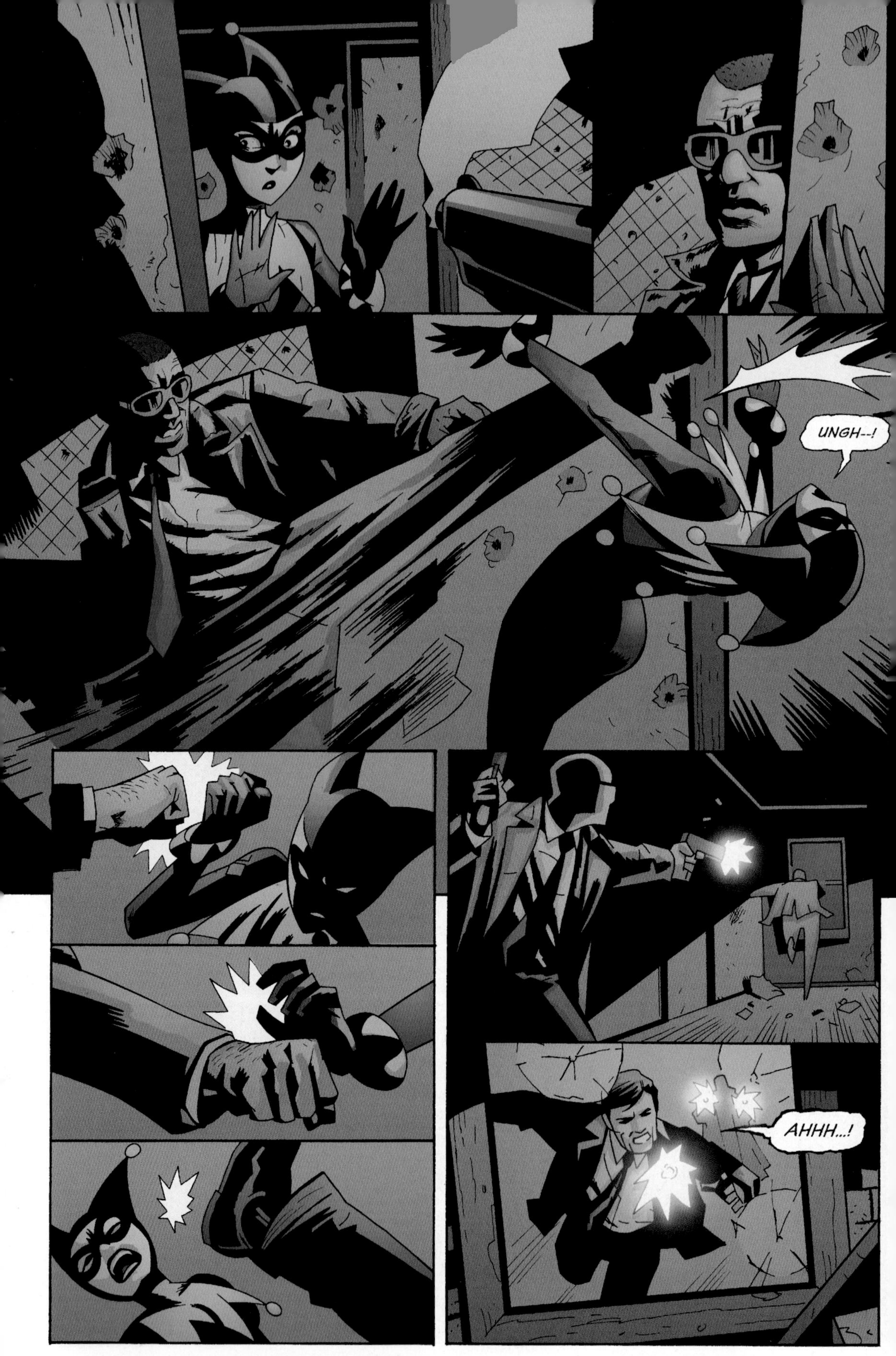
UNGH--!
AHHH...!

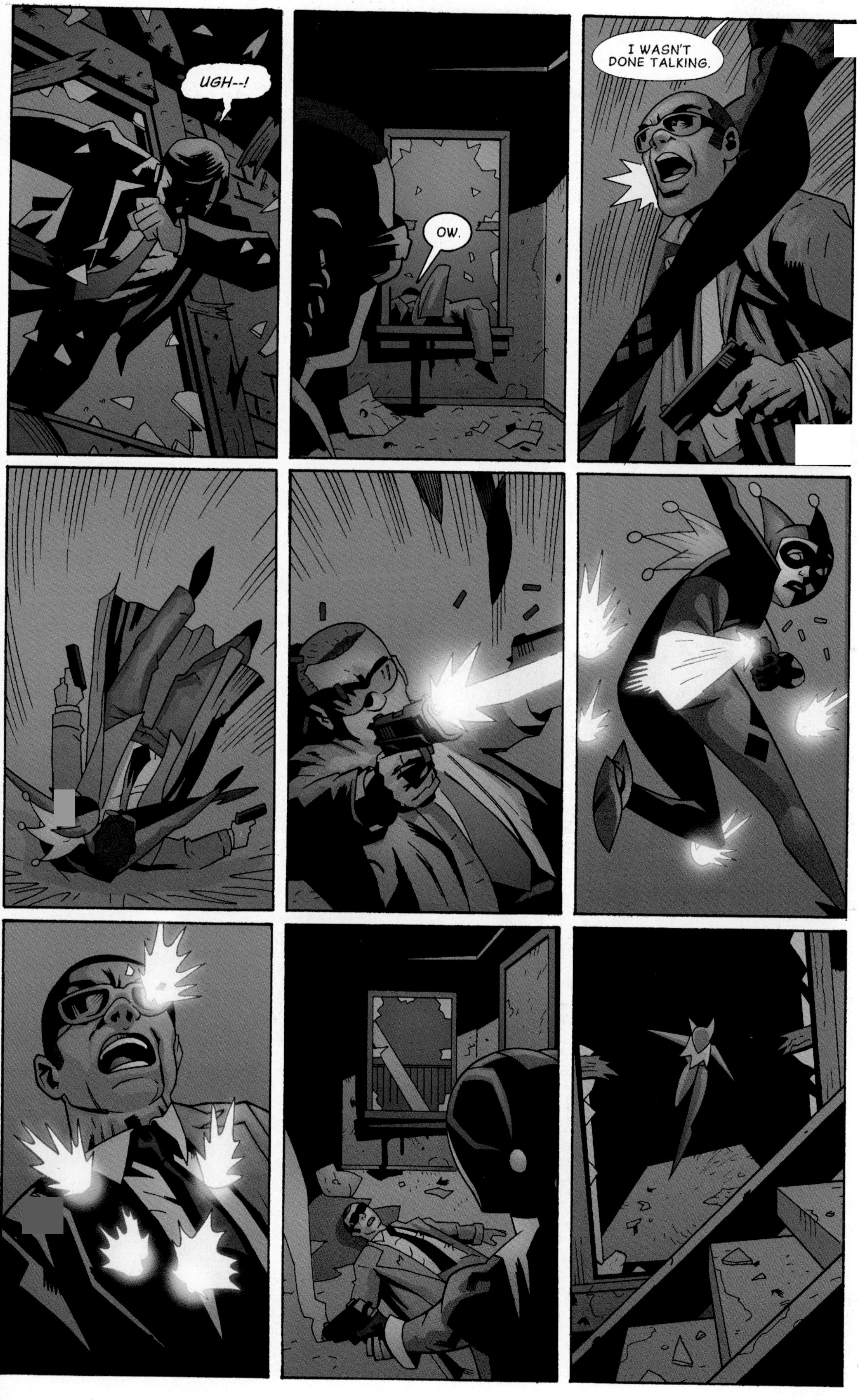
UGH--!
OW.
I WASN'T DONE TALKING.

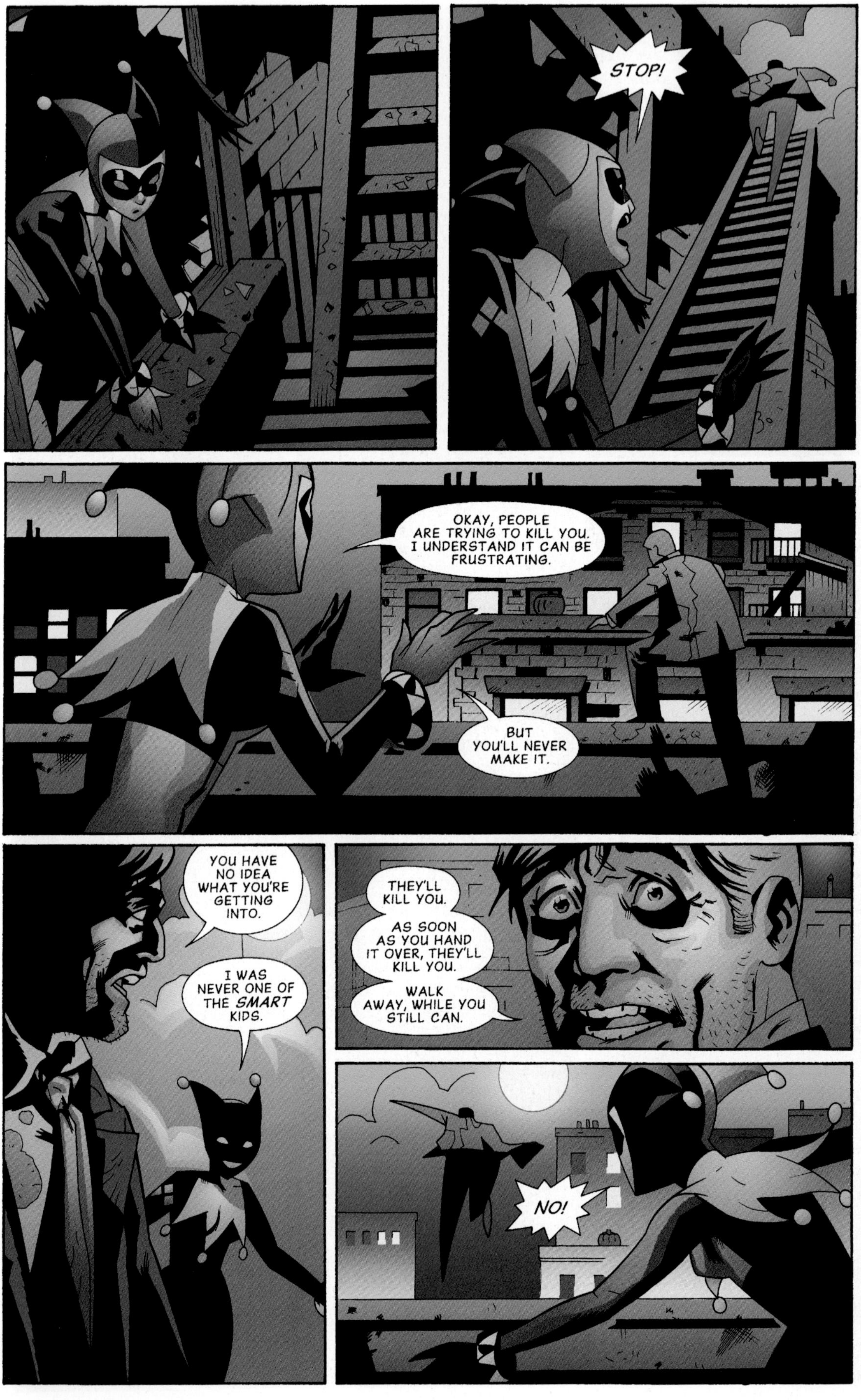
STOP!
OKAY, PEOPLE ARE TRYING TO KILL YOU. I UNDERSTAND IT CAN BE FRUSTRATING.
BUT YOU'LL NEVER MAKE IT.
YOU HAVE NO IDEA WHAT YOU'RE GETTING INTO.
I WAS NEVER ONE OF THE *SMART* KIDS.
THEY'LL KILL YOU.
AS SOON AS YOU HAND IT OVER, THEY'LL KILL YOU.
WALK AWAY, WHILE YOU STILL CAN.
NO!

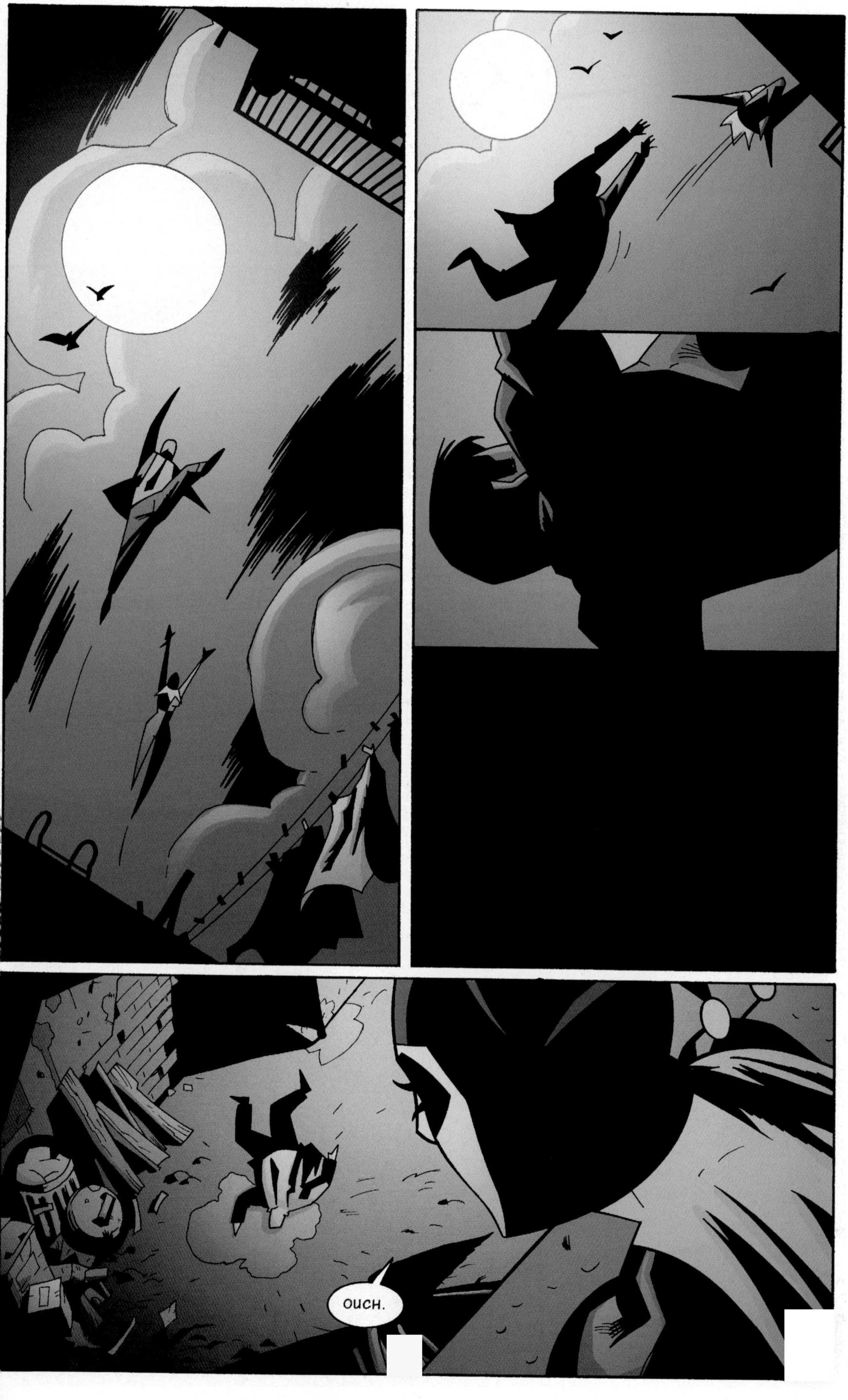
OUCH.

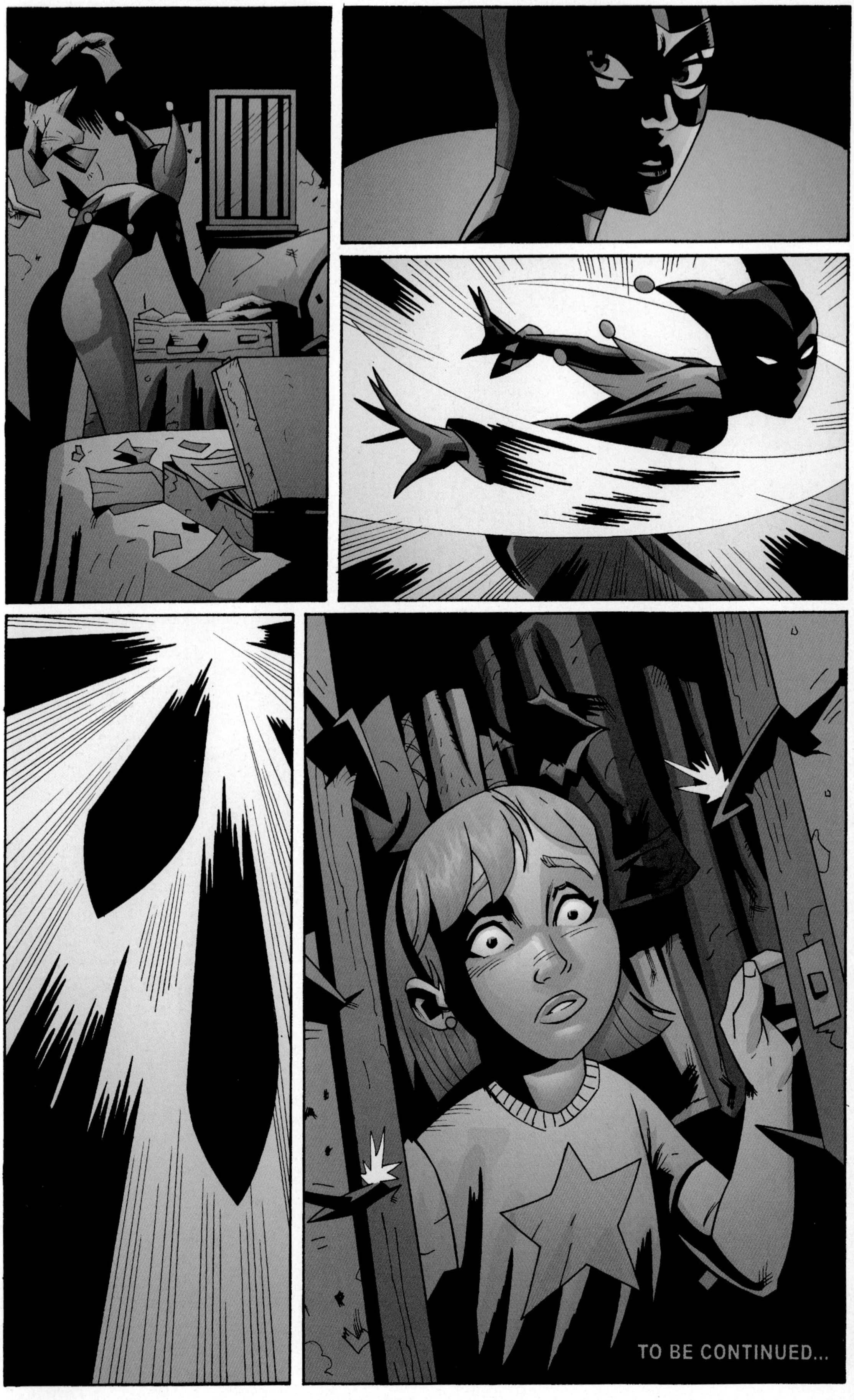
TO BE CONTINUED...

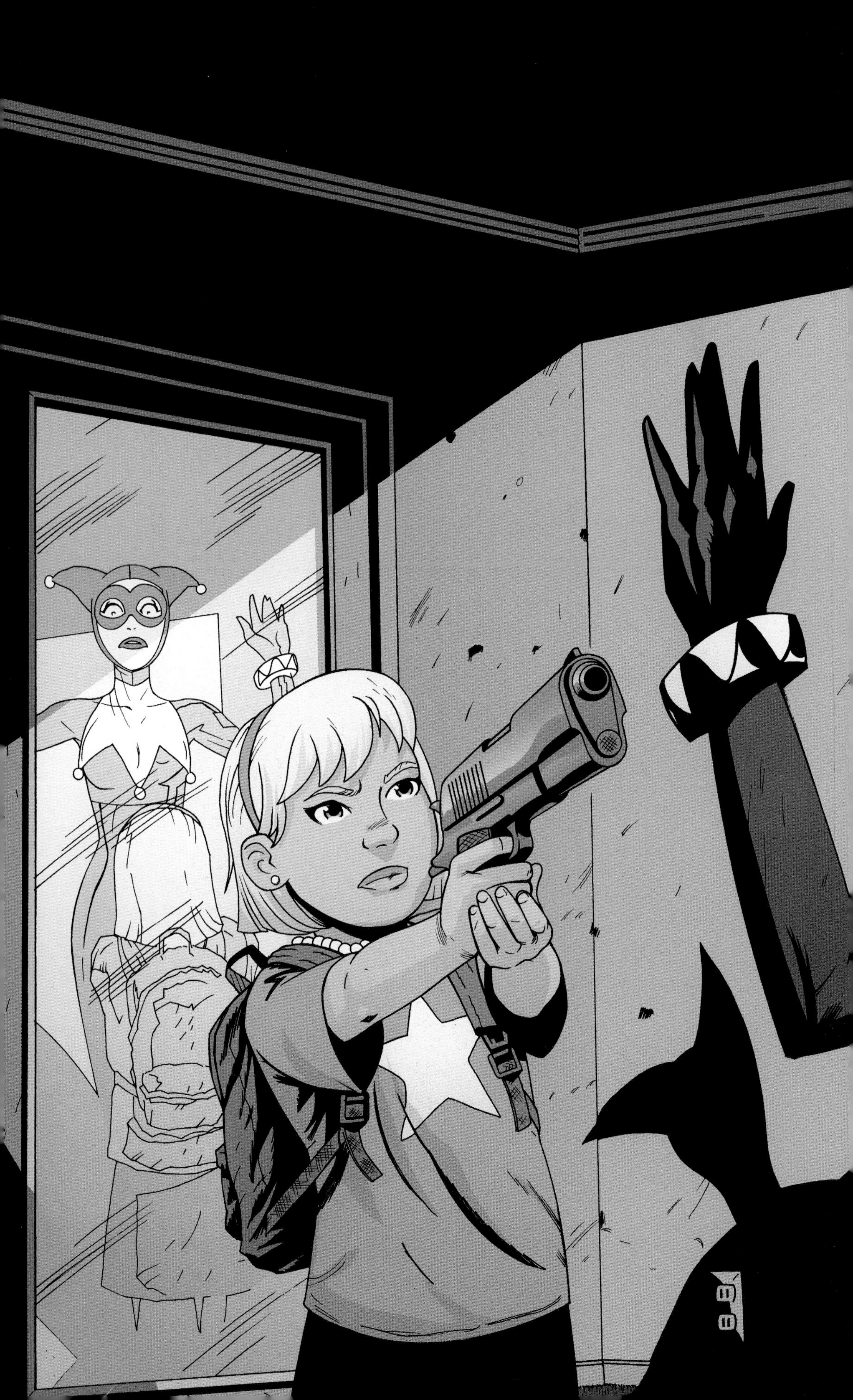

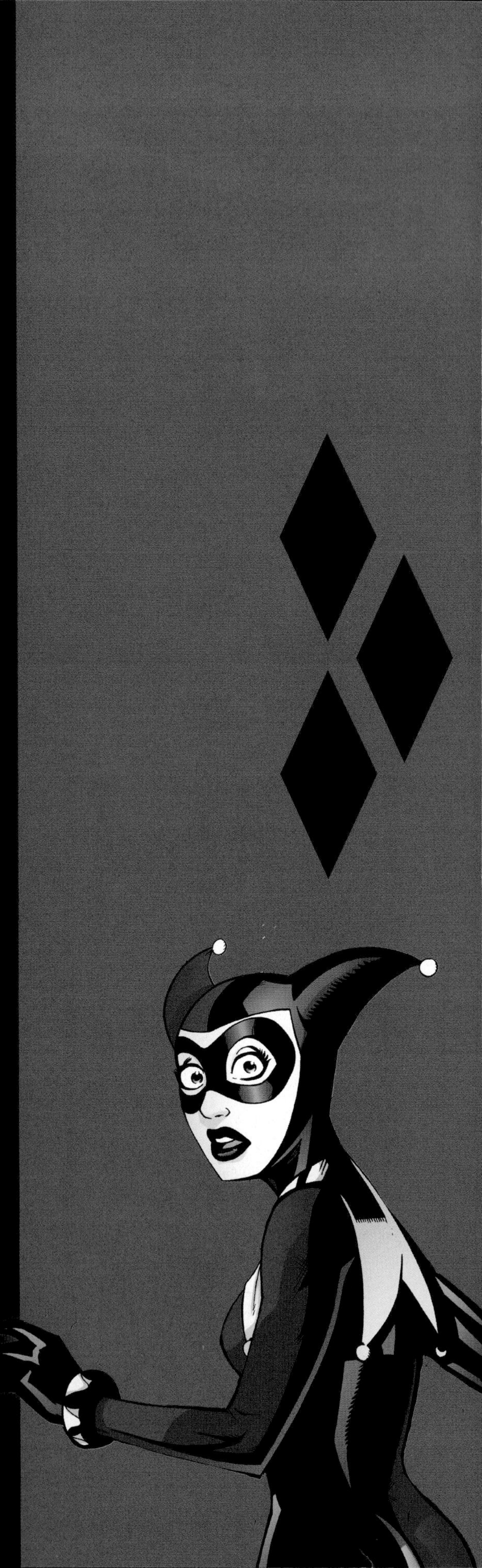

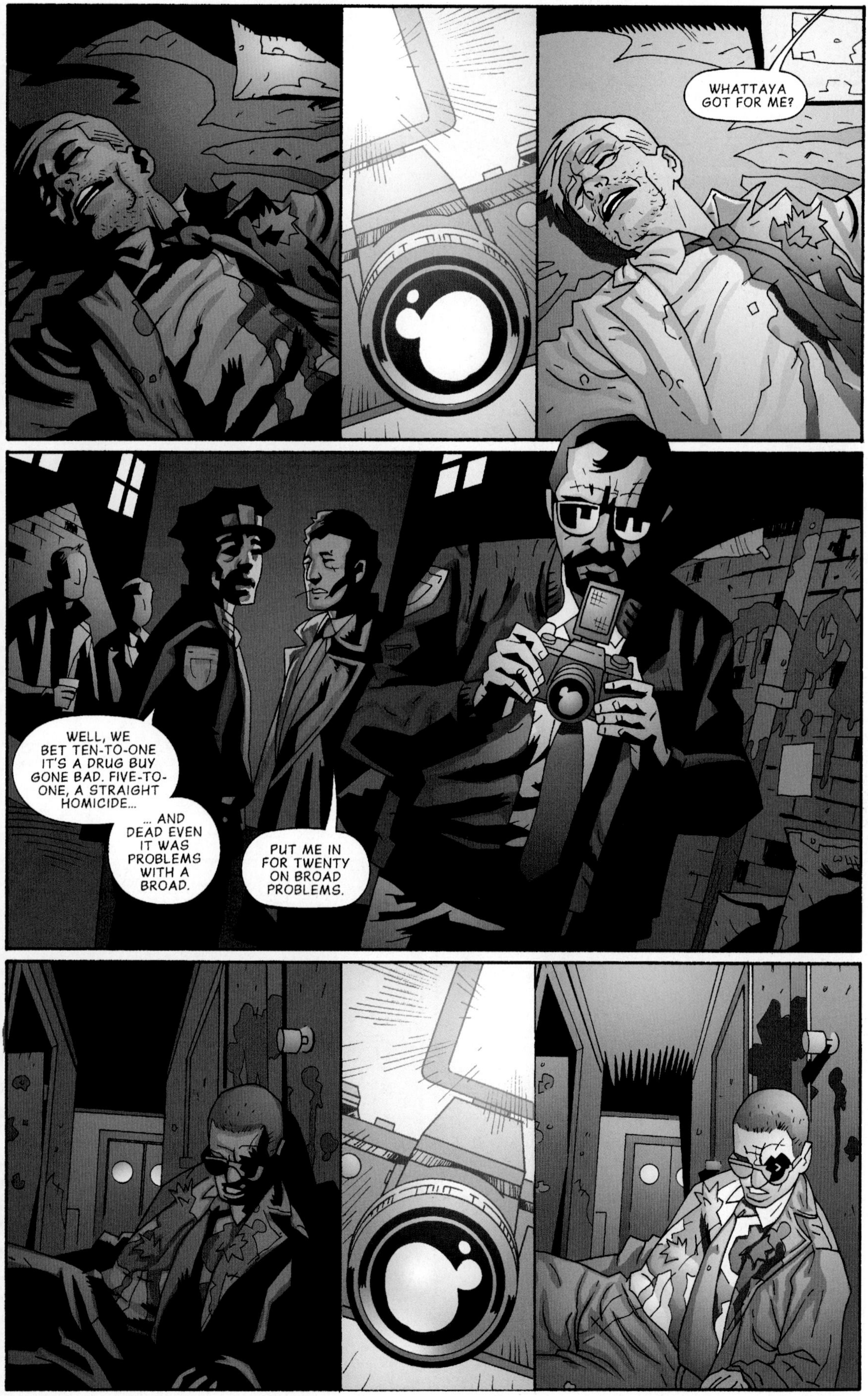
WHATTAYA GOT FOR ME?
WELL, WE BET TEN-TO-ONE IT'S A DRUG BUY GONE BAD. FIVE-TO-ONE, A STRAIGHT HOMICIDE...
... AND DEAD EVEN IT WAS PROBLEMS WITH A BROAD.
PUT ME IN FOR TWENTY ON BROAD PROBLEMS.

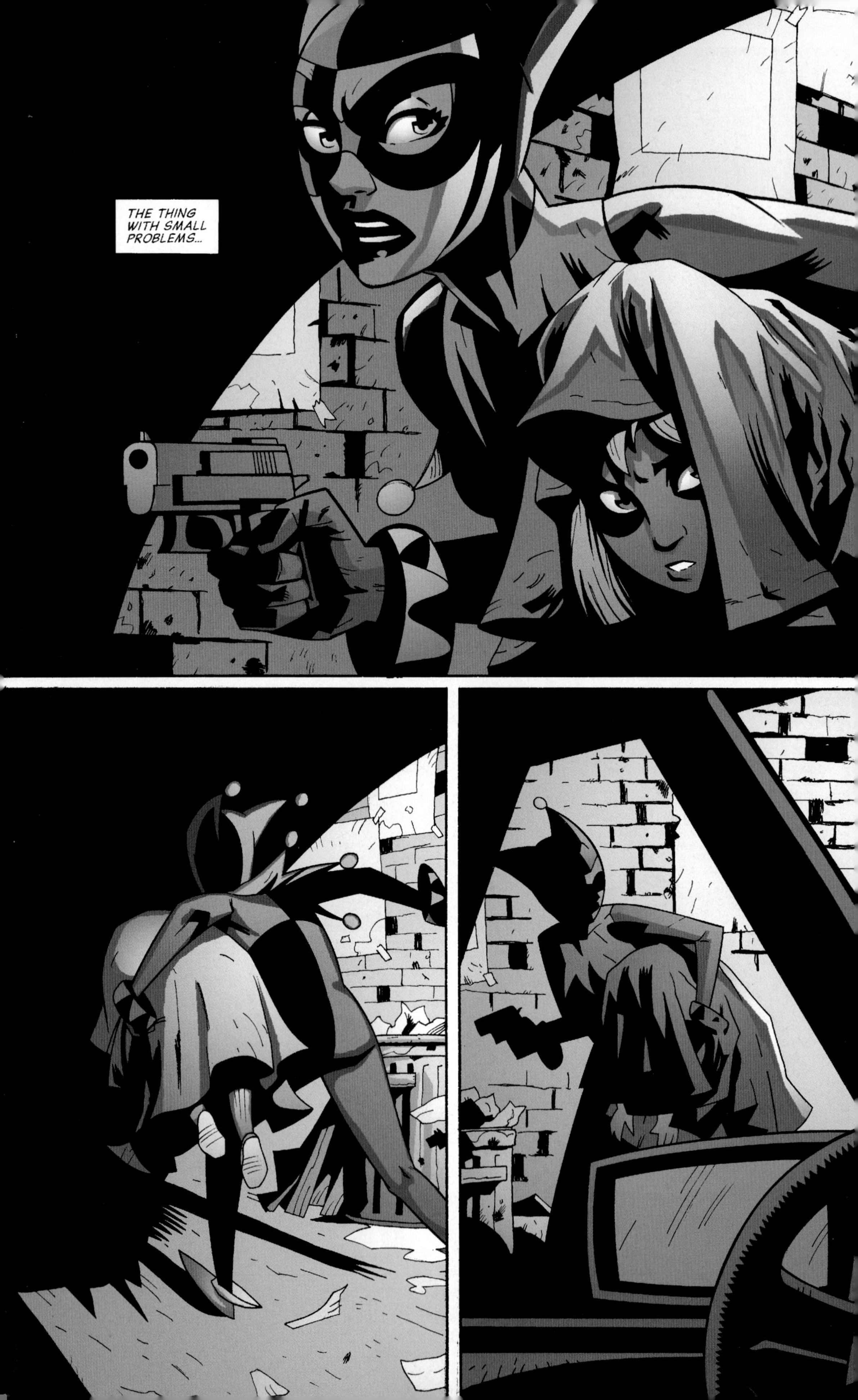
THE THING WITH SMALL PROBLEMS...

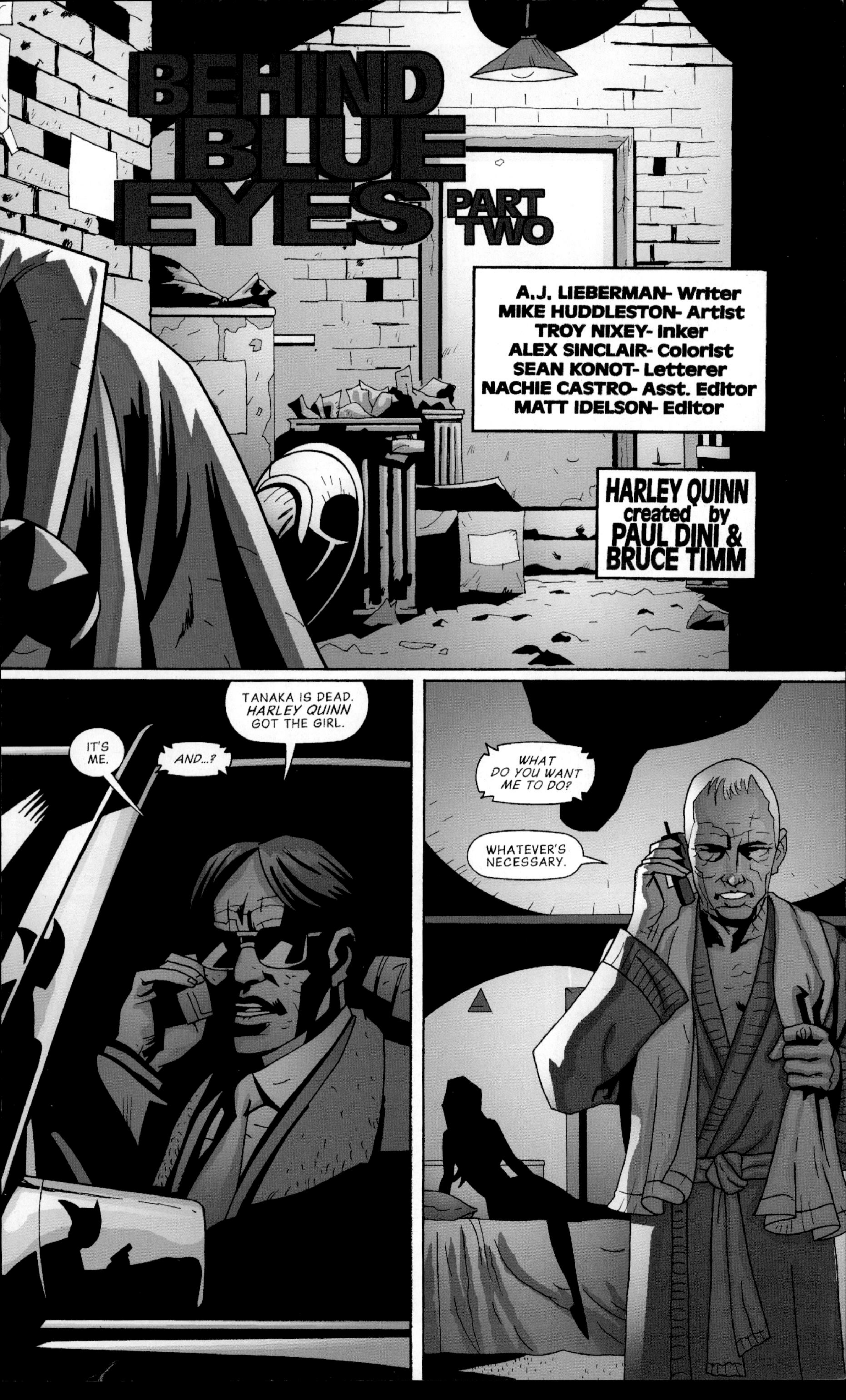
BEHIND BLUE EYES PART TWO
A.J. LIEBERMAN- Writer
MIKE HUDDLESTON- Artist
TROY NIXEY- Inker
ALEX SINCLAIR- Colorist
SEAN KONOT- Letterer
NACHIE CASTRO- Asst. Editor
MATT IDELSON- Editor
HARLEY QUINN created by PAUL DINI & BRUCE TIMM
IT'S ME.
AND...?
TANAKA IS DEAD. HARLEY QUINN GOT THE GIRL.
WHAT DO YOU WANT ME TO DO?
WHATEVER'S NECESSARY.

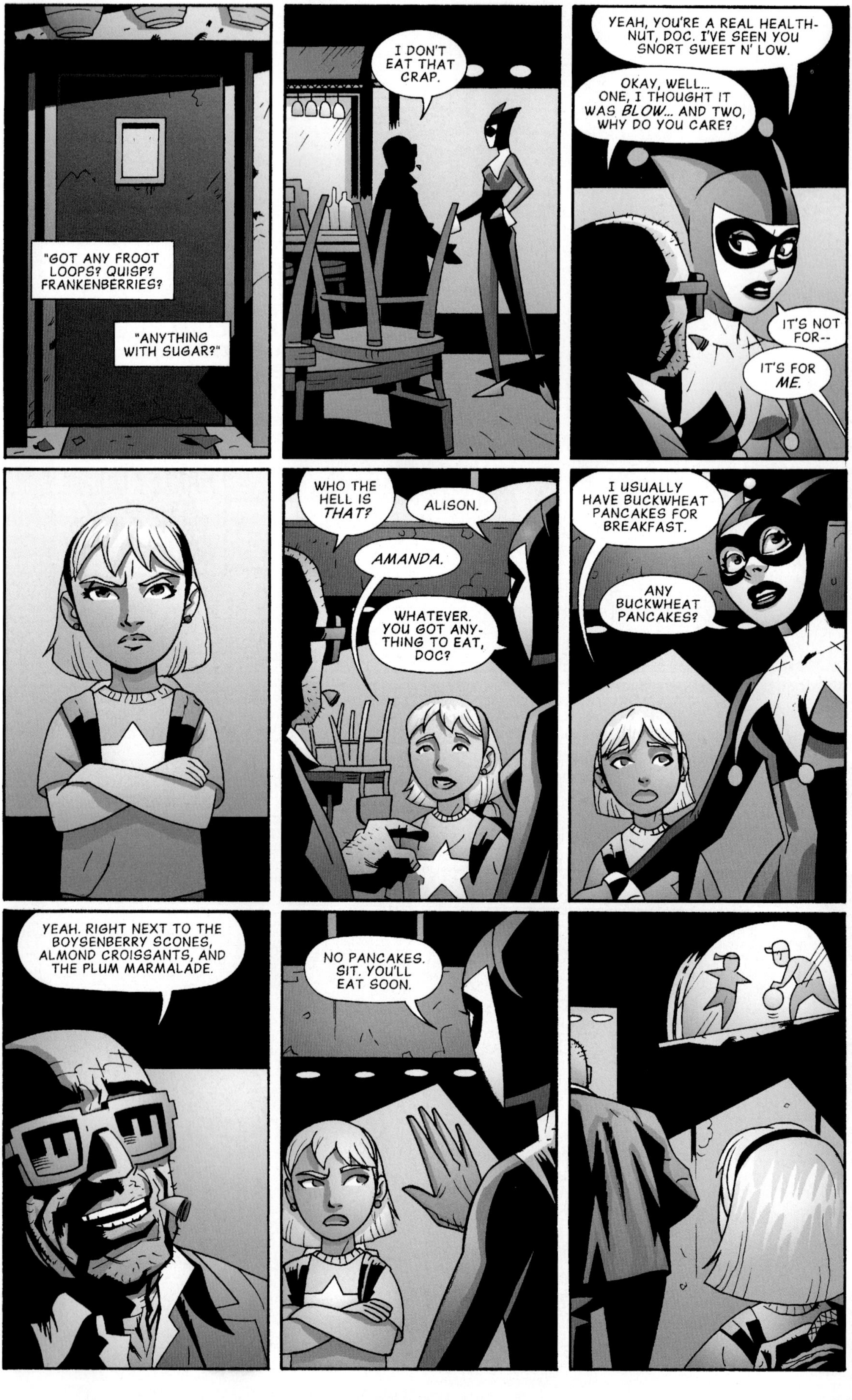
"GOT ANY FROOT LOOPS? QUISP? FRANKENBERRIES?
"ANYTHING WITH SUGAR?"
I DON'T EAT THAT CRAP.
YEAH, YOU'RE A REAL HEALTH-NUT, DOC. I'VE SEEN YOU SNORT SWEET N' LOW.
OKAY, WELL... ONE, I THOUGHT IT WAS BLOW... AND TWO, WHY DO YOU CARE?
IT'S NOT FOR--
IT'S FOR ME.
WHO THE HELL IS THAT?
ALISON.
AMANDA.
WHATEVER. YOU GOT ANY-THING TO EAT, DOC?
I USUALLY HAVE BUCKWHEAT PANCAKES FOR BREAKFAST.
ANY BUCKWHEAT PANCAKES?
YEAH. RIGHT NEXT TO THE BOYSENBERRY SCONES, ALMOND CROISSANTS, AND THE PLUM MARMALADE.
NO PANCAKES. SIT. YOU'LL EAT SOON.

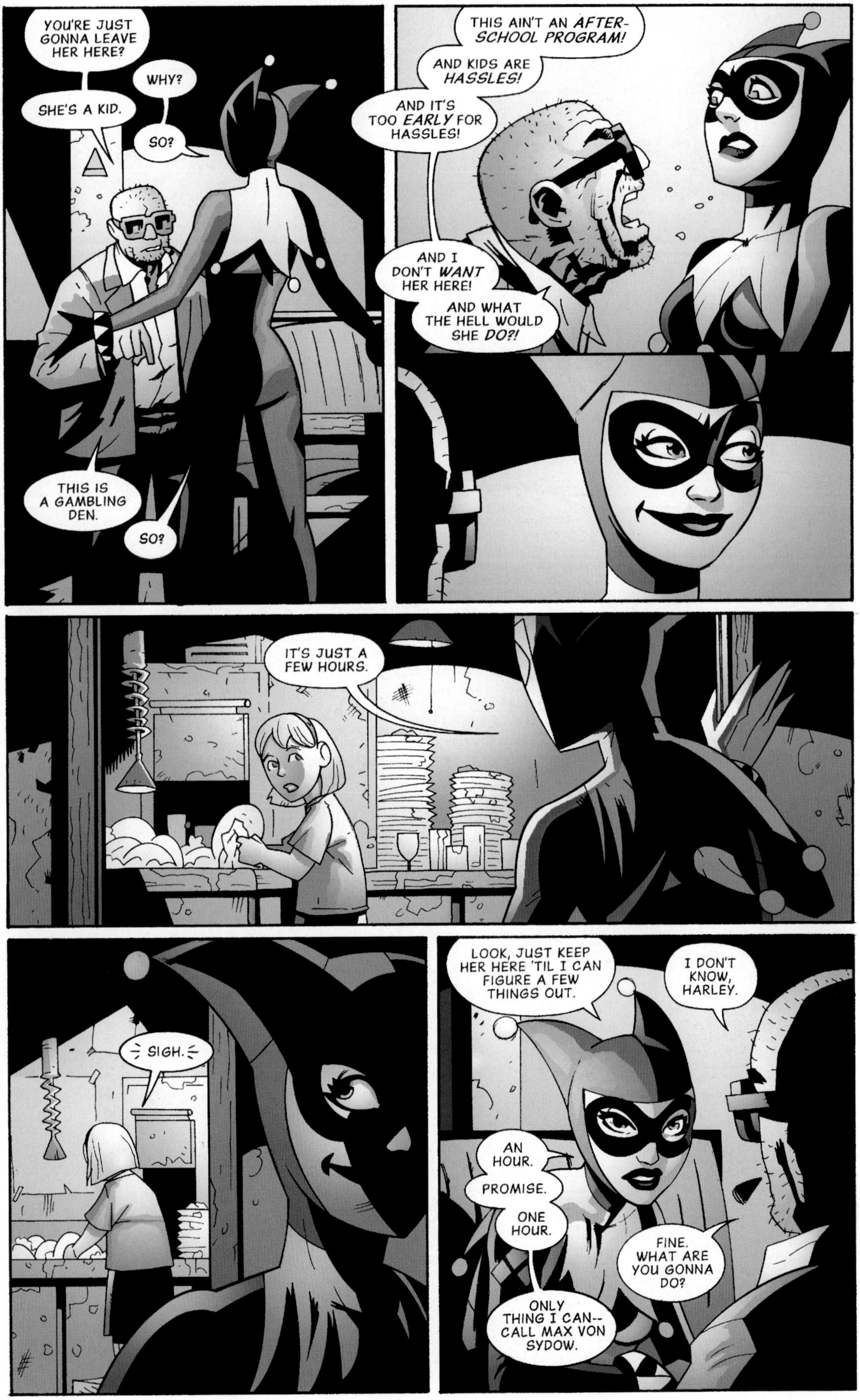
YOU'RE JUST GONNA LEAVE HER HERE?
WHY?
SHE'S A KID.
SO?
THIS IS A GAMBLING DEN.
SO?
THIS AIN'T AN AFTER-SCHOOL PROGRAM!
AND KIDS ARE HASSLES!
AND IT'S TOO EARLY FOR HASSLES!
AND I DON'T WANT HER HERE!
AND WHAT THE HELL WOULD SHE DO?!
IT'S JUST A FEW HOURS.
SIGH.
LOOK, JUST KEEP HER HERE 'TIL I CAN FIGURE A FEW THINGS OUT.
I DON'T KNOW, HARLEY.
AN HOUR.
PROMISE.
ONE HOUR.
FINE. WHAT ARE YOU GONNA DO?
ONLY THING I CAN-- CALL MAX VON SYDOW.

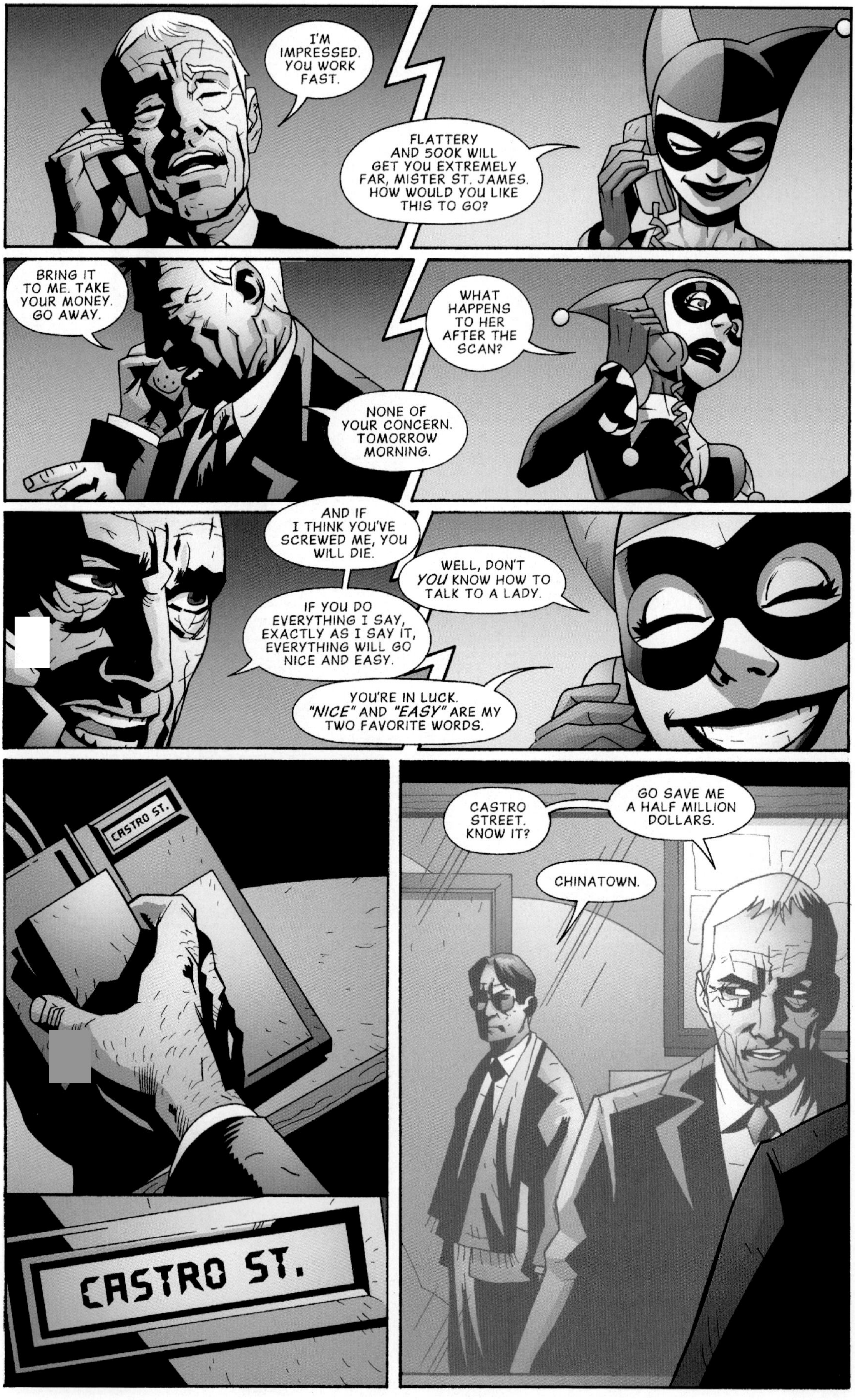
I'M IMPRESSED. YOU WORK FAST.
FLATTERY AND 500K WILL GET YOU EXTREMELY FAR, MISTER ST. JAMES. HOW WOULD YOU LIKE THIS TO GO?
BRING IT TO ME. TAKE YOUR MONEY. GO AWAY.
WHAT HAPPENS TO HER AFTER THE SCAN?
NONE OF YOUR CONCERN. TOMORROW MORNING.
AND IF I THINK YOU'VE SCREWED ME, YOU WILL DIE.
WELL, DON'T *YOU* KNOW HOW TO TALK TO A LADY.
IF YOU DO EVERYTHING I SAY, EXACTLY AS I SAY IT, EVERYTHING WILL GO NICE AND EASY.
YOU'RE IN LUCK. *"NICE"* AND *"EASY"* ARE MY TWO FAVORITE WORDS.
CASTRO ST.
CASTRO ST.
CASTRO STREET. KNOW IT?
CHINATOWN.
GO SAVE ME A HALF MILLION DOLLARS.

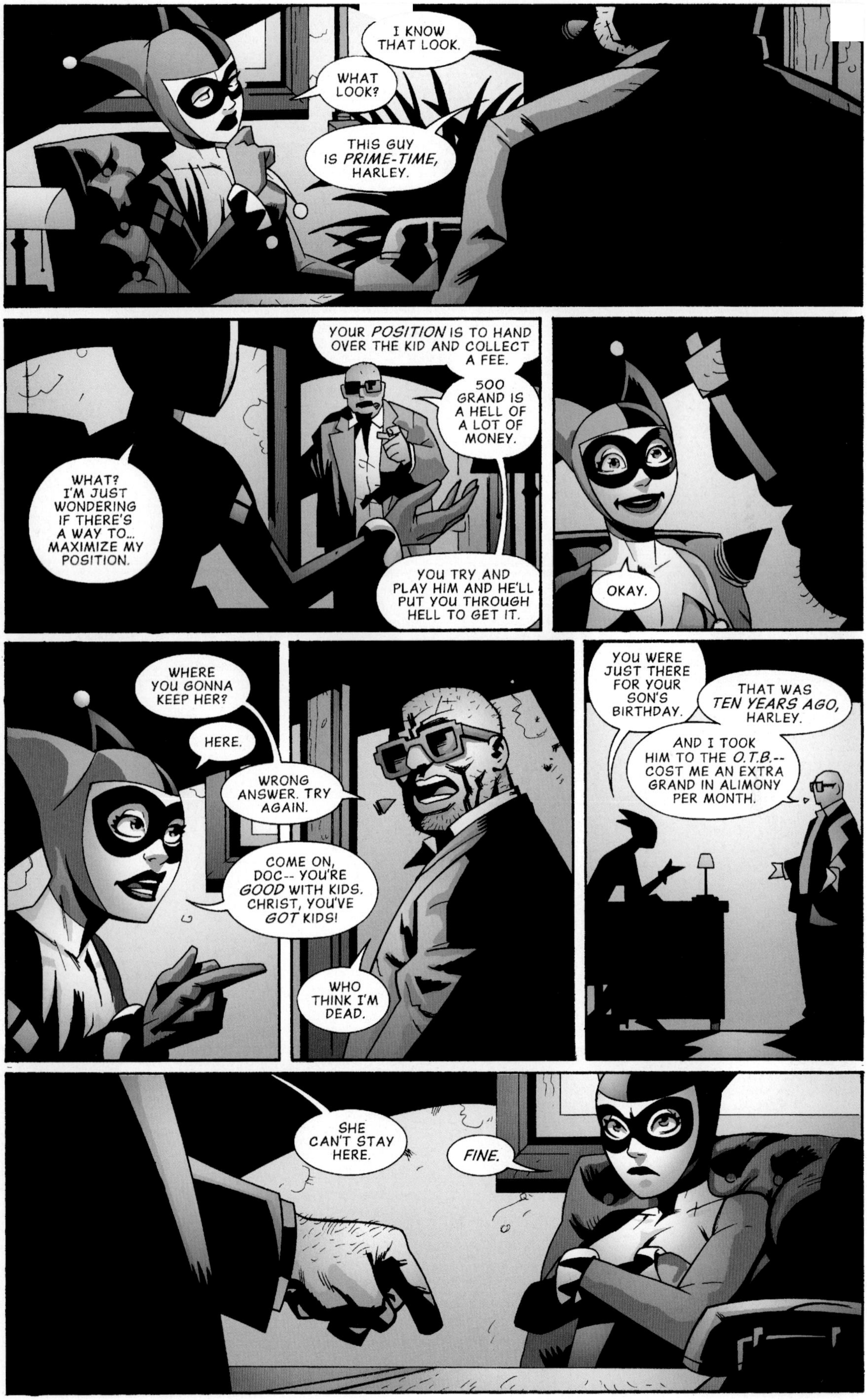
I KNOW THAT LOOK.
WHAT LOOK?
THIS GUY IS PRIME-TIME, HARLEY.
YOUR POSITION IS TO HAND OVER THE KID AND COLLECT A FEE.
500 GRAND IS A HELL OF A LOT OF MONEY.
WHAT? I'M JUST WONDERING IF THERE'S A WAY TO... MAXIMIZE MY POSITION.
YOU TRY AND PLAY HIM AND HE'LL PUT YOU THROUGH HELL TO GET IT.
OKAY.
WHERE YOU GONNA KEEP HER?
HERE.
WRONG ANSWER. TRY AGAIN.
COME ON, DOC-- YOU'RE GOOD WITH KIDS. CHRIST, YOU'VE GOT KIDS!
WHO THINK I'M DEAD.
YOU WERE JUST THERE FOR YOUR SON'S BIRTHDAY.
THAT WAS TEN YEARS AGO, HARLEY.
AND I TOOK HIM TO THE O.T.B.-- COST ME AN EXTRA GRAND IN ALIMONY PER MONTH.
SHE CAN'T STAY HERE.
FINE.

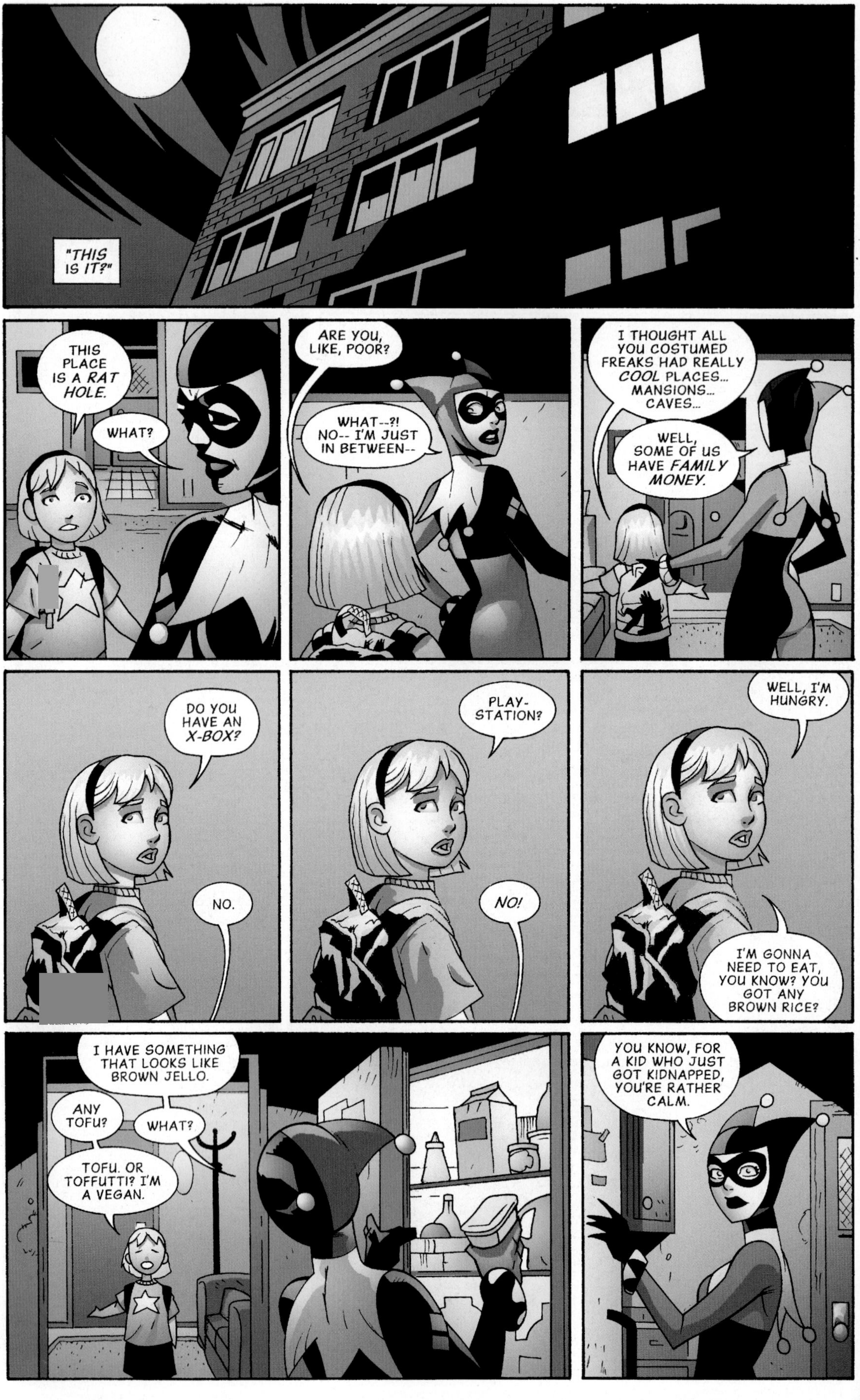
"THIS IS IT?"
THIS PLACE IS A RAT HOLE.
WHAT?
ARE YOU, LIKE, POOR?
WHAT--?! NO-- I'M JUST IN BETWEEN--
I THOUGHT ALL YOU COSTUMED FREAKS HAD REALLY COOL PLACES... MANSIONS... CAVES...
WELL, SOME OF US HAVE FAMILY MONEY.
DO YOU HAVE AN X-BOX?
NO.
PLAY-STATION?
NO!
WELL, I'M HUNGRY.
I'M GONNA NEED TO EAT, YOU KNOW? YOU GOT ANY BROWN RICE?
I HAVE SOMETHING THAT LOOKS LIKE BROWN JELLO.
ANY TOFU?
WHAT?
TOFU. OR TOFFUTTI? I'M A VEGAN.
YOU KNOW, FOR A KID WHO JUST GOT KIDNAPPED, YOU'RE RATHER CALM.

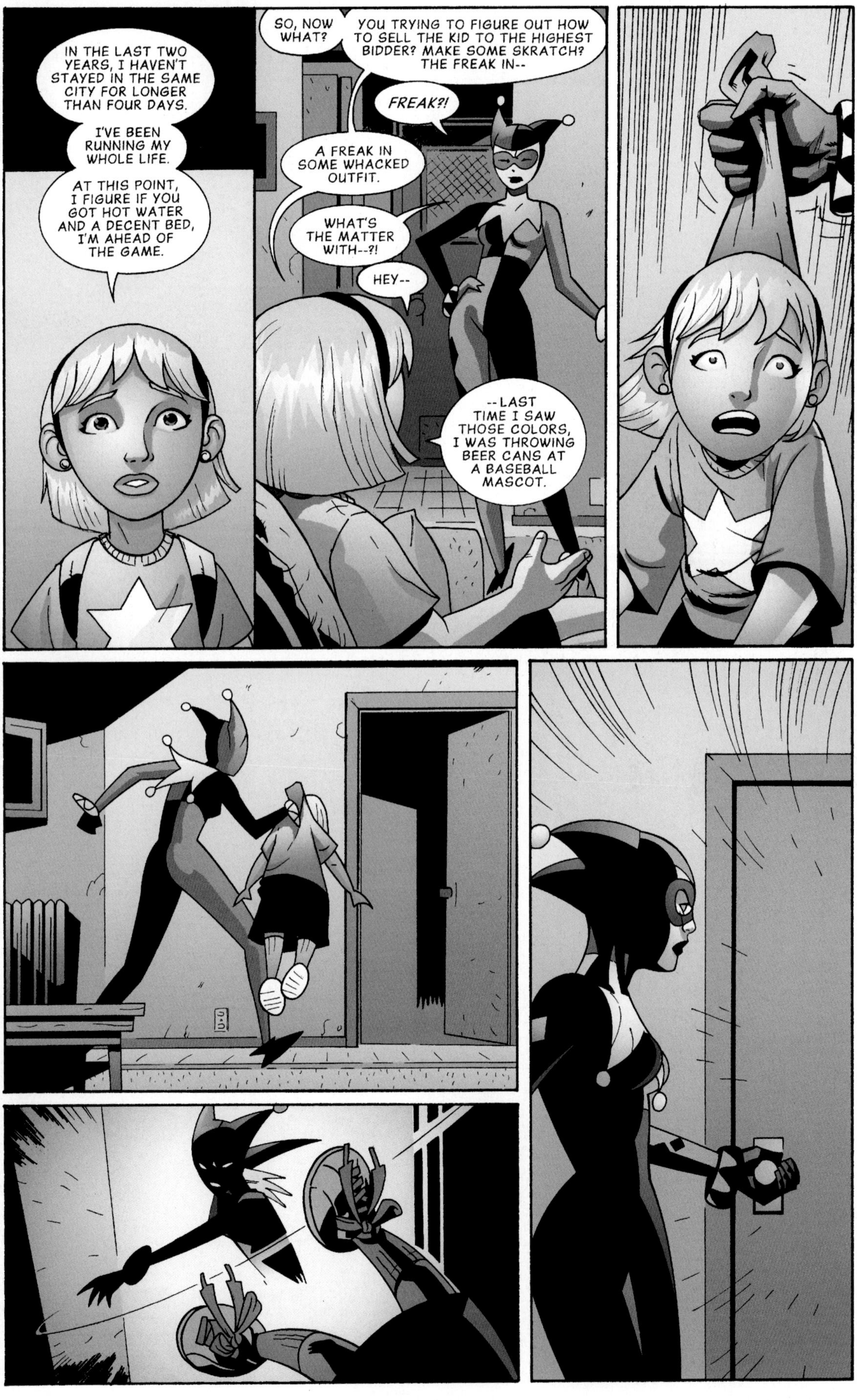
IN THE LAST TWO YEARS, I HAVEN'T STAYED IN THE SAME CITY FOR LONGER THAN FOUR DAYS.
I'VE BEEN RUNNING MY WHOLE LIFE.
AT THIS POINT, I FIGURE IF YOU GOT HOT WATER AND A DECENT BED, I'M AHEAD OF THE GAME.
SO, NOW WHAT?
YOU TRYING TO FIGURE OUT HOW TO SELL THE KID TO THE HIGHEST BIDDER? MAKE SOME SKRATCH? THE FREAK IN--
FREAK?!
A FREAK IN SOME WHACKED OUTFIT.
WHAT'S THE MATTER WITH--?!
HEY--
--LAST TIME I SAW THOSE COLORS, I WAS THROWING BEER CANS AT A BASEBALL MASCOT.

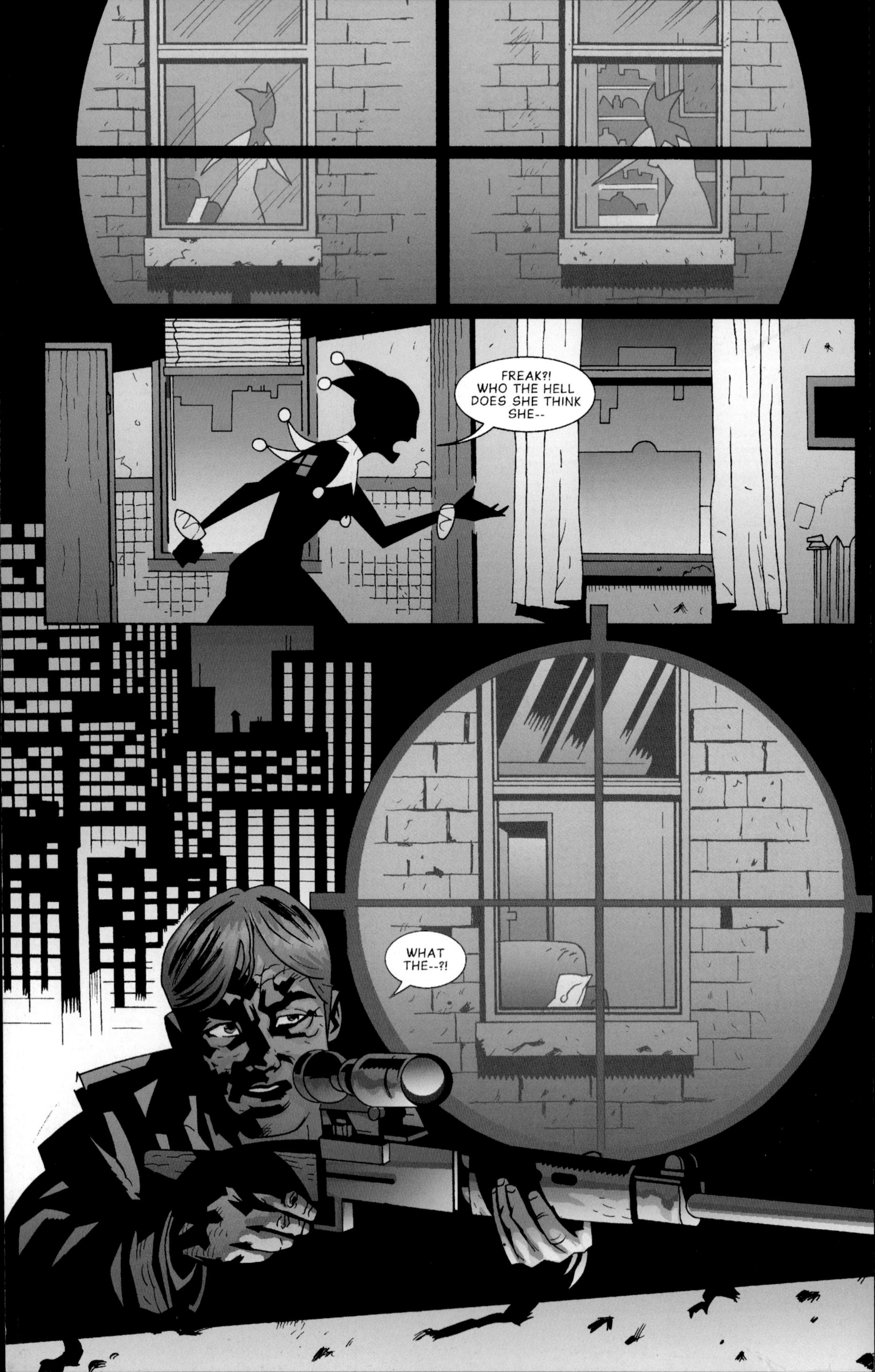
FREAK?! WHO THE HELL DOES SHE THINK SHE--
WHAT THE--?!

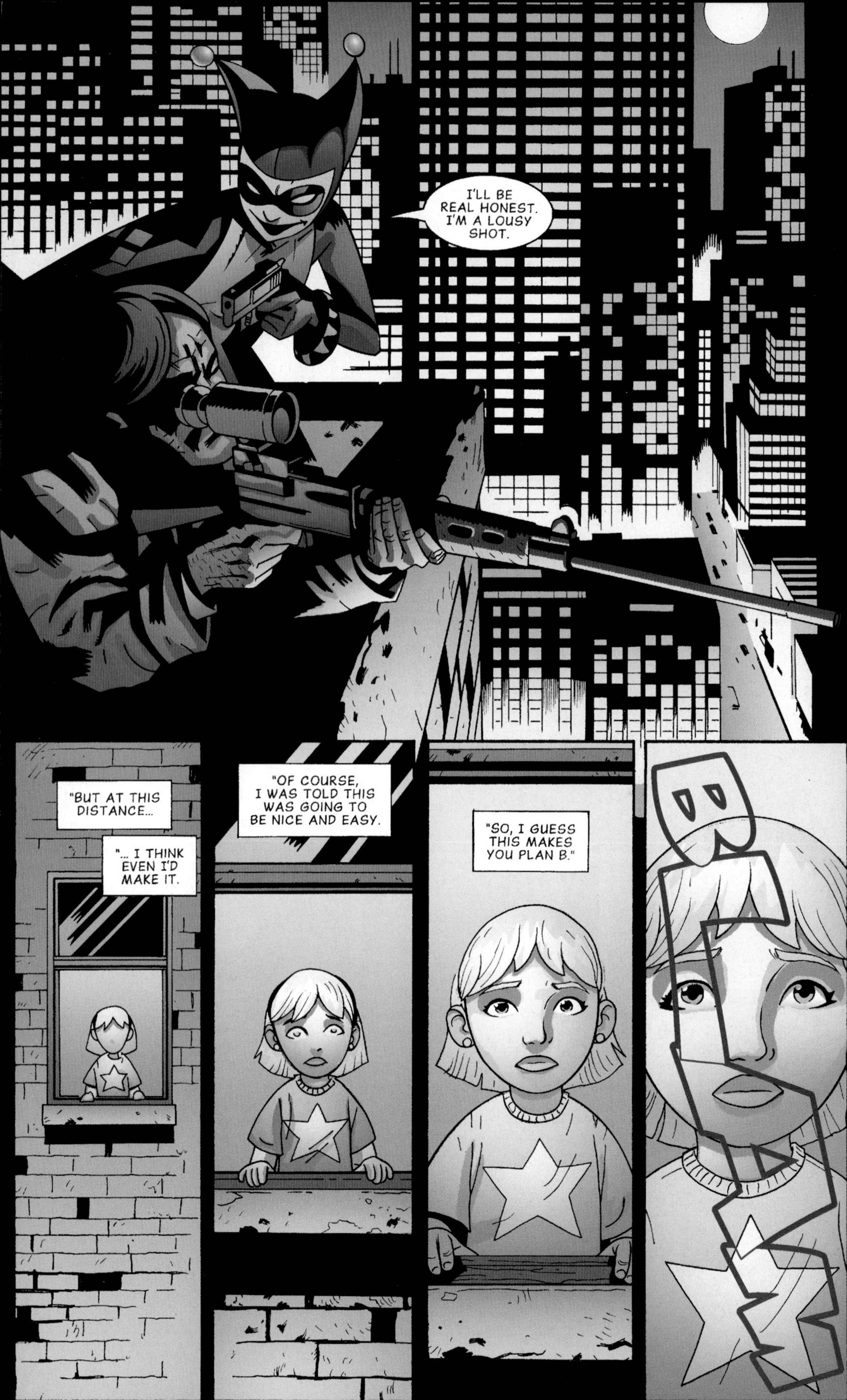
I'LL BE REAL HONEST. I'M A LOUSY SHOT.
"BUT AT THIS DISTANCE...
"... I THINK EVEN I'D MAKE IT.
"OF COURSE, I WAS TOLD THIS WAS GOING TO BE NICE AND EASY.
"SO, I GUESS THIS MAKES YOU PLAN B."

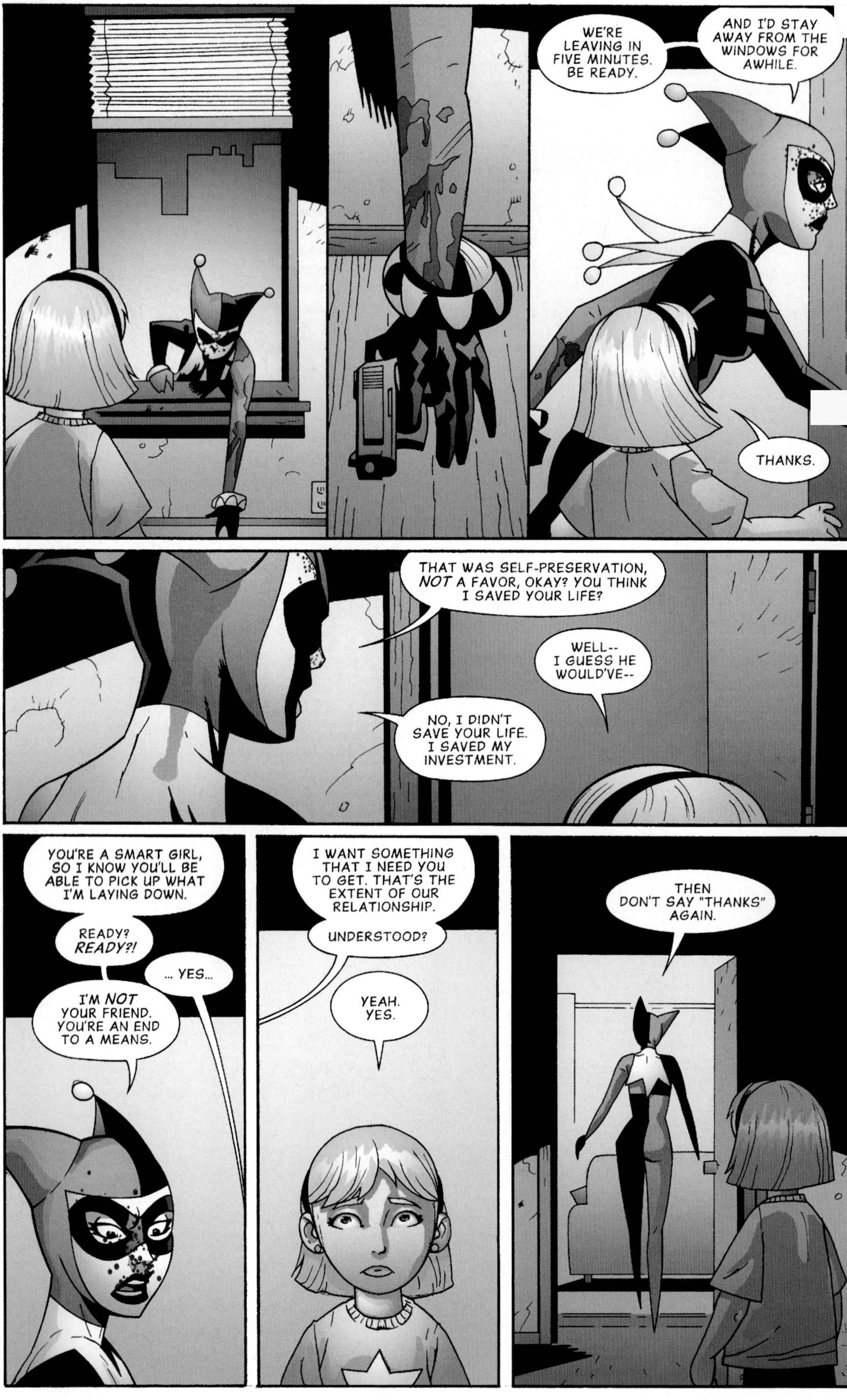
WE'RE LEAVING IN FIVE MINUTES. BE READY.
AND I'D STAY AWAY FROM THE WINDOWS FOR AWHILE.
THANKS.
THAT WAS SELF-PRESERVATION, *NOT* A FAVOR, OKAY? YOU THINK I SAVED YOUR LIFE?
WELL-- I GUESS HE WOULD'VE--
NO, I DIDN'T SAVE YOUR LIFE. I SAVED MY INVESTMENT.
YOU'RE A SMART GIRL, SO I KNOW YOU'LL BE ABLE TO PICK UP WHAT I'M LAYING DOWN.
READY? *READY?!*
... YES...
I'M *NOT* YOUR FRIEND. YOU'RE AN END TO A MEANS.
I WANT SOMETHING THAT I NEED YOU TO GET. THAT'S THE EXTENT OF OUR RELATIONSHIP.
UNDERSTOOD?
YEAH. YES.
THEN DON'T SAY "THANKS" AGAIN.

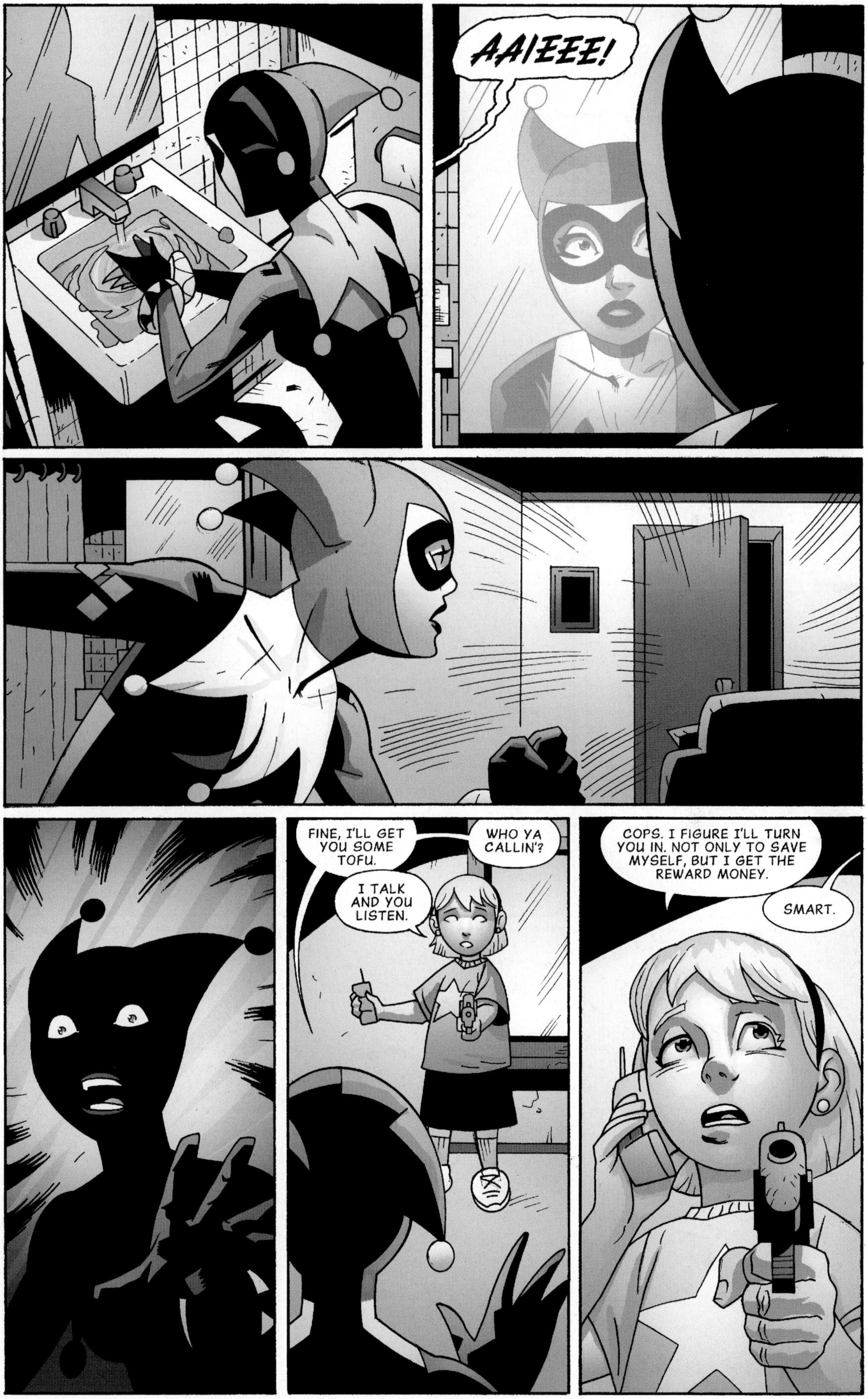
AAIEEE!
FINE, I'LL GET YOU SOME TOFU.
WHO YA CALLIN'?
I TALK AND YOU LISTEN.
COPS. I FIGURE I'LL TURN YOU IN. NOT ONLY TO SAVE MYSELF, BUT I GET THE REWARD MONEY.
SMART.

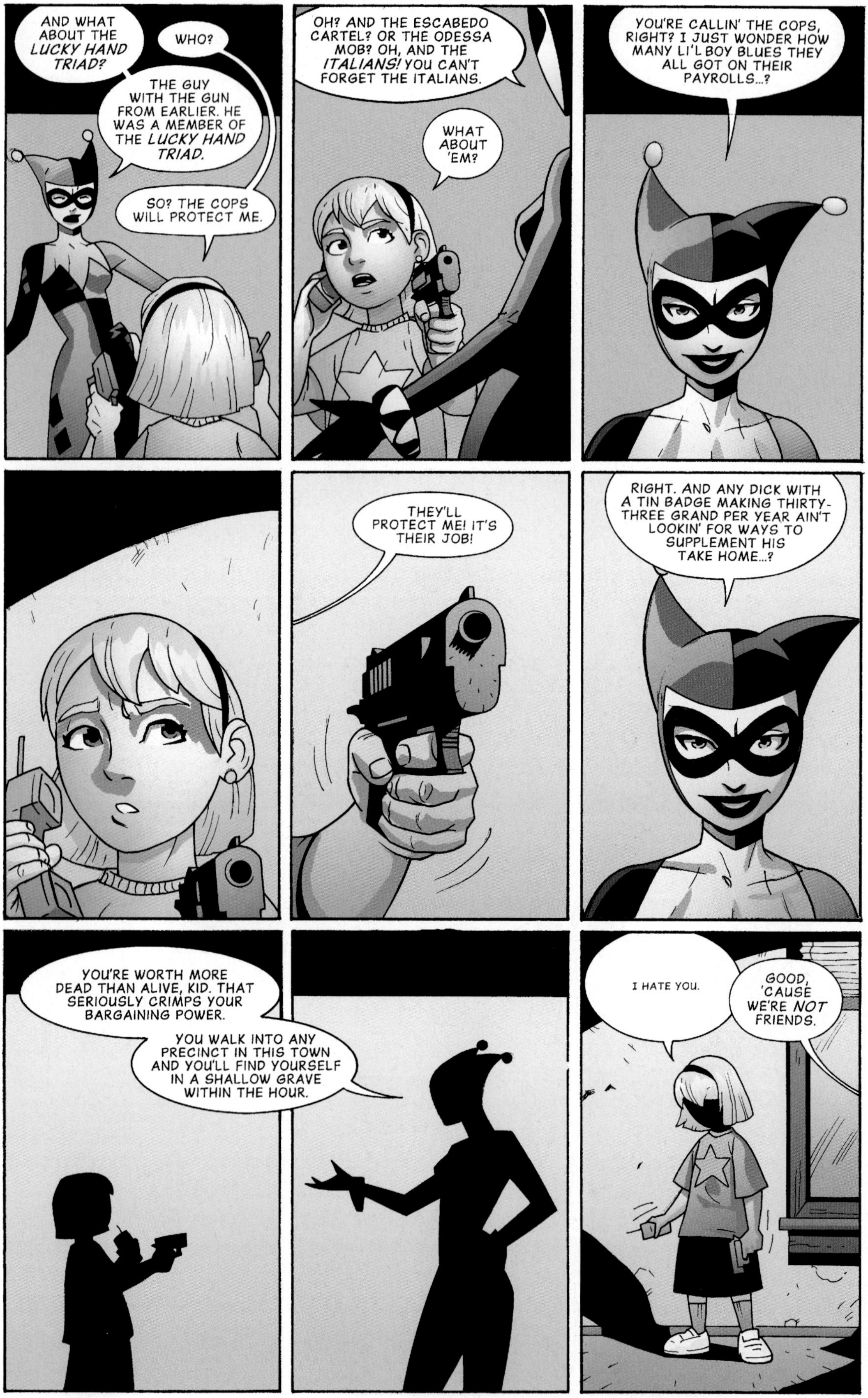
AND WHAT ABOUT THE LUCKY HAND TRIAD?
WHO?
THE GUY WITH THE GUN FROM EARLIER. HE WAS A MEMBER OF THE LUCKY HAND TRIAD.
SO? THE COPS WILL PROTECT ME.
OH? AND THE ESCABEDO CARTEL? OR THE ODESSA MOB? OH, AND THE ITALIANS! YOU CAN'T FORGET THE ITALIANS.
WHAT ABOUT 'EM?
YOU'RE CALLIN' THE COPS, RIGHT? I JUST WONDER HOW MANY LI'L BOY BLUES THEY ALL GOT ON THEIR PAYROLLS...?
THEY'LL PROTECT ME! IT'S THEIR JOB!
RIGHT. AND ANY DICK WITH A TIN BADGE MAKING THIRTY-THREE GRAND PER YEAR AIN'T LOOKIN' FOR WAYS TO SUPPLEMENT HIS TAKE HOME...?
YOU'RE WORTH MORE DEAD THAN ALIVE, KID. THAT SERIOUSLY CRIMPS YOUR BARGAINING POWER.
YOU WALK INTO ANY PRECINCT IN THIS TOWN AND YOU'LL FIND YOURSELF IN A SHALLOW GRAVE WITHIN THE HOUR.
I HATE YOU.
GOOD, 'CAUSE WE'RE NOT FRIENDS.

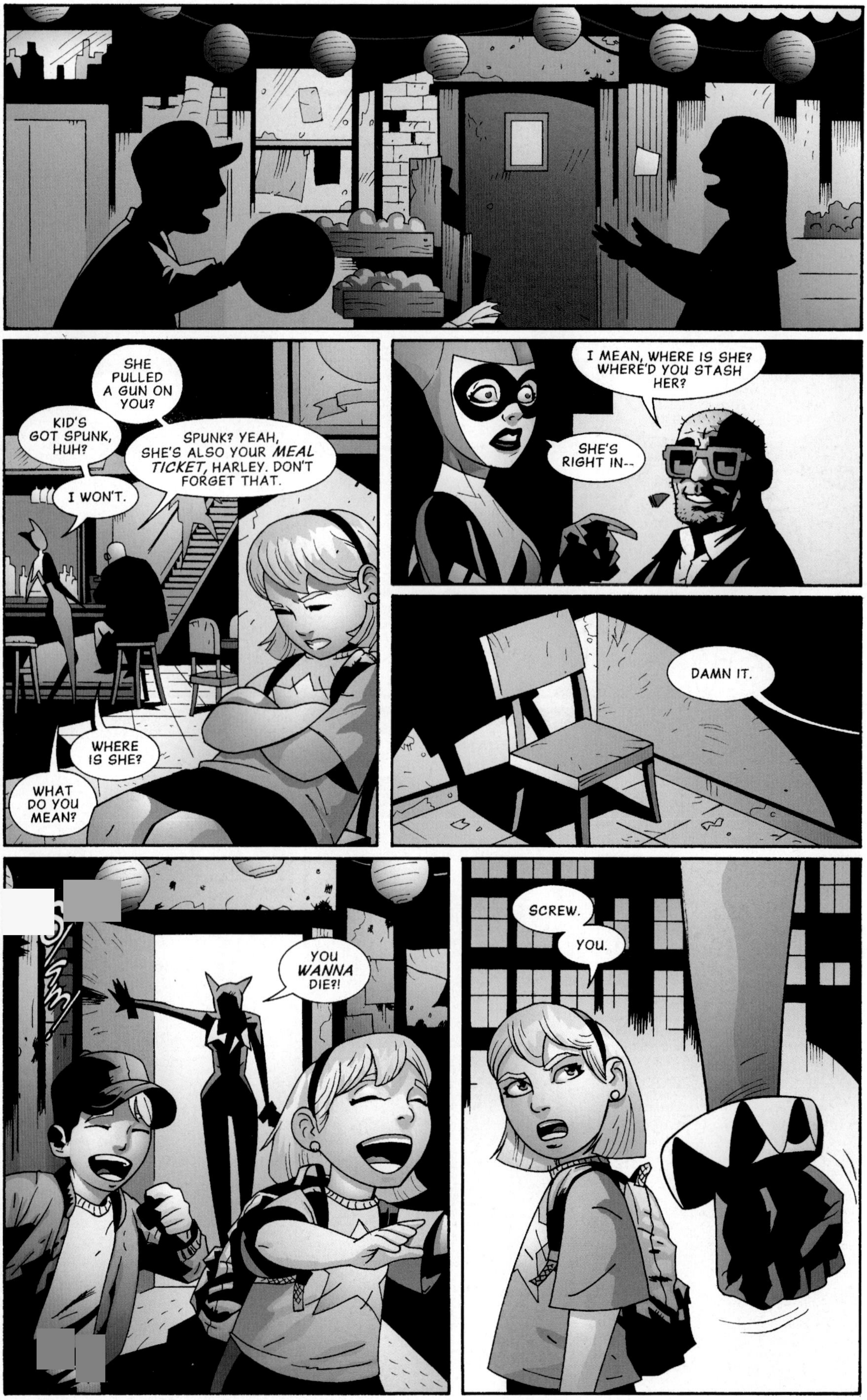
SHE PULLED A GUN ON YOU?
KID'S GOT SPUNK, HUH?
SPUNK? YEAH, SHE'S ALSO YOUR *MEAL TICKET,* HARLEY. DON'T FORGET THAT.
I WON'T.
WHERE IS SHE?
WHAT DO YOU MEAN?
I MEAN, WHERE IS SHE? WHERE'D YOU STASH HER?
SHE'S RIGHT IN--
DAMN IT.
YOU *WANNA* DIE?!
SCREW.
YOU.

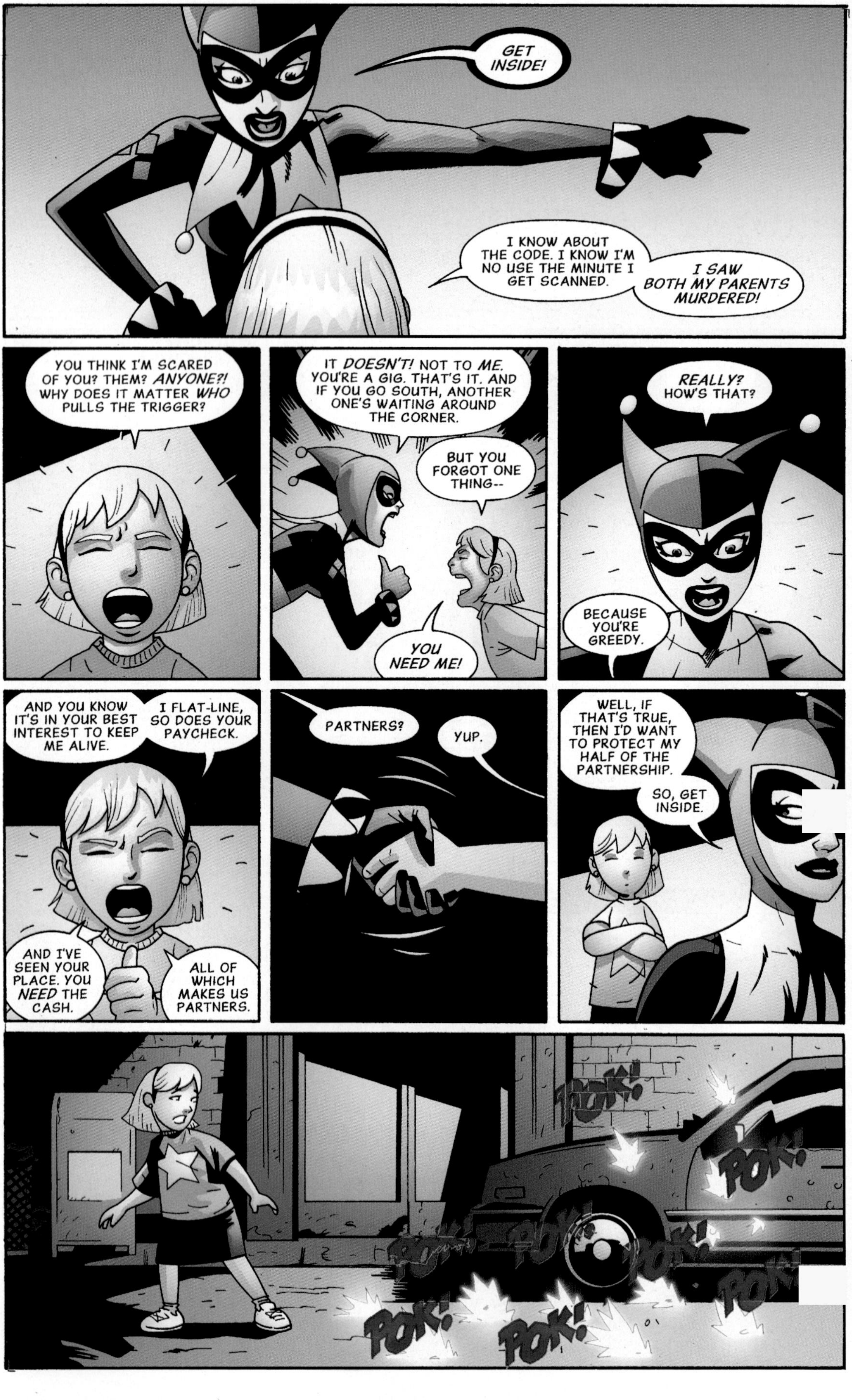
GET INSIDE!
I KNOW ABOUT THE CODE. I KNOW I'M NO USE THE MINUTE I GET SCANNED.
I SAW BOTH MY PARENTS MURDERED!
YOU THINK I'M SCARED OF YOU? THEM? ANYONE?! WHY DOES IT MATTER WHO PULLS THE TRIGGER?
IT DOESN'T! NOT TO ME. YOU'RE A GIG. THAT'S IT. AND IF YOU GO SOUTH, ANOTHER ONE'S WAITING AROUND THE CORNER.
BUT YOU FORGOT ONE THING--
YOU NEED ME!
REALLY? HOW'S THAT?
BECAUSE YOU'RE GREEDY.
AND YOU KNOW IT'S IN YOUR BEST INTEREST TO KEEP ME ALIVE.
I FLAT-LINE, SO DOES YOUR PAYCHECK.
AND I'VE SEEN YOUR PLACE. YOU NEED THE CASH.
ALL OF WHICH MAKES US PARTNERS.
PARTNERS?
YUP.
WELL, IF THAT'S TRUE, THEN I'D WANT TO PROTECT MY HALF OF THE PARTNERSHIP.
SO, GET INSIDE.
POK!
POK!
POK!
POK!
POK!
POK!
POK!
POK!
POK!

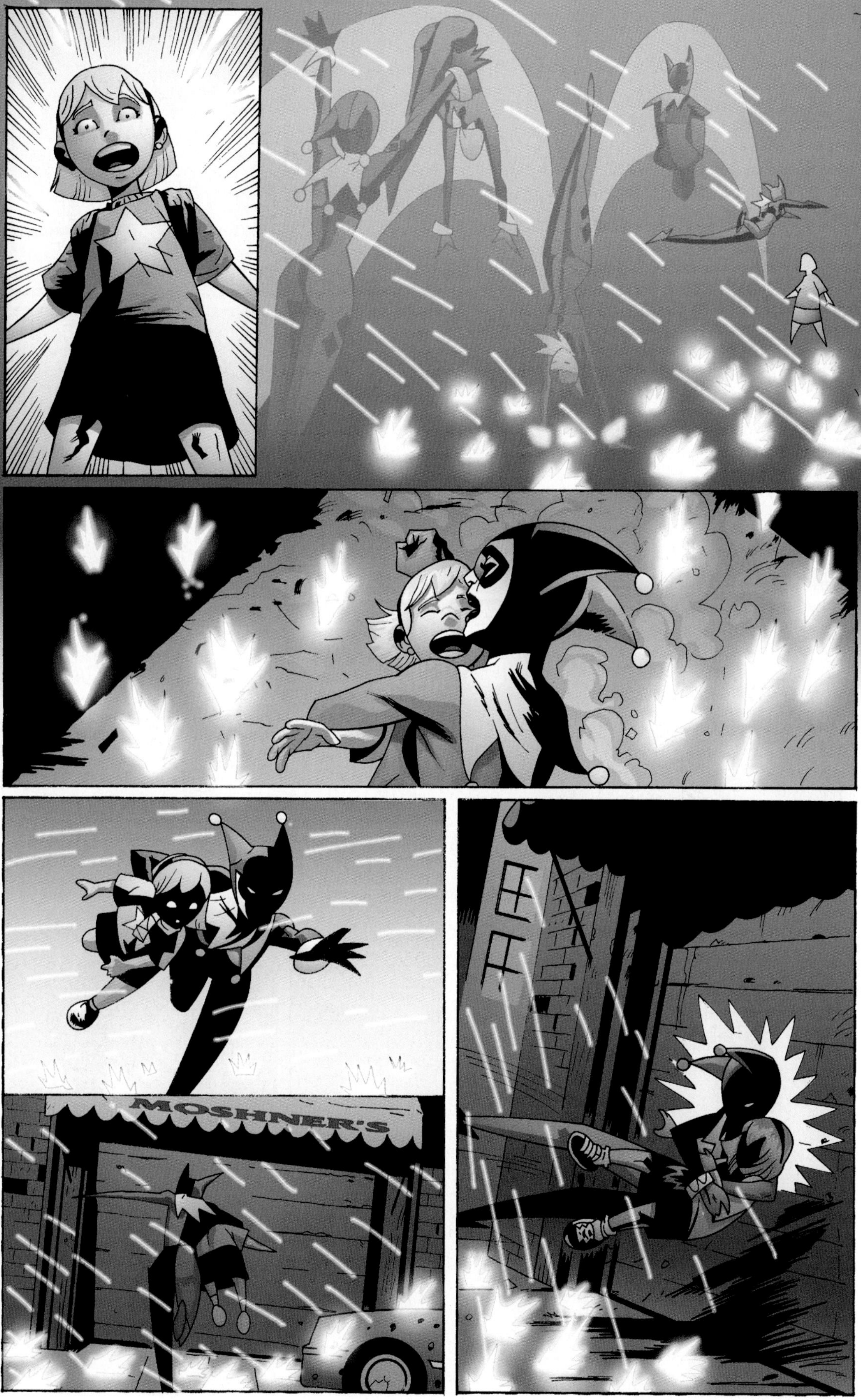
MOSHNER'S

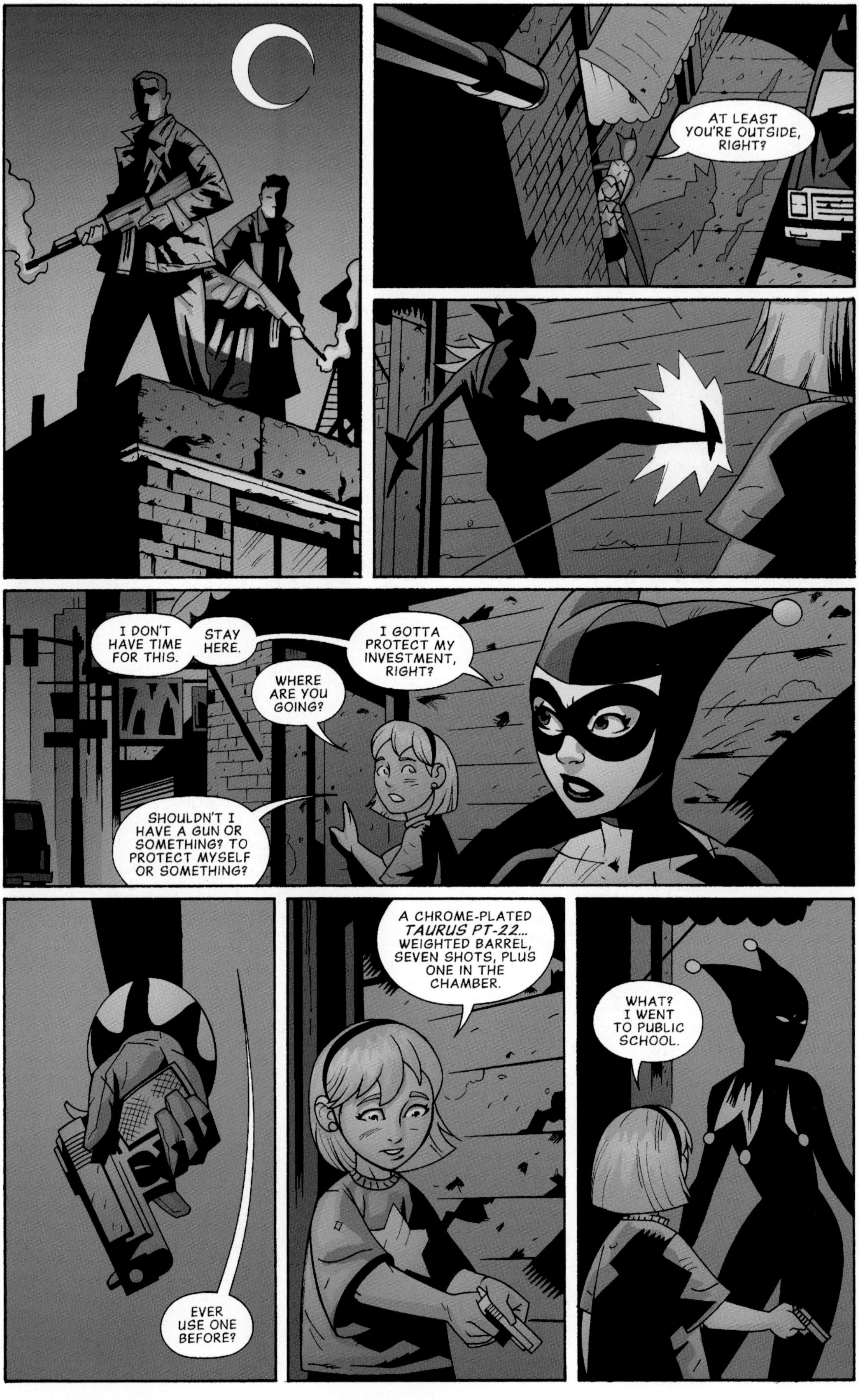
AT LEAST YOU'RE OUTSIDE, RIGHT?
I DON'T HAVE TIME FOR THIS.
STAY HERE.
I GOTTA PROTECT MY INVESTMENT, RIGHT?
WHERE ARE YOU GOING?
SHOULDN'T I HAVE A GUN OR SOMETHING? TO PROTECT MYSELF OR SOMETHING?
EVER USE ONE BEFORE?
A CHROME-PLATED *TAURUS PT-22*... WEIGHTED BARREL, SEVEN SHOTS, PLUS ONE IN THE CHAMBER.
WHAT? I WENT TO PUBLIC SCHOOL.

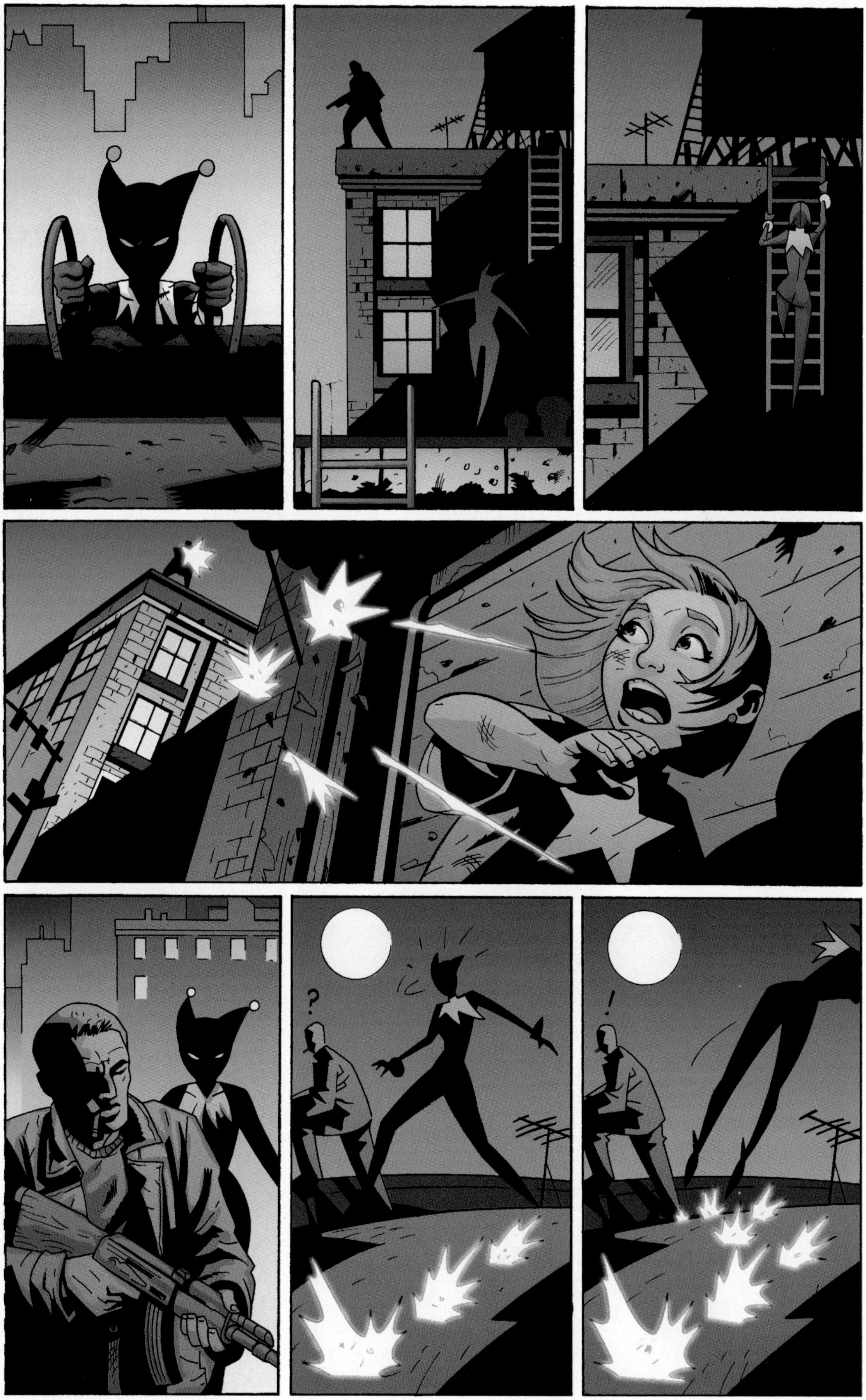
?
!

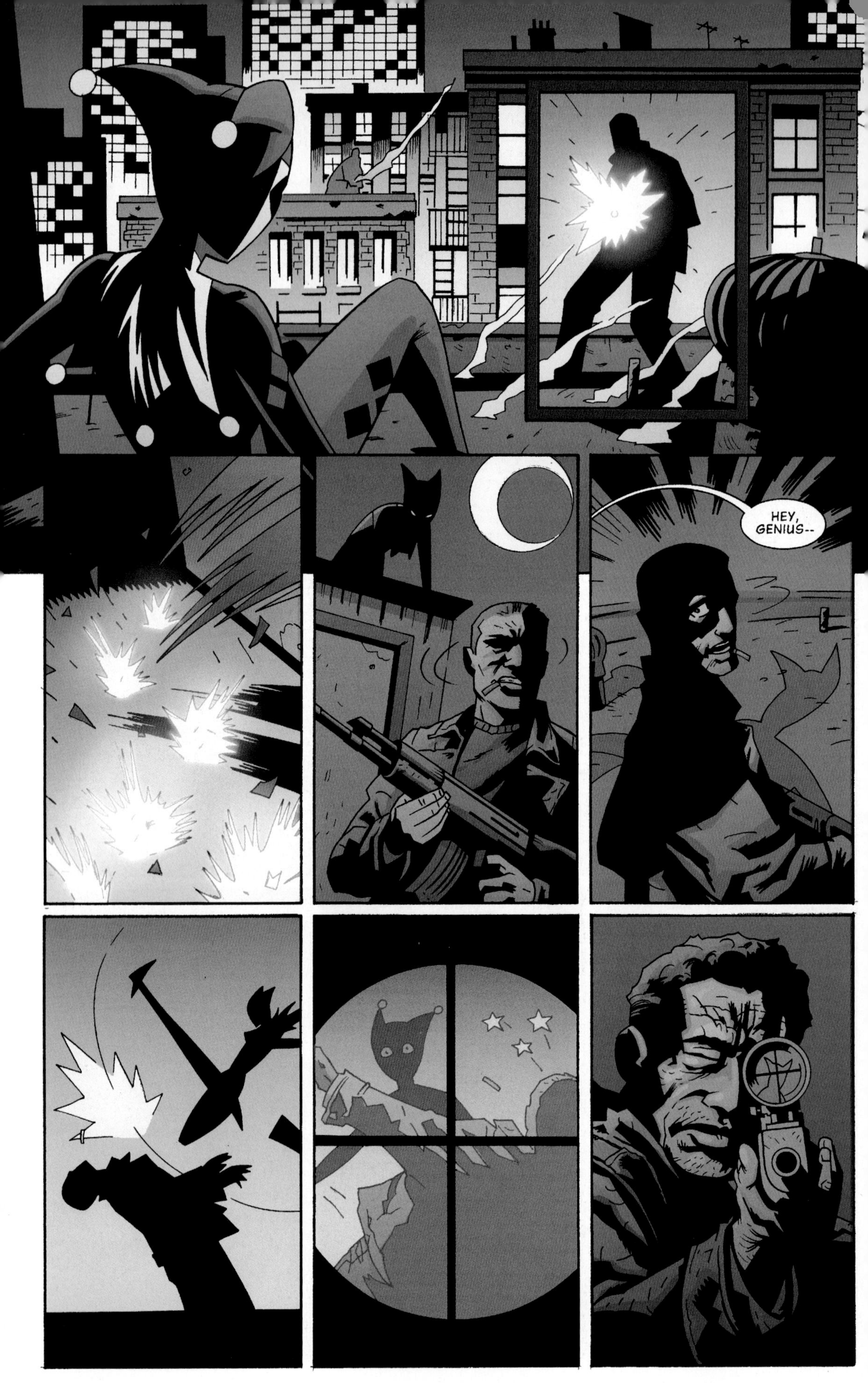
HEY, GENIUS--

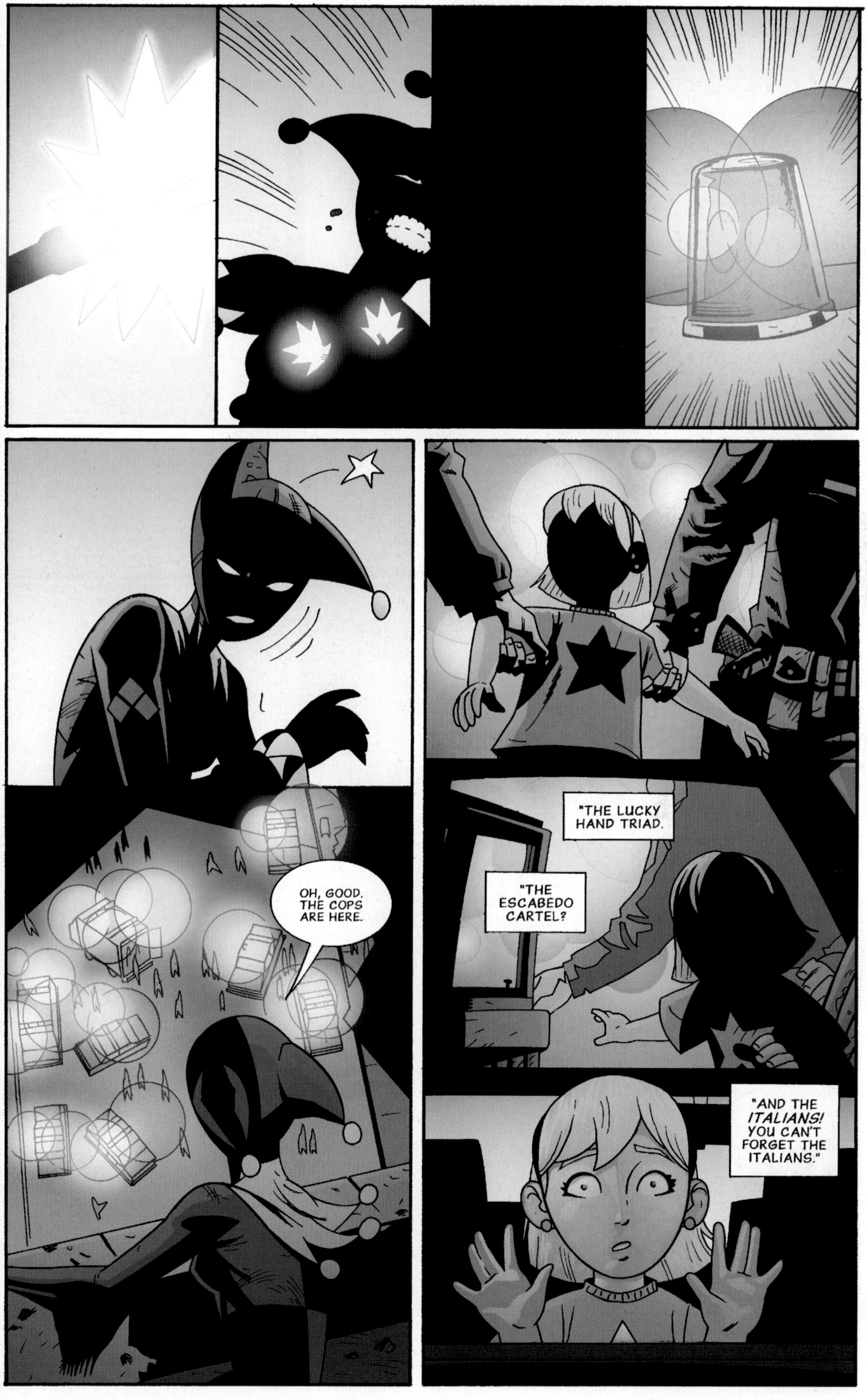
OH, GOOD. THE COPS ARE HERE.
"THE LUCKY HAND TRIAD.
"THE ESCABEDO CARTEL?
"AND THE ITALIANS! YOU CAN'T FORGET THE ITALIANS."

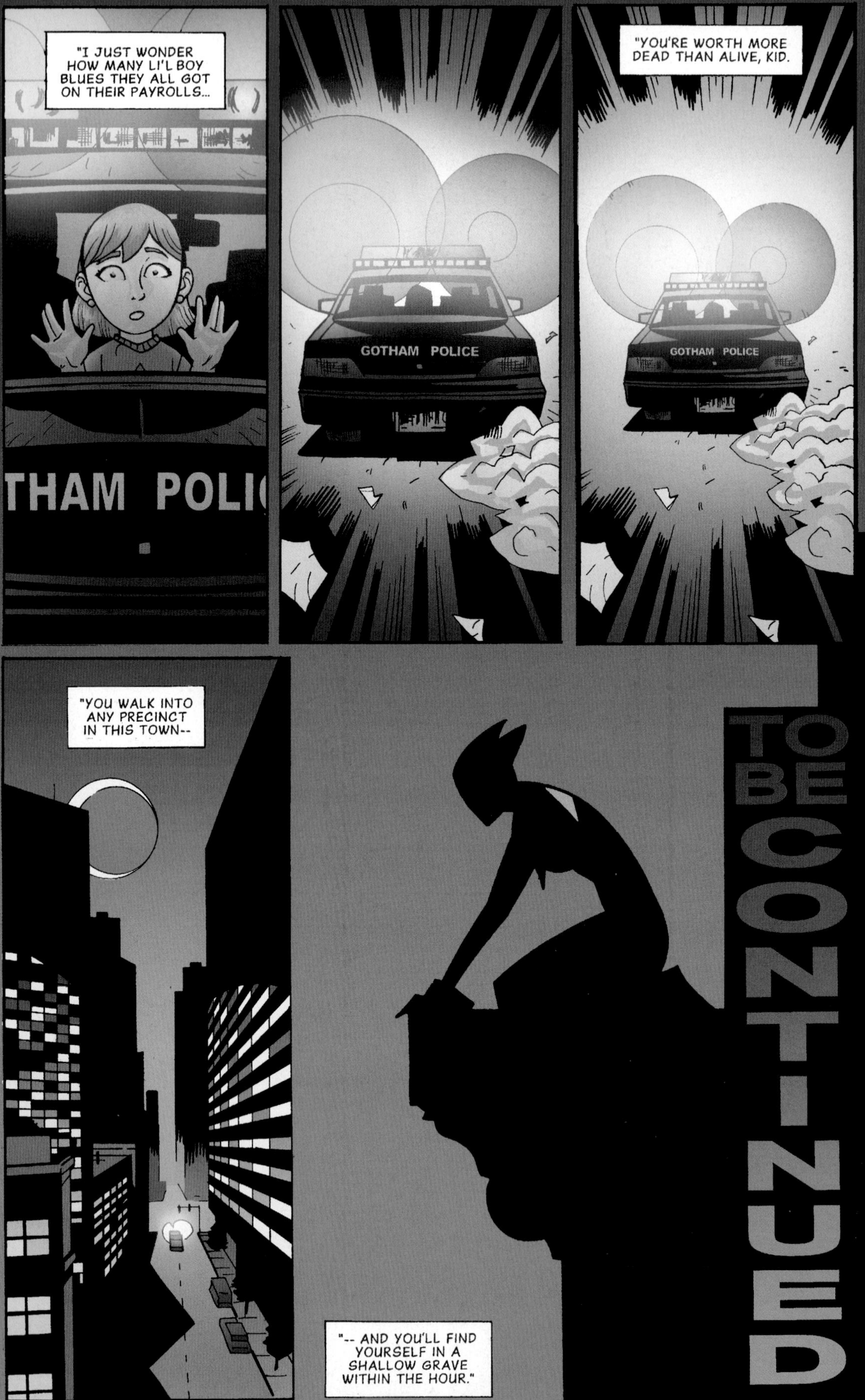
"I JUST WONDER HOW MANY LI'L BOY BLUES THEY ALL GOT ON THEIR PAYROLLS...
THAM POLI
GOTHAM POLICE
"YOU'RE WORTH MORE DEAD THAN ALIVE, KID.
GOTHAM POLICE
"YOU WALK INTO ANY PRECINCT IN THIS TOWN--
"-- AND YOU'LL FIND YOURSELF IN A SHALLOW GRAVE WITHIN THE HOUR."
TO BE CONTINUED

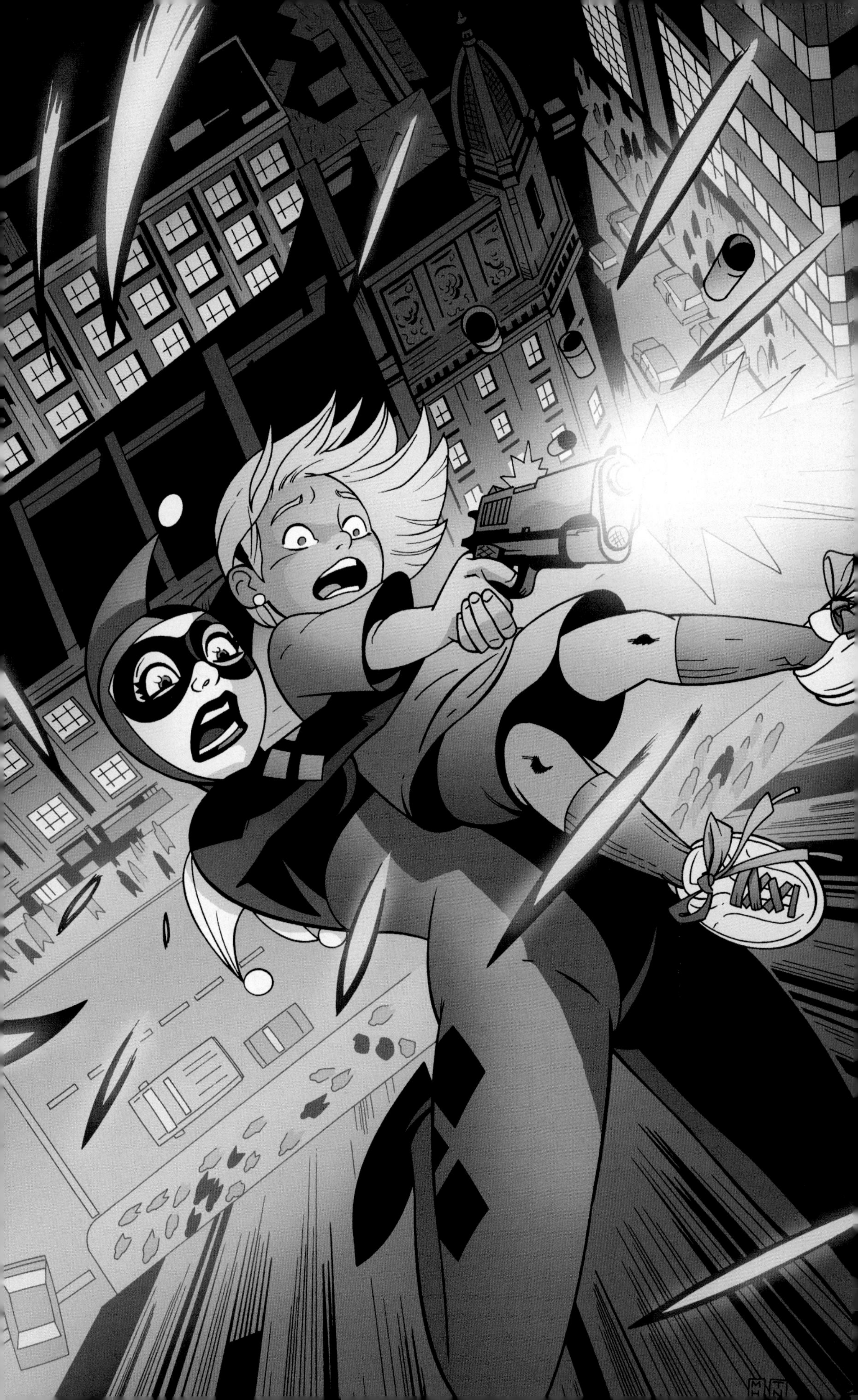

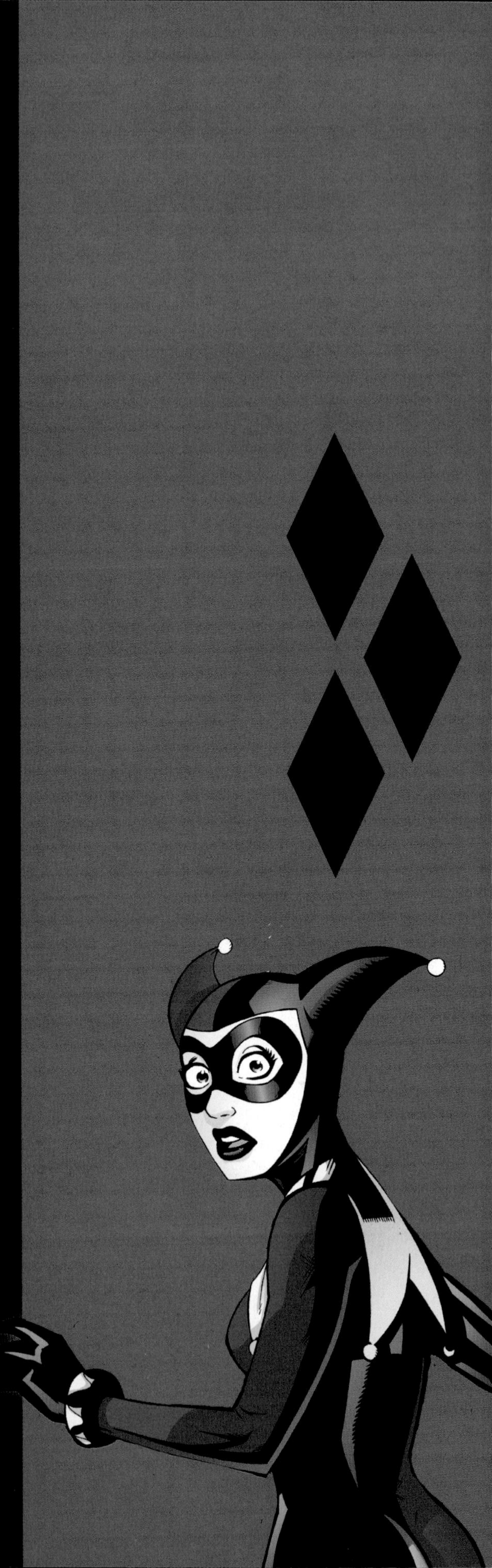

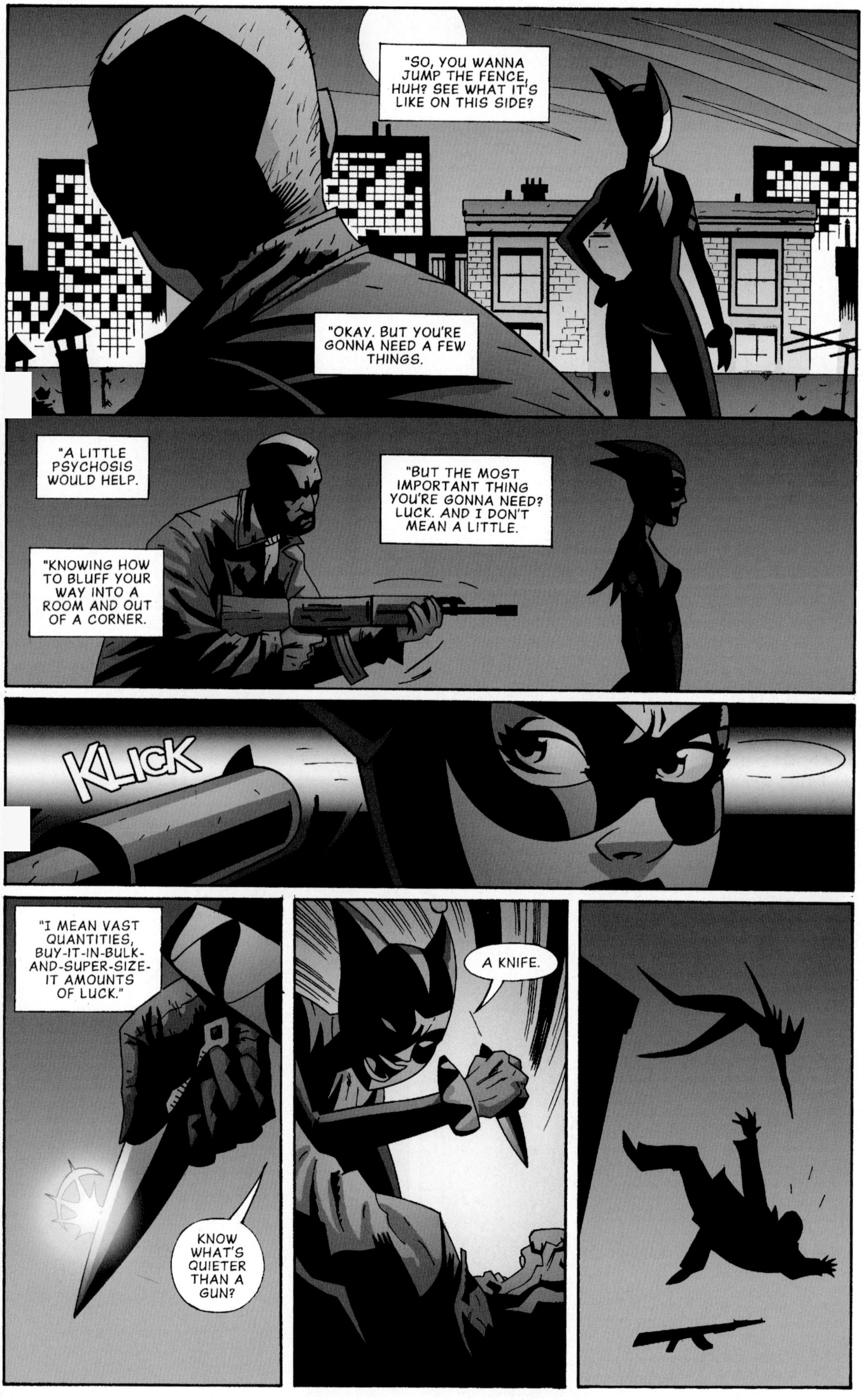
"SO, YOU WANNA JUMP THE FENCE, HUH? SEE WHAT IT'S LIKE ON THIS SIDE?
"OKAY. BUT YOU'RE GONNA NEED A FEW THINGS.
"A LITTLE PSYCHOSIS WOULD HELP.
"KNOWING HOW TO BLUFF YOUR WAY INTO A ROOM AND OUT OF A CORNER.
"BUT THE MOST IMPORTANT THING YOU'RE GONNA NEED? LUCK. AND I DON'T MEAN A LITTLE.
KLICK
"I MEAN VAST QUANTITIES, BUY-IT-IN-BULK-AND-SUPER-SIZE-IT AMOUNTS OF LUCK."
KNOW WHAT'S QUIETER THAN A GUN?
A KNIFE.

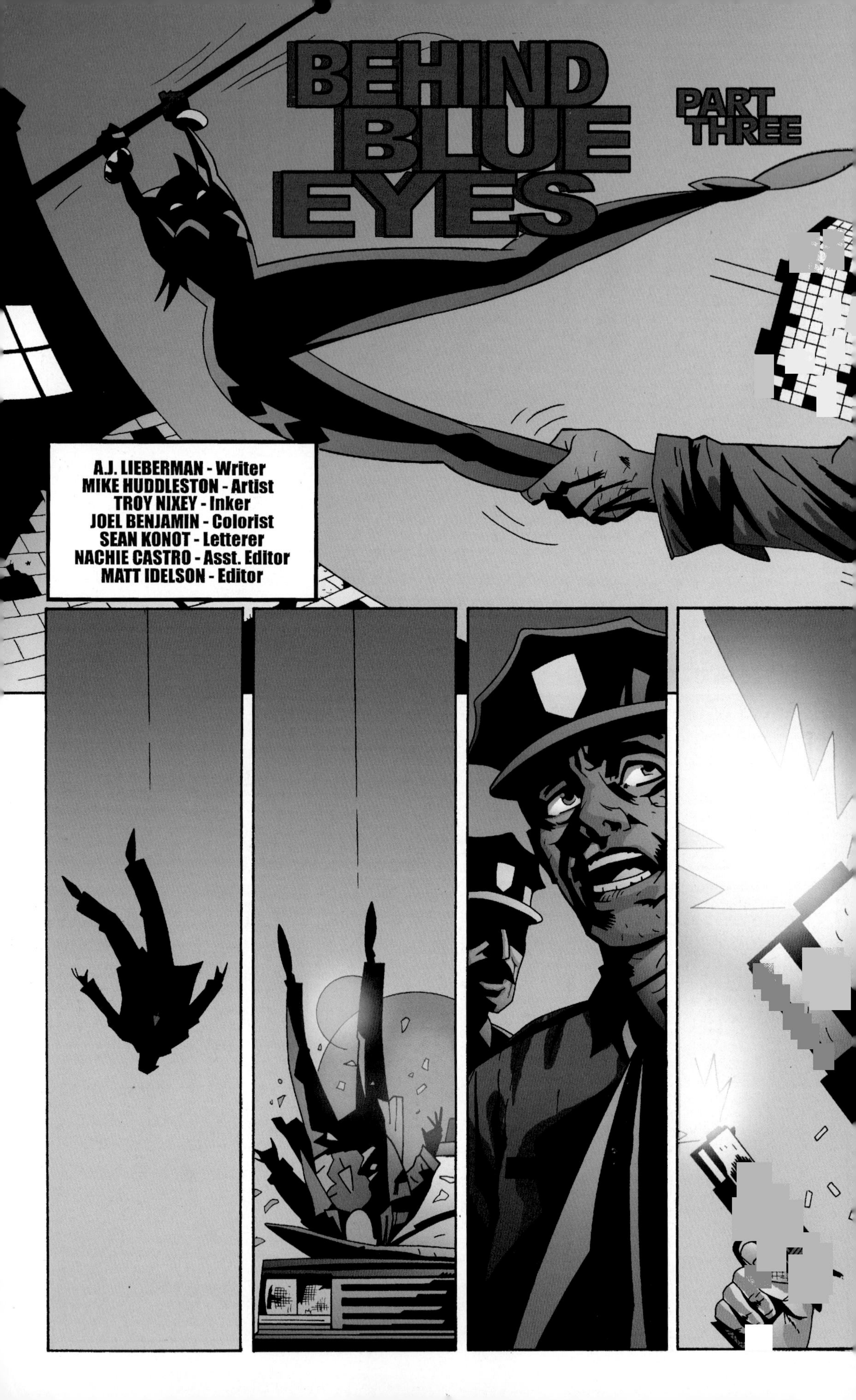

BEHIND BLUE EYES
PART THREE
A.J. LIEBERMAN - Writer
MIKE HUDDLESTON - Artist
TROY NIXEY - Inker
JOEL BENJAMIN - Colorist
SEAN KONOT - Letterer
NACHIE CASTRO - Asst. Editor
MATT IDELSON - Editor

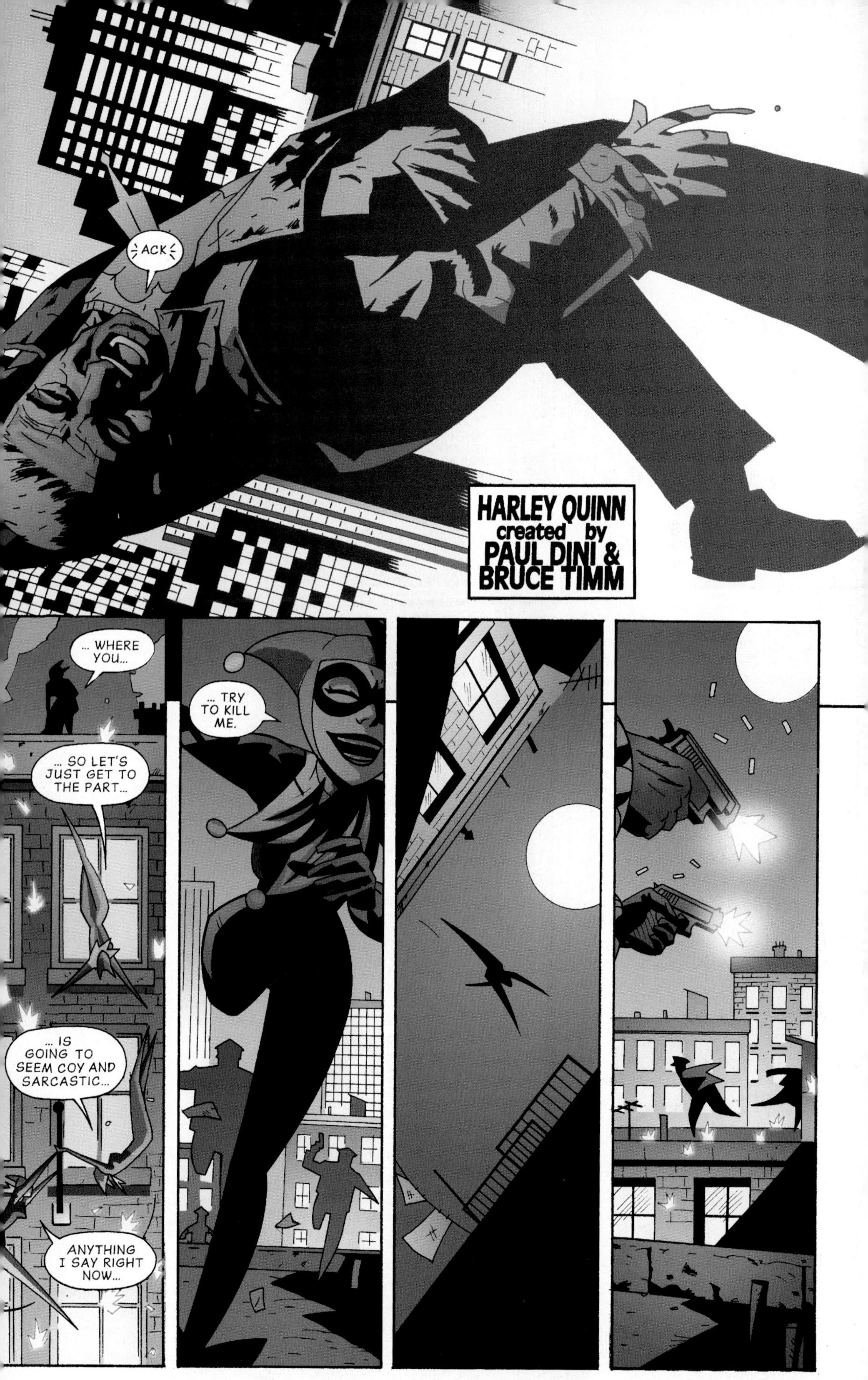
ACK
HARLEY QUINN created by PAUL DINI & BRUCE TIMM
... WHERE YOU...
... SO LET'S JUST GET TO THE PART...
... IS GOING TO SEEM COY AND SARCASTIC...
ANYTHING I SAY RIGHT NOW...
... TRY TO KILL ME.

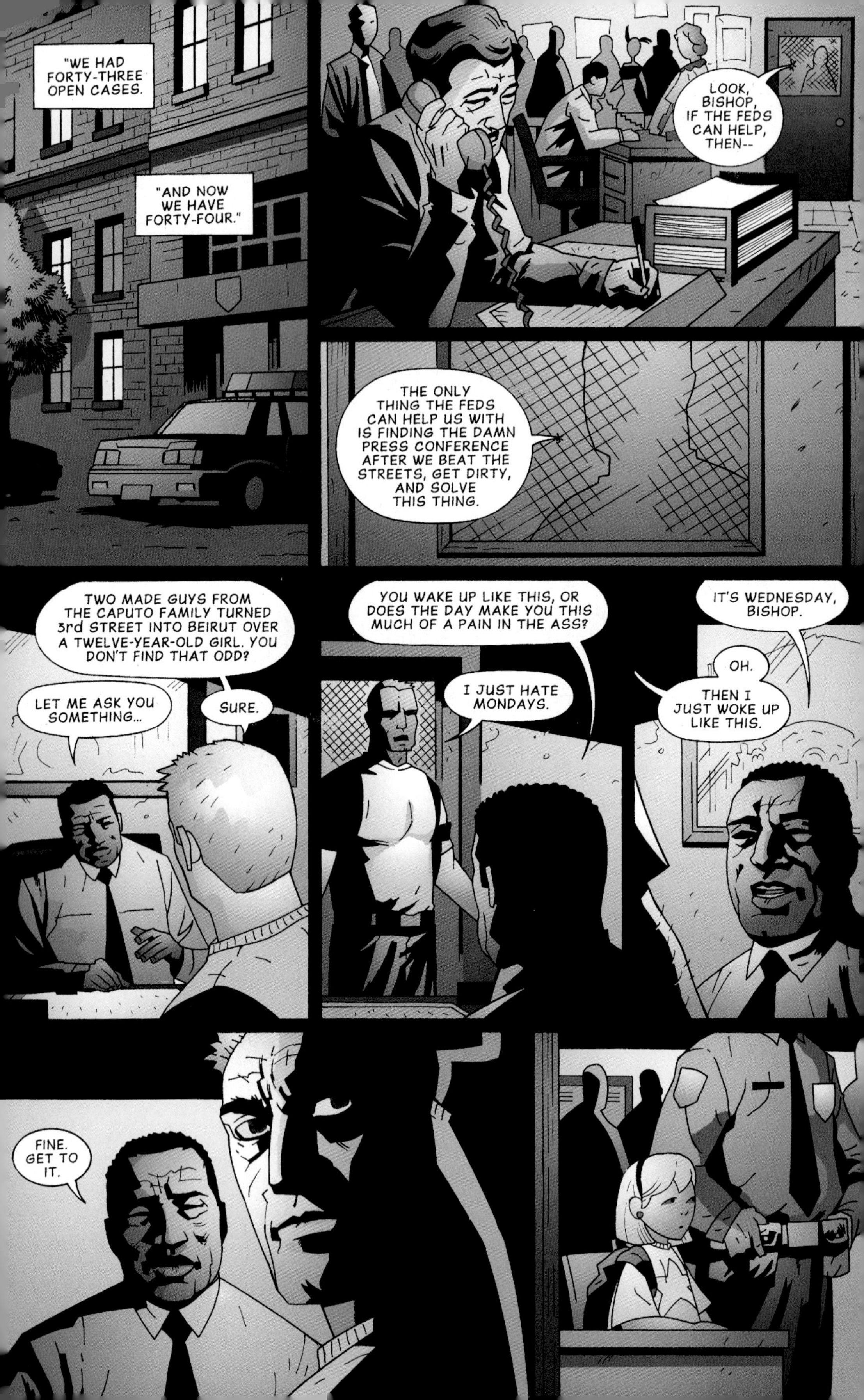
"WE HAD FORTY-THREE OPEN CASES.
"AND NOW WE HAVE FORTY-FOUR."
LOOK, BISHOP, IF THE FEDS CAN HELP, THEN--
THE ONLY THING THE FEDS CAN HELP US WITH IS FINDING THE DAMN PRESS CONFERENCE AFTER WE BEAT THE STREETS, GET DIRTY, AND SOLVE THIS THING.
TWO MADE GUYS FROM THE CAPUTO FAMILY TURNED 3rd STREET INTO BEIRUT OVER A TWELVE-YEAR-OLD GIRL. YOU DON'T FIND THAT ODD?
SURE.
LET ME ASK YOU SOMETHING...
YOU WAKE UP LIKE THIS, OR DOES THE DAY MAKE YOU THIS MUCH OF A PAIN IN THE ASS?
I JUST HATE MONDAYS.
IT'S WEDNESDAY, BISHOP.
OH.
THEN I JUST WOKE UP LIKE THIS.
FINE. GET TO IT.

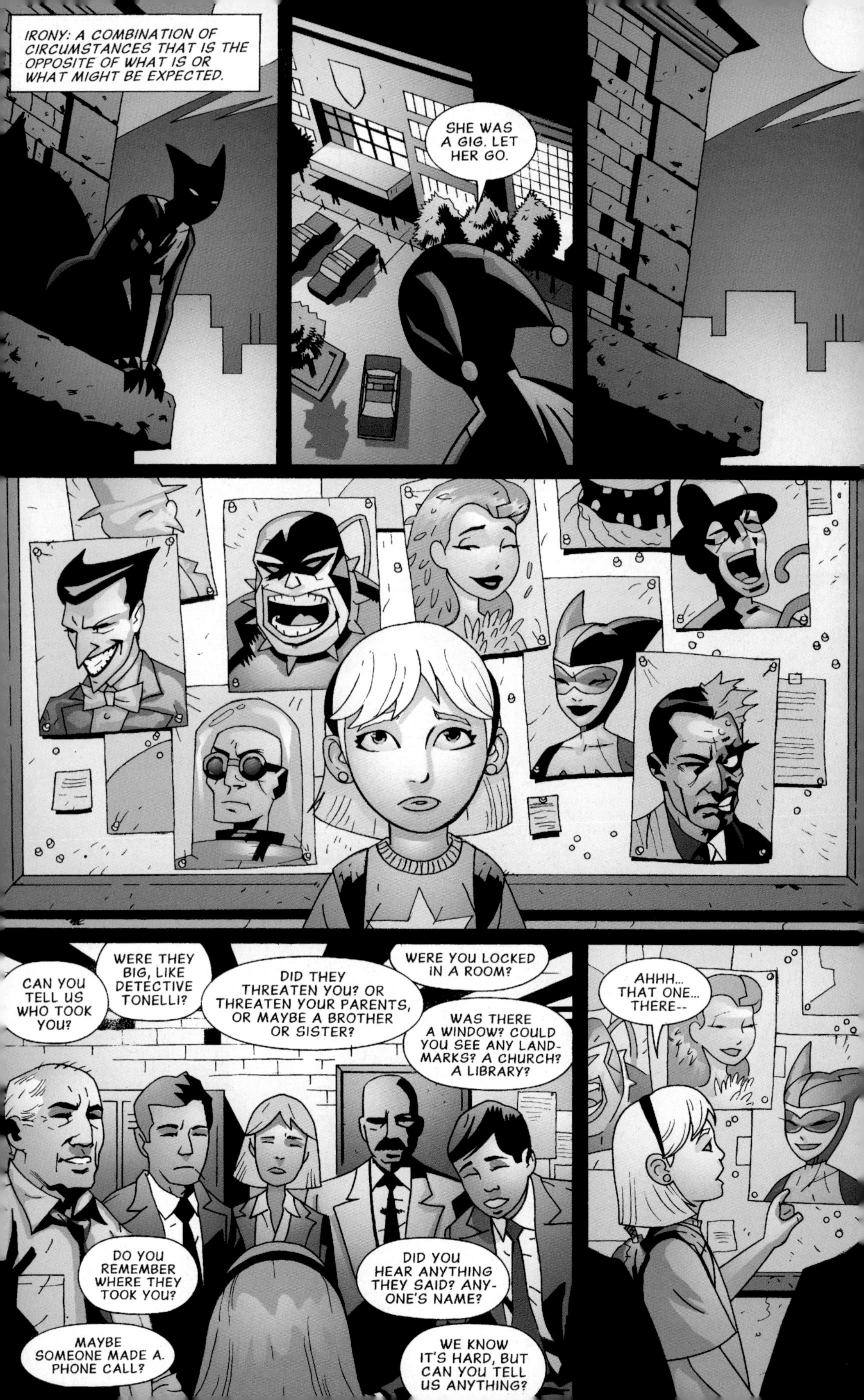
IRONY: A COMBINATION OF CIRCUMSTANCES THAT IS THE OPPOSITE OF WHAT IS OR WHAT MIGHT BE EXPECTED.
SHE WAS A GIG. LET HER GO.
CAN YOU TELL US WHO TOOK YOU?
WERE THEY BIG, LIKE DETECTIVE TONELLI?
DID THEY THREATEN YOU? OR THREATEN YOUR PARENTS, OR MAYBE A BROTHER OR SISTER?
WERE YOU LOCKED IN A ROOM?
WAS THERE A WINDOW? COULD YOU SEE ANY LAND-MARKS? A CHURCH? A LIBRARY?
DO YOU REMEMBER WHERE THEY TOOK YOU?
MAYBE SOMEONE MADE A PHONE CALL?
DID YOU HEAR ANYTHING THEY SAID? ANY-ONE'S NAME?
WE KNOW IT'S HARD, BUT CAN YOU TELL US ANYTHING?
AHHH... THAT ONE... THERE--

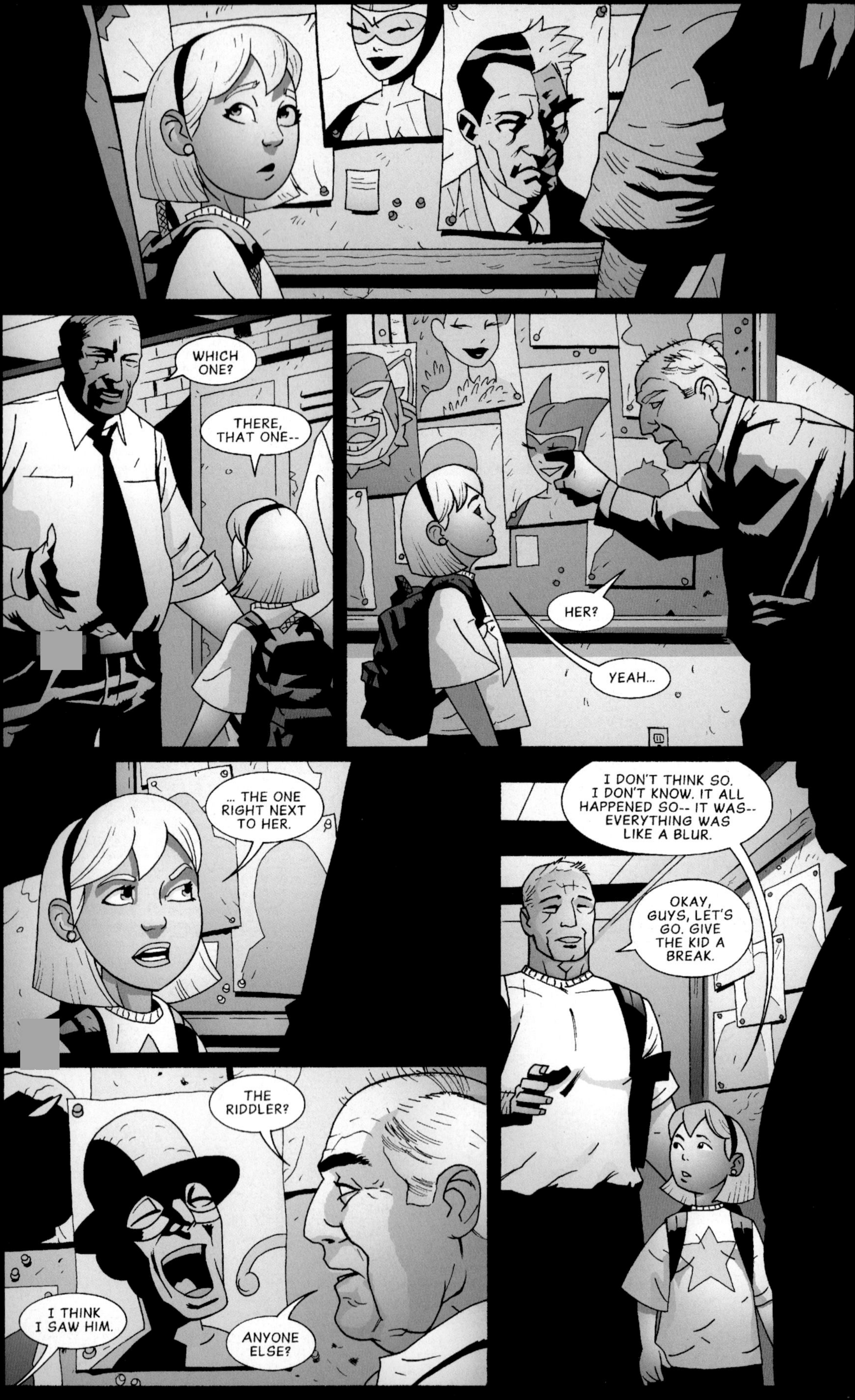
WHICH ONE?
THERE, THAT ONE--
HER?
YEAH...
... THE ONE RIGHT NEXT TO HER.
THE RIDDLER?
I THINK I SAW HIM.
ANYONE ELSE?
I DON'T THINK SO. I DON'T KNOW. IT ALL HAPPENED SO-- IT WAS-- EVERYTHING WAS LIKE A BLUR.
OKAY, GUYS, LET'S GO. GIVE THE KID A BREAK.

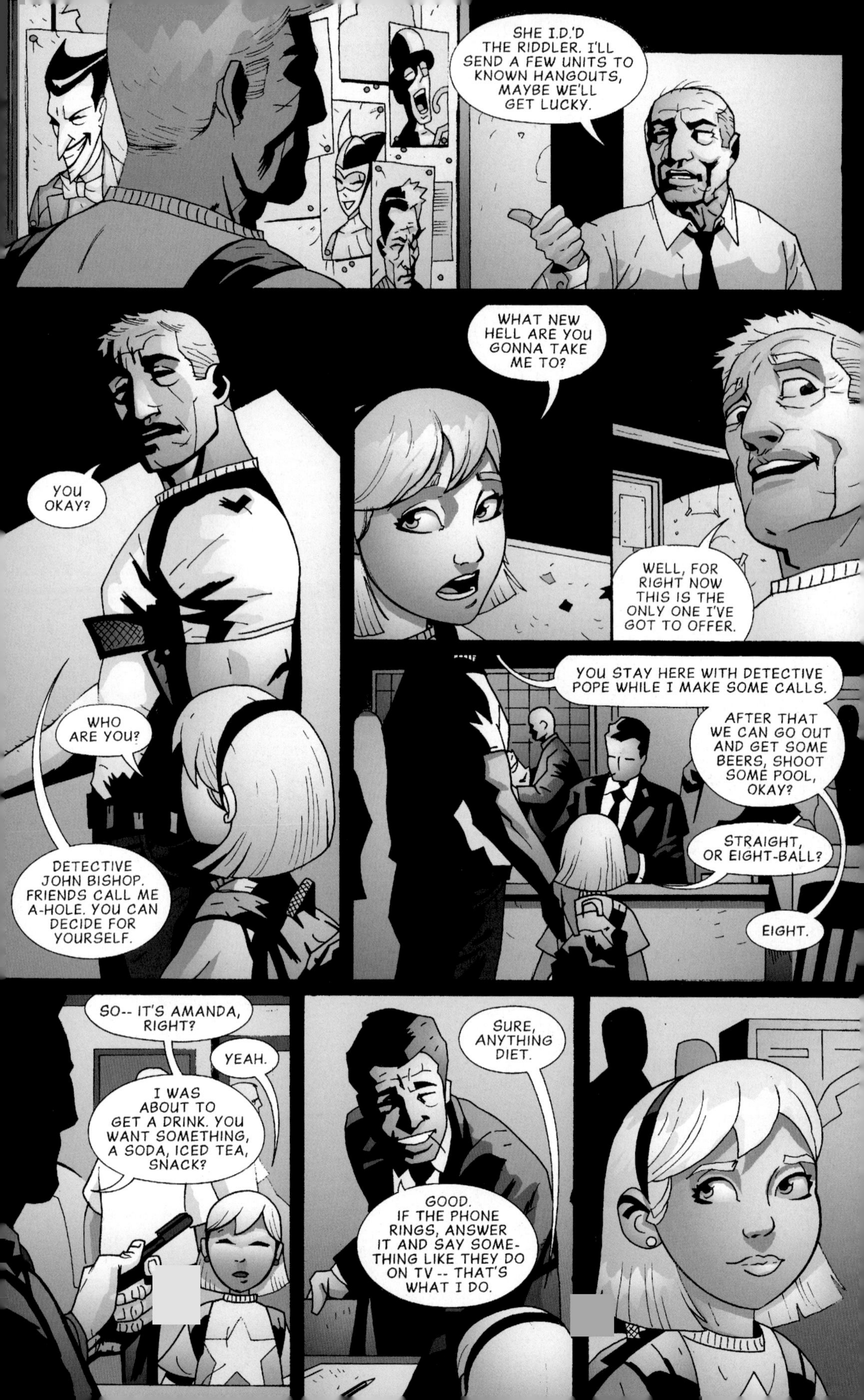
SHE I.D.'D THE RIDDLER. I'LL SEND A FEW UNITS TO KNOWN HANGOUTS, MAYBE WE'LL GET LUCKY.
YOU OKAY?
WHAT NEW HELL ARE YOU GONNA TAKE ME TO?
WELL, FOR RIGHT NOW THIS IS THE ONLY ONE I'VE GOT TO OFFER.
WHO ARE YOU?
DETECTIVE JOHN BISHOP. FRIENDS CALL ME A-HOLE. YOU CAN DECIDE FOR YOURSELF.
YOU STAY HERE WITH DETECTIVE POPE WHILE I MAKE SOME CALLS.
AFTER THAT WE CAN GO OUT AND GET SOME BEERS, SHOOT SOME POOL, OKAY?
STRAIGHT, OR EIGHT-BALL?
EIGHT.
SO-- IT'S AMANDA, RIGHT?
YEAH.
I WAS ABOUT TO GET A DRINK. YOU WANT SOMETHING, A SODA, ICED TEA, SNACK?
SURE, ANYTHING DIET.
GOOD. IF THE PHONE RINGS, ANSWER IT AND SAY SOME-THING LIKE THEY DO ON TV -- THAT'S WHAT I DO.

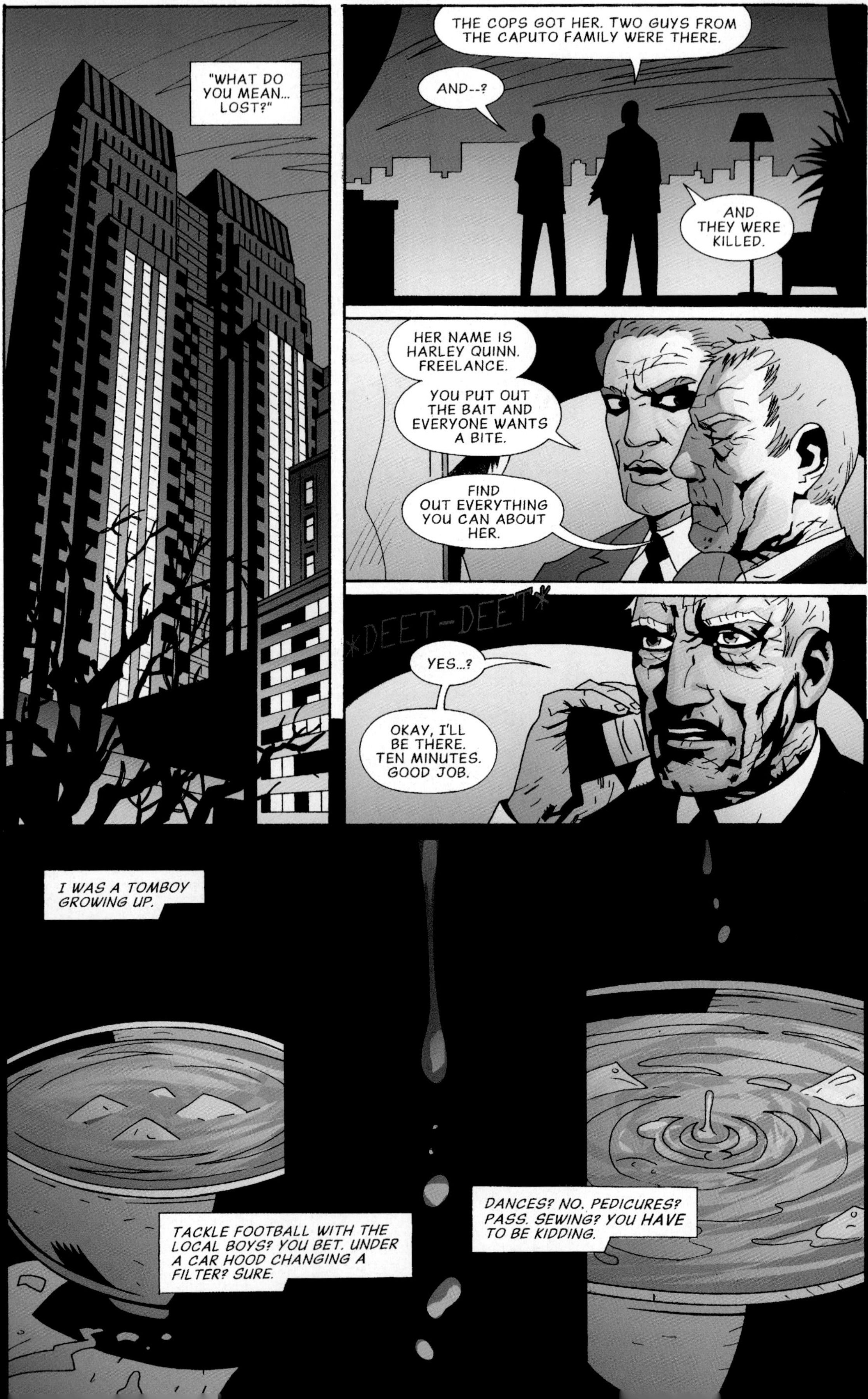
"WHAT DO YOU MEAN... LOST?"
THE COPS GOT HER. TWO GUYS FROM THE CAPUTO FAMILY WERE THERE.
AND--?
AND THEY WERE KILLED.
HER NAME IS HARLEY QUINN. FREELANCE.
YOU PUT OUT THE BAIT AND EVERYONE WANTS A BITE.
FIND OUT EVERYTHING YOU CAN ABOUT HER.
DEET-DEET
YES...?
OKAY, I'LL BE THERE. TEN MINUTES. GOOD JOB.
I WAS A TOMBOY GROWING UP.
TACKLE FOOTBALL WITH THE LOCAL BOYS? YOU BET. UNDER A CAR HOOD CHANGING A FILTER? SURE.
DANCES? NO. PEDICURES? PASS. SEWING? YOU HAVE TO BE KIDDING.

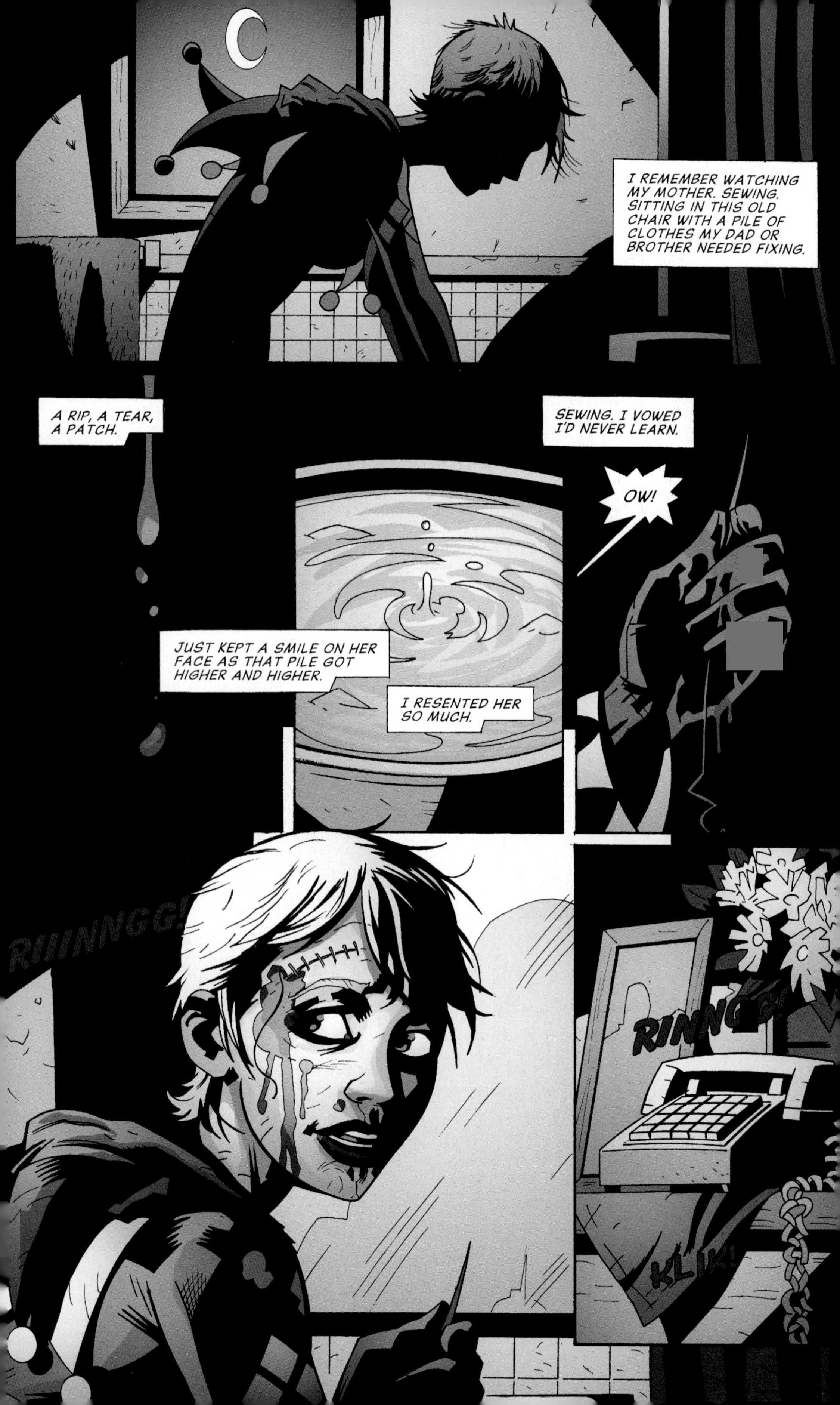
I REMEMBER WATCHING MY MOTHER. SEWING. SITTING IN THIS OLD CHAIR WITH A PILE OF CLOTHES MY DAD OR BROTHER NEEDED FIXING.
A RIP, A TEAR, A PATCH.
SEWING. I VOWED I'D NEVER LEARN.
OW!
JUST KEPT A SMILE ON HER FACE AS THAT PILE GOT HIGHER AND HIGHER.
I RESENTED HER SO MUCH.
RIIINNGG!
KLIK!

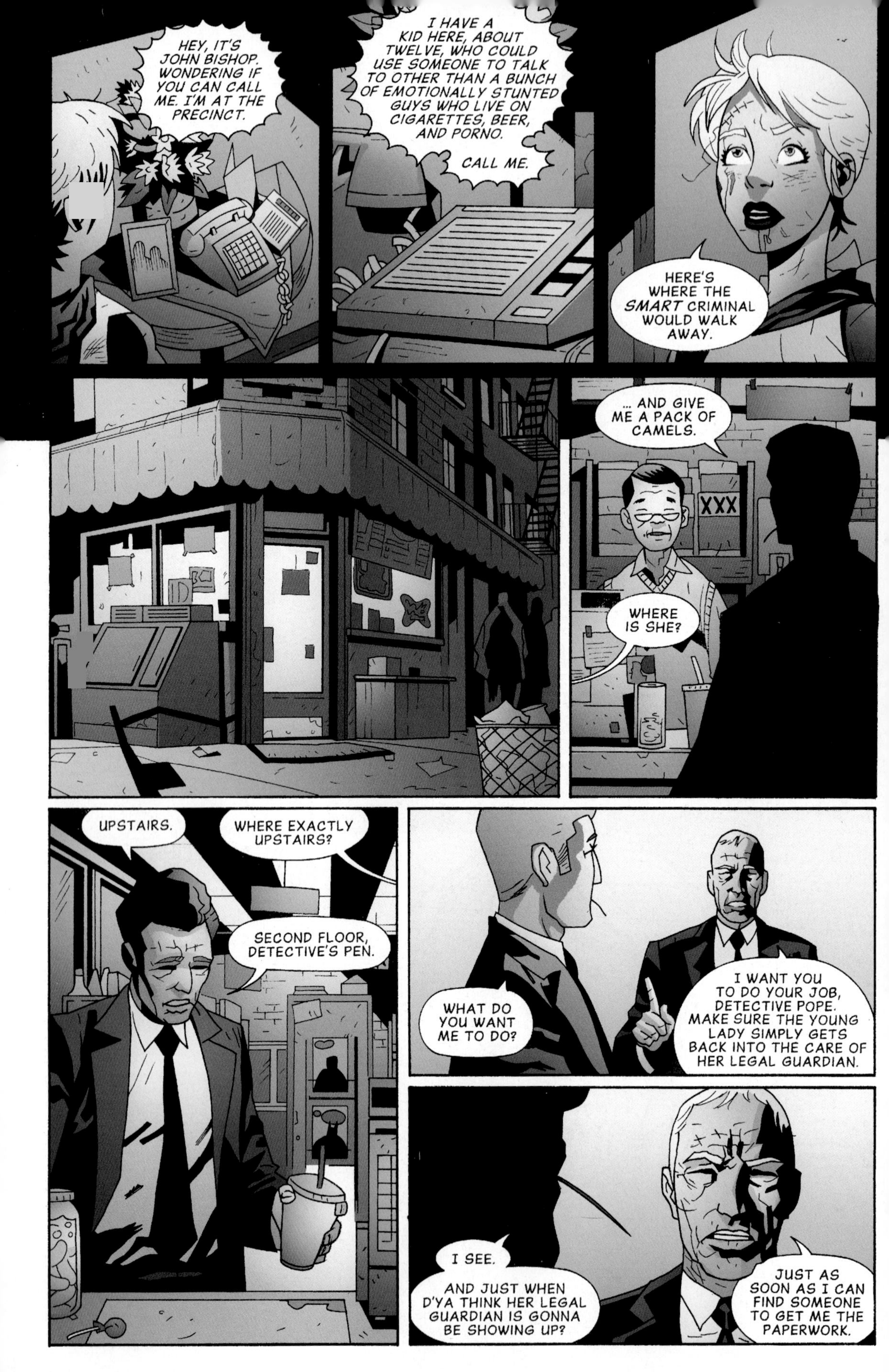

HEY, IT'S JOHN BISHOP. WONDERING IF YOU CAN CALL ME. I'M AT THE PRECINCT.
I HAVE A KID HERE, ABOUT TWELVE, WHO COULD USE SOMEONE TO TALK TO OTHER THAN A BUNCH OF EMOTIONALLY STUNTED GUYS WHO LIVE ON CIGARETTES, BEER, AND PORNO.
CALL ME.
HERE'S WHERE THE SMART CRIMINAL WOULD WALK AWAY.
... AND GIVE ME A PACK OF CAMELS.
XXX
WHERE IS SHE?
UPSTAIRS.
WHERE EXACTLY UPSTAIRS?
SECOND FLOOR, DETECTIVE'S PEN.
WHAT DO YOU WANT ME TO DO?
I WANT YOU TO DO YOUR JOB, DETECTIVE POPE. MAKE SURE THE YOUNG LADY SIMPLY GETS BACK INTO THE CARE OF HER LEGAL GUARDIAN.
I SEE.
AND JUST WHEN D'YA THINK HER LEGAL GUARDIAN IS GONNA BE SHOWING UP?
JUST AS SOON AS I CAN FIND SOMEONE TO GET ME THE PAPERWORK.

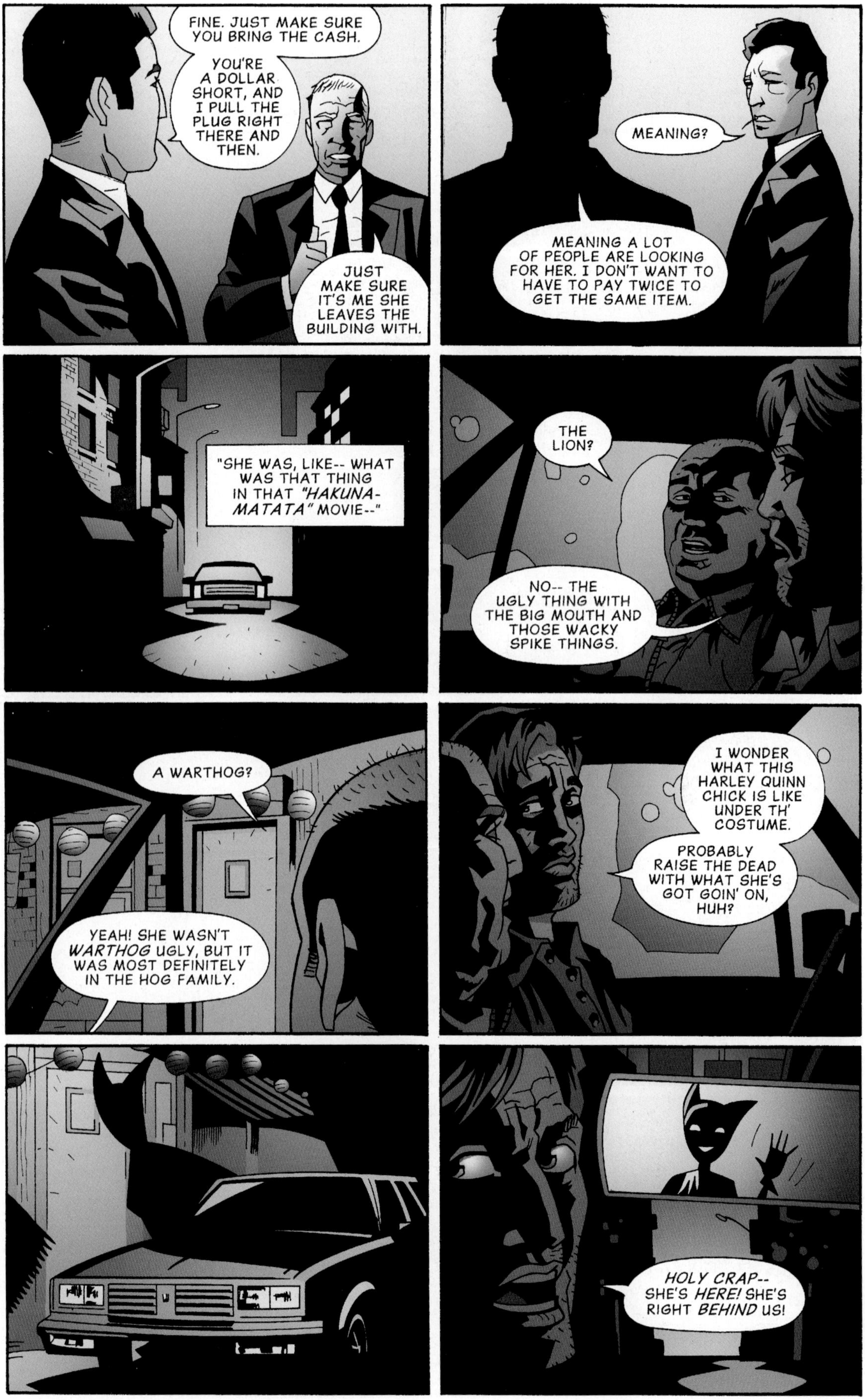
FINE. JUST MAKE SURE YOU BRING THE CASH.
YOU'RE A DOLLAR SHORT, AND I PULL THE PLUG RIGHT THERE AND THEN.
JUST MAKE SURE IT'S ME SHE LEAVES THE BUILDING WITH.
MEANING?
MEANING A LOT OF PEOPLE ARE LOOKING FOR HER. I DON'T WANT TO HAVE TO PAY TWICE TO GET THE SAME ITEM.
"SHE WAS, LIKE-- WHAT WAS THAT THING IN THAT *"HAKUNA-MATATA"* MOVIE--"
THE LION?
NO-- THE UGLY THING WITH THE BIG MOUTH AND THOSE WACKY SPIKE THINGS.
A WARTHOG?
YEAH! SHE WASN'T *WARTHOG* UGLY, BUT IT WAS MOST DEFINITELY IN THE HOG FAMILY.
I WONDER WHAT THIS HARLEY QUINN CHICK IS LIKE UNDER TH' COSTUME.
PROBABLY RAISE THE DEAD WITH WHAT SHE'S GOT GOIN' ON, HUH?
HOLY CRAP-- SHE'S *HERE!* SHE'S RIGHT *BEHIND* US!

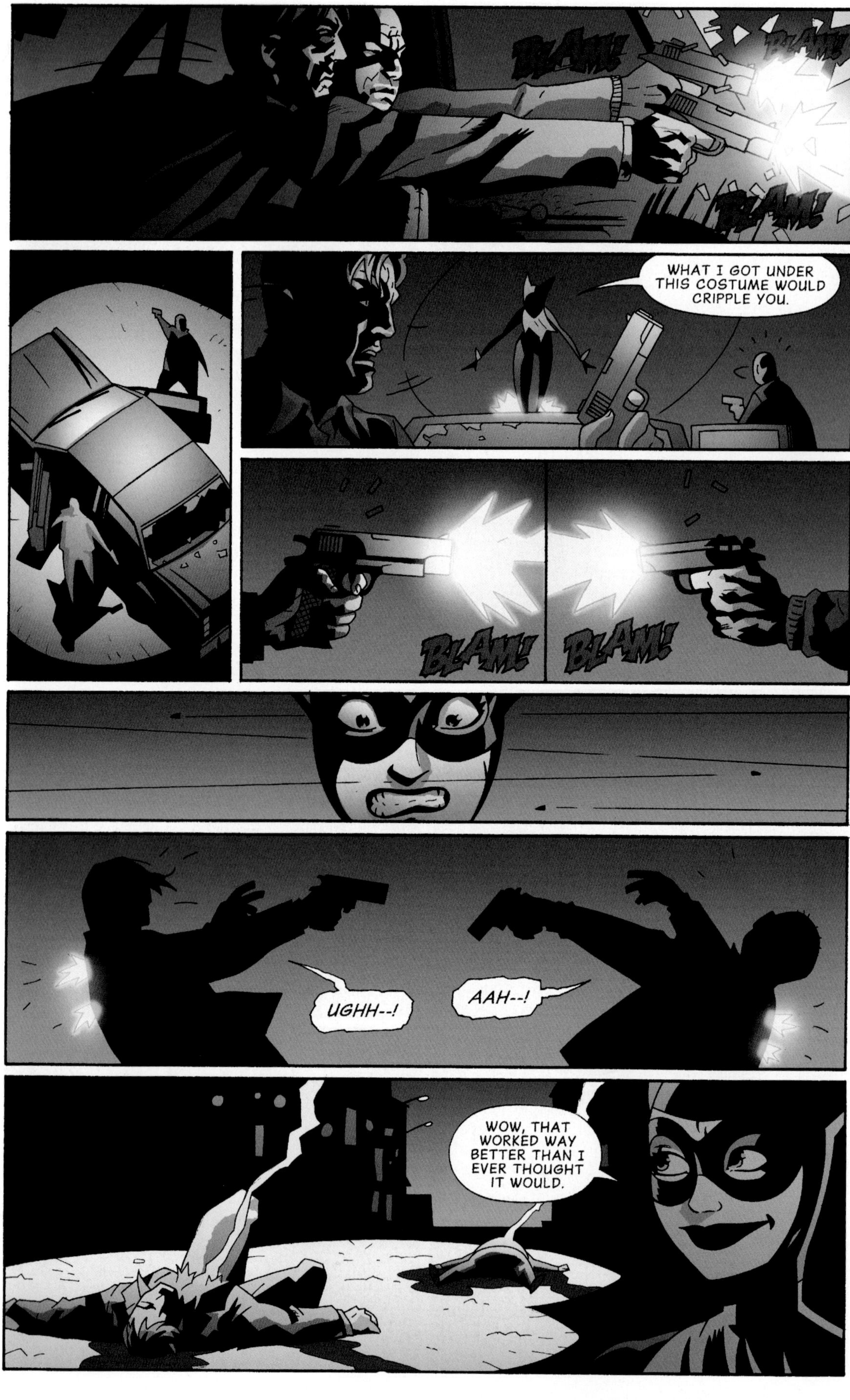

BLAM!
BLAM!
BLAM!
WHAT I GOT UNDER THIS COSTUME WOULD CRIPPLE YOU.
BLAM!
BLAM!
UGHH--!
AAH--!
WOW, THAT WORKED WAY BETTER THAN I EVER THOUGHT IT WOULD.

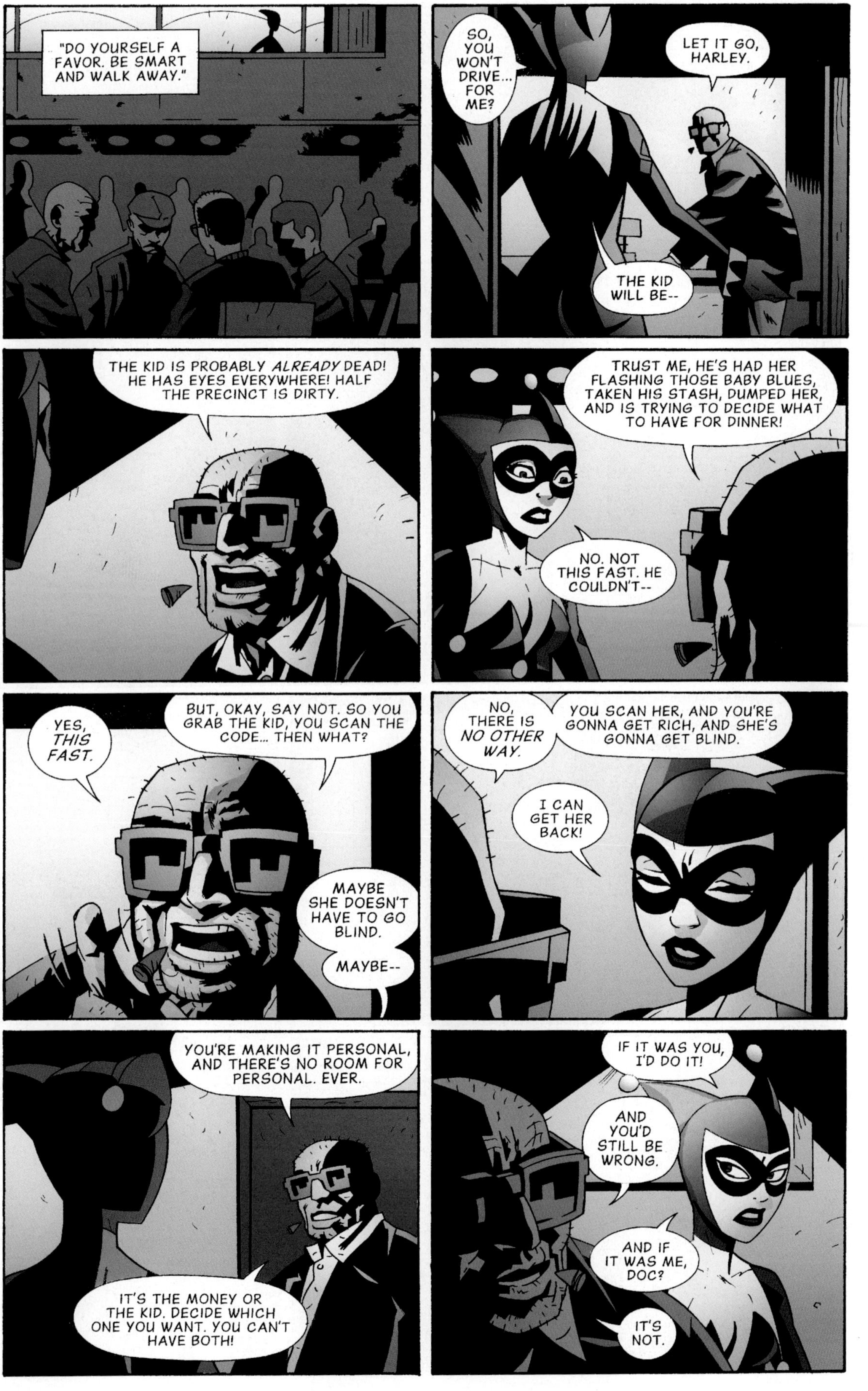
"DO YOURSELF A FAVOR. BE SMART AND WALK AWAY."
SO, YOU WON'T DRIVE... FOR ME?
LET IT GO, HARLEY.
THE KID WILL BE--
THE KID IS PROBABLY *ALREADY* DEAD! HE HAS EYES EVERYWHERE! HALF THE PRECINCT IS DIRTY.
TRUST ME, HE'S HAD HER FLASHING THOSE BABY BLUES, TAKEN HIS STASH, DUMPED HER, AND IS TRYING TO DECIDE WHAT TO HAVE FOR DINNER!
NO. NOT THIS FAST. HE COULDN'T--
YES, *THIS FAST.*
BUT, OKAY, SAY NOT. SO YOU GRAB THE KID, YOU SCAN THE CODE... THEN WHAT?
MAYBE SHE DOESN'T HAVE TO GO BLIND.
MAYBE--
NO, THERE IS *NO OTHER WAY.*
YOU SCAN HER, AND YOU'RE GONNA GET RICH, AND SHE'S GONNA GET BLIND.
I CAN GET HER BACK!
YOU'RE MAKING IT PERSONAL, AND THERE'S NO ROOM FOR PERSONAL. EVER.
IT'S THE MONEY OR THE KID. DECIDE WHICH ONE YOU WANT. YOU CAN'T HAVE BOTH!
IF IT WAS YOU, I'D DO IT!
AND YOU'D STILL BE WRONG.
AND IF IT WAS ME, DOC?
IT'S NOT.

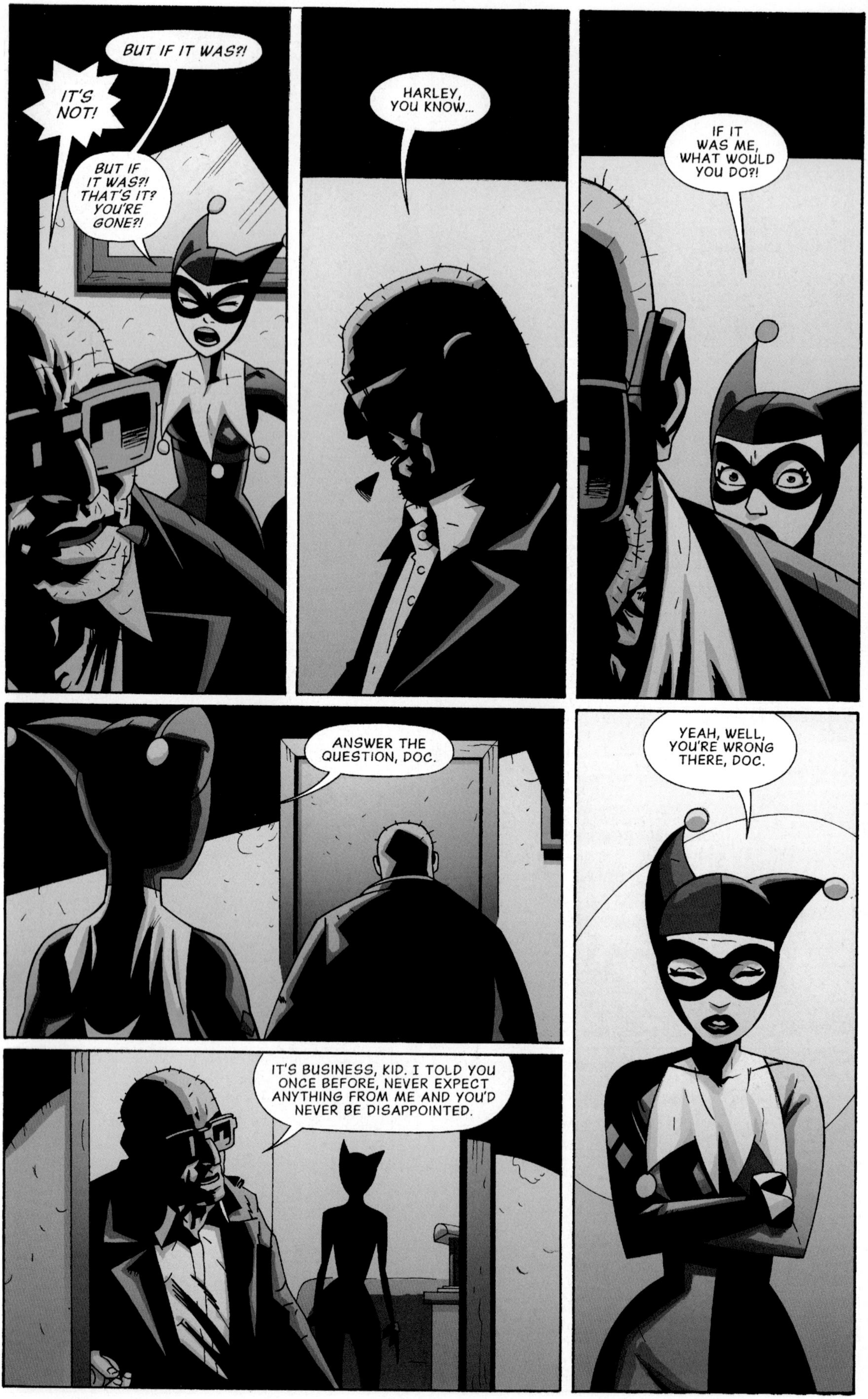
BUT IF IT WAS?!
IT'S NOT!
BUT IF IT WAS?! THAT'S IT? YOU'RE GONE?!
HARLEY, YOU KNOW...
IF IT WAS ME, WHAT WOULD YOU DO?!
ANSWER THE QUESTION, DOC.
IT'S BUSINESS, KID. I TOLD YOU ONCE BEFORE, NEVER EXPECT ANYTHING FROM ME AND YOU'D NEVER BE DISAPPOINTED.
YEAH, WELL, YOU'RE WRONG THERE, DOC.

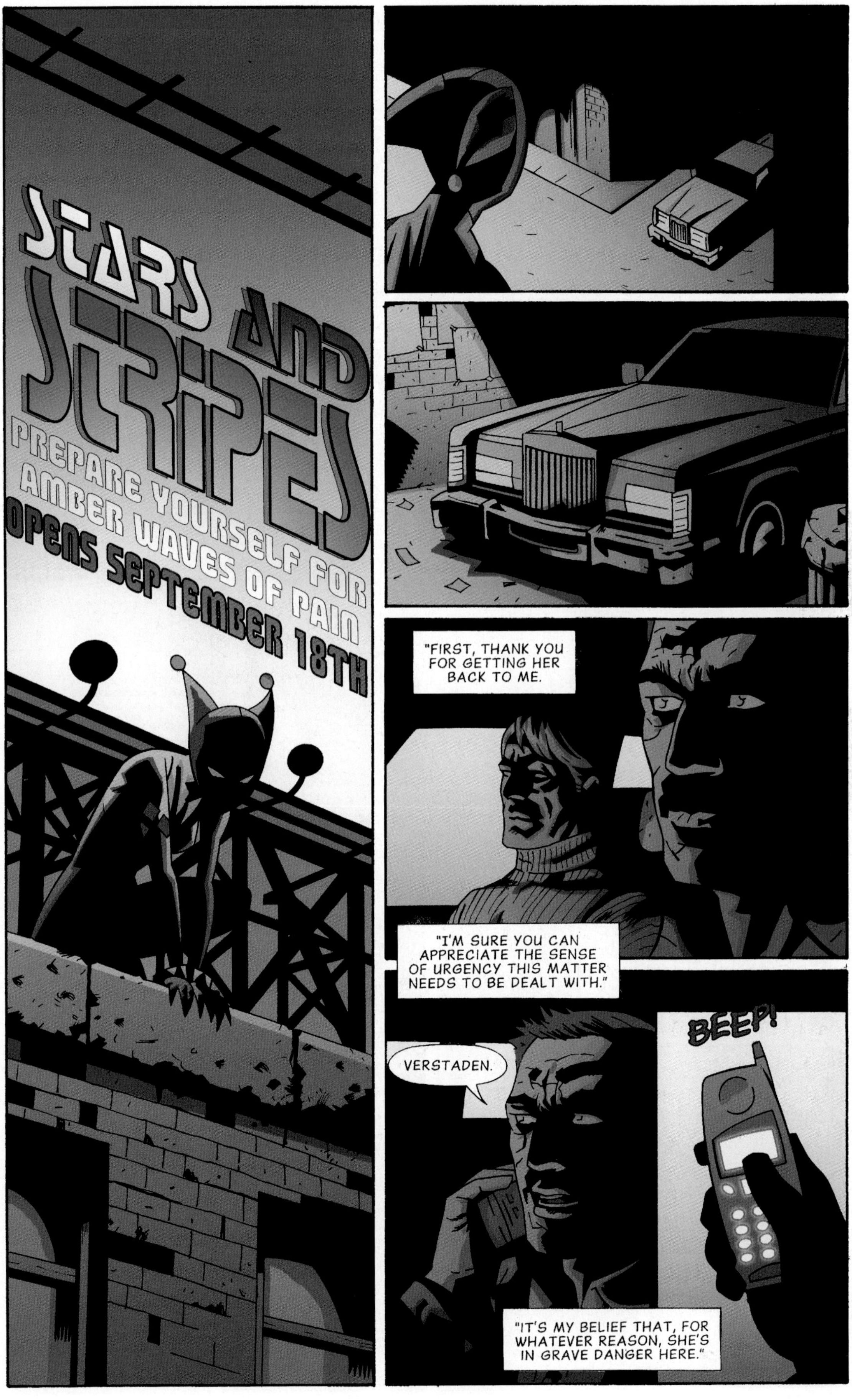
STARS AND STRIPES
PREPARE YOURSELF FOR
AMBER WAVES OF PAIN
OPENS SEPTEMBER 18TH
"FIRST, THANK YOU FOR GETTING HER BACK TO ME.
"I'M SURE YOU CAN APPRECIATE THE SENSE OF URGENCY THIS MATTER NEEDS TO BE DEALT WITH."
VERSTADEN.
BEEP!
"IT'S MY BELIEF THAT, FOR WHATEVER REASON, SHE'S IN GRAVE DANGER HERE."

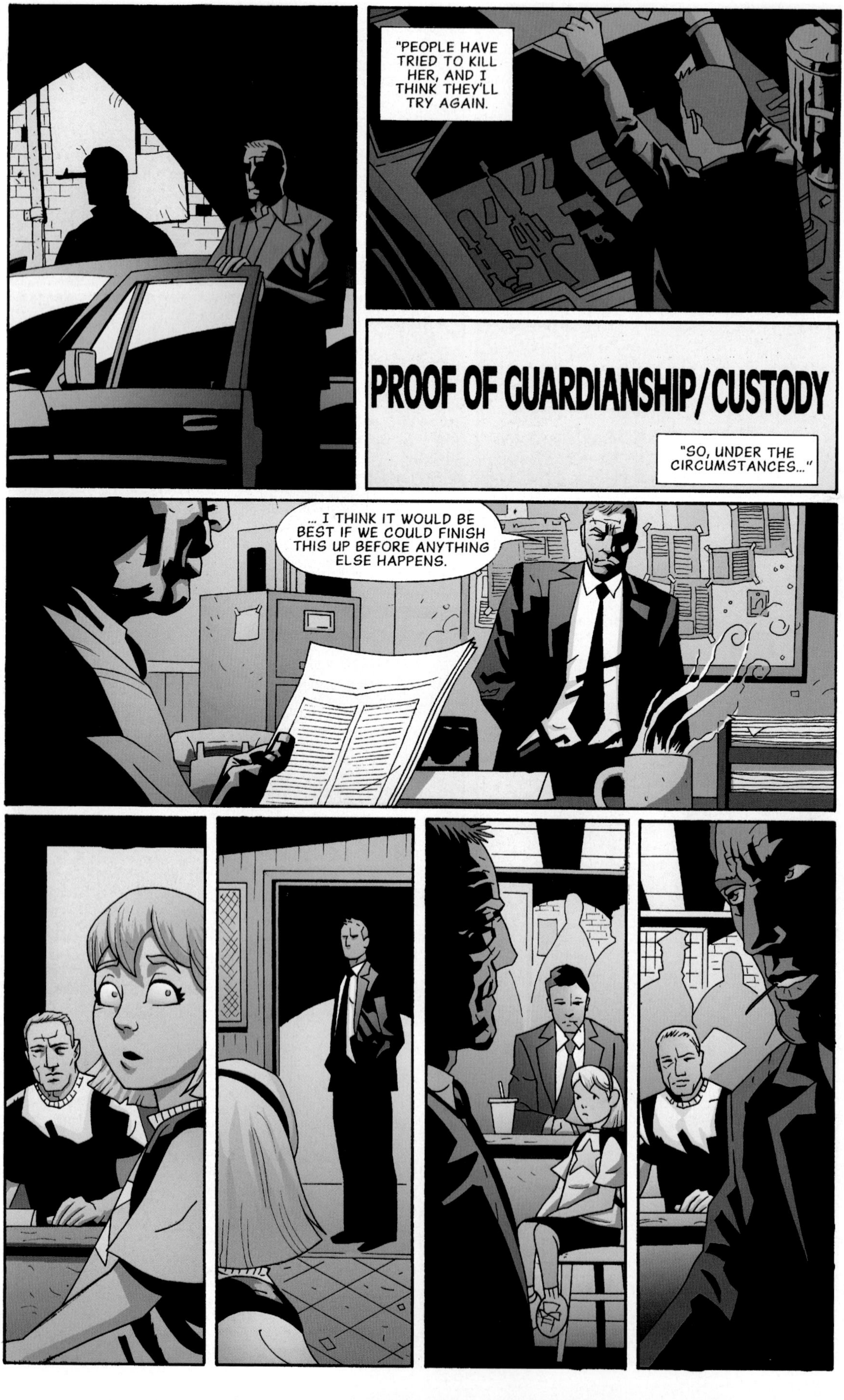
"PEOPLE HAVE TRIED TO KILL HER, AND I THINK THEY'LL TRY AGAIN.
PROOF OF GUARDIANSHIP/CUSTODY
"SO, UNDER THE CIRCUMSTANCES..."
... I THINK IT WOULD BE BEST IF WE COULD FINISH THIS UP BEFORE ANYTHING ELSE HAPPENS.

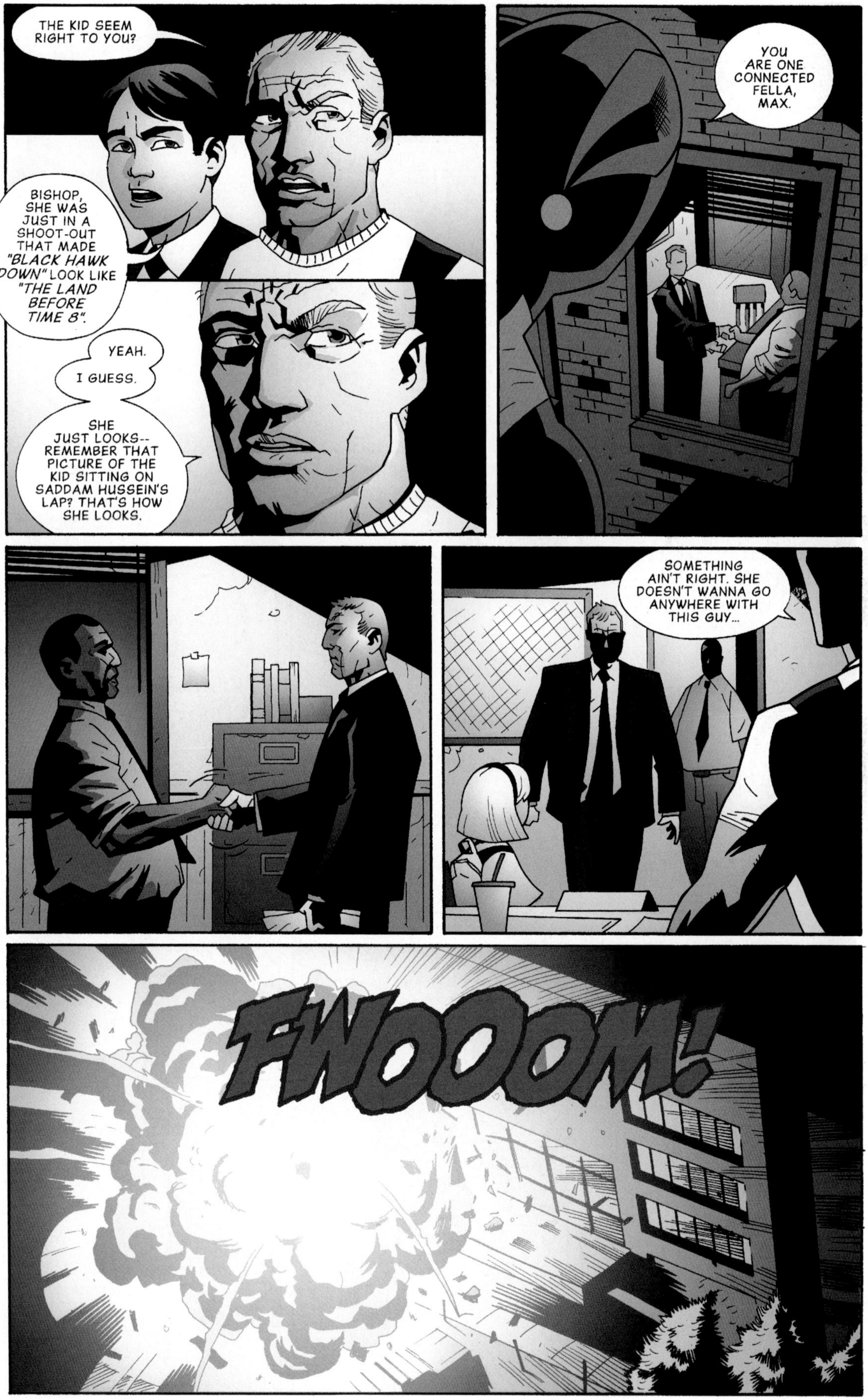
THE KID SEEM RIGHT TO YOU?
BISHOP, SHE WAS JUST IN A SHOOT-OUT THAT MADE "BLACK HAWK DOWN" LOOK LIKE "THE LAND BEFORE TIME 8".
YEAH.
I GUESS.
SHE JUST LOOKS-- REMEMBER THAT PICTURE OF THE KID SITTING ON SADDAM HUSSEIN'S LAP? THAT'S HOW SHE LOOKS.
YOU ARE ONE CONNECTED FELLA, MAX.
SOMETHING AIN'T RIGHT. SHE DOESN'T WANNA GO ANYWHERE WITH THIS GUY...
FWOOOOM!

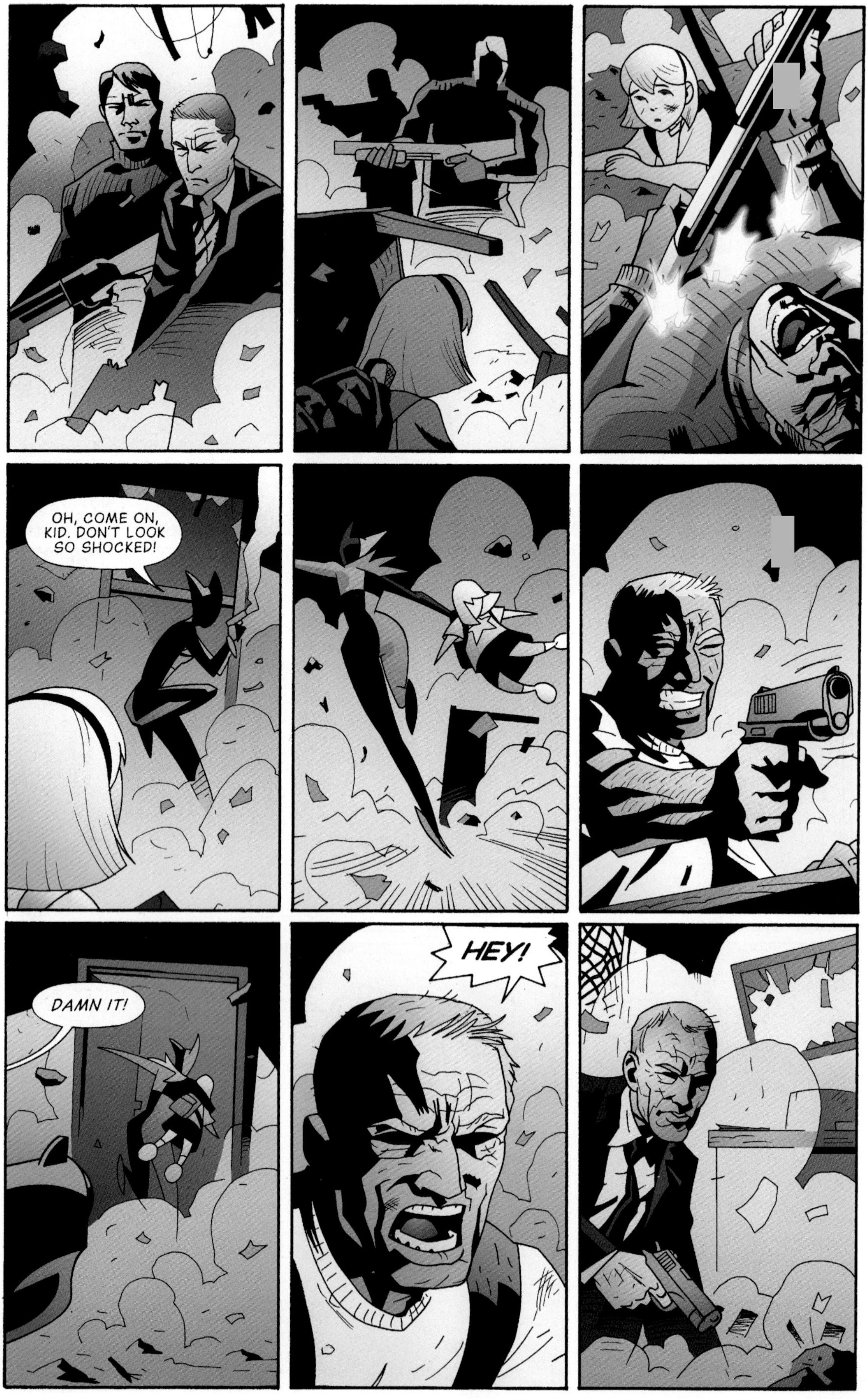
OH, COME ON, KID. DON'T LOOK SO SHOCKED!
DAMN IT!
HEY!

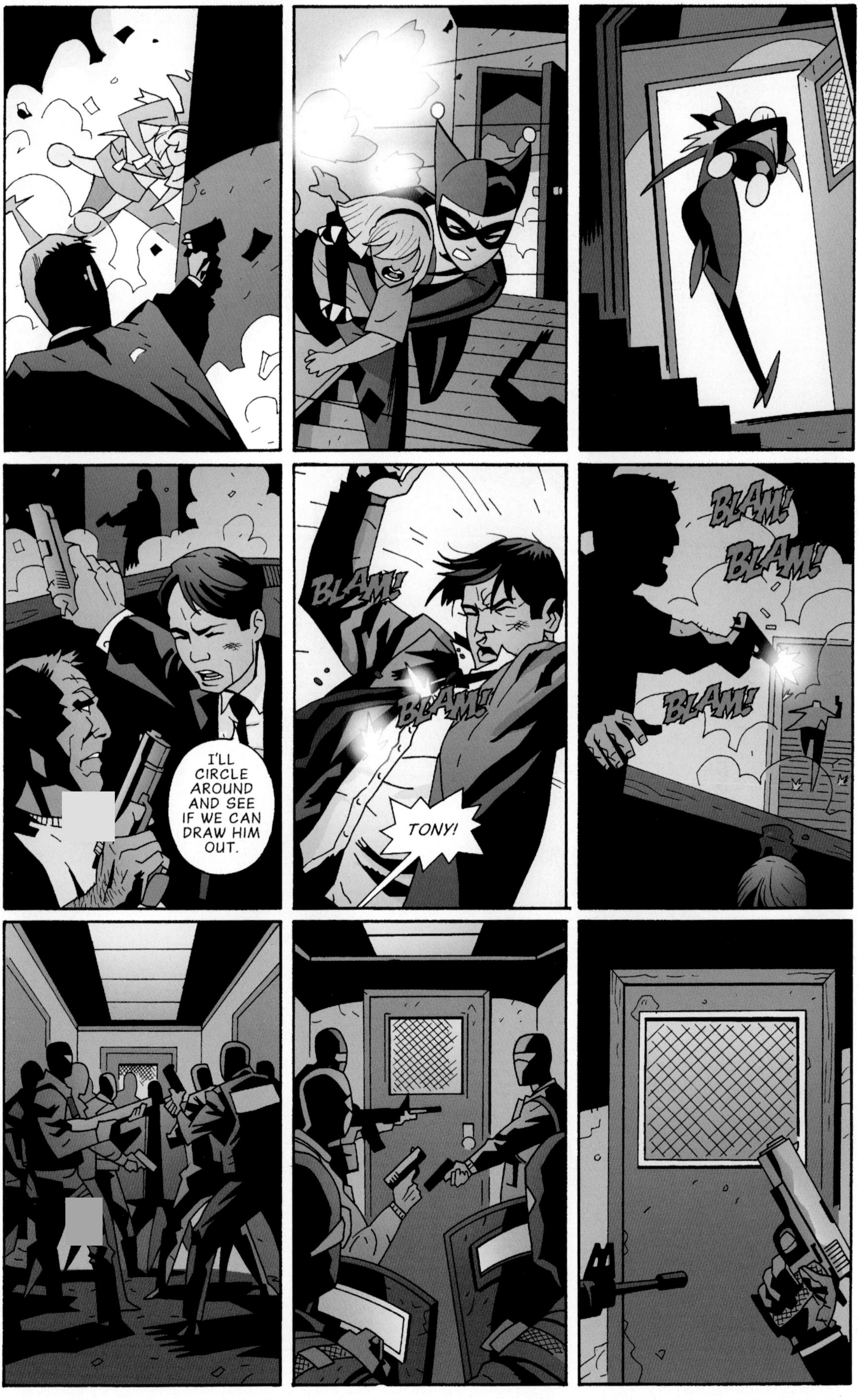
I'LL CIRCLE AROUND AND SEE IF WE CAN DRAW HIM OUT.
BLAM!
BLAM!
TONY!
BLAM!
BLAM!
BLAM!

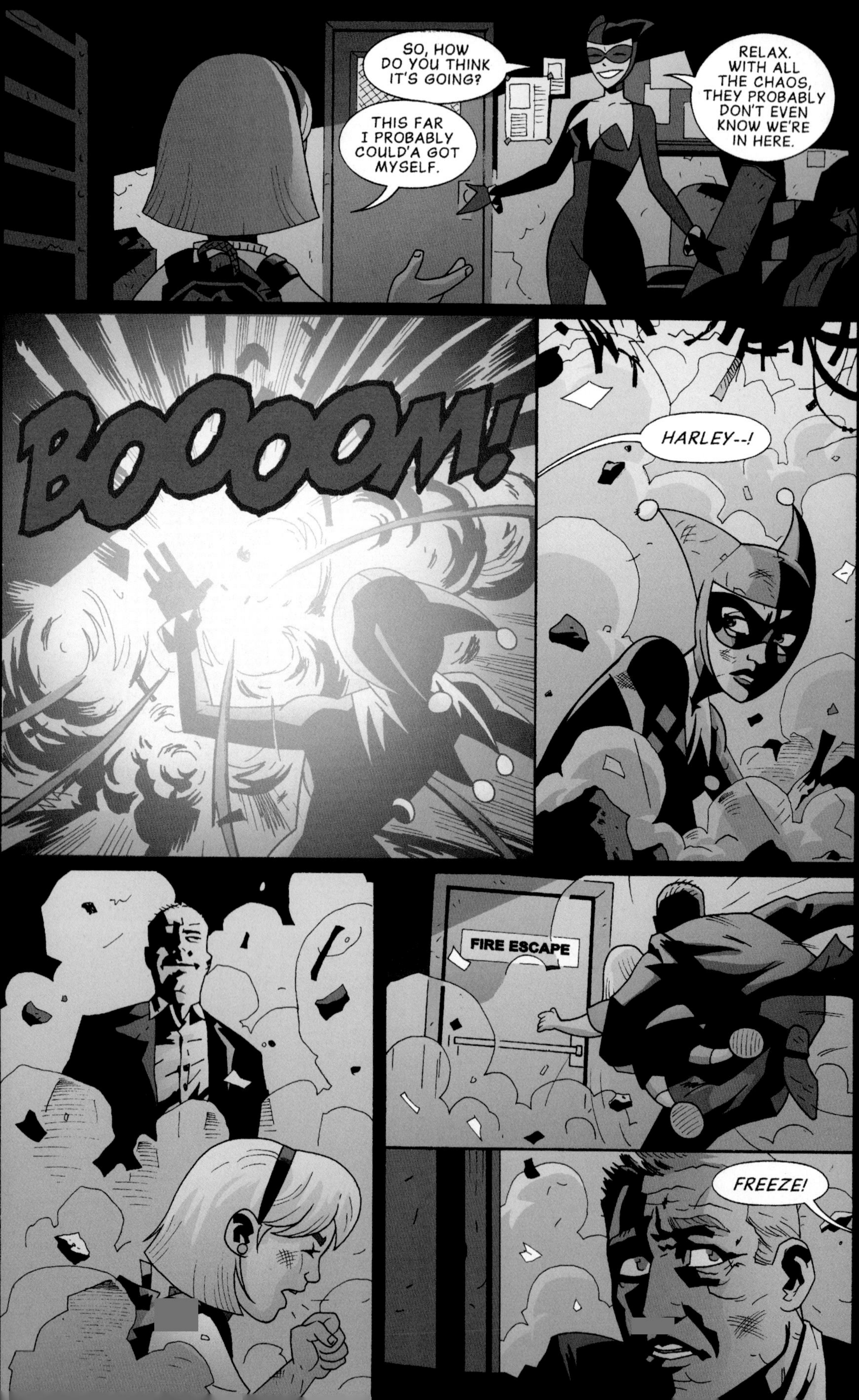

SO, HOW DO YOU THINK IT'S GOING?
THIS FAR I PROBABLY COULD'A GOT MYSELF.
RELAX. WITH ALL THE CHAOS, THEY PROBABLY DON'T EVEN KNOW WE'RE IN HERE.
BOOOOM!
HARLEY--!
FIRE ESCAPE
FREEZE!

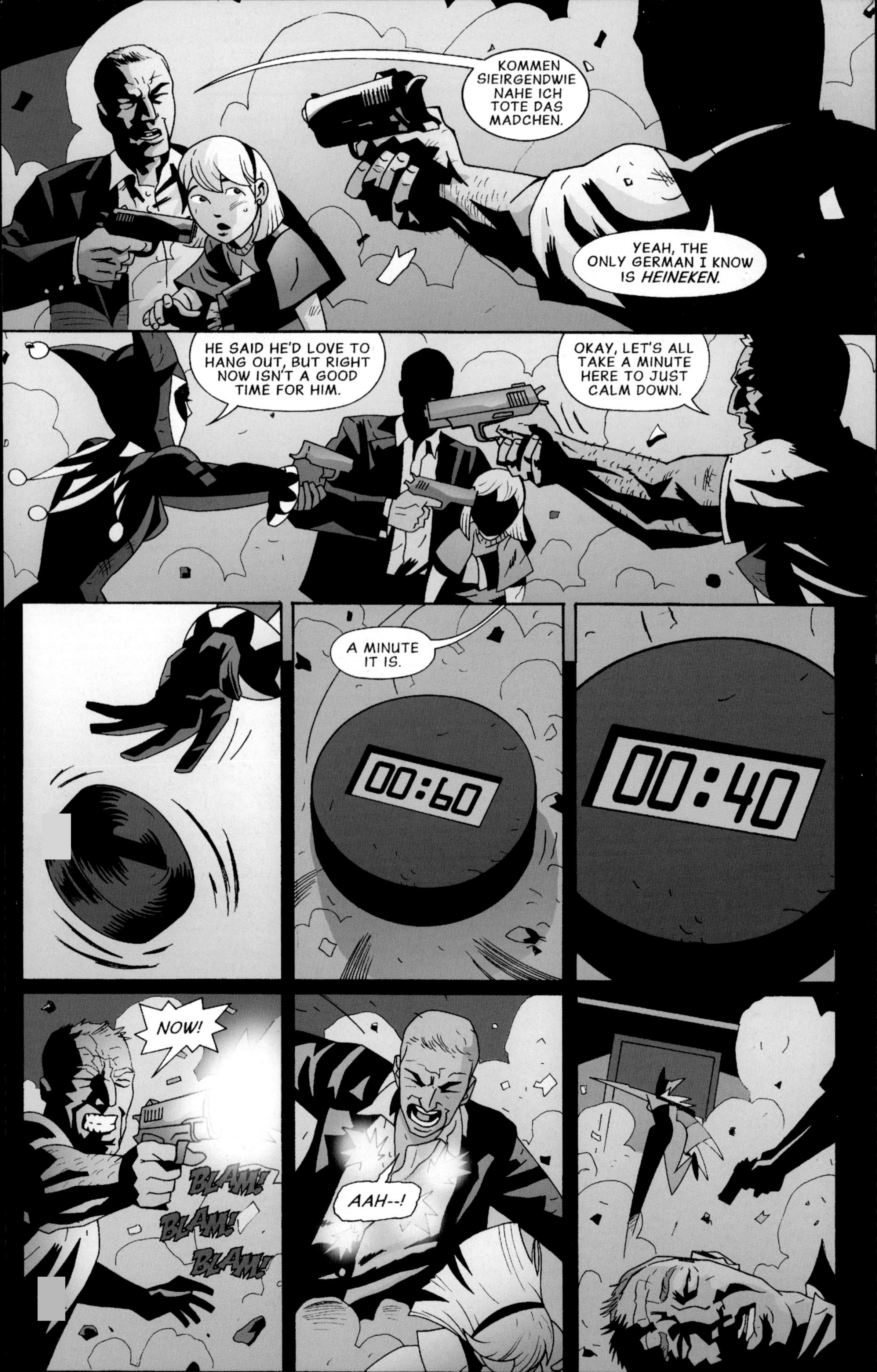
KOMMEN SIEIRGENDWIE NAHE ICH TOTE DAS MADCHEN.
YEAH, THE ONLY GERMAN I KNOW IS *HEINEKEN.*
HE SAID HE'D LOVE TO HANG OUT, BUT RIGHT NOW ISN'T A GOOD TIME FOR HIM.
OKAY, LET'S ALL TAKE A MINUTE HERE TO JUST CALM DOWN.
A MINUTE IT IS.
00:60
00:40
NOW!
BLAM!
BLAM!
BLAM!
AAH--!

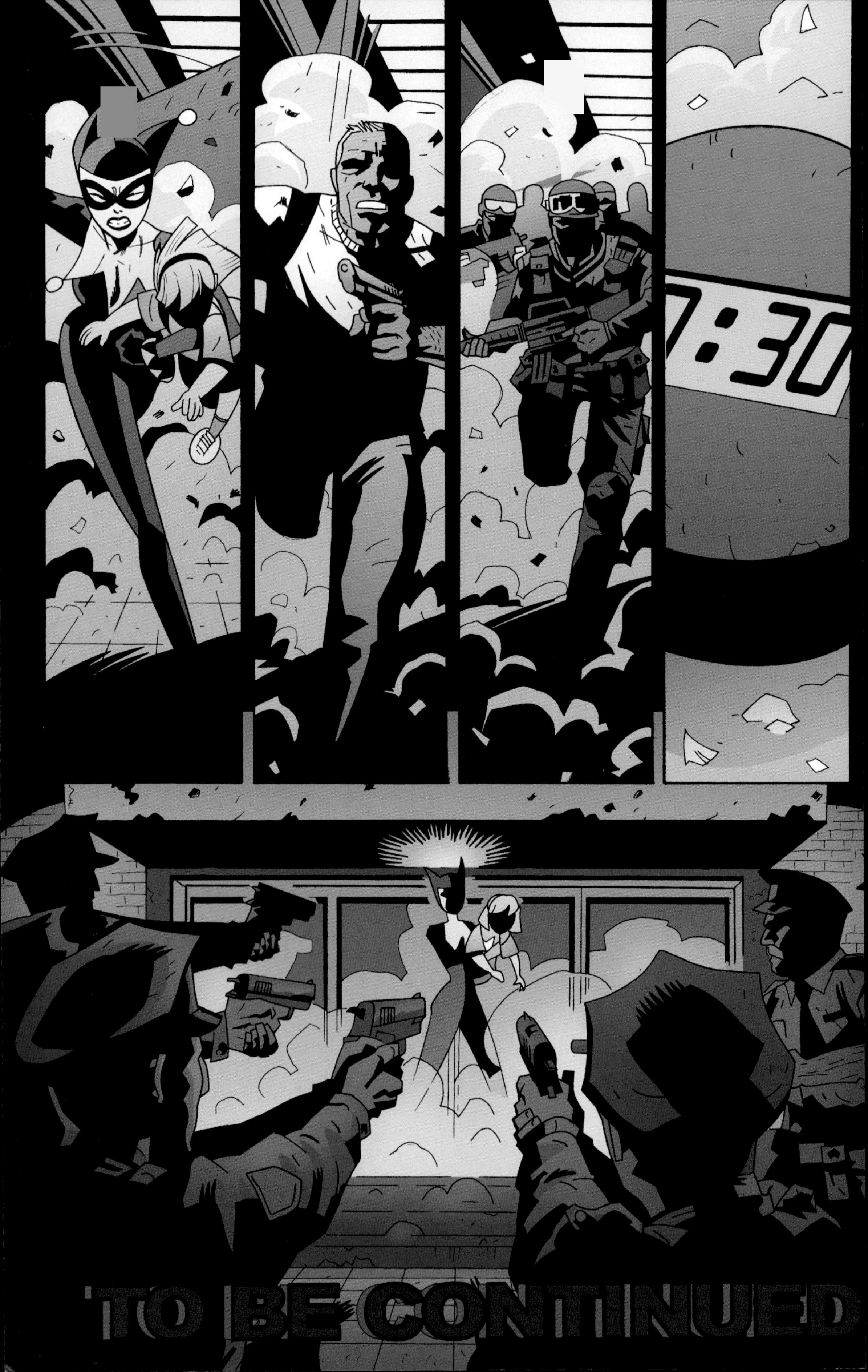
:30
TO BE CONTINUED

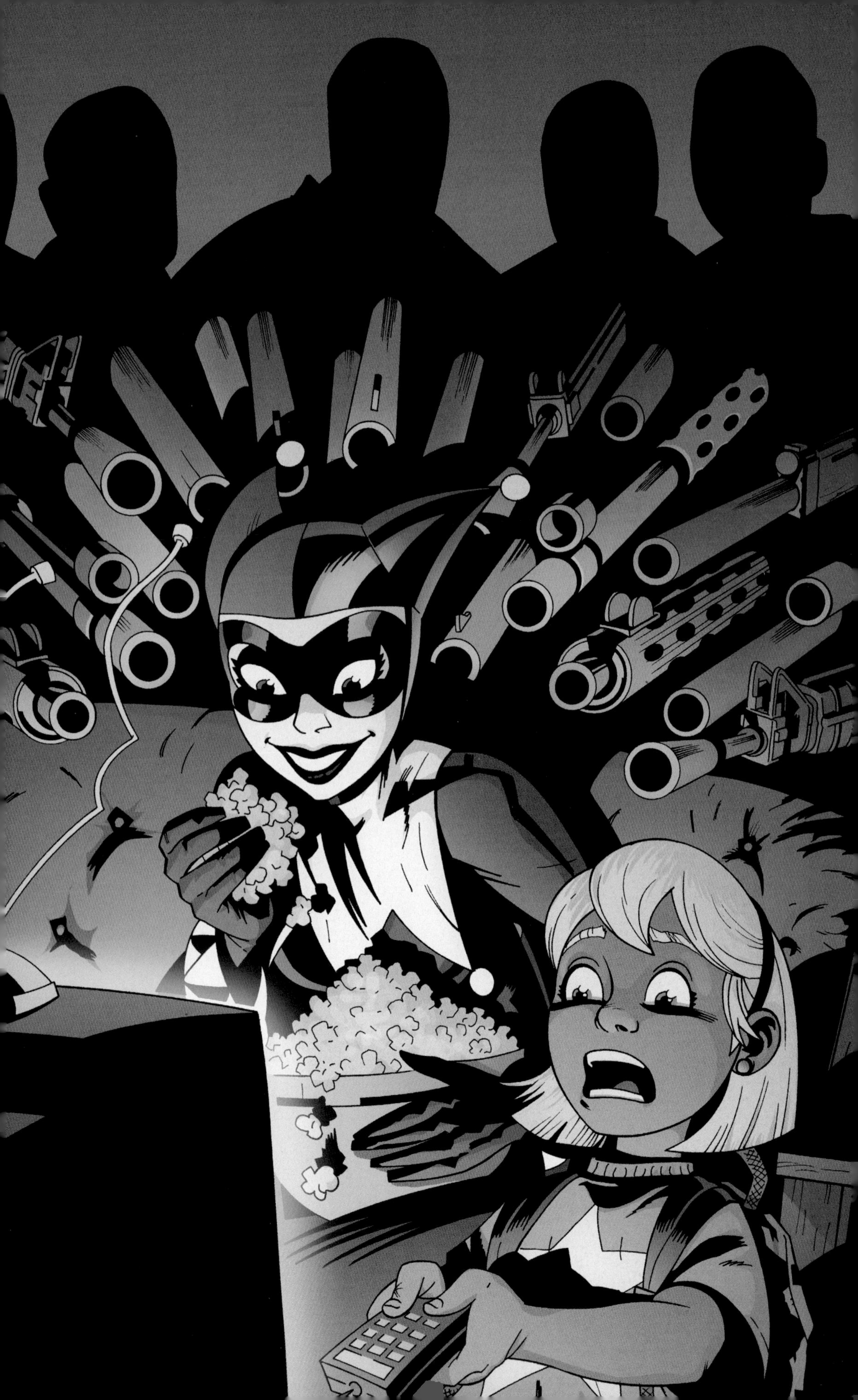

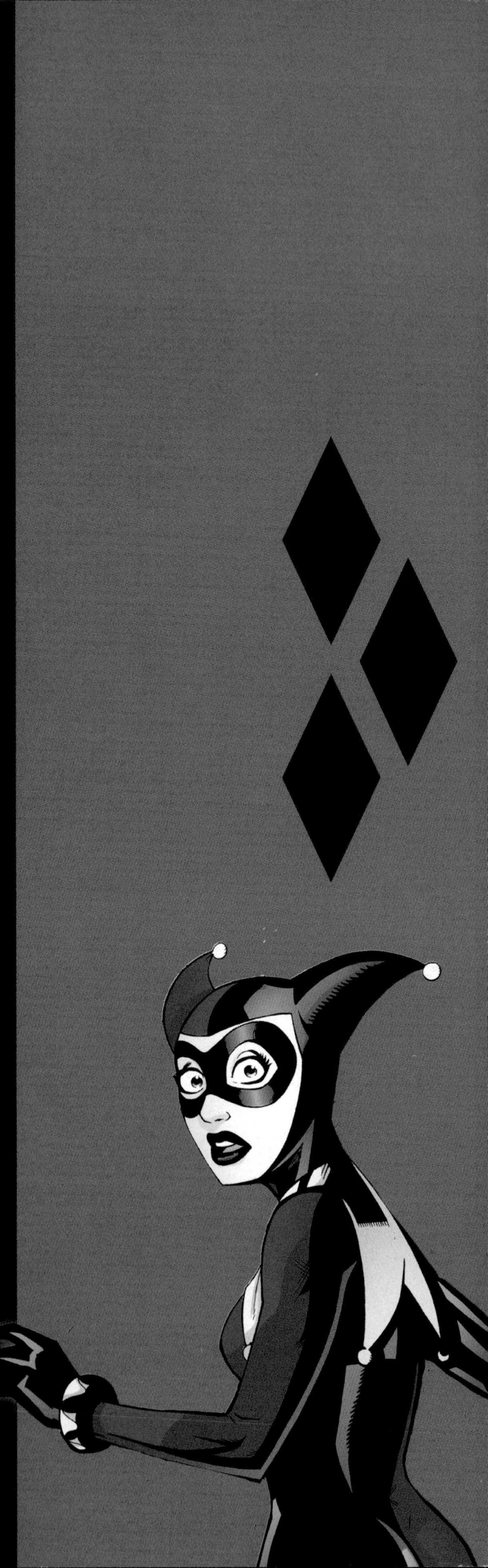

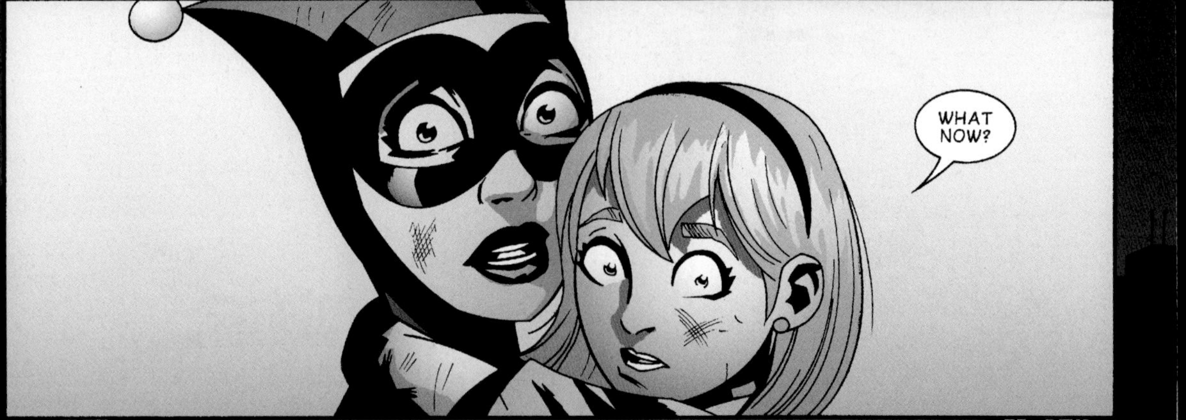
WHAT NOW?

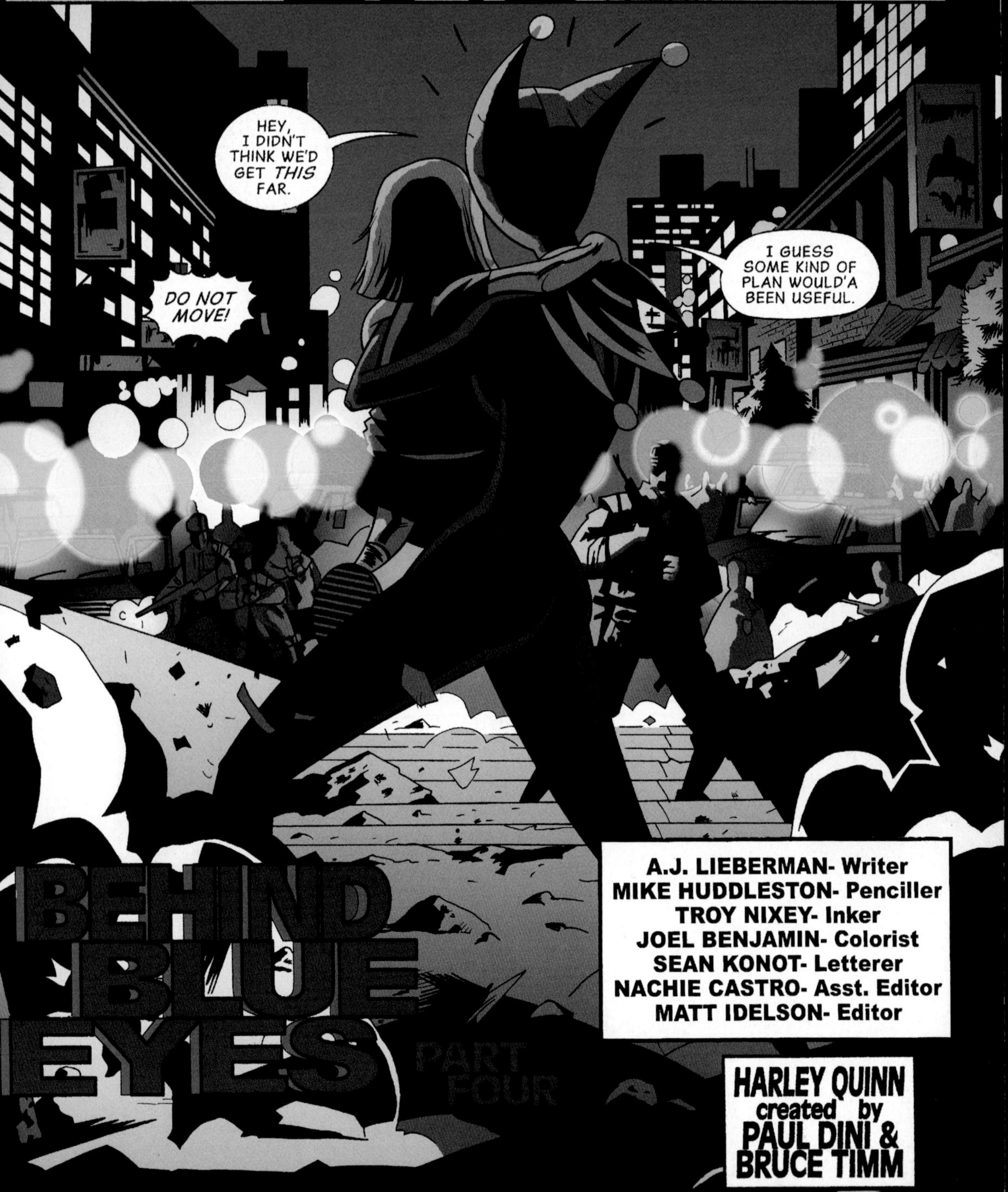
HEY, I DIDN'T THINK WE'D GET *THIS* FAR.
I GUESS SOME KIND OF PLAN WOULD'A BEEN USEFUL.
DO NOT MOVE!
BEHIND BLUE EYES
PART FOUR
A.J. LIEBERMAN- Writer
MIKE HUDDLESTON- Penciller
TROY NIXEY- Inker
JOEL BENJAMIN- Colorist
SEAN KONOT- Letterer
NACHIE CASTRO- Asst. Editor
MATT IDELSON- Editor
HARLEY QUINN created by PAUL DINI & BRUCE TIMM

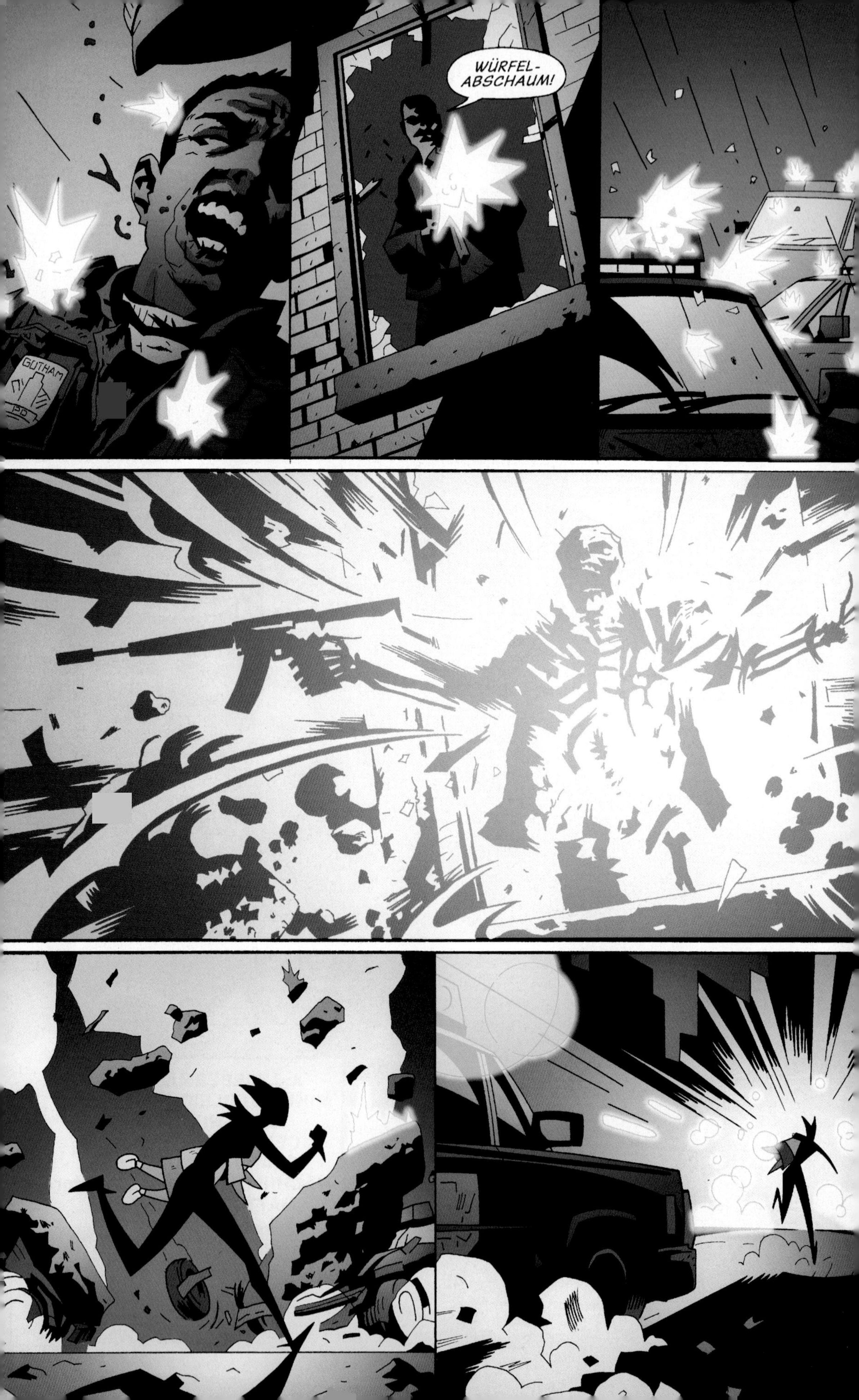
WÜRFEL-
ABSCHAUM!
GOTHAM
PD

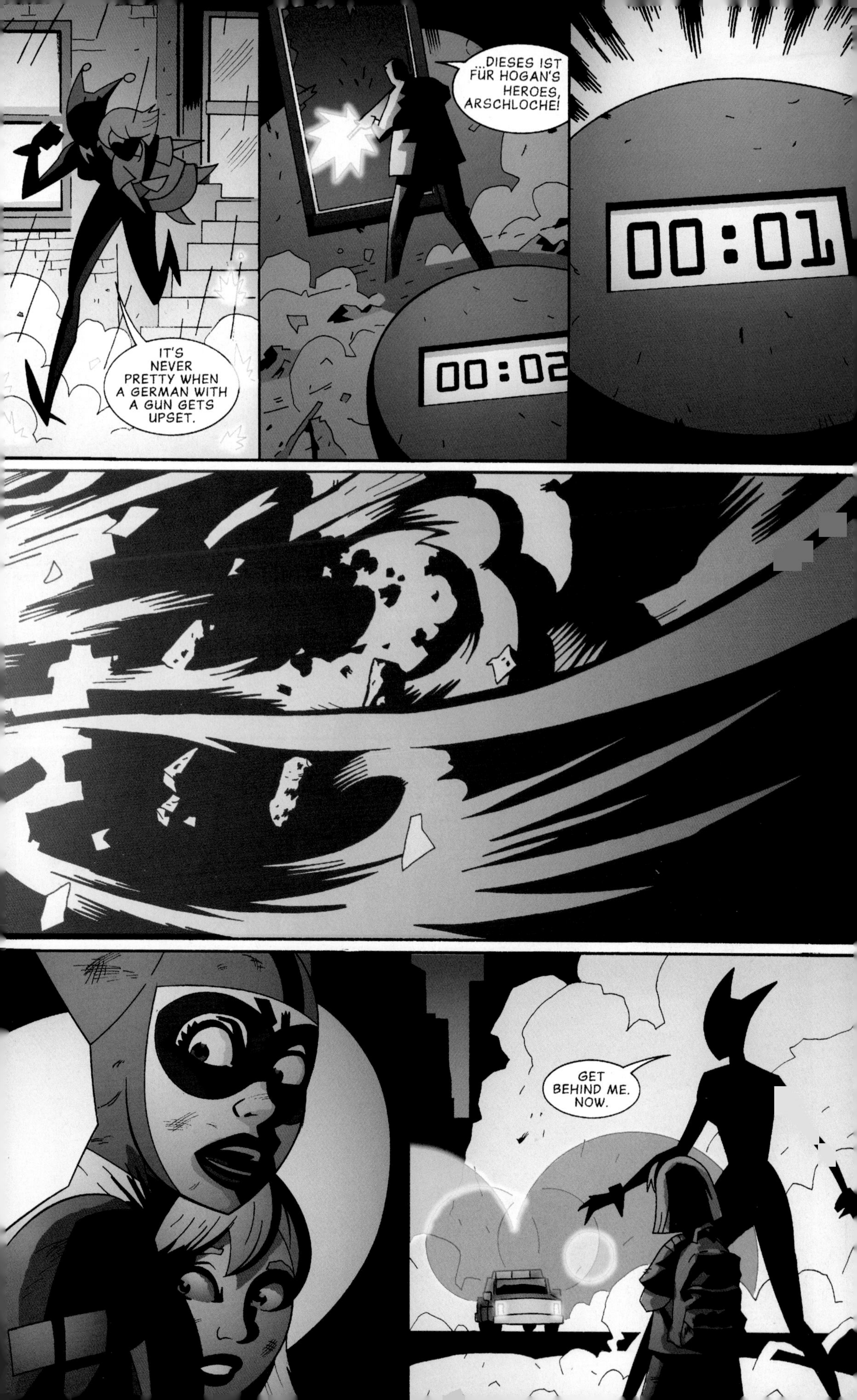
IT'S NEVER PRETTY WHEN A GERMAN WITH A GUN GETS UPSET.
...DIESES IST FÜR HOGAN'S HEROES, ARSCHLOCHE!
00:02
00:01
GET BEHIND ME. NOW.

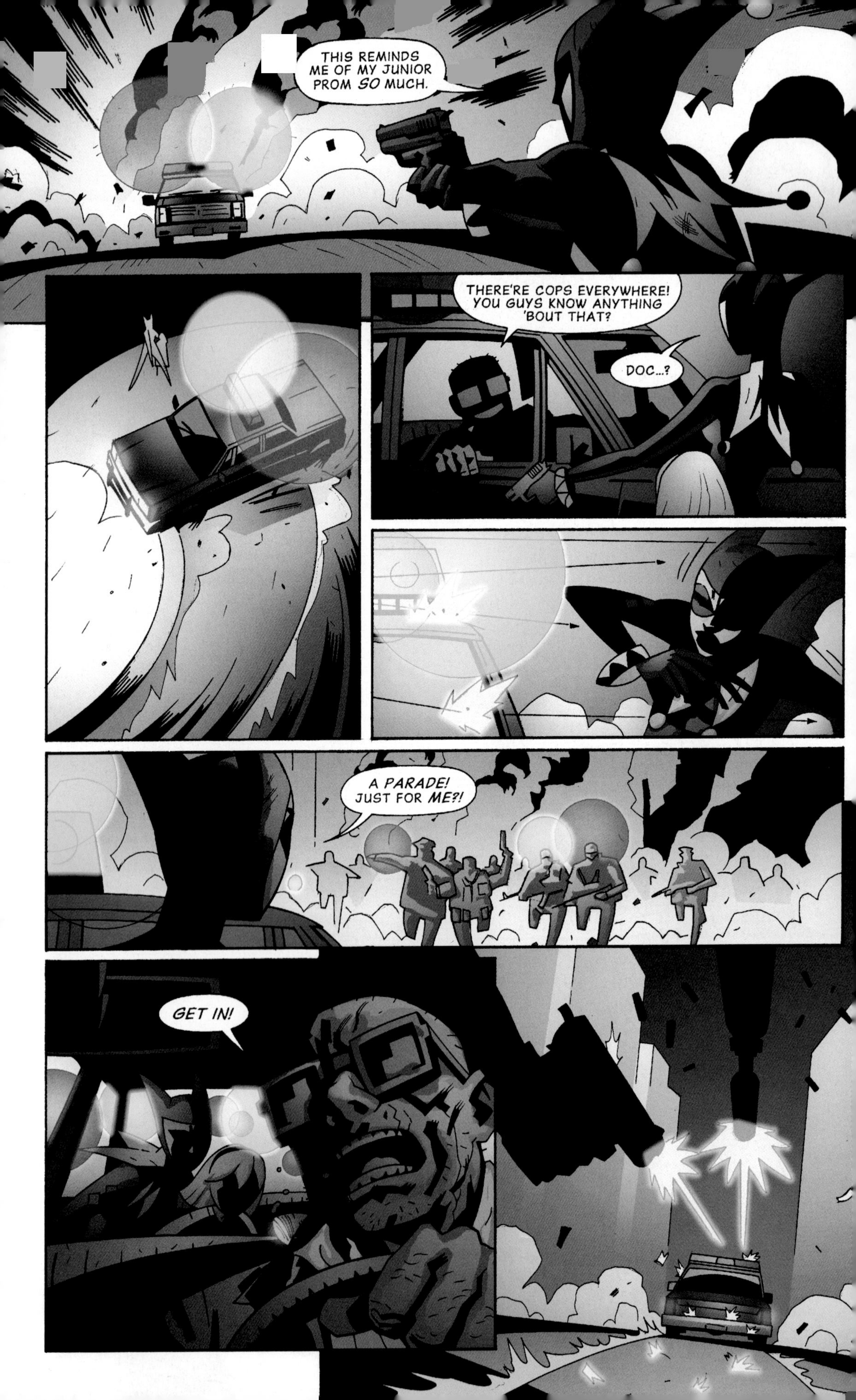
THIS REMINDS ME OF MY JUNIOR PROM SO MUCH.
THERE'RE COPS EVERYWHERE! YOU GUYS KNOW ANYTHING 'BOUT THAT?
DOC...?
A PARADE! JUST FOR ME?!
GET IN!

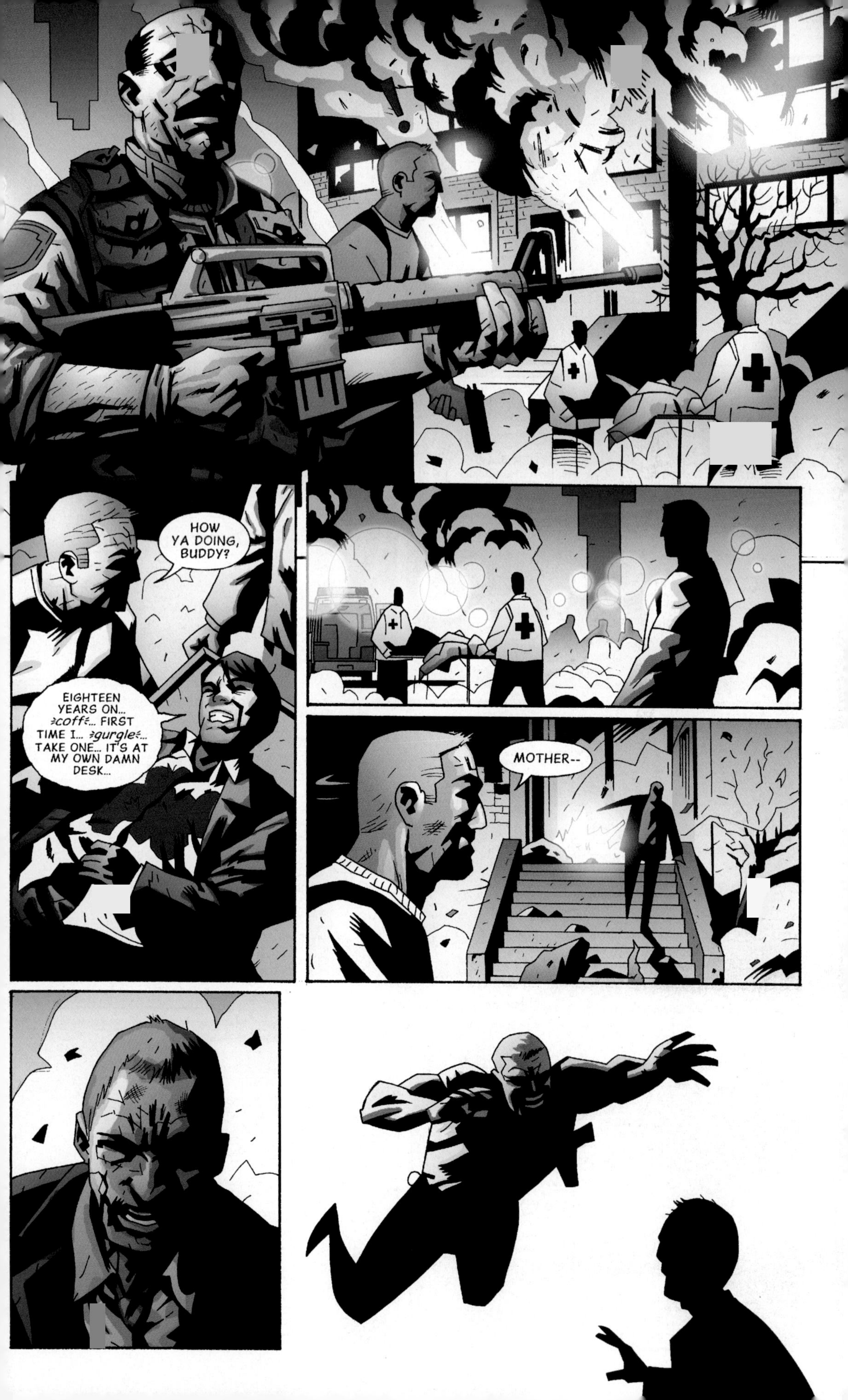
HOW YA DOING, BUDDY?
EIGHTEEN YEARS ON... *coff*... FIRST TIME I... *gurgle*... TAKE ONE... IT'S AT MY OWN DAMN DESK...
MOTHER--

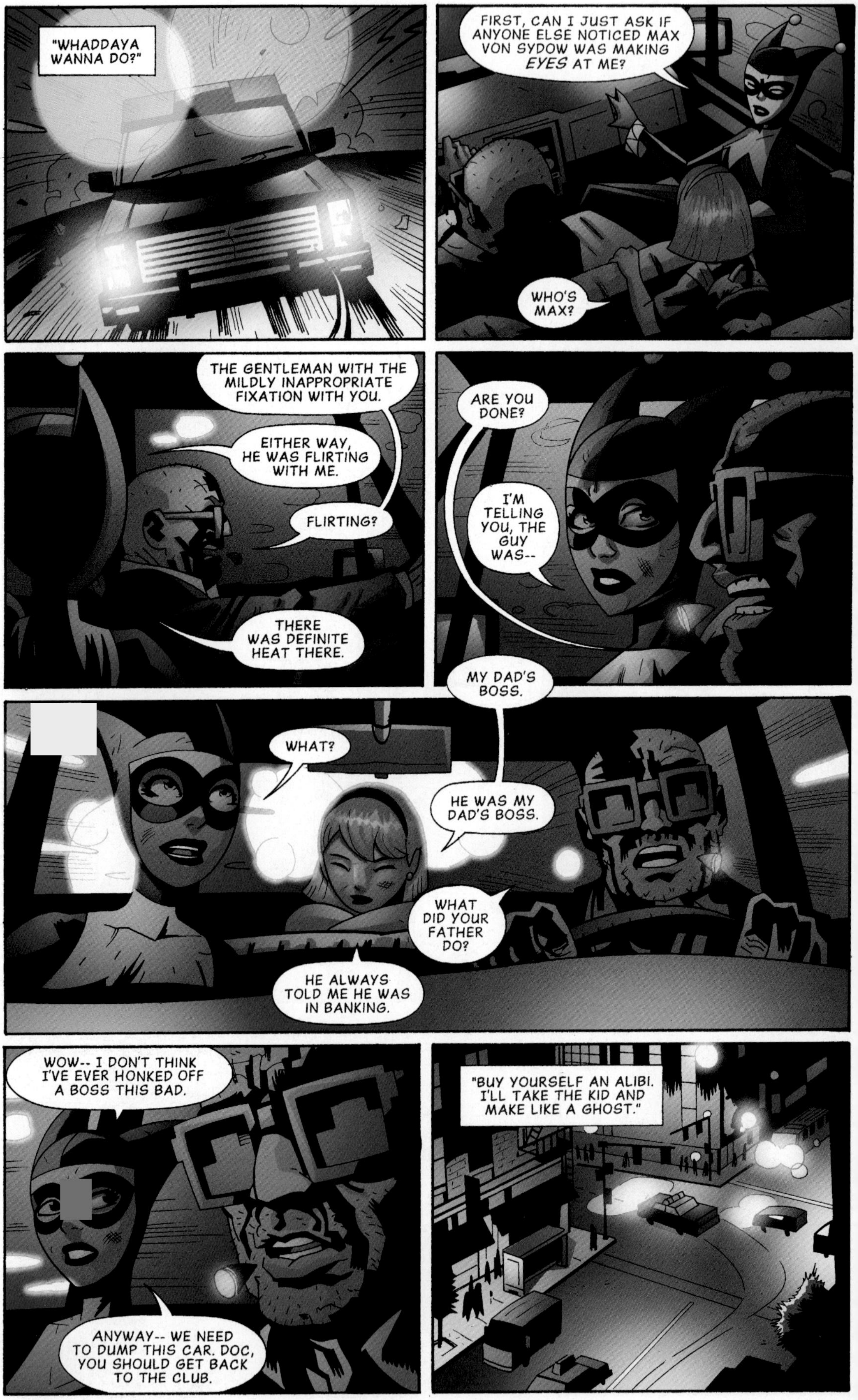
"WHADDAYA WANNA DO?"
FIRST, CAN I JUST ASK IF ANYONE ELSE NOTICED MAX VON SYDOW WAS MAKING *EYES* AT ME?
WHO'S MAX?
THE GENTLEMAN WITH THE MILDLY INAPPROPRIATE FIXATION WITH YOU.
EITHER WAY, HE WAS FLIRTING WITH ME.
FLIRTING?
THERE WAS DEFINITE HEAT THERE.
ARE YOU DONE?
I'M TELLING YOU, THE GUY WAS--
MY DAD'S BOSS.
WHAT?
HE WAS MY DAD'S BOSS.
WHAT DID YOUR FATHER DO?
HE ALWAYS TOLD ME HE WAS IN BANKING.
WOW-- I DON'T THINK I'VE EVER HONKED OFF A BOSS THIS BAD.
ANYWAY-- WE NEED TO DUMP THIS CAR. DOC, YOU SHOULD GET BACK TO THE CLUB.
"BUY YOURSELF AN ALIBI. I'LL TAKE THE KID AND MAKE LIKE A GHOST."

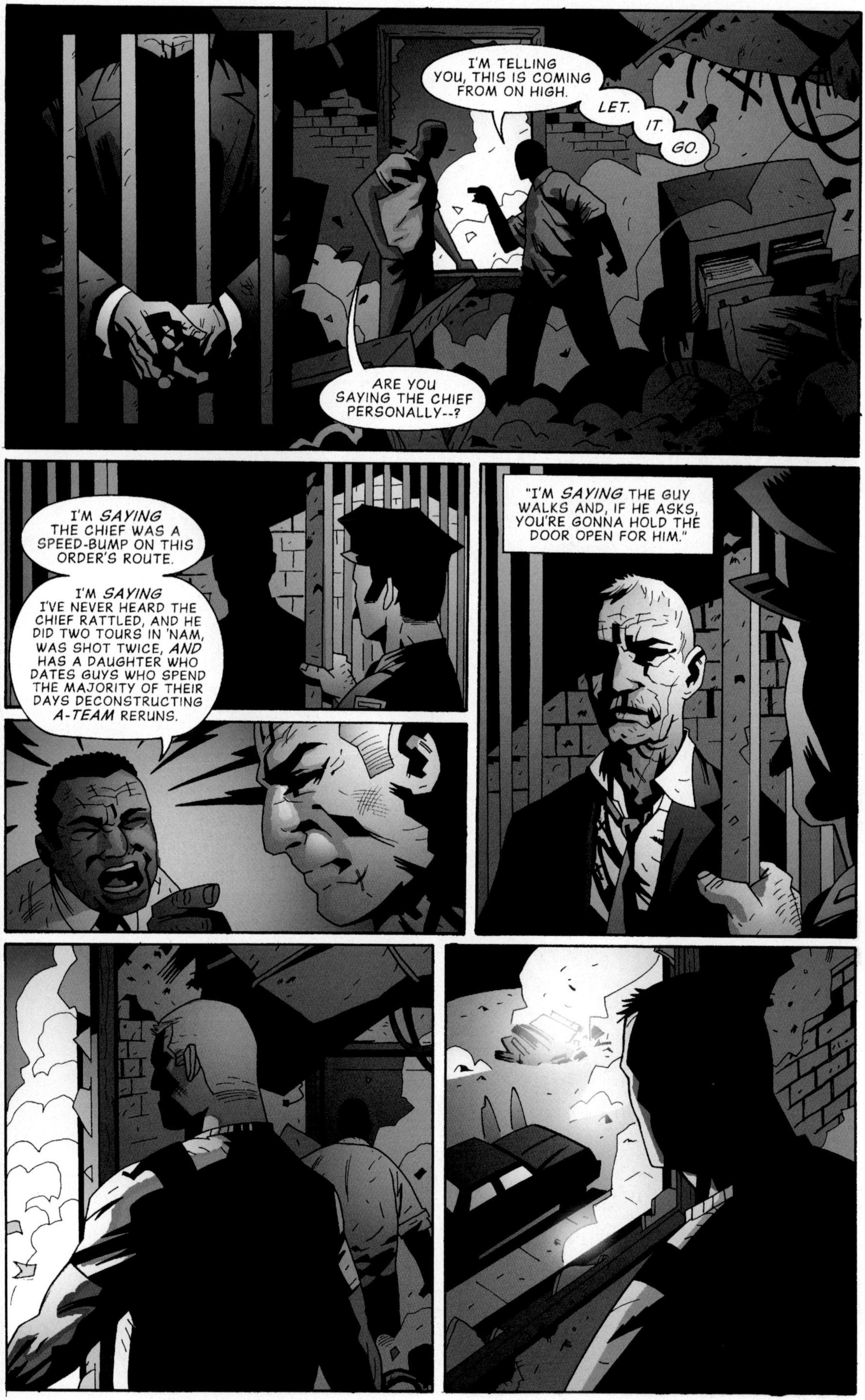
I'M TELLING YOU, THIS IS COMING FROM ON HIGH.
LET. IT. GO.
ARE YOU SAYING THE CHIEF PERSONALLY--?
I'M SAYING THE CHIEF WAS A SPEED-BUMP ON THIS ORDER'S ROUTE.
I'M SAYING I'VE NEVER HEARD THE CHIEF RATTLED, AND HE DID TWO TOURS IN 'NAM, WAS SHOT TWICE, AND HAS A DAUGHTER WHO DATES GUYS WHO SPEND THE MAJORITY OF THEIR DAYS DECONSTRUCTING A-TEAM RERUNS.
"I'M SAYING THE GUY WALKS AND, IF HE ASKS, YOU'RE GONNA HOLD THE DOOR OPEN FOR HIM."

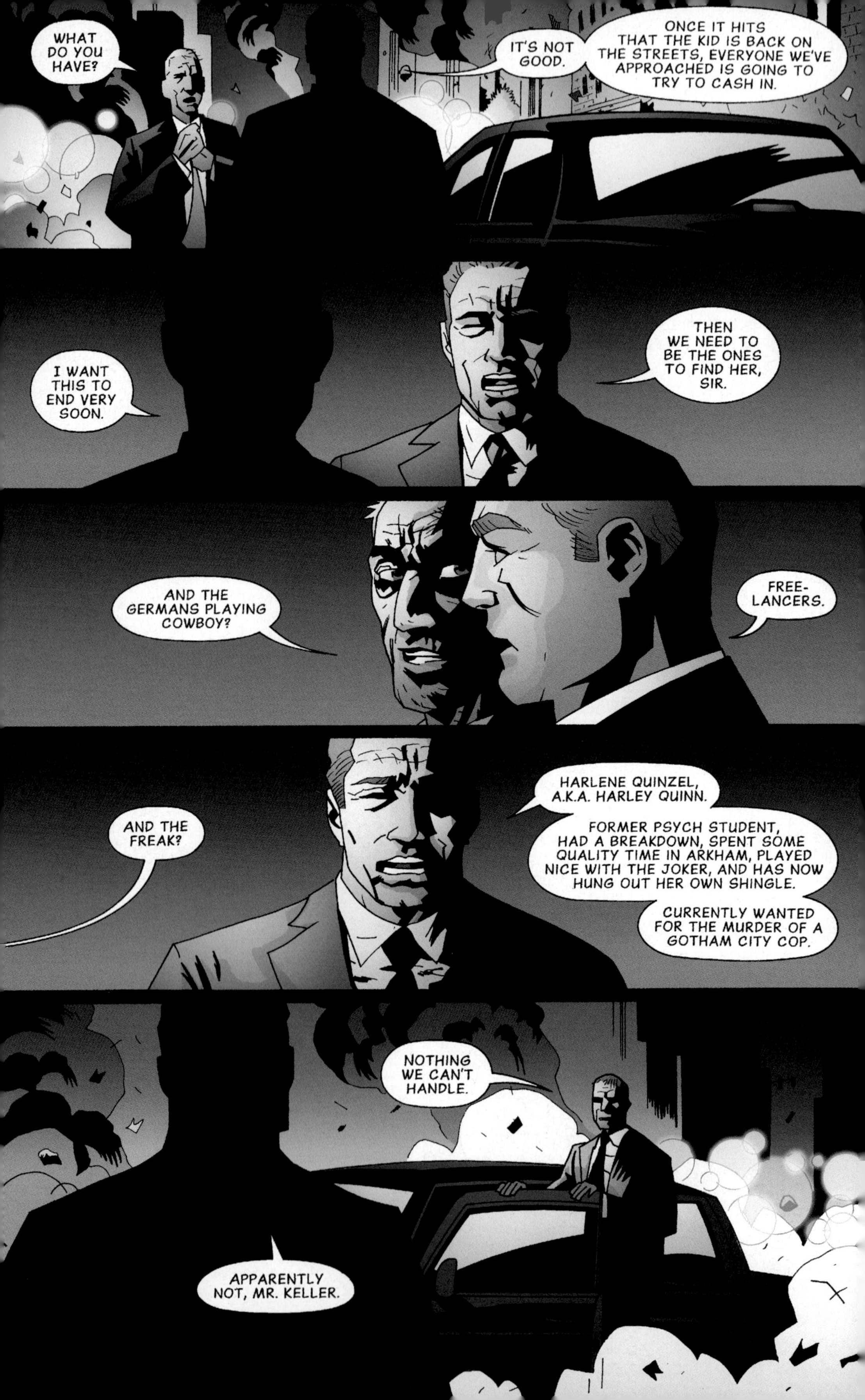
WHAT DO YOU HAVE?
IT'S NOT GOOD.
ONCE IT HITS THAT THE KID IS BACK ON THE STREETS, EVERYONE WE'VE APPROACHED IS GOING TO TRY TO CASH IN.
I WANT THIS TO END VERY SOON.
THEN WE NEED TO BE THE ONES TO FIND HER, SIR.
AND THE GERMANS PLAYING COWBOY?
FREE-LANCERS.
AND THE FREAK?
HARLENE QUINZEL, A.K.A. HARLEY QUINN.
FORMER PSYCH STUDENT, HAD A BREAKDOWN, SPENT SOME QUALITY TIME IN ARKHAM, PLAYED NICE WITH THE JOKER, AND HAS NOW HUNG OUT HER OWN SHINGLE.
CURRENTLY WANTED FOR THE MURDER OF A GOTHAM CITY COP.
NOTHING WE CAN'T HANDLE.
APPARENTLY NOT, MR. KELLER.

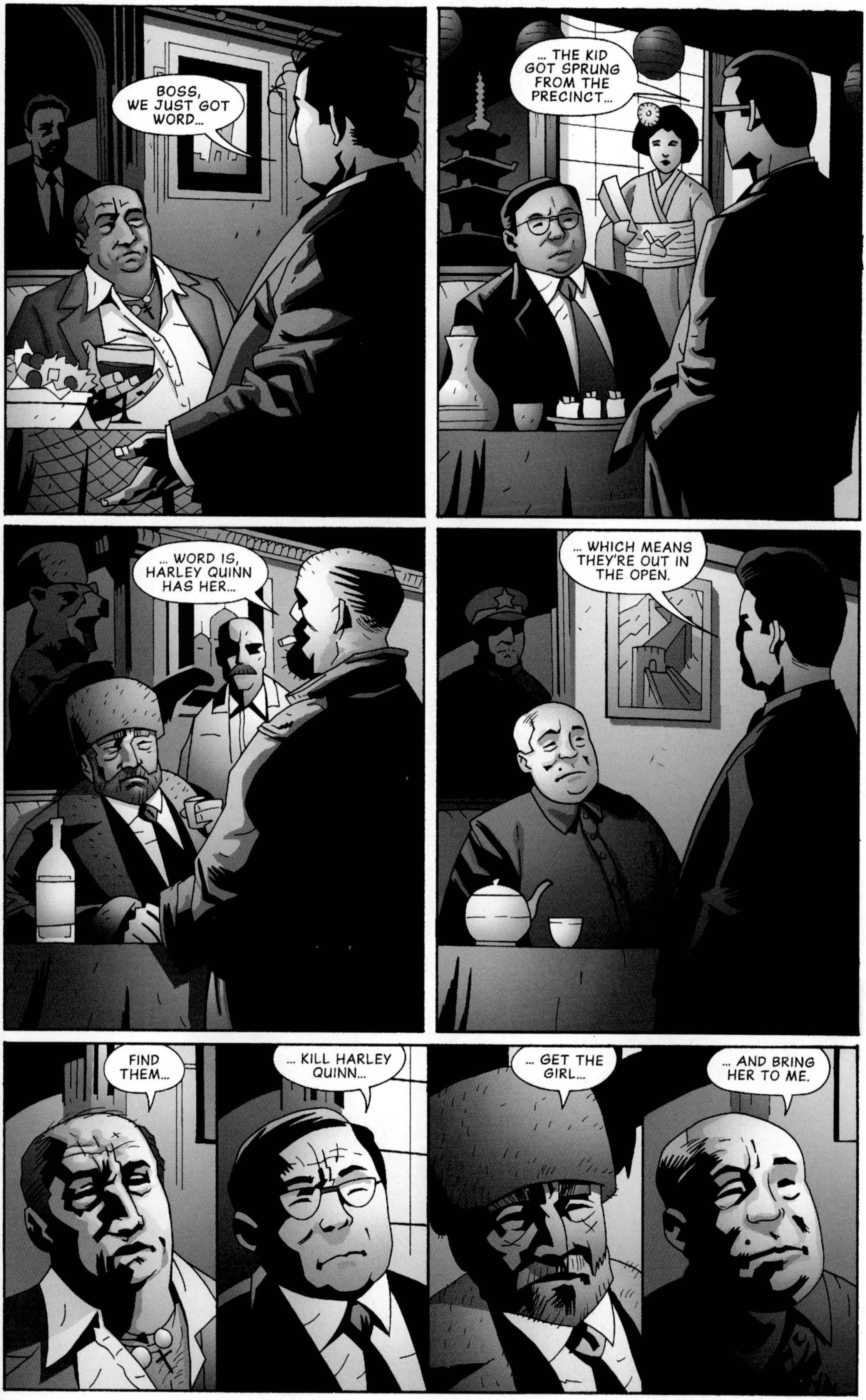
BOSS, WE JUST GOT WORD...
... THE KID GOT SPRUNG FROM THE PRECINCT...
... WORD IS, HARLEY QUINN HAS HER...
... WHICH MEANS THEY'RE OUT IN THE OPEN.
FIND THEM...
... KILL HARLEY QUINN...
... GET THE GIRL...
... AND BRING HER TO ME.

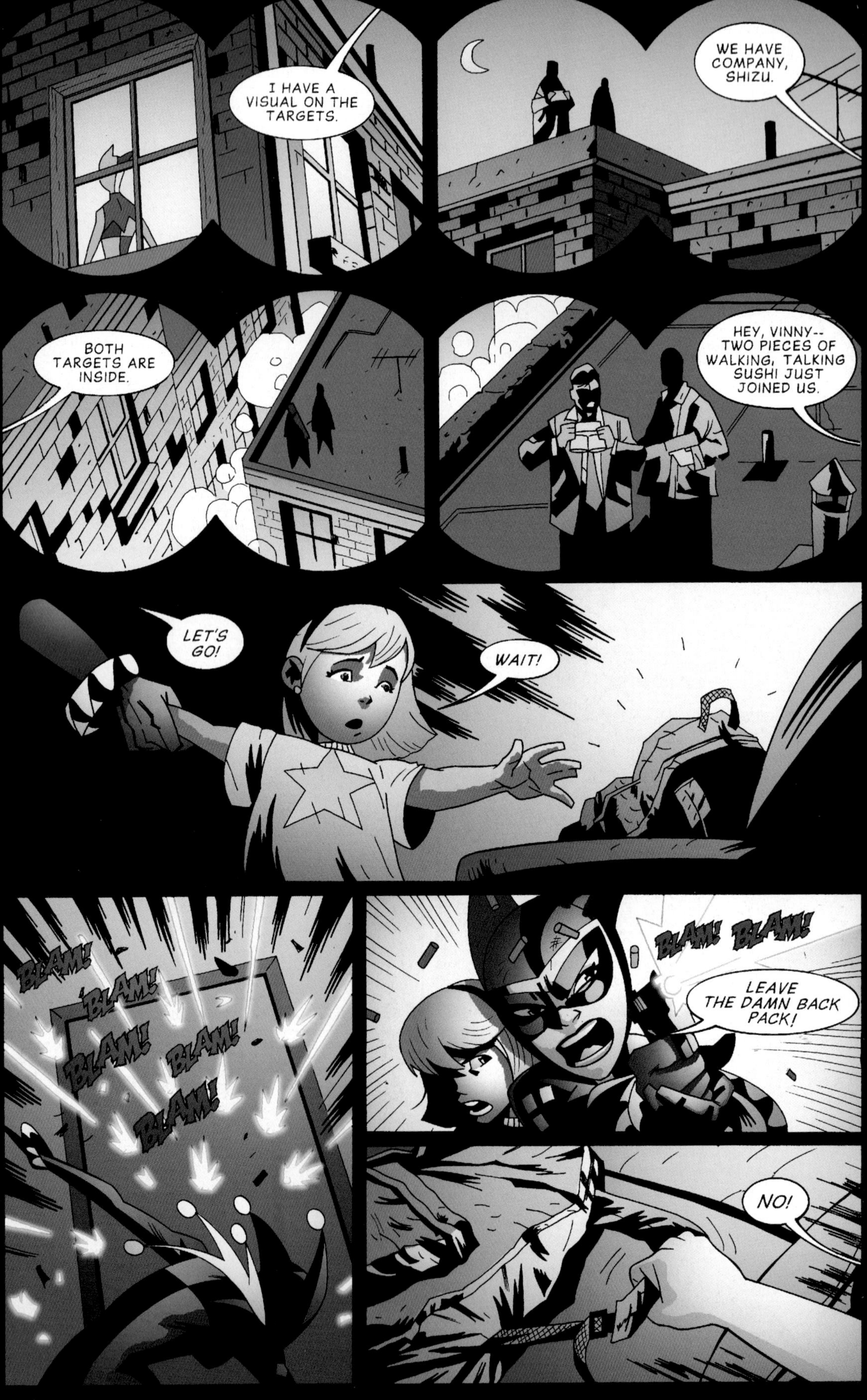
I HAVE A VISUAL ON THE TARGETS.
WE HAVE COMPANY, SHIZU.
BOTH TARGETS ARE INSIDE.
HEY, VINNY-- TWO PIECES OF WALKING, TALKING SUSHI JUST JOINED US.
LET'S GO!
WAIT!
BLAM!
BLAM!
BLAM!
BLAM!
BLAM!
BLAM! BLAM!
LEAVE THE DAMN BACK PACK!
NO!

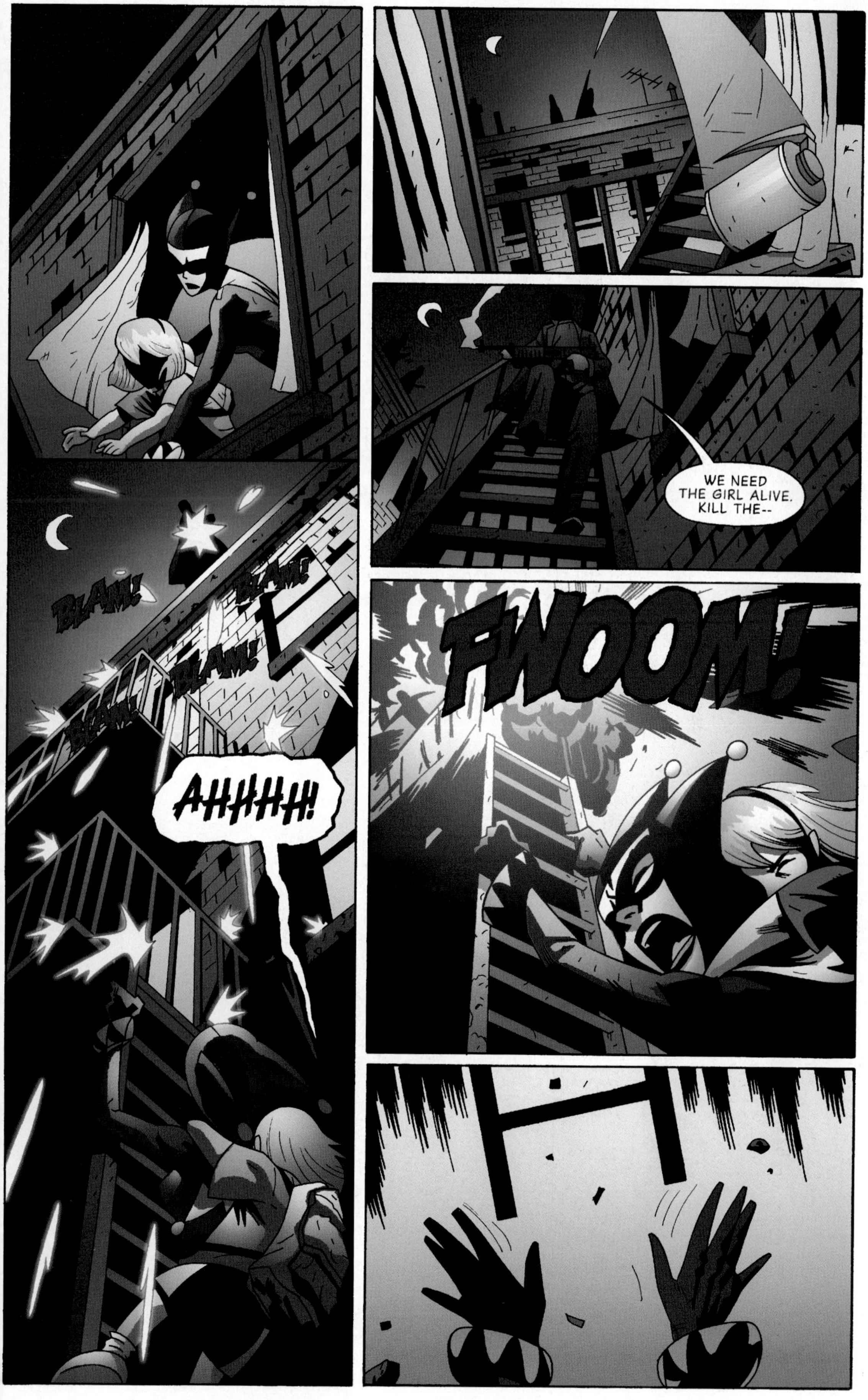
BLAM!
BLAM!
BLAM!
BLAM!
AHHHH!
WE NEED THE GIRL ALIVE. KILL THE--
FWOOM!

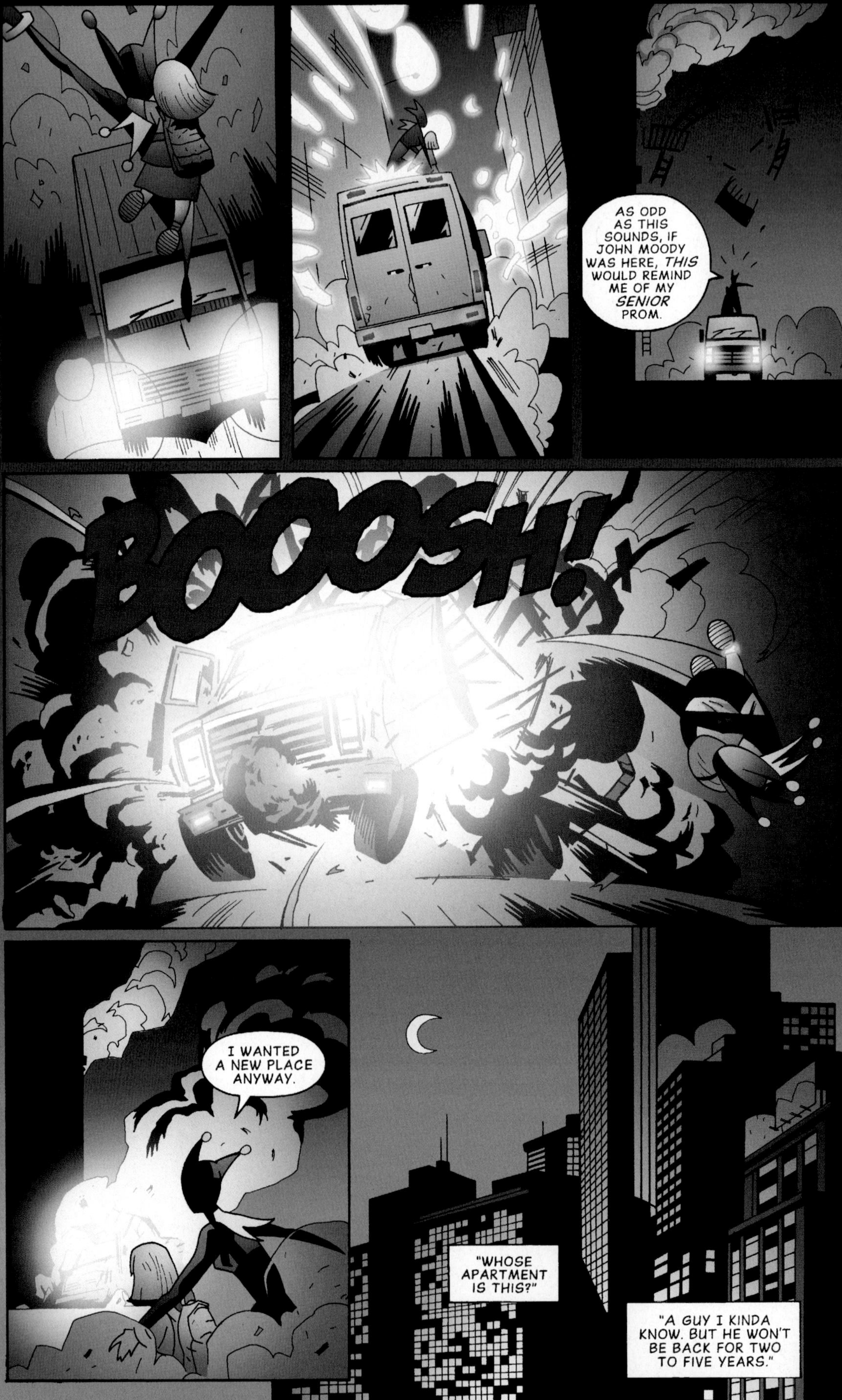

AS ODD AS THIS SOUNDS, IF JOHN MOODY WAS HERE, *THIS* WOULD REMIND ME OF MY *SENIOR* PROM.
BOOOSH!
I WANTED A NEW PLACE ANYWAY.
"WHOSE APARTMENT IS THIS?"
"A GUY I KINDA KNOW. BUT HE WON'T BE BACK FOR TWO TO FIVE YEARS."

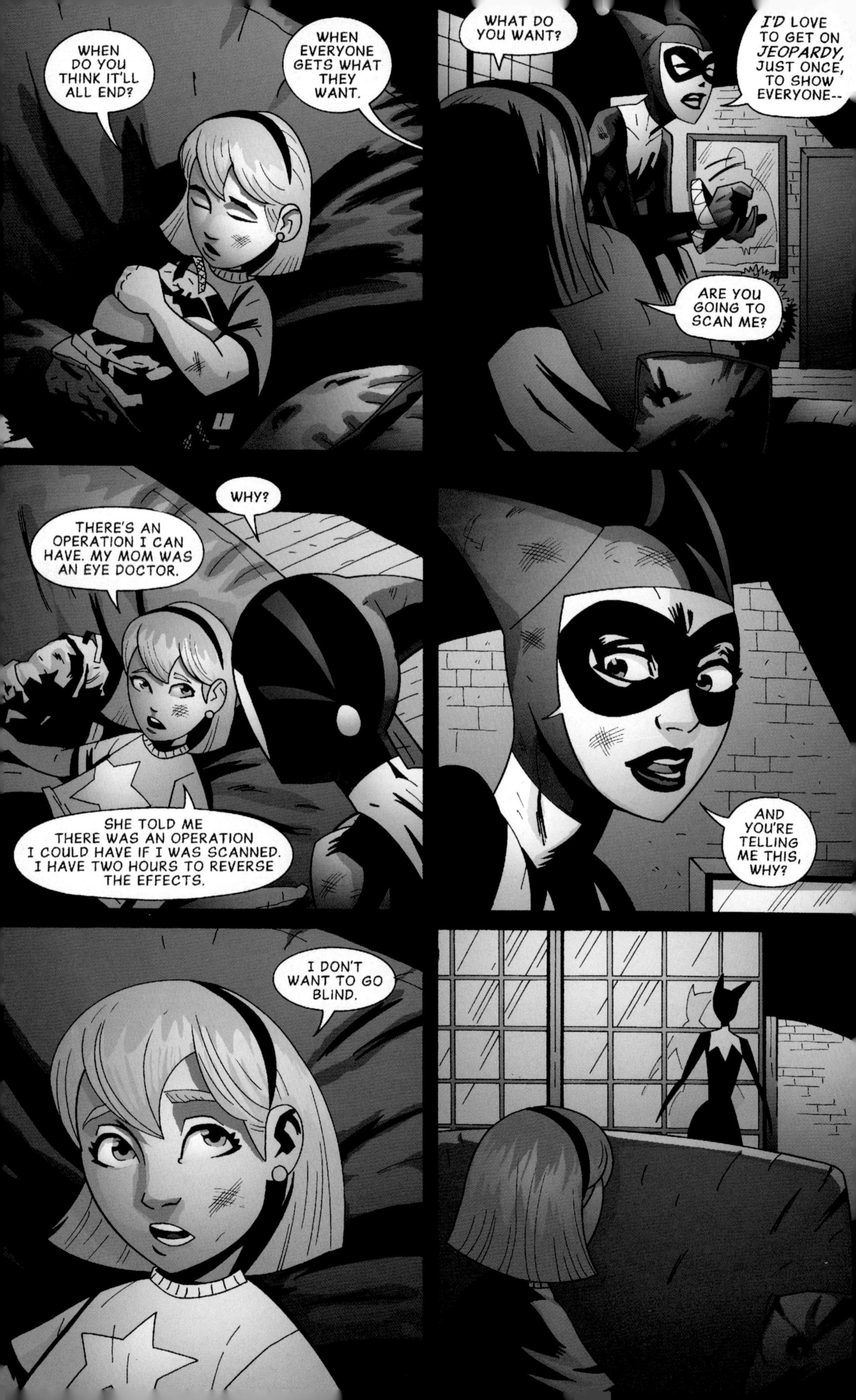
WHEN DO YOU THINK IT'LL ALL END?
WHEN EVERYONE GETS WHAT THEY WANT.
WHAT DO YOU WANT?
I'D LOVE TO GET ON JEOPARDY, JUST ONCE, TO SHOW EVERYONE--
ARE YOU GOING TO SCAN ME?
WHY?
THERE'S AN OPERATION I CAN HAVE. MY MOM WAS AN EYE DOCTOR.
SHE TOLD ME THERE WAS AN OPERATION I COULD HAVE IF I WAS SCANNED. I HAVE TWO HOURS TO REVERSE THE EFFECTS.
AND YOU'RE TELLING ME THIS, WHY?
I DON'T WANT TO GO BLIND.

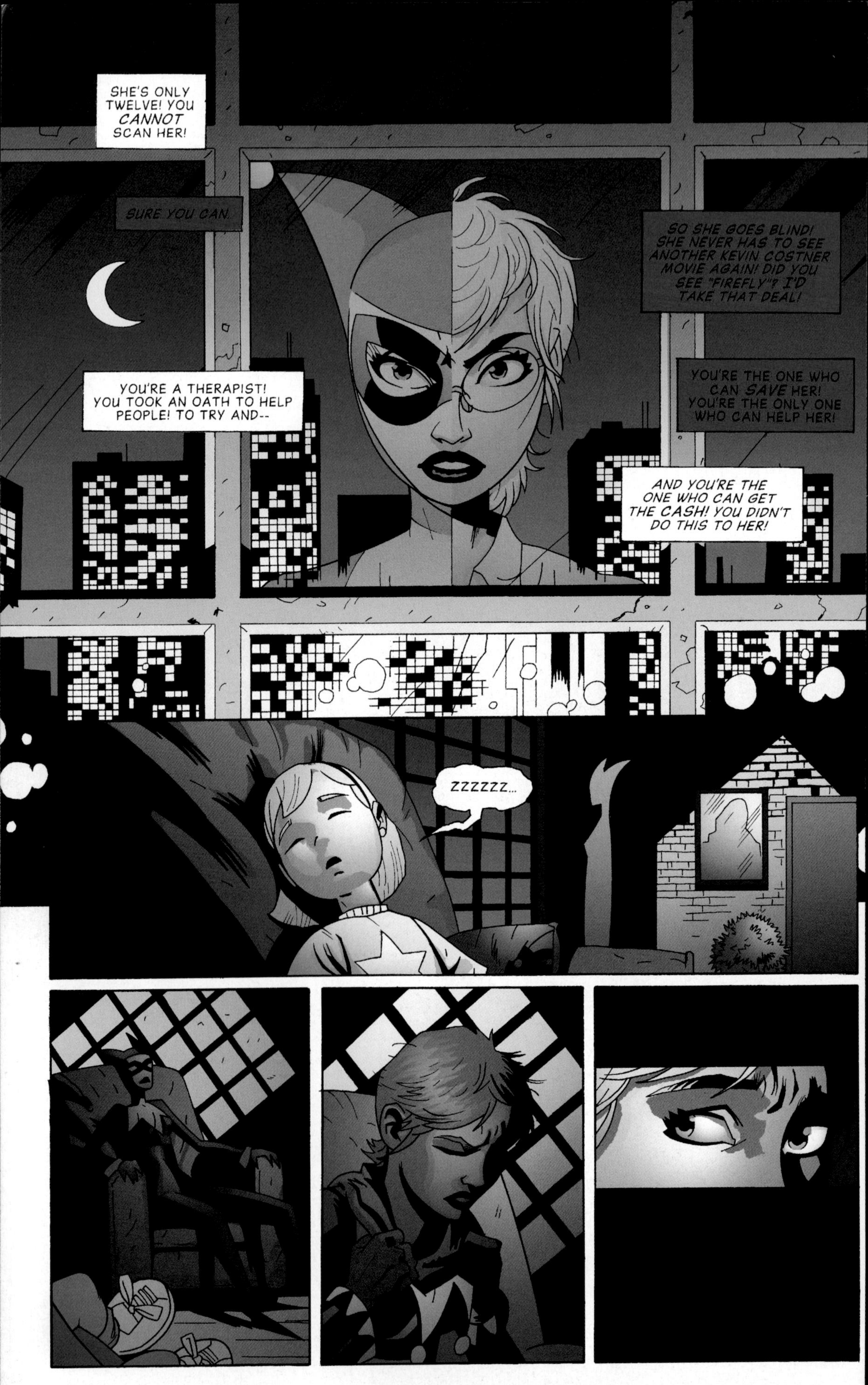
SHE'S ONLY TWELVE! YOU CANNOT SCAN HER!
SURE YOU CAN.
SO SHE GOES BLIND! SHE NEVER HAS TO SEE ANOTHER KEVIN COSTNER MOVIE AGAIN! DID YOU SEE "FIREFLY"? I'D TAKE THAT DEAL!
YOU'RE A THERAPIST! YOU TOOK AN OATH TO HELP PEOPLE! TO TRY AND--
YOU'RE THE ONE WHO CAN SAVE HER! YOU'RE THE ONLY ONE WHO CAN HELP HER!
AND YOU'RE THE ONE WHO CAN GET THE CASH! YOU DIDN'T DO THIS TO HER!
ZZZZZZ...

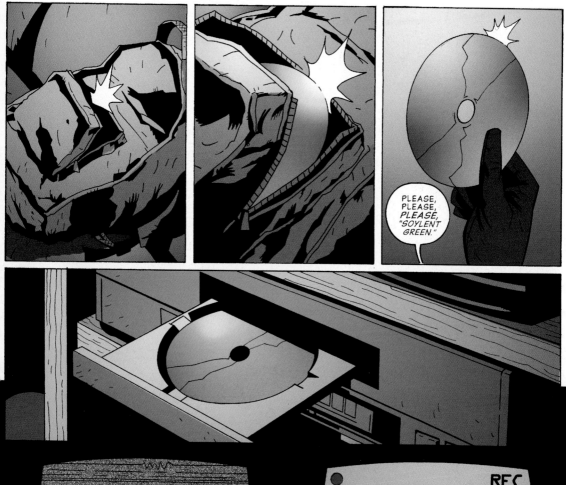

PLEASE, PLEASE, PLEASE, "SOYLENT GREEN."

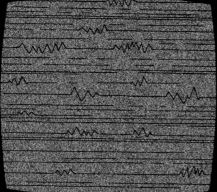

EVIL.

REC

IT'S AMAZING HOW IT CAN TAKE THE FORM OF ANYTHING IT WANTS.

I NOW KNOW THE NIGHTMARE STARTED THE DAY I PUT THIS RING ON.

IT WAS GIVEN TO ME BY THE MAN WHO IS TRYING TO KILL YOU.

I'M GOING TO TELL YOU EVERYTHING. MOST OF IT YOU'RE TOO YOUNG TO UNDERSTAND.

BUT THAT WON'T ALWAYS BE THE CASE. AND I WANT YOU TO KNOW THE TRUTH.

I WANT YOU TO KNOW THAT WHAT WE DID TO YOU WAS OUT OF LOVE.

IF YOUR MOTHER AND I DID ANYTHING WRONG, YOU NEED TO KNOW WE WERE DOING IT FOR THE RIGHT REASONS.

I THOUGHT IF HE WAS FACED WITH YOU, YOUR PURITY WOULD STOP HIM. THAT ONCE THE CODE WAS LACED ONTO YOUR RETINA, HE WOULD REALIZE IT WAS OVER. THAT HE WOULD NEVER KILL YOU JUST TO GET THAT CODE.

I PRAY WE WERE RIGHT.

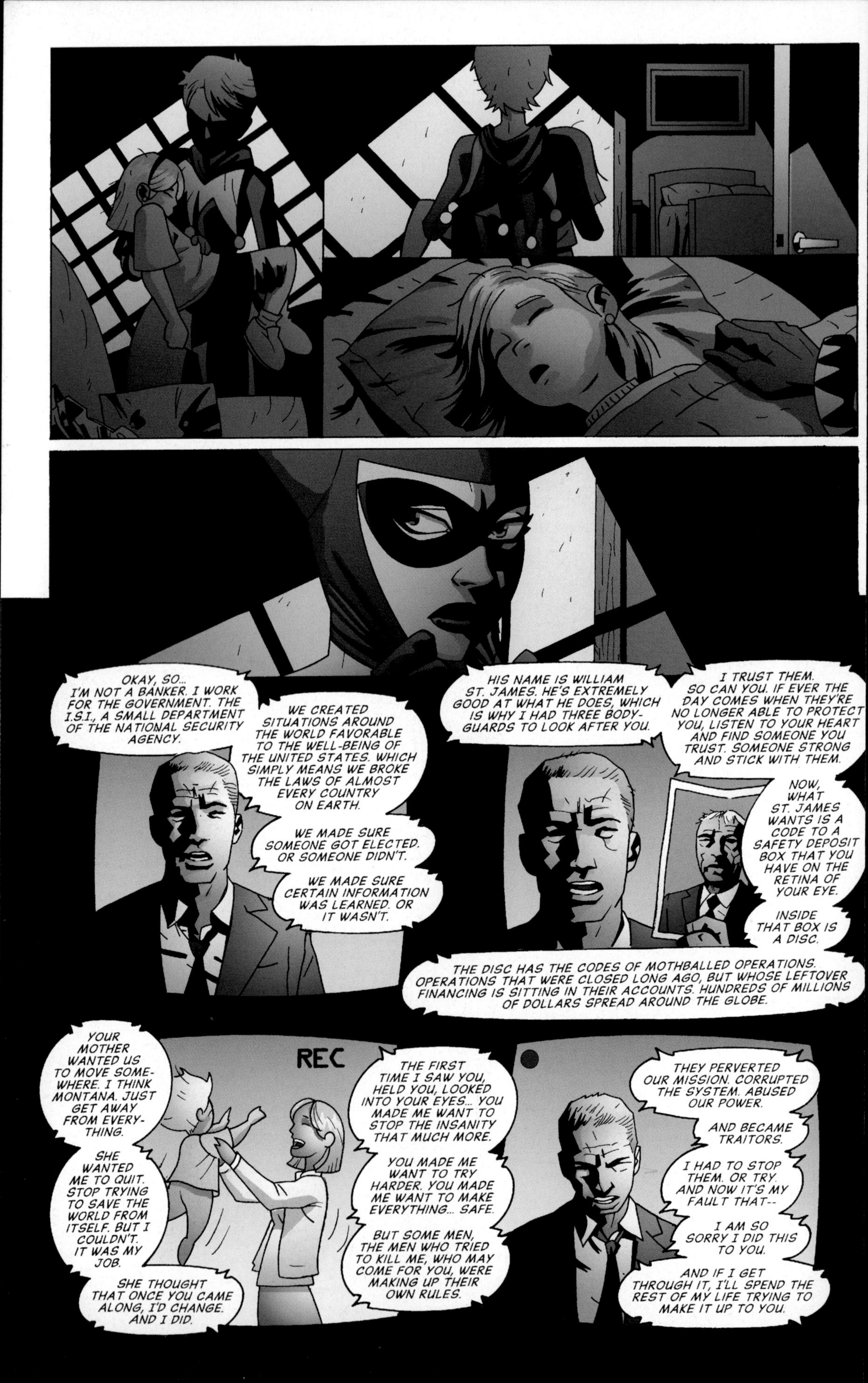
OKAY, SO... I'M NOT A BANKER. I WORK FOR THE GOVERNMENT. THE I.S.I., A SMALL DEPARTMENT OF THE NATIONAL SECURITY AGENCY.
WE CREATED SITUATIONS AROUND THE WORLD FAVORABLE TO THE WELL-BEING OF THE UNITED STATES. WHICH SIMPLY MEANS WE BROKE THE LAWS OF ALMOST EVERY COUNTRY ON EARTH.
WE MADE SURE SOMEONE GOT ELECTED. OR SOMEONE DIDN'T.
WE MADE SURE CERTAIN INFORMATION WAS LEARNED. OR IT WASN'T.
HIS NAME IS WILLIAM ST. JAMES. HE'S EXTREMELY GOOD AT WHAT HE DOES, WHICH IS WHY I HAD THREE BODY-GUARDS TO LOOK AFTER YOU.
I TRUST THEM. SO CAN YOU. IF EVER THE DAY COMES WHEN THEY'RE NO LONGER ABLE TO PROTECT YOU, LISTEN TO YOUR HEART AND FIND SOMEONE YOU TRUST. SOMEONE STRONG AND STICK WITH THEM.
NOW, WHAT ST. JAMES WANTS IS A CODE TO A SAFETY DEPOSIT BOX THAT YOU HAVE ON THE RETINA OF YOUR EYE.
INSIDE THAT BOX IS A DISC.
THE DISC HAS THE CODES OF MOTHBALLED OPERATIONS. OPERATIONS THAT WERE CLOSED LONG AGO, BUT WHOSE LEFTOVER FINANCING IS SITTING IN THEIR ACCOUNTS. HUNDREDS OF MILLIONS OF DOLLARS SPREAD AROUND THE GLOBE.
YOUR MOTHER WANTED US TO MOVE SOME-WHERE. I THINK MONTANA. JUST GET AWAY FROM EVERY-THING.
SHE WANTED ME TO QUIT. STOP TRYING TO SAVE THE WORLD FROM ITSELF. BUT I COULDN'T. IT WAS MY JOB.
SHE THOUGHT THAT ONCE YOU CAME ALONG, I'D CHANGE. AND I DID.
REC
THE FIRST TIME I SAW YOU, HELD YOU, LOOKED INTO YOUR EYES... YOU MADE ME WANT TO STOP THE INSANITY THAT MUCH MORE.
YOU MADE ME WANT TO TRY HARDER. YOU MADE ME WANT TO MAKE EVERYTHING... SAFE.
BUT SOME MEN, THE MEN WHO TRIED TO KILL ME, WHO MAY COME FOR YOU, WERE MAKING UP THEIR OWN RULES.
THEY PERVERTED OUR MISSION. CORRUPTED THE SYSTEM. ABUSED OUR POWER.
AND BECAME TRAITORS.
I HAD TO STOP THEM. OR TRY. AND NOW IT'S MY FAULT THAT--
I AM SO SORRY I DID THIS TO YOU.
AND IF I GET THROUGH IT, I'LL SPEND THE REST OF MY LIFE TRYING TO MAKE IT UP TO YOU.

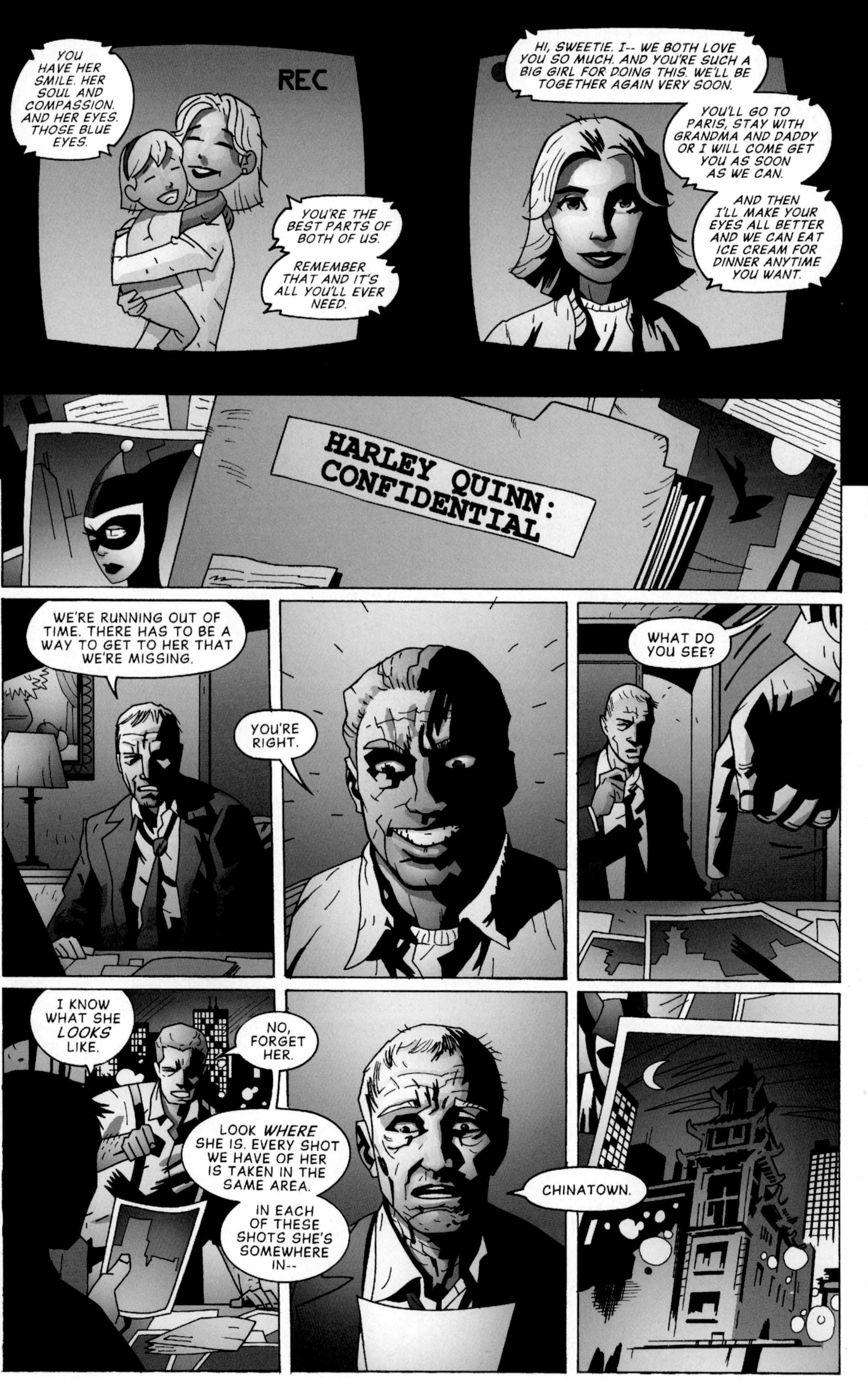
REC
YOU HAVE HER SMILE. HER SOUL AND COMPASSION. AND HER EYES. THOSE BLUE EYES.
YOU'RE THE BEST PARTS OF BOTH OF US.
REMEMBER THAT AND IT'S ALL YOU'LL EVER NEED.
HI, SWEETIE. I-- WE BOTH LOVE YOU SO MUCH. AND YOU'RE SUCH A BIG GIRL FOR DOING THIS. WE'LL BE TOGETHER AGAIN VERY SOON.
YOU'LL GO TO PARIS, STAY WITH GRANDMA AND DADDY OR I WILL COME GET YOU AS SOON AS WE CAN.
AND THEN I'LL MAKE YOUR EYES ALL BETTER AND WE CAN EAT ICE CREAM FOR DINNER ANYTIME YOU WANT.
HARLEY QUINN: CONFIDENTIAL
WE'RE RUNNING OUT OF TIME. THERE HAS TO BE A WAY TO GET TO HER THAT WE'RE MISSING.
YOU'RE RIGHT.
WHAT DO YOU SEE?
I KNOW WHAT SHE *LOOKS* LIKE.
NO, FORGET HER.
LOOK *WHERE* SHE IS. EVERY SHOT WE HAVE OF HER IS TAKEN IN THE SAME AREA.
IN EACH OF THESE SHOTS SHE'S SOMEWHERE IN--
CHINATOWN.

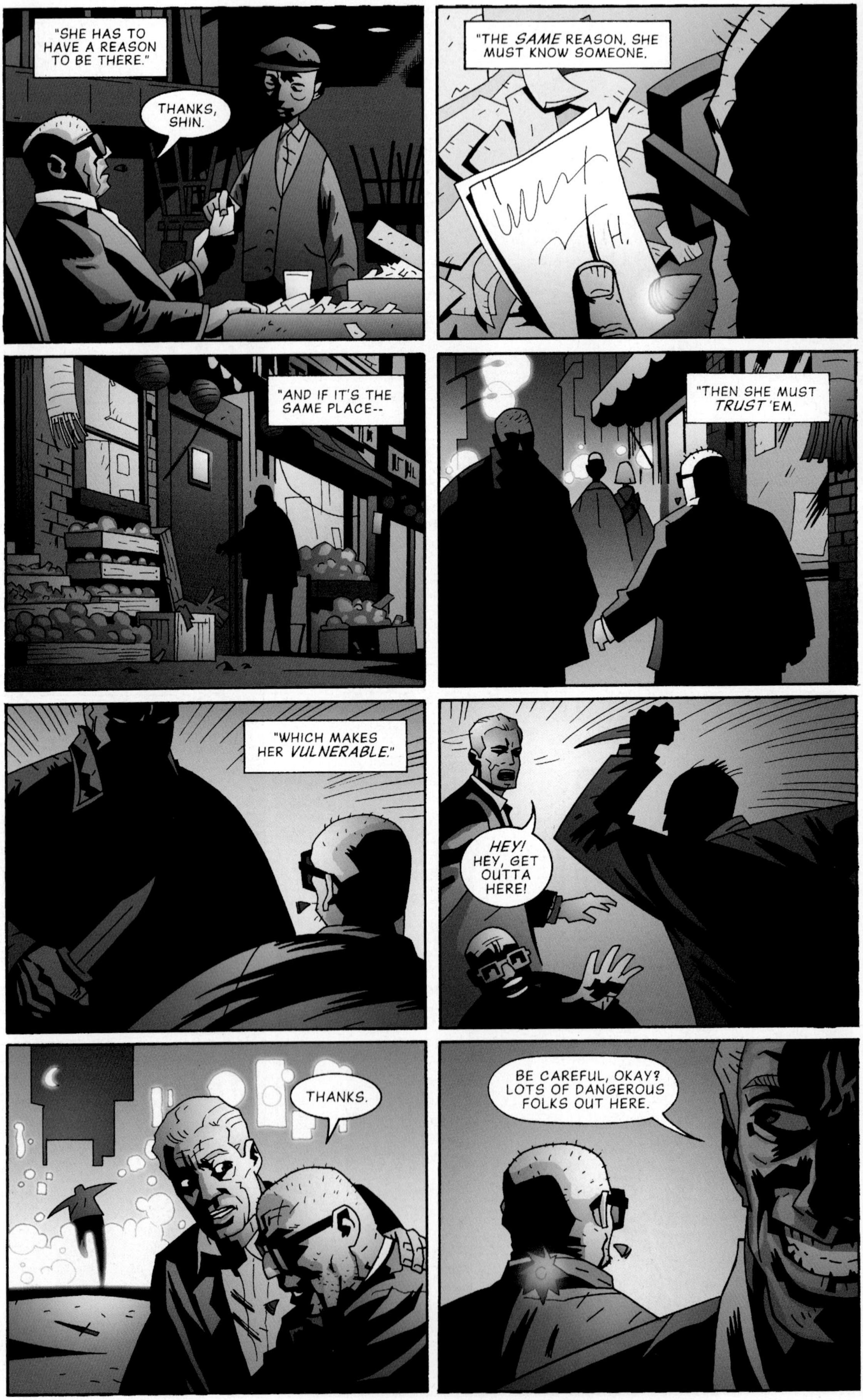
"SHE HAS TO HAVE A REASON TO BE THERE."
THANKS, SHIN.
"THE SAME REASON. SHE MUST KNOW SOMEONE.
"AND IF IT'S THE SAME PLACE--
"THEN SHE MUST TRUST 'EM.
"WHICH MAKES HER VULNERABLE."
HEY! HEY, GET OUTTA HERE!
THANKS.
BE CAREFUL, OKAY? LOTS OF DANGEROUS FOLKS OUT HERE.

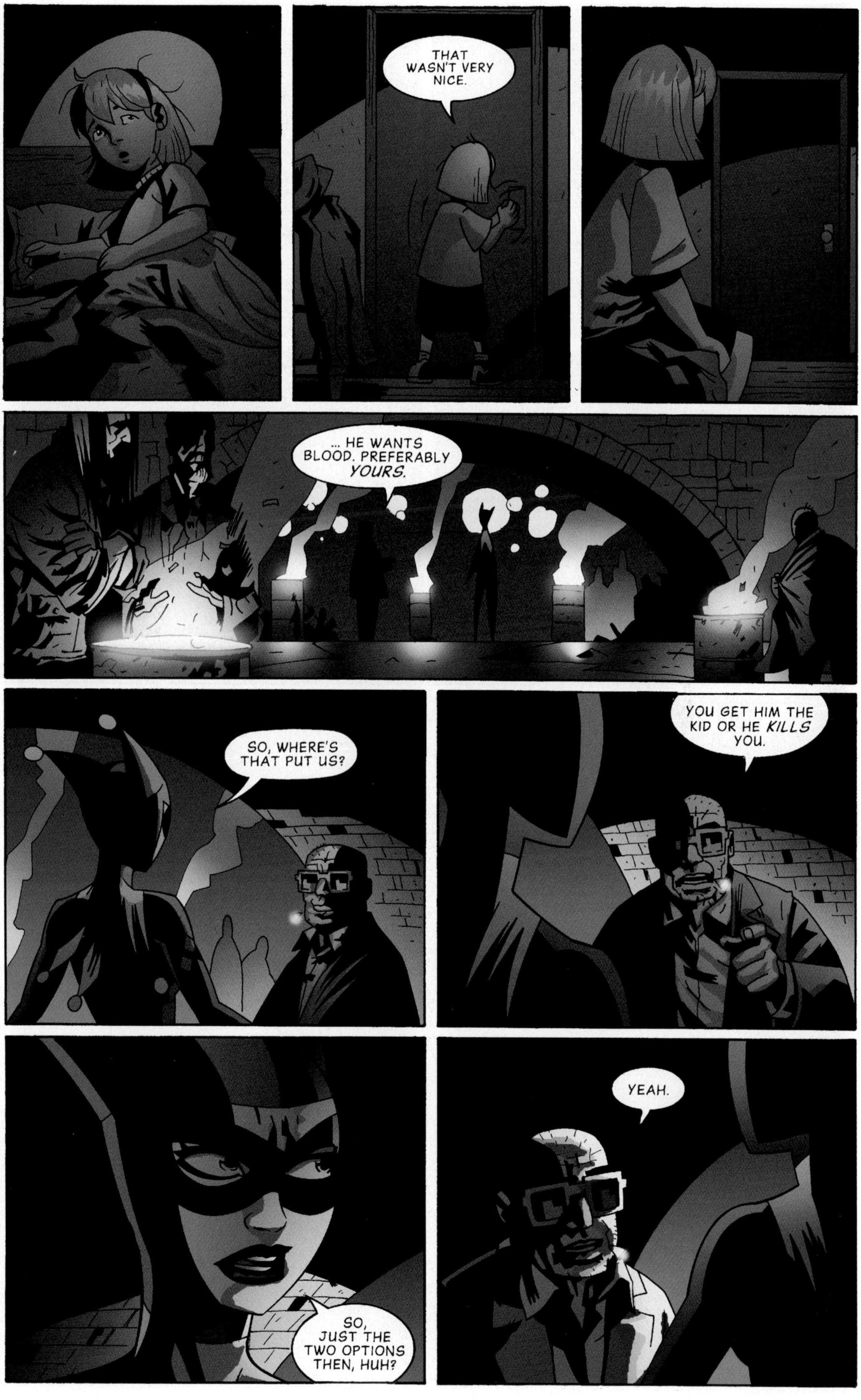
THAT WASN'T VERY NICE.
... HE WANTS BLOOD. PREFERABLY YOURS.
SO, WHERE'S THAT PUT US?
YOU GET HIM THE KID OR HE KILLS YOU.
SO, JUST THE TWO OPTIONS THEN, HUH?
YEAH.

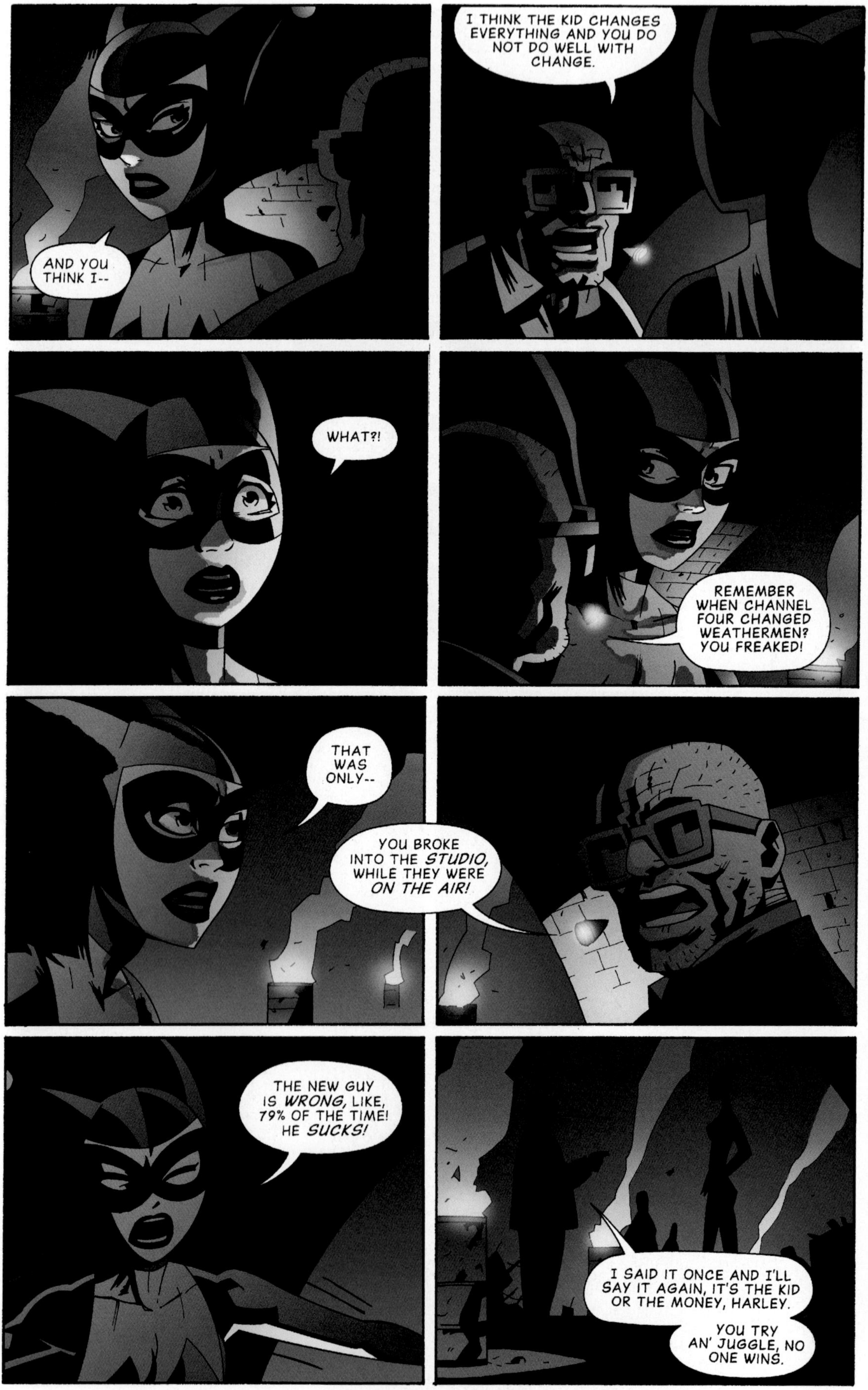

AND YOU THINK I--
I THINK THE KID CHANGES EVERYTHING AND YOU DO NOT DO WELL WITH CHANGE.
WHAT?!
REMEMBER WHEN CHANNEL FOUR CHANGED WEATHERMEN? YOU FREAKED!
THAT WAS ONLY--
YOU BROKE INTO THE STUDIO, WHILE THEY WERE ON THE AIR!
THE NEW GUY IS WRONG, LIKE, 79% OF THE TIME! HE SUCKS!
I SAID IT ONCE AND I'LL SAY IT AGAIN, IT'S THE KID OR THE MONEY, HARLEY.
YOU TRY AN' JUGGLE, NO ONE WINS.

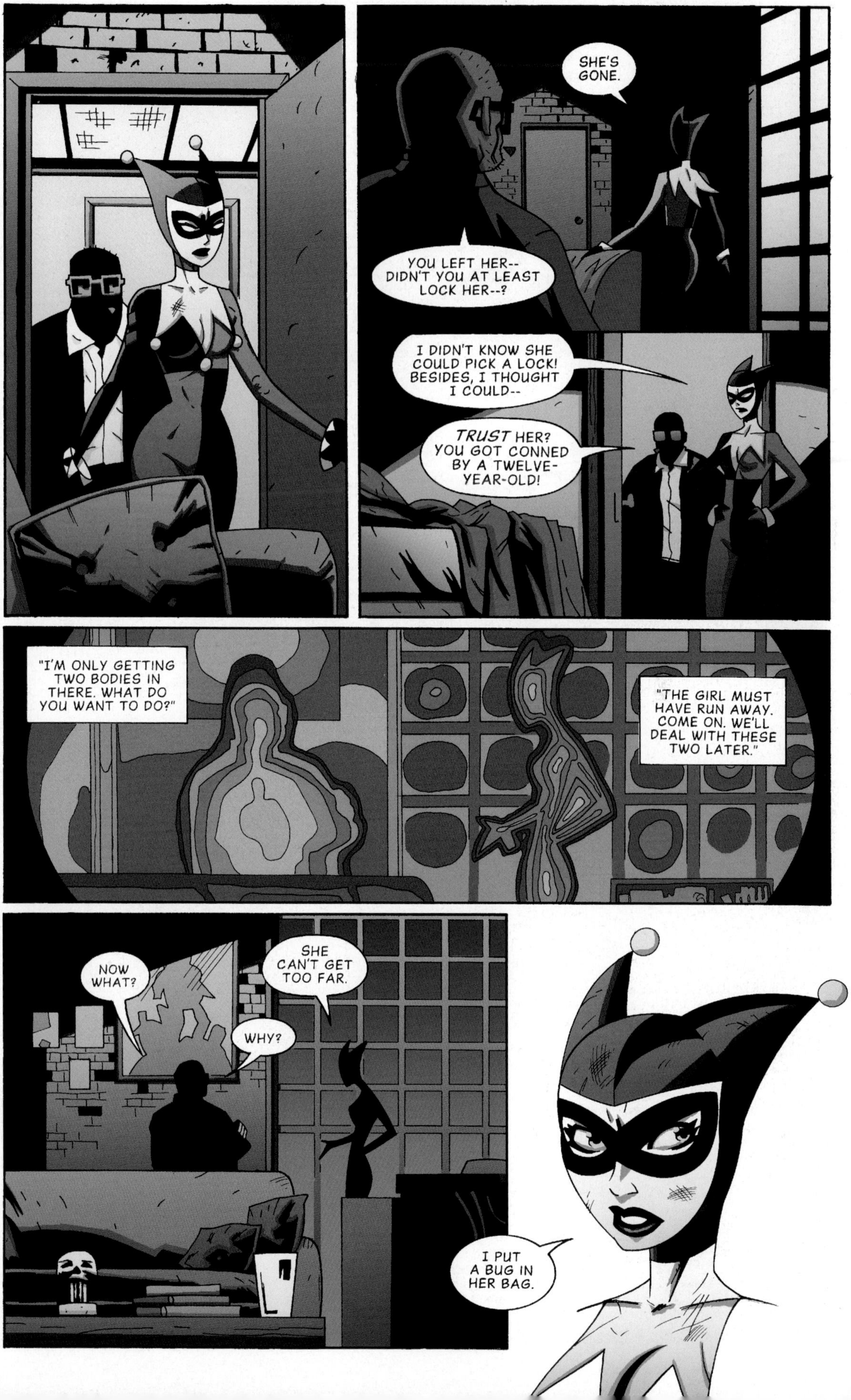
SHE'S GONE.
YOU LEFT HER-- DIDN'T YOU AT LEAST LOCK HER--?
I DIDN'T KNOW SHE COULD PICK A LOCK! BESIDES, I THOUGHT I COULD--
TRUST HER? YOU GOT CONNED BY A TWELVE-YEAR-OLD!
"I'M ONLY GETTING TWO BODIES IN THERE. WHAT DO YOU WANT TO DO?"
"THE GIRL MUST HAVE RUN AWAY. COME ON. WE'LL DEAL WITH THESE TWO LATER."
NOW WHAT?
SHE CAN'T GET TOO FAR.
WHY?
I PUT A BUG IN HER BAG.

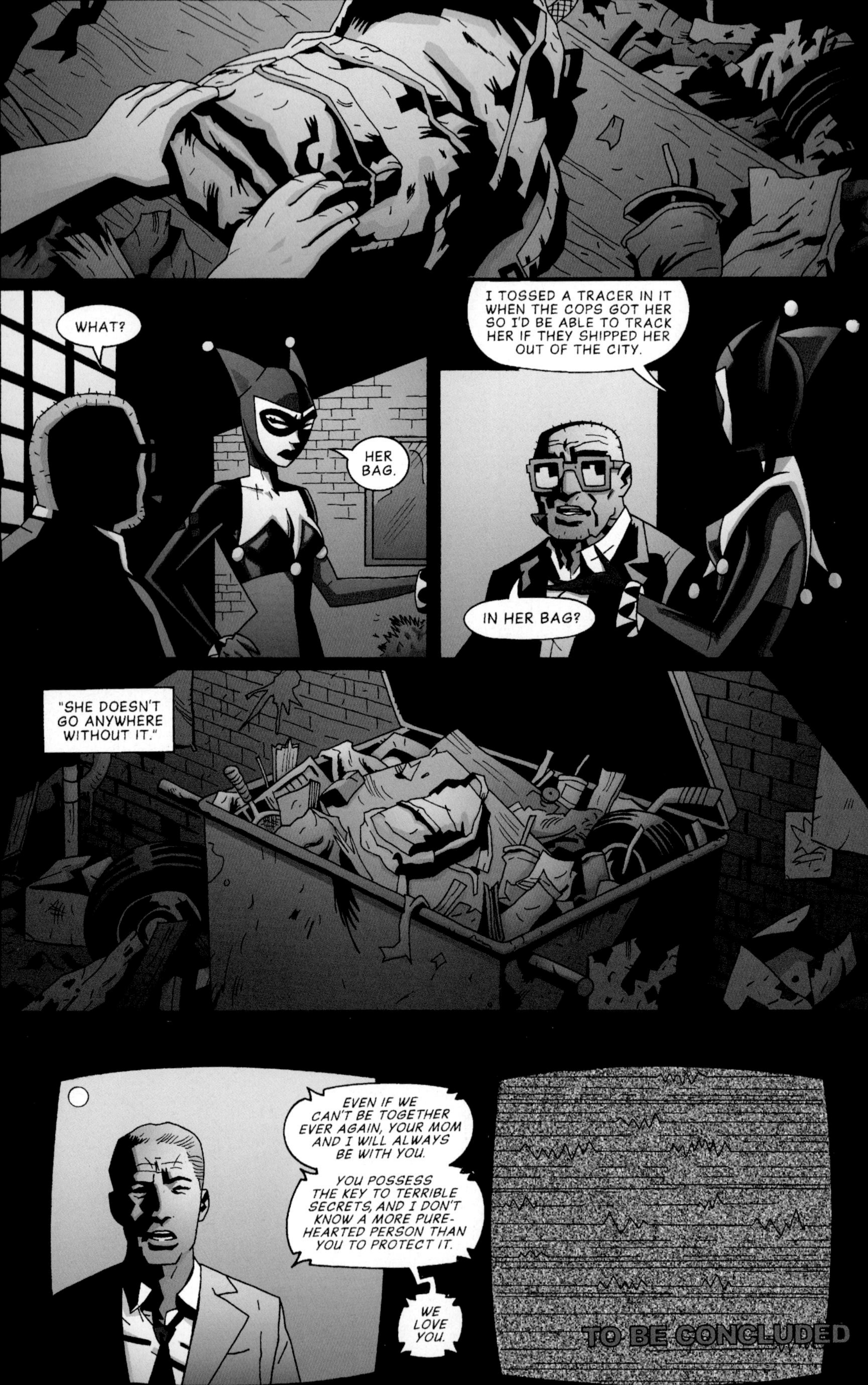
WHAT?
HER BAG.
I TOSSED A TRACER IN IT WHEN THE COPS GOT HER SO I'D BE ABLE TO TRACK HER IF THEY SHIPPED HER OUT OF THE CITY.
IN HER BAG?
"SHE DOESN'T GO ANYWHERE WITHOUT IT."
EVEN IF WE CAN'T BE TOGETHER EVER AGAIN, YOUR MOM AND I WILL ALWAYS BE WITH YOU.
YOU POSSESS THE KEY TO TERRIBLE SECRETS, AND I DON'T KNOW A MORE PURE-HEARTED PERSON THAN YOU TO PROTECT IT.
WE LOVE YOU.
TO BE CONCLUDED

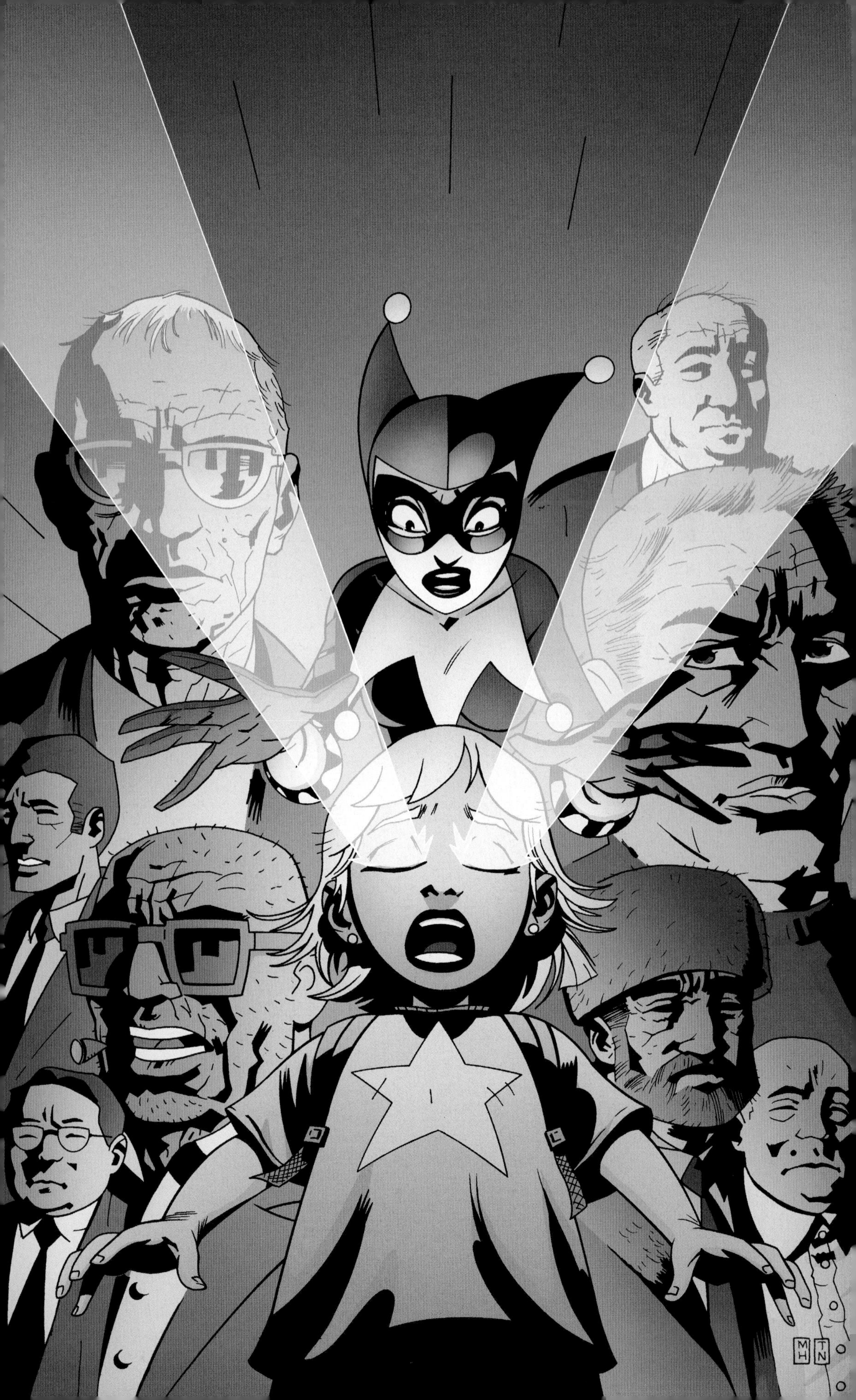

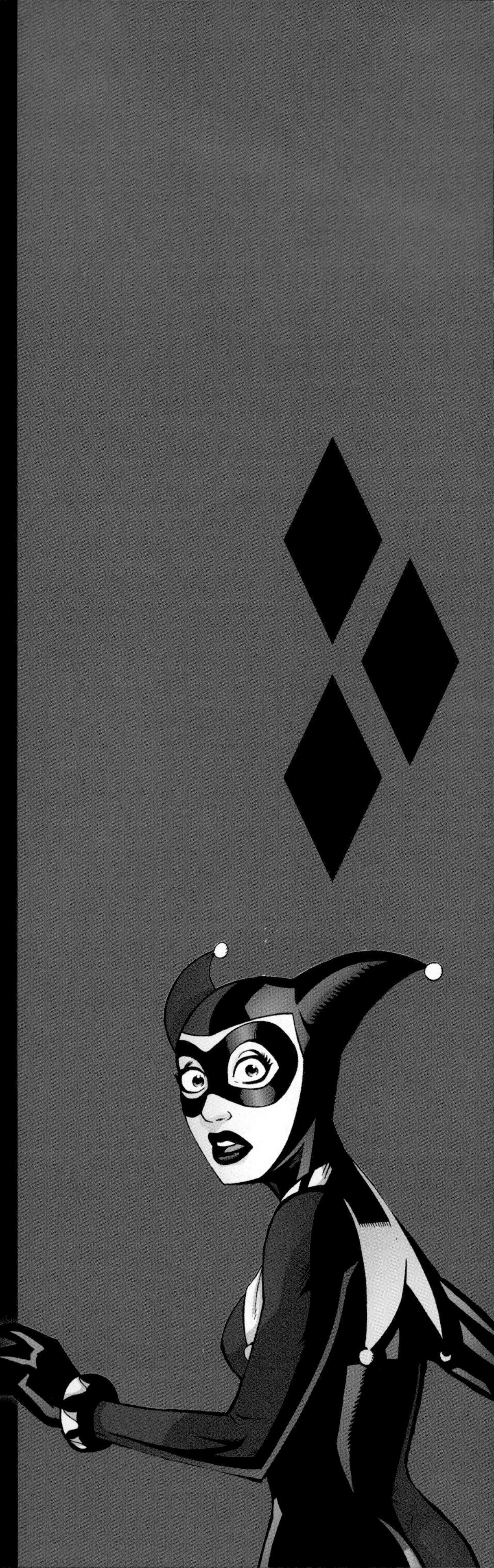

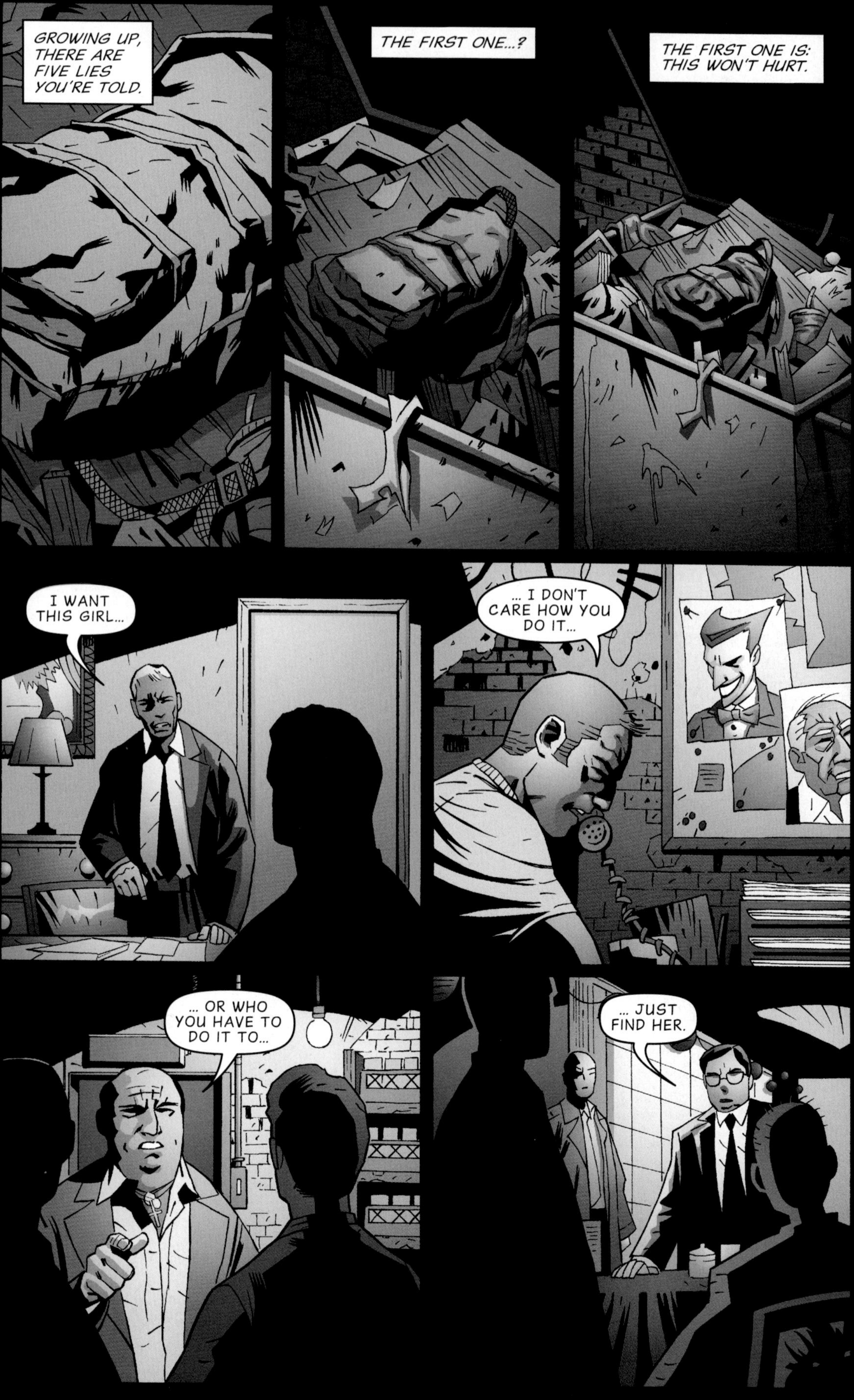
GROWING UP, THERE ARE FIVE LIES YOU'RE TOLD.
THE FIRST ONE...?
THE FIRST ONE IS: THIS WON'T HURT.
I WANT THIS GIRL...
... I DON'T CARE HOW YOU DO IT...
... OR WHO YOU HAVE TO DO IT TO...
... JUST FIND HER.

BEHIND BLUE EYES

PART FIVE

A.J. LIEBERMAN- Writer
MIKE HUDDLESTON- Penciller
TROY NIXEY- Inker
JOEL BENJAMIN- Colorist
SEAN KONOT- Letterer
NACHIE CASTRO- Asst. Editor
MATT IDELSON- Editor

HARLEY QUINN
created by
PAUL DINI &
BRUCE TIMM

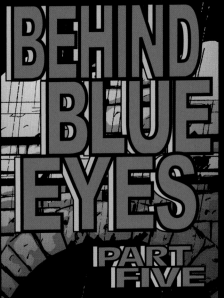

WHAT'S THE WORD?

RAZZLES.

WHAT?!

REMEMBER *RAZZLES?* MOODY AND I WERE JUST TRYIN' TO FIGURE OUT IF THEY WERE A CANDY OR A GUM OR MAYBE--

OR MAYBE I COULD JUST TELL YOU WHAT I'VE FOUND.

THAT WOULD WORK, TOO.

THE GUY'S A GHOST. HE DOESN'T HAVE A RECORD.

I DON'T CARE ABOUT *PARKING TICKETS* OR--

NO, I MEAN THE GUY DOESN'T *EXIST.* ON PAPER, ANYWAY. I FOUND NOTHING... AND I CAN FIND *ANY*THING.

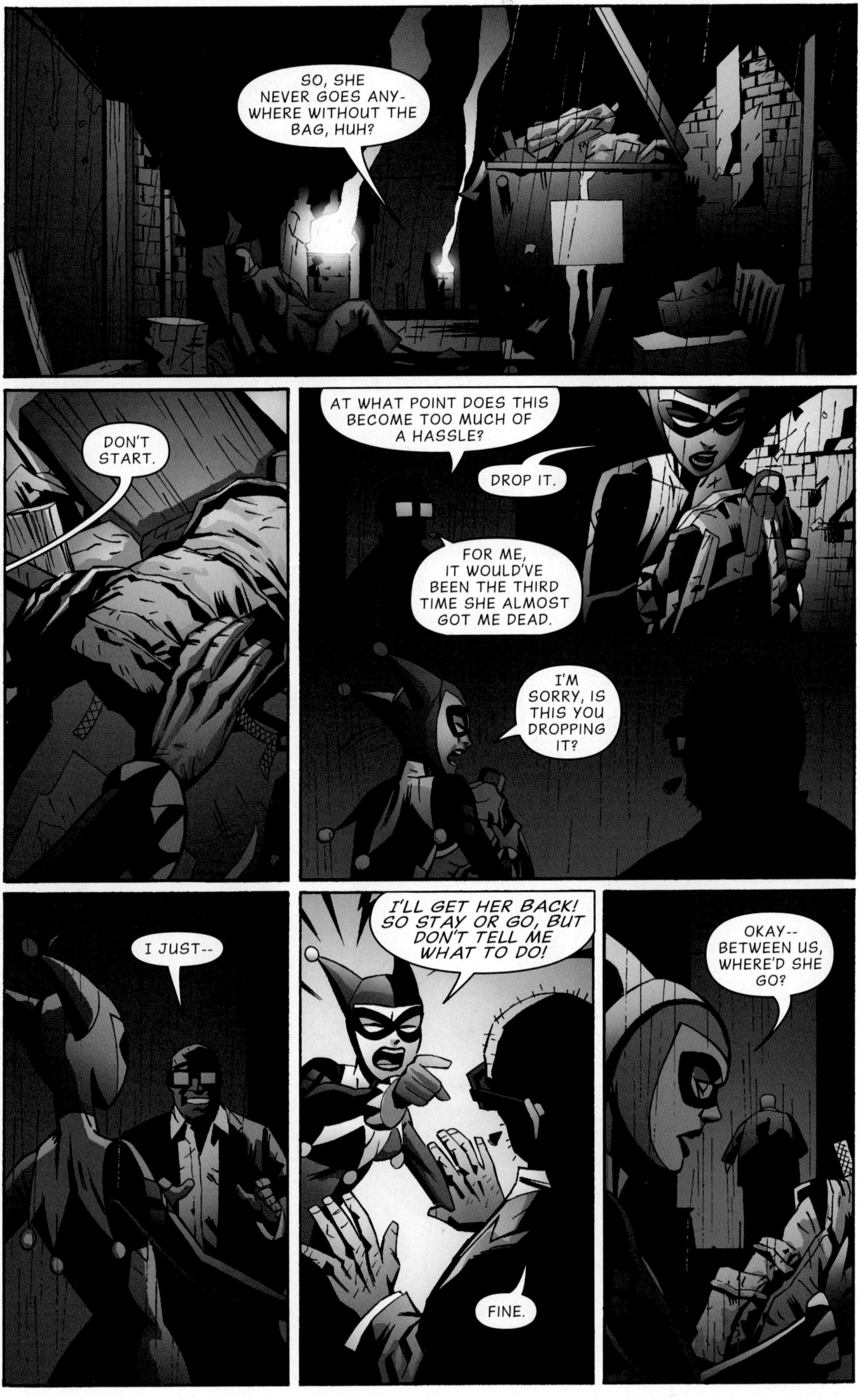
SO, SHE NEVER GOES ANY-WHERE WITHOUT THE BAG, HUH?
DON'T START.
AT WHAT POINT DOES THIS BECOME TOO MUCH OF A HASSLE?
DROP IT.
FOR ME, IT WOULD'VE BEEN THE THIRD TIME SHE ALMOST GOT ME DEAD.
I'M SORRY, IS THIS YOU DROPPING IT?
I JUST--
I'LL GET HER BACK! SO STAY OR GO, BUT DON'T TELL ME WHAT TO DO!
FINE.
OKAY-- BETWEEN US, WHERE'D SHE GO?

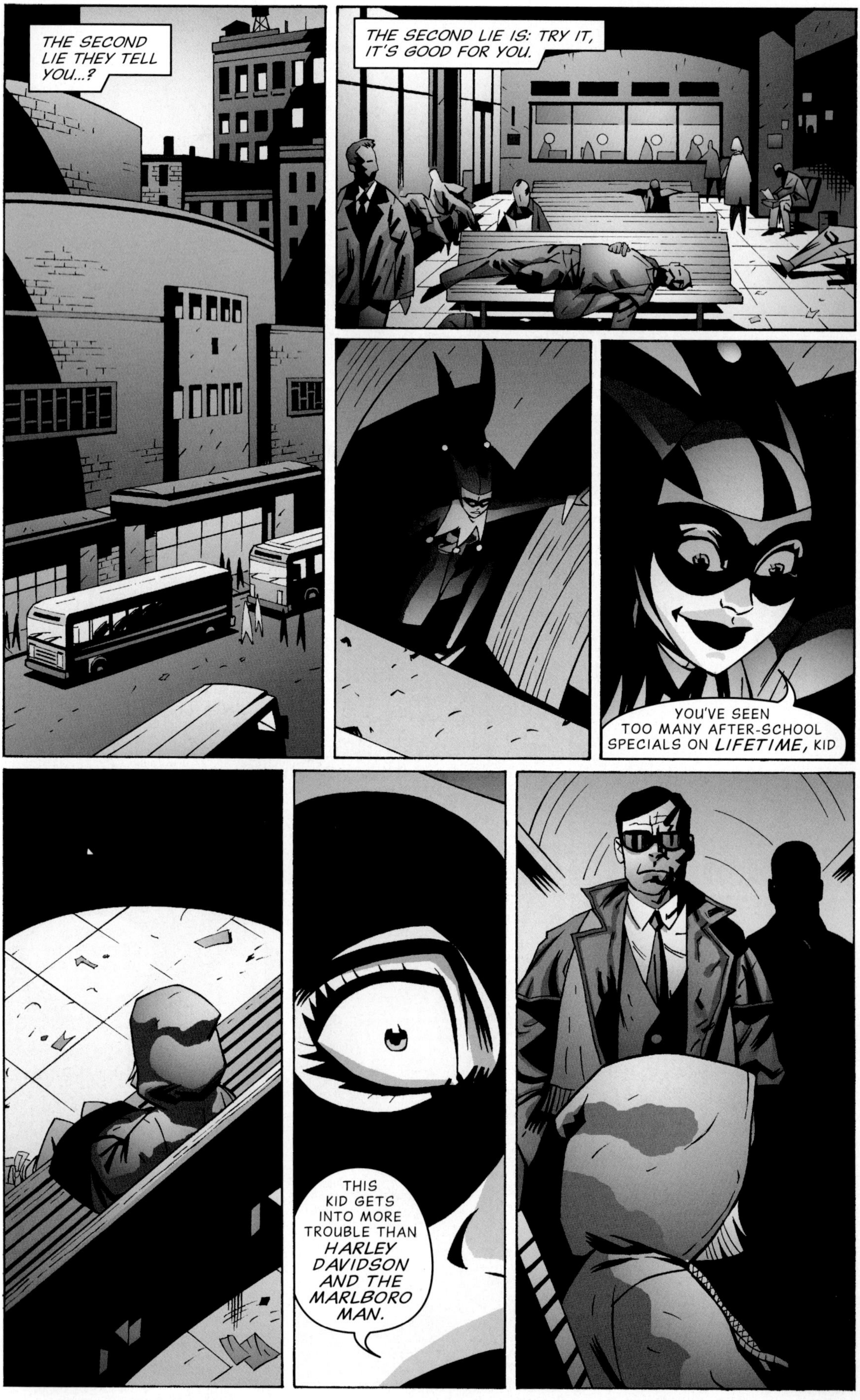
THE SECOND LIE THEY TELL YOU...?
THE SECOND LIE IS: TRY IT, IT'S GOOD FOR YOU.
YOU'VE SEEN TOO MANY AFTER-SCHOOL SPECIALS ON *LIFETIME*, KID
THIS KID GETS INTO MORE TROUBLE THAN *HARLEY DAVIDSON AND THE MARLBORO MAN.*

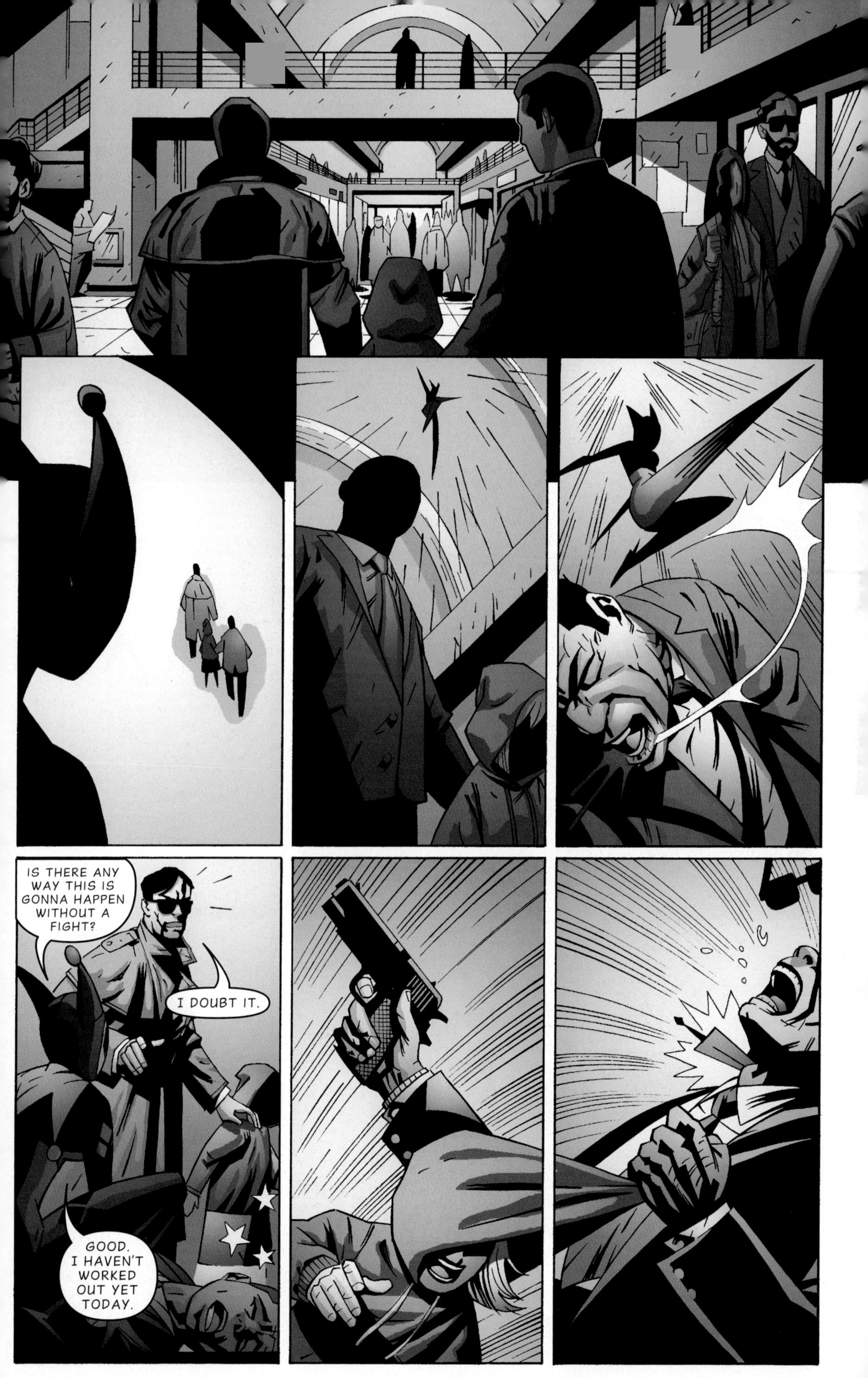
IS THERE ANY WAY THIS IS GONNA HAPPEN WITHOUT A FIGHT?
I DOUBT IT.
GOOD. I HAVEN'T WORKED OUT YET TODAY.

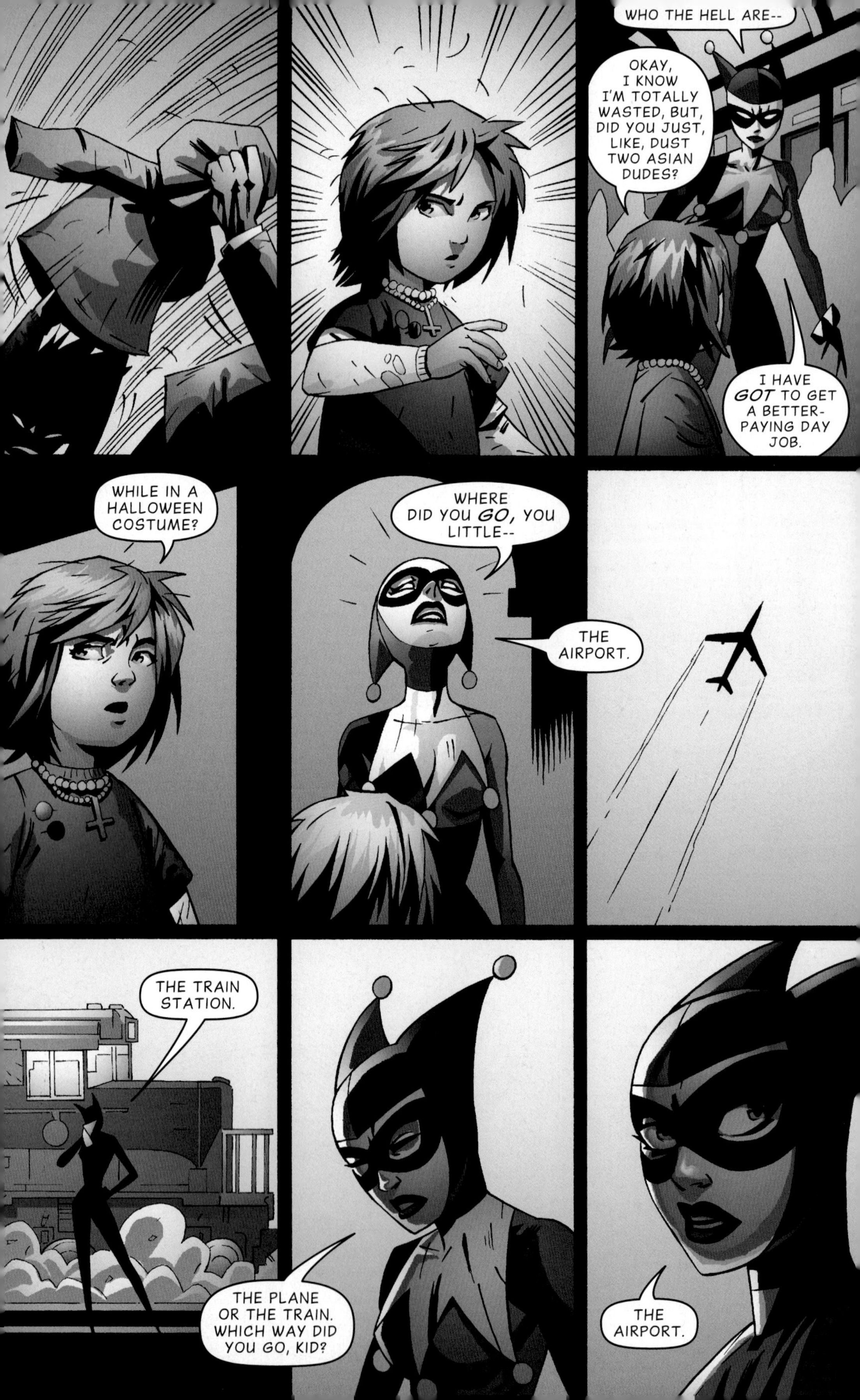
WHO THE HELL ARE--
OKAY, I KNOW I'M TOTALLY WASTED, BUT, DID YOU JUST, LIKE, DUST TWO ASIAN DUDES?
I HAVE GOT TO GET A BETTER-PAYING DAY JOB.
WHILE IN A HALLOWEEN COSTUME?
WHERE DID YOU GO, YOU LITTLE--
THE AIRPORT.
THE TRAIN STATION.
THE PLANE OR THE TRAIN. WHICH WAY DID YOU GO, KID?
THE AIRPORT.

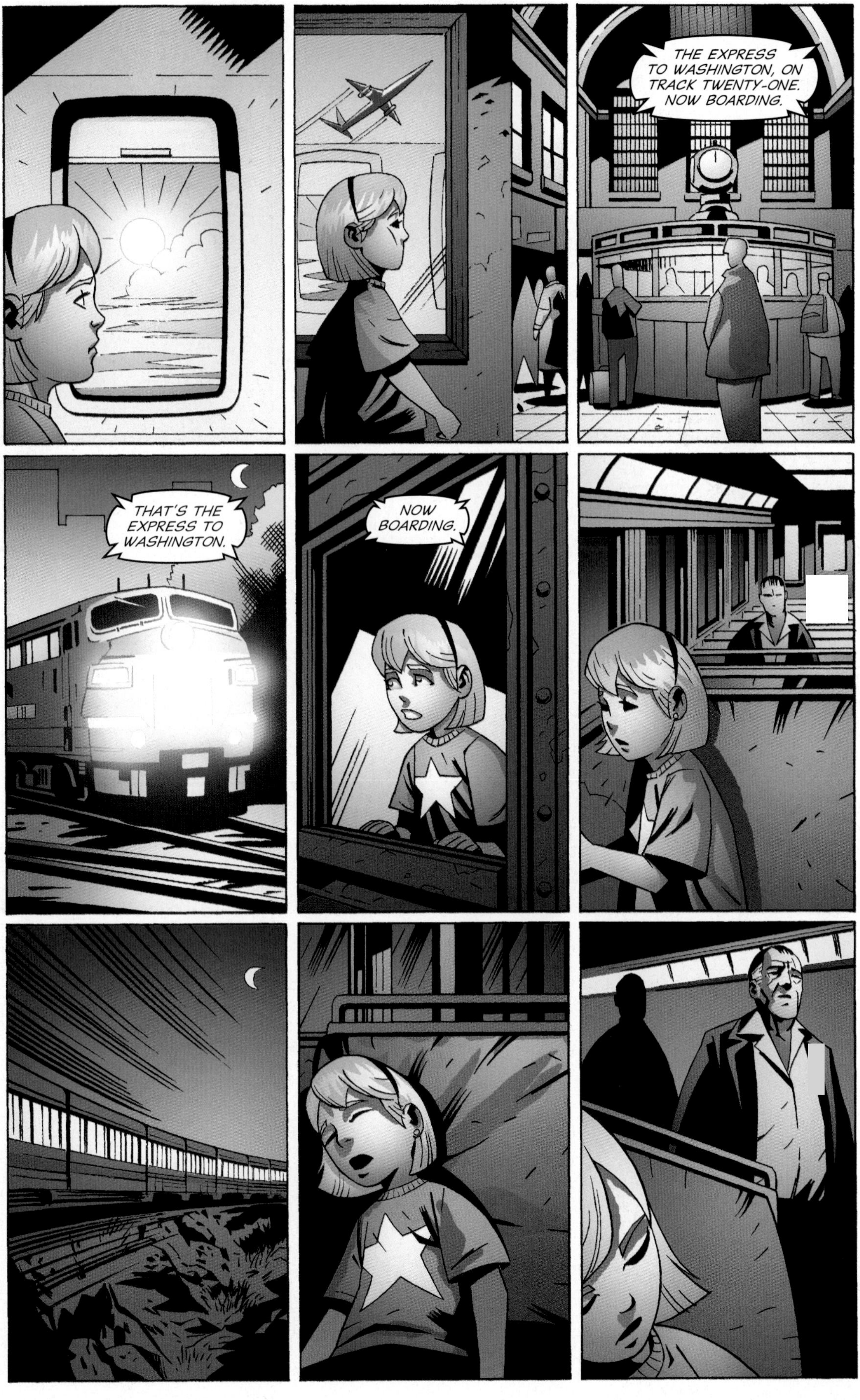
THE EXPRESS TO WASHINGTON, ON TRACK TWENTY-ONE. NOW BOARDING.
THAT'S THE EXPRESS TO WASHINGTON.
NOW BOARDING.

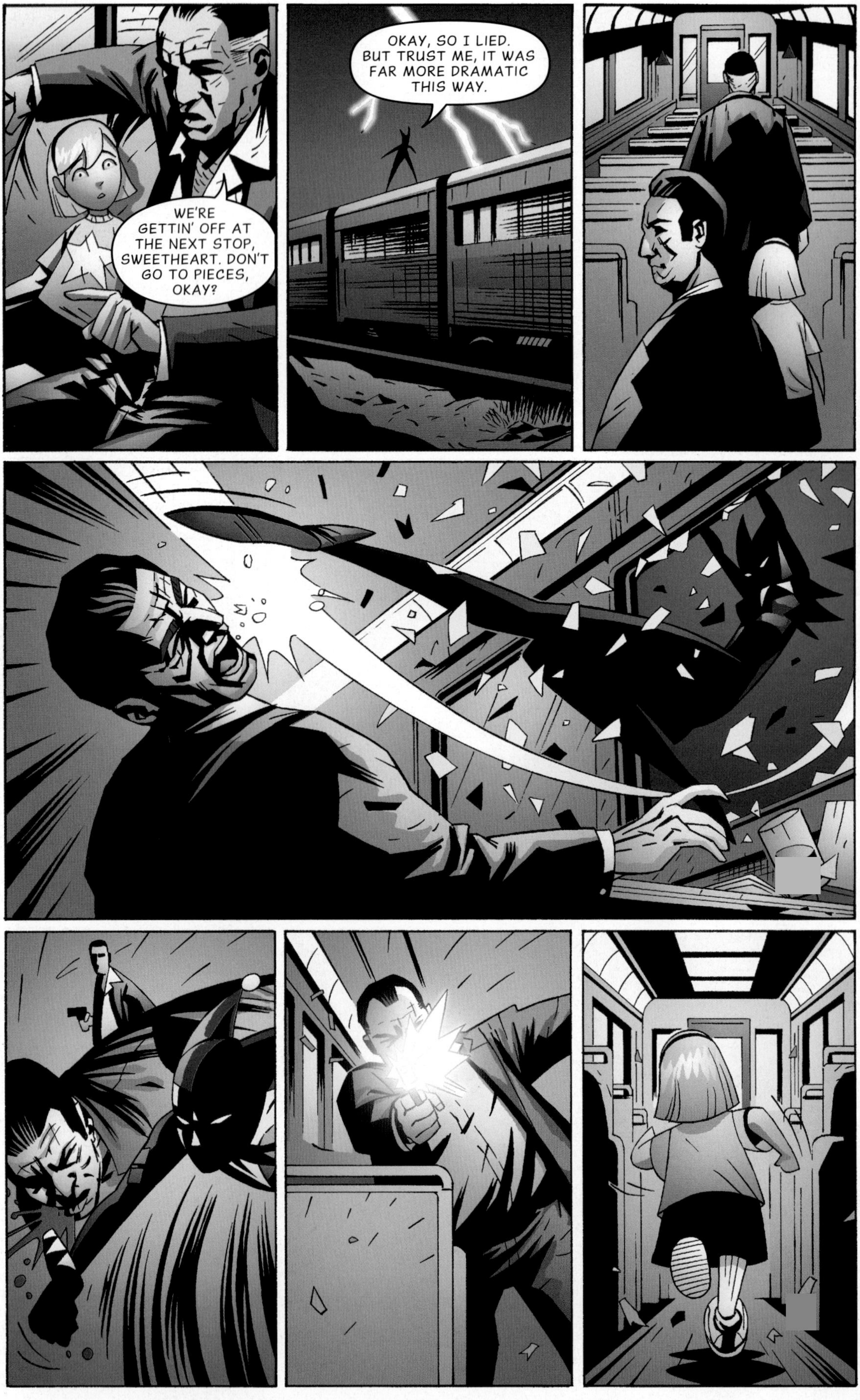
WE'RE GETTIN' OFF AT THE NEXT STOP, SWEETHEART. DON'T GO TO PIECES, OKAY?
OKAY, SO I LIED. BUT TRUST ME, IT WAS FAR MORE DRAMATIC THIS WAY.

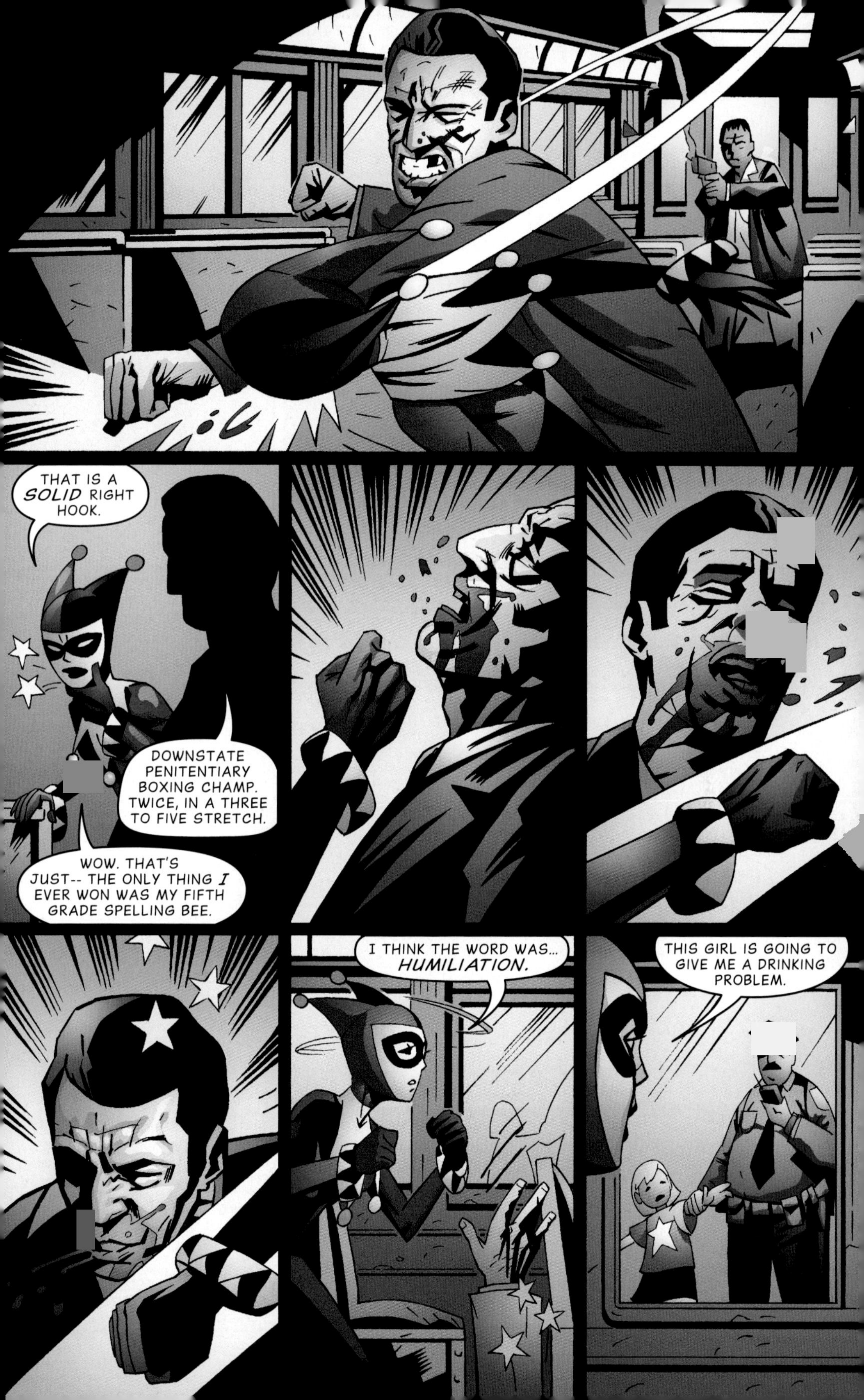
THAT IS A *SOLID* RIGHT HOOK.
DOWNSTATE PENITENTIARY BOXING CHAMP. TWICE, IN A THREE TO FIVE STRETCH.
WOW. THAT'S JUST-- THE ONLY THING *I* EVER WON WAS MY FIFTH GRADE SPELLING BEE.
I THINK THE WORD WAS... *HUMILIATION.*
THIS GIRL IS GOING TO GIVE ME A DRINKING PROBLEM.

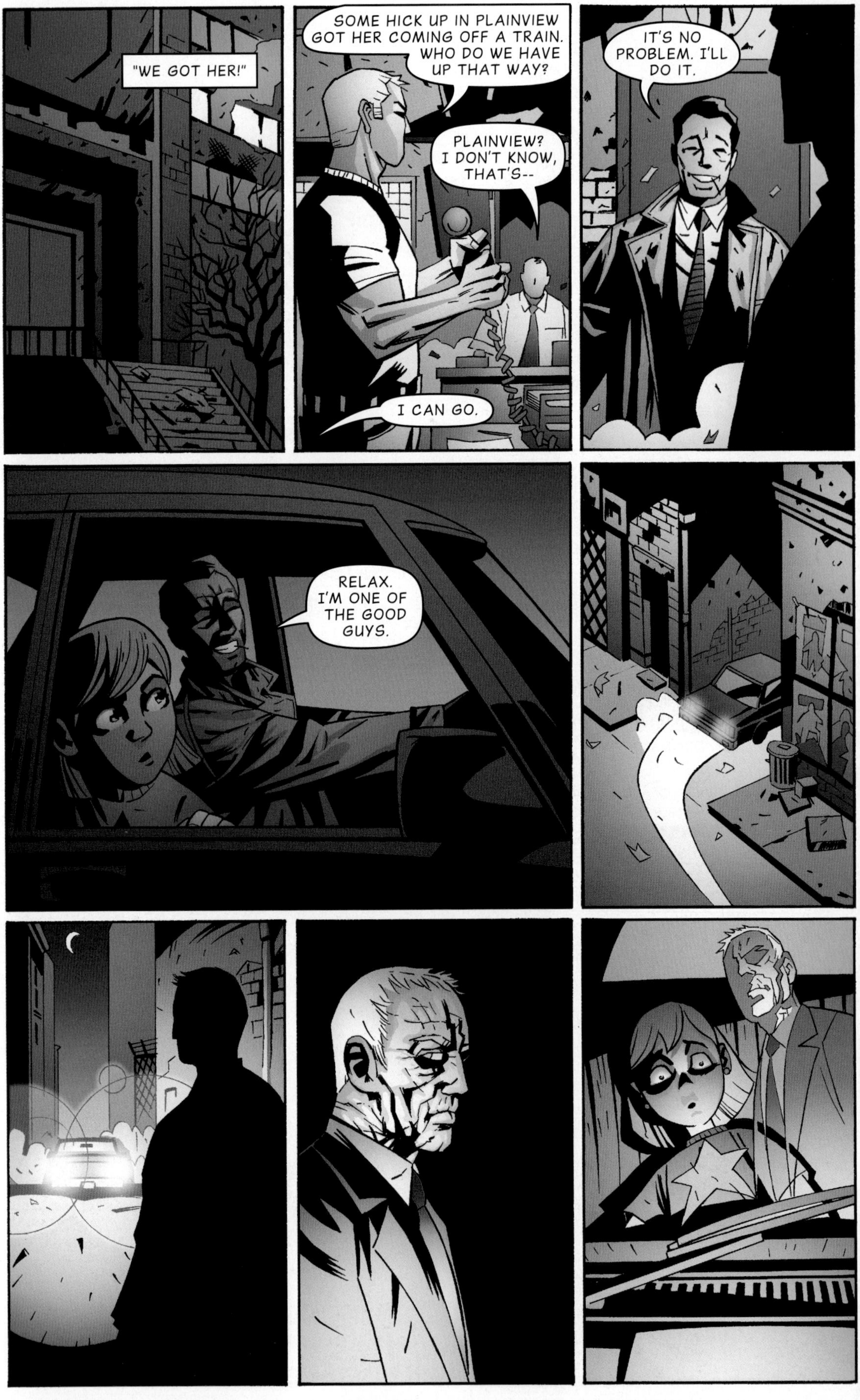
"WE GOT HER!"
SOME HICK UP IN PLAINVIEW GOT HER COMING OFF A TRAIN. WHO DO WE HAVE UP THAT WAY?
PLAINVIEW? I DON'T KNOW, THAT'S--
I CAN GO.
IT'S NO PROBLEM. I'LL DO IT.
RELAX. I'M ONE OF THE GOOD GUYS.

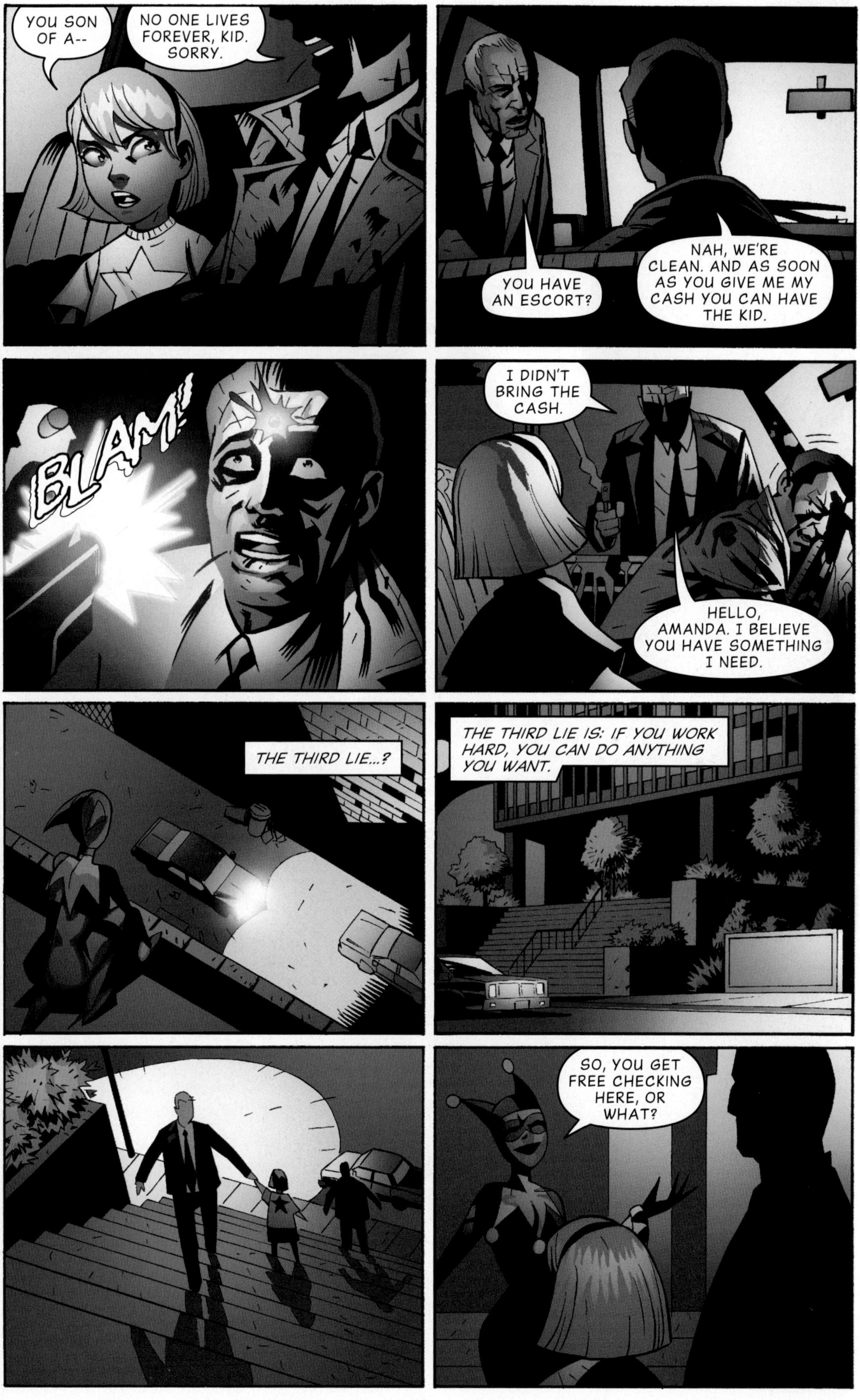
YOU SON OF A--
NO ONE LIVES FOREVER, KID. SORRY.
YOU HAVE AN ESCORT?
NAH, WE'RE CLEAN. AND AS SOON AS YOU GIVE ME MY CASH YOU CAN HAVE THE KID.
BLAM!!
I DIDN'T BRING THE CASH.
HELLO, AMANDA. I BELIEVE YOU HAVE SOMETHING I NEED.
THE THIRD LIE...?
THE THIRD LIE IS: IF YOU WORK HARD, YOU CAN DO ANYTHING YOU WANT.
SO, YOU GET FREE CHECKING HERE, OR WHAT?

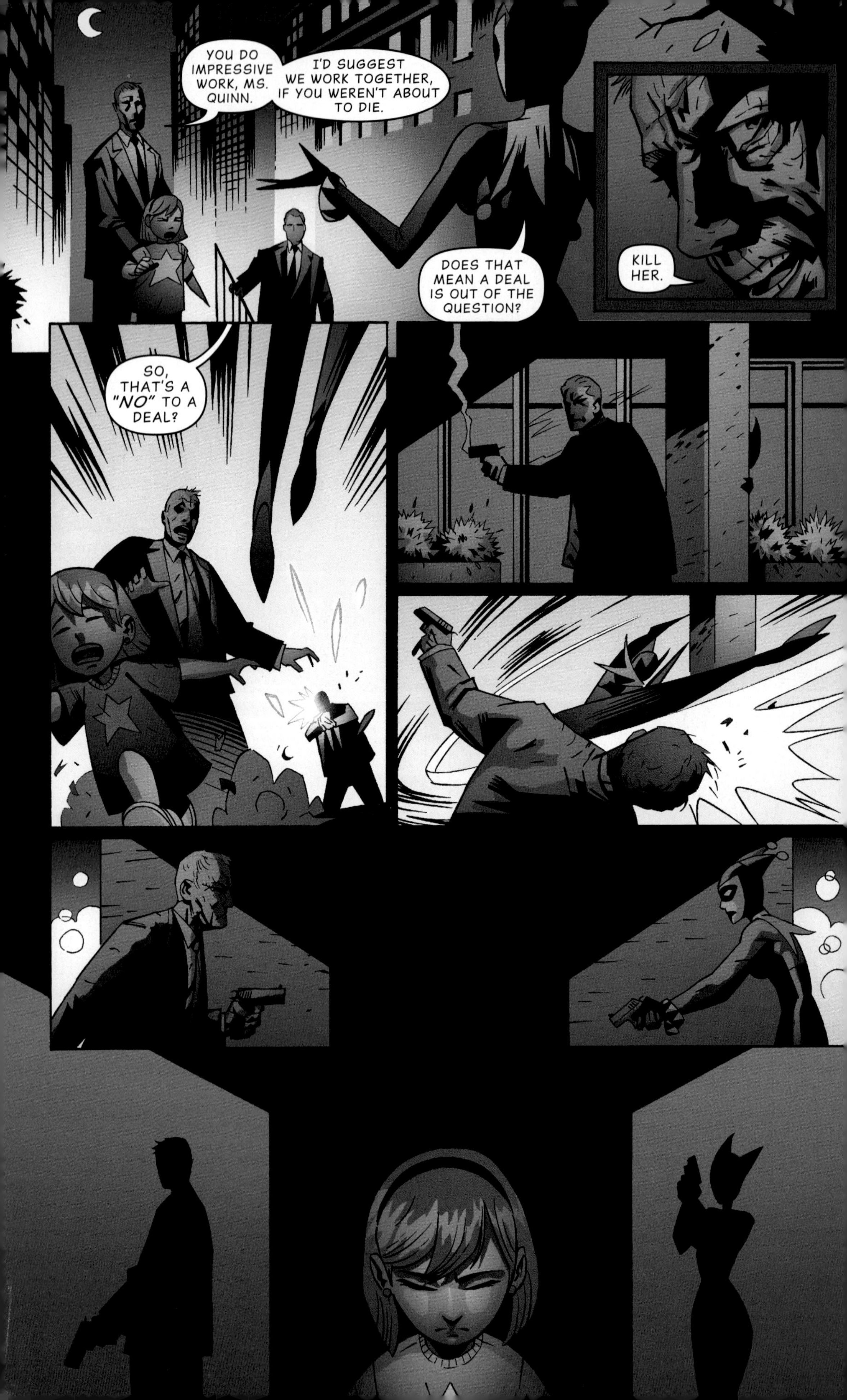
YOU DO IMPRESSIVE WORK, MS. QUINN.
I'D SUGGEST WE WORK TOGETHER, IF YOU WEREN'T ABOUT TO DIE.
DOES THAT MEAN A DEAL IS OUT OF THE QUESTION?
KILL HER.
SO, THAT'S A "NO" TO A DEAL?

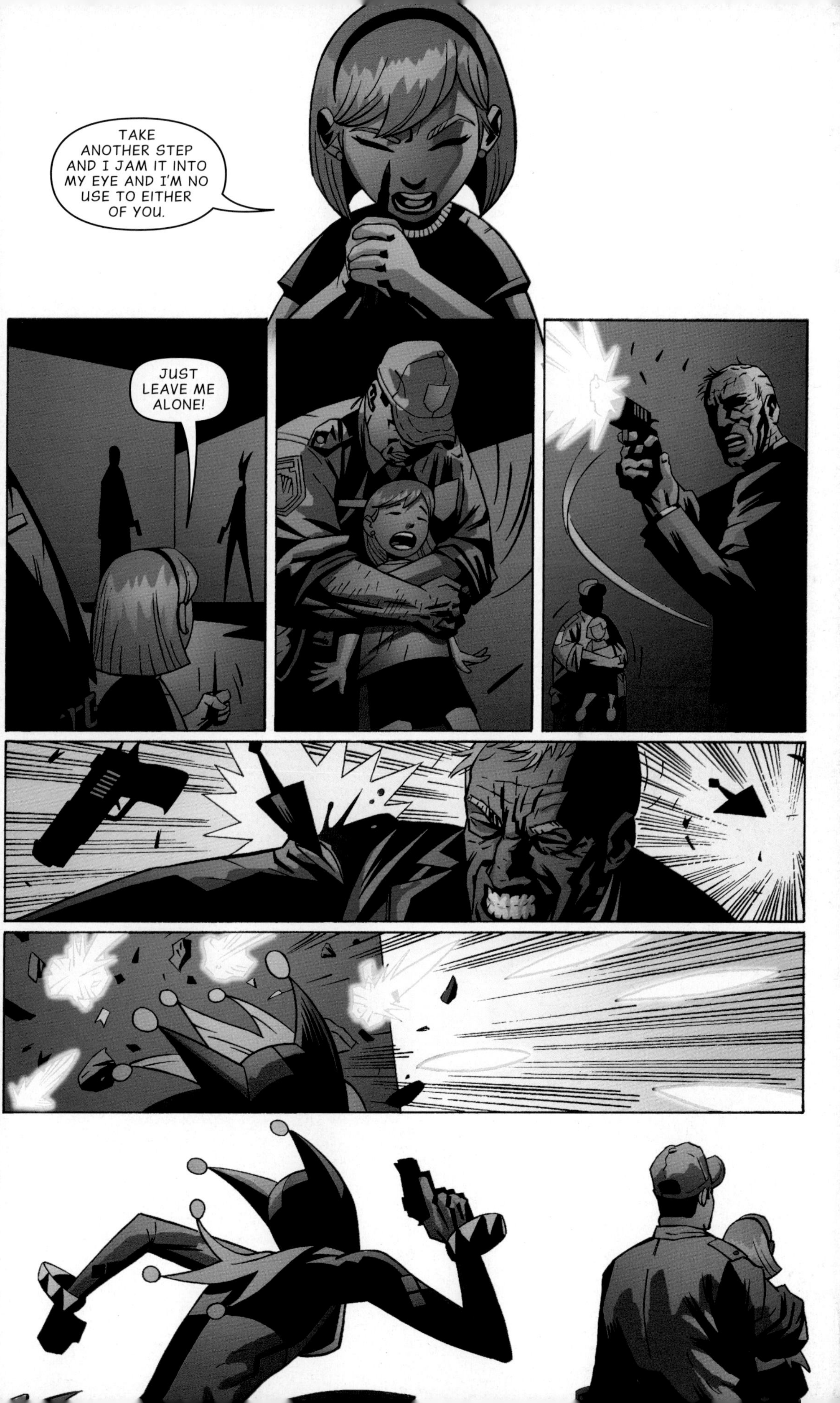
TAKE ANOTHER STEP AND I JAM IT INTO MY EYE AND I'M NO USE TO EITHER OF YOU.
JUST LEAVE ME ALONE!

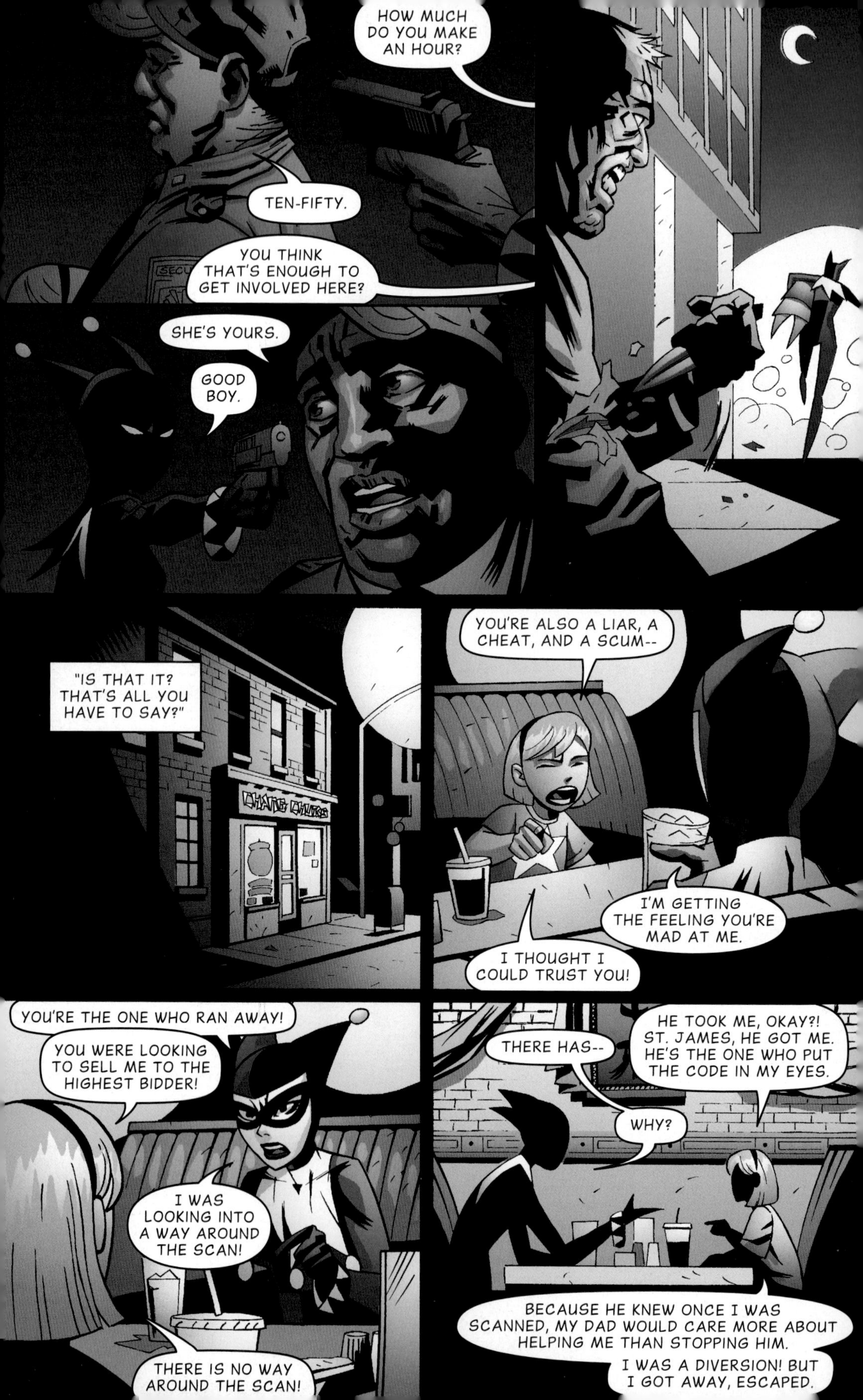
HOW MUCH DO YOU MAKE AN HOUR?
TEN-FIFTY.
YOU THINK THAT'S ENOUGH TO GET INVOLVED HERE?
SHE'S YOURS.
GOOD BOY.
"IS THAT IT? THAT'S ALL YOU HAVE TO SAY?"
YOU'RE ALSO A LIAR, A CHEAT, AND A SCUM--
I'M GETTING THE FEELING YOU'RE MAD AT ME.
I THOUGHT I COULD TRUST YOU!
YOU'RE THE ONE WHO RAN AWAY!
YOU WERE LOOKING TO SELL ME TO THE HIGHEST BIDDER!
I WAS LOOKING INTO A WAY AROUND THE SCAN!
THERE IS NO WAY AROUND THE SCAN!
THERE HAS--
HE TOOK ME, OKAY?! ST. JAMES, HE GOT ME. HE'S THE ONE WHO PUT THE CODE IN MY EYES.
WHY?
BECAUSE HE KNEW ONCE I WAS SCANNED, MY DAD WOULD CARE MORE ABOUT HELPING ME THAN STOPPING HIM.
I WAS A DIVERSION! BUT I GOT AWAY, ESCAPED.

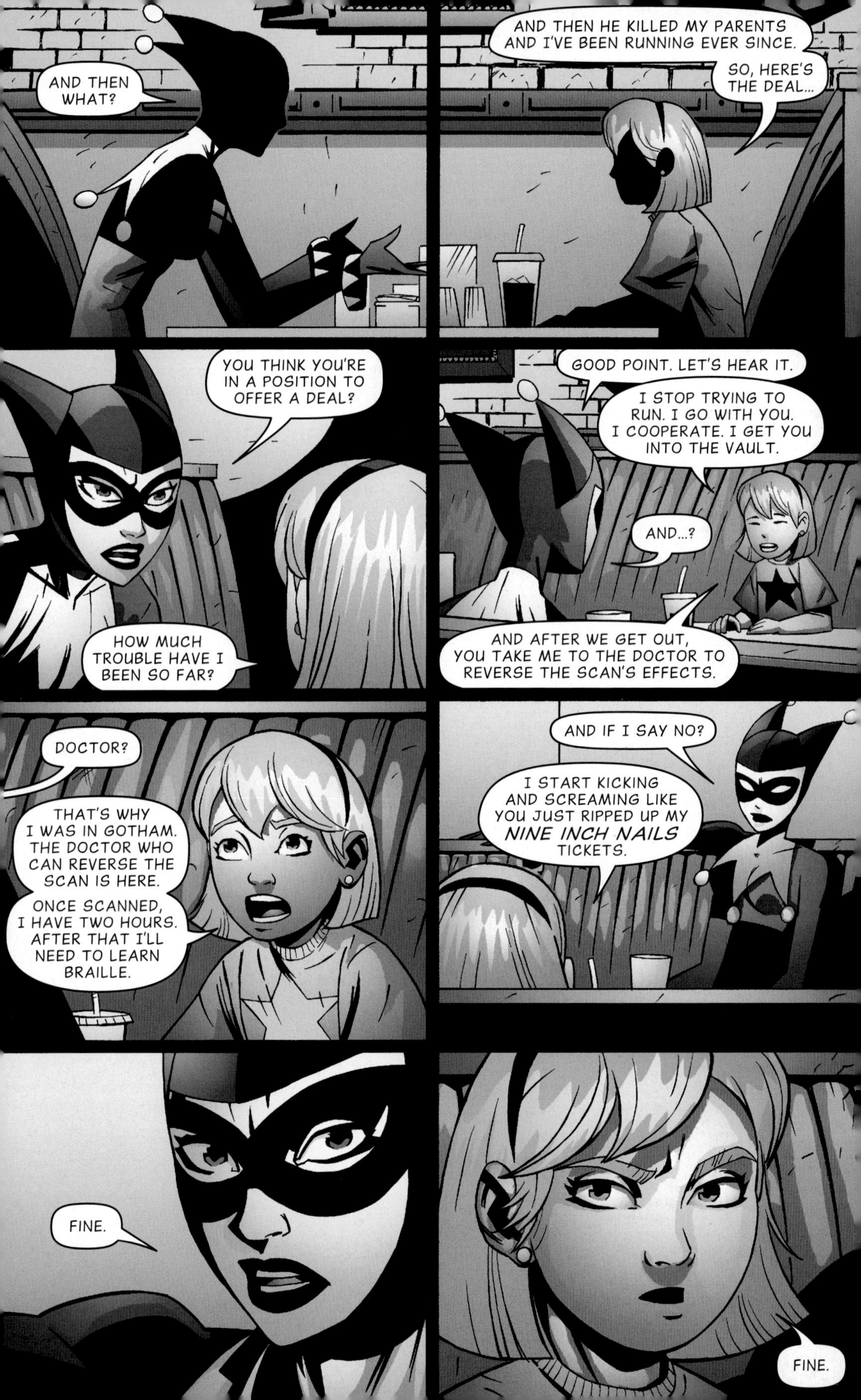
AND THEN WHAT?
AND THEN HE KILLED MY PARENTS AND I'VE BEEN RUNNING EVER SINCE.
SO, HERE'S THE DEAL...
YOU THINK YOU'RE IN A POSITION TO OFFER A DEAL?
HOW MUCH TROUBLE HAVE I BEEN SO FAR?
GOOD POINT. LET'S HEAR IT.
I STOP TRYING TO RUN. I GO WITH YOU. I COOPERATE. I GET YOU INTO THE VAULT.
AND...?
AND AFTER WE GET OUT, YOU TAKE ME TO THE DOCTOR TO REVERSE THE SCAN'S EFFECTS.
DOCTOR?
THAT'S WHY I WAS IN GOTHAM. THE DOCTOR WHO CAN REVERSE THE SCAN IS HERE.
ONCE SCANNED, I HAVE TWO HOURS. AFTER THAT I'LL NEED TO LEARN BRAILLE.
AND IF I SAY NO?
I START KICKING AND SCREAMING LIKE YOU JUST RIPPED UP MY *NINE INCH NAILS* TICKETS.
FINE.
FINE.

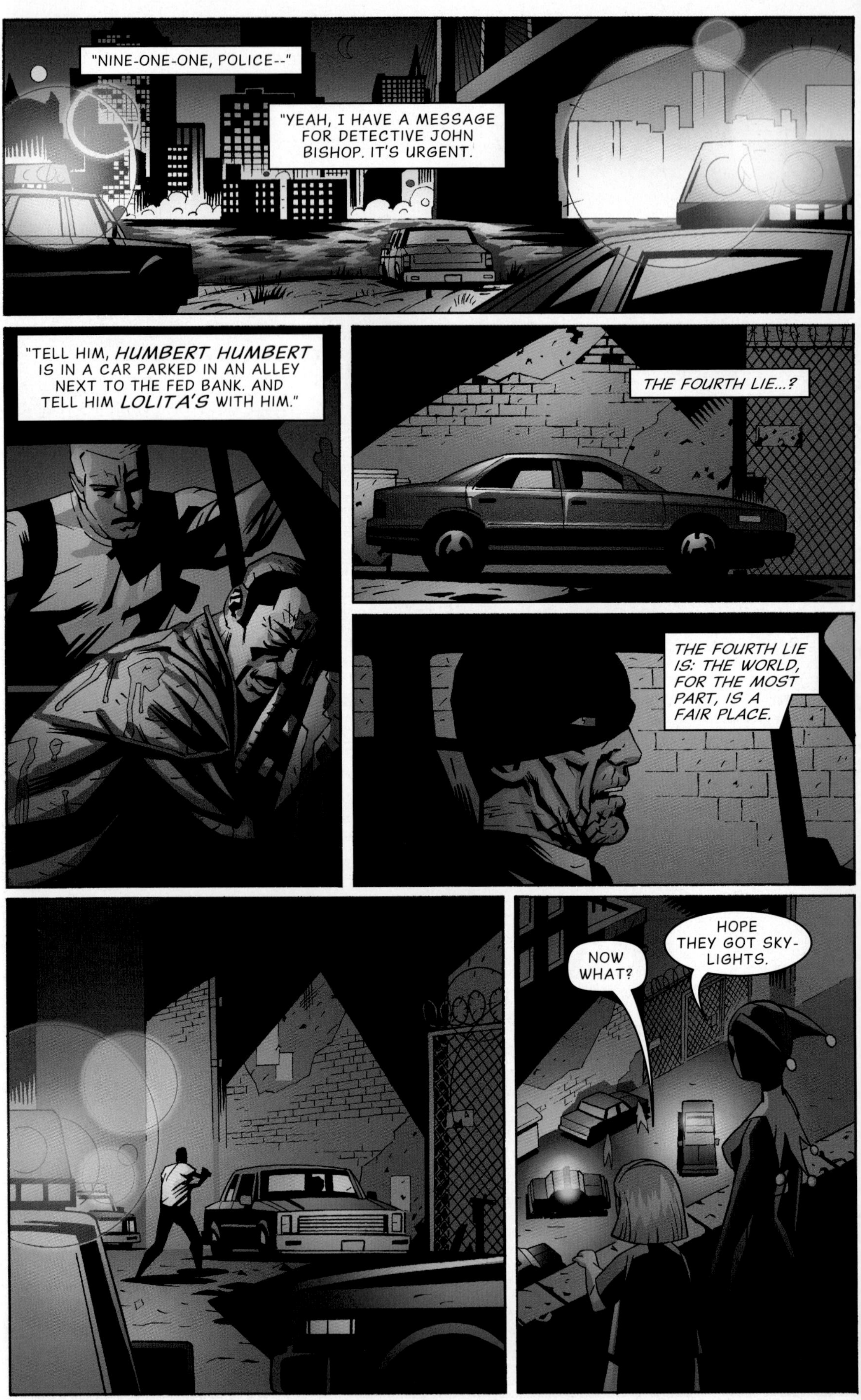
"NINE-ONE-ONE, POLICE--"
"YEAH, I HAVE A MESSAGE FOR DETECTIVE JOHN BISHOP. IT'S URGENT.
"TELL HIM, HUMBERT HUMBERT IS IN A CAR PARKED IN AN ALLEY NEXT TO THE FED BANK. AND TELL HIM LOLITA'S WITH HIM."
THE FOURTH LIE...?
THE FOURTH LIE IS: THE WORLD, FOR THE MOST PART, IS A FAIR PLACE.
NOW WHAT?
HOPE THEY GOT SKY-LIGHTS.

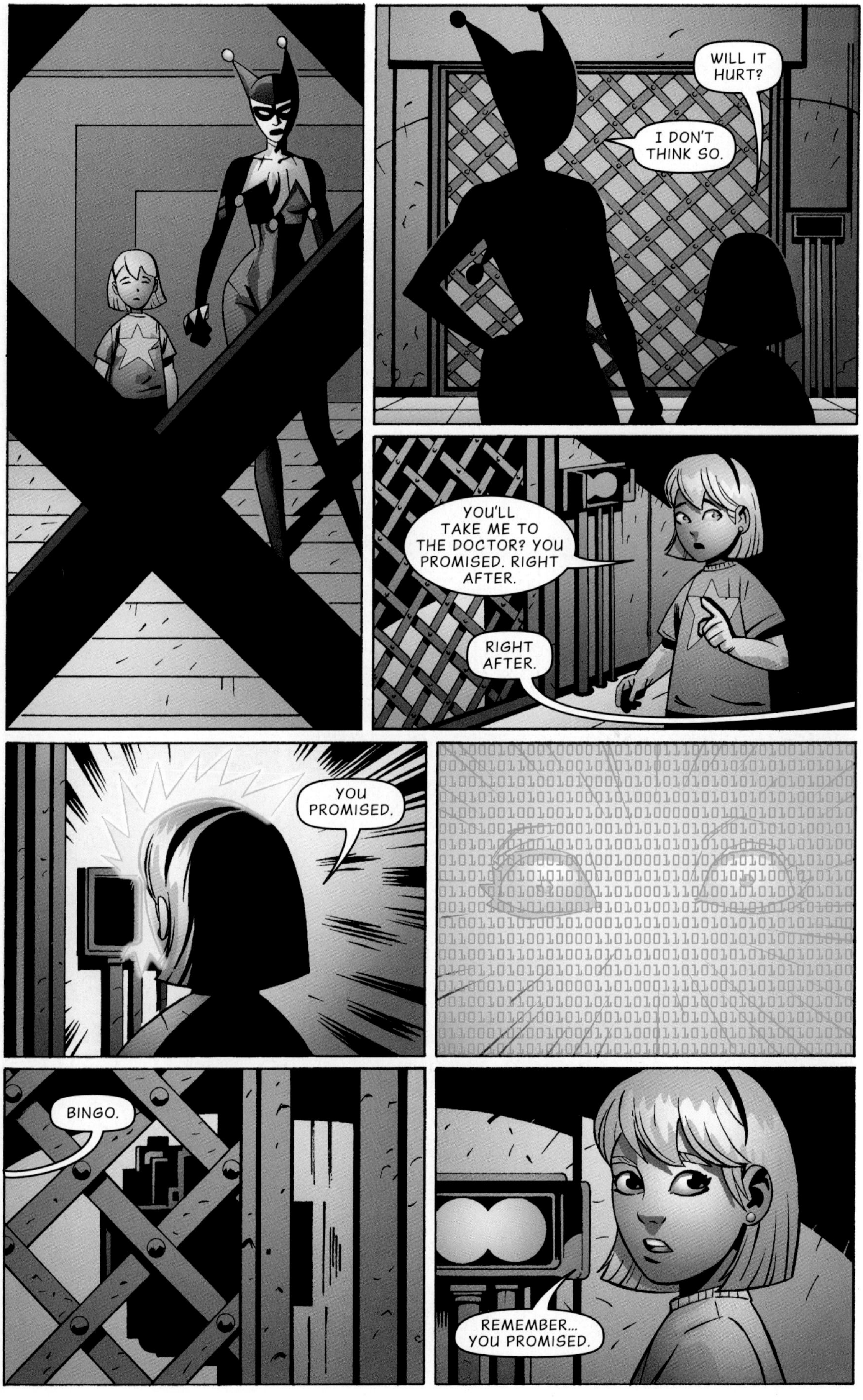
WILL IT HURT?
I DON'T THINK SO.
YOU'LL TAKE ME TO THE DOCTOR? YOU PROMISED. RIGHT AFTER.
RIGHT AFTER.
YOU PROMISED.
BINGO.
REMEMBER... YOU PROMISED.

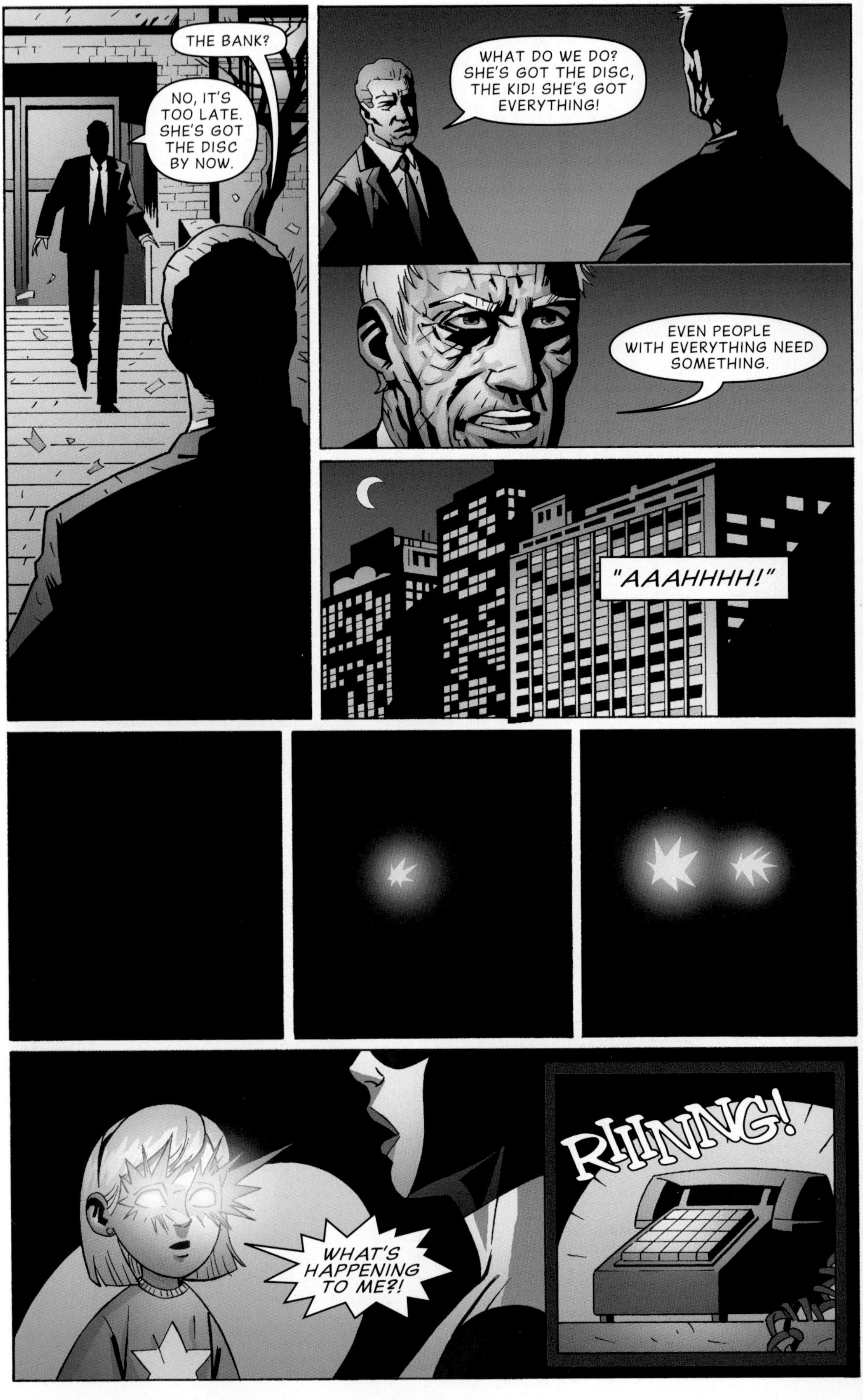
THE BANK?
NO, IT'S TOO LATE. SHE'S GOT THE DISC BY NOW.
WHAT DO WE DO? SHE'S GOT THE DISC, THE KID! SHE'S GOT EVERYTHING!
EVEN PEOPLE WITH EVERYTHING NEED SOMETHING.
"AAAHHHH!"
WHAT'S HAPPENING TO ME?!
RIIINNG!

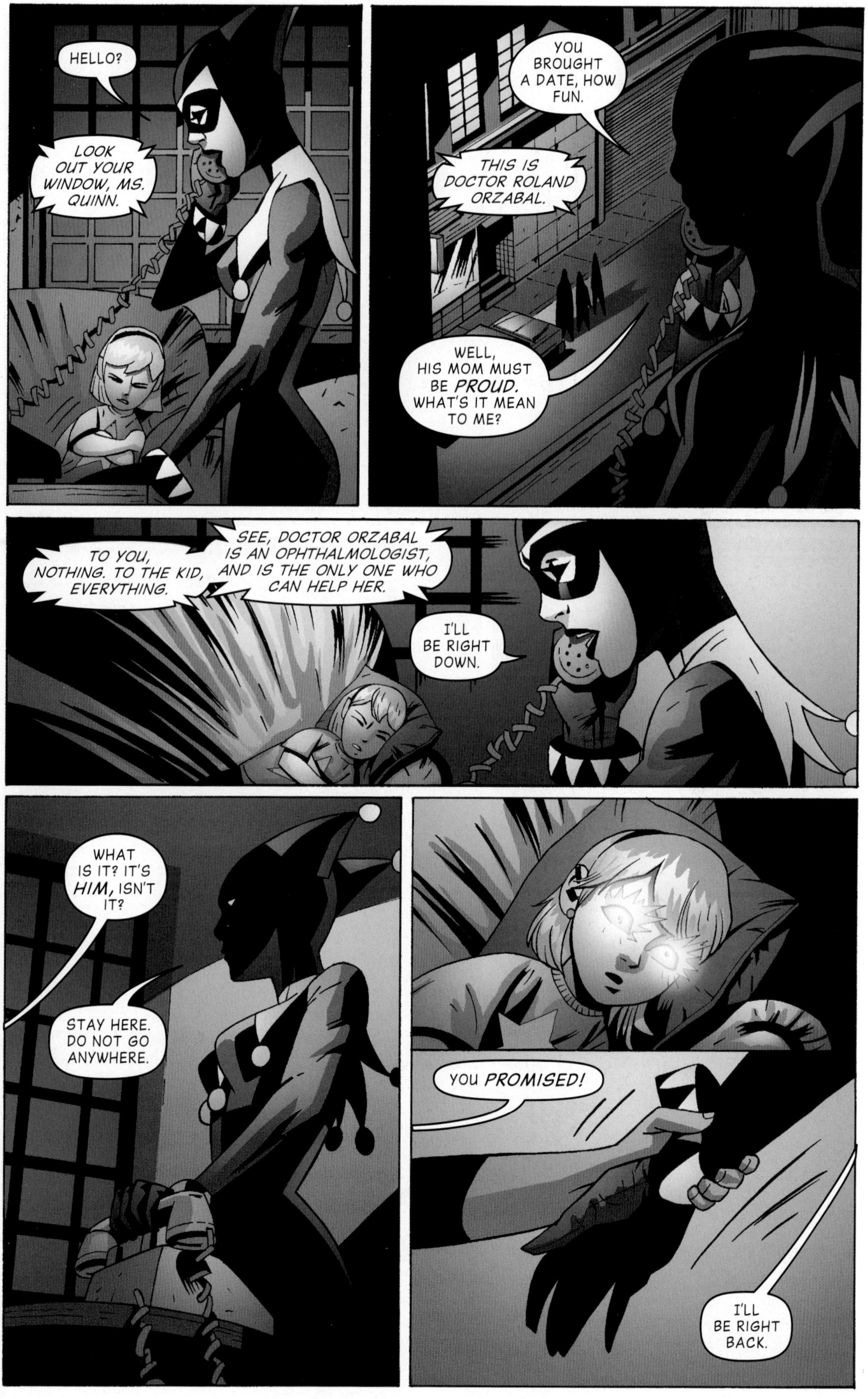
HELLO?
LOOK OUT YOUR WINDOW, MS. QUINN.
YOU BROUGHT A DATE, HOW FUN.
THIS IS DOCTOR ROLAND ORZABAL.
WELL, HIS MOM MUST BE PROUD. WHAT'S IT MEAN TO ME?
TO YOU, NOTHING. TO THE KID, EVERYTHING.
SEE, DOCTOR ORZABAL IS AN OPHTHALMOLOGIST, AND IS THE ONLY ONE WHO CAN HELP HER.
I'LL BE RIGHT DOWN.
WHAT IS IT? IT'S HIM, ISN'T IT?
STAY HERE. DO NOT GO ANYWHERE.
YOU PROMISED!
I'LL BE RIGHT BACK.

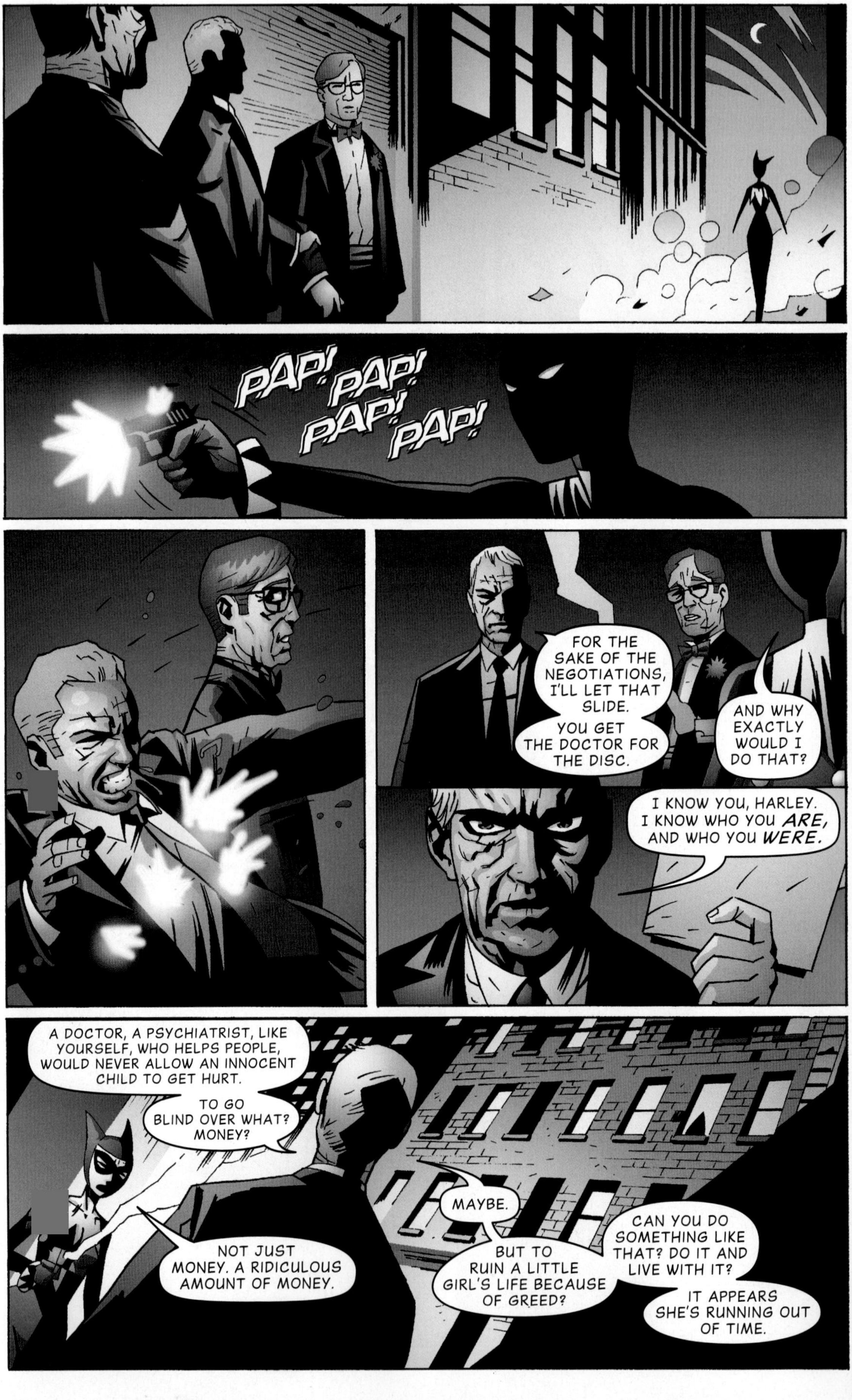
PAP! PAP! PAP! PAP!
FOR THE SAKE OF THE NEGOTIATIONS, I'LL LET THAT SLIDE.
YOU GET THE DOCTOR FOR THE DISC.
AND WHY EXACTLY WOULD I DO THAT?
I KNOW YOU, HARLEY. I KNOW WHO YOU *ARE,* AND WHO YOU *WERE.*
A DOCTOR, A PSYCHIATRIST, LIKE YOURSELF, WHO HELPS PEOPLE, WOULD NEVER ALLOW AN INNOCENT CHILD TO GET HURT.
TO GO BLIND OVER WHAT? MONEY?
NOT JUST MONEY. A RIDICULOUS AMOUNT OF MONEY.
MAYBE.
BUT TO RUIN A LITTLE GIRL'S LIFE BECAUSE OF GREED?
CAN YOU DO SOMETHING LIKE THAT? DO IT AND LIVE WITH IT?
IT APPEARS SHE'S RUNNING OUT OF TIME.

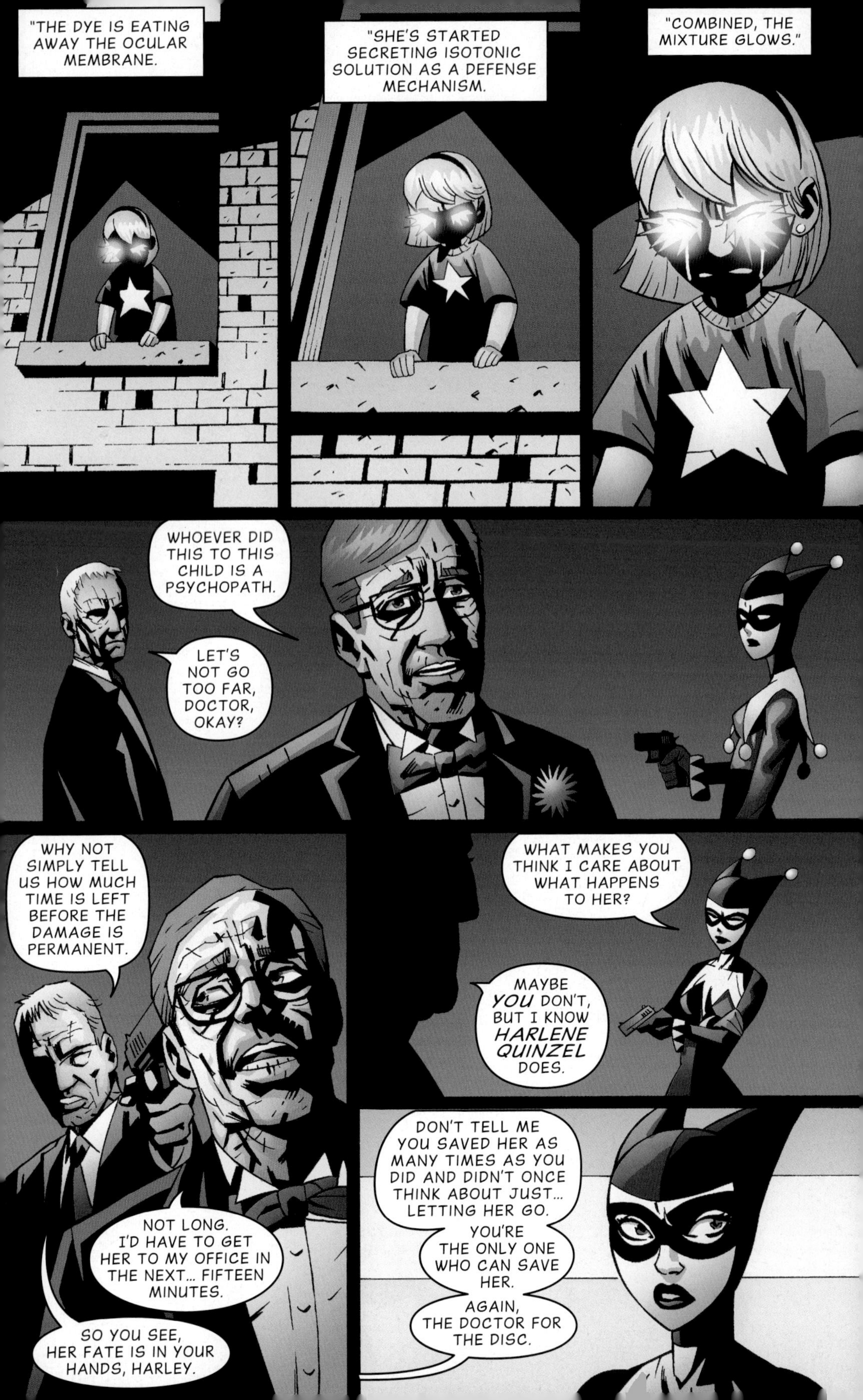
"THE DYE IS EATING AWAY THE OCULAR MEMBRANE.
"SHE'S STARTED SECRETING ISOTONIC SOLUTION AS A DEFENSE MECHANISM.
"COMBINED, THE MIXTURE GLOWS."
WHOEVER DID THIS TO THIS CHILD IS A PSYCHOPATH.
LET'S NOT GO TOO FAR, DOCTOR, OKAY?
WHY NOT SIMPLY TELL US HOW MUCH TIME IS LEFT BEFORE THE DAMAGE IS PERMANENT.
NOT LONG. I'D HAVE TO GET HER TO MY OFFICE IN THE NEXT... FIFTEEN MINUTES.
SO YOU SEE, HER FATE IS IN YOUR HANDS, HARLEY.
WHAT MAKES YOU THINK I CARE ABOUT WHAT HAPPENS TO HER?
MAYBE *YOU* DON'T, BUT I KNOW *HARLENE QUINZEL* DOES.
DON'T TELL ME YOU SAVED HER AS MANY TIMES AS YOU DID AND DIDN'T ONCE THINK ABOUT JUST... LETTING HER GO.
YOU'RE THE ONLY ONE WHO CAN SAVE HER.
AGAIN, THE DOCTOR FOR THE DISC.

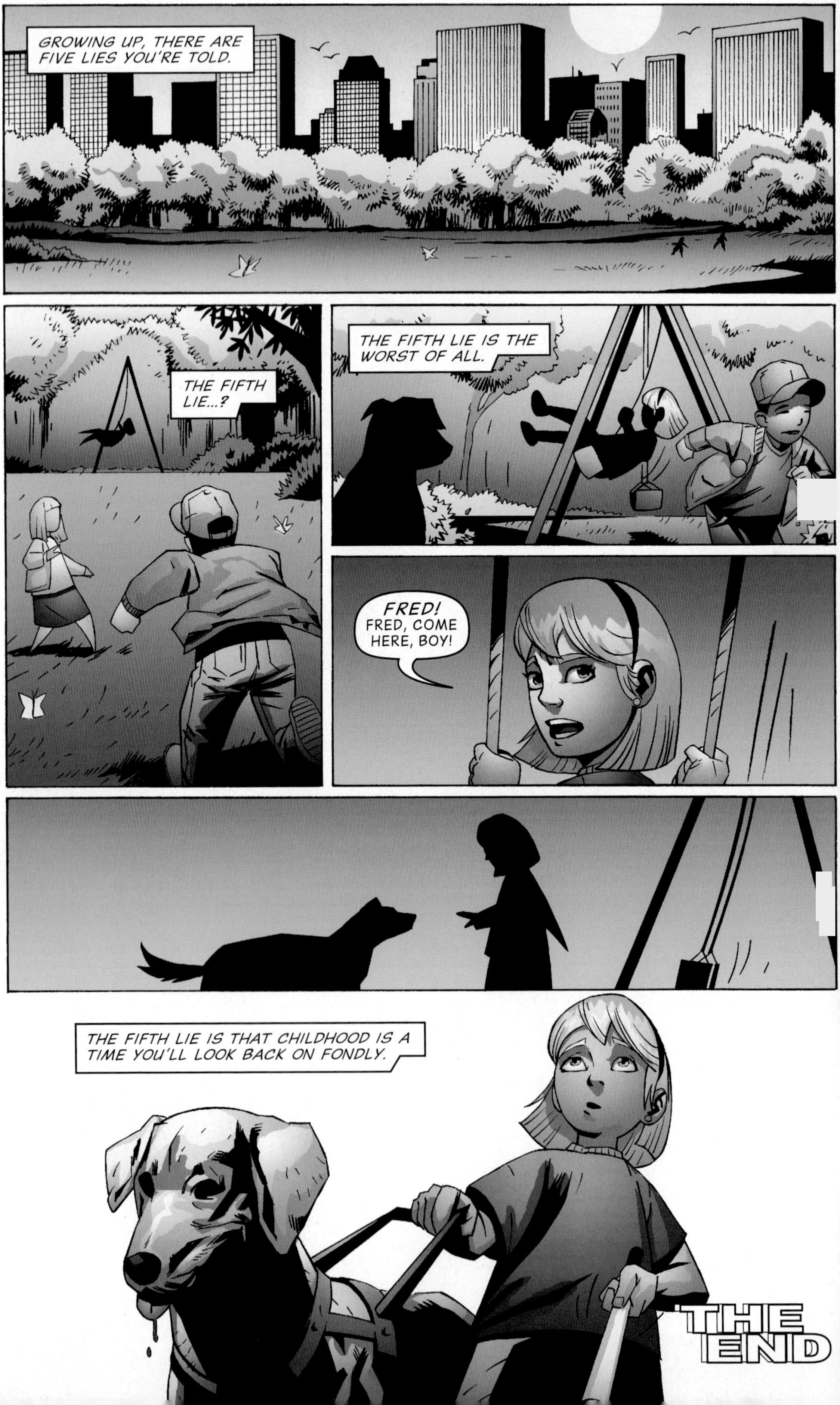
GROWING UP, THERE ARE FIVE LIES YOU'RE TOLD.
THE FIFTH LIE...?
THE FIFTH LIE IS THE WORST OF ALL.
FRED! FRED, COME HERE, BOY!
THE FIFTH LIE IS THAT CHILDHOOD IS A TIME YOU'LL LOOK BACK ON FONDLY.
THE END

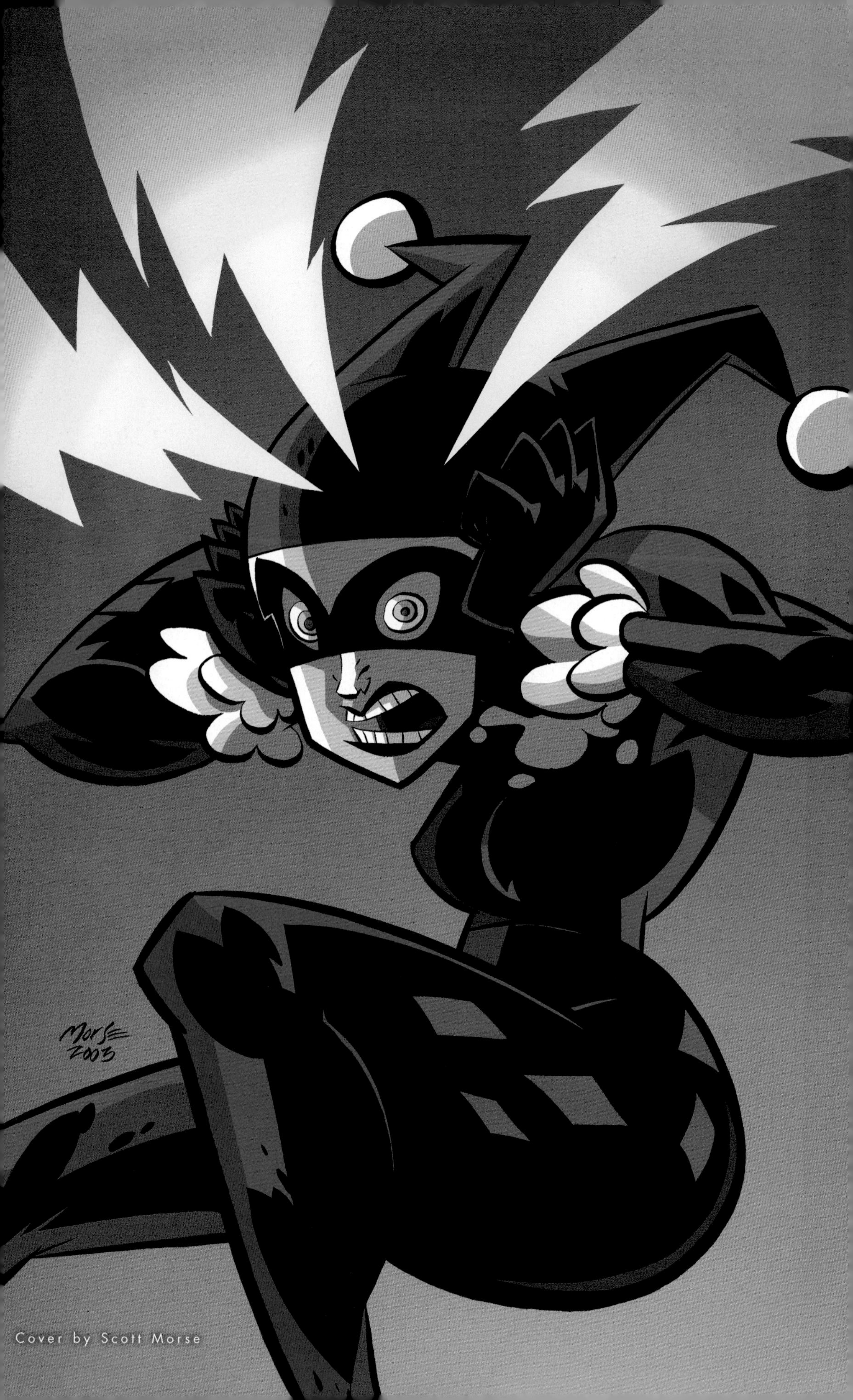
MORSE
2003

Cover by Scott Morse

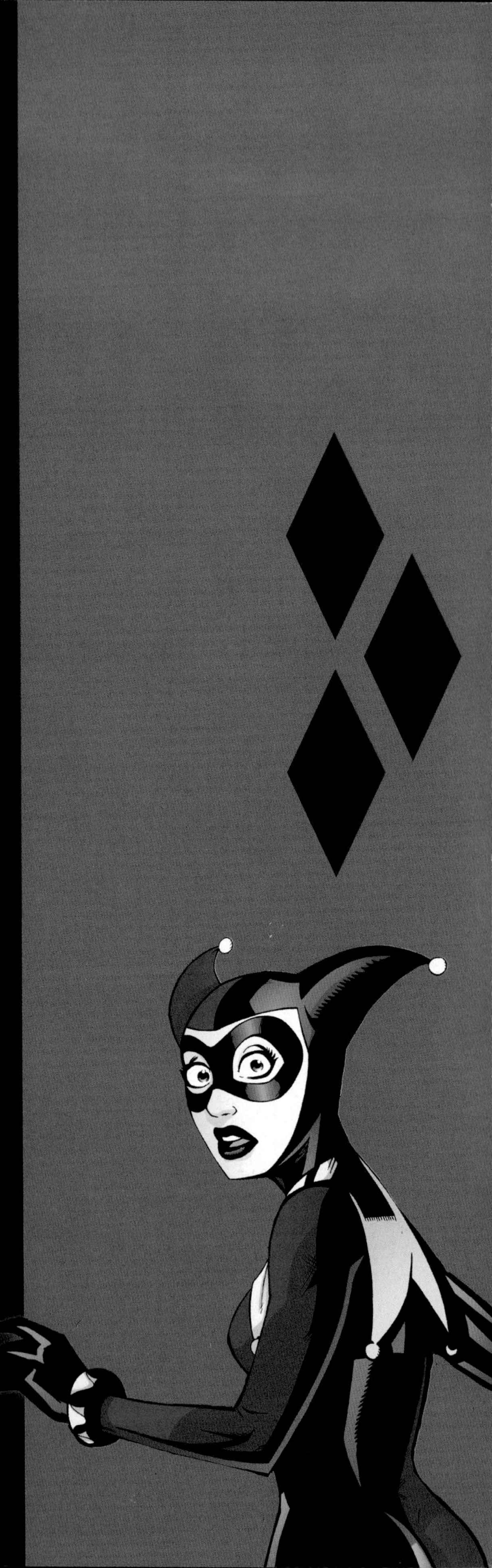

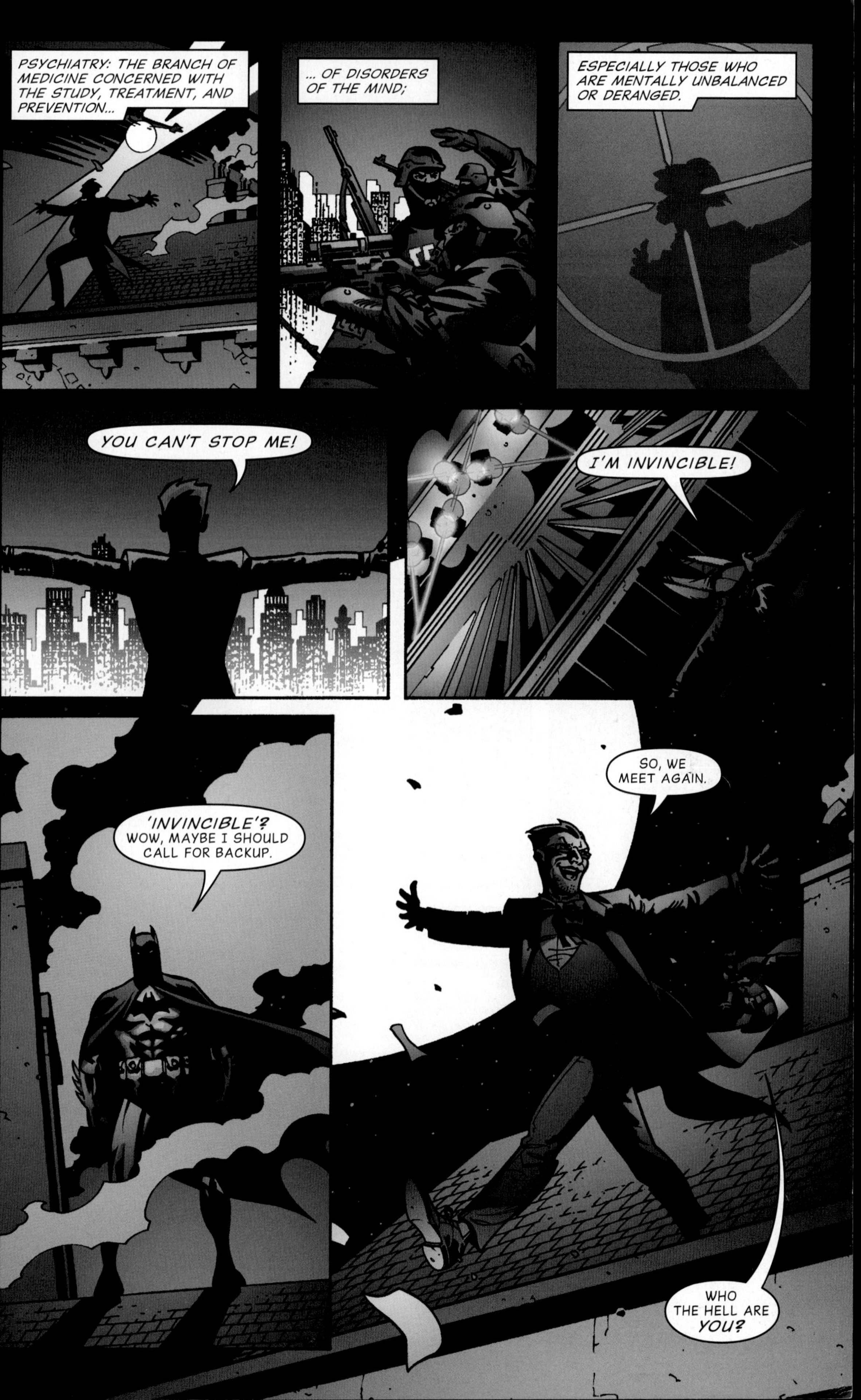
PSYCHIATRY: THE BRANCH OF MEDICINE CONCERNED WITH THE STUDY, TREATMENT, AND PREVENTION...
... OF DISORDERS OF THE MIND;
ESPECIALLY THOSE WHO ARE MENTALLY UNBALANCED OR DERANGED.
YOU CAN'T STOP ME!
I'M INVINCIBLE!
'INVINCIBLE'? WOW, MAYBE I SHOULD CALL FOR BACKUP.
SO, WE MEET AGAIN.
WHO THE HELL ARE YOU?

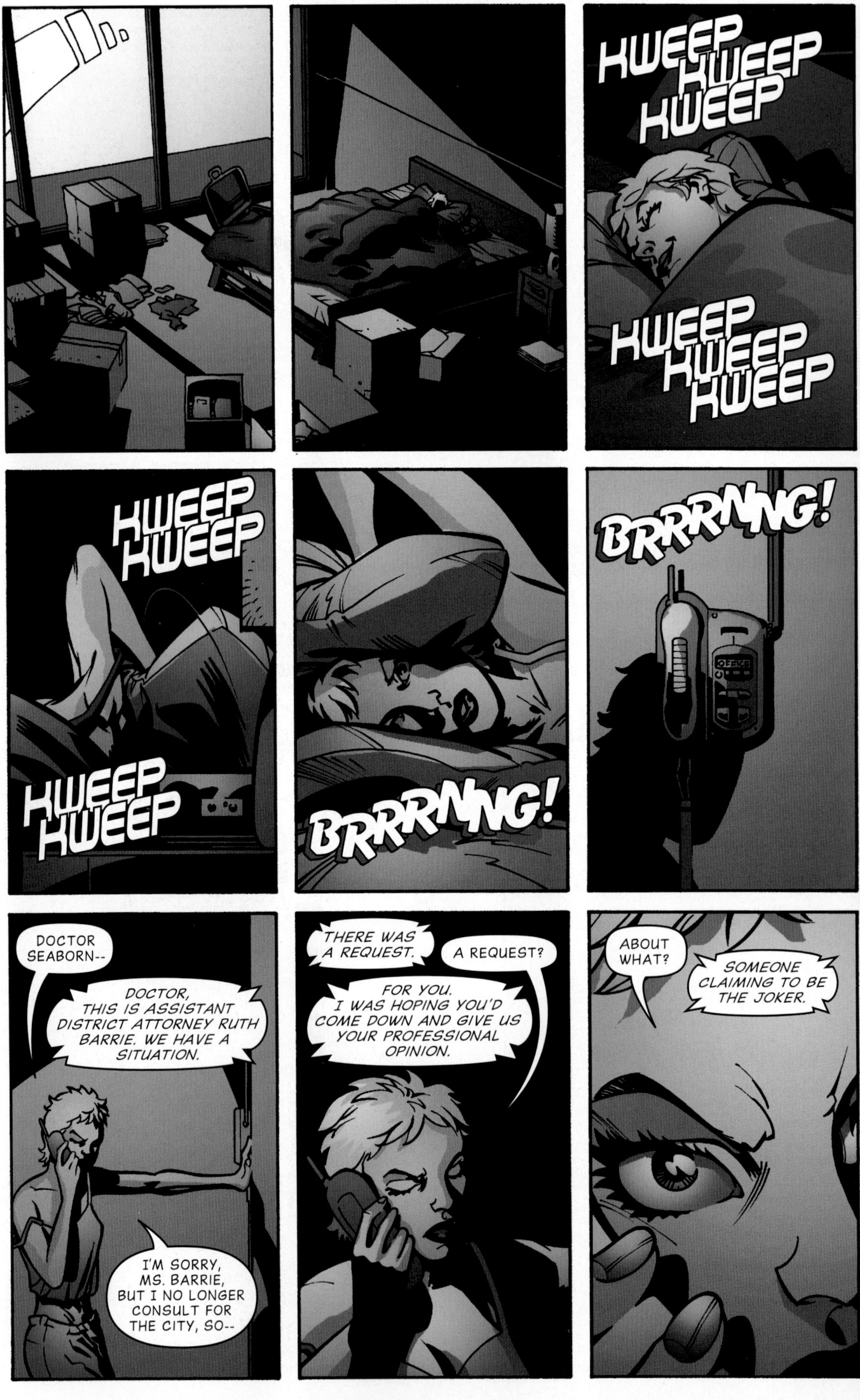

KWEEP KWEEP KWEEP
KWEEP KWEEP KWEEP
KWEEP KWEEP
KWEEP KWEEP
BRRRNNG!
BRRRNNG!
DOCTOR SEABORN--
DOCTOR, THIS IS ASSISTANT DISTRICT ATTORNEY RUTH BARRIE. WE HAVE A SITUATION.
I'M SORRY, MS. BARRIE, BUT I NO LONGER CONSULT FOR THE CITY, SO--
THERE WAS A REQUEST.
A REQUEST?
FOR YOU. I WAS HOPING YOU'D COME DOWN AND GIVE US YOUR PROFESSIONAL OPINION.
ABOUT WHAT?
SOMEONE CLAIMING TO BE THE JOKER.

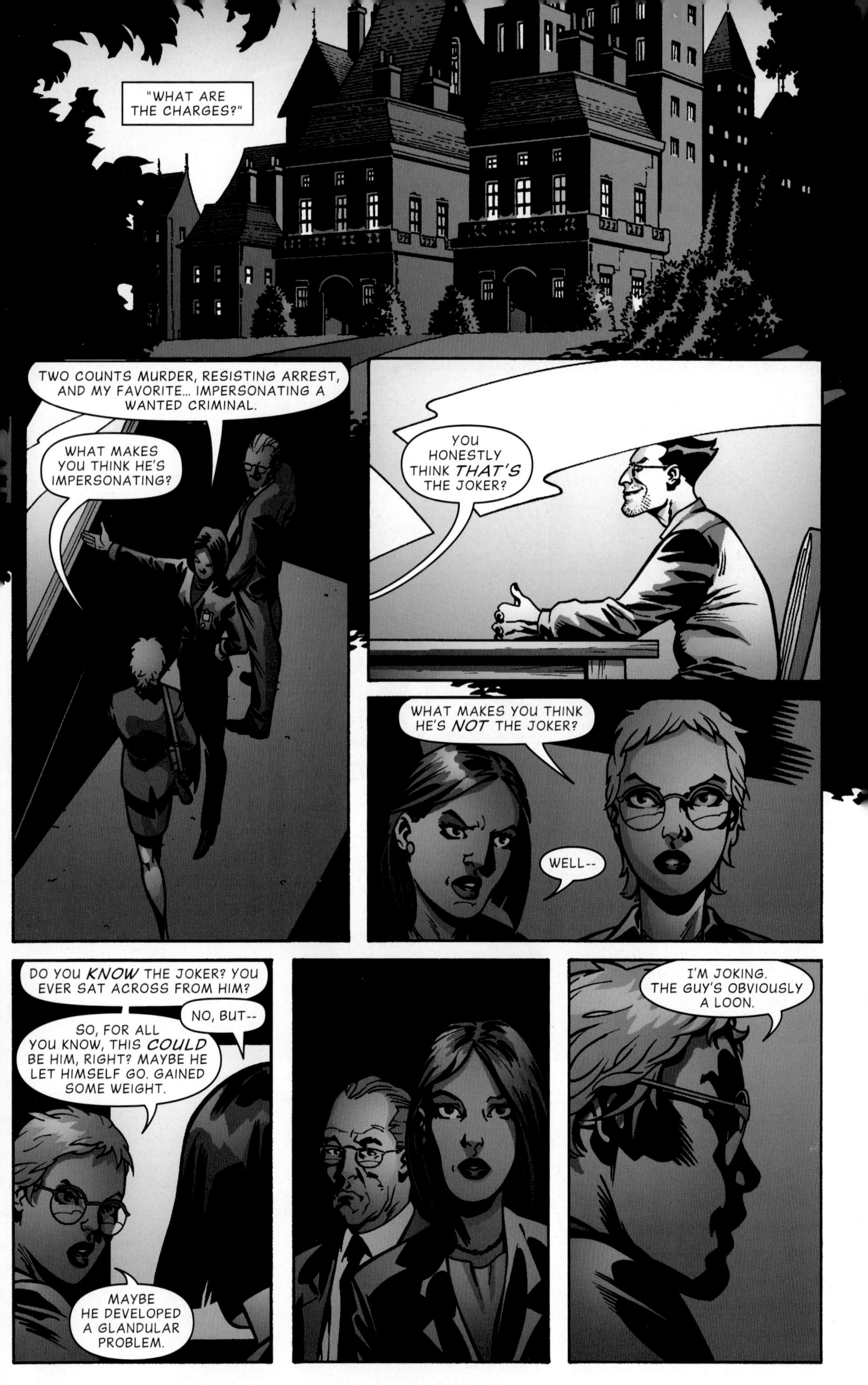
"WHAT ARE THE CHARGES?"
TWO COUNTS MURDER, RESISTING ARREST, AND MY FAVORITE... IMPERSONATING A WANTED CRIMINAL.
WHAT MAKES YOU THINK HE'S IMPERSONATING?
YOU HONESTLY THINK *THAT'S* THE JOKER?
WHAT MAKES YOU THINK HE'S *NOT* THE JOKER?
WELL--
DO YOU *KNOW* THE JOKER? YOU EVER SAT ACROSS FROM HIM?
NO, BUT--
SO, FOR ALL YOU KNOW, THIS *COULD* BE HIM, RIGHT? MAYBE HE LET HIMSELF GO. GAINED SOME WEIGHT.
MAYBE HE DEVELOPED A GLANDULAR PROBLEM.
I'M JOKING. THE GUY'S OBVIOUSLY A LOON.

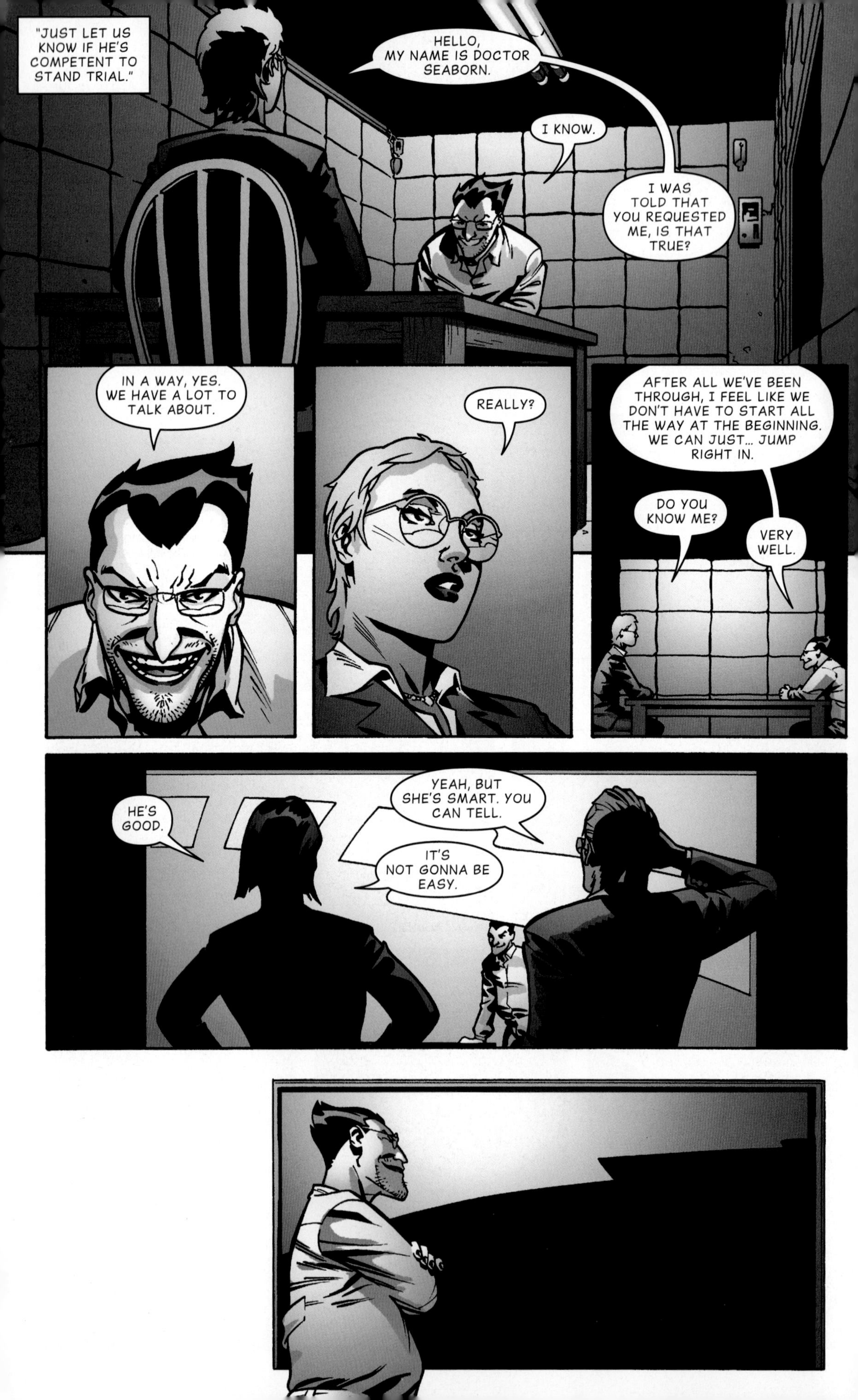
"JUST LET US KNOW IF HE'S COMPETENT TO STAND TRIAL."
HELLO, MY NAME IS DOCTOR SEABORN.
I KNOW.
I WAS TOLD THAT YOU REQUESTED ME, IS THAT TRUE?
IN A WAY, YES. WE HAVE A LOT TO TALK ABOUT.
REALLY?
AFTER ALL WE'VE BEEN THROUGH, I FEEL LIKE WE DON'T HAVE TO START ALL THE WAY AT THE BEGINNING. WE CAN JUST... JUMP RIGHT IN.
DO YOU KNOW ME?
VERY WELL.
HE'S GOOD.
YEAH, BUT SHE'S SMART. YOU CAN TELL.
IT'S NOT GONNA BE EASY.

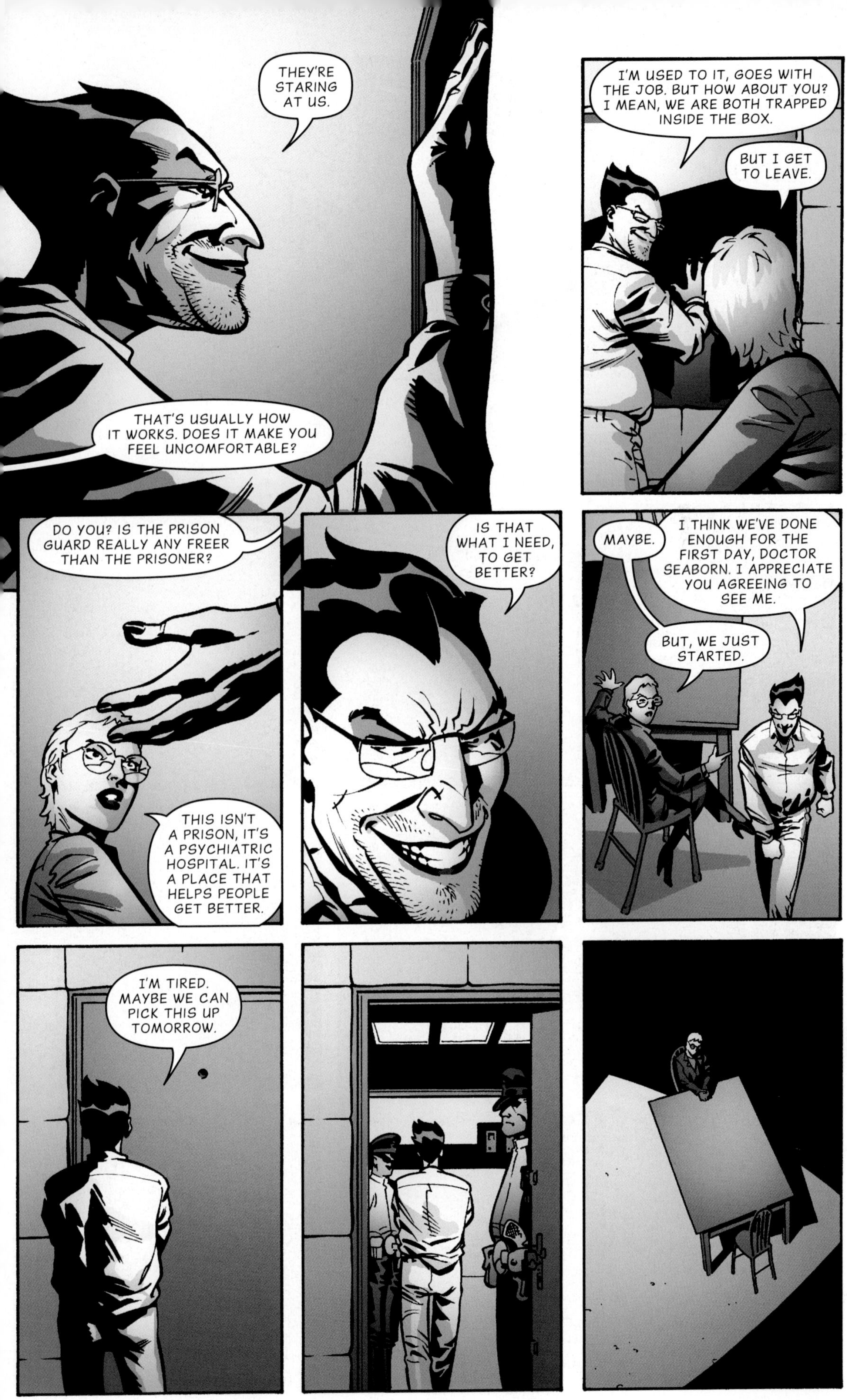
THEY'RE STARING AT US.
THAT'S USUALLY HOW IT WORKS. DOES IT MAKE YOU FEEL UNCOMFORTABLE?
I'M USED TO IT, GOES WITH THE JOB. BUT HOW ABOUT YOU? I MEAN, WE ARE BOTH TRAPPED INSIDE THE BOX.
BUT I GET TO LEAVE.
DO YOU? IS THE PRISON GUARD REALLY ANY FREER THAN THE PRISONER?
THIS ISN'T A PRISON, IT'S A PSYCHIATRIC HOSPITAL. IT'S A PLACE THAT HELPS PEOPLE GET BETTER.
IS THAT WHAT I NEED, TO GET BETTER?
MAYBE.
I THINK WE'VE DONE ENOUGH FOR THE FIRST DAY, DOCTOR SEABORN. I APPRECIATE YOU AGREEING TO SEE ME.
BUT, WE JUST STARTED.
I'M TIRED. MAYBE WE CAN PICK THIS UP TOMORROW.

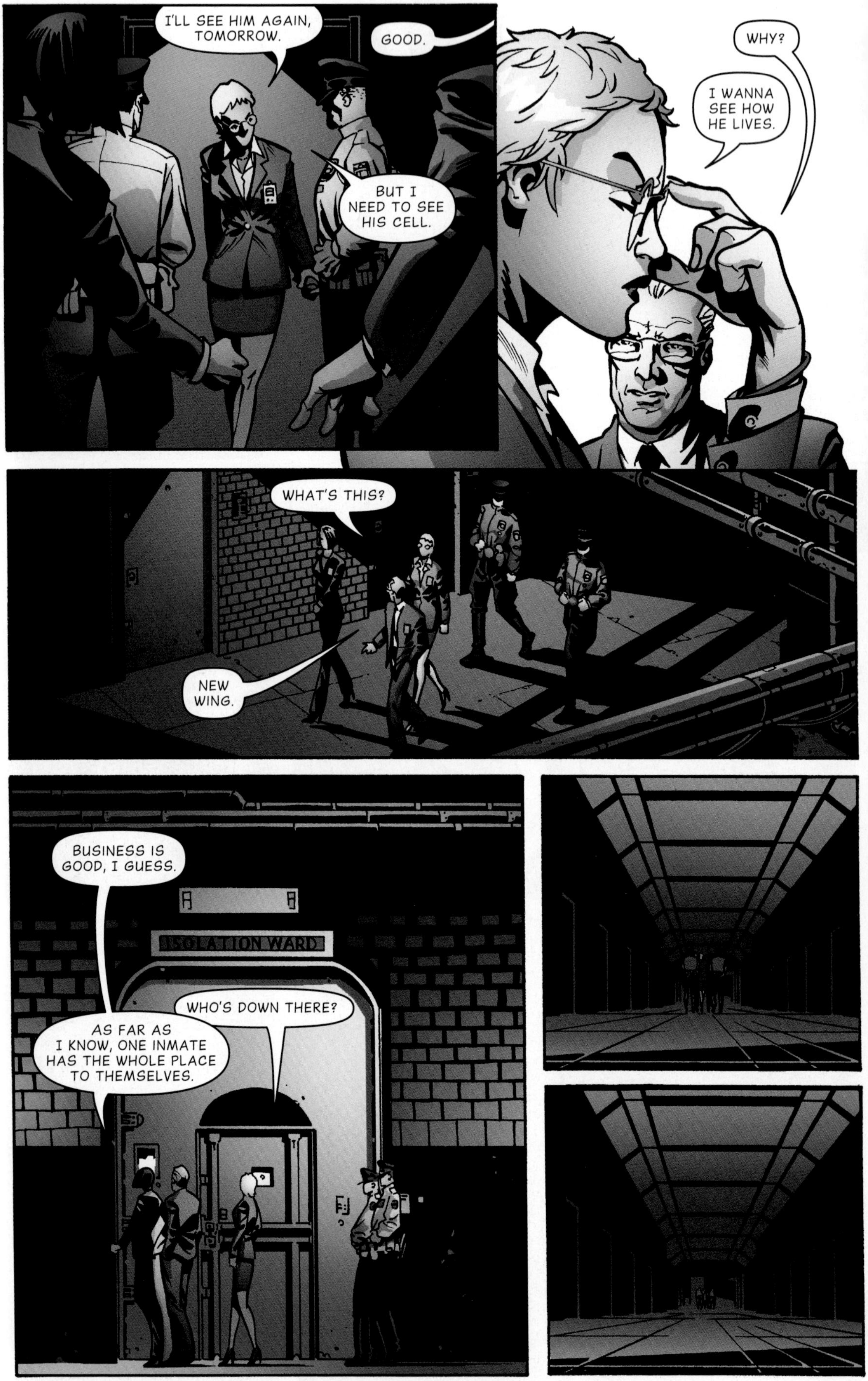
I'LL SEE HIM AGAIN, TOMORROW.
GOOD.
BUT I NEED TO SEE HIS CELL.
WHY?
I WANNA SEE HOW HE LIVES.
WHAT'S THIS?
NEW WING.
BUSINESS IS GOOD, I GUESS.
ISOLATION WARD
WHO'S DOWN THERE?
AS FAR AS I KNOW, ONE INMATE HAS THE WHOLE PLACE TO THEMSELVES.

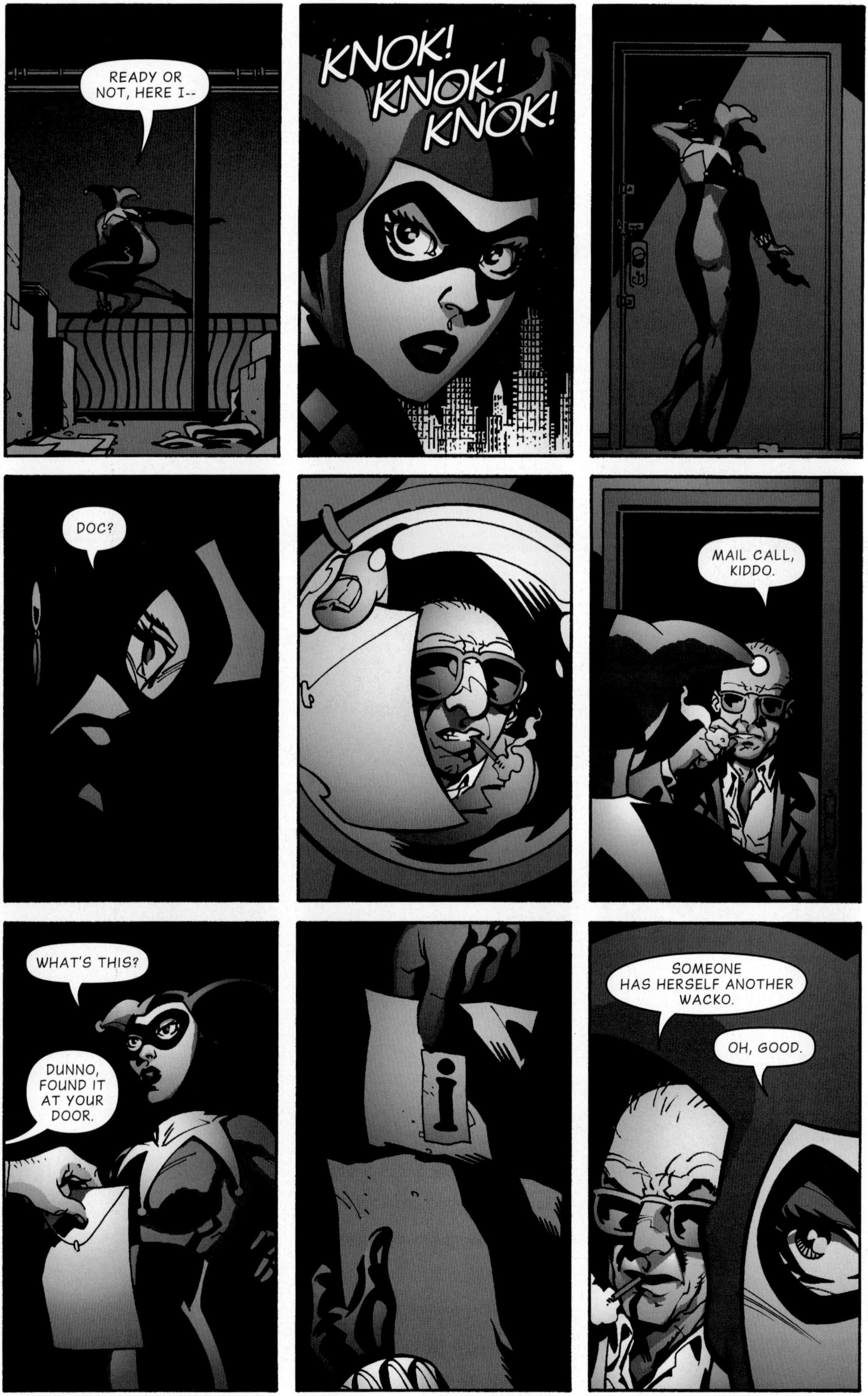
READY OR NOT, HERE I--
KNOK! KNOK! KNOK!
DOC?
MAIL CALL, KIDDO.
WHAT'S THIS?
DUNNO, FOUND IT AT YOUR DOOR.
SOMEONE HAS HERSELF ANOTHER WACKO.
OH, GOOD.

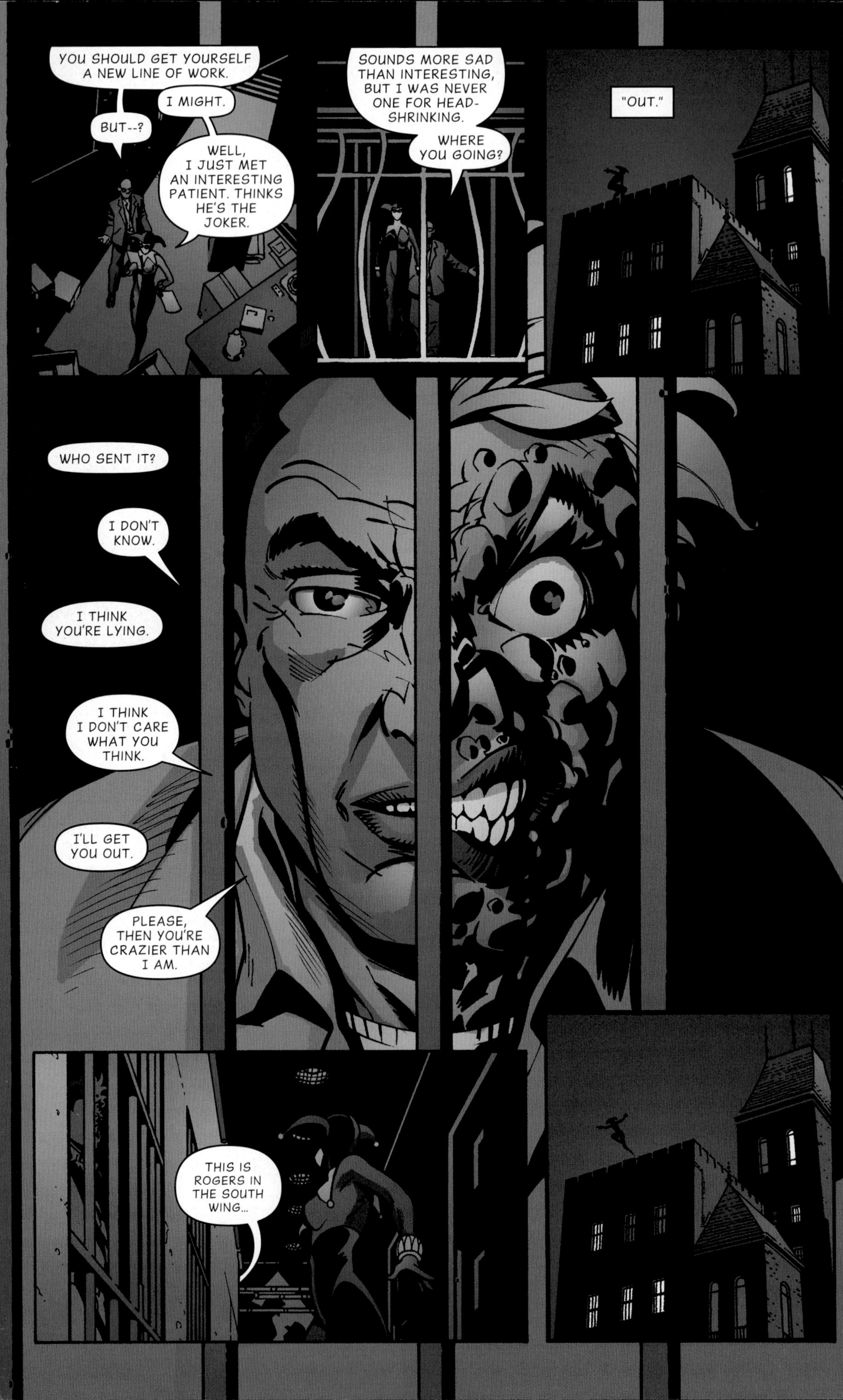
YOU SHOULD GET YOURSELF A NEW LINE OF WORK.
BUT--?
I MIGHT.
WELL, I JUST MET AN INTERESTING PATIENT. THINKS HE'S THE JOKER.
SOUNDS MORE SAD THAN INTERESTING, BUT I WAS NEVER ONE FOR HEAD-SHRINKING.
WHERE YOU GOING?
"OUT."
WHO SENT IT?
I DON'T KNOW.
I THINK YOU'RE LYING.
I THINK I DON'T CARE WHAT YOU THINK.
I'LL GET YOU OUT.
PLEASE, THEN YOU'RE CRAZIER THAN I AM.
THIS IS ROGERS IN THE SOUTH WING...

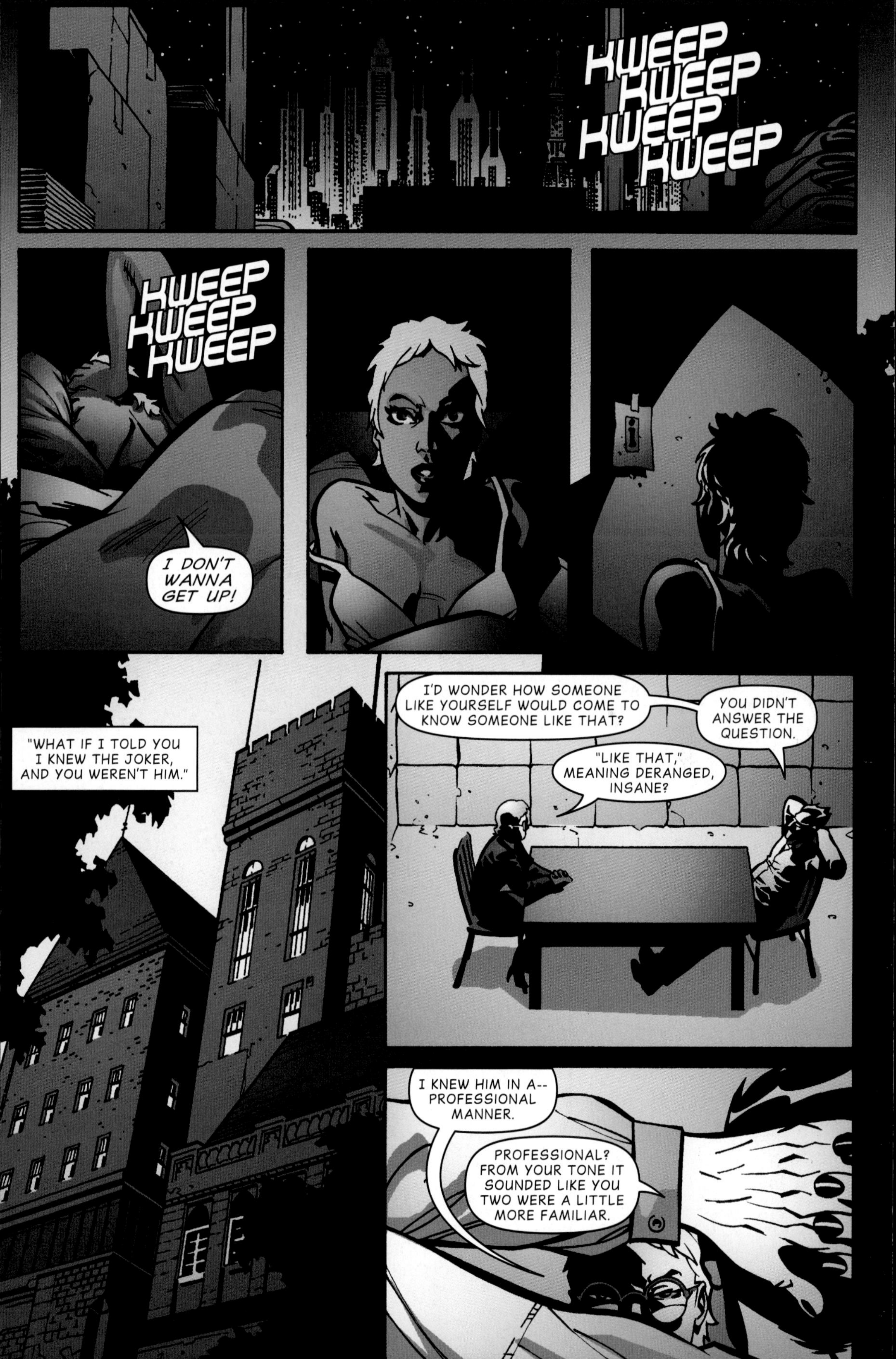
KWEEP KWEEP KWEEP KWEEP
KWEEP KWEEP KWEEP
I DON'T WANNA GET UP!
"WHAT IF I TOLD YOU I KNEW THE JOKER, AND YOU WEREN'T HIM."
I'D WONDER HOW SOMEONE LIKE YOURSELF WOULD COME TO KNOW SOMEONE LIKE THAT?
YOU DIDN'T ANSWER THE QUESTION.
"LIKE THAT," MEANING DERANGED, INSANE?
I KNEW HIM IN A-- PROFESSIONAL MANNER.
PROFESSIONAL? FROM YOUR TONE IT SOUNDED LIKE YOU TWO WERE A LITTLE MORE FAMILIAR.

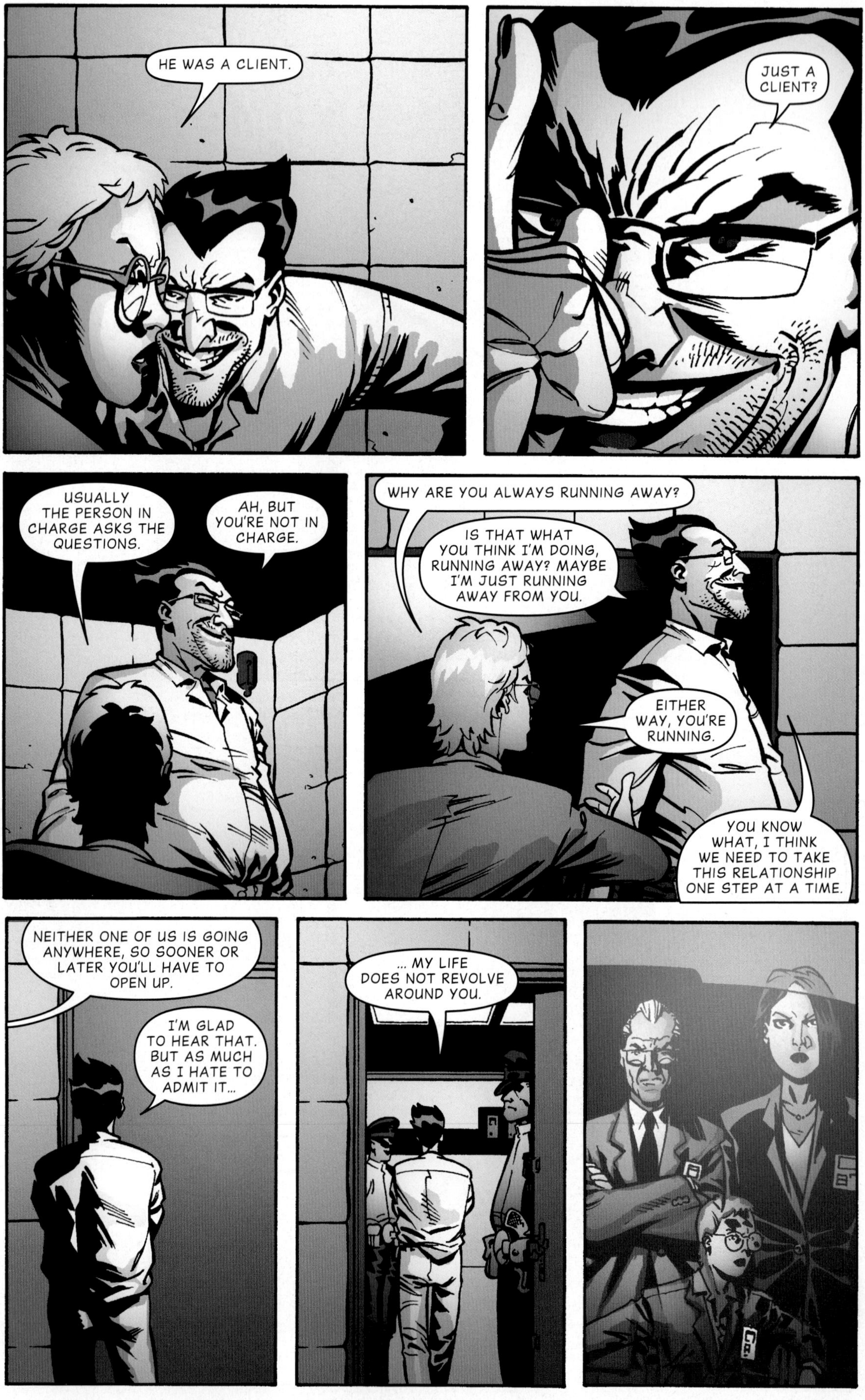
HE WAS A CLIENT.
JUST A CLIENT?
USUALLY THE PERSON IN CHARGE ASKS THE QUESTIONS.
AH, BUT YOU'RE NOT IN CHARGE.
WHY ARE YOU ALWAYS RUNNING AWAY?
IS THAT WHAT YOU THINK I'M DOING, RUNNING AWAY? MAYBE I'M JUST RUNNING AWAY FROM YOU.
EITHER WAY, YOU'RE RUNNING.
YOU KNOW WHAT, I THINK WE NEED TO TAKE THIS RELATIONSHIP ONE STEP AT A TIME.
NEITHER ONE OF US IS GOING ANYWHERE, SO SOONER OR LATER YOU'LL HAVE TO OPEN UP.
I'M GLAD TO HEAR THAT. BUT AS MUCH AS I HATE TO ADMIT IT...
... MY LIFE DOES NOT REVOLVE AROUND YOU.

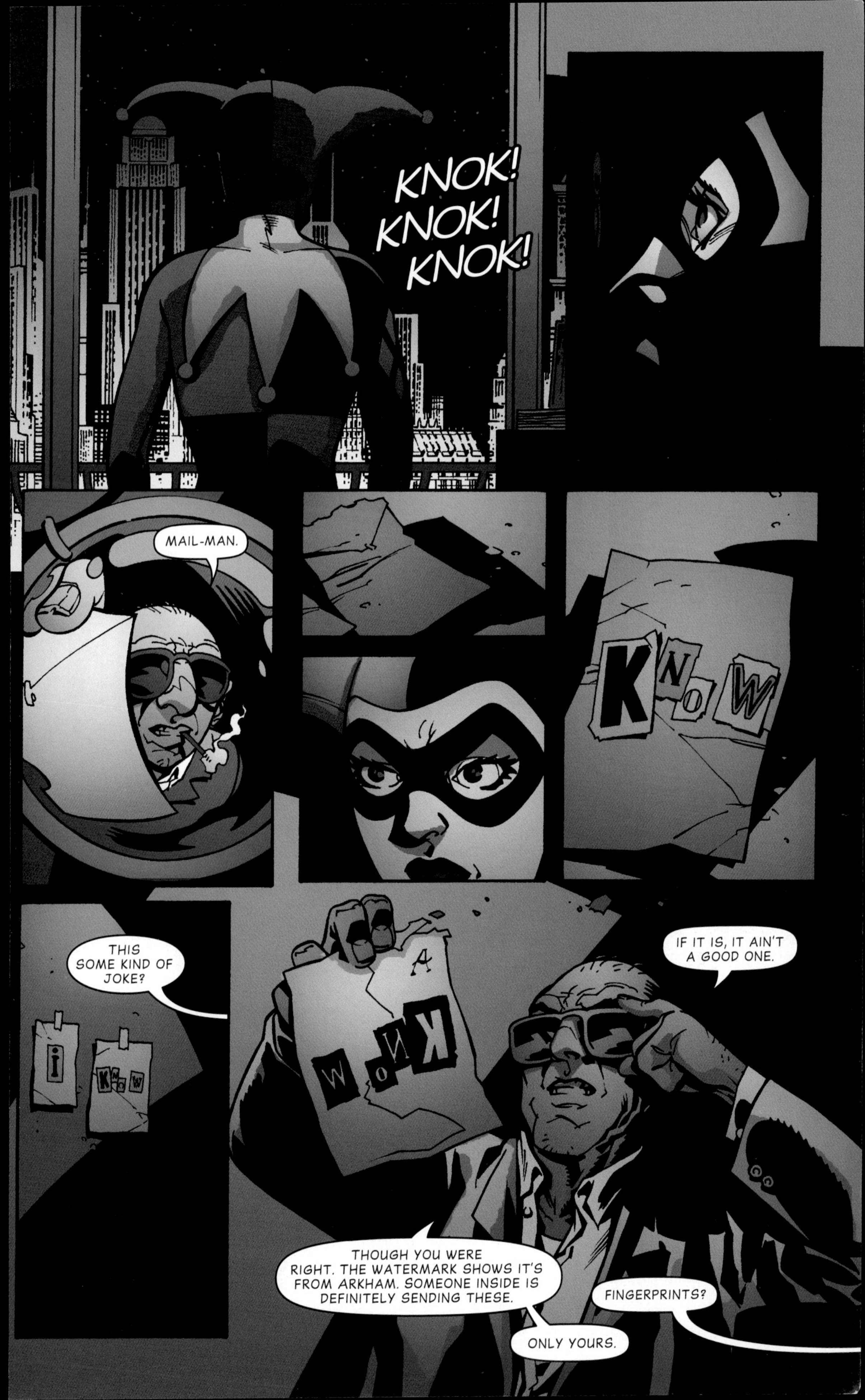
KNOK! KNOK! KNOK!
MAIL-MAN.
KNOW
THIS SOME KIND OF JOKE?
IF IT IS, IT AIN'T A GOOD ONE.
A KNOW
THOUGH YOU WERE RIGHT. THE WATERMARK SHOWS IT'S FROM ARKHAM. SOMEONE INSIDE IS DEFINITELY SENDING THESE.
FINGERPRINTS?
ONLY YOURS.

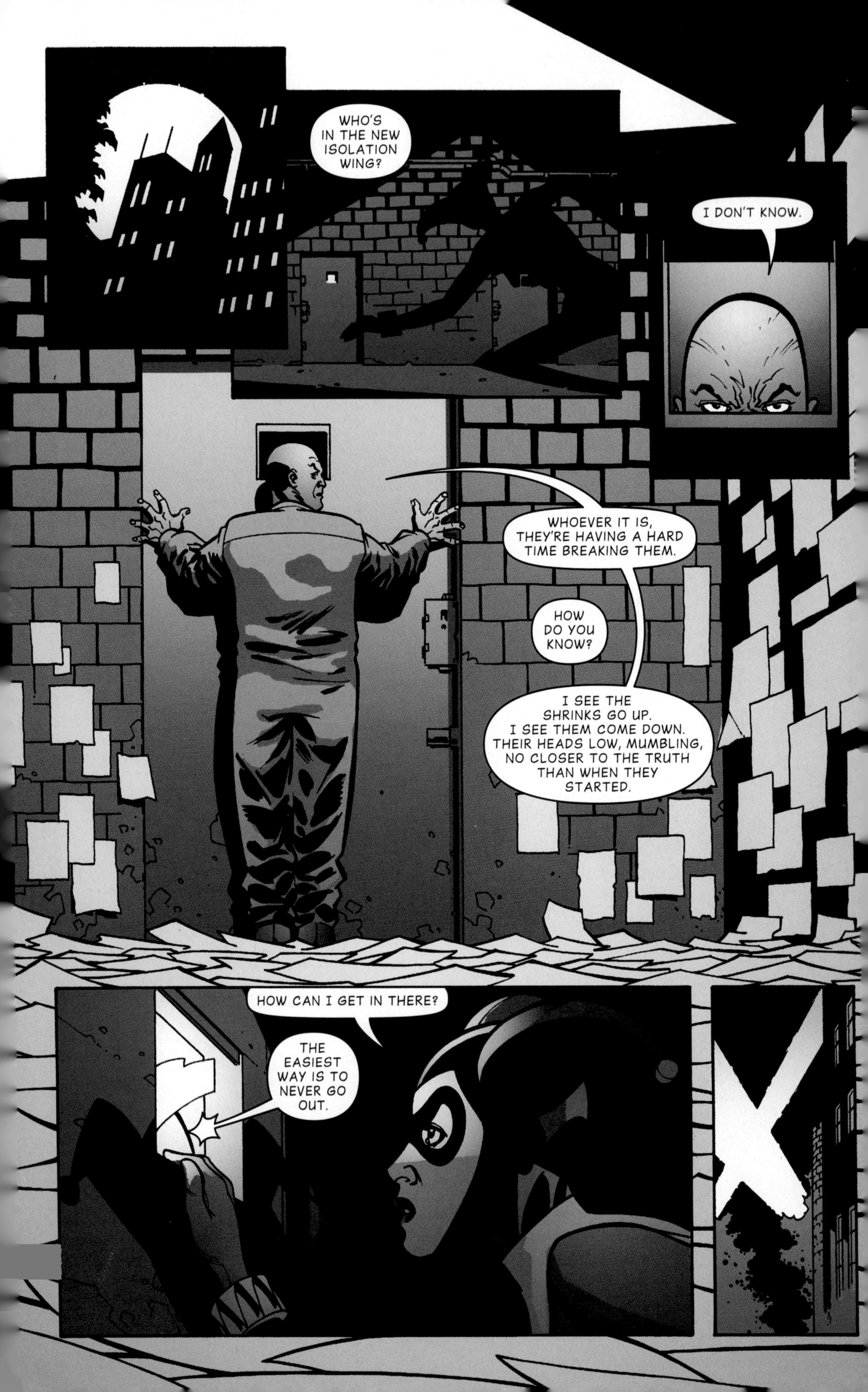
WHO'S IN THE NEW ISOLATION WING?
I DON'T KNOW.
WHOEVER IT IS, THEY'RE HAVING A HARD TIME BREAKING THEM.
HOW DO YOU KNOW?
I SEE THE SHRINKS GO UP. I SEE THEM COME DOWN. THEIR HEADS LOW, MUMBLING, NO CLOSER TO THE TRUTH THAN WHEN THEY STARTED.
HOW CAN I GET IN THERE?
THE EASIEST WAY IS TO NEVER GO OUT.

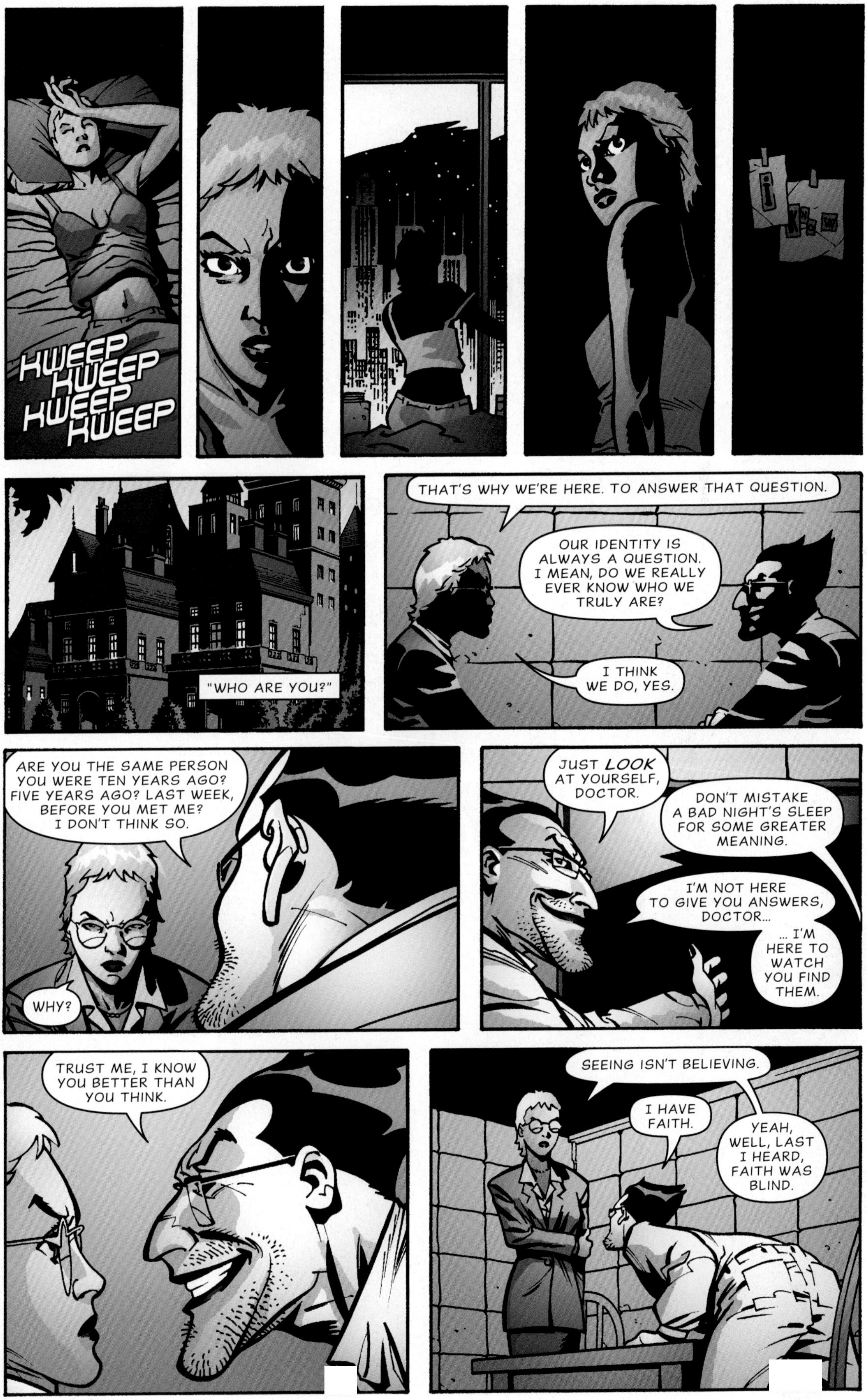
KWEEP
KWEEP
KWEEP
KWEEP
"WHO ARE YOU?"
THAT'S WHY WE'RE HERE. TO ANSWER THAT QUESTION.
OUR IDENTITY IS ALWAYS A QUESTION. I MEAN, DO WE REALLY EVER KNOW WHO WE TRULY ARE?
I THINK WE DO, YES.
ARE YOU THE SAME PERSON YOU WERE TEN YEARS AGO? FIVE YEARS AGO? LAST WEEK, BEFORE YOU MET ME? I DON'T THINK SO.
WHY?
JUST LOOK AT YOURSELF, DOCTOR.
DON'T MISTAKE A BAD NIGHT'S SLEEP FOR SOME GREATER MEANING.
I'M NOT HERE TO GIVE YOU ANSWERS, DOCTOR...
... I'M HERE TO WATCH YOU FIND THEM.
TRUST ME, I KNOW YOU BETTER THAN YOU THINK.
SEEING ISN'T BELIEVING.
I HAVE FAITH.
YEAH, WELL, LAST I HEARD, FAITH WAS BLIND.

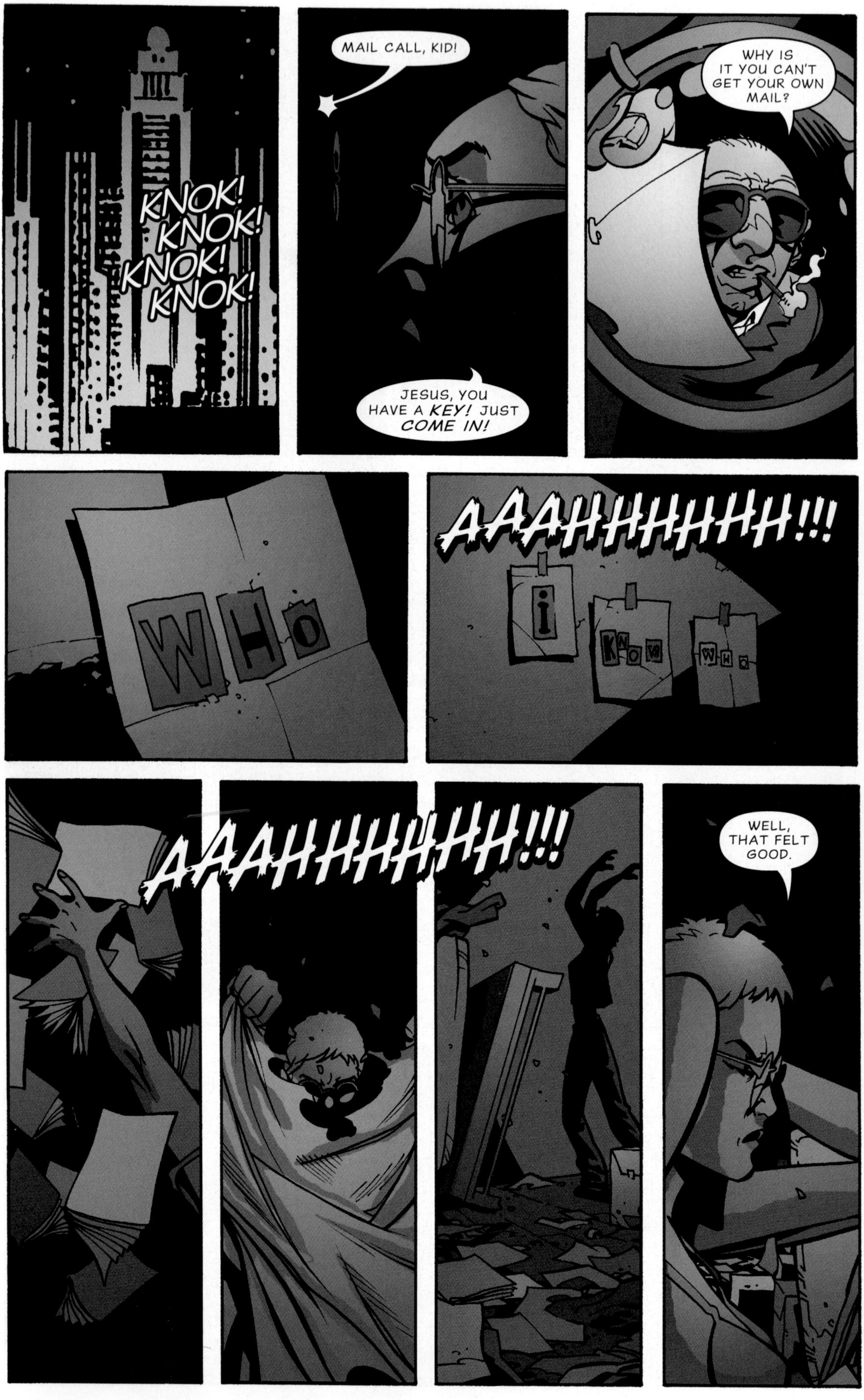
KNOK! KNOK! KNOK! KNOK!
MAIL CALL, KID!
JESUS, YOU HAVE A KEY! JUST COME IN!
WHY IS IT YOU CAN'T GET YOUR OWN MAIL?
WHO
AAAHHHHHH!!!
I KNOW WHO
AAAHHHHHH!!!
WELL, THAT FELT GOOD.

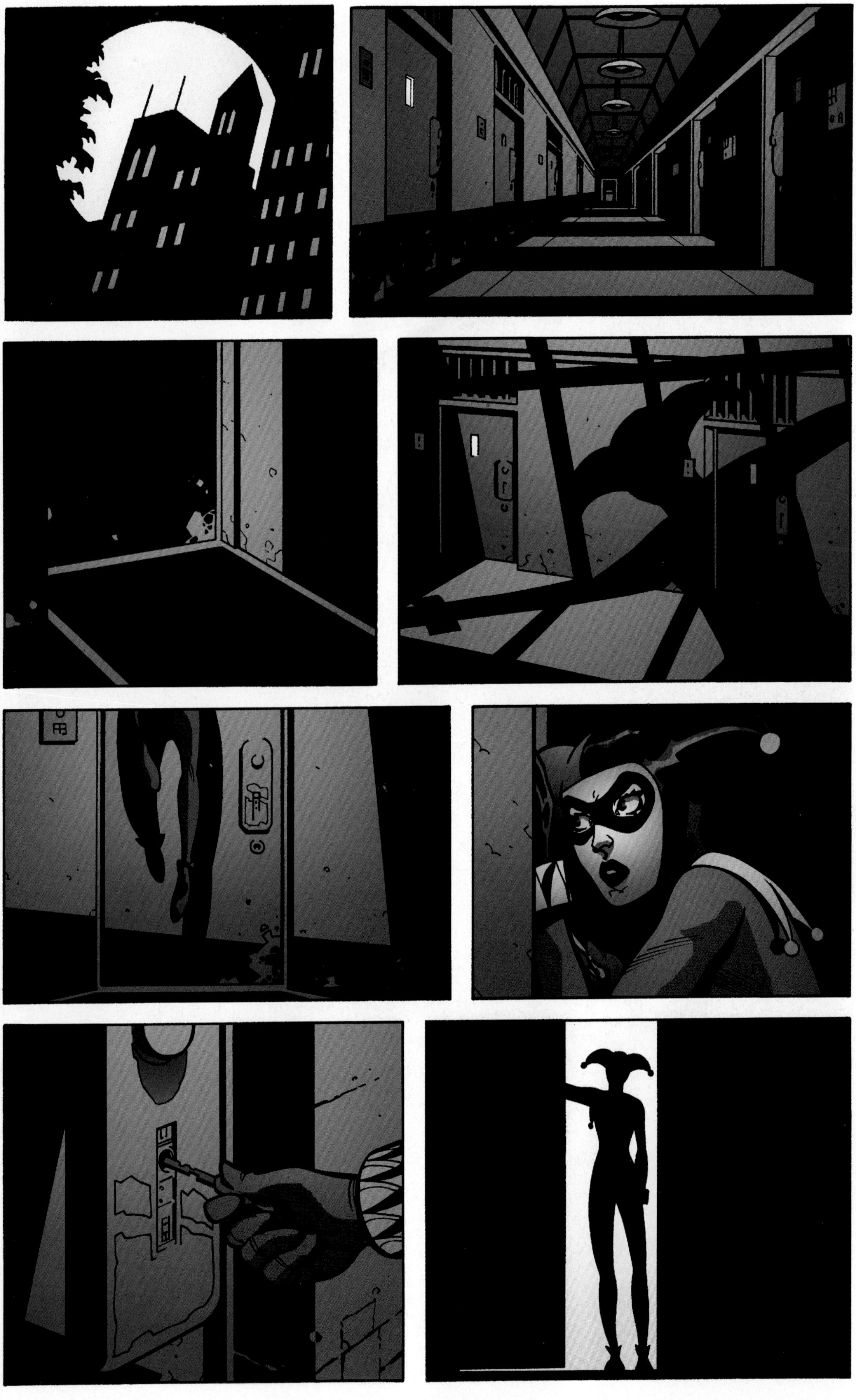

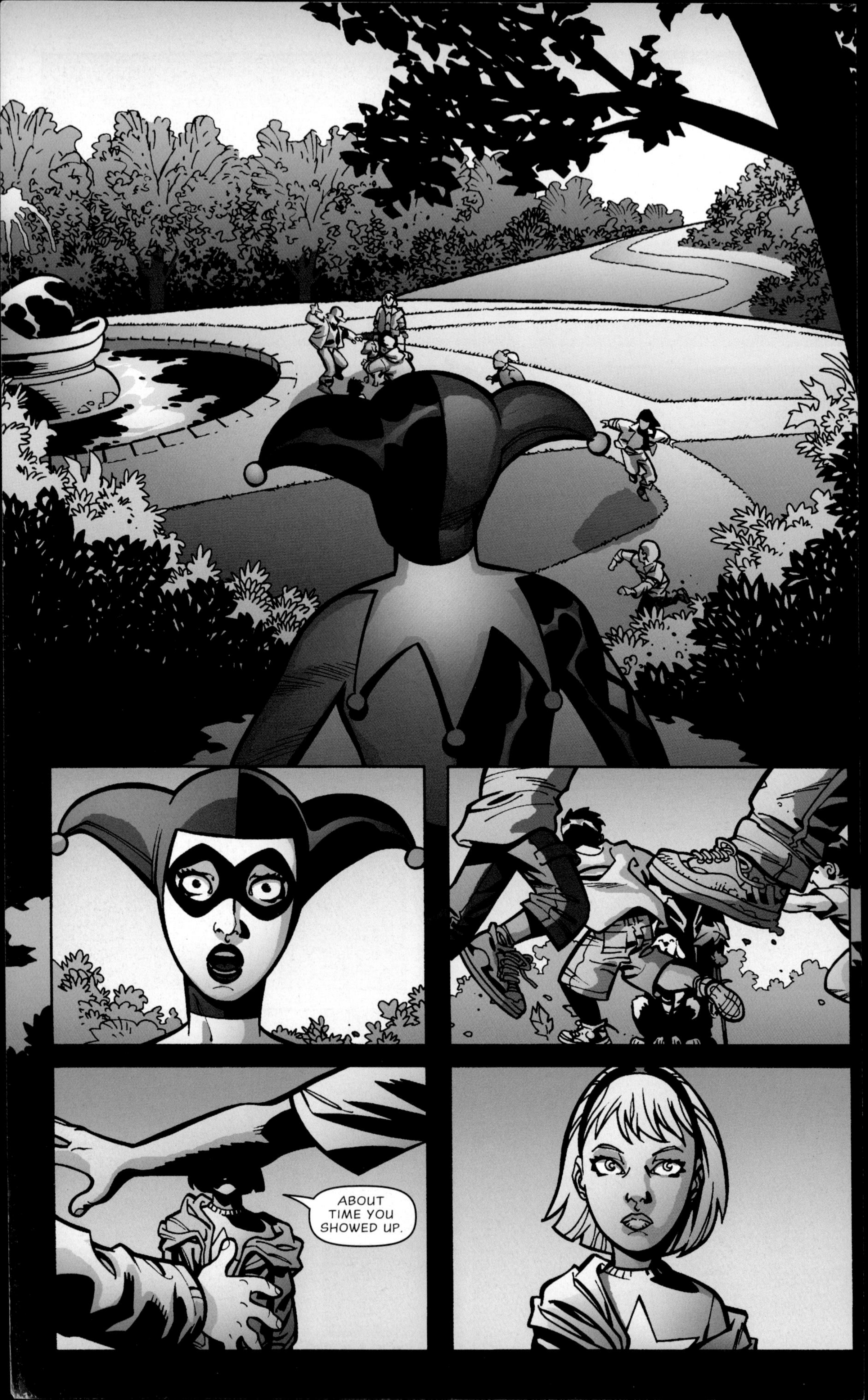
ABOUT TIME YOU SHOWED UP.

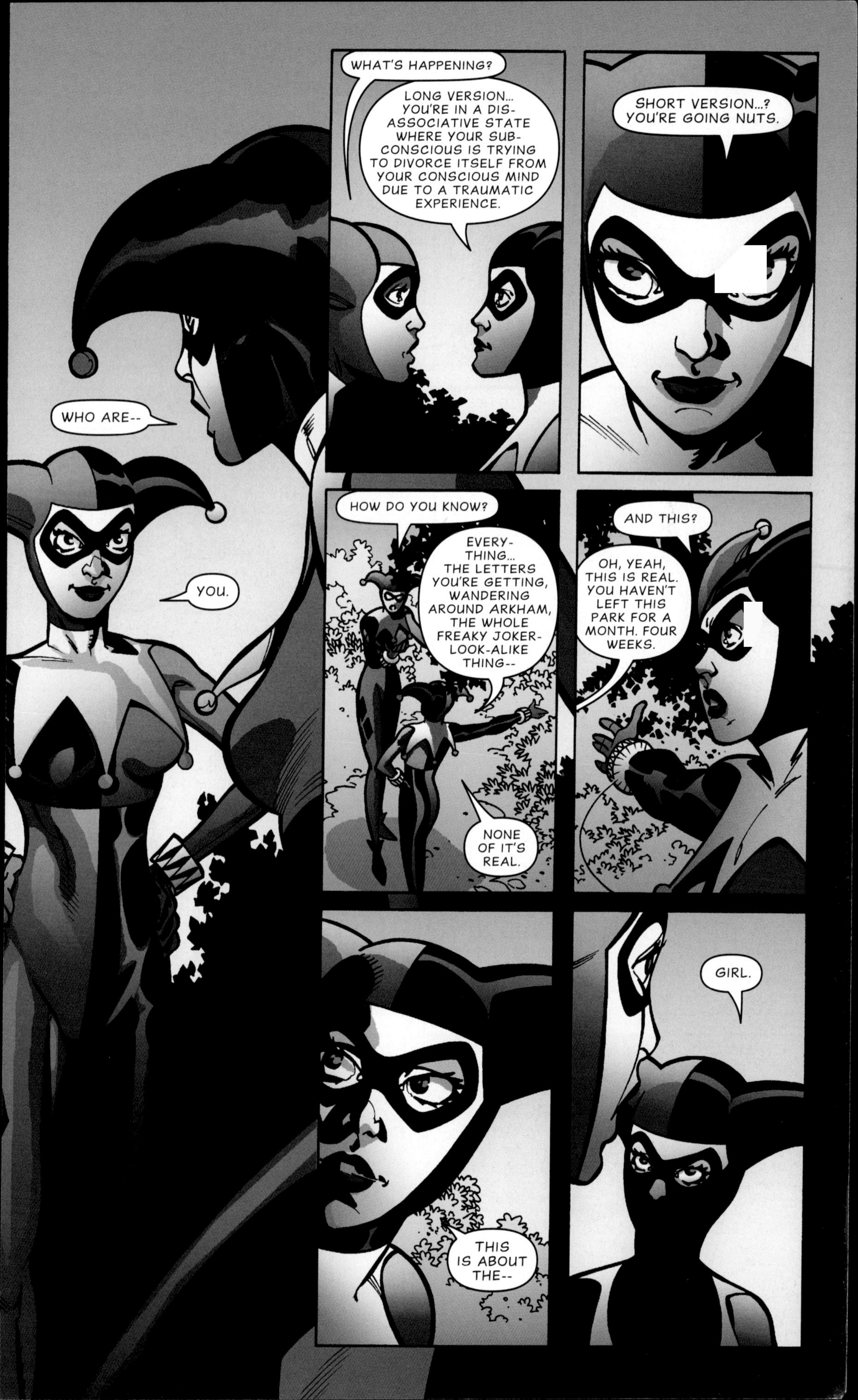
WHO ARE--
YOU.
WHAT'S HAPPENING?
LONG VERSION... YOU'RE IN A DIS-ASSOCIATIVE STATE WHERE YOUR SUB-CONSCIOUS IS TRYING TO DIVORCE ITSELF FROM YOUR CONSCIOUS MIND DUE TO A TRAUMATIC EXPERIENCE.
SHORT VERSION...? YOU'RE GOING NUTS.
HOW DO YOU KNOW?
EVERY-THING... THE LETTERS YOU'RE GETTING, WANDERING AROUND ARKHAM, THE WHOLE FREAKY JOKER-LOOK-ALIKE THING--
NONE OF IT'S REAL.
AND THIS?
OH, YEAH, THIS IS REAL. YOU HAVEN'T LEFT THIS PARK FOR A MONTH. FOUR WEEKS.
THIS IS ABOUT THE--
GIRL.

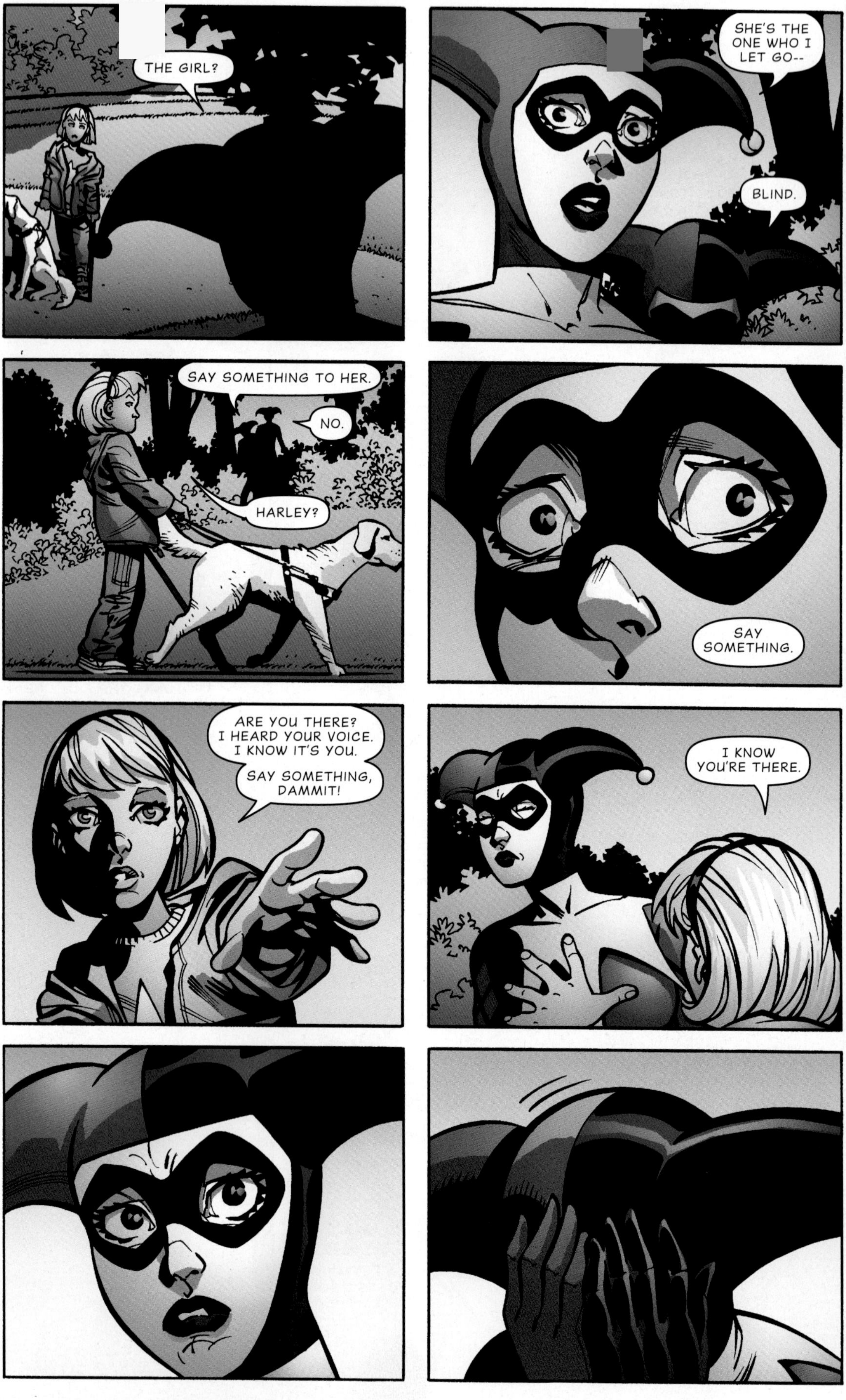
THE GIRL?
SHE'S THE ONE WHO I LET GO--
BLIND.
SAY SOMETHING TO HER.
NO.
HARLEY?
SAY SOMETHING.
ARE YOU THERE? I HEARD YOUR VOICE. I KNOW IT'S YOU.
SAY SOMETHING, DAMMIT!
I KNOW YOU'RE THERE.

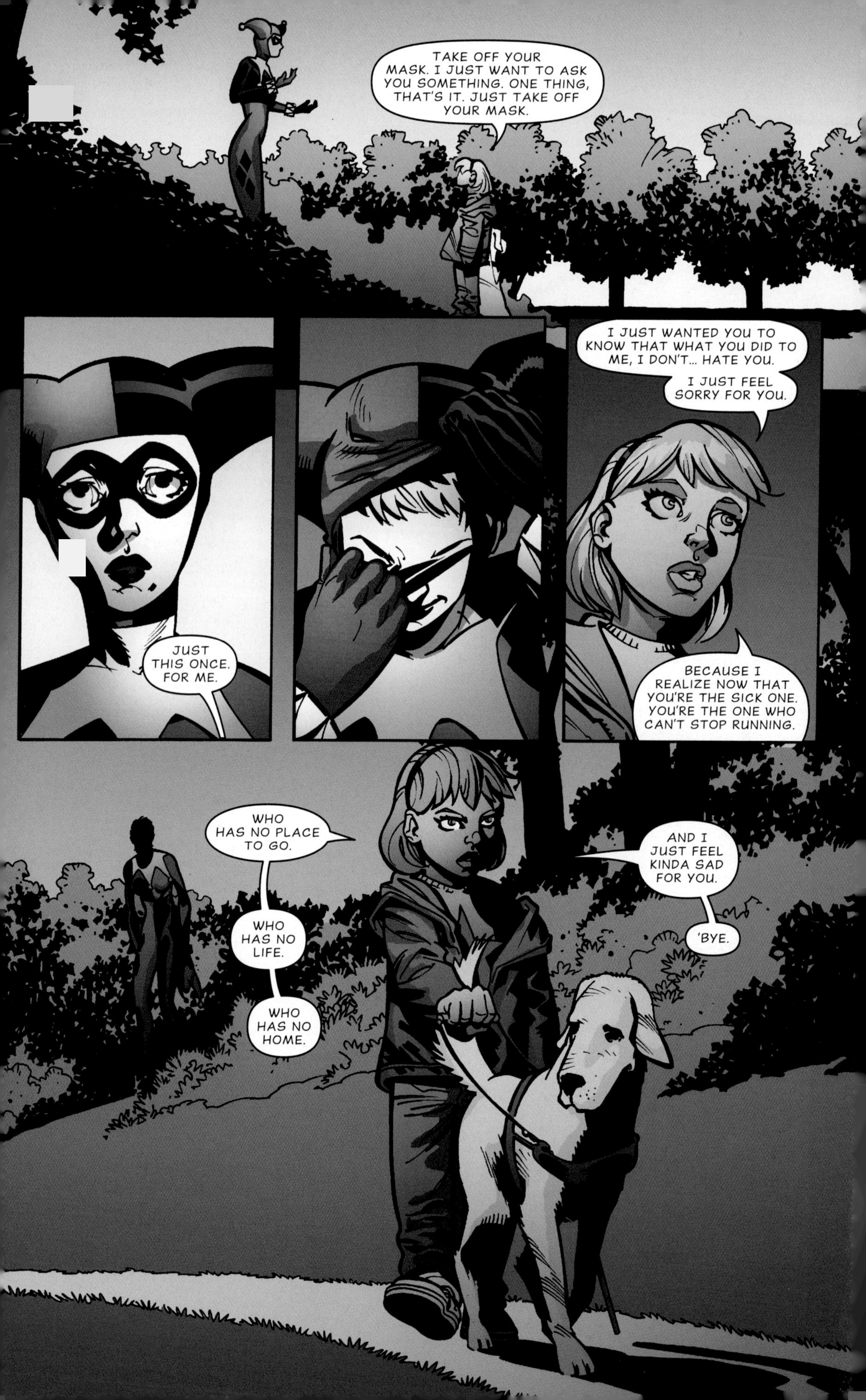
TAKE OFF YOUR MASK. I JUST WANT TO ASK YOU SOMETHING. ONE THING, THAT'S IT. JUST TAKE OFF YOUR MASK.
JUST THIS ONCE. FOR ME.
I JUST WANTED YOU TO KNOW THAT WHAT YOU DID TO ME, I DON'T... HATE YOU.
I JUST FEEL SORRY FOR YOU.
BECAUSE I REALIZE NOW THAT YOU'RE THE SICK ONE. YOU'RE THE ONE WHO CAN'T STOP RUNNING.
WHO HAS NO PLACE TO GO.
WHO HAS NO LIFE.
WHO HAS NO HOME.
AND I JUST FEEL KINDA SAD FOR YOU.
'BYE.

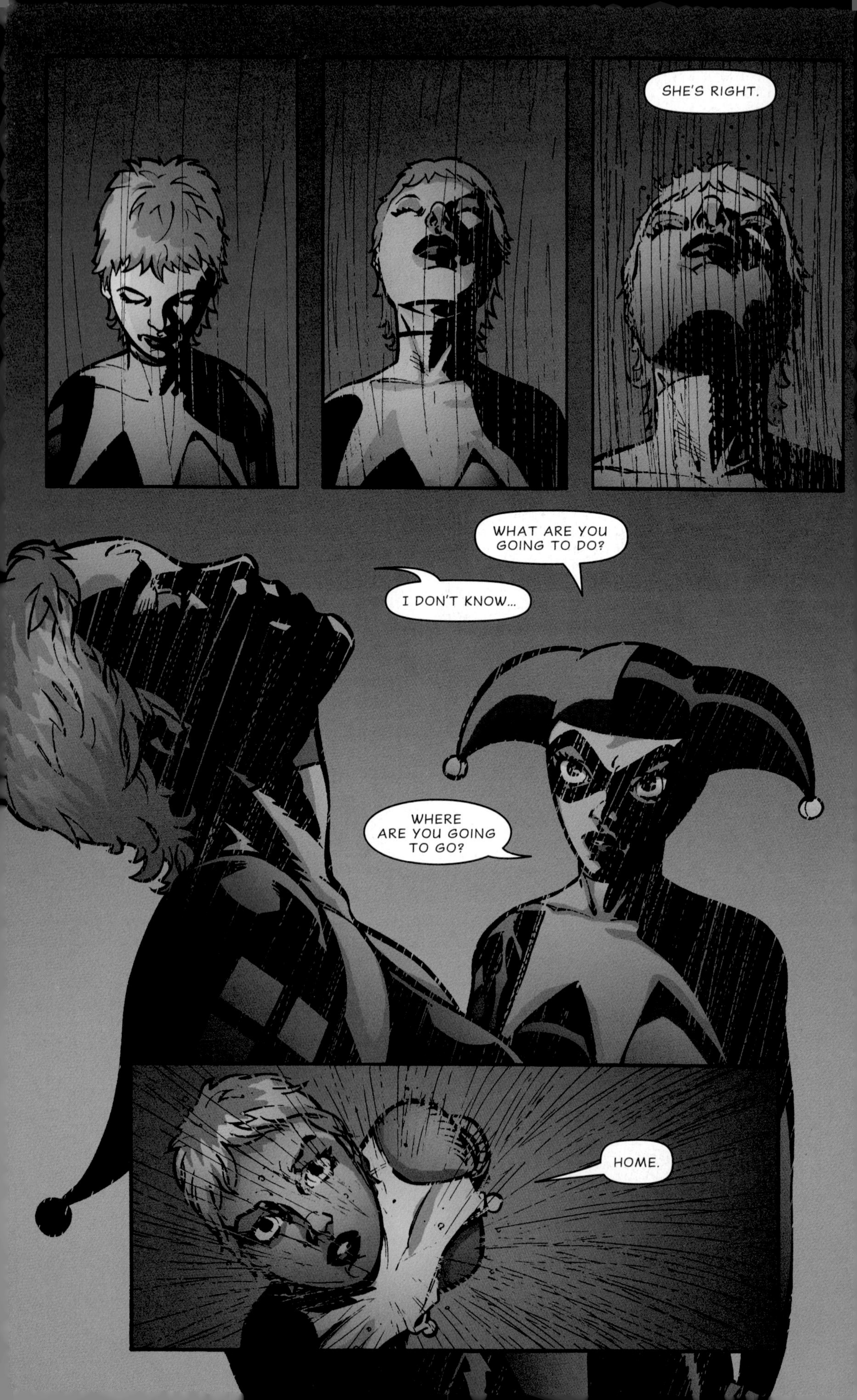

SHE'S RIGHT.
WHAT ARE YOU GOING TO DO?
I DON'T KNOW...
WHERE ARE YOU GOING TO GO?
HOME.

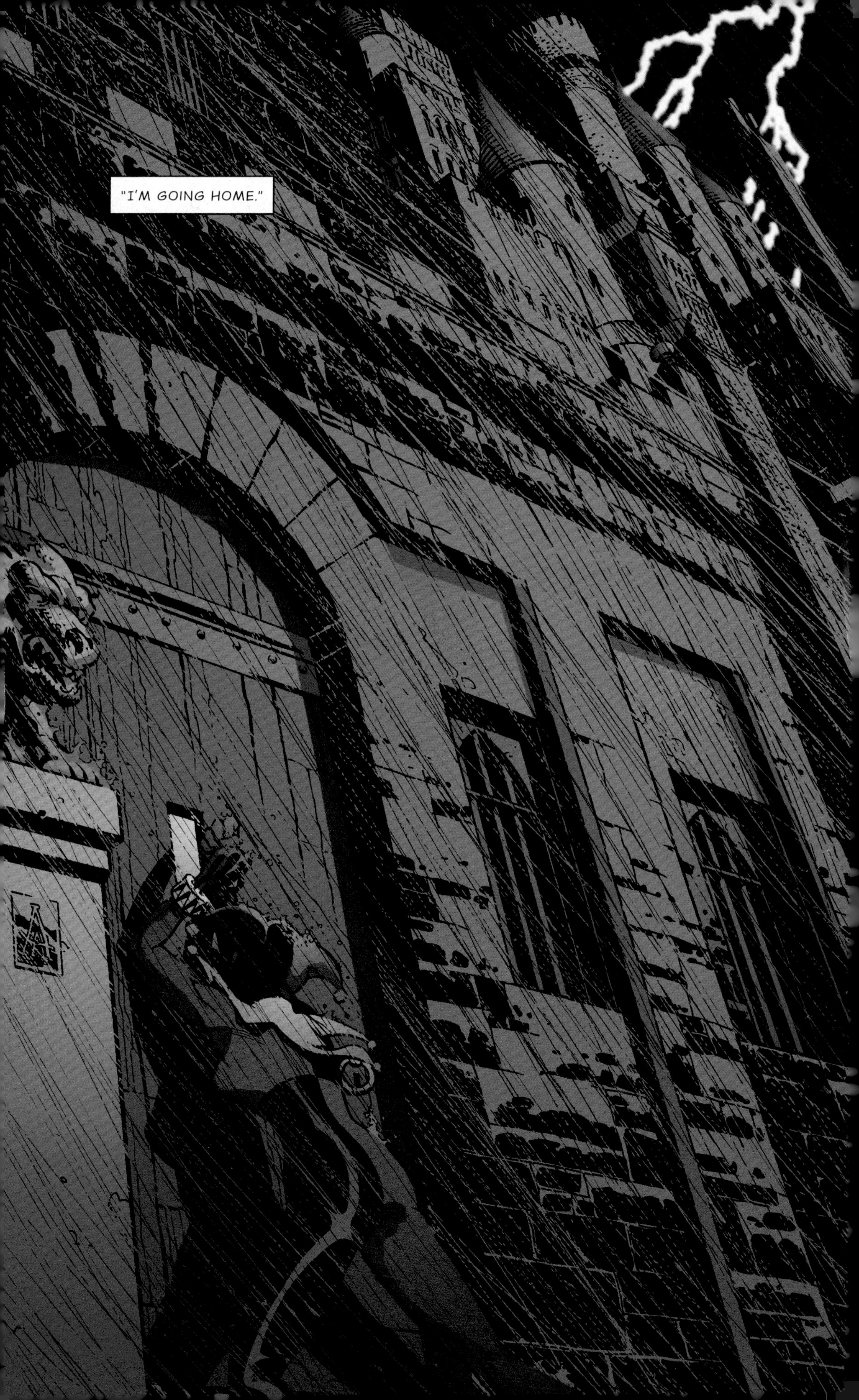
"I'M GOING HOME."

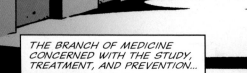

PSYCHIATRY:

THE BRANCH OF MEDICINE CONCERNED WITH THE STUDY, TREATMENT, AND PREVENTION...

... OF DISORDERS OF THE MIND;

ESPECIALLY THOSE WHO ARE MENTALLY UNBALANCED OR...

... DERANGED.

A.J. LIEBERMAN
Writer

CHARLIE ADLARD
Artist

JOEL BENJAMIN
Colorist

SEAN KONOT
Letterer

NACHIE CASTRO
Asst. Editor

MATT IDELSON
Editor

HARLEY QUINN
created by
PAUL DINI & BRUCE TIMM

DC COMICS™

"A pretty irresistible hook. What if the good guys assembled a bunch of bad guys to work as a Dirty Dozen-like superteam and do the dirty work traditional heroes would never touch (or want to know about)?"—THE ONION/AV CLUB

START AT THE BEGINNING!

SUICIDE SQUAD
VOLUME 1: KICKED IN THE TEETH

**SUICIDE SQUAD
VOL. 2: BASILISK
RISING**

**SUICIDE SQUAD
VOL. 3: DEATH IS FOR
SUCKERS**

**DEATHSTROKE VOL. 1:
LEGACY**

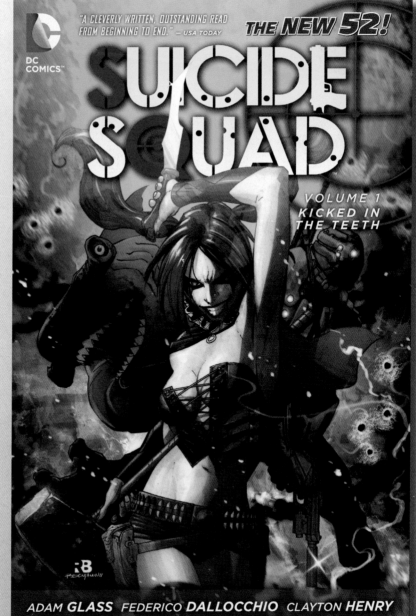

"A CLEVERLY WRITTEN, OUTSTANDING READ FROM BEGINNING TO END." — USA TODAY

THE NEW 52!

DC COMICS™

SUICIDE SQUAD

VOLUME 1
KICKED IN
THE TEETH

ADAM GLASS FEDERICO **DALLOCCHIO** CLAYTON **HENRY**

© 2012 DC Comics. All Rights Reserved.

DC COMICS™

"[Writer Scott Snyder] pulls from the oldest aspects of the Batman myth, combines it with sinister-comic elements from the series' best period, and gives the whole thing terrific forward-spin."—ENTERTAINMENT WEEKLY

START AT THE BEGINNING!

BATMAN VOLUME 1: THE COURT OF OWLS

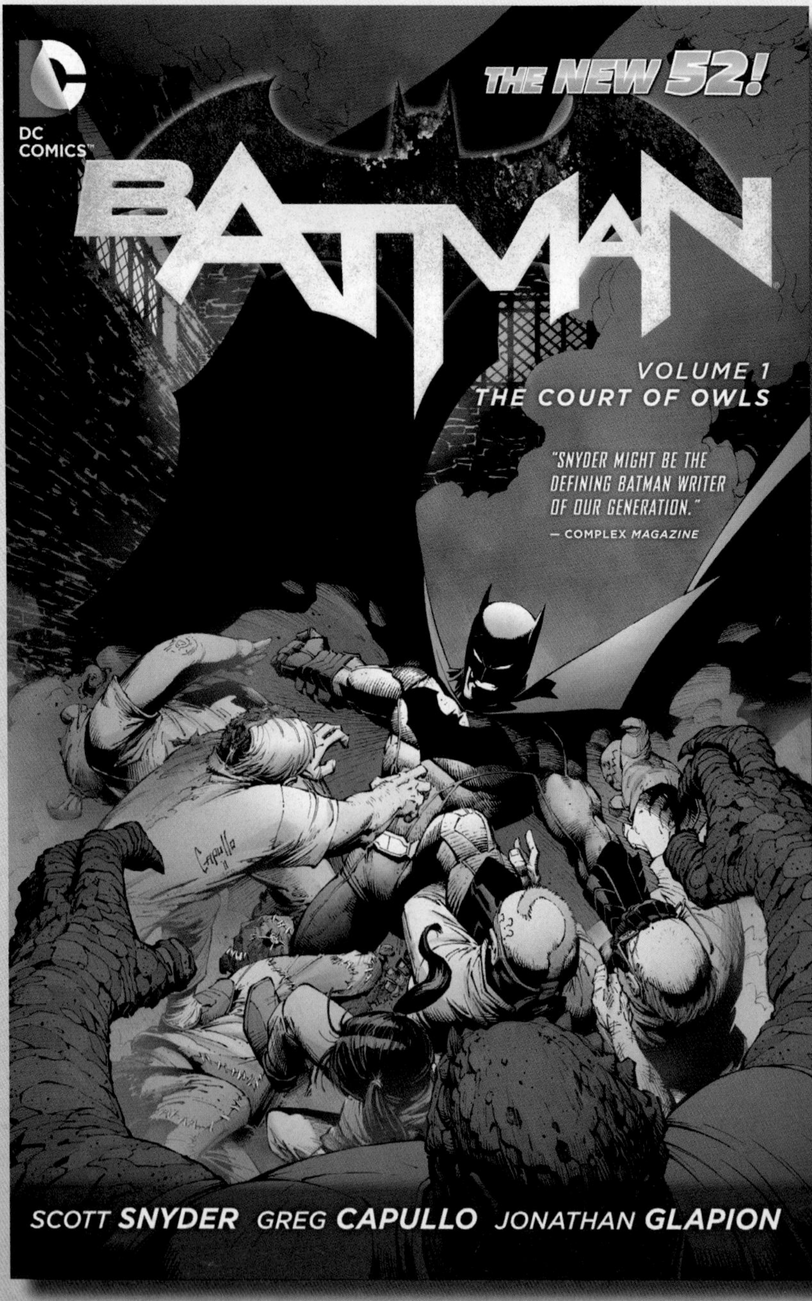

BATMAN VOL. 2: THE CITY OF OWLS

with SCOTT SNYDER and GREG CAPULLO

BATMAN VOL. 3: DEATH OF THE FAMILY

with SCOTT SNYDER and GREG CAPULLO

BATMAN: NIGHT OF THE OWLS

with SCOTT SNYDER and GREG CAPULLO

DC COMICS™

THE NEW 52!

BATMAN

VOLUME 1
THE COURT OF OWLS

"SNYDER MIGHT BE THE DEFINING BATMAN WRITER OF OUR GENERATION."
— COMPLEX MAGAZINE

SCOTT SNYDER   GREG CAPULLO   JONATHAN GLAPION

DC COMICS™

"Rock solid."—IGN

"This is the kind of Batman story I like to read: an actual mystery with an emotional hook."
—THE ONION/AV CLUB

START AT THE BEGINNING!

BATMAN & ROBIN
VOLUME 1: BORN TO KILL

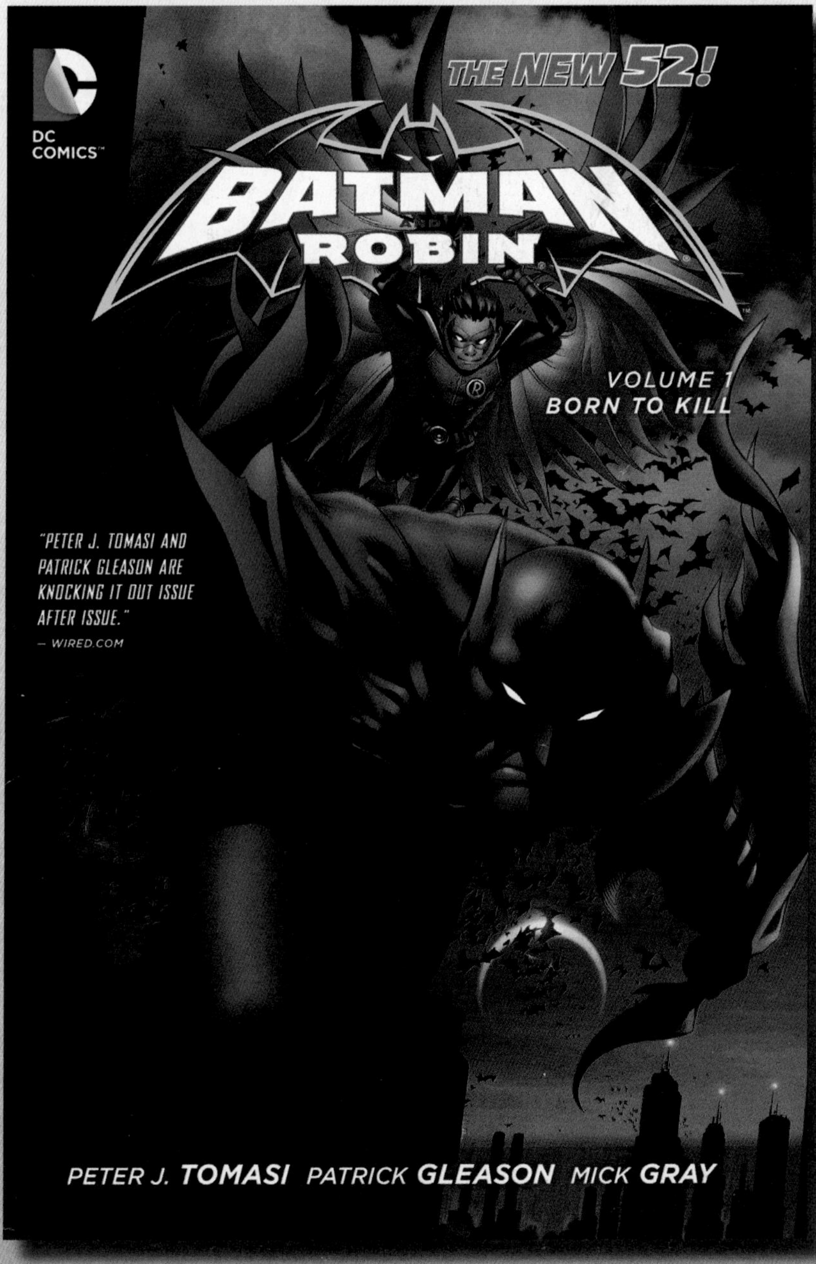

BATMAN & ROBIN VOL. 2: PEARL

BATMAN & ROBIN VOL. 3: DEATH OF THE FAMILY

BATMAN INCORPORATED VOL. 1: DEMON STAR

"PETER J. TOMASI AND PATRICK GLEASON ARE KNOCKING IT OUT ISSUE AFTER ISSUE."
— WIRED.COM

THE NEW 52!

PETER J. **TOMASI** PATRICK **GLEASON** MICK **GRAY**

© 2012 DC Comics. All Rights Reserved.

DC COMICS™

"Chaotic and unabashedly fun."—IGN

"I'm enjoying HARLEY QUINN a great deal; it's silly, it's funny, it's irreverent."
—COMIC BOOK RESOURCES

HARLEY QUINN

VOLUME 1: HOT IN THE CITY

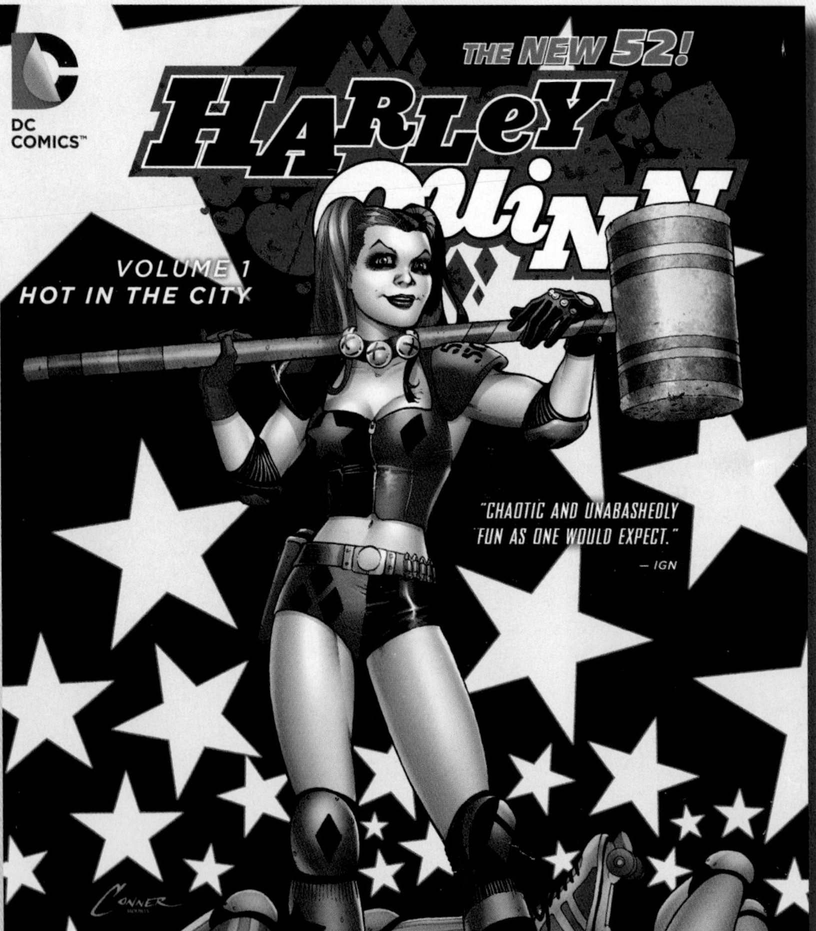
DC COMICS™
THE NEW 52!
HARLEY QUINN
VOLUME 1
HOT IN THE CITY
"CHAOTIC AND UNABASHEDLY FUN AS ONE WOULD EXPECT." — IGN
AMANDA CONNER JIMMY PALMIOTTI CHAD HARDIN
STEPHANE ROUX ALEX SINCLAIR PAUL MOUNTS

SUICIDE SQUAD VOL. 1: KICKED IN THE TEETH

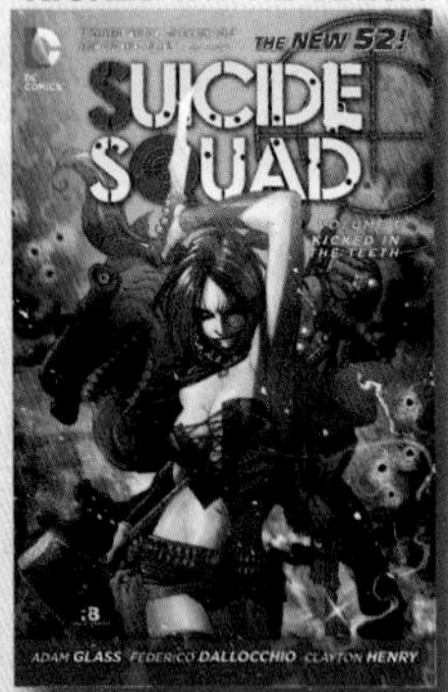
THE NEW 52!
SUICIDE SQUAD
ADAM GLASS FEDERICO DALLOCCHIO CLAYTON HENRY

with ADAM GLASS and FEDERICO DALLOCCHIO

HARLEY QUINN: PRELUDES AND KNOCK-KNOCK JOKES

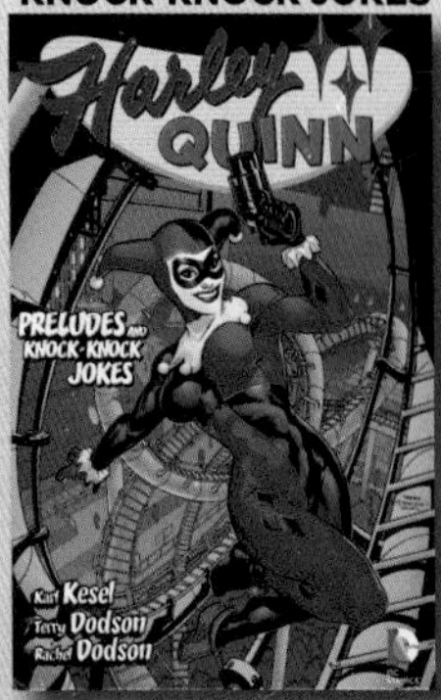
Harley QUINN
PRELUDES and KNOCK-KNOCK JOKES
Karl Kesel
Terry Dodson
Rachel Dodson

with KARL KESEL and TERRY DODSON

BATMAN: MAD LOVE AND OTHER STORIES

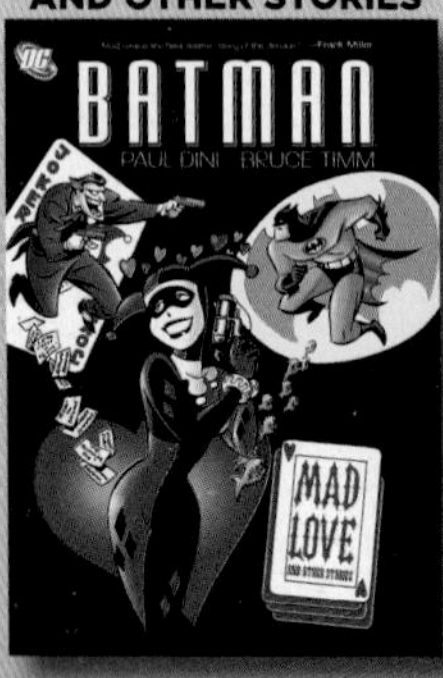
BATMAN
PAUL DINI BRUCE TIMM
MAD LOVE

with PAUL DINI and BRUCE TIMM